WHERE POWER
LIES

ALSO BY LANCE PRICE

The Spin Doctor's Diary
Time and Fate

WHERE POWER LIES

Prime Ministers v the Media

LANCE PRICE

**SIMON &
SCHUSTER**

London · New York · Sydney · Toronto

A CBS COMPANY

First published in Great Britain by Simon & Schuster UK Ltd, 2010
A CBS COMPANY

1 3 5 7 9 10 8 6 4 2

Simon & Schuster UK Ltd
1st Floor
222 Gray's Inn Road
London WC1X 8HB

www.simonandschuster.co.uk

Simon & Schuster Australia
Sydney

PICTURE CREDITS
Getty: 1, 3, 4, 5, 6, 10, 11, 12, 14, 17, 19, 20, 26, 27, 28, 29
Corbis: 2, 13, 30
Political Cartoon Gallery: 7
Mirrorpix: 8
Lebrecht Music & Arts: 9
Solo Syndication: 15, 16
Daily Telegraph: 23, 31
Rex: 24
Steve Bell: 25
Gerald Scarfe: 32

A CIP catalogue record for this book
is available from the British Library.

ISBN: 978-1-84737-253-6

Typeset in Bembo by M Rules
Printed in the UK by CPI Mackays, Chatham ME5 8TD

CONTENTS

PART TWO: PRIME MINISTERS V. THE MEDIA:
TWENTY-FOUR-HOUR NEWS AND THE
MEDIA DEMOCRACY

To my parents, Jean and Colin

Public sentiment is everything. With public sentiment nothing can fail. Without it nothing can succeed. He who moulds opinion is greater than he who enacts laws.

Abraham Lincoln

Whoever controls the media, controls the mind.

Jim Morrison

ACKNOWLEDGEMENTS AND NOTES

If the former German chancellor Konrad Adenauer was right that 'history is the sum total of things that could have been avoided' then there is a great deal in the pages that follow which future prime ministers and their sparring partners in journalism might wish to avoid. Almost without exception, the many people who agreed to be interviewed in the course of my research shared the hope that relations between Downing Street and the media can be put on a more sensible footing in the future than they have been in the past. I am grateful to them all for their time and valuable insights. Most cannot be named for obvious reasons. They include current and former Downing Street staff, special advisers and civil servants from permanent-secretary level down, government directors of communication past and present, and senior correspondents and editors from most national newspapers. Those who were willing and able to speak on the record are named in the text. The contributions of the others were no less appreciated. I would like to thank Sir Trevor Lloyd-Hughes, in particular, for allowing me to be the first author to see and quote from his unpublished memoirs.

Professors Peter Hennessy and Ivor Gaber offered thoughtful observations on the early drafts. With the benefit of his long experience Anthony Howard helped me avoid some historical blunders. Many others suggested productive avenues of research and provided useful nuggets of information and other practical support. They include Professors Brian Brivati and Bob Franklin, Peter Kellner, Ben Brogan,

John Rentoul, Steve Richards, Nicholas Jones, Matthew Parris, Julian Glover, Robert Peston, Julia Hobsbawn, Matt Aston, Scott Gill, Scott Solder, Malcolm Crayton, Dave Piggin, Chris Poole and Marnix Elsenaar. Thanks to Tim Benson at the Political Cartoon Gallery in London for his help with the illustrations.

I am indebted to Andrew Gordon for getting the project started and to my editor Mike Jones, Rory Scarfe, Karl French, Gina Rozner and the rest of the team at Simon and Schuster. My agent Broo Doherty showed her characteristic patience and good sense throughout and her access to supplies of excellent red wine didn't go amiss either. Thanks, Tom. The staff at the British Library were courteous and efficient throughout the long months of research. It almost became a second home. At my first home my civil partner James put up with my absences, and my distractedness when I was around, with as much good humour and understanding as anybody could ask for.

Where Power Lies became more ambitious in scope as it went along but even now it is far from a complete record of the history of either Downing Street or the media in the period it covers. It concentrates on the relationship between the two. If at times there appears to be an ele-phant in the room, or even several at once, it is in the interests of keeping the text to a manageable length and sticking as much as possible to the point. Highly significant developments on which prime ministers and journalists had a great deal to say barely feature, if at all. They include the Irish question, the women's movement, the end to colonialism, and numerous wars. Where other events – the general strike, the abdica-tion crisis, Suez, Iraq – do receive more attention it is because they shed important light on the endless tussle between the power of Downing Street and the power of the media. The same goes for the efforts of the parties in opposition to enlist journalists in their attempt to gain power. There could be a whole book in that, but here they fea-ture only when, as with Neil Kinnock's defeat in 1992, their experience has a direct impact on subsequent attitudes within Number 10.

Some prime ministers get more attention than others, but then some took the media a great deal more seriously than others. A. J. P. Taylor observed that 'history gets thicker as it approaches recent times' and so it does here. Part One, which covers the period before the advent of 24-hour news and the government response to it, includes the history of thirteen premierships. Part Two outlines the experience of just four. Downing Street's preoccupation with the media has grown enormously in recent years, but the fundamentals of the relationship have changed less than might be imagined. David Lloyd George eyed the media of his day just as warily as Gordon Brown and David Cameron do now. And the question of where power really lies is as significant as ever it was.

INTRODUCTION:
THE POWER AND THE GLORY

The men who create power make an indispensable contribution to the nation's greatness, but the men who question power make a contribution just as indispensable, especially when the questioning is disinterested, for they determine whether we use power or power uses us.

John F. Kennedy, 1963

The British are not given to revolutions. Even the 'Glorious Revolution' of 1688, which brought to an end the absolute power of monarchs and ushered in our parliamentary democracy, was something of a myth. It wasn't really a revolution at all. There was no popular uprising. Power changed hands at the top thanks to a *coup d'état* and a foreign invasion. The Bill of Rights that the 'revolution' helped establish made precious little difference to the lives of ordinary Britons. In 2009 we witnessed an Inglorious Revolution. This time the people did rise up, although their anger was played out in the media not on the streets. It was the greatest shock to the political system since the days of David Lloyd George almost a century ago. In normal circumstances the British prefer to let democracy look after itself. It is sometimes referred to as 'Britain's gift to the world' but sadly we all too often take it for granted. Most of the time voters are happy to put their cross on a ballot paper every four or five years and then let parliament get on with the job. A disturbingly large number of people don't bother to vote at all.

It takes something pretty serious to shake us out of our complacency. In the early years of the twentieth century, when Lloyd George was in high office, it was the attempt by the House of Lords to block social reform and the absence of votes for women. Early in the twenty-first century, however, it was expenses claims for bath plugs, moats and duck ponds that provoked so much fury. Yet they were just the symbols. The scandal over MPs' allowances was about more than that. Representative democracy relies on the assumption that those we elect can be trusted to behave responsibly and in the public interest until the next time they come looking for our votes. Now it seemed they could not. In the view of the *Sunday Times*, 'The disclosures over MPs' expenses have turned a general lack of respect for politicians, which some put down to the decline of deference, into open contempt. We may have thought MPs were merely incompetent; now we know many are no better than fraudsters, thieves and benefit cheats.'[1] MPs of all parties hung their heads in shame. Reputations were destroyed and careers brought to a premature end. The most high-profile casualty was no less a figure than the Speaker of the House of Commons, Michael Martin. He became the first holder of that august post to be forced from office since 1695, when the Glorious Revolution was still being played out.

Those who had transgressed dared not ask for sympathy and would have received little if they had tried. The public believed the power they had entrusted in their members of parliament had been abused. Their faith in the entire system of government was undermined. It was not just individuals but institutions that were perceived to have failed. Constitutional reform, the demand for radical change in the way Britain is run, was turned overnight from the obsession of a tiny minority to a national concern. Power – who had it, where they got it from, how it was exercised and how it could be taken away – was no longer something voters could safely ignore from one election to the next. The integrity of parliament, not something to which most people had given much thought until now, had been shown to be a myth. Some wondered how much else that they had taken for granted was just as illusory.

For once journalists, who are usually to be found in opinion surveys

languishing with politicians and estate agents among those least deserv-
ing of the public's trust, were spared. The shaft of light that had
exposed parliament's failings came from the media, and in particular a
paper usually thought of as a pillar of the Establishment, the *Daily
Telegraph*. Those MPs who tried to raise questions about newspaper
ethics, chequebook journalism or the purchase of stolen information,
were wasting their breath. The public didn't want to hear. The media
had done what the media was supposed to do: expose wrongdoing in
high places and hold the powerful to account. Those commentators
who sought to inject a note of caution about their own trade were few
and far between. 'What aspect of the restoration of trust in politics
would be in the media's interest?' asked Martin Kettle in the *Guardian*.
'The answer is no part of it at all. A media that have become progressively less engaged with serious political argument and progressively
more focused on personal frailty, foible and failure is one of the shapers
of the nation's political problem, not the deliverer from it.'[2] More
common was the sense that journalists had earned the right to side
with the public in an unprecedented level of scorn for all politicians,
from the prime minister down. Words written even before the scandal by the *Guardian's* more outspoken columnist Charlie Brooker no
longer sounded so extreme: 'The politicians have finally shut us out of
their game for good and we have nowhere left to turn. We're not part
of their world any more. We don't even speak the same language.
We're the ants in their garden. The bacteria in their stools. They have
nothing but contempt for us. They snivel and lie and duck questions . . . while demanding we respect their authority.'[3]

Having declared the political system broken, the media then set
about discussing how to fix it. Acres of newsprint and hours of broadcasting time were spent analysing not just the claims for duck ponds
and second homes, but the balance of power at Westminster itself.
Should parliament and its scrutiny committees have more; the executive, the prime minister and the party whips less? Should the voters
be able to unseat MPs in exceptional circumstances? Should parliament
be made more representative by changing the electoral system? By
contrast, few questions were asked about the power of the media and,
in the circumstances, understandably so. Left to its own devices,

parliament would never have revealed the full story of how its members were exploiting the self-regulating system of expenses and allowances. It took a newspaper campaign to expose the inglorious conduct of MPs. If they couldn't be trusted then there would have to be much greater transparency about what really goes on at Westminster. And transparency is something journalists, those valiant pursuers of the truth, strongly support. Except, that is, when it comes to themselves.

If we are to make the most of this rare period of genuine public interest in where power lies in Britain, the relationship between the media and politics cannot be ignored. If for no other reason than that so many people in both professions would prefer to keep their dealings with each another away from public scrutiny. In the two volumes of Margaret Thatcher's memoirs, running to almost 1,500 pages, there is not a single reference to Rupert Murdoch. It will be interesting to note if he does any better when Tony Blair comes to write his. When I published *The Spin Doctor's Diary*, an account of my time as a Downing Street media adviser during Blair's first term, it was my entries about Mr Murdoch to which the Whitehall censors most objected. At all levels in the media, from global proprietors down to individual reporters, there is a similar aversion to transparency. When it suited it, the *Daily Telegraph* could brush aside questions about its purchase of stolen information by saying that the first rule of journalism is never to discuss your sources. A few months later, in July 2009, it was alleged that the *News of the World* had been tapping into the mobile-phone messages of thousands of politicians and celebrities. The paper's editor at the time this was going on, Andy Coulson, was now the Conservative party's director of communications. He told MPs he had no recollection of any such abuses when he was in charge and 'I am not sure there is an awful lot more I could have done' to prevent them[4]. In the weeks before the expenses furore broke, Downing Street had been engulfed by another scandal: the revelation that Gordon Brown's most trusted media adviser, Damian McBride, had sent an email containing salacious gossip about senior Conservatives and their wives to a Labour-supporting blogger. McBride was forced to resign within hours. He had been given the stories by his contacts in the media but that didn't stop them condemning 'slurs, none of which have any substance'.[5]

During my own time in Downing Street I took a call from a well-respected political editor who made an extraordinary offer. In return for some private information that he wanted, information that reflected badly on the Conservative party, he would say in print that it had come from 'senior Tory sources'. In other words he would not merely hide where his information came from, he would lie about it. To my shame I agreed. He got his story and the fingerprints of Downing Street were well and truly hidden. There are, of course, journalists of great integrity just as there are politicians who have never abused the trust of their electors, but neither profession can claim an unblemished record for honesty.

Where Power Lies is an attempt to shed a little more light on the cloud-covered territory where the worlds of journalism and politics overlap. I have spent long enough criss-crossing that rocky terrain to know that it can never be mapped with complete accuracy. Anybody hoping for clear and unambiguous signposting should turn back now. It is a place where private conversations, off-the-record briefings, nods, winks and gestures of a less friendly nature are often the language of choice. But the territory is too important to be left to those of us who already know our way around. This book is largely free of the perpendicular pronoun, although I get a walk-on part in chapters nine and ten and a small supporting role in chapter eleven, but the reader deserves to know where the author is coming from. For seven years I was a BBC political correspondent doing my best to treat all views equally. From 1998 I was first a special adviser at 10 Downing Street, where I deputised for Alastair Campbell, and then the Labour party's director of communications. During those three years the only views that counted for me were Tony Blair's. Since 2001 I have been a freelance commentator, liberated at last to say just what I think. So *Where Power Lies* is not 'a spin doctor's guide to prime ministers and the media'. Far from it. There's no doubt I contaminated my impartiality when I went to work at Number 10, and perhaps some of my integrity, too. But I also got a glimpse of how government really works, and of where power really lies, that not every journalist is privileged to see.

Flaubert said our ignorance of history makes us vilify our own age.[6] So *Where Power Lies* also attempts to put the relationship between politics and the media that we see today into an historical context. It opens in the darkest days of the First World War, when the press was widely believed to have been part of a conspiracy to replace one prime minister, Herbert Asquith, with another, David Lloyd George. It ends with Gordon Brown, who faced similar accusations of having used his allies in the media to help undermine his predecessor and force him from office. Whatever the truth, it is clear that there were journalists on both occasions who were not content to be mere bystanders. One senior newspaper correspondent was refreshingly frank about his own role in recent events when he said to me: 'One of the most interesting things about the first draft of history of the New Labour government and of Gordon Brown in particular is the extent to which the media, and particularly the journalists who were involved with Gordon, are going to tell the true story about how we were all implicated in the dirty business of Gordon Brown. How we all colluded in advancing Gordon Brown's interests.' He even went as far as to describe what went on as 'treachery'. He might have added that he, and others like him, wasted little time in turning against the man they had helped into Downing Street once they decided he didn't measure up to the job after all.

A similar fate befell David Lloyd George, who was built up by the press when it suited it and then discarded when it no longer had any use for him. Again, in the 1960s, Harold Wilson went from being the darling of the media to believing they were out to destroy him. These men, and many others besides, soon learned that consistency and loyalty are not attributes for which journalists are famous. Stanley Baldwin, a Conservative prime minister in the twenties and thirties whom powerful press barons really did try to destroy, said they aimed for 'power without responsibility – the prerogative of the harlot down the ages'. The words were written for him by Rudyard Kipling, but nobody has ever put it better. When the unusually honest correspondent I referred to above, a thoughtful and serious man, spoke of 'treachery' it was because he agreed with Baldwin that prime ministers should be chosen by open and democratic means. Yet he was ready

to admit that he, like many journalists in his position, was easily flattered and rather enjoyed it when a man who aspired to lead the
country came looking for his help.

The independence of the British media may be a myth but it is one
that has been around for a very long time. It was no one man's creation, but was described best by the legendary editor of *The Times*,
John Delane, in 1852. In his view the proper relationship between the
press and politicians was unambiguous. 'The purpose and duties of the
two powers are constantly separate, generally independent, sometimes
diametrically opposed . . . To perform its duties with entire independence, and consequently with the utmost political advantage, the
press can enter into no close or binding alliances with the statesmen of
the day, nor can it surrender its permanent interests to the convenience
of the ephemeral power of any government.'[7] I suspect most journalists today would say 'hear, hear' to that. I doubt if any would claim it
was an accurate description of how the relationship works in reality. In
truth, the two powers are constantly intertwined, rarely independent,
sometimes even working in harness. To maximise their commercial
advantage and to exert the greatest political influence, journalists enter
into all manner of secret alliances with politicians, including the prime
minister of the day, surrendering any claim to genuine independence
and often bolstering rather than scrutinising those in government or
aspiring to government.

The media, or at least those in the media who help cover what goes
on at Westminster, don't merely observe the political system; they are
part of it. They don't just scrutinise the exercise of power – a recent
study claimed that a new form of 'monitory democracy' has now
evolved[8] – they are elements of the machinery through which it is
exercised. If as voters we have a right to know what our elected representatives are up to – and we do – then as readers, viewers and
listeners we have a right to know how those who inform us and influence our opinions behave also. Only then can we start to make sense
of all the allegations and counter-allegations of spin, bullying and the
illegitimate use of power and influence that both sides hurl at each
other at regular intervals.

Tony Blair and Gordon Brown didn't invent spin. The media was manipulated ruthlessly by or on behalf of David Lloyd George, Neville Chamberlain, Winston Churchill, Margaret Thatcher and most of the other prime ministers covered here. Anybody who thinks Rupert Murdoch has too much influence for a man whom nobody elected should take a look at what press barons like Lord Northcliffe and Lord Beaverbrook tried to do in the twenties and thirties. And while 'client journalism'[9] was a term first coined under New Labour to describe those who willingly enter the service of a politician or faction, it could have been used just as well at almost any point in the past hundred years. There were journalists and editors no less willing to give up their independence to serve Lloyd George, to protect Churchill, to idolise Margaret Thatcher or, far worse, to appease Adolf Hitler at the behest of Chamberlain. In the summer of 1918 the following advertisement appeared in the pages of *The Times*: 'PUBLICITY. – Experienced Journalist undertakes, with good results, Newspaper Publicity work for public men, philanthropic or business enterprises. – R.M., Fleet Street, E.C.4.' Today there is no need to advertise. Politicians and their advisers seek out and cultivate those who will do their publicity work for them.

Some cross the line unambiguously. Many of the most effective ministers of information and prime-ministerial press secretaries started their professional lives as journalists. Sir Bernard Ingham and Alastair Campbell are only the latest. They do it, in part at least, because politics can be addictive and power a notorious aphrodisiac. As Bill Deedes, who was an information minister under Harold Macmillan and later editor of the *Daily Telegraph*, put it somewhat quirkily, 'There is a great invisible struggle going on as to who really has the most power – the government or the newspapers. We don't even admit this to our own wives . . . There's a high sex drive on both sides.'[10]

Charles Hill, another former cabinet minister, who joined the ranks of the media, as chairman of the BBC, referred to the relationship as being like that between a husband and wife. 'The husband – the government – is older, and heavier than his wife, serious minded, a bit pompous, rather humourless and slow of speech . . . the wife – the press – is livelier, shrewder and more perceptive, wise to the ways of the world, quick of tongue and addicted to gossip. Of course, husband

and wife bicker: she often drives him to distraction. But he cannot do without her and he knows it.'[11] That sounds very sexist and rather dated now, but it is also a little too comfortable, implying that it's only natural for them to get into bed together.

The American writer H. L. Mencken famously said the relationship should be akin to that between a dog and a lamp-post, although he didn't say which was the dog and which the lamp-post. Animal imagery is always popular in the context of both professions. To Denis Thatcher journalists were 'reptiles'. Tony Blair characterised them as 'feral beasts'. For all their similarities, journalists and politicians are breeds apart. When they get too close it is like the coming together of a horse and a donkey. They might get some satisfaction out of it but the result is rarely attractive and invariably sterile. The only question, to be crude, is: who's screwing who? It's a question people have been asking ever since David Lloyd George first turned the gentler art of mutual flattery and persuasive discourse into the cruder practices of bullying and spin. With characteristic stubbornness the unwholesome by-products of unnatural relations between politicians and the media have delivered well-aimed kicks to the democratic system ever since.

In 1916, the year Lloyd George became prime minister, a man by the name of Kennedy Jones was elected to the House of Commons for the first time. Jones had helped found the *Daily Mail* alongside Alfred Harmsworth, later Lord Northcliffe, so when he wrote a book, *Fleet Street and Downing Street*, he knew what he was talking about. 'The root of the trouble,' he said, 'lies in the fact that each seeks to employ the other for its own ends, and each is aware of it. And so the two streets assume a semi-contemptuous attitude, each exaggerating its own value and importance and belittling the work and abilities of the other.'[12] His analysis of the way it worked and the risks it posed for the prime minister of the day are no less pertinent today. 'A daily paper thrives on news. The government and its departments have in their possession news – valuable news. This is the way and these the means whereby Downing Street by skilful manipulation has always sought to dominate Fleet Street. In neither street is there any deficiency of brains. Fleet Street is conscious of how it may be worked, but knows its worth and puts a price on its publicity. If Downing Street refuses to pay what it may consider an exorbitant fee there is trouble. The two spring apart like a broken bow, and henceforth, until the fracture is mended a perpetual jangle ensues.' It is a jangle that has regularly disturbed the peace at Westminster ever since those words were written.

Some of the prime ministers covered here understood the media particularly well because they had worked as professional journalists themselves, among them David Lloyd George, Ramsay MacDonald and Winston Churchill. The young Harold Wilson applied for a job on the *Guardian*, and even Ted Heath was once news editor of the *Church Times*, although it wasn't something he bragged about later. No doubt Tony Blair and Gordon Brown could have made a living writing for newspapers, although probably at different ends of the market. They all preferred to go into politics because they believed that was where the real power – the power to make things happen and change people's lives – lay. The power of the media, such as it was, deserved respect but never held the same attraction.

Those who control so much of the news fascinate those who make so much of the news and vice versa. Prime ministers believe they are in office to exercise power but they live with the fear that men whom nobody elected might snatch it from them. At the root of that fear is a deeper anxiety. Who is best able to reflect and to shape public opinion? As Kennedy Jones understood, 'There is an obvious similarity between the politician and the journalist, in that for his success each is dependent on gauging aright the popular mind.'[13] Which is why any modern prime minister will use whatever means he can get away with to secure a good press. As James Harding, editor of *The Times*, acknowledged, 'spin is not, in and of itself, a sin. There is something Luddite about the popular tendency to bemoan modern, media-savvy politics and remember with misplaced nostalgia a lost age of intelligent public debate. To rail against focus groups and polling, artful speechwriters and rapid rebuttal, targeted messaging and expensive advertising, is to wish that politics can live out of time. The politician who eschews spin is as self-denying as the farmer who shuns fertiliser.'[14] As long ago as 1919 Kennedy Jones was warning of the dangers that spin, although he wouldn't have recognised the word, presented for journalists. Trouble would follow whenever 'Fleet Street lends itself for any reason whatsoever to the manipulations of Downing Street, and allows its daily news to be garnished by the clever fingers of the Government or the ministers of the day.'[15] Today that news is garnished constantly and not always in a manner that Jones could have predicted. Clever fingers are put to work to try to whip up the kind of stories Number 10 believes the voters want to read. No longer content to dole out the valuable news at its disposal to those journalists who can be trusted to repackage it appropriately, Downing Street now creates valueless news in order to satisfy a perceived demand. Like candyfloss, stories are spun from very little to appear larger and more eye-catching than they really are. Along the way the distinction between the public interest and what interests the public is quickly forgotten.

The intention may have been to try to reconnect what politicians say with what the majority of the public are thought to care about, but the consequence led directly to the disillusionment with all politics that was expressed so vocally in Britain during the expenses crisis. James Harding had already predicted as much when he warned that, 'Spin reinforced a vicious circle of suspicion in politics, while a calculating politician, a cynical media, and a distrusting public reinforced one another to hollow out the national conversation.'[16]

Governments have become so alarmed that the public are switching off from politics that prime ministers will now engage with any passing media fancy rather than risk appearing remote. What started almost tongue-in-cheek when Tony Blair called for the release from prison of a person who didn't actually exist, *Coronation Street*'s Deirdre Rachid, has become a matter of habit. Gordon Brown clearly thought somebody would be impressed that he had taken time out from dealing with the global economic crisis and the expenses scandal to call Simon Cowell and ask after the health of the talent-show contestant Susan Boyle.[17] By indulging the whims of popular journalism Downing Street has squandered its greatest asset – the authority of the office of prime minister. Where once the prime minister's words had scarcity value and were listened to with care, they are now devalued to such an extent that they jostle for attention alongside those of anybody else with access to the media. Worse. When they are heard they are often treated as toxic, never to be taken at face value, only to be handled as one, almost certainly unreliable, version of the truth.

It is tempting to put all the blame on the politicians, but Professor David Marquand makes a persuasive case for pinning a sizeable share of responsibility on the emergence of a 'new media elite, more arrogant and self-serving, less civilised and far more aggressive than the ones it had replaced . . . Like Beaverbrook and Northcliffe, Murdoch and lesser moguls such as the latest Lord Rothermere and (until his disgrace) Conrad Black sought power without responsibility. They faced fewer obstacles than their predecessors had done. They had no other elites to contend with and, in the fluid cultures of the late twentieth and early twenty-first centuries, there was an insatiable appetite for easily digested information, titillation and opinion, the commodities in which they dealt.'[18] On this analysis the media stand alongside Downing Street as the two great powers in the land. Little wonder, then, that they are so obsessed with one another.

It is true that, if we exclude the increasingly common presence of babies and young children in the Downing Street flat, the media are unique in their ability to keep prime ministers awake at night. They are also proof that Lord Hailsham's aphorism about 'the elective dictatorship'[19] is only partly true. Dictators close down newspapers they don't like; prime ministers just wish they could. It's more than thirty years since Hailsham gave the lecture that brought the phrase to prominence. Since then prime-ministerial power has only increased further. The position carries with it more executive authority than any other in the democratic world. When our system is described as 'presidential' it underestimates the truth. With a secure majority in the House of Commons and the support or acquiescence of the cabinet, the prime minister is subject to few of the checks and balances that constrain, for example, the President of the United States. The other powers in the land, the House of Lords, the courts, the monarchy, can all be overruled if necessary. Mercifully the military never flexes it muscles, no matter how unhappy its leaders may be with their civilian bosses. And even when the occupant of Downing Street is a devout Christian the Church can be safely ignored.

There is one thing that will make a prime minister stop and think before taking action and that is a bad headline or the fear of one. We should probably be grateful for that. A free and vigorous media is essential in any democracy, and all the more so when there are few other constraints on the executive. The prime-ministerial beauty sleep remains undisturbed by thoughts of overmighty bishops or monarchs, and over that first cup of coffee it is not the proceedings of the previous day's debates in the Upper House or the court reports that are scanned for danger signs. If there is a threat it is more likely to be contained within the daily summary produced by the government's media-monitoring unit.

This document, which runs to several pages, is the single most widely read report inside Number 10 and throughout Whitehall. That fact alone tells us almost all we need to know about the sensitivity of the government to what the media have to say. The politicians and civil servants aren't scanning the report to discover the news. If they are any good at their jobs they know most of that already. They are looking to see what the media have to say about the performance of the government, its ministers and, most significantly, the prime minister. We have become used to a media that devotes fewer and fewer resources to finding out and telling us what's going on in the world and more and more to either predicting what might happen or commenting on what already has. If anything this should make prime ministers sleep a little easier. There are so many columnists and commentators now, all of them competing to have something original to say, that the influence of any one individual or newspaper is greatly reduced. The impact of the internet has accelerated a trend that was already well under way. The days of 'The Thunderer', when an editorial in *The Times* could shake empires, are long gone and thank goodness. Prime ministers do worry about what the papers say, however, or at least they have people to worry for them, because in the broad fabric of competing opinions a common thread almost always emerges. Collectively the media can help define a premiership. They can't fabricate its defining characteristics but they can amplify them. As the former *Daily Mirror* director Hugh Cudlipp, one of the great figures of twentieth-century popular journalism, recognised: 'A newspaper may successfully accelerate but never reverse the popular attitude which common sense has commended to the public.'[20]

For a new prime minister, time is of the essence. Walter Mondale, whose presidential ambitions in the United States were swept aside by the 'great communicator' Ronald Reagan, put it well when he said, 'Political image is like mixing cement. When it's wet you can move it around and shape it, but at some point it hardens and there's almost nothing you can do to reshape it.'[21] Thus Thatcher was strong but wouldn't listen. Major was weak and had no firm beliefs. Blair was willing to say anything to court popularity. Gordon Brown is an interesting case. The cement appeared to have set, leaving him looking forever like a man who had struggled and failed to measure up to the job he'd always coveted. Then the world changed around him and he had a rare opportunity to reshape his image into something less belittling. For a while he seemed to have some success but then found himself being sucked back into the same mould.

This obsession with image has led some, like Professor Bob Franklin, to believe that 'Britain has become a "media democracy" in which politicians and policies are packaged for media marketing and public consumption'.[22] In 1997 Richard Eyre, then director of the National Theatre, suggested that 'all politics has declined to the condition of show business, and all politicians have been obliged to become performers. They choose their costumes carefully, their décor fastidiously; their fellow actors and agents; they study their scripts, they rehearse, they put on make-up and they give performances; they adapt their acting styles from the would-be intimacy of the small screen to the not-to-be-avoided histrionics of the public platform; and sometimes, often disastrously, they improvise.'[23] Roy Hattersley was already out of date when he put the opposite view a year earlier: 'Performance, the theatre of politics, is an essentially supplementary activity.'[24] He quoted Stephen Sondheim on grand opera to ask, 'What sort of show is it that regards the singer as more important than the song?' Sadly we now know the answer. It is the show that has been on the road for so long that its big numbers have been reduced to the status of lift music. Nobody is listening any more.

Why has this happened? Because most prime ministers, encouraged by the legions of press advisers and pollsters that surround them, have come to believe that journalists are far more powerful than they really are. That belief has, in itself, strengthened the media and weakened the office of prime minister. And, in the process, far from winning the approval of the media, it has earned politicians in general and prime ministers in particular a mixture of ridicule and contempt. Having seen politicians demean themselves as they scrabble for their favour, the media have reported the sound bites and broadcast the pretty pictures but lost any respect they might once have had for those who supply them. It is hardly surprising that the public has followed suit.

Yet it is a consistent feature of the long battle for supremacy between Downing Street and the media that those prime ministers who fretted most about getting the support of the media not only failed to keep it, but also performed less well in office as a consequence of trying. Harold Wilson may have won four general elections out of five but much too much of his time was wasted obsessing about what journalists wrote and plotting his revenge on those who displeased him. Even in the 1960s his friends thought he was going 'mildly off his rocker'[25] in the process, long before there was any evidence of actual dementia. Anthony Eden and John Major were also among the worst offenders. Memoirs and diaries from the time of their administrations, in the 1950s and 1990s respectively, are full of references to their constant preoccupation with what was being said about them. Gordon Brown has demonstrated an excessive sensitivity to media criticism, sometimes publicly and much more often in private. And like the others he has been a less successful prime minister as a consequence. Tony Blair's relationship with journalists was the most fascinating of all. He often said that complaining about the media was like complaining about the weather. It didn't make it any better. Blair used journalists to help him achieve much that he set out to do, but failed to pursue some of his most ambitious dreams in part, at least, because he thought the attempt would cost him too much support in the media.

In their different ways, and in the face of very different challenges, the prime ministers of the past hundred years who had the greatest impact were also those who fretted least about the media: Margaret Thatcher because she didn't need to, Winston Churchill because he had more important things to do, and Clement Attlee because he simply wasn't interested. Both Thatcher and Churchill had the benefit of powerful friends in Fleet Street willing to do much of their work for them. They themselves recognised the importance of a good image but had no intention of ceding to journalists one ounce of real power. Indeed, Thatcher used the media to increase her own strength and gathered journalists as courtiers to help win her battles and vanquish her foes, all at a modest cost to her that was the best bargain in British politics. Her success has had a profound effect on everyone who has occupied Downing Street since her tearful exit in 1990. John Major, Tony Blair and Gordon Brown all believed that her success in winning so much support, not to say adulation, in the press was the key to her electoral success. As a result they exaggerated the power of the media and paid a heavy price for it. The election of 1992 had a profound effect on each of them, too. That contest, in which John Major triumphed against the odds, was followed by the claim that 'It's The *Sun* Wot Won It'.[26] It was by no means the first such assertion by the press. In close to half the general elections since the First World War one newspaper or another has claimed to have swung the result. If you believed every press baron's boast then Lloyd George, Attlee and Wilson, to name but three, would never have become prime minister without them. The history that follows weighs up the evidence but not once is the case for media supremacy proven. It doesn't make for such a catchy headline but elections are won or lost by parties and their rival candidates for the post of prime minister not by the media.

It is between elections when the media wields its greatest influence. Here there is clear evidence of proprietors and editors trying to exercise real political power that went way beyond the entirely honourable pursuit of campaigning journalism. Wealthy newspaper owners have not been content with throwing their weight behind a particular cause or even a particular party. On occasions they have entered the political fray themselves, launching campaigns with candidates in by-elections and massive propaganda offensives designed to reverse government policy and even force a change of government itself. More often than not they have been humiliated. When it comes to individuals, they have certainly succeeded in hounding ministers from office, sometimes with good cause, sometimes not. As for prime ministers, however, they have always failed. The media alone have never created a prime minister and never destroyed one. Where they have succeeded all too often is in convincing prime ministers that they, the media, are more powerful than they really are. You can't blame them for trying but more fool the politicians for believing it. As Eleanor Roosevelt said, admittedly in a different context, 'No one can make you feel inferior without your consent.'[27]

It is when prime ministers feel they owe something to the media that the weakness sets in. David Lloyd George was never given to feelings of inferiority, but after he ousted Herbert Asquith in a coup in which the newspapers were key players he never escaped their grasp. Peter Hennessy observed that, 'by the change of administration in 1997, sensitivity towards the media had infected governmental life so deeply and comprehensively that its contagion affected and distorted virtually every aspect'. But if we want to look for the moment when the virus of media fixation first entered the political bloodstream then the darkest days of the First World War are as good a place as any to start. It was then that the struggle for supremacy was first joined in earnest, a struggle that even now remains unresolved.

PART ONE

PRIME MINISTERS V. THE MEDIA:

THE CONTEST TURNS PROFESSIONAL

1

WAR AND PEACE: LLOYD GEORGE (1916–22)

Politicians are like monkeys. The higher they climb the more revolting are the parts they expose.

Gwilym Lloyd-George

When David Lloyd George supplanted Herbert Asquith in December 1916, Downing Street opened its doors for the first time to the modern age of the media-conscious prime minister. Previous holders of the post had without doubt cultivated an image and revelled in the attention of the press. The dandy Benjamin Disraeli, the war hero Lord Wellington, the precocious and aloof William Pitt the Younger were all in their own ways larger-than-life politicians. What made Lloyd George different was that, while the others drew strength from how they were perceived, he depended on his image for his very survival. It was his making and ultimately it was his undoing. Historically his misfortune is to be forever associated with that image, and in particular the less edifying aspects of it, rather than for his many achievements. Prime ministers can never escape responsibility for how they are remembered and Lloyd George is certainly no exception. He made no objection when people expected great things of him and had no cause for complaint when they felt let down. His oratory was mesmerising but he, like so many others with an instinctive gift for communication, found that what he did mattered more than what he said. Many of the defining characteristics of what we now call 'spin' first emerged during his time in high office and, as ever, there was a price to pay.

Lloyd George had a clear strategy for dealing with the press: 'What you can't square, you squash. What you can't squash, you square.'[1] He had little choice. Having deposed the Liberal leader, Herbert Asquith, he became a prime minister without a party. Without any of the usual ties of loyalty to sustain him in office, he kept the part as long as he looked the part. He was the first also to learn the hard way that journalists love nothing better than to build you up in order to knock you down. As Bernard Ingham, Margaret Thatcher's press secretary, put it eighty years after Lloyd George's fall from grace, 'common sense (and hard experience) teaches that the media worm always eventually turns on a government and consumes even the hand that feeds it'.[2]

It all started so well. At the outset of his premiership Lloyd George was nothing short of a national celebrity. His face was everywhere, in the papers, on posters, in films and in endless cartoons. There was a star quality about him that captivated some and deeply unsettled others. With his great fluency, his easy manner, the twinkle in his eye and his unstuffy, direct way of speaking he reached out to and inspired people who didn't normally pay much attention to politicians. In many ways he was the Tony Blair of his day.

In some respects the similarities between the two men are uncanny. Once in power Lloyd George tore up the rulebook. He was a man in a hurry, interested only in what would get things done. He was soon accused of running a presidential style of government, of circumventing the traditional civil service and relying heavily on his personal advisers. He wanted to break the mould of the old party system where he had never felt comfortable and took a positive pleasure in just being different. All of which was manna to Fleet Street. Here was a prime minister who gave them what they wanted, good copy. He made news with almost everything he said and everything he did. The newspapers lapped it up and he courted them as none of his predecessors had ever done.

Like other prime ministers who enjoyed, for a while at least, powerful support in the press, Lloyd George was a strong and determined war leader. The reason normally loyal Conservative newspapers, as well as others sympathetic to his own Liberal party, backed him was the belief that he would do better than Asquith at waging all-out war. It was not what he went into politics to do. As chancellor, his determination to push through a Budget to fund radical social reforms, including the first old-age pensions and sickness benefits, helped break the blocking powers of the House of Lords. He brought the same resolution to the conduct of the war, believing in victory at almost any cost. In the face of bloody reverses and unimaginable horrors on the battlefields of France and Belgium he never lost the will to fight to the end.

Like Blair, when he finally resigned in 1922 Lloyd George was seen to be tarnished goods. He was a huge figure on the international stage, preoccupied with the politics of the big powers but devoting much time and energy to trying to find a peaceful settlement in Ireland, the Middle East and, yes, even what is now Iraq. But at home his government had lost its authority and was haemorrhaging credibility. Personally he was mired in scandal over the granting of honours, from peerages to humble knighthoods, in return for cash. The press lords had done very nicely out of his honours lists without even having to dip into their pockets but that didn't restrain them from self-righteous indignation. When the newspapers turned on him he had few friends left to sympathise with his plight. His enemies, some of whom had been happy to serve under him when the going was good, shook their heads sagely and said he had supped with the devil and was now paying the price. If the newspaper proprietors with whom he had both flirted and sparred proved to be fair-weather friends, then more fool him.

We shouldn't get too carried away by the parallels. At least Tony Blair won a general election fair and square to get the top job. The media may have fallen for his charms, but it was the voters who gave him his mandate. Whereas, to his dying day Asquith believed Lloyd George had ousted him in a coup driven by the newspapers. The claims of some arrogant press barons helped convince him he was right. But the media didn't make Lloyd George prime minister any more than they would, eighty years later, put Blair into Downing Street. What they did for both was to give them crucial support while they established themselves in office. To Blair, who had little love for the party he led, and to Lloyd George, who was disowned by the Liberals the moment he entered Number 10, the support of the press provided important breathing space. It was raw politics that brought each of them down. Lloyd George fell because the Conservative party that had supported him as an expedient no longer had any use for him. He may have disappointed the traditionalists in his own party but at least he was a great believer in the traditions of parliament. So much so that he remained an MP for twenty-three years after resigning as prime minister. Tony Blair quit the Commons the very same day.

The press tired of both men, as they always do of such individuals, but in the eighty years that separated their two governments the nature of the media changed out of all recognition. Fortunately for Lloyd George he governed in a more respectful age, one when private vices rarely made it on to the front pages. He wouldn't have survived five minutes with the popular press of today. He was the first man of truly humble origins, and, incidentally, the first and only Welshman, to make it to the top of what Disraeli first dubbed 'the greasy pole'. He was always conscious that he lacked the private means that sustained so many of his colleagues and shamelessly lined his own pockets once he got there, leaving office far wealthier than when he entered it. Shame was not a word that appeared to feature in his private lexicon. In the drawing rooms of polite society, where he never fitted in, he was known as 'the goat'. His personal life reflected his general disregard for the rules of convention. He lived openly with his mistress, his secretary Frances Stevenson, and saw little reason to curb his enthusiasm for sexual philandering other than to keep his wife, who stayed at home in Wales for much of the time, from erupting. Yet none of it appeared in the press.

Later in life he hosted a private dinner at a London hotel. The guests included Sir Oswald Mosley, the British fascist leader. Mosley remarked, 'this will hit the roof if it gets out'. Lloyd George was unruffled as ever, replying, 'My dear boy, if everything I have done in this hotel during the last forty years had got out, you have no idea how many times I would have had to retire from politics.'[3] The relationship between the press and politics then and now is as different as a top hat to a hoodie.

Today's newspapers may be partisan, prurient and prejudiced, but in the first quarter of the twentieth century many were either the playthings of proprietors or the prostitutes of parties. From the point of view of the political classes, they were not so much domesticated animals as part of the family. Many of the great titles – some we would still recognise, others that have long since disappeared – were joined at the hip to either the Conservative or Liberal establishments. In some cases this reflected the views of the millionaire press barons who controlled them. Others didn't just lap up the propaganda of the side they supported out of loyalty, they were as good as owned by them, subsidiary holdings of the party organisations. Before long this shabby business would be on the wane. Newspapers would become more expensive to own and the parties' pockets weren't deep enough to keep up. With a wider readership came advertising revenues that bought political independence. Relations between Downing Street and Fleet Street were soon to get a great deal more fractious, but when Lloyd George was catapulted into Downing Street in December 1916, press support was still a commodity that could be bought and sold.

Newspapers were rarely profitable and so were easy pickings for wealthy men. The Liberal chief whip and the Tory party chairman saw it as part of their jobs to find well-heeled supporters to act as front men, investing in titles that would otherwise go under or, worse still, fall into the hands of the other side. So the Liberals effectively owned the *Westminster Gazette*, a very influential evening paper despite having few readers outside London, the *Daily News*, less overtly political but more widely read, and the best-selling *Daily Chronicle*. The Tories had the snobbish *Morning Post*, the *Pall Mall Gazette*, the *Daily Telegraph* and the *Observer* as well as dozens of regional titles including the *Yorkshire Post*. Conservative-party money was also sunk into the *Daily Express* through a Canadian-born Tory MP by the name of Max Aitken.

Aitken was an extraordinary character, now remembered as one of the great press barons of the twentieth century but then more interested in playing kingmaker than proprietor. He may have been a

Conservative but it was Lloyd George who turned him into him Lord
Beaverbrook in 1917. On Christmas Day the new prime minister sat
down to lunch with Sir George Riddell, chairman of the *News of the
World*. 'I see that Max Aitken has got his peerage,' remarked the newspaperman. Lloyd George laughed heartily. 'Yes, my first peer! He had
a great deal to do with the formation of the government.'[4] Lloyd
George enjoyed the company of men like Beaverbrook and Riddell.
Their trade fascinated him. A few years later Beaverbrook penned
some reflections on Lloyd George and his dealings with the press. 'Mr
Lloyd George,' he observed, 'falls into the class neither of the sensitive nor of the indifferent. He is himself too much a part of the
movements of popular opinion to be unduly resentful of its blame or
to be scornful of its praise. He frankly accepts press criticism as one
of the most important presentations of the national mind . . . He likes
a good press like a shopkeeper likes a good customer.' And in words
that could be used to describe many of those who became prime minister after him, Lloyd George was judged to be 'over-subtle in
studying the press . . . He reads too much into what is often merely
the result of haste, accident or coincidence. He searches for a motive
in every paragraph.'[5]

Beaverbrook will feature heavily in the story of the battles between
Downing Street and Fleet Street over the next thirty years but at first
it was by no means clear in which of the two streets he would make
his name. He got involved in newspapers only because he was very
rich and his Tory masters wanted his money to help them buy influence. He wrote a cheque for £25,000 to the editor of the *Express* on
the steps of the Monte Carlo casino in 1911 at the request of Andrew
Bonar Law, a fellow Canadian and leader of the Conservative party.
The same year the Tories offered him a knighthood. He was told it was
'for the purpose of rewarding me for services to come',[6] an unusual
interpretation of the honours system to say the least. They wanted to
keep him sweet so that they could use his money again for the same
purpose. But he was a slippery character and in 1916 he took a controlling interest in the *Express* on his own behalf not the party's. The
date was significant, which is why he kept what he'd done secret. It
coincided with the coup that put Lloyd George into power. Had it

been made public, Asquith and his supporters would have had yet more evidence for their theory of a press conspiracy.

Not all newspapers relied on party money. The *Manchester Guardian*, then owned and edited by the magisterial C. P. Scott (who first declared that 'comment is free but facts are sacred'), was Liberal out of conviction and its support all the more valuable for not being bought. On the other side the *Daily Mail* and *The Times* backed the Tories without being paid to do so. They were owned by the other great press baron of the time, Alfred Harmsworth, 1st Viscount Northcliffe, the father of modern popular journalism.

In his last few years Lord Northcliffe's grasp on reality would slip away from him. Before his death in 1922 he was to be found driving about in his blue Rolls-Royce, firing off shots from his revolver at imaginary enemies, ranting about assassination attempts with poisoned ice cream and calling his editors at all times of the night to demand that they sack most of their staff. In 1916 he was merely power crazy. He didn't much like politicians and he was very happy to be thought both cleverer and more powerful than they were. Northcliffe once tried on Napoleon's hat and wasn't joking when he said he'd make a better emperor. Merely deposing prime ministers was clearly well within his assessment of his own strength and ability. The morning after Lloyd George's victory Northcliffe rang his younger brother Cecil, then MP for Luton. Had he seen that day's *Morning Post*? The paper's headline was in the form of a question. 'Who Killed Cock Robin?' it asked, referring to Asquith's demise. 'You did!' replied Cecil, telling his brother exactly what he wanted to hear.

Yet in his more considered moments, even Northcliffe was forced to admit that Asquith's days were numbered with or without the influence of the press. There was intrigue, certainly, but the main players were politicians not newspapermen. The papers didn't make Lloyd George prime minister but the events of 1916 proved a major turning point nonetheless and they are worth looking at in detail. For the first time the media played a significant, though not decisive, role in deciding who should occupy Number 10. The struggle for supremacy between Fleet Street and Downing Street was suddenly much more evenly balanced. From then on, like two arm wrestlers who refuse to give up, first one then the other might appear to have the upper hand but neither would ever walk away the undisputed winner.

Lloyd George's accession was no ordinary transfer of power. It was a coup against the serving prime minister in the middle of a war. The myth that newspapers can make or break prime ministers was born with Asquith's own conviction that an overmighty press had been responsible for his demise. He did what all powerful men do when they come a cropper: he looked for somebody else to blame. Lloyd George had certainly cultivated the press although he claimed never to have wanted the job but only to change the way the war was being run. In April 1916 he had invited C. P. Scott to his house outside London and had shown the great man a letter. It was his resignation from Asquith's government. Scott was duly impressed and urged him to go to the back benches where he could be more effective in opposing the current strategy. The letter was never sent, but by the time the crisis came to a head eight months later Scott and others who had been taken into Lloyd George's confidence had no doubt that his opposition to Asquith was principled and not opportunistic. Despite all the newspaper criticism of his war strategy, or lack of it, Asquith continued to get enough personal support in the Liberal-owned press to mislead him about the strength of his position. He was a politician from a different age, hopelessly ill equipped for the task in hand. Eventually he had to go because his policy was wrong, not because the papers said it was.

Asquith had always been dismissive of journalists, saying even of those who supported him 'the Liberal press is written by boobies for boobies'.[7] He was aloof and had nothing of the common touch. Above all, he was a gent when his rival was clearly anything but. Asquith's bland but easy style had worked well in peacetime. Now that the country was waging a war of unprecedented brutality he looked out of place. He enjoyed country weekends out of town with his formidable second wife, Margot, and on weeknights MPs couldn't help but notice that he was a bit the worse for drink. They nicknamed him 'Squiffy' and the word soon entered the popular vocabulary. He had a proud record of domestic reform to his name, but he liked to work by lengthy discussion and compromise. And that, thought Lloyd George and his standard bearers in Fleet Street, was no way to run a war.

We have become used to seeing contemporary political crises played out in the TV and radio studios and in December 1916 it was to the media of the day that the main players turned to watch the latest instalments in the crisis unfold. Fleet Street became a player in its own right because the politicians made it one. It was hardly surprising, then, if, in the aftermath, the press exaggerated its own role in what had happened and the losing side chose to believe it. One reason events took Asquith by surprise was that there weren't supposed to be sides. Since May 1915 the Conservative party had been in coalition with the Liberals to demonstrate national unity and aid the war effort. He had hoped that the two parties would bring their supporters in the press together too in the kind of patriotic alliance of opinion that all wartime premiers crave. Unfortunately for Asquith, one man in particular stood outside that cosy consensus and his newspapers were so widely read that they were able to drag Fleet Street opinion in quite a different direction.

Lord Northcliffe had a healthy contempt for much of what went on at Westminster and was interested only in producing successful and popular newspapers. Whenever he allowed himself to get too close to those in power he always regretted it. J. A. Spender, editor of the *Westminster Gazette*, recalled a train journey with him after the war. 'He spoke bitterly about the ingratitude of politicians and their tortuous ways, and said that journalists had far better stick to their newspapers and give them a wide berth.'[8] Northcliffe controlled half the circulation of the entire London press with papers at both ends of the market. The *Daily Mail*, which remains in the hands of his descendants even now, was then a broadsheet but already intent on barking its strident views as aggressively as it could. It was hugely successful and had the largest daily circulation in the country. *The Times* was less widely read but often considered to be 'the voice of the nation'. Northcliffe, not unlike Rupert Murdoch, put his stamp very firmly on the mass-circulation paper while letting *The Times* enjoy a greater measure of editorial freedom. But unlike Murdoch he gave his editors hell on a daily basis. When he didn't get his way he was capable of furious rages. His refusal to follow any party line and his willingness to attack without mercy anybody who he felt was letting the country down made him at the same time feared, despised and mistrusted. Beaverbrook, who would vie with him for the credit for deposing Asquith, although by different means, said simply that he was the greatest figure who ever strode down Fleet Street.

In 1916 the influence of Northcliffe and his fellow proprietors was at a peak as a direct result of the war. As the casualty lists from the front started to be published, newspaper readership rose significantly. The creation of the coalition government had largely closed down debate about the war at Westminster, creating a vacuum the papers were more than ready to fill. In Lloyd George's own assessment, 'the press has performed the function which should have been performed by parliament'.[9]

The papers had been in a truculent mood almost from the outbreak of war thanks to the first serious attempt by a British government at media management. Lloyd George may have been the first prime minister to suffer from a fixation with the media, but Herbert Asquith had been the first to try to fix what they wrote in a systematic way. He learned a lesson that many future prime ministers would have to relearn. If you make life difficult for journalists and try to tell them what they should be reporting, they will make life twice as difficult for you when they get the chance. Realising that public opinion was likely to play a far bigger role in this conflict than it ever had previously, Asquith's government had set up two agencies to control access to official information. The first was the 'press bureau', designed as the conduit through which 'all information relating to the war which any of the departments of state think right to issue is communicated to the press'. The second was the Foreign Office news department. Both were presented as attempts to help journalists by giving them easier access to the facts. Except that it didn't work like that. News desks were getting more information about how the war was going from their sources in Berlin and elsewhere than they were from either agency at home. The Liberal editors protested in private, but the Tory press was on the rampage. Asquith met a delegation of editors to hear their complaints and, according to one, conceded there was some evidence 'of news and particularly bad news being kept back or mutilated'. Nothing much changed as a result of the meeting except that the stock of goodwill towards the prime minister depleted still further. J. A. Spender of the *Westminster Gazette* was the nearest thing Asquith had to a real friend in

Fleet Street and even he agreed that the system had been 'corrupting to the press, and a fatal snare to politicians'.

The quest for reliable information, and for the secrets the censors didn't want published, brought Northcliffe into contact with a young Australian by the name of Keith Murdoch. Murdoch's son would later eclipse him in the history of the trade but it is not hard to see where Rupert's flair for self-promotion and thirst for power came from. Keith Murdoch had been with the ANZAC troops at Gallipoli, in part as a journalist, but also as an agitator and unofficial representative of the man who would go on to become Australia's prime minister, another Welshman, Billy Hughes. Murdoch's accounts of the incompetence and corruption of the British officer class were not exactly dispassionate or even-handed and were largely based on generalisations. In one famous letter he described 'high officers and conceited young cubs who are plainly only playing at war'.[10] But Northcliffe was delighted. He used Gallipoli as an example of Asquith's ineffectual war leadership and after the troops were successfully evacuated at the end of 1915 *The Times* even hailed Murdoch as 'the journalist who stopped a war'.[11]

On the Western Front Northcliffe had a different issue with which to fight back against the censors. No amount of obfuscation could cover up the fact that Britain's troops in the trenches were desperately short of munitions. Through the *Daily Mail* in particular, Northcliffe blamed Asquith and, even more so, his war secretary, Lord Kitchener. Kitchener may have been the poster boy of the war – YOUR COUNTRY NEEDS YOU! and all that – but he was failing to deliver and Northcliffe's papers said so in no uncertain terms. To attack the prosecution of a war while it's still going on is to invite the charge of giving succour to the enemy, and so it was for Northcliffe. Copies of the *Daily Mail* were ceremoniously burned at the London Stock Exchange and the paper was banned from the service clubs of Pall Mall after a particularly sharp attack on Lord Kitchener. Northcliffe was convinced the war secretary was retaliating by having people spy on him, tap his phones and open his letters. Whether this was true or an early sign of his paranoia, Northcliffe wasn't a man to be silenced by intimidation, real or imagined.

In any case he knew that most Tory MPs and some Liberals,

including Lloyd George, agreed with him. The unofficial alliance against his own leader between Lloyd George and the press was already starting to take shape by the time Asquith announced the formation of his grand coalition with the Conservatives in May 1915. Lloyd George was made minister of munitions but, despite Northcliffe's campaign, Kitchener kept his job in overall control of the war effort. Asquith wasn't going to let Northcliffe or anybody else decide the composition of his government, although by the autumn of 1915 he was ready to dismiss Kitchener in his own time. Ironically, it was the press who stopped him doing so. On 6 November 1915 the *Globe* had the scoop that Kitchener was for the chop. Like some of the best scoops, it was true at the time. The government, as governments do, felt obliged to deny it and then went further, banning the newspaper from publishing for two weeks. When it reappeared it had to print a statement to the effect that there were 'no grounds of dissension between Kitchener and his colleagues'. It was balderdash, as everybody in the know was aware. The government was denying the truth and bullying the press into printing what it knew to be false.

There's no evidence that Lloyd George had given the *Globe* the story but only collective cabinet responsibility prevented him from agreeing publicly that Kitchener should be sacked. Conservative members of the coalition suffered the same constraints. In A. J. P. Taylor's words, 'this was the perfect government, if the object of politics be to silence criticism'.[12] But it didn't last long. Many on the back benches in all parties were deeply unhappy with the conspiracy of silence at the top. They were not convinced Asquith's coalition would bring the end to the war any closer. That Lloyd George was getting on quickly with the job of increasing the supply of shells did not go unnoticed in the tea rooms of Westminster or a mile or so away in the newsrooms of Fleet Street. People were starting to ask what he could do for the war effort as a whole if he was given the chance.

Asquith was living on borrowed time but he alone seemed oblivious to the fact. Again it is worth quoting his closest newspaper ally, J. A. Spender: 'Asquith never could be got to see that his peacetime method of silence and magnanimity and leaving-the-country-to-judge would not avail him in war, and in spite of many urgings he would neither meet his press critics and conciliate them nor reply to them in public. Everyone in the world, certainly everyone in Fleet Street, seemed to know what was afoot in the autumn and winter of 1916, but it was useless to take warnings to Downing Street. Asquith was still persuaded that all his geese were swans, and all his colleagues loyal, and that anything which appeared to suggest to the contrary was either a heated imagination or the malicious gossip of Fleet Street.'[13]

Lloyd George was playing an altogether different game. While Asquith shunned journalists, Lloyd George courted them. And how. Tony Blair famously flew to the other side of the world to charm Rupert Murdoch. Lloyd George didn't have to go so far but he too was accused of flirting with his party's traditional enemies. The *Daily Mail* was ready to back anybody who would take the fight to the enemy with conviction and Northcliffe had his eye on Lloyd George. It had the makings of a dangerous alliance. Sir George Riddell warned Lloyd George to his face that 'the Liberal journalists are very suspicious of you. They hate Northcliffe so much that they will not scruple to attack you and your policy if you identify with him.'[14]

Lloyd George was media savvy enough to be aware of the risks. In all likelihood the Conservative papers would drop him and go back to their natural allies just as soon as it suited them. He knew the Tory establishment despised him. According to the editor of the *Daily News*, A. G. Gardiner, he had long been seen by them as yet another affliction that threatened society, 'sometimes it was the black death, sometimes the small-pox, now it was Mr Lloyd George'.[15] They remembered that he'd been virtually a pacifist during the Boer War and had always championed the poor against the rich. He was in danger of alienating his true supporters to win the fickle backing of new ones. Already his support for all-out war against Germany had led his radical friends to believe the Conservatives had captured him and it made him very uncomfortable.

To redress the balance Lloyd George did his best to court C. P. Scott at the *Manchester Guardian*. Scott thought of himself as the conscience of true Liberalism and wasn't easily persuaded but eventually he succumbed. Lloyd George also made it his business to befriend Robert Donald, editor of the ultra-Liberal *Daily Chronicle*, who would become an even more valuable ally when the time came. He even invested much time trying to win over W. Robertson Nicholl, the editor and publisher of the non-conformist *British Weekly*, a journal with a derisory readership but one made up of just the kind of people who had once adored the Welsh Wizard.

At the other end of the circulation graph, Lloyd George had strong supporters among those who controlled the best-selling Sunday papers: not only Riddell at the *News of the World*, even then a hugely popular and profitable title, but also Sir Henry Dalziel, proprietor of *Reynolds' News*. Riddell was another of those curious Fleet Street grandees who, like Beaverbrook, was willing to trade proximity to power for the promise that nothing he learned there would be published without permission. He was also very generous with his own money. Peter Mandelson would have to resign from Tony Blair's cabinet over a home loan from a ministerial colleague. Lloyd George made it to be prime minister despite accepting both a car and the lease on a five-bedroom house from a Fleet Street editor. And without an expenses form or allowance claim in sight.

In terms of newspaper influence the laid-back prime minister was now massively outgunned by his wily, hyperactive lieutenant. To a modern eye it looks like nothing other than a man carefully laying the ground until the time came to strike. The nearest parallel is perhaps Michael Heseltine, another Welshman, working the media assiduously while he waited to launch his bid to topple Margaret Thatcher. Lord Buckmaster, the solicitor-general, who was in charge of the press bureau, complained that 'many of the more powerful newspapers' had been benefiting from a kind of backstairs patronage making 'the proper execution of my duties extremely difficult'. In his assessment, 'there were people anxious to secure newspaper support who, in return for press favours, were friends of the newspapers when difficulties arose'.[16] Lloyd George wasn't the only suspect but his Liberal colleagues couldn't help but notice the favourable comments he was getting in traditionally Conservative papers. He professed his loyalty to Asquith and no smoking gun has ever been produced to show that he was actively plotting to take over the top job. Perhaps, with his seemingly inexhaustible supplies of self-confidence, he was merely happy to take things as they came.

Whatever his intentions his name started appearing in public print as a possible alternative leader. The *Observer* set the ball rolling in January 1915, questioning Asquith's ability to lead the country to victory and comparing him unfavourably to the likes of Lloyd George and Winston Churchill, then a Liberal MP out of favour with the leadership. The *Morning Post*, another Tory paper, took up the call but it was only when the *Daily Chronicle*, firmly in the Liberal camp, published a leader entitled 'The Intrigue Against The Prime Minister' on 23 March that things really started to hot up. By the end of the year Northcliffe was writing about the need for a 'genius' to turn the war around and it was obvious whom he had in mind.

Once again Lloyd George was suspected of colluding with the enemy. Frances Stevenson, his secretary and mistress, wrote in her diary of 23 October 1915, 'The unfortunate part is, that although the Northcliffe press are absolutely right in their estimate of the situation, yet the very mention of Northcliffe makes all the Liberals see red, so that their judgement is absolutely warped by party hatred and jealousy.'[17] She was almost certainly reflecting his own views, as she was again on 31 January 1916: 'Northcliffe's few harmless visits to D [David] have been magnified in the City into endless secret conclaves, & I must say I think this has done D a little harm with his Liberal friends, for Northcliffe is not trusted, nor does he deserve to be.' A. G. Gardiner, editor of the *Daily News*, worked himself up into a frenzy of indignation at what he believed was going on. In an open letter to Lloyd George he wrote, 'If we inquire what is the link between you and Lord Northcliffe we shall find that it is in the common belief in the idea of dictatorship . . . You cannot walk in step with Mr Asquith and Lord Northcliffe at the same time.'[18] Even his good friend Sir George Riddell, just a few days after giving him the lease to the house near London that would become his metropolitan base, wrote in his dairy, 'There is no doubt that LG and Northcliffe are acting in close consort . . . a strong but dangerous combination . . . It looks as if LG and Northcliffe are working to dethrone Mr. A.'[19]

It didn't help Lloyd George in his protestations of innocence that he had started a practice which goes on to this day, that of employing a personal and somewhat thuggish spin doctor to help push his agenda.

It would be another decade before 10 Downing Street employed its first press officer so it is little wonder that eyebrows were raised. William Sutherland, known as 'Bronco Bill', was a secretary in the Ministry of Munitions whom Lloyd George asked to keep an eye on what the press was saying about him and do what he could to influence opinion in his favour. 'Bronco Bill' never published a diary and, unlike some of his successors, he kept a low public profile. His antics soon came to the attention of Westminster insiders, however, and he quickly earned an 'egregious reputation for rumbustious intriguing'. The Conservatives alleged that he 'regularly, and crudely, manipulated the public account of events to enhance Lloyd George's personal popularity'.[20] The best-documented example involved the doctoring of a communiqué signed with the engineering union to give the false impression that Lloyd George had settled a strike single-handedly, but it seems clear from the hatred he aroused that his talents were used a great deal more widely and to good effect.

Sutherland didn't have the notoriety of Alastair Campbell or Bernard Ingham, although he did go on to become an MP in his own right. And unlike either Campbell or Ingham, he was immortalised in verse. Hilaire Belloc, no less, who'd been a Liberal MP himself but had no time for the rougher breed of politicians like Lloyd George and the long-forgotten Handel Booth, MP for Pontefract, wrote:

> When dirty Mr George desired to soothe
> The still more dirty Mr Handel Booth,
> He found convenient to his dirty hand
> The really filthy William Sutherland.[21]

At first Sutherland didn't need any black arts to ensure that his boss was still the flavour of the month in Fleet Street. The clamour had moved on from the lack of shells to the need for conscription and Northcliffe was, as ever, the most vociferous. He had demanded a coalition but now he had one he felt cheated. According to Margot Asquith, he 'went about saying that he had made the coalition and can smash it whenever he likes'. He took an early swipe in April 1916 when he gave financial and editorial support to an anti-coalition by-election candidate in Wimbledon. His man lost but it wouldn't be the last time a press baron would try to hit a prime minister where it really hurts, in the ballot box.

Luck can play a critical role in politics and in the summer of 1916 even the fates seemed to favour Lloyd George. He came close to earning the least sought-after award in British politics, 'The Best Prime Minister We Never Had'. In June he was due to sail with his arch-enemy Kitchener to Russia, which was faltering in its support for the war against Germany, but a domestic crisis over Ireland kept him from going. HMS *Hampshire* struck a mine off Scapa Flow and went down with few survivors. Hearing of Kitchener's death, Northcliffe, never one for sentimentality, declared, 'Providence is on the side of the British Empire after all.'[22]

Asquith, who was in the country playing bridge when the ship went down, reluctantly put Lloyd George into the dead man's shoes as secretary for war. It was not a comfortable place to be. A new name was about to be added to the list of suicidal and bloody tactical disasters of the Great War. The Somme. It seems, like Kitchener before him, that Lloyd George believed it could be the knockout blow. When instead it led to the greatest loss of life ever suffered by the British Army in a single day, the fact that he had inherited the strategy meant he avoided most of the political fallout. If anything it made the calls for change at the top all the more urgent and he was the undeclared candidate of change.

Things were rapidly moving to a climax. Everybody but Asquith could see that something would have to give. Finally, he was presented with a demand that proved too much to stomach even to a man for whom compromise was a way of life. The plan, strongly supported by Lloyd George in private and Northcliffe in public, was for a war council of just three people so the conflict would no longer be run by committee. The problem was that the prime minister wasn't on the list of proposed members. He put up a fight, albeit a rather half-hearted one, until he was persuaded that a large section of his own party and the Tory leadership as well were backing Lloyd George to chair the council, in effect reducing Asquith to little more than a figurehead. Max Aitken, who had just secretly bought a controlling share in the

Express, helped push the Tory leader, Bonar Law, into the Lloyd George camp. This was the basis of his claim to have helped choose the new prime minister. In fact, opinion in both parties was much less clear-cut than Aitken and others tried to persuade Asquith to believe. There was a great deal of spinning going on, although the guilty parties wouldn't have recognised the term. In those days spinning was happily confined to the textile industry.

It all happened over the first weekend in December 1916. On the Sunday, *Reynolds' News* fired the opening shot. The headlines, 'Grave Cabinet Crisis', 'Lloyd George To Resign', told their own story without the source needing to be revealed. Asquith believed the stories anyway. So when Bonar Law warned him to expect Tory resignations from the government as well, he panicked and agreed to Lloyd George's demands.

Then, the following day, Asquith changed his mind. When his fellow Liberal ministers, who'd been kept in the dark, read their morning papers they had a collective fit. A number of the Tory big beasts quickly made it clear that while they weren't happy, they weren't backing Lloyd George either. What infuriated Asquith most was a singularly well-informed leading article in *The Times* supporting his rival's take on events. He was convinced, almost certainly wrongly, that Lloyd George had all but written it himself and was now conspiring with Northcliffe not merely to turn him into a figurehead but to depose him altogether.

In any event it was the perception that mattered. Asquith wrote to Lloyd George, saying, 'Such productions as the first leading article in today's *Times*, showing the infinite possibilities for misunderstanding & misrepresentation of such an agreement as we considered yesterday, make me at least doubtful as to its feasibility. Unless the impression is at once corrected that I am being relegated to the position of an irresponsible spectator of the war, I cannot possibly go on.'

In other words, 'Get your tanks off my lawn'.

The deal was off. Lloyd George promptly resigned and that evening Asquith followed suit. This was his 'put up or shut up' moment of the kind John Major would later engineer with far greater success. Asquith didn't believe either Lloyd George or Bonar Law would be able to form a government and expected to be back in office just as soon as that had been established. It was a fatal miscalculation. The King sent for Bonar Law, who said he would only take the job if Asquith would join his government. Asquith refused. It was over to Lloyd George, who quickly secured the support first of the small but growing Labour party and then, with Bonar Law's help, of most of the Tory grandees who had turned their noses up at him previously. Urgent sounding showed that he would be able to command a majority among back-benchers of all parties in parliament and on the evening of 7 December Lloyd George kissed hands with the King before becoming prime minister. Most of his former Liberal colleagues followed Asquith out of the government.

It was a sensational story and the papers couldn't help but make the most of their own role in it. The *Daily Mail* promptly declared itself 'The Paper That Is Combing Them Out'. Northcliffe wrote a signed article in *The Times* saying how fortunate the new prime minister had been to have his support. 'I do not know Mr Lloyd George in private life,' he insisted, 'I am not in agreement with him in many public affairs . . . [but] I believe he will be at the head of the government that wins the war.'[23] One particularly astute contemporary observer, Kennedy Jones, recognised that, 'What *The Times* did was to raise the shout at exactly the right moment – this is clever journalism – "The dam's going." And the dam went.'[24] It was the politicians, not the press, that put Lloyd George in Downing Street, but no previous incumbent had ever made it to that distinguished address owing so much to the media.

Once there, Lloyd George's priority was, of course, winning the war. He also had to decide what to do about the press. Having unpre-dictable and unprincipled proprietors going around claiming he was there only thanks to them wasn't going to help him establish his authority. Aitken was still more politician and fixer than media mogul at this stage and he was ready to help the new prime minister even though he came from a different party. It was Northcliffe who was the real problem and he soon sent a clear signal of where he thought the balance of power now lay. Lloyd George asked Aitken to call with the message that 'the prime minister would like to see Lord Northcliffe at

No.10 Downing Street'. The line went silent. Eventually the reply came back: 'Lord Northcliffe sees no advantage of any interview between him and the prime minister at this juncture'.[25]

There was speculation that Lloyd George might solve his problem by bringing Northcliffe and others into the government as ministers. There was a certain logic to it. After all, the papers never stopped demanding that the nation come together to fight the Germans. Northcliffe soon made clear, however, that he wasn't interested in a job. It was just as well, as at least half the cabinet would have refused to serve with him. Aitken, on the other hand, was very interested indeed but he had been a singularly undistinguished Tory MP and nobody apart from himself really thought he was cabinet material. What he got instead, and largely because Bonar Law wanted his seat in the Commons for somebody else, was a peerage. No prime minister until Margaret Thatcher came along gave so many honours to their supporters in the media, and none of her appointments raised as much of a stink as the elevation of Max Aitken to become the 1st Baron Beaverbrook. It was hard to see what he had done to deserve it. The *Morning Post* suggested he should have taken the title Lord Bunty, after the popular West End comedy *Bunty Pulls the Strings*. Even King George V objected but to no avail. Beaverbrook claimed, somewhat unconvincingly, to be a reluctant peer although later he would refer to the House of Lords as 'the real and rightful Newspaper Proprietors Association'.[26]

The leading Conservative, Austen Chamberlain, whose half-brother Neville would become prime minister twenty years later, expressed the unease felt by many of his colleagues when he told the Commons that the new government 'have surrounded themselves quite unnecessarily with an atmosphere of suspicion and distrust because they have allowed themselves to become too intimately associated with these great newspaper proprietors'. Yet for all his intimacy with the press, Lloyd George quickly learned that newspaper support is an ephemeral commodity and that, no matter what they say about you on your way up, once you get to be prime minister you have to earn good headlines each and every day because nobody is giving them away. The solidly Liberal papers followed the party establishment and continued to stand with Asquith, who was reconfirmed as leader despite his downfall. The Tory papers held back waiting to see if the new prime minister would shape up and especially whether things would improve on the battlefield.

Lloyd George set about mending fences, 'squaring' wherever he could, inviting editors to Downing Street and stroking their egos. Even his harshest critic, A. G. Gardiner of the *Daily News*, conceded that the prime minister had been 'extremely agreeable' when they met. Lloyd George started to make discreet inquiries to see if, in the tradition of the times, he couldn't buy a stake in a paper or two himself, but as yet he didn't have access to the necessary funds. And he made full use of the new Lord Beaverbrook, even though 'the Beaver', as he soon came to be known, owed his first loyalty to Bonar Law. Beaverbrook did what he could to improve relations with Northcliffe but with, at best, mixed success.

It was Beaverbrook's idea to ask Northcliffe to head the British war mission in the United States. According to Riddell, 'Beaverbrook told Lloyd George that a friendly arrangement with Northcliffe was vital to his administration, that Lloyd George had no party, that he depended upon the press, and that as he had lost the support of one important section he must secure the support of another.'[27] At first the answer was 'no', then, the following month, 'with more regret and reluctance than I can express', Northcliffe agreed. Britain was desperate to get the Americans into the war and helpfully Northcliffe left behind instructions that while he was away 'not one line of criticism of the United States . . . should appear in the *Daily Mail* . . . or any other publication associated with the *Daily Mail*'. Getting him out of the way had been a masterstroke, not only because he proved very good at the job, but also because in the summer of 1917 there was little sign that things were getting better for the government either politically or militarily.

Later that year Northcliffe returned, his job ostensibly done, and showed every sign of going back to his old ways. His brother, Lord Rothermere, owner of the *Daily Mirror*, was brought inside the government tent in his place and given control of a new independent air ministry. Again it had been Beaverbrook's idea. Then, in 1918, Beaverbrook received his own reward. On 10 February he was made minister of information with a seat in the cabinet as chancellor of the

Duchy of Lancaster. On the same day Northcliffe was back as director of enemy propaganda. He had already been given a leg up the nobility ladder in the New Year's honours when Lloyd George had promoted him from a baron to a viscount. Northcliffe insisted he wasn't becoming a minister and nor would he, but there was no doubt he was being 'squared'. Lloyd George told C. P. Scott, 'It was necessary to "harness" him in order to find occupation for his superfluous energies . . . "if I was to avoid a public quarrel with him" . . .'[28]

The government had already gone in for a bit of media 'squashing', including banning the foreign sales of one newspaper because it advocated a negotiated peace with Germany. Now it had two press lords, a description that had only recently come into circulation as a term of abuse, as its leading propagandists. The appointments caused grave disquiet in parliament and at the Palace but Lloyd George weathered the storm. Slowly but surely he felt he was getting the press where he wanted it. Fortunately both men proved energetic and effective at their jobs, although not even their inflated egos could claim all the credit for the unexpected collapse of Germany.

The year 1918 saw Lloyd George at his peak. Success at last on the battlefield brought him popularity at home and with it, inevitably, better coverage in the newspapers. The Liberal press was still suspicious of him, however, and with an eye to the future the prime minister still looked for a paper he could rely on unconditionally. It finally came when a syndicate of wealthy supporters effectively bought him the *Daily Chronicle*. The paper had outraged Lloyd George by appointing a former general and prominent critic of the government as its military correspondent. Lloyd George got his revenge but he paid a heavy price for it. The financiers of the deal were to be rewarded with honours, a blatant bribe. Lloyd George was on the slippery slope to his own destruction. In the short term, however, victory was his. On paper the *Chronicle*'s new owner was Sir Henry Dalziel, but as the recently ennobled Lord Riddell wrote in his dairy, 'L.G. is to have full control of the editorial policy through Sir H. Dalziel, who will in effect be his agent.'[29]

Lloyd George was already thinking of an autumn election. The war was effectively won, although the armistice wouldn't be signed until

11 November. With that in mind he tossed a few more honours the way of journalists, ostensibly for their help with the propaganda effort. And he turned his attention more than ever to political propaganda. The number of voters in Britain had been hugely increased, from around seven million electors to twenty million by the 1918 Representation of the People Act, which gave the vote to all men (but not women) over the age of twenty-one. Without opinion polls to consult, nobody could be quite sure what impact to expect. Soldiers returning from the front would be a key constituency and Northcliffe offered to use his overseas edition of the *Daily Mail* to put the government's case. Lloyd George should have guessed there would be strings attached and there were. Northcliffe wanted nothing less than a veto on the incoming government. He wrote, 'My exact position may be summed up in the following words: I do not propose to use my newspapers and personal influence . . . unless I know definitely, and in writing, and can consciously approve, the personal constitution of the government.'[30] The astonishing thing is that Northcliffe ever believed he had the power to make such an outrageous demand. With admirable restraint Lloyd George said he 'would not dream' of complying.

The election was a personal triumph. He had persuaded Bonar Law to keep the coalition together and have a 'coupon election'. Those candidates with the coupon, proof of their loyalty to the outgoing government, swept the country. Asquith's Liberals and many leading Labour figures who had refused to sign up were annihilated. Again the press barons sought the credit. Rothermere wrote to Lloyd George saying, 'Without the aid of the press, it is a fair thing to say that the present coalition government could not have survived'.[31] He didn't think the prime minister had shown enough gratitude, but others thought Lloyd George had been far too generous. Honours continued to shower down on Fleet Street. F.E. Guest, the Coalition Liberal chief whip, complained that Beaverbrook was demanding yet more titles to reward helpful journalists, 'This is very unprincipled of our friend Max, but not an excessive price to pay for his full support.'[32]

Lloyd George made the most of his victory. He was now an international statesman negotiating at Versailles for a new world order. If the press barons wanted to pretend he was in their debt he was too busy to care very much. When Northcliffe demanded a seat at the peace conference the prime minister would have none of it. He told Riddell, 'I would rather cease to be prime minister than be at the beck and call of Northcliffe, Rothermere, Beaverbrook & Co.'[33] The result was predictable enough. The Northcliffe titles accused the government of 'betrayal' at Versailles, throwing away the victory for which so many had sacrificed their lives. Lloyd George squared up to put his adversary in his place. He told the Commons that the owner of *The Times* was 'deluded' and 'labouring under a deep sense of disappointment'. Then he went in for the kill. Tapping his forehead to indicate what he really thought of Northcliffe's state of mind, he went on, 'when that kind of diseased vanity is carried to the point of sowing dissention between great allies, then I say that not even that kind of disease is justification for so black a crime against humanity'.[34]

Even as Lloyd George felt strong enough to launch such a blistering attack, 'Bronco Bill' Sutherland knew he must still watch his master's back. Northcliffe was beyond the pale, but not so his younger brother. Riddell recorded in his diary that, 'Sir William Sutherland, the PM's parliamentary secretary and press manager, is very thick with Rothermere and Beaverbrook. Rothermere has made him a director of the *Mirror* . . . Sutherland has not a good word to say for any member of the cabinet except Lloyd George. They are all duds or worn out. Rothermere expresses the same opinion in his articles. This creates a very bad impression among the public, who are coming to think that the government consists of one man surrounded by a lot of duffers.'[35]

Before long Sutherland would move on to pursue his own parliamentary career, but like many a loyal spin doctor he would continue to stir the pot from time to time when he thought it would help. His successor, as befitted his name, was a rather more cerebral character. Sir Geoffrey Shakespeare was more diplomatic in his approach than 'Bronco Bill' but he understood the 'square and squash' strategy well. He described the 'squash' element in words that might just as easily have been uttered, with more contemporary expletives, by Alastair Campbell. 'If the Press are constantly attacking, you go for them in a big way, in public of course. Hit them as hard as you possibly can, because proprietors and editors don't like being attacked; they're not accustomed to it and start squealing like stuck pigs . . . and readers . . . say to themselves: "So that's why the *Daily Whatnot* keeps boring away about the PM."[36]

Shakespeare took over at a time when Lloyd George and his ministers had started to see the press as not merely unreliable but also potentially subversive. The war may have been won but national security was still uppermost in the prime minister's mind. The cabinet had already discussed the possibility of seizing printing presses to keep any paper that might be so tempted from publishing military secrets.[37] Now, with the perceived danger of home-grown insurrection after the Soviet takeover in Russia, the government had the security services investigate the journalistic staff of the left-wing *Daily Herald*. Nothing was found that could possibly have warranted a prosecution.

On the political front, too, Lloyd George was starting to see threats from all sides. He was still a prime minister without a party and hoped to rectify that by persuading the Tories to merge with his own rump of the Liberals. He thought they might call themselves the National Democratic party. Nobody bought the idea except the *Daily Chronicle*, the paper he had already purchased for himself, so he set about buying himself a political future as best he could. The 'Lloyd George Fund' became the biggest slush fund in British political history. It was an open secret that a knighthood could be had for £15,000, right up to a viscountcy at £120,000. At the top end that was the equivalent of the £2 million that today constitutes the more generous contributions to party funds, except that in 2010 they are openly declared and any connection with an honour is rigorously denied. The British economy was going through tough times in the early twenties but David Lloyd George, who had sole control of how the fund was spent, was doing very nicely, although it is usually forgotten that half the profits from the sale of honours went to his coalition partners, the Conservative party.

Lloyd George now had the resources to fund parliamentary candidates of his own. But he wasn't the only one. Lord Rothermere was so affronted at what he saw as government profligacy at a time of recession that he founded the 'Anti-Waste League', defeating the coalition in a by-election in Dover in January 1921. Rothermere and his *Daily*

Mirror never posed a serious threat, but while his fund had made Lloyd George financially secure he was starting to feel vulnerable on several fronts. Winston Churchill, whom he had brought back into government, was manoeuvring. Beaverbrook warned that Churchill, who made it his business to maintain good relations with proprietors and editors, was becoming more and more of a Tory and was even talking of ousting Lloyd George in favour of a new Conservative-led coalition. The papers were attacking the government daily, and on graver issues than cutting waste in Whitehall. Among them were the failed attempts to bring peace to Ireland, the contentious issue of free trade versus protectionism, and the uncertain future in Europe. His policy of reconciliation with Soviet Russia alarmed most of the wealthy proprietors who had hoped he would be a bulwark against socialism not its ally. A consensus was starting to emerge that the government's days were numbered and the Conservatives were due for a comeback.

In March 1922 Beaverbrook urged Lloyd George to hold a confidence vote in parliament. 'In the course of your speech the main object of the attack should be the opposing newspapers. The press is always unpopular with members of the Commons and you would rally a lot of sympathy.'[38] Lloyd George did as he was advised and earned himself a little more time, but Beaverbrook was disappointed by his performance. He found him 'really woolly in outlook, and confused in argument . . . The glitter of his supreme office held him in chains.'

Beaverbrook's own loyalties were shifting in any event, both professionally and politically. He was by now more interested in the *Daily Express*, which was finally making good money. Northcliffe was dying and, although Beaverbook denied it, there were rumours that he was thinking of buying *The Times* as well. He still supported Lloyd George over Ireland but otherwise his natural Tory sympathies drew him back towards his old friend Andrew Bonar Law. Even before the issue that would destroy the coalition, whether to support Greece against the Turkish belligerence in the Near East, Lloyd George could see the writing on the wall. And so he planned yet another astonishing twist in his relations with the press. He would join it.

With or without Beaverbrook, the prime minister hoped to do a deal with Northcliffe's heirs after his death. He wanted to take over *The*

Times and have himself installed as its editor. It would have been sweet revenge. The paper had only recently described him as 'the most mistrusted man in the world'.[39] He told Lord Riddell, 'I want to get out and am looking for a soft place on which to fall . . . I want to get control of *The Times*. That would give me great power and would enable me to compel the Conservatives to pay due regard to my views and policies.'[40] And according to his mistress, Frances Stevenson, 'D says he would not mind resigning if he could become editor of *The Times* at a decent salary & with a decent contract.'[41]

That he wanted the job was an extraordinary tribute to the paper's importance; that he failed was evidence of his waning prestige. He couldn't muster enough support and failed to put together a sufficiently attractive bid. *The Times* was not to be the vehicle for his future ambitions and, as he had anticipated, the Conservatives were no longer ready to accommodate him either. The editor of *The Times* from 1919 to 1922, Henry Wickham Steed, urged Bonar Law to go for the highest office. The mercurial Beaverbrook now gave the same advice. On the Turkish question they all saw eye to eye. Bonar Law was no wordsmith but he wrote in *The Times* – or perhaps Beaverbrook wrote it for him – 'We cannot alone act as the policemen of the world.'[42] The Conservative party resolved to fight the coming election on its own and, faced with the inevitable, Lloyd George resigned.

Even in defeat he wasn't finished with the media. He made an enormous sum from the *Daily Telegraph* for his memoirs and became one of the highest-earning columnists in the land. Politically, however, it was all over. His resurrection was often predicted but it never materialised. He died more than twenty years later towards the end of another great war, having finally joined the House of Lords himself. During his time in government the relationship between Downing Street and the media had changed decisively and irrevocably. The press had grown in strength and independence. Downing Street had started to become habituated to many of the techniques of media manipulation that persist to this day. 'Bronco Bill' Sutherland was the first of the modern Machiavellian spin doctors. Influencing the broad mass of public opinion through the media became part of the prime-ministerial job description just as a clutch of 'press barons' emerged with highly exaggerated ideas of their own importance. They had claimed the power to unseat a prime minister and choose his successor and had demanded the right to veto cabinet appointments. And while they hadn't succeeded there was no telling what they might try to do if their arrogance wasn't checked. Both sides were flexing their muscles as never before. The arm wrestlers had locked palms and they haven't let go yet.

2

'TIS PITY SHE'S A WHORE: BONAR LAW, BALDWIN, MACDONALD (1922–31)

Freedom of the press in Britain means freedom to print such of the proprietor's prejudices as the advertisers don't object to.

Hannen Swaffer

With the resignation of David Lloyd George media influence in Downing Street took a nosedive. Party politics was back with a vengeance and self-confident prime ministers, deeply rooted in their parties, are usually the least likely to be swayed by the gusts and squalls of newspaper opinion. Not that the press barons stopped trying to impose their views on the politicians; if anything their arrogance and audacity only increased, but the harder they campaigned the less success they had.

While the political scene was getting back to normal after six years of highly personalised government, the media world was in a state of flux. The year Andrew Bonar Law finally became prime minister after leading the Conservative party for most of the past decade also saw the establishment of the British Broadcasting Company Ltd, although it would be another five years before the BBC received public funding and much longer before it could be said to have any real political influence. In Fleet Street the financial and institutional links between newspapers and the parties were breaking down. The only exception was on the left. In September 1922 the Trades Union Congress bought into the *Daily Herald* and the paper declared it 'now belongs to and is under the control of the organised Labour movement'.[1] That movement was gearing up to wrest the initiative for social and political reform from the Liberals and the heirs to Lloyd George have never yet managed to grab it back. For Labour to have its own paper for the first time was part of its move from protest to power. It also reflected much bigger changes in society as a whole, not the least the extension of voting rights to working men (women would have to wait until 1928). Better education also meant more and better-informed newspaper readers. This had an impact on papers of all political persuasions. The press enjoyed a rapidly expanding circulation, making newspapers far more likely to respond to the demands of their advertisers, who now funded them, rather than the politicians. The latter knew all about pipers and tunes but didn't have the resources to compete.

A different breed of political leader now faced a Fleet Street with fewer reasons than ever to cooperate, far less collude, with Downing Street. The prime ministers who saw Britain through the rest of the twenties faced formidable problems but they didn't see the press as part of the solution for dealing with them, although some of their lieutenants were still keen to bully and manipulate journalists when they got the chance. Some of the bigger egos in Fleet Street found it harder to adjust to the new climate. They still liked to think of themselves as having the power to make or break prime ministers. Henry Wickham Steed at *The Times* counted bringing down the Lloyd George coalition as one of the achievements of his editorship. Lord Beaverbrook, too, believed he had helped make his old friend Bonar Law prime minister, although he was realistic enough to acknowledge that he hadn't created the opportunity but only taken advantage of it. As A. J. P. Taylor concluded, 'at most, Beaverbrook imposed resolution upon the irresolute'.[2]

Bonar Law was resolute about one thing, however. He may not have been hungry for the honour, but having got the top job he was going to do things very differently from his predecessor, not least in terms of what he called 'trafficking with the press'. One newly appointed minister in his government, F. Stanley Jackson, was told in no uncertain terms that he must sever all connections with the *Yorkshire Post*, still a Tory-owned paper, in which he was a sleeping partner. He wasn't alone. It was made clear to all those taking office that being a minister was now incompatible with any newspaper directorship.

The clearest indication that Bonar Law meant to do things differently came during a celebrated meeting at Downing Street with Lord Rothermere. Rothermere had recently failed to get control of *The Times* but he had inherited the *Daily Mail*, the country's largest-selling paper, from his brother and still had the *Daily Mirror* and a healthy stable of regional titles. What he wanted now was more personal, an earldom for himself and a place in the cabinet for his son, the MP Esmond Harmsworth. Bonar Law's reaction soon became the stuff of legend and, as often happens, became somewhat distorted in the retelling. In most accounts he pretended not to have heard what Rothermere had said and simply called for his visitor's car to be sent round. Whether he was startled by the impudence or knew enough of the arrogance of proprietors not to be surprised is unclear, but either way he was furious. The account of one man who was on the scene within seconds suggests the prime minister had told Rothermere just what he thought. J. C. C. Davidson, the prime minister's private secretary, recalled going 'into Bonar's room and Rothermere was like a bear with a sore head; he pushed past me angrily and I knew what had happened. Bonar, in spite of his gentleness, could be as tough as hell when he wanted to be . . . He told me he had sent Rothermere away with a flea in his ear, and I urged him to write down at once an exact description of the interview.'[3] This the prime minister did and told Davidson later that he was quite prepared to reveal exactly what had happened if Rothermere ever got difficult. The career of the press baron was held back rather than advanced and Bonar Law had the satisfaction of seeing Rothermere's papers support him in the forthcoming general election regardless.

J. C. C. Davidson was the nearest thing Bonar Law had to a press officer. He was a highly fastidious man but widely liked by the editors. Nobody wanted to go back to the days of Lloyd George, and Davidson saw the antics of the former prime minister not only as a lesson from which to learn but also as a guide to his own relations with the media: 'I had Lloyd George and the circus at No 10 as a warning – a warning not only to me and to Bonar, but also to the people who were the great figures in the press and had been let down by Lloyd George and his circus.'[4]

Bonar Law occupied Downing Street for only 209 days. Ill health would soon force him out of a job it seems he never really wanted. After his funeral service in Westminster Abbey in 1923, Asquith remarked that it was 'fitting that we should have buried the unknown prime minister by the side of the unknown soldier'. There is no way of knowing whether, had his health been better, he would have become a great holder of the office. If he had, it would not have been through any efforts at self-promotion. To the frustration of his friends, Bonar Law was forever searching for a bushel under which to hide his light. When Beaverbrook told him he should start talking and behaving like a great man he replied, 'If I am a great man, then all great men are frauds.'[5] Lloyd George called his successor 'honest to the verge of simplicity', a backhanded compliment if ever there was one. Like John Major after Margaret Thatcher and Gordon Brown after Tony Blair, Bonar Law both by instinct and political calculation wanted to signal that change was in the air.

Beaverbrook was no doubt right when he warned his friend that he would need to look after his propaganda. Bonar Law didn't have the modern prime minister's habit of considering how his words might play before he uttered them. He had wanted to announce at the outset that he would serve only for a year until it was pointed out to him that he'd be a lame duck before he started. Instead he prepared for an election in which the watchwords would be a promise of 'tranquillity and stability'. Clearly he had little intention of lighting up the political firmament. He would be the only holder of the office unlikely to complain about being thought of as the unknown prime minister. Again like Major and Brown, he promised to turn his back on a style of government that concentrated power in the hands of its leader and to return to more conventional ways of working. Although it's hard to imagine any prime minister these days promising, as he did, to leave ministers to get on with their jobs without interference from Number 10 – and meaning it. And few who have taken over mid-term have followed in Bonar Law's footsteps by calling an immediate election. He did so despite fearing the Conservatives would lose and that he might not even hold his own seat. In the event the quiet man of politics was not to be underestimated, other than by himself, and he secured a Tory majority of seventy-seven.

Labour was now the second party with 142 MPs, despite having little or no support in the mainstream press. The fear of a socialist takeover continued to preoccupy many Establishment minds, not just those of the press barons. Some had reluctantly supported Lloyd George, while holding their noses, in the hope that the working-class firebrand could keep more dangerous radicals in check. With him gone the need to respond to the growing militancy of the Labour movement outside parliament would impose new strains on relations between Fleet Street and Downing Street. The press was happy to play up the 'red threat' but less happy to see its own freedoms challenged as part of the response.

Bonar Law got a taste of what was to come when he refused to meet a delegation of the unemployed who were marching on London and insisting on seeing the prime minister. He took the view that it was the minister of labour's job and he didn't propose to interfere. All might have been well had he not taken the extra precaution of having the criminal records of some of the marchers checked out. When he read the violent and provocative language they were given to using he saw the prospect of public disorder on the streets of London. He had his staff tell the Fleet Street editors of his fears, which they duly did, while omitting, whether deliberately or not is unclear, to include the *Daily Herald* among those he informed. When Labour MPs got to hear of it they accused the prime minister of going back on his election promise not to tamper with the press. He was able to defuse the row by saying truthfully that he hadn't ordered the *Daily Herald* to be treated any differently and that if he'd known they were being excluded he'd have insisted they get the same briefings. The row subsided but only temporarily. Before long, parliament, the press and the Labour movement would all have cause to reflect on the vulnerability of the freedom of expression, whether on the streets or in the media, in an increasingly divided society.

Bonar Law then chose to exercise his own right to free expression in a most unconventional way for a prime minister, especially one committed to doing things the old-fashioned way. He sent his inexperienced new chancellor of the exchequer, Stanley Baldwin, off to America to try to renegotiate Britain's war debt. He feared it would reduce the country's standard of living for a generation if its terms could not be made less onerous. Baldwin returned with a modest improvement that Bonar Law felt was inadequate, saying he would be 'the most cursed prime minister that ever held office in England'[6] if he accepted it. Frustrated, but unwilling or unable to get the cabinet to overturn the deal, he even considered resigning. After consulting Beaverbrook he relented but let off steam in another way, writing a lengthy attack on his own government's policy and having it published in *The Times*. These days prime ministers have articles published in their own names without having penned a word of them. Bonar Law did the opposite. Only days earlier he had warned his colleagues against writing letters or articles for the press, so putting his own name to it would have opened him up to the charge of hypocrisy, not to mention causing a constitutional furore. So the prime minister's renunciation of his own government's policy appeared under the byline 'A Colonial Correspondent'.

Andrew Bonar Law has the rare distinction of never having bribed a journalist with an honour. The 1923 New Year's honours list was devoid of the kind of payback peerages that had so sullied Lloyd George's administration. Rothermere had no choice but to await a more biddable prime minister before trying once again to secure his promotion up the ladder of nobility, but he didn't give up the more immediate quest for political power. Knowing what he did of Bonar Law's fastidiousness and of his friendship with Beaverbrook, it seems extraordinary that Rothermere should have written to the latter in April 1923 to propose a deal. He could not have been less subtle. 'If Bonar places himself in my hands,' he wrote, 'I will hand him down to posterity at the end of three years as one of the most successful prime ministers in history, and if there is a general election I will get him returned again. This may sound boastful but I know exactly how it can be done.'[7] There can be little doubt how Bonar Law would have responded had he seen the letter, but the promises it contained would soon be rendered meaningless in any case.

The political prospects for the Bonar Law government looked healthy with or without the help of Lord Rothermere, but the prime minister's own health was another matter. His throat was giving him so much pain that he found himself unable to speak in the Commons on occasion. And while Beaverbrook's *Daily Express* wrote that he 'walked like an athlete' at the wedding of the Duke of York to Elizabeth Bowes-Lyon, the future Queen Mother, Bonar Law knew he was too sick to carry on. On his doctor's advice he embarked on a Mediterranean cruise. He would return only to tender his resignation, a desperately ill man whose throat cancer would kill him within five months.

All that was left for him to do was to advise the palace on his successor, although he was reluctant to interfere even in so important a matter as this. Beaverbrook was busy interfering on his behalf, however, eager as ever to play his favourite role of kingmaker. George V was left with the clear but erroneous impression that the prime minister wanted Stanley Baldwin to succeed him. Bonar Law had expressed no such preference; far less asked that it be passed on to the Palace. It was the last time for many, many years that Beaverbrook would enjoy any such influence. Bonar Law's parting words to him were 'You are a curious fellow'.[8] All future occupants of Number 10 bar one – Winston Churchill, who liked curious fellows – thought he was something far worse and would have nothing to do with him. His energies would now go exclusively into his newspapers and his personal campaigns, primarily that for free trade within the British Empire, a cause his best friend in politics had done nothing to advance. Not only did Bonar Law abstain from flattering any press barons, he didn't bend to their policy demands either.

If Bonar Law had kept Fleet Street at arm's length during his brief premiership his successor would go on to give interfering press barons a collective bloody nose from which they would never fully recover. That would have to wait until Baldwin had spent long enough in

Downing Street to become heartily sick of their efforts to push him about, although right from the outset he regarded most journalists with undisguised disdain. For many in Fleet Street the feelings were mutual. As he admitted himself, he was inexperienced and unprepared when the job of prime minister came to him unexpectedly in 1923. His first government would be even shorter-lived than Bonar Law's and rather less distinguished. Little wonder that the likes of Rothermere and Beaverbrook soon came to the conclusion that they were both cleverer and more powerful men than he was.

In time they would discover how wrong they were as Baldwin repeatedly got the better of them. There is no finer example of a prime minister with the temperament and self-confidence to tell the press to get on with their own jobs and leave him to get on with his. And while he threw away his first government's majority and would later be held responsible for the failure to start rearming in the face of Nazi belligerence, his record in office is now generally considered to have been more impressive than he was given credit for at the time.

Baldwin owed nothing to the media. The newspapers had been divided over who should succeed Bonar Law. Many had supported Lord Curzon, whom they believed with some justification to be far better qualified. *The Times* was more helpful, arguing that having a prime minister in the Lords was no longer tenable. Geoffrey Dawson, who returned to the editor's chair in 1923, would become the nearest thing Baldwin had to a confidant in Fleet Street. Beaverbrook sent out mixed signals, despite having made Baldwin's case to the Palace ostensibly on behalf of Bonar Law. It may be that he was waiting to see which way the wind was blowing before committing himself. J. C. C. Davidson claimed that Beaverbrook had belatedly come down in favour of Curzon. His memoirs recount a phone call to Downing Street in which Beaverbrook said the party establishment would best unite under Curzon, '. . . to which I replied, "I am sorry Max, but it's too late; Baldwin has just come back from the palace and is busy in the cabinet room making the new government." There was a roar like a lion and it sounded as though the telephone had been thrown across the room and crashed against the wall. This is an absolutely true account of what happened.'[9]

Another diarist of the period, Leo Amery, suggests that as soon as Baldwin was installed Lord Rothermere too was up to his old games, trying to get preferment for himself and his son in return for the backing of his newspapers. Once again he came up against a man who was in no mood to deal. Baldwin told him bluntly that 'there was no question of him getting any of the things he wanted'.[10] According to his own son, Baldwin simply didn't like the kind of popular papers Rothermere and Beaverbrook excelled in producing. He found them inaccurate, tendentious and 'possessing an influence, not necessarily political, that aimed somewhat lower than the best . . . only a journalism of the more sober, unsensational, and what might be called old-fashioned type would appeal to him'.[11] Baldwin used rather more evocative language when he said, 'The Press? I would as soon have ink squirted over me by a cuttlefish, as their praise has no more effect than their blame.'[12]

What was yet to be tested was whether a prime minister who treated the popular press with such disdain could prosper. Millions of ordinary voters got their only news of what he was doing and saying through the pages of papers like the *Mail* and the *Express*. That seemed to matter little to Baldwin. *The Times* described the new prime minister as 'singularly free from self-advertisement' and they meant it as a compliment. Beaverbrook saw weakness in the same trait, suggesting that Baldwin would have to learn to 'work the press in his own interest – an art for which apparently he has no inclination or talent'.[13] He certainly had no desire to play the press manipulation game in the way Beaverbrook understood it, but Baldwin had a canny sense of his own image nonetheless and knew how to use it to his advantage. It suited him to allow people to believe he was an unsophisticated country farmer at heart. It was an act that lulled many into underestimating him until he proved what a sharp operator he really was. The Tory grandee Austen Chamberlain, who might have taken over from Bonar Law himself in different circumstances, was never taken in. Personal rivalry no doubt coloured his vision but he wrote that '. . . the Stanley Baldwin whom we know does not fit in at any point with the picture which the public have made of him for themselves. They think him a simple, hardworking, unambitious man, not a "politician" in the

abusive sense in which they so often use the word . . . and we know
him as self-centred, selfish and idle, yet one of the shrewdest politicians,
but without a constructive idea in his head . . .'[14] So when Baldwin
told Davidson that he would 'rather take a single ticket to Siberia than
become prime minister' it was probably just a little disingenuous. And
when he replied to journalists who offered him their congratulations
on his way into Downing Street for the first time that he would rather
have their prayers, it may also have been part of the act.[15] If they prayed
for him at all they clearly didn't do it hard enough. Within a few
months his own misjudgements would see the majority he had inherited wiped out and his detractors nodding their heads in satisfaction
that they'd been right all along.

Baldwin decided to go to the country on the issue that had divided
the Tory party for a decade or more: protectionism. The growth of
unemployment, and the very real fear of more to come, persuaded him
to bounce the cabinet into supporting trade barriers to protect British
jobs. His speech in Plymouth on 25 October 1923 announcing the
shift appeared to come out of the blue, but this was not just the
impetuous action of an inexperienced leader. H. A. Gwynne, the veteran editor of the Conservative-supporting *Morning Post*, had warned
him that David Lloyd George was busy planning a comeback. His aim
was to create a new centre party, including those of the Tory old guard
like Chamberlain who had little time for Baldwin. Gwynne warned
that the new party would get widespread newspaper backing if it
embraced Imperial protection. Lloyd George was on a speaking tour
in America at the time, but Gwynne wrote to the prime minister
saying he had 'declared that he was coming back to sweep the country on an Empire policy. So [we] will have to hustle with ours.'[16]
Davidson's diary confirms that Baldwin feared Lloyd George would get
powerful support in the shape of 'the mischievous influence of the press
lords. Rothermere and Beaverbrook still hoped in some measure for
the revival of a centre party. There were a good many comings and
goings . . . at Beaverbrook's house at Leatherhead.'[17]

Ten days after Baldwin's speech, the ship carrying Lloyd George
docked at Southampton. The Liberal MP Sir Alfred Mond rushed
aboard 'for fear Beaverbrook should capture him' first. Mond wanted

to persuade Lloyd George that, now Baldwin had declared his hand, all Liberals, whatever their previous differences, should come together in defence of free trade. He succeeded. Baldwin was far less troubled by a reunited Liberal party than he was by a potentially disastrous split in his own. He was convinced Labour would emerge as the long-term challenger to the Conservatives and he was right, although he didn't expect it to happen as soon as it did. In later life he gave varying explanations for his policy shift, although courting popularity in the press was never one of them. It was probably a mixture of political tactics and a genuine belief that the time for protection had come. The number of people out of work had risen to over two million in 1923. In his Plymouth speech he declared that 'the unemployment problem is the most critical problem of our country. I can fight it. I am willing to fight it. I cannot fight it without weapons.'[18] Nor, he believed, could he fight it without a mandate from the people.

Not even the King could dissuade Baldwin from going ahead with a December election on the issue. The Tory press was wary. According to Beaverbrook, 'Hardly more than one responsible Conservative organ thought a precipitate general election on this issue advisable. The others were only dragged in by the hair of their heads.'[19] Even *The Times*, which was the most supportive, could only praise 'the sincerity of [Baldwin's] conviction . . . shown by the readiness with which he is prepared to risk the highest position in the state.'[20] The *Manchester Guardian* looked on gleefully, describing 'Civil War in the Tory Press' and observing 'How different from the days when the newspaper posters and caricatures of the popular Tory press furnished the chief ammunition of the party!'[21] Nonetheless the Conservatives anticipated a fairly easy win and an increased majority. Instead they came back with ninety-two fewer seats than the opposition parties combined. The fact that they were still the largest single party in parliament was little consolation. Baldwin had gambled and lost. It was the classic hung parliament and with nobody sure who would be able to form a workable government MPs went off for Christmas with Baldwin still, nominally at least, prime minister.

Why had he got it so wrong? One reason was that, like all politicians at the time, he was flying blind. It would be at least another decade

before opinion polling would emerge as a rough science first in the
United States and then in Britain. It would be half a century or more
before the techniques of focus groups and voter ID would enable a
prime minister to judge with any accuracy the likely popularity of any
policy before it was announced. In the 1920s Downing Street had to
rely on the imperfect assessments of MPs and the party machines of
how the electorate might react, plus raw political instinct. Then, as
now, they could read the newspapers to try to gauge public opinion
but, then as now, the press reflected what it wanted the public to think
as much as anything else.

In the wake of the result the Conservative party took a long hard
look at its methods of influencing the press. For most of their history,
the Tories have managed to stay one step ahead in the political communications war and the 1920s were no exception. They hit on the
idea of a research department that would produce briefing material not
just for those papers who traditionally supported them but – and this
was the novelty – for those read by the people they needed to win
over. 'For the purposes of political propaganda for the working classes,'
said the proposal, 'the evening papers, especially in the provinces, and
the Sunday newspapers provide the best media.'[22] The need for what
would later become known as 'strategic communications' was already
apparent.

The Tories had good reason to look to the working classes.
Industrial militancy was on the rise and the big domestic political issues
were jobs, housing and the provision of education for all. Slums still
disfigured most British cities and the school leaving age remained at
fourteen. Even for those lucky enough to have work, conditions in the
factories and mines were often deplorable. Labour was the real winner
of the 1923 election, despite coming second in terms of seats. No party
could command a majority in the Commons. *The Times* advocated a
Tory–Liberal coalition, but Baldwin knew he had lost. The only
halfway workable solution to the uncertain verdict of the electorate was
for Labour to form a minority government. Ramsay MacDonald duly
became Britain's first Labour prime minister on 22 January 1924. He
was in office but not really in power and his main objective was to
show that his party could govern at all. He and his ministers hired dress

suits from Moss Bros and settled in to make the best of what was widely expected to be yet another short-lived administration.[23]

MacDonald took office with advantages and disadvantages in terms of his relations with the press. On the negative side the biggest problem was obvious. No newspaper other than the *Daily Herald*, which the Labour movement owned anyway, supported him. He was a vain man, sensitive to criticism, and had to endure the kind of highly personal abuse that Labour leaders have attracted disproportionately since the party was founded. He had already suffered the ignominy of having his birth certificate published in the influential right-wing journal *John Bull*. Until then even MacDonald himself hadn't known he was illegitimate. According to the long-serving *Sunday Times* journalist James Margach, who met MacDonald and was still reporting on politics when Margaret Thatcher was in Downing Street, Labour's first prime minister 'was hounded, in campaigns of personal venom, more widely than any other premier'.[24] On the positive side MacDonald was very much at ease with journalists. He was one himself, having kept his political career afloat in an age when MPs earned a relative pittance by writing comment pieces for a wide range of national and regional papers. He would visit London's press club even after becoming PM. He spoke their language even if they had been noticeably reluctant to listen to his during the election campaign. In a way that would become all too familiar over the next seventy years the Labour party complained of blatant bias. MacDonald wrote that '. . . the way that the *Daily News* and the *Westminster Gazette* behaved was contemptible. We expect nothing better from the *Daily Mail* and such miserable products.'[25]

MacDonald appointed just about the most moderate cabinet that he could. His chancellor, Philip Snowden, was pathologically averse to spending public money and the King need hardly have wasted his breath advising the government to follow a course of 'prudence and sagacity'.[26] Yet press lords like Lord Rothermere feared not just for the country's future, but for their own pockets. He predicted that Labour would shake the economy to its foundations within two months and in the process cut newspaper advertising revenues in half. In fact, if Beaverbrook's *Daily Express* was in any way typical, 1924 was a bumper year.

Rothermere and Beaverbrook didn't always see eye to eye, but they were as one in the need to look for a new saviour after the calamitous performance of Baldwin. They hit on Winston Churchill, now out of parliament after losing his seat. He had first entered the Commons as a Tory and then switched sides to become a very independently minded Liberal MP and minister. The two press lords promised him their full support if he would stand as an independent in a forthcoming by-election in Westminster. They hoped and believed that he would return to the Tory fold. Their hopes would eventually be realised but not just yet. He agreed to stand but his illustrious backers didn't have quite the powers to sway public opinion that they imagined and, despite their efforts, he lost, albeit narrowly. Baldwin, foreshadowing language he would use to great effect a decade later, told the owner of the *Spectator* that he found it 'horrible . . . to see the press prostituted . . . and used as the medium of a private vendetta'. He said he was 'indifferent to Beaverbrook's attacks . . . He lowers everything he touches . . . He was spoiled by my predecessors.'[27]

While the Tories in opposition concentrated on building up their machinery for dealing with the press, Labour lacked the resources to follow suit. There was no strategy to counter the widespread hostility the party faced. Without the benefit of professional media advice MacDonald had to trust to his own instincts. According to the Labour MP George Lansbury, he was not lacking in guile. Lansbury, who would later succeed MacDonald as party leader, told Beatrice Webb he found him 'more adept at intrigue and word-twisting and word-spinning than even Lloyd George himself'. She confessed that she did not 'have the remotest idea whether the P.M. is a genius, a mere spinner of words, or a sufficiently able man to make a good job of the country's business, on more or less Labour lines', although she was resigned to the fact that 'he was never a socialist.'[28] At the end of his brief first tenure in office MacDonald's instincts would let him down badly, but in an earlier and far less serious case he conducted himself with exemplary skill.

MacDonald's reputation was being damaged by the 'Affair of the Daimler and the Biscuits'.[29] The prime minister had never owned a car and went everywhere by bus, tram or the tube. If pushed he might splash out on a taxi. So eyebrows were raised when he was spotted driving around London in a fancy Daimler. The *Daily Mail*, a paper that clearly believes working-class politicians like Ramsay MacDonald and John Prescott shouldn't have one posh car, never mind two, put its journalists on the trail of where he'd got the money. It could only be corruption. Lo and behold, MacDonald had suddenly acquired rather a lot of shares in the biscuit company McVitie and Price. Its chairman, Sir Alexander Grant, an old friend, had only just been knighted to boot. The fact that this was at the request of the outgoing Tory government was quietly overlooked by the *Mail*. For weeks MacDonald's speeches were interrupted by heckles of 'biscuits!' and he decided he had to act. He adopted the wise strategy of putting all the facts on the table and inviting the public to decide if he'd done anything wrong. The car had indeed been provided by Grant, who had started life a poor man himself and didn't believe it was good for Britain to have its premier waiting around on underground platforms. Although MacDonald would benefit from them while in office, both the Daimler and the shares would, moreover, revert to the company as soon as he stopped being prime minister. By the standards of the day that was acceptable to public opinion. The affair even helped persuade Whitehall to start providing official ministerial cars for the first time. In a nice additional touch, having decided to put his side of the story MacDonald ignored the massed ranks of the national press who were clamouring outside the door of his Scottish home waiting for a statement and gave an interview instead to a trusted acquaintance on the *Aberdeen Free Press*. Downing Street 1, Fleet Street 0.

MacDonald might have expected such treatment from the *Daily Mail*, but he thought the few friends he had in the media were treating him shabbily, too. In his opinion even the *Daily Herald* couldn't be relied upon and was flirting too much with the communist left. He didn't mince his words in a letter to the editor, Hamilton Fyfe, saying the paper had become 'a dumping-ground for rubbish which would be put in the waste-paper basket for anyone who knew his business or who was not out for mischief'. So began the long tradition of Labour prime ministers taking out their frustration on those papers closest to them politically. Fyfe gave as good as he got. Calling MacDonald 'petulant', he suggested 'It should help for a prime minister to keep in touch with the sentiments and convictions, the reactions and perplexities of those who have put him where he is . . . Isn't it just possible that you have something to learn too?'[30]

The Labour government picked a bigger fight with the paper that really did speak for the communist left, the *Workers' Weekly*, which would go on to become the *Daily Worker* in 1930. MacDonald, who was his own foreign secretary, had scored a considerable diplomatic success in his efforts to negotiate a fairer agreement over the thorny issue of war reparations. As part of a much wider settlement he proposed an Anglo-Soviet treaty, opposed vigorously by Lloyd George, Asquith and the Liberals whose votes he relied on to stay in power. Perhaps conscious of the damage that could be done by a press campaign based on the 'red scare', the cabinet decided to take action against the *Workers' Weekly* for an article calling on British soldiers to 'let it be known that, neither in the class war nor in a military war, will you turn your guns on your fellow workers'.[31] That, in the assessment of the director of public prosecutions, was incitement to mutiny. The acting editor, J. R. Campbell, was duly charged under the Mutiny Act of 1797. It was not a smart move. For a start Campbell had been disabled fighting for Britain in the First World War. Furthermore, the papers had little trouble pointing to similar statements made by Labour MPs themselves, none of whom had been prosecuted. MacDonald quickly intervened to order the prosecution stopped, but that only made matters worse. The Tories now leapt in, accusing him of interfering with the course of justice, which he clearly was. The Communist party said they wanted the prosecution to continue and promised to call MacDonald as a defence witness. The prime minister denied having been consulted then denied having denied it. Never mind that previous Tory and Liberal cabinets had discussed the political expediency of prosecutions, this was not going well. It was all about politics and very little to do with justice. The Liberals had found common cause with the Tories, who were ready to bring the experiment in Labour government to an end, and MacDonald, who was tiring of leading a minority administration, had little inclination to resist. After losing a critical vote in the Commons, Labour headed into a general election in the worst possible climate. The party had proved itself competent in office but now had to go to the country with the 'red scare' once again uppermost in people's minds. It was a situation the Tories and their friends in the press were more than willing to exploit to the full.

From the start the campaign was dominated by the threat of Bolshevism in the UK. According to *The Times*, Labour's plan for a national system of electricity generation was similar to a project 'dear to Lenin'. Women were advised to watch out for communist agents disguised as health visitors and were warned that communism destroyed marriage. And just in case anybody failed to get the message, some Conservative candidates spelt it out in black and white – a vote for Labour was a vote for communism.[32]

The scene was set for the most notorious example of media complicity in election dirty tricks of the twentieth century, the Zinoviev letter. The affair didn't cost Labour the election – the Tories would almost certainly have won with or without it – but it did deliver the party a body blow. The audacity of the forged letter and the willingness of the Tory press to seize on it uncritically were bad enough. MacDonald's feeble and confused response then added an extra degree of self-inflicted humiliation. Not for nothing is it the most frequently cited example of Labour's vulnerability to a ruthless and unprincipled Tory establishment.

The one innocent party in the whole affair was Grigori Zinoviev himself. Just as Molotov will be for ever remembered for the cocktail he never mixed (or threw), so Zinoviev will always be associated with the letter he never wrote. Yet the forgery was plausible enough for people to believe that the good comrade, who was president of the Communist International, could easily have penned it. It was addressed to the British Communist party and urged on them various acts of sedition, including within the armed forces. It also touched on the proposed Anglo-Soviet pact, saying it would 'assist in the revolutionising of the international and British proletariat not less than a successful rising in any of the working districts of England'. In other words, MacDonald's foreign policy was doing the Soviets' work for them. The manner of the letter becoming public has never been fully explained.

The Foreign Office released it during the election campaign but only once they knew it was already in the hands of both Conservative Central Office and the *Daily Mail*. The senior civil servant who authorised its release said with some justification that he had no choice because he knew the press was onto it.

The *Daily Mail* had a field day. 'Civil War Plot By Socialists' it cried. 'Moscow Order to Our Reds. Great Plot Disclosed Yesterday.' The paper was still a broadsheet with room for such expansive headlines. 'Lenin Says Vote Labour' would be today's equivalent. A close reading of the story only made things look worse for MacDonald. It included the government's response to the letter, including the complaint that it constituted a 'direct interference from outside in British domestic affairs'. No suggestion there that it was a forgery. What the paper didn't know was that MacDonald had known about the letter for two weeks and had helped draft the reply while out on the stump. Yet when he was asked about it he refused to comment, which made him look shifty to say the least. Even the most impartial reader would have been forgiven for thinking that the government had been hoping to keep it quiet until after the election.

By the time he did respond, two days later, MacDonald still wouldn't say whether he thought the letter was genuine, although he claimed later that he had had his doubts from the outset. At a rally in Cardiff he called it a 'big stunt', 'a new Gunpowder Plot' and a 'great chance for Tory propagandists'. 'I am also informed,' he went on, 'that the Conservative headquarters had been spreading abroad for some days that . . . a mine was going to be sprung under our feet, and that the name of Zinoviev was to be associated with mine . . . how can I . . . avoid the suspicion – I will not say the conclusion – that the whole thing is a political plot?'[33] He did the decent thing by refusing to condemn the Foreign Office for giving credence to its authenticity, but that just muddied the waters further.

In all probability the letter was forged by 'White' Russian émigrés hostile to the Soviet regime, quite possibly with a little help from within His Majesty's secret services. Whoever it was, they showed a better grasp of how to handle a media sensation in the midst of an election campaign than did the prime minister or the Labour party.

MacDonald, to be fair, had precious little help of any sort from the party during the campaign. He barely had anybody to carry his bags, never mind advise him on his press relations. But if he had ever taken the time to sit down and think about what he should say if and when the letter became public, there was precious little evidence of it.

At first sight the most astonishing feature of the 1924 election was that, despite all of this, Labour's vote actually increased from 4.4 million to 5.4 million. The real story, however, was the Liberal collapse. They fielded 113 fewer candidates than the year before and lost 118 seats, including that of their leader, Herbert Asquith. The Conservatives had a majority of over 200 in the new parliament and all mutterings about Baldwin's leadership were silenced. He was back with a vengeance and dependent upon nobody, least of all the journalists he so despised.

Still fresh in Baldwin's mind was an incident earlier in the year that had served only to confirm his suspicion that the gentlemen of the press couldn't be relied upon to behave like gentlemen at all. After making a series of policy speeches on 'New Conservatism' he agreed to give a rare newspaper interview to expand on his ideas. The lucky recipient was the *People*. It was owned by a Tory backbencher, which may have lulled Baldwin into a false sense of security. For whatever reason, he gave one of the most indiscreet interviews ever conducted by a party leader. Or, at least, the most indiscreet ever to be published attributably. Baldwin failed to take the most elementary precautions. He established no ground rules before speaking and asked for no sight of the finished product before the paper went to press. He almost never read the papers himself, knew little and cared less about how journalists went about their business. No doubt Conservative Central Office should have protected him better, but that doesn't alter his own responsibility for the PR disaster that followed.

After some mildly interesting stuff about how any future government would have to be 'socialistic' in the sense that previous generations had used the word, he went on to talk about his political colleagues and rivals. Lloyd George, Churchill and the Tory grandee Lord Birkenhead were, he said, a 'sinister and cynical combination'. He said he was surrounded by 'intriguers' who simply wanted to go back to the 'old dirty kind of politics'. Birkenhead received the sharpest rebuke. 'If his health does not give way, he will be a liability to the party.' As for Beaverbrook and Rothermere, 'I care not what they say or think. They are both men I would not have in my house.'[34]

Baldwin said much later that he thought the interview was over before he uttered the offending remarks. He had been relaxing and having a cup of tea with the journalist when he made them. He felt betrayed. Later still the reporter F. W. Wilson told James Margach that he'd told his editor that Baldwin hadn't meant the words to be on the record but he had been overruled and ordered to write them up anyway. Nobody came out of the affair well. Baldwin wrote to Churchill with less than total honesty asking him to 'accept my assurance that the offensive remarks were never uttered by me'.[35] Unfortunately his mannerisms and speaking style had been captured all too accurately for anybody seriously to doubt it was authentic Baldwin. He never gave another set-piece interview to any newspaper or magazine or spoke to the parliamentary lobby journalists as a group either on or off the record, although Margach remembered him continuing to treat individuals he really did know well with frankness and generosity.

Baldwin was more at home with a medium he discovered he could master and where there was no possibility of his words being taken out of context, the radio broadcast. The 1924 election was the first in which party leaders were given the chance to address the nation, or that tiny percentage of the nation able to tune in and hear them, over the airwaves. MacDonald failed totally to grasp the opportunity, allowing himself to be broadcast live from a public meeting in Glasgow. His oratory was more than capable of wowing them in the hall, but on the radio it sounded raucous and remote. Baldwin spoke in a much quieter, more intimate way from a BBC office and, by contrast, came across as the sweet voice of reason.

It wasn't an act. He really did believe that turning down the rhetoric and bringing people together was the best way to deal with problems. His cabinet appointments reflected his desire to unite rather than divide. His comments to the *People* notwithstanding, there were jobs for both Birkenhead and Churchill. The latter, who had finally re-entered the Commons and returned to the Tory fold as Rothermere and Beaverbrook had hoped he would, was made chancellor of the exchequer, another example of Baldwin's willingness to take bold risks when the circumstances allowed. Churchill apparently thought he was being offered a far more lowly post, chancellor of the Duchy of Lancaster, and would have been more than happy with that.

Baldwin started as he meant to go on, concentrating on the business in hand, much of it economic, and leaving the 'stunt press', as he called it, to get on with whatever the press needed to do. He felt no gratitude for the help the Tory papers had given him in the election and this continued to rankle with the barons of Fleet Street. Davidson recalled Birkenhead remarking that 'after the help which the *Daily Mail* had given in the election, the statement that the election had not been won by the stunt press was taken as a gratuitous insult by Rothermere, who had worked very hard to win the election. Rothermere never ceases to refer to this in conversation.'[36] Rothermere predicted, or perhaps more accurately willed, that the Baldwin government would fail sooner rather than later. He continued to court Churchill and the chancellor had no qualms about maintaining contact with a man whose horns he found harder to detect than did the prime minister. A bit of old-fashioned schmoozing helped Churchill get a good press for the government's economic policies and overall the Tories were getting an easy ride. In the assessment of Geoffrey Dawson at *The Times*, 'on the whole the cabinet is very popular and unprovocative'.[37]

Unprovocative it may have been but it was about to be provoked sorely. During 1925 there was much criticism in the press about the huge subsidies being sunk into the struggling coal industry. He couldn't say so publicly but Baldwin was buying off the prospect of an ugly strike that he didn't feel ready to confront. Margaret Thatcher would do much the same thing sixty years later before she was ready for the final showdown. In both cases it was a calculated short-term tactic and in both cases it worked. The strike Baldwin eventually had to deal with was far shorter than Thatcher's but no less a turning point. Britain has only ever had one general strike and this was it. It was an unprecedented challenge not just for Downing Street but also for Fleet Street. Many in the press and in the government thought it was some kind of final showdown with the forces of communism, although it was actually a relatively straightforward industrial dispute. The mines were losing money. The mine owners wanted to cut wages and impose longer hours. The miners were having none of it and they had the support of other key unions.

Baldwin didn't have the kind of thirst for a fight that Margaret Thatcher would later demonstrate. He wasn't looking to break the power of the unions. His hand was forced at the beginning of May 1926 in the unlikely surroundings of the compositors' room at Rothermere's *Daily Mail*. The paper's editor, Thomas Marlowe, was already a bogeyman of the left for publishing the Zinoviev letter. Now he had written an editorial, 'For King and Country', which described the threatened general strike as 'a revolutionary movement intended to inflict suffering on the great mass of innocent persons in the community'. The compositors, without the approval of their union, refused to set it in type. It gave the hardliners in the cabinet, including Birkenhead and Churchill, the excuse they needed. Churchill in particular grasped the opportunity for a confrontation with unbridled enthusiasm. Taking the fight to the enemy and prosecuting it without restraint was in his nature. As the strike spread he wanted to take over the BBC and turn it into a propaganda agency. The prime minister, in an effort to channel his chancellor's energies in a direction less likely to inflame the situation, asked him instead to set up the *British Gazette* to keep the public informed now that the TUC had officially called out the printers. Of 1,870 newspapers in Britain, only forty were able to carry on publishing during the strike. This, perhaps more than anything else, led middle-class opinion to believe that revolution might indeed be in the air.[38] Some TUC leaders argued that the printers should not be called out for this very reason. But the majority relished the opportunity to stand up to the press barons for once. A future editor of the *New Statesman*, Kingsley Martin, described the prevalent view from the left: 'The freedom of the press today means the autocratic right of Lord Beaverbrook, Lord Rothermere and a few other private persons to select news and impose the suggestions they desire upon as large a part of the population as they can persuade to buy their brand of news . . .'[39]

The real purpose of the *British Gazette*, of course, had little to do with press freedom and everything to do with putting across the government's view during the strike. Churchill set about the task with gusto, commandeering newsprint, taking over the printing presses of the *Morning Post* and publishing articles calling for 'unconditional surrender'. Davidson warned Baldwin at the time that 'he thinks he is Napoleon'. No detail was left to chance and Churchill was even to be found changing the punctuation when it didn't suit him. He managed in the process to upset just about everybody. The unions accused him of 'a poisonous attempt to bias the public mind'.[40] The Fleet Street editors complained that his commando-style raids on their paper stocks were making it impossible for them to try to get back to normal publishing. Baldwin apparently had his doubts, too, if Geoffrey Dawson's diary is to be replied upon. On 7 May he wrote: 'I lunched at the House of Commons . . . and had a long talk there afterwards with the prime minister mainly on my own subject of publicity which in my view (and he agreed) was being mishandled by Winston . . .'

The BBC under John Reith didn't need to be taken over; it did everything the government wanted anyway. From inside Number 10 Davidson recorded that Reith 'never doubted that the BBC should back the constitutional government to the full and, although he allowed the use of news from trade union sources as long as the reports were objective and true, he instructed the stations that they were not to broadcast anything calculated to extend the area of the strike. In practice . . . my unofficial control was complete.'[41] MacDonald, now leader of the opposition, wasn't allowed to broadcast during the strike and even the archbishop of Canterbury was kept off the airwaves when he wanted to call for reconciliation. The government dominated the communications battle with ruthless determination. The general strike, which lasted just eight days, was successfully portrayed as a threat to the constitution rather than a dispute over working men's wages. The miners fought on alone for six months before being comprehensively defeated and Baldwin too had his physical and mental strength sapped by the whole affair. He may have won but he hadn't developed a taste for confrontation.

The prime minister was not alone in his discomfort. British society was in a nervous and uncertain state. Press 'freedom' was far from the only traditional value that had been called into question, but it was an important one. Owners like Beaverbrook were not exactly consumed with self-doubt, the world hadn't changed that much, but they did feel the need to explain themselves before the court of public opinion. The phrase 'power without responsibility' had been attributed to them more than once in parliament and elsewhere. Beaverbrook took up his pen to answer back in an article entitled 'Has The Press Any Power?'. In it he turned the accusation on its head, or tried to. 'The proprietor of a popular newspaper has responsibility without power, and he stands at the bar of popular opinion. Not once every five years, but every morning of every day.' Curiously he sent the article to Rothermere for publication in the *Sunday Pictorial* and, for whatever reason, it was never published.[42]

The press barons were feeling sore, not least because of the constant rebuffs from Baldwin. The appointment of J. C. C. Davidson as Conservative party chairman in 1927 went some way to helping matters. It was also a highly significant moment in the history of relations between Downing Street and the media. He would take a lot of stick for the Tories' political setbacks in the years to come, but in many ways that was the point. From this moment on, Conservative prime ministers would have a powerful individual outside of government but close at hand nonetheless to do much of their dirty work with the media. Labour prime ministers (there would never be another Liberal) rarely had such a valuable adjunct and were the poorer for it. Davidson was too busy to dwell on the significance of his new role but he meant to ensure that the Central Office press operation remained streets ahead of its rivals. He took control of the 'lobby press service', which served up political 'news' to over two hundred weekly and daily papers outside London. It had a remarkable strike rate. In June 1927 alone, 353 leading articles appeared in the newspapers based almost exclusively on Tory propaganda provided by the service.[43]

While his staff at Conservative Central Office worked on the generally Tory-owned provincial press, Davidson himself concentrated on the London-based editors and proprietors. His courteous and diplomatic manner smoothed some ruffled feathers but he never underestimated his task in trying to get old friends back in the prime minister's nest. Lloyd George, who had finally replaced Asquith as leader of the Liberals, and Churchill remained attractive alternatives for newspapers in search of decisive and charismatic leadership. And the days of unquestioning loyalty from any newspaper were over. Even discounting the tendency for journalists to overstate their own independence, it is interesting to note that, according to H. A. Gwynne, editor of the *Morning Post* and president of the Institute of Journalists, by 1928 it was 'difficult, if not impossible, at times to give the correct political label to any newspaper'.[44] As if to prove his point Rothermere set a cat amongst the pigeons by soon afterwards writing that 'a socialist majority might prove salutary.'[45] Any such sentiments didn't last long. Rothermere was soon joining Beaverbrook in dreaming once more of some kind of centre party. The Tories had been doing badly in by-elections and a general election was due in 1929. Baldwin would have to defend his majority with the media lukewarm towards him at best.

It was to be the 'Safety First' election, remembered for perhaps the least inspiring slogan ever promoted by a governing party. Baldwin had no bright new ideas to put before the electorate and hoped that his reputation for quiet, moderate leadership would be enough. It wasn't. Unemployment was moving inexorably higher and the Tories looked complacent in the face of it. Labour had a stronger emotional claim to care about the issue and the Liberals, supported by the work of John Maynard Keynes, the best intellectual claim to a solution. Baldwin did, however, have the best organisation and the most money at his disposal. The Tory party was getting more professional in its campaigning with every election. 'Safety First' had been the recommendation of an advertising agency, Benson's, although it matched perfectly Baldwin's instincts. The party might just as well have saved its money because it did more harm than good and was blamed afterwards – along with Davidson himself – for the Tories' unexpected defeat.

If organisation and professionalism were all that counted Labour should have been trounced rather than emerging as the largest party for the first time in history. MacDonald was constantly frustrated at the lack of facilities and support offered to him as leader. Things had improved a great deal since the 'red scare' election five years earlier but in terms of communications Labour was still in the dark ages.

MacDonald knew he needed somebody to mind his back with the press if he was to avoid getting caught out again. He asked the social-ist writer and academic R. H. Tawney to be a 'companion who would read the newspapers before breakfast and then discuss with me the lines for my speeches during the day'.[46] Labour's real success was in per-suading the politically uncommitted, including many women who got the vote for the first time in the Reform Act of 1928, that it was both 'time for a change' (that old chestnut) and that a Liberal vote was a wasted vote (which the electorate swallowed, too). Labour had 287 MPs in the new parliament, the Tories 260 and the Liberals just 59. Lloyd George had received more supportive coverage than MacDonald, prompting Margot Asquith to observe, 'the boosting in the press of Ll.G. shows how *very* little power it has'.[47] Baldwin had the consolation of seeing his son, Oliver, enter the House of Commons, although the pleasure was offset by the fact that he was one of the new Labour members.

MacDonald was once again a prime minister without a majority but after the trouncing they had just received the Liberals were unlikely to provoke another election any time soon. As the economy worsened both Lloyd George and Baldwin were content to let Labour try to sort it out in the confident expectation that the party would fail and normal service would be restored soon enough. In the crash of 1929, like the credit crunch eighty years later, it was the lot of Labour to try to rescue capitalism from its own failures. Like Gordon Brown, MacDonald believed socialism – however each chose to define it – would be built on the success of capitalism not its failure, but MacDonald had none of Brown's experience to help see him through. He was wedded to some old-fashioned economic values, like not spending money you hadn't earned, and he wasn't going to let go of them. The most orig-inal thinking on the Labour benches came from a man who would later be jailed in his new incarnation as leader of the British Union of Fascists, Oswald Mosley. Among his proposals was the freeing up of credit to encourage economic expansion. One of the great 'what ifs' of British politics is how things might have turned out differently had the Labour party or the media received his ideas with more enthusi-asm. Mosley resigned the Labour whip in 1931. He and his blackshirts would briefly get the support of the capricious Lord Rothermere. But politically he was out in the cold long before he found himself inside in the warm at His Majesty's pleasure.

Mosley wasn't the only man with ambitions to break the mould of the British political system. Lord Beaverbrook was another. He had been busy turning the *Daily Express* into a popular newspaper more than capable of giving Rothermere's *Daily Mail* a run for its proprietor's money. A hallmark of the *Express*'s success was Beaverbrook's belief that it should tell the news of the day in an accessible and lively form that ordinary readers could readily digest. By the end of the twenties he had proved that the formula worked. He told Davidson his aim was 'to move further and further from party politics and more and more in the direction of old age devoted to contemplation and repose'.[48] Davidson knew well enough that Beaverbrook was too restless a spirit for that and in 1929 Beaverbrook duly revived his campaign for free trade within an Empire protected by high trade barriers against the rest of the world. Realising that his influence over the main parties was negligible, he soon decided to launch his own United Empire party that would contest parliamentary seats. Media megalomania was rearing its ugly head once more and not for the first or last time Beaverbrook wondered if he might end up becoming prime minister himself. He wrote to an American friend, 'I have a very great fear that my present complications may land me at 10 Downing Street.'[49]

The *Daily Express* became the mouthpiece for the campaign – the 'crusader' emblem is still on the masthead to this day. The vehicle for achieving its aims was to be the by-election, much favoured by political insurgents down the ages. In October 1930 an Empire Crusade candidate, Vice-Admiral A. E. Taylor, won the South Paddington by-election in London by 941 votes. The following year in Islington Beaverbrook's candidate again polled more votes than the Tory and helped Labour hold the seat.[50] Baldwin's leadership was again on the line. He might never have gone on to become prime minister for a third time had he not decided to stand, fight and deliver what remains the most celebrated blow against overmighty press barons to this day. The next by-election, in the St George's ward of Westminster on 19 March 1931, was the showdown. Beaverbrook's cause was

supported by Rothermere, who had a habit of joining any press barons'
alliance when he could cause most mischief and gain most publicity by
doing so. Both saw the issue at stake unambiguously as the leadership
of the Conservative party and the future direction of the country. It
was, in the words of James Margach, who observed it first hand, 'Fleet
Street's biggest challenge of all time, with the ultimate, and astonishing objective of taking over No 10 Downing Street and forming their
own government'. Had they succeeded, 'the press would have emerged
as the supreme national political force with Downing Street reduced
to the status of a Fleet Street outpost.'[51] Such an outcome was unthinkable and Margach exaggerates the risk, although not the arrogance of
two men who really did seem to think they were more powerful than
the prime minister.

Baldwin, who didn't like to pick fights but hated even more to lose
them, enlisted the help of a relative, Rudyard Kipling, to arm him with
the killer phrase. Kipling, better known as the author of 'Britain's
favourite poem'[52] – 'If you can keep your head when all about you are
losing theirs . . .' etc. – saved his cousin's neck with a riposte that seemed
to say it all. In a reference to the *Daily Express* and the *Mail*, Baldwin
told a by-election meeting that 'What the proprietorship of these papers
is aiming at is power, and power without responsibility – the prerogative of the harlot throughout the ages.'[53] Hearing those words, the
editor of the *Express*, Beverley Baxter, threw down his pen saying,
'That's the finish. There can be no answer to that.' Although the article Baxter wrote about the speech omitted the killer line and merely
observed that Baldwin had attacked the *Daily Mail* and after doing so
'looked furtively at his audience and licked his lips'.[54] Less frequently
quoted from the speech is Baldwin's view that the two papers 'are the
engines of propaganda for the constantly changing policies, desires, personal wishes, personal likes and dislikes of two men. What are their
methods? Their methods are direct falsehood, misrepresentation, half-
truths, the alteration of a speaker's meaning by publishing a sentence
apart from the context . . .' Mr Baxter swiftly proved him right.

The issue was now 'press dictatorship' not Baldwin's leadership. Two
days later the Tory candidate, Duff Cooper, was duly elected to
parliament. Rarely has a single speech had such an immediate and

dramatic effect. The sentiments had been expressed many times before, but the timing was critical. Without it even a narrow Tory win would have left Baldwin vulnerable. With it his party could scarcely ditch him without appearing to have buckled to the will of unelected bullies. Kipling had every reason to be delighted with the impact of his words. He was a fastidious man and his opinion of popular journalism was lower, if anything, than his cousin's. Twenty years earlier he had been close friends with Beaverbrook, who was godfather to one of his children. But he'd had cause even before the Empire Crusade to call him a 'harlot' to his face. Kipling had asked for an explanation of the idiosyncratic political views of the *Express*, only to be told, 'I want power. Kiss 'em one day, kick 'em the next.'[55] It was a foolish boast and he got what was coming to him, a hefty kick in return from Baldwin, a man he had once again underestimated.

There's nothing a sitting prime minister enjoys more than watching the leader of the opposition being knocked about mercilessly. It was a pleasure that gave MacDonald considerable comfort from 1929 to 1931. He may not have had a majority but he had the other parties where he wanted them. The reverse may also be true. They had him where they wanted him, responsible for trying to find a response to an economic crisis that was not of his making and for which the conventional solution was to bear down on the least well off, including the unemployed. He was no more inclined to experiment with any truly radical 'socialist' alternative than any subsequent Labour prime minister. And the party's first prime minister was influenced by the right-wing press just as later ones would be. After reading some of the many stories of dole cheats and other supposed fraudsters in the papers he is said to have referred frequently in conversation to women driving up to benefit offices in fur coats to claim payments not due to them.[56] Other stories troubled him less, in particular those planted by some on the left of his own party suggesting that the foreign secretary, Arthur Henderson, would make a better leader. MacDonald remarked in his diary merely that 'the old games of Byzantine times go on'.[57] More widely MacDonald was getting a better press than he had ever enjoyed before, which is not saying much, although this was a product more of the disarray in the Tory party than any great affection for

Labour. Despite the doom-laden fears of Rothermere, newspapers were doing well. Even the left's own paper, the *Daily Herald*, was prospering, with new presses and a populist touch that would soon bring it within striking distance of the circulation of the *Express*.

MacDonald read the papers, undoubtedly, but he also made sure he now had others to read them for him, too. Indeed, his second government was responsible for another of the landmarks in relations between Downing Street and the media that look more significant in retrospect than they did at the time. In 1930 Number 10 employed its first ever full-time press secretary. George Steward, who came across the road from the Foreign Office news department, was given the rather more cumbersome title of 'chief press liaison officer of His Majesty's government' but there is a direct line from him to the communications director of today. At first the Labour administration had tried using its party press officer, William Henderson, MP for Enfield and the foreign secretary's son, to manage its media relations. It may well have been Henderson junior that MacDonald was referring to when he wrote in his diary about 'paragraphs issued by members of L.P. publicity staff saying I am to resign & that intellectuals of party want [Arthur] Henderson'[58]. Whether or not he was doing a bit of briefing on his father's behalf, William Henderson wasn't feeding the media beast sufficient red meat about the government's intentions. Journalists complained that as a party man he wasn't privy to the right information and the lobby asked for 'the provision of regular machinery for facilitating press inquiries'.[59] So the Downing Street press office was born, and with it the habit of spoon-feeding political journalists at their own request.

George Steward would remain the Number 10 spokesman throughout the turbulent years in the run-up to the Second World War. His period in the job started with the country's economy under threat and ended with its future as an independent nation in the balance. It was a far from glorious period for the British press but it opened with a sensational story. Labour's first ever prime minister, faced by demands for cuts in unemployment benefits to balance the budget and restore international confidence, dramatically abandoned his party and formed a National government with the opposition. His cabinet had refused to support the cuts, although the policy had the strong backing of the chancellor, Philip Snowden. Under normal circumstances the prime minister would have resigned and called an election. But the circumstances were not normal. MacDonald came under huge pressure from a diverse a group of interests including the King, *The Times* and both opposition leaders to head a coalition to get the country out of its mess. Snowden and a handful of other ministers joined him in deserting the Labour party. The majority went into opposition, along with the TUC, the *Daily Herald* (which called it a 'surrender to the city') and the rest of the Labour movement. Four days later, on 28 August 1931, MacDonald and the other 'traitors' were expelled from Labour's ranks. The period of relatively normal party politics that had begun with the downfall of David Lloyd George was at an end. Only illness prevented Lloyd George from joining the National government himself; it was just the kind of dramatic reordering of the furniture of which he wholeheartedly approved.

3

A FAREWELL TO ARMS: MACDONALD AGAIN, BALDWIN AGAIN, CHAMBERLAIN 'NEVER AGAIN' (1931–40)

The press creates. The press destroys.
King Edward VIII

In the 1930s Britain had never been more in need of an independ-ent and critical media. The challenges of mass unemployment and the rise of fascism posed enormous questions. Could they be turned back and, if so, at what cost? Were Britain's democratic institutions appropriate to the task? What would be the consequences of failure? But, except in left-wing journals with modest circulations, like the *New Statesman* and *The Week*, few journalists were asking them. The mainstream press was at its most pusillanimous when it should have been at its most aggressive. The battle for supremacy with the politi-cians was in abeyance because one side all but left the field. Several reasons were apparent at the start of the decade, although a newfound respect for parliament was not among them. Stanley Baldwin's 'harlots' speech had certainly had an impact. Beaverbrook and Rothermere and the other leading proprietors opted to make money rather than making trouble. They lost interest in politics and detected no appetite among their readers for more of it. Another reason was that politics, despite the crises at home and abroad, really did seem boring. The coalition had an overwhelming majority and none of the parties outside it, including Labour under its new leader in parliament, George Lansbury, stood the remotest chance of forming an alternative government. In Fleet Street, only the *Daily Herald* was left with an independent political party holding distinctive views to support. And even at the *Herald* the pursuit of readers took precedence over the pursuit of socialism. One observer suggested that the only way to get any socialism into the paper would be to 'write in on the back of a bathing beauty'.[1]

Coalitions are rare in Britain. There hasn't been one since the Second World War. The liberal intelligentsia may complain about the injustices of one-party governments based on less than half the votes in a general election, but most of the time the rest of the country yawns and looks the other way. From 1931, however, there was an extraordinarily long period in which Britain was governed by one coalition after another. It ended only in 1945. They were all 'National' governments in name, although until the outbreak of war they were heavily weighted in favour of the Conservatives and the official Labour party remained in opposition. The media largely supported the calls for national unity in the face of the economic challenge of the Depression and then, with their habitual disregard for consistency, complained at the consequences. As the decade progressed the papers frequently bemoaned that parliament had gone to sleep while volunteering to help hold a large rag of chloroform over the mouth of the body politic.

By the end of the decade *The Times* and its editor, Geoffrey Dawson, would stand accused of the worst offences of collusion with Downing Street to silence opposition to appeasement. In 1931 Dawson's most serious offence was vacillation. That summer, when the country still had a minority Labour government, Dawson wrote to the King saying of MacDonald that it 'was his business to get the country out of the mess' and that Labour staying in office 'was the only course that would have a permanent effect in reversing a policy of extravagance'.[2] Having opposed coalition government in print as well as in private he changed his mind as soon as one was formed. One advantage of the National government he declared, to justify his conversion, was that it made a general election in such turbulent times unnecessary. Then, when it became clear that both MacDonald and Baldwin favoured an election which they intended to fight together appealing for a 'doctor's mandate' to cure the sickly state of the economy, Dawson changed tack again. He wrote a leader advocating an election and found a loud echo of support from other editors and many Tory MPs. Throughout all his twists and turns Dawson was in close contact with both MacDonald and Baldwin and neither had any reason to be dissatisfied with what they got in return for confiding in him. Baldwin had always found Dawson to be a man he could do business with, an unusual quality in a newspaperman from his point of view. MacDonald, who was now a traitor in the eyes of the Labour movement, could at least take some comfort from the fact that the Establishment, and *The Times* represented nothing if not that, was now embracing him.

In the run-up to the election of 1931, MacDonald took pains to meet several of the editors and found most of them supportive. When the campaign began, only the *Daily Herald*, institutionally loyal to the Labour party, and the *Manchester Guardian* were hostile to the coalition. The latter was forthright, saying, 'this sham unity, this temporary and embarrassing alliance of tigers and sheep, is worth less than nothing'. The paper didn't say who were the tigers and who the sheep. Once the campaign began it was the claws of MacDonald and his colleagues, now huddling together inside a new and tiny 'National Labour' party, which proved sharpest. Philip Snowden, the chancellor, went on the radio to call his former party's programme 'Bolshevism run mad', knowing full well it had a great deal in common with the platform he'd campaigned on himself two years earlier. One Labour MP who stayed loyal to his party rather than MacDonald recalled fighting hostile and wholly inaccurate propaganda from his former leaders to the effect that 'Labour would steal money from people's post office savings bank accounts to put it into national insurance if elected'.[3] MacDonald was 'working the patriotic racket', he said, and using the union jack as if he owned it. Tony Blair and Peter Mandelson weren't the first to hit on that particular ploy. The official Labour opposition complained that the BBC, along with the rest of the Establishment, was now hostile. The allocation of party election broadcasts suggests they were right. The National government members were given eleven, Labour just three.

It all had the inevitable result of a massive parliamentary majority for the coalition on the back of 60 per cent of the popular vote. Of the members of the previous Labour cabinet who stayed loyal to the party, all but one lost their seats. MacDonald was curiously ambivalent about the result, recording in his diary, 'It has turned out all too well'. Even he knew that the Tory party had used him. 'It saw its advantage and took it, & unfortunately the size of the victory has weakened me. Once again I record that no honest man should trust in too gentle-manly a way the Conservative wirepullers.'[4] MacDonald still had Downing Street but the new government was predominantly a Conservative one. Like Lloyd George before him he was conscious that he had few true friends in the media. He had lost the *Daily Herald* and the Tory press would offer him support only as long as he was useful to them. He didn't have a thug like 'Bronco Bill' Sutherland to call on but he knew he needed help. Sir Robert Donald, former editor of the *Morning Chronicle*, was recruited to chair the National Labour party's publicity committee and was able to make a bit of difference at the margins, while George Steward got to work as the Number 10 press spokesman representing the government as a whole. Steward was a highly regarded civil servant with a good understanding of how the media of his time worked but he was employed in a purely reactive capacity, to respond to press inquiries and answer questions rather than to go out and actively sell the government's achievements, such as they were. By the end of the 1930s he was being significantly more proac-tive on behalf of Chamberlain's appeasement policy, but at the outset he contented himself with establishing regular briefings at Downing Street for journalists in the Westminster 'lobby' and trying (but failing) to stop them making approaches to ministers without going through him first.[5] He was a gatekeeper not a proselytiser and would have con-sidered it quite improper to be asked to be anything else.

The size of the majority swiftly stifled political debate and even if Steward had wanted to excite the interest of the media he'd have had

an uphill task. The papers were now much more interested in offering an outlandish array of advertising and promotional gimmicks,
including giveaway silk stockings, sets of Dickens' novels and free
insurance policies to registered readers. 'The reader no longer bought
newspapers. Newspapers bought readers,' as A. J. P. Taylor noted.[6]
After the Labour rump elected Lansbury, a former editor of the *Daily
Herald*, as its leader, both the prime minister and leader of the opposition were men who had earned their livings as journalists. Between
them, however, they failed to generate much excitement in their
former profession.

One reason, according to Taylor, was the sudden rise in the popularity of cinema with the arrival of 'the talkies'. 'The cinema was the
essential social habit of the age . . . Glittering cinema palaces went up
everywhere, even in the most impoverished areas . . . cinema provided
a substitute for real life and helped people to become watchers rather
than doers . . . real life was itself turned into a spectacle. The newsreels,
which were then part of every programme, presented current events
in the same intense, dramatic way.' As so often the Tories spotted the
potential for propaganda before anybody else. In the 1931 election they
sent a fleet of twenty-two 'cinema vans' around the country showing
what were in effect the first party election broadcasts in support of their
candidates.[7] Economic arguments didn't make for good viewing any
more than they do today. Even so, after the acres of press comment and
hours of economic analysis generated by the world economic crisis of
2008 onwards, it is perhaps surprising that the great depression, with
which it was so often compared, excited comparatively little debate.
Even the great hunger marches of the early thirties did little to excite
the interest, far less sympathy, of the media. On 27 October 1932 a
crowd estimated at around 100,000 people gathered in London's Hyde
Park to greet eighteen contingents of marchers from some of the most
depressed areas of Britain. A petition with a million signatures
demanded the abolition of means testing but was confiscated by the
police before it could be delivered to Downing Street. The marchers
had received scant publicity on their way to the capital and when they
arrived 'they were met by an almost blanket condemnation in the press
as a threat to public order'.[8]

The politicians were largely left alone to get on with the job and there was little appetite for a blame game about the causes of the Depression. Economic peaks and troughs were generally considered to be inevitable and mainstream opinion didn't expect ministers to start waving magic wands. MacDonald was, like Gordon Brown, a Scot brought up as a socialist, with an austere chancellor at his side. Unlike Brown he had no grand plan, and felt under no pressure to come up with one. Rather, he looked forward to a 'natural recovery' and simply hoped for the best. He was fortunate enough still to be around when things did indeed start to improve. Unemployment peaked towards the end of 1932 and during 1933 it fell by half a million. The weak pound boosted exports, interest rates were low, and this, along with a general world economic recovery, helped Britain over the worst.

By then some in Fleet Street were finally starting to wonder if it wasn't time to take a bit more notice of what the politicians had been doing while the papers were giving away encyclopaedias. One executive on the *Daily Express*, R. D. Blumenfeld, was moved to observe that 'from devoting too much attention to the sayings and doings of our legislators, the press has now gone to the other extreme, and devotes too little'.[9] Not surprisingly, he blamed the politicians. 'All reality has departed from party politics, and the shadow-fights at Westminster have ceased to interest anybody. Never in my long experience as a journalist has parliament been so lacking in forcible and picturesque personalities, or so out of touch with the feeling of the nation, as at the present time.'

Wise heads in the Conservative and Liberal parties saw dangers in the sullen mood that had descended on Fleet Street. The left may have been excluded politically but it had a vigorous and extremely successful national newspaper and when an election came around it would have everything to fight for. Having established its place in the market, the *Herald* was already taking more interest in the daily hardships of its readers. By comparison, the other papers had gone off the boil. The ageing J. L. Garvin, still editing the *Observer* after twenty-five years, warned its owner, Lord Astor, that 'the meaning of the *Daily Herald* is not realised by one Conservative in 10,000. A few years ago Labour had no big daily – an immense handicap. Now the *Daily Herald* has more readers than the *Daily Mail* and never ceases a relentless propaganda.'[10] The Tory press on the other hand couldn't muster the enthusiasm to say much in the government's favour. *The Times* supported the coalition, especially in foreign affairs, but while there may have been a solid Conservative majority, among its ministers the Tory papers saw little in the same old faces around the cabinet table to inspire their imagination.

Over at the *Daily Mail* Rothermere flirted with Mosley and fascism. On 8 January 1934 the paper declared 'Hurrah for the Blackshirts!'. A week later it called the British Union of Fascists 'a well organised party of the right ready to take over responsibility for national affairs with the same directness of purpose and energy as Hitler and Mussolini have displayed'. In May Rothermere ordered that the paper attack 'the apathetic sexagenarians of Downing Street' for lacking Mosley's zeal.[11] Only in June, when the BUF used brutal force to eject hecklers from a massive rally at London's Olympia and the *Daily Mail's* advertisers started to take fright did Rothermere back off. By the end of the year he was more inclined to look to Lloyd George, now a septuagenarian but ever hopeful of a comeback, as the great hope for the future.

Beaverbrook at the *Express* was a self-confessed 'political hobgoblin', but he was never tempted by fascism. Instead he used the paper to pursue a variety of lost causes and tried to appeal to a younger readership that had little interest in the grey old men in and around Number 10. He would have been happy to destroy the government and even to support Lloyd Gorge once again if he thought he could do it. Frances Stevenson, still at the old man's side although she would have to wait another nine years before he would marry her after the death of his wife, recalled a meeting with Beaverbrook. Lloyd George asked him if he hated MacDonald. 'No!' thundered Beaverbrook, with a diabolical look on his face. 'Baldwin!'[12] In the same period Margot Asquith, widow of Lloyd George's former rival, complained, 'How sad it is that we have no really good Liberal newspaper.'[13] She and others saw the *News Chronicle*, once their house journal, as more sympathetic to socialism than liberalism and the *Manchester Guardian* in much the same light.

One thing that might have reignited some interest in the established parties was a break-up of the coalition and a return to something more like adversarial politics. MacDonald had no interest in that because he had no party to speak of, but by the mid-1930s many Tories had good reason to believe that it would quickly result in a single-party Conservative government. The left may have done well in the propaganda war during the crisis of capitalism, they argued, but that didn't mean the country had turned socialist. Baldwin, Mr 'Safety First', wasn't convinced. He had been comfortable playing second fiddle to MacDonald within the National government and didn't see any reason to risk the coalition's thumping majority unnecessarily. Labour had been securing some impressive swings in by-elections and Baldwin, who had misread the popular mood before, didn't want to risk doing so again. So instead the Conservatives opted to strengthen their hold on the administration with a job swap between Baldwin and MacDonald, who was now sixty-eight with failing eyesight and memory. To put it politely, his mind was not what it had been and it was clear to everybody that his days of political usefulness were numbered. On 16 May 1935 he was persuaded to tender his resignation to the King and Stanley Baldwin returned to Downing Street soon afterwards as prime minister once more. MacDonald took Baldwin's old job of leader of the House of Commons but his career was effectively over. A general election was held at bay a little longer, until October, when the National parties agreed to fight it together once again.

Foreign affairs rarely feature heavily in elections but by 1935 the rise of Hitler in Germany and Mussolini in Italy already posed a real challenge to the current world order, sufficient at the very least to demand some political debate at home. Instead there was an early example of the conspiracy of silence to come. All the parties were nervous of the issue and Baldwin found a formulation with which none could argue: 'all sanctions short of war' and support for the League of Nations. Ministers judged that for most voters there were more pressing domestic concerns, including jobs and the lack of affordable housing. The newspapers, equally mindful that their readers were more interested in bread-and-butter issues, were happy to keep the international situation off the front pages.

On the eve of the election the Labour opposition chose a new leader, Major Clement Attlee, and he had the satisfaction of seeing the party treble its number of MPs to 154. The success of the *Daily Herald* and the de-politicisation of much of the rest of Fleet Street undoubtedly played their part. Nonetheless, the National parties had a huge majority, almost entirely made up of Tories, and the newspaper owners had little reason to feel guilty for having downplayed the political debate. Only later would it become clear just how cynically Baldwin, in particular, had been in his calculation not to trouble the electorate with events in mainland Europe.

Within a few years the election of 1935 would be cited to place Baldwin among the 'Guilty Men' accused of failing to prepare Britain for the fight against fascism. This was the title of a polemic against the pre-war appeasers written by Michael Foot (then a journalist working for Beaverbrook) and others in 1940. It charged Baldwin with failing to warn the nation of the dangers ahead and of wilfully neglecting the need to rearm. Baldwin himself had revealed his responsibility when, in 1936, he told the Commons with, in his own words, 'appalling frankness' that as early as 1933 'I and my friends were all very worried about what was happening in Europe', but that having recently lost a by-election to a pacifist Labour candidate he found himself in an uncomfortable position. 'Supposing I had gone to the country and said that Germany was rearming and we must rearm, does anybody think that this pacific democracy would have rallied to that cry at that moment? I cannot think of anything that would have made the loss of the election from my point of view more certain.'[14] In other words, claimed 'Cato', the pseudonym chosen by Foot and his friends (Cato had cleaned out the Roman sewers), he had put the interests of his party before those of his country.[15] Baldwin's words were listened to with interest by a young journalist on the *Daily Telegraph* by the name of W. F. Deedes. At the end of a long career in journalism and politics, Bill Deedes would look back and reflect that 'Baldwin hanged himself politically with that admission, yet he was right. As a reporter in those times I knew what a "pacific democracy" we were. I was also just old enough in the 1920s to sense how deeply the slaughter of 1914–18 had implanted in hearts and minds the resolution "Never Again".'[16]

Soon after the election Baldwin found he could ignore the threat from the Continent no longer. Mussolini, not Hitler, was the first to make bellicose noises and the British government's timorous response nearly destroyed it. A leak to the press in Paris showed how Britain and France were willing to sacrifice a nation's independence − that of Abyssinia (now called Ethiopia) − in order to appease a belligerent dictator. The so-called Hoare–Laval Pact, named after the British and French foreign ministers who agreed it, would have rewarded Mussolini's sabre-rattling in the Horn of Africa with territorial concessions that made a mockery of the system of international diplomacy. Given that all parties had pledged to back the principle of collective at the election, the leak led to an avalanche of criticism, joined on this occasion even by *The Times*, and a backbench Tory revolt that came close to burying Baldwin.

The press had woken from its slumbers and the prime minister was forced to dissociate himself from the pact and lose his foreign secretary into the bargain. His own credibility had suffered badly. The Abyssinia affair had left him physically exhausted but when his doctor prescribed a week's rest at Chequers while parliament was still sitting, J. C. C. Davidson warned him, 'Every mongrel is yapping, believing that a very tired fox has gone to ground . . . with no fight left in him.'[17] They were wrong. Baldwin survived the furore and had one last gargantuan fight ahead of him, one that he threw himself into with uncharacteristic vigour. He also had the satisfaction of once more defeating Rothermere and Beaverbrook into the bargain and getting the better of a troublesome backbencher with a distasteful habit of courting the press by the name of Winston Churchill.

The prime minister might not have been too good at standing up to dictators but when it came to British kings he felt on stronger ground. The unexpected death of King George V in January 1936 and the succession of his son as King Edward VIII set in train a crisis that created some bizarre alliances cutting across the worlds of politics and journalism. At the best of times the attitude of the British media towards the royal family is an extraordinary mix of subservience and prurience that defies all logic. Even today it is considered unacceptable for a journalist, however politely, to ask Britain's head of state a direct question, other than perhaps 'How are you today, Ma'am?' In 1936 a somewhat less respectful question was starting to be asked. Was the new king really going to marry a divorced American woman by the name of Mrs Wallis Simpson? The only reason the question wasn't on everybody's lips was that the press, far from telling its readers what was going on, was keeping from them facts that were the talk of Establishment circles. Elsewhere in the world, especially in the United States, the papers were speculating wildly. Back home even the communist *Daily Worker* kept mum.

Behind this wall of self-censorship a lot of not-so-subtle manoeuvring was going on, much of it accompanied by good food and champagne. In early November the wealthy Tory MP Sir Henry 'Chips' Channon, a passionate supporter of Edward's, arranged a dinner so as to introduce the monarch to Lord Beaverbrook 'with an idea of taming the press'.[18] Channon was a great believer in using his social connections to achieve political ends and he could see better than the monarch the troubles that lay ahead. In private Baldwin was vehemently opposing the marriage, which he believed would not only break all conventions, but also split the Empire. Churchill, no friend of Baldwin's, was also fêted by 'Chips'. Churchill had come close to supporting Beaverbrook's candidate against the official Conservative in the 'harlots' by-election of 1931 and had spent the past few years languishing on the back benches, writing books about his ancestors and fighting a lonely campaign against Indian independence. Churchill was an instinctive and impassioned royalist and Channon even thought he might have the makings of an alternative prime minister at the head of a new king's party. The woman at the centre of the storm that was yet to break, Mrs Wallis Simpson, did some discreet lobbying of her own and worked on one man in particular to great effect. Esmond Harmsworth had taken over the day-to-day running of the *Daily Mail* from his brother, Rothermere, and a few days after being lunched at Claridge's by the undoubtedly seductive Mrs Simpson the paper praised the King in a manner that was judged by Channon to be 'so fulsome and exaggerated as to be almost dangerous'.[19]

Five days later Channon recorded in his dairy: 'The Battle for the Throne has begun. On Wednesday evening (I know all that follows to be true, though not six people in the kingdom are so informed), Mr Baldwin spent one hour and forty minutes at Buckingham Palace with the King and gave him his ultimatum that the government would resign, and that the press could no longer be restrained from attacking the King, if he did not abandon all idea of marrying Mrs Simpson. Mr Baldwin had hoped, and thought to frighten the monarch, but found him obstinate, in love and rather more than a little mad; he refused point blank, and asked for time to consult his friends. "Who are they?" Mr Baldwin demanded. The audience was not acrimonious, but polite, sad and even affectionate, I am told. "Lord Beaverbrook," the King retorted. The prime minister gasped and departed.'[20]

It was the kind of intrigue in which Beaverbrook revelled and none of what he knew found its way into his newspapers. He told the King that it wasn't the support of the more downmarket papers that he needed, in any case, but *The Times* and the *Daily Telegraph*, and they could not be relied upon. Nor, it seemed, could other pillars of the Establishment. The archbishop of Canterbury, Dr Cosmo Lang, said nothing publicly but was said privately to be unhappy about conducting either the marriage ceremony or the coronation. The compromise advocated by some, a 'morganatic' marriage that would make Wallis Simpson the King's wife without her becoming Queen, was no more acceptable to him.

In the end it was another cleric, the aptly named Right Reverend Blunt, who helped bring matters to a head. Blunt was bishop of Bradford and on 1 December he gave a sermon on the King's need of divine grace. 'We hope that he is aware of his need. Some of us wish that he gave more positive signs of his awareness,' said the innocent prelate. Alarm bells rang at the Palace. Edward feared *The Times* would use the address as an opportunity to reveal what the bishop was so worried about and attack Mrs Simpson personally. He thought that the best way to prevent that was to get Baldwin to intervene on his behalf. He clearly shared the dangerous belief that the British prime minister could dictate what the 'voice of the nation' said. Baldwin rather sheepishly phoned Dawson and said that while he didn't claim to have any 'control over *The Times* or any other newspaper' he would like to know what he intended to print. Dawson reassured him that, far from planning to attack Mrs Simpson, he 'hoped we should never have to mention her'.[21]

It wasn't *The Times* the King had to worry about. The paper reported the bishop's remarks but with only the most oblique comment about the need for 'the English people's idea of kingship' to be reflected at the coronation. The following day it got a little braver reporting, on page 14, 'Cabinet Problems' and observing, 'The prime minister spent an even busier and more anxious day than usual yesterday.' There was a vague hint about a union 'incompatible with the throne' but no more. It was the *Daily Mirror* that broke the story wide open. With extraordinary secrecy it prepared a bombshell for its final edition on 3 December, giving the rest of Fleet Street no time to catch up.

The decision was taken by the *Mirror*'s director, Guy 'Bart' Bartholomew. He couldn't be sure of the agreement of the paper's chairman, John Cowley, so he waited for him to go home before reappearing in the office in his pyjamas. At 3.53 a.m. he watched as the new front page rolled off the presses with a huge picture of Mrs Simpson and the headline, 'The King Wants To Marry Mrs Simpson, Cabinet Advises No'.[22] The paper came down firmly on the King's side and demanded that Baldwin come clean with the country. 'Until this week,' it said, 'the *Daily Mirror* rigidly refrained from commenting on or publishing news of this situation. We have been in full possession of the facts but we resolved to withhold them until it was clear that the problem could not be solved by diplomatic methods. This course we took with the welfare of the nation and the empire at heart. Such is the position now that the nation, too, must be placed in possession of the facts.'

The rest of the Fleet Street followed up the story the next day. The *Mail* and the *Express* also voiced their support for the King against the prime minister. The *Telegraph* took the opposite view while in *The Times* Dawson produced what the diarist and MP Harold Nicolson called 'an amalgam of tortuous and pompous nothings'.[23] Neither Downing Street nor Fleet Street could be sure how the public would react. Until now, nobody had asked them or even told them there was a question in need of an answer. The *Mirror* had warned Baldwin that

'The Country Will Give You The Verdict' but before the country had the chance the King decided for himself. 'Our cock won't fight,' declared Beaverbrook.[24] On 5 December King Edward told Baldwin he intended to abdicate in favour of his brother and go abroad as the Duke of Windsor.

'The tired fox' had seen off the combined strength of the King, Churchill and what he had taken to calling 'the Devil's press' of Beaverbrook and the Rothermere clan. In the end the conspiracy of silence had damaged rather than helped the King, leaving him precious little chance to make his case to his people. 'The press creates. The press destroys,' he wrote later, but by his own estimation those papers that supported him had a combined readership of about 12.5 million while those against him had 8.5 million.[25] J. C. C. Davidson reflected that the combined strength of the *Daily Mail* and the *Daily Express* had 'no real weight, and it was very striking how the British people refused absolutely to be stirred up by a pro-King hysteria at the behest of the old Rothermere–Beaverbrook Alliance'.

When Baldwin had first entered Downing Street in 1923 he had been determined not to let the press call the shots. He stood down five months after the abdication, in May 1937, content to see that it had not. The remaining years of the decade would be no more comfortable for the media. Their willingness to keep the truth from the public was demonstrated again very swiftly. And the fate of a king was as nothing compared to the stakes for which Baldwin's successor would soon be gambling. When Baldwin resigned at a time of his own choosing, a rare enough luxury for a British prime minister, he was replaced without a contest by the chancellor of the exchequer, Neville Chamberlain. In the process, a man contemptuous of the media was succeeded by one with a dangerous obsession with controlling them. And while Baldwin had something of a walk-on part in the cast of *Guilty Men*, Chamberlain would be centre stage. Standing right alongside him would be many gentlemen of the press.

The journalist James Margach, who knew Chamberlain well and saw him in action at close hand, described him as 'the first prime minister to employ news management on a grand scale'. Not content with merely arguing his case, Chamberlain 'abandoned persuasion, turning instead to the use of threats and suppression to coerce the press into co-operation . . . He made the most misleading and inaccurate statements which he was determined to see published so as to make his policies appear credible and successful. Quite simply, he told lies.'[26] Margach worked on the true-blue *Sunday Times* and was one of Chamberlain's confidants. He was willing to accept his share of the responsibility on behalf of his own profession. He concluded that the sorry episode proved how 'the integrity and independence of journalism is in grave jeopardy when the media become active participants in the affairs of the government and Whitehall'.

It was one thing for much of Fleet Street to suspend its critical fac-ulties during the economic crisis and even to show an excess of discretion over the monarchy, but for the press to stifle debate while dictatorship spread across much of Europe and built up armed forces that would threaten the peace of the world was quite another. That is not to say that Hitler, Mussolini and Franco never made it into the papers; of course they did. But when Downing Street sought the help of the press to reassure the public and downplay the threat to Britain too many editors and proprietors were willing to comply. It was the darkest period in relations between Number 10 and the media, not because they were at loggerheads but because they were too cosy, too complacent and too ready to join in a conspiracy of misinformation. Few on either side of the supposed divide emerged from the period with their reputations enhanced. The media were subjected to the most sustained campaign of official bullying and lying they had ever seen and almost in unison they rolled over and asked for more.

Of course had appeasement worked, had Hitler backed down, then the judgement of history would be different. A bit of deception on behalf of both Downing Street and the media would have been for-given. And whatever else they are charged with, neither Chamberlain nor his friends in Fleet Street deserve to be accused of having anything other than the country's best interests at heart. Yet, notwithstanding the best efforts of a minority of politicians and journalists who refused to go along with it, the country was systematically deceived about the dangers it faced. *The Times*, in particular, deliberately and wilfully colluded with Downing Street to hide the truth. It misled not only its own readers, but also those abroad who believed the paper still spoke for the nation as a whole. Geoffrey Dawson, whom Margach called 'the patron saint of appeasement', was far from the only sinner but his failure to uphold the integrity of his profession was the starkest. He was well aware of the words of his nineteenth-century predecessor John Delane about the dangers of the press entering into alliances with statesmen,★ but he chose to follow a different path.

Neville Chamberlain was already sixty-eight by the time he became prime minister. Had he never succeeded to the top job he would have been remembered as an effective and principled minister with a record of which to be proud. As he ruefully observed to the archbishop of Canterbury shortly before his death in 1940, 'few men can have known such a tremendous reverse of fortune in so short a time'.[27] Chamberlain cared deeply about how he was perceived and took unprecedented pains to establish good relations with the press long before he entered Number 10. In 1930 he became Conservative party chairman, a post that carried with it responsibility for propaganda. He founded the Conservative research department to produce the material necessary to make that propaganda effective. He clearly had a taste and a talent for the relatively new business of political communications. He also knew how to use it for his own advancement as well as that of his party. When he left Central Office to resume his ministerial career he kept control of the CRD and it became known as 'Neville Chamberlain's private army'.[28] His aide-de-camp was Major Joseph Ball, a behind-the-scenes political fixer who had been made party publicity officer in 1927. Ball had unusual credentials for the job, to say the least. He had been head of MI5's investigation branch during the First World War and was described by J. C. C. Davidson as having wide experience 'in the seamy side of life and the handling of crooks'. Sadly for history, Ball had all his papers burned before his death, either in an effort to cover his tracks or in the belief that the actions of his political masters should tell their own story.[29]

According to Davidson, Ball was instrumental in running 'a little

★See p. 7.

intelligence service of our own. We had agents in certain key centres
and also had agents actually in the Labour party headquarters.'[30] In fact,
the spy was at Labour's printers, Oldhams, where the *Daily Herald* also
had its presses. Copies of Labour party leaflets and documents were
regularly collected and sent on to Conservative Central Office.[31] In the
1935 election the Tories obtained a copy of Clement Attlee's radio
address before he delivered it, enabling them to put together a detailed
and rapid reaction to what he said. Ball was knighted for his efforts the
following year, although inevitably no mention was made of his under-
cover work in the citation. Richard Cockett, now writing for *The
Economist*, has unearthed startling evidence of Ball's activities, including the secret purchase of the weekly newspaper *Truth*, which he used
to publish pro-Chamberlain stories and undermine the prime minister's rivals, both inside and outside the Tory party. Chamberlain
certainly knew all about that, confiding to his sister that the paper was
'secretly controlled by Sir Joseph Ball'.[32]

   Once Chamberlain was prime minister, Ball was set loose to do far
more damage. This he did alongside the hitherto uncontroversial
Downing Street press spokesman George Steward. Until now Steward's
contribution to the art of media manipulation had been confined to
building up the dependence of lobby journalists on briefings from
Number 10, like junkies in need of their twice-daily fix. MacDonald
and Baldwin had let him get on with it, rarely if ever getting involved
directly, but Chamberlain went to the opposite extreme. As chancellor of the exchequer he had chosen to brief the lobby himself on many
occasions and had come to think of it as his own private preserve. As
prime minister he continued to keep a close eye on what all the political journalists were writing while concentrating his personal energy
on those closest to his way of thinking, lunching with them regularly
at a Westminster club. Margach called it the closest government-press
exercise he ever experienced and it continued even as the international
situation became more and more threatening. All that changed as the
skies over Europe darkened was Chamberlain's manner, which went
from being cosy and relaxed to cold and arrogant. Even those journalists from government-supporting papers would get short shrift if
they asked difficult questions, often being told that they were falling for

'Jewish-Communist propaganda'.[33] Unusually for a Conservative, Chamberlain spent comparatively little time trying to court the proprietors. The only man he saw regularly was Lord Kemsley, owner of the *Sunday Times* (where Margach was employed), the *Daily Sketch* and various papers outside London. It was a relationship that paid dividends. Chamberlain would see the *Sunday Times'* political editor every Friday at Downing Street and every Sunday his views would be faithfully reproduced.

Meanwhile, Ball and Steward were doing some far less straightforward briefing, designed to put pressure not just on the media at home but also on the dictators abroad. Ball, with his MI5 background, liked to have friends in key centres of influence and power, and that included the Italian embassy in London. Steward had a good contact at the German embassy, the press attaché, Dr Hesse. Through these unofficial channels Hitler and Mussolini would receive intelligence about Chamberlain's views and intentions that was often at odds with the official government line. In Ball's case this was certainly disreputable and duplicitous, but for Steward to act in this way as a civil servant was wholly improper and, Cockett argues, even treasonable if he didn't have the defence of doing Chamberlain's bidding. The crucial question is a familiar one. How much did the prime minister know about what was going on? From the evidence, both direct and circumstantial, the answer seems to be 'a great deal'. His own expertise at press handling suggests he must have been able to detect the hand of those who worked on his behalf. Manipulation of the news was an integral part of his foreign policy and his personal dealings with journalists involved him directly in what we would now call the 'spin operation'. He was too dependent on its success to be able to claim ignorance.

Neville Chamberlain didn't have it all his own way. Ranged against him were individuals every bit as determined to use their own media contacts to put over a very different take on events. Winston Churchill may have been a mere backbencher in 1937 but he was a former chancellor and a formidable campaigner who openly called for an anti-fascist alliance and British rearmament in the face of German expansionism. The very fact that he had no platform as a minister made him even more dependent on the press to put over his views and, incidentally, given his expensive tastes, to provide a much-needed boost to his income. He made good money from Beaverbrook's *Evening Standard* until his contract was torn up without warning in 1938. He then moved to the *Daily Telegraph*, the paper that, along with the *Yorkshire Post*, supported his anti-German position most consistently. Churchill's campaign was sustained by a regular stream of leaks from within government, information provided by civil servants horrified at the Downing Street policy of playing down the threat to peace. These public servants were in breach of their contracts and duties just as much as George Steward, but having been proved right by history they have been exonerated while he stands condemned.

These days we are used to the idea of 10 Downing Street having to compete with another department of state – often the Treasury – actively, even aggressively, putting its own spin on events. Chamberlain was the first prime minister to have to confront such a challenge on a regular basis, although in his case the rival operation was being run from the Foreign Office. Anthony Eden, Chamberlain's first foreign secretary, was no appeaser and he struggled unsuccessfully to establish a *modus operandi* with the prime minister before resigning in 1938. While in office Eden had a powerful ally in Sir Robert Vansittart who, as permanent secretary, was in charge of running the department. Vansittart defied Downing Street with remarkable audacity before being removed from the scene, kicked upstairs in the best traditions of the civil service. Chamberlain hoped his removal would mean that 'in Rome and Berlin the rejoicings will be loud and deep'.[34] Vansittart used every method at his disposal, official or unofficial, to undermine Chamberlain's policy and the wonder is that he managed to do so for so long. He made little effort to disguise his views or indeed his activities. He believed it was his duty to try to warn politicians, in particular Churchill, whom he saw openly in his office, and the public that the Nazi threat was a great deal more serious than Downing Street maintained. Fortunately for Vansittart the Foreign Office had an already well-developed press operation. Its news department was run by another anti-appeaser, Rex Leeper (who would later suffer the same fate as his boss), and enjoyed excellent contacts with the diplomatic correspondents.

The Foreign Office had been building up a relationship with these

journalists for years and most of its clients, like the lobby correspondents who relied on Steward, were quite happy to open their
notebooks and take what was on offer. The consequence of this rival
briefing, the extent of which would always be denied by both sides,
was that a careful reader might detect two rather different accounts of
the balance of power within Europe in the same paper on the same
day, one from the political staff, the other from the diplomatic correspondent. It would have been even more confusing had most editors
and proprietors not ensured it was the Downing Street line that dominated the front pages and leader columns. Chamberlain was winning
the propaganda war so convincingly that he was prepared to put up
with the irritation of the Foreign Office, at least for a while. Although
it is a tribute to the persistent efforts of the Foreign Office news
department to defy him that Chamberlain eventually took the extraordinary step of asking Ball to set up a new organisation, the 'British
Association for International Understanding', to 'provide accurate and
unbiased information about foreign affairs'.[35]

One crucial reason for the success of Chamberlain's aggressive media
management tactics, quite apart from the fact that he was prime minister and so carried the biggest clout, was that he was a man of strong
convictions at a time when so many others were uncertain about what
could or should be done. A clear lead, pursued with consistency and
determination, is always attractive to journalists and Chamberlain
offered just that. He was also sure, as were most editors, that his policy
had popular support. The memories of the last war were too vivid, too
recent and too horrific for anyone to wish to see another. Perverse
though it may sound, Chamberlain had a touch of Margaret Thatcher
about him in his certainty and self-confidence. Like her he subscribed
to the view that 'there is no alternative', and nobody, including
Churchill, Eden, Vansittart or indeed any of the committed anti-fascists
on the left, had a clear strategy of their own for resisting Hitler. They
didn't share Chamberlain's view that Germany could be brought back
into the fold of civilised nations through persuasion, but nor did they
advocate all-out war to stop him. It is significant, too, that they didn't
question Chamberlain's integrity, only his judgement.

With his gift for theatricality, the prime minister quoted

Shakespeare's *Henry IV* as he left Britain to negotiate with Hitler. He hoped to be able to return and say, 'Out of this nettle, danger, we pluck this flower, safety.' After Munich he believed he had succeeded and the dramatic speech most often associated with him was delivered from a Downing Street window on 30 September 1938. He waved the agreement he had signed with Hitler and told the cheering crowd, 'here is the paper which bears his name upon it as well as mine . . .'. It was, he said, 'peace with honour. I believe it is peace for our time.' His parliamentary private secretary, Alec Douglas-Home, said his mistake haunted him for the last years of his life. But had he been right it would be remembered as one of the great political speeches of all time. Even his severest critics, Michael Foot and the other authors of *Guilty Men*, acknowledged that, 'Nobody can accuse Mr Chamberlain of being a wilful liar. He said those things because he believed them. He was absolutely satisfied that when Hitler signed that little piece of paper, the heart of a man who had built up his regime by treachery, lies and deception, had changed.'[36]

Whether the cheering crowds truly reflected the state of public opinion is impossible to say with certainty but the first ever monthly opinion poll from Gallup in October 1938 showed strong support for the prime minister. That may not be entirely surprising given the diet of news people were being fed. J. L. Garvin of the *Observer* wrote to Lord Astor that 'the daily press no longer gives any true idea of the feeling of this country'.[37] It would be wrong to believe that the entire press was singing from the government's hymn sheet, but most of it was. In a few isolated cases, notably the *Daily Telegraph*, the *Glasgow Herald* and the *Yorkshire Post*, Churchill and his friends were given ample space to express their views. The left and liberal press, including the *Manchester Guardian*, *News Chronicle* and *Daily Herald*, retained a healthy scepticism. But in most other papers, the contributions of the diplomatic correspondents notwithstanding, the government view was treated less critically than at any other time in modern history.

Not all the distortion that appeared in the press was inspired by Chamberlain or Downing Street. As ever, some powerful proprietors used the papers they owned to promote their own prejudices. Lord Rothermere may have dropped his support for Sir Oswald Mosley and his blackshirts, but had he not fallen ill he might have found himself interned for his openly voiced enthusiasm for Hitler. Under his direct orders the *Daily Mail* not only excused Nazi excesses, but also suggested that many of the attributes of Nazism, from its proud nationalism to its passion for youth and vigour, should be imported to Britain. Beaverbrook had his own, more peace-loving aspirations. He was never tempted by fascism and as a life-long admirer of Churchill ensured the *Daily Express* was a strong supporter of British rearmament. Yet Beaverbrook was essentially an isolationist. He didn't believe in war against Germany and he didn't believe it was going to happen either. After Munich he ordered the paper to carry a front-page banner announcing that 'Britain will not be involved in a European war this year, or next year either'.[38] It expressed his hope as much as his belief and he persisted in it longer than most, even when the evidence was mounting against him. He later claimed that his 'newspaper was invited by the government itself to make these declarations, the purpose being to influence opinion favourably so that there might be delay and time for consideration',[39] but he clearly hadn't taken much persuading.

It is the *The Times* that the government most frequently asked to help influence opinion and which most readily agreed to doctor the news it carried so as not to give offence to Hitler or provoke him into rebuffing Chamberlain's entreaties for peace. Geoffrey Dawson was described by Lord Northcliffe as early as 1919 as 'naturally pro-German. He just can't help it.' According to A. J. P. Taylor, in the late 1930s, Dawson 'turned the *Times* into a propaganda sheet and did not hesitate to suppress, or to pervert, the reports of his own correspondents'.[40] He as good as admitted as much himself, telling one of his staff in 1937 that he had been doing all he could not to offend Germany and had tried 'night after night, to keep out of the paper anything that might have hurt their susceptibility'.[41] Indeed, he told a friend, 'I spend my nights dropping in little things which are intended to soothe them.'[42]

It wasn't merely little things, however. In September 1938 *The Times* carried a notorious editorial that was directly inspired by Lord Halifax, who had replaced Eden as foreign secretary and was at this stage a strong supporter of appeasement. Dawson was allowing his paper to be used as a pawn in the government's negotiations. Chamberlain wanted to test the proposition that persuading Czechoslovakia to give up its German-speaking territories might satisfy Hitler's territorial ambitions. He wasn't ready to make the case publicly so he used *The Times* to do it for him. George Steward had already been to the German embassy to tell the ambassador privately that the 'British government were prepared to demand the most far-reaching sacrifices from Czechoslovakia if only Germany would adhere to peaceful methods in settling the Czech question'.[43] The article in *The Times* argued that it was impractical to apply the principle of self-determination rigidly and that it might be in the Czechs' own interest to let the Sudetenland go to Germany. Rab Butler, who was then a junior foreign-office minister, later confirmed that he believed Halifax had inspired the article.[44] The Foreign Office went through the motions of distancing itself from what *The Times* had said but the German press attaché, Dr Hesse, reported back to Berlin that 'no part of the article has been disavowed' by Chamberlain.

There were good reasons for the government to want to use *The Times* in this way. The paper was read in Berlin, sometimes by Hitler himself, and was considered to be the voice of the British nation more frequently abroad than at home. (Some in the German press had noted that if you spelled Times backwards you got 'Semit', proving that it was part of a Marxist-Jewish conspiracy.) It was impressed upon Dawson by Chamberlain, Halifax and the British ambassador in Berlin, Sir Nevile Henderson, that what appeared in his paper could have a direct impact on Hitler's actions. Halifax met Hitler and his propaganda chief Dr Josef Goebbels in November 1938 and had been shocked by how exercised both men were on the subject of the press. Hitler told him that 'Nine tenths of all tension was produced simply and solely by it.'[45] Goebbels was even more excitable, talking about little else. He asked Halifax to do something 'to put a stop in the British press to personal criticism of Hitler'. Halifax took what he had heard to heart, writing to Henderson on his return to London that he was hopeful about relations with Germany 'if only we can get the press in both countries tame'. When, a year later, that optimism was to be proven wrong, Henderson made the extraordinary claim that 'History will judge the press generally to have been the principal cause of war.'[46] That was nonsense but there's no doubt Halifax and Chamberlain believed that muting media criticism of Germany was a vital foreign-policy objective. The BBC was persuaded to drop a series of talks on the 'German colonial problem' and Halifax met Dawson shortly after his return from Berlin to impress upon him once more the importance of his newspaper to peace in Europe. There is no doubt that Dawson, supported by his deputy, Robin Barrington-Ward, felt a real sense of responsibility. It was Barrington-Ward who wrote many of the leading articles calling for an understanding with the Nazis. He did so not because either he or Dawson was pro-Nazi, but because they were genuinely convinced there was no alternative policy available. Barrington-Ward wrote in his diary, 'Appeasement is a misleading term, even though it has had official sanction. *The Times* has declined to use it, implying as it does a policy of "buns to the bear" instead of an endeavour to secure by negotiation the removal of the causes of war.'[47]

If the Sudetenland wasn't 'buns to the bear' it's hard to see what would have been. But it wasn't just events inside Germany and its neighbours that were deliberately distorted both by *The Times* and by Downing Street. Chamberlain ensured that any signs of dissent within his own government were minimised even if it meant undermining the reputations of profoundly honourable men. Other prime ministers have been accused of sanctioning briefings against critics within their own parties but none had as much success with the tactic as Chamberlain. When Anthony Eden resigned as foreign secretary in February 1938, in a dispute over Chamberlain's interference in his responsibilities, few in the press had much sympathy for him. Sir Joseph Ball told Chamberlain he had taken 'certain steps privately' to destroy Eden's case for resigning and they certainly worked. He put it about that Eden was exhausted and couldn't cope with the strain of the job. According to the *Manchester Guardian*, 'the government press' presented a 'curiously distorted picture' of the resignation and 'for the most part . . . preserved a unity of silence that could hardly be bettered in a totalitarian state'.[48] The same fate would befall Duff Cooper when he resigned as first lord of the Admiralty in the wake of Munich. Cooper made a powerful resignation speech in the Commons that much impressed Churchill, among others. The report by *The Times*'s gallery reporter Anthony Winn, said as much. Except that it never appeared in the paper. Dawson spiked it and wrote his own account of the occasion, under the byline 'From our Lobby Correspondent' that dismissed the speech as a 'damp squib'.[49] Winn resigned from the paper without making a public fuss. Margach, who knew him, called the incident 'about the worst example of editorial distortion deliberately engineered to give comfort and support to a prime minister'. A few weeks later *The Times* offered its readers special Christmas cards with a photograph of Chamberlain just back from Munich waving to the crowd from the Buckingham Palace balcony in the company of the King and Queen.

Ball didn't waste the skills he had learned with MI5 merely on the media. Eden and Cooper had a small but enthusiastic band of supporters on the Tory back benches. Some would meet weekly at the house of the MP Ronald Tree in Queen Anne's Gate, close to the House of Commons. Many, many years later Tree wrote a book that shed a bit more light on Ball's methods. The house across the street was rented by two journalists, Victor Gordon-Lennox, diplomatic correspondent of the *Daily Telegraph*, no friend of the appeasers, and Helen Kirkpatrick of the *Chicago Daily News*. Tree recalled, 'One day Helen rang me and asked me if I knew that my phone was tapped. I had noticed some odd clickings when I picked up the receiver to ask for a number, but I had not realised that the government thought us to be so dangerous. Some time later, during the war, I came across Sir Joseph Ball at the Ministry of Information, a dislikeable man with an unenviable reputation for doing some of Chamberlain's "behind-the-scenes" work. We got into conversation and he had the gall to tell me that he himself had been responsible for having my telephone tapped.'[50]

It is reasonable to suppose that Ball didn't tell the prime minister of this bit of freelance dirty tricks. When political henchmen get their fingers particularly dirty they normally protect their masters from any association by keeping them in the dark about the details. Nor is it possible from the records to know exactly how much Chamberlain knew of his own press secretary's involvement with the German ambassador to London. What is clear is that in the aftermath of Munich Chamberlain was determined to quell all opposition to his policies. Rex Leeper, who after the departures of Eden and Vansittart had continued to use the Foreign Office news department to counter Downing Street's complacency, was himself sidelined with a posting in Bucharest in the summer of 1939. George Steward told Dr Hesse with alarming frankness that Chamberlain held the Foreign Office responsible for trying 'to sabotage his plans and commit Great Britain to warlike actions against Germany'. Berlin was told that the prime minister had got his way over Munich only by 'ignoring the provisions of the British constitution and customary cabinet usage'.[51] Steward's behaviour would have continued unchecked had MI5 not had its own source inside the embassy who told the Foreign Office what the Downing Street press secretary was up to. When Halifax, who by now was starting to have his doubts about the effectiveness of appeasement, relayed the information to Chamberlain the prime minister claimed to be 'aghast at the news'. He couldn't have been that aghast, however. Steward kept his job until May 1940 when, in the first year of the war, Chamberlain resigned and Churchill took his place.

Chamberlain was not only being disingenuous with his foreign secretary, he was deceiving the lobby and even lying to parliament. According to Margach, the prime minister 'constantly attempted to mislead political correspondents in the most calculated fashion, by telling us what later proved to be the most grotesque version of the truth. He persisted in giving optimistic forecasts of international prospects which were lies.'[52] He had strengthened his grip on the government's propaganda machine but too many inconvenient facts were starting to emerge for even the prime minister to suppress. As evidence of Hitler's bad faith mounted, Halifax came to accept that war could no longer be avoided. Increasing numbers of MPs started to doubt the government's reliability and integrity as a source of information. In answer to a question in parliament about what official or unofficial advice ministers had been giving newspaper owners on their coverage of foreign policy, Chamberlain replied that 'no such advice had been tendered . . . neither officially nor unofficially'.[53] He lied.

Throughout the early spring of 1939 Chamberlain continued to

ooze optimism both in public and in private. And the political correspondents continued to report his upbeat assessments under the usual
cloak of lobby anonymity. The prime minister didn't even bother to
tell his foreign secretary when he had the journalists in for another of
his pep talks on 9 March. There is no record of exactly what he said,
but it was to the effect that a golden age of peace and prosperity was
just around the corner. When the newspapers appeared the following
day, foreign officials were aghast at what one called the 'ridiculous rain-
bow story' that was attributed to 'an authoritative source'. Nobody had
any doubt where it had come from and Halifax was moved to complain to Chamberlain. The prime minister wrote back that he was
'horrified at the result of my talk to the press' which was intended only
as a 'general background'. The prime minister promised 'faithfully not
to do it again'.[54]

On 15 March 1939 everything changed. Hitler's armies marched
into Czechoslovakia and Chamberlain's optimism was seen for the self-
deluding and dangerous nonsense that it was. Even *The Times* observed
that 'German policy no longer seeks the protection of a moral case'.[55]
The mood in parliament was increasingly restive and MPs were ready
to point the finger at the paper for giving Hitler comfort in the past.
The monolith of the pro-Chamberlain press began to crack. Rival
papers relished in reprinting the notorious *Times* leader of the previous
September. Yet, astonishingly, not only was Chamberlain ready to persist with his old techniques, but Dawson was willing to go the extra
mile with him. After Britain gave its solemn guarantee to defend
Poland's independence on 31 March *The Times* pointed out that this
didn't mean a guarantee to defend Poland's existing borders.
Chamberlain told the parliamentary lobby on the eve of the Easter
recess that they could have a good holiday because there would be no
more shocks from the dictators. This time he found them in a different mood. Almost at the eleventh hour the London press started to
show some independence and a readiness to take Chamberlain on.
Editorials speculated about a general election or the formation of a war
cabinet. Several called for Churchill to be brought into the government.
The *Sunday Pictorial* put his picture on its front page as 'the man that
Hitler fears'.[56] *The Times*, loyal to the last, called the campaign to enlist

Churchill 'mischievous and futile'.[57] Not for long it wasn't. The German–Soviet pact was signed on 24 August and on 1 September Hitler invaded Poland. The very same day Winston Churchill was invited to join the government. Chamberlain's policy lay in ruins.

In his radio address to the nation on 3 September announcing the declaration of war, Chamberlain told the British people, 'You can imagine what a bitter blow it is to me that all my long struggle to win peace has failed. Yet I cannot believe that there is anything more, or anything different, that I could have done, and that would have been more successful. Up to the very last it would have been quite possible to have arranged a peaceful and honourable settlement between Germany and Poland. But Hitler would not have it.' In the Commons he went further. 'This is a sad day for all of us, and to none is it sadder than for me. Everything that I have worked for, everything that I hoped for, everything I have believed in during my public life has crashed into ruins.' There was no time and little inclination to ruminate on the way in which he had enlisted the media in his struggle. The circumstances were extraordinary but there were lessons in his failure that would carry forward to more normal times. A prime minister used to reading his own views repeated back to him, with the added bonus of being told how wise they are, may mistake good notices for good policy and a consensus in the media for an equally broad agreement in the country. Chamberlain's efforts to dictate the headlines were dangerous not just for himself, but, far more importantly, for the country. Churchill put it succinctly on the eve of war when he said, 'Criticism in the body politic is like pain in the human body. It is not pleasant, but where would the body be without it?' Britain was weaker militarily, morally and politically as a result of the collusion between Downing Street and Fleet Street. But this was not the moment to give up on propaganda, rather to direct it towards a very different objective. Those who remembered the clumsy efforts of the government to control the media in the First World War entered the second with understandable trepidation.

4

PUT OUT MORE FLAGS: CHURCHILL (1940–45)

Propaganda is all very well, but it is events that move the world.
Winston Churchill

For two years Neville Chamberlain had been cajoling the media to suppress their critical faculties and trust him in the cause of peace. He can hardly have been surprised that when he now urged them to do the same in the cause of war they were far from sympathetic. The newspapers had been manipulated, bullied and lied to by Downing Street and the prime minister had made fools of them. Far from helping to prepare their readers for the hardship and sacrifices of war and explaining the brutal realities that made conflict unavoidable, most papers had given over their pages to endless words of reassurance, suggesting it wasn't going to happen. Chamberlain's failure was their failure. They had forfeited the trust of the people just as he had done, although they stood a better chance of regaining it. Chamberlain's prime ministership would soon be over, but no editor or journalist felt the need to resign. His ultimate decline and fall was to them another story and they would be around to write his obituaries, both political and personal, and usher in the new regime.

When, in the autumn of 1939, Chamberlain had the novel

experience of an almost universally hostile press he put it down to the fact that 'papers must live and . . . they sell better if they abuse the government than if they praise them'. With even more extraordinary self-assurance he told the cabinet in November that the criticism '. . . bore no relation to any spontaneous feeling of indignation in the country. The explanation of so unpatriotic a course of conduct on the part of newspaper proprietors lay in the degeneration of our press. We have now a very different press from that which, in past ages, had been a bulwark of the liberty of the subject'.[1]

In September 1939 Britain moved from an illusory peace to an illusory war. The opening months of the Second World War became known as the phoney war or, with an added touch of humour, the bore war. At least the government was now starting seriously to prepare for the very real battles ahead rather than seeking to avoid them. Those preparations included putting in place a new propaganda machinery, more overt in its intentions but scarcely more comfortable for the media than what had gone before. Without exception war provokes tension between journalists and the government no matter how united the country might be in opposing the enemy. Ministers believe they have a right to impose their views and tend to interpret media criticism as something akin to treason. New structures for disseminating information are established, almost invariably involving the military, and any hesitation about using the law to keep the media in line quickly evaporates. So it was in 1939. Even the ultra-loyal J. C. C. Davidson would be moved to describe the plans for the wartime propaganda machinery as something '. . . of which any totalitarian state would be proud'.[2] That might have been true if the new Ministry of Information had been more effective. Instead, it got off to a very bad start and was better known to journalists as the ministry of aggravation.

The plans for the ministry had been drawn up by Rex Leeper before his removal as head of the Foreign Office news department. Under Leeper's scheme the ministry would be responsible for distributing all information concerning the prosecution of the war and for propaganda at home and abroad. All other departments would have to go through the MOI and no news activity was to be undertaken without its knowledge. In theory that would reduce the power not only of

individual departments, but also of Downing Street to operate independently. No doubt it looked good on paper but it was never going
to work in practice. Only a week into the war the new ministry was
made to look ridiculous when news leaked through the Paris media
that a British Expeditionary Force was on French soil. At first the War
Office confirmed it, without going through the MOI. Then it got cold
feet and called in the police to confiscate the first editions of the
London papers. Raiding newspaper offices was bad enough but the
police then set about stopping trains and pulling over cars driving out
of London in order to confiscate any early editions people might be
carrying. There was uproar in Fleet Street. Ministers were roused from
their beds in the middle of the night to answer calls from furious journalists and the confiscation order was withdrawn. In the coming days
editors bombarded Downing Street with complaints. Francis Williams,
editor of the *Daily Herald* and a future Number 10 press secretary,
pointed out that the presence of British troops had been broadcast
twice by French radio. Lord Macmillan, the minister in charge of the
MOI, reported that the newspapers were 'in a state of revolt'. The War
Office's only defence was 'The newspapers might have published more
details. You can't expect us to trust the newspapers.'[3] If the government
wanted to keep the media onside it was going to have to find a more
effective way of doing so.

The parliamentary lobby journalists wrote to the prime minister
urging him to go back to the system of confidential briefings to trusted
individuals that had given them their privileged access to information
and given Downing Street the ability to influence public opinion
under the cloak of anonymity. They may have been angry at the way
the system had been abused by Chamberlain but they were willing to
risk more of the same rather than see information handed out on the
record to all and sundry, or, worse still, suppressed. Chamberlain could
see the attraction of their argument and, despite complaints from journalists outside the lobby, the exclusive right of the MOI to disseminate
news was quickly removed. Arguably the media had let slip an opportunity to turn information about the activities of government from a
commodity to be traded in secret into one available publicly and
openly. It's doubtful, however, that persisting with the original plans

would have led to the public being any better informed about the conduct of the war. The ministry had never been intended as a step
towards open government. The attitude of those within its walls was
well reflected in a memo written in September 1939 entitled 'The
Preservation of Civilian Morale'. In it an unnamed official wrote,
'. . . the people must feel that they are being told the truth. Distrust
breeds fear much more than knowledge of reverses. The all-important
thing for publicity to achieve is the conviction that the worst is
known . . . the people should be told that this is a civilians' war, or a
People's War, and therefore they are to be taken into the government's
confidence as never before'. So far, so good. But it went on to ask,
'. . . what is truth? We must adopt a pragmatic definition. It is what is
believed to be the truth.' The government would be wise therefore 'to
tell the truth and, if a sufficient emergency arises, to tell one big,
thumping lie that will then be believed'.[4]

There was even a suggestion that the ministry should prepare standard headlines and hand them out to editors, who would then be
compelled to use them. The plan was shelved because of technical difficulties, which is just as well. The ministry had drafted in temporary
staff from a variety of backgrounds but few were journalists. Williams
feigned regret that 'sadly the world never learned what headlines a committee of retired admirals, civil servants, professors and ex-ambassadors
might come up with'. After a brief flirtation with the idea that it could
be all-powerful, the ministry quickly realised it was not even going to
be able to control what news the government released, never mind how
it was headlined in the press. What it got instead was a dreadful muddle,
intended to meet everyone's objections but in the end merely alienating them all. Ministries, including the service departments, could make
their own announcements but these would be simultaneously released
at the Ministry of Information. This was a nightmare for the censors,
who didn't always see material until after it had gone out. Journalists
were also invited to submit their copy to the censors before it was published in order to ensure it didn't contain information that might be
useful to the enemy. The scheme was voluntary, except for material des-
tined to go abroad. Newspapers at home could publish what they liked
but they could be prosecuted if they published anything of value to

Britain's enemies. It was a system 'based on bluff, goodwill and the fear that something worse would follow if it broke down'.[5]

Not surprisingly the complaints from journalists continued unabated. Chamberlain decided he needed a ministerial heavyweight in charge of the ministry. He thought first of Leslie Hore-Belisha, then at the War Office. The foreign secretary, Lord Halifax, among others, queried the idea on the grounds that Hore-Belisha was Jewish. John Colville, a civil servant who had recently joined the Number 10 staff and whose diaries are an invaluable record of the period, noted that 'the fact that he is a Jew would make him a target for the Nazis, who would represent all British propaganda as an inspiration of Judaism. This argument has impressed . . . the PM.'[6] Lord Beaverbrook had been under consideration for the job but said he wasn't interested in an organisation that was bureaucratic, cautious and 'seemingly intent only on preaching a supine confidence to the British public'.[7] Eventually it went to Sir John Reith, the former director general of the BBC, who had been running Imperial Airways since 1938. Not everybody in the ministry was excited by the prospect. Somebody put up a notice 'Demise of Lord Macmillan. No Reiths by request'.[8] The fears proved short-lived. Reith came in with gusto, determined to win back for the ministry many of the powers it had lost, but he had no time to do anything about it. Chamberlain himself resigned just a few weeks later and Reith, who thought Churchill was a 'horrid fellow', was out the job scarcely before he'd begun it.

By May 1940 the bore war was over and the real war was going badly. The slapdash and chaotic administration of the information ministry was symptomatic of a malaise that went far wider. The papers were crying out for action abroad and for somebody to get a grip at home. There were no well-defined war aims beyond 'smashing Hitler' and the government didn't look as if it could muster the energy or the imagination to start taking the fight to the enemy. Chamberlain, who had a knack for the sound bite if nothing else, declared that 'Hitler has missed the bus' but that was no substitute for a strategy. Chamberlain and Halifax seemed to think that Nazi Germany would just wear itself out and sue for peace before very long. The prime minister's critics saw things very differently and they had many allies in the press. Brendan

Bracken MP, one of Churchill's oldest friends and now his parliamentary private secretary, told a *Manchester Guardian* correspondent, 'We are not winning this war, we are on the way to losing it.'[9] In the end it would be an unsuccessful military operation that would bring Chamberlain down, even though it had been promoted by Churchill against the prime minister's instincts. The failure to prevent the Nazis taking control of Norway gave the anti-Chamberlain forces the excuse they needed to move in for the kill. The Norway campaign was a PR disaster as well as a military one. Colville recorded listening to the news on the radio 'which was derived almost entirely from German sources: scarcely a word from our own . . . Sir John Reith feels bitterly on the subject – but nobody will supply him with the necessary material.'[10]

When it came to the political fallout, journalists had no shortage of material for their stories. The prime minister's allies did their best to argue that he bore no responsibility for the defeat, but they could do little to stop the tide of opinion shifting against Chamberlain. Even Dawson in *The Times* called for 'a stock-taking both of the structure and of the personnel of the government'.[11] It wasn't the pressure in the media that brought down Chamberlain or lifted up Churchill in his place, although as usual some egotistical proprietors would claim otherwise. On the eve of the Norway Debate in the Commons the prime minister was 'very depressed about the press attacks on him' but with his 'curious vanity and self-esteem' he didn't anticipate defeat.[12] Indeed, he won the vote, but the government's majority was cut from 200 to 81 and there were calls of 'Resign!' when the figures were announced. It was parliament not the press that delivered the fatal blow. 'In the name of God, go!' declared the Tory MP Leo Amery, quoting Oliver Cromwell, in the debate's most dramatic intervention.[13] David Lloyd George showed that, even at the age of seventy-seven, there was life in him yet, telling Chamberlain 'there is nothing which can contribute more to victory in this war than that he should sacrifice the seals of office'. Forty-one of the government's backbenchers voted with the opposition at the end of the debate and another sixty abstained. Chamberlain had lost his authority and two days later he resigned. But for a piece of high political theatre, Lord Halifax, whose decency and popularity helped absolve him for his early support for appeasement, might have taken over. Chamberlain, Churchill and Halifax had a meeting to try to resolve the issue of whom to recommend to the Palace. When Churchill was given the opportunity to confirm that he would serve under Halifax he said nothing at all for a full two minutes, which must have been torture for a man never normally lost for words. The others in the room got the message. No government without Churchill in it would have been acceptable to the country, never mind the media. Attlee was then consulted and, once he reported back that the Labour party would join the coalition under Churchill and take ministerial positions for the first time since MacDonald's defection in 1931, the matter was settled.

Had Chamberlain governed at a time more suited to his talents, which were as a domestic reformer, he would very probably be remembered to this day as a great prime minister. His fascination for the media might also have been put to better use, making the case for compassionate conservatism rather than for appeasement. And had his attempts to avert war not failed then Churchill would almost certainly never have become prime minister at all. In safer times his reputation for being hot-headed and unpredictable would have made him too risky a proposition. Many thought as much even in May 1940. When he made his first appearance in the Commons as PM he got more cheers from the Labour benches than he did from the Tories. Churchill told the House that he had 'nothing to offer but blood, toil, tears and sweat'. His policy? 'Victory at all costs.'[14] Life was about to be made a lot easier for the headline writers but a lot tougher for everybody else.

If the Conservative benches were still unsure about the new prime minister so too were some sober heads in Fleet Street. The change at the top was a huge story, but while the editors had little doubt Churchill would supply them with good copy they were in a mood to wait and see whether he would also provide good government. The reappointment of many of the old faces to senior positions, including Halifax, who stayed as foreign secretary, and Chamberlain, who became lord president, didn't inspire confidence in a brave new beginning. The Labour ministers who joined the new coalition, notably Clement Attlee, Herbert Morrison and Ernest Bevin, had yet to prove their

value. There were two significant appointments lower down the ministerial ladder, however, both of them very well known to journalists.
Lord Beaverbrook, who had remained close to Churchill throughout his
years in the wilderness, became minister of aircraft production. He
feigned reluctance, citing his asthma and lack of executive experience
in Whitehall. But he soon accepted and was described as being 'so
pleased to be in the government that he is like the town tart who has
finally married the Mayor!'.[15] The relationship was perhaps not quite
that intimate, but, according to his biographer, 'Beaverbrook was now
Churchill's only personal friend in political circles'.[16] Churchill wanted
him around to keep him cheerful, but he also valued his reputation for
cutting though the bureaucracy and getting things done in a hurry.
Churchill rightly concluded that he would be more effective getting
planes built than advising on the media, where in any case Beaverbrook
had at least as many enemies as friends. One military man observed that
'Beaverbrook as minister of aircraft production is still Beaverbrook the
press king: he attaches supreme importance to the numbers of aircraft
he can produce, as he formerly did to the numbers of the *Daily Express*
he could sell. "Circulation" is his paramount interest.'[17] It was an
inspired choice, though not a popular one with all his ministers. Attlee,
who loathed Beaverbrook with a rare intensity for such a calm man,
thought Churchill needed him as 'a stimulant or drug'.[18]

The job of information minister went instead to Duff Cooper,
another controversial appointment. Robin Barrington-Ward, who
would succeed to the editor's chair at *The Times* in 1941, described
him as having an 'asinine ignorance of newspaper practice'.[19] Cooper
had a miserable time in the job, in no small part because he couldn't
get the prime minister to take a serious interest in the issue of press
relations. 'When I appealed for support from the PM, I seldom got it',
he wrote later. 'He was not interested in the subject. He knew that
propaganda was not going to win the war.'[20]

Winston Churchill had extensive experience as a journalist,
although mainly of the more swashbuckling kind. On the whole he
liked newspapermen, even if he thought most were suitable only for
the tradesman's entrance. He read more newspapers with greater
attention than almost any other prime minister. Barrington-Ward

described him as having the press 'rather on the brain'.[21] His mind was too restless and too fertile not to want to keep up to date with what the media were saying. Baldwin's indifference to what journalists wrote would have struck him as bizarre, but so too would Chamberlain's belief that he had a right to interfere in both the news they reported and the views they expressed. Churchill would often get extremely irritated with what he read and would obsess unnecessarily over details that need not concern a prime minister at any time, never mind one waging a world war. He would wait up until the early hours when the next morning's papers were delivered to Downing Street and have plenty to say about what was in them. Arthur Christiansen, then editor of the *Daily Express*, recorded that a 'motor-cycle despatch rider called at the *Express* office every night to collect the first edition for him as soon as it came off the presses. Often Beaverbrook used to call me long after midnight to say that the PM had been on the telephone complaining about some tiny item in the early edition.'[22] Colville was present on one occasion when 'Winston was furious because the morning papers, which he likes to see before going to bed, had not arrived. In his emotion he upset his whisky and soda all over his papers.'[23] Yet for the most part Churchill was prepared to let the journalists get on with their jobs so long as they would let him get on with his. Beaverbrook would encourage him to see Fleet Street editors at Downing Street but the encounters were rarely a success and were soon discontinued. Christiansen was among those invited and said Churchill 'always struck me as being in a thoroughly bad humour on these occasions . . . he looked smaller than any of us but twice as ferocious . . . the cigar would be laid aside and in his sibilant stammer he would demand, "Pray, gentlemen, what can I say to you?"'

He may not have had a lot to say to them but what he said about them, in public at least, was generally positive. In the middle of the war he declared that 'Our vast influential press has known how to combine independence and liveliness with discretion and patriotism.'[24] He believed in a free press but then he believed in a lot of things and not all of them were compatible in wartime. What Churchill believed in first and foremost was victory 'at all costs', even the cost of denying freedoms he might otherwise defend.

Early in his premiership he was willing to consider a severe crack-down on the liberty of the press. The chief of the naval staff was among those urging compulsory censorship of military information. He wrote Churchill a memo warning that 'mischievousness, commercial competition, political antagonisms, professional jealousies and desire of individuals to secure "a scoop" all play their part in assisting the enemy and retarding the efforts of the Allies'.[25] The prime minister was willing to listen to the argument for censorship but he also asked for the opinions of those he knew would disagree. Barrington-Ward was consulted and he responded with just the right arguments to get through to Churchill. If British papers were reduced to propaganda sheets then the public would turn to other sources, including German radio broadcasts in English. He also gently reminded the prime minister of how helpful a free press had been to him in the First World War in exposing the shortage of shells. The matter went to the war cabinet where Cooper pointed out that the government had never yet had cause to use the powers it already possessed to prosecute newspapers for aiding the enemy under the so-called D-Notice system designed to protect information vital to Britain's defence. Cooper's final argument brought to mind Lloyd George's view that the press had to be 'squashed or squared'. 'The press are very sensitive and must either be humoured or completely squashed. The great argument against the latter method would be the shock it would give to public confidence.' Churchill agreed to a toughening of D-Notices instead, forcing editors to obey specific requests from the government, although even this was reversed after heavy lobbying from Fleet Street. The power to censor the media wholesale would be kept in reserve, for use only in the event of an invasion.

The press, by promising to be on its best behaviour, had seen off the danger of direct government control. The Ministry of Information, which could have made their lives so difficult, became known instead as 'Minnie', 'a fusspot, dreaded not so much for what she did as what she might do'.[26] The mainstream media had fought an effective rear-guard action to protect their liberties. It was a campaign based more on self-interest than high principle and didn't extend to protecting those who wished to use the right to free expression to propound more extreme views. In Churchill's first few weeks as prime minister the export of both fascist and communist journals was banned with barely a peep from the defenders of free speech. The *Daily Worker*, owned by the British Communist party, was warned that worse would follow unless it stopped campaigning for 'revolutionary defeatism'. Anti-fascists in the CP had been wrestling with their consciences ever since the 1939 Hitler–Stalin pact and the non-communist left had little sympathy with them. It was the Labour MP Herbert Morrison who, as home secretary, eventually banned the paper altogether at the end of January 1941, sending in the police to close down the printing presses. The ban was only lifted when Russia switched sides and joined the war against Germany the following year.

The threat posed by the *Daily Worker* was pretty modest. It had a small circulation and half its readers were uneasy with its editorial line anyway. The same could not be said for the *Daily Mirror*, the paper which did most during the war years to raise Churchill's hackles. The *Mirror* was a very popular paper indeed, especially so with servicemen and their wives and families back home. The fact that it was the forces' favourite paper helped explain why it was read with such interest, and often dismay, in Downing Street. Its popularity was only partly to do with its outspokenness. The then editor of the *Daily Herald* put his rival's success down every bit as much to the cartoons featuring Jane, 'a young lady of pleasant appearance who was involved day by day in startling adventures causing her to divest herself of most of her clothes and display her charming figure to her admirers in only the scantiest of underclothes'.[27] Be that as it may, politics mattered to the *Mirror*. It had consistently opposed appeasement and once the war started it wanted it to be pursued relentlessly. It was one of the few papers to be openly enthusiastic about Churchill's appointment as prime minister and was prepared to trumpet his successes in a language the ordinary man and woman understood. Its editorial after the Dunkirk evacuations was 'Bloody Marvellous', which should have pleased Churchill as much as the *Sun*'s 'Gotcha!' would Margaret Thatcher during the Falklands conflict. In wartime, however, prime ministers have a habit of taking supportive headlines as their due while only really taking notice of the critical ones. The *Daily Mirror* could be every bit as

forthright when it thought things were going badly. The paper was dismayed when Churchill's first administration included so many of the
old 'muddlers' like Chamberlain who had been running the war like
'the village vicar's wife runs a gymkhana at a charity fete'.[28]

Soon after Churchill took over the Mirror Group, director Cecil
Harmsworth King, a nephew of Lord Northcliffe, was called to
Downing Street to be given a rap over the knuckles by the prime minister for 'political bickering'. King did his best to point out that
Chamberlain was unpopular in the country and his papers were merely
reflecting public opinion, only to be told that Churchill 'didn't see the
public had any right to take such a line'.[29] King and his colleagues
thought the *Daily Mirror* and *Sunday Pictorial* could act as pressure
valves, allowing the public to let off steam about the frustrations of war
without exploding, but they certainly didn't have the same effect on
Churchill. King's diary described the prime minister fulminating in the
Commons and describing 'the tone of "certain organs of the Press" as
"so vicious and malignant" that it would be "almost indecent if applied
to the enemy." It rather sounds as if this were aimed at our two
papers . . .'[30] A few days later Attlee and Beaverbrook were deputed by
the cabinet to warn the Newspaper Proprietors Association that if criticism of an 'irresponsible kind' didn't stop there could be censorship
of both news and views. Attlee seemed a little embarrassed by the
whole thing, explaining that he was expressing the government's view
not his own. At a subsequent meeting with King, Attlee couldn't say
what was meant by 'irresponsible criticism', although King managed
to throw away his advantage by claiming that Chamberlain had lost the
premiership not as a result of events in parliament but 'by public opinion led by the press', and in particular of course the *Daily Mirror*.[31]

Other papers had come under similar pressure. Bevin, the ex-trade
unionist turned minister for labour, was despatched to use his influence
with the *Daily Herald*. The Liberals had also joined the coalition and
they were asked to work on their friends in the media, including the
News Chronicle. Chamberlain's eventual resignation from the cabinet on
genuine health grounds in October helped calm things a little. King
agreed that his papers should 'pipe down for a few weeks'. The cease-
fire didn't last long. In January Churchill was at it again. King was told

'that our policy was a very clever form of fifth columnism – praising the PM, pressing for an intensification of our war effort, but at the same time magnifying grievances, vilifying ministers and generally creating a distrust by the nation for its leaders'.[32] The prime minister had even had somebody look into the ownership of the *Mirror*, presumably suspecting some communist shareholding although none existed. Churchill wasn't content with berating King to his face. He had his secretary send over cuttings that had offended him along with letters referring to their 'malevolence' and 'spirit of hatred and malice'. He started to accuse the paper of actually wanting to see Britain lose the war and of speaking out as it did so that 'large numbers of readers would be brought into a state of despondency and resentment, of bitterness and scorn, which at the proper moment, when perhaps some disaster had occurred or prolonged tribulations had wearied the national spirit, could be suddenly switched over into naked defeatism, and a demand for a negotiated peace'.[33] Churchill continued with the correspondence for weeks without giving an inch in the face of King's protestations that he and his colleagues wanted 'to give you personally all the support possible'.[34]

The most notorious clash between Downing Street and the *Mirror* came a year later and was caused not by a news article but by a cartoon. Singapore had just been lost to the Japanese and the cartoonist Philip Zec depicted a sailor clinging to some wreckage in dark seas.* The paper's uncompromising columnist 'Cassandra' provided the caption which read, 'The price of petrol has been increased by one penny – Official'.[35] The same issue carried an editorial which mocked the army's leaders as 'brass buttoned, boneheads, socially prejudiced, arrogant and fussy [with] . . . a tendency to heart disease, apoplexy, diabetes and high blood-pressure'. The cartoon was ambiguous but, according to Francis Williams, whose source was presumably Attlee, Churchill thought he knew exactly what the paper was up to. 'In his view the cartoon was deliberately meant to imply that seamen were risking their lives in order that bigger profits could be made by the oil companies. It was, he declared, bound to have a strong effect in deterring seamen

---

*See plate 8.

from agreeing to serve on oil tankers. The leading article he regarded as a gross and improper libel on the higher officers in the army, and incidentally on the government which appointed them, and one calculated to spread alarm and despair in the ranks and make men unwilling to fight in the belief that they were being led to their deaths by aged and stupid incompetents. He demanded that instant action should be taken to suppress a paper guilty of such practices.'[36]

The job of taking action was passed to Herbert Morrison who called in the editor and threatened him with the same fate that had befallen the *Daily Worker*. It was, said Morrison, 'the unanimous decision of the cabinet'. The cartoon was 'worthy of Goebbels at his best'. The editor thought the paper was being closed down immediately until Morrison made clear it was just a final warning. 'If you are closed, it will be for a long time. We shall act with a speed that will surprise you.'[37] When Morrison went on to say as much in a statement to the House, most other newspapers rose up in varying degrees of indignation. *The Times*, now edited by Barrington-Ward, promised to discharge its duty to its readers undeterred.

The charge that the *Mirror's* owners and staff wanted Britain defeated or forced into a humiliating truce was clearly nonsense. Cudlipp would later record his pleasure when the examination of Nazi files after the war revealed an order to arrest immediately all *Mirror* directors as soon as London was occupied. Too much prime ministerial and parliamentary time had been given over to fulminating against the *Mirror's* alleged infamies, although the government did succeed in its objectives to the extent that, in the words of the most detailed history of the political press, 'For the rest of the war, the *Daily Mirror* minded its ways without quite mending them. Morrison's admonition did its work and possibly served to chasten other would-be offenders.'[38]

The Battle of the Mirror had been led by Downing Street. The Ministry of Information had played a relatively minor role in the skirmishes, generally trying to calm Churchill down and discourage him from carrying out his threat to suppress one of the most popular papers in the land. 'Minnie' was still a problem, satisfying neither the prime minister nor the media. Churchill finally hit on the solution by appointing one of his closest allies to take her over. The MP Brendan

Bracken, a flame-haired and loquacious Irishman, was another of the rogues Churchill liked to have around him. Like Beaverbrook, Bracken enjoyed a career that spanned newspaper management and politics and often both at once. As the prime minister's parliamentary private secretary one of Bracken's jobs had been to sit up late at night drinking with him in Downing Street, helping Churchill talk through the big issues of the day. It was a position of considerable power but little responsibility, as befitted a future owner of the *Financial Times*, and one he was reluctant to give up in order to run a ministry that nobody loved.

Duff Cooper, on the other hand, had no reluctance at all about giving up the job. The press had abused him for much of the past year. He had prised little of value out of the service ministries to offer them and when he tried to restrict access to sensitive information they turned on him personally. Even before his appointment the ministry had started sending out investigators to try to research public opinion a bit more scientifically, but when the papers got to hear of it they dubbed them 'Cooper's Snoopers'. It didn't help that they had been asking women about their corsets, even if the government could ill afford the unnecessary waste of steel. Abuse from the media is often the lot of those placed in charge of handling press relations. If the prime minister is supportive it can be bearable, but Churchill wasn't. All Cooper had ever got from him were gruff instructions about what he was *not* to do. No explicit discussion of war aims, no precise details to be given of the effects of air raids, no attempts to lift morale by raising expectations of a better life to come after the war. When Rudolf Hess, Hitler's deputy, flew to Britain on an apparently covert mission, nobody bothered to tell the head of the information ministry until two days later. The media had to rely on German sources, leading the *Daily Express* to publish the headline 'Hess Is Dead' when he wasn't.[39] Cooper, who had been made to look incompetent, called the ministry a 'misbegotten freak' and said, 'the PM is not really interested in propaganda and still less in information'.[40] Before he left the job Cooper warned the prime minister that the ministry was in peril. 'There is a danger of it ceasing to be an object of ridicule in order to become one only of pity.'

Little wonder then that Bracken's normally buoyant mood was so deflated by his appointment. He rose to the task, however. He had 'a somewhat romantic approach to the truth'[41] having used lavish helpings of Irish blarney to cover up his lowly origins and lack of formal education. Yet when it came to helping the press he was strongly in favour of telling it straight and giving the media as much information as he could. He happily referred to the service departments and the Foreign Office as 'the oysters' as he tried to prise more information out of them. His campaign became known as the 'Battle of Bloomsbury' after the ministry's headquarters at Senate House in that part of London. Bracken's staff loved him and he quickly earned the respect of most journalists, who recognised that he understood their business and didn't regard them either as a necessary evil or as just another weapon in the war against Germany. They were grateful to him for easing the censorship rules so that the only reason for suppressing news would be if it would give valuable information to the enemy that they did not already possess. Bracken had no intention of suffering the same fate as his predecessors, being driven to distraction by the job he'd been handed. He aimed to put an end to the constant skirmishes between the government and the media and he succeeded well enough to be able to say towards the end of the war that his ministry was 'even less exciting than the British Museum'.[42] His great advantage, one he shared with all the most successful post-war press secretaries, was that he was known to have a very close relationship with the prime minister. It meant that ministers and civil servants alike were far less likely to challenge him, and it gave him real credibility with journalists. He was also, like Bernard Ingham and Alastair Campbell, a larger-than-life character. He could use a bit of bluster and bullying and get away with it and he could turn on the charm when it suited him. Unlike Ingham and Campbell he was very clubbable and while he was no shirker he didn't share their capacity for hard work and attention to detail. It was his deputy, Cyril Radcliffe, who did much of the nitty-gritty, leaving Bracken free to be there when Churchill needed him as a friend and a prop.

Brendan Bracken's greatest propaganda asset was Winston S. Churchill. It didn't matter that much if papers like the *Daily Mirror* questioned the effective running of the war if Churchill could stand up on a regular basis and find the right language to show there was a strong man in charge. If it came to a choice between the carping criticism of the *Mirror* and the inspiring rhetoric of the prime minister there was never much doubt whom the public would listen to and believe. Under Bracken the Ministry of Information stopped trying to take responsibility for the nation's morale. That was Churchill's job. Bracken believed the government 'must stop appealing to the public or lecturing it. One makes it furious, the other resentful.'[43] He decided to stop ministers appearing on the BBC whenever they felt they had something important to impart. Bracken recognised that only a very few politicians had the knack of sounding convincing on the radio and he got Churchill to support him in insisting that all ministerial broadcasts be cleared with the ministry first. The BBC did not have a comfortable war. The government took new powers to control what was broadcast and while many of these were kept in reserve the BBC's editors had to cope with a level of official interference that would now be unthinkable. Today's ministers might rather like the idea of the corporation being obliged to carry their press statements in full but the public can be thankful such rules didn't outlast the war. There was no guarantee that the statements would be accurate. Allied losses during the Battle of Britain were under-reported and the statistics for damage caused by the Blitz frequently massaged. The fact that BBC broadcasts could be heard in Germany with relative ease helped ministers justify such deceptions, but Bracken insisted it was more important to retain the trust of the British public than to try to systematically deceive the enemy. Churchill is famously quoted as saying that the truth was 'so precious that in war-time she should always be surrounded by a bodyguard of lies',[44] but under Bracken's direction she was allowed out alone more often than she had been for some time.

While Churchill had one of his friends with genuine expertise in propaganda working loyally and effectively within the government, by early 1942 he had lost another. Lord Beaverbrook had been an unconventional minister, detested by many of his colleagues, but Churchill valued his honest counsel and was willing to put up with his temperamental behaviour and his habit of threatening to resign whenever he couldn't always get his own way. His success in boosting aircraft production and as a link-man with Russia made him think he was indispensable and, in all but name, the deputy prime minister. Attlee, who actually was deputy prime minister from February 1942, clashed with him repeatedly. Years later when asked to write an appreciation of Beaverbrook for use after his death, Attlee refused, saying, 'He was the only evil man I ever met. I could find nothing good to say about him'.[45] Nobody has ever been able to explain why Attlee felt quite so strongly, although Beaverbrook's constantly shifting loyalties and will-ingness to entertain all manner of conspiracies was undoubtedly a factor. Churchill thought he could handle him, however, but in early 1942 his authority was at a low ebb. The war was going badly both in the Far East and Africa and there was open speculation in parliament and in the press about the prime minister's future. Beaverbrook was suspected of seeing himself as a potential successor. After the *Daily Mail* had run a 'violently anti-Churchill, anti-government leader' that had caused fury in Downing Street, Sir Henry 'Chips' Channon, detected talk among MPs 'about the formation of a so-called "Centre party" composed of Liberals, disgruntled Conservatives etc., with Beaverbrook at its head'.[46]

Only in Beaverbrook's wildest dreams could he ever have become prime minister. He was on the way out not up. After saying he didn't want to serve in a government with Attlee as deputy prime minister, Beaverbrook's resignation was finally accepted. Only his arrogance could have blinded him to the fact that Churchill needed the leader of the Labour party more than he needed him. Churchill had earlier warned him, 'If we part now, we part for ever.'[47] There was a touch of the petulant lover about Beaverbrook at times and when, to his evident shock, he learned he was no longer wanted he wrote immediately asking instead for a trial separation, 'four months' leave of absence so that I may deal with the papers in the interest of your direction of the war'. Beaverbrook left the government nominally on health grounds but really as a result of a power battle he couldn't win. He even went so far as to recall Baldwin's description of him in the 1930s aiming for 'power without responsibility'. He complained that as a minister 'I was carrying on my shoulders a great deal of responsibility without sufficient power.'[48] No press baron before or since has enjoyed so much real political power as Lord Beaverbrook but still it was not enough.

Out of office, he continued with his old ways and seemed to have forgotten his offer to support Churchill's interests in the press. The *Daily Express* started to campaign for a second front in the war in Europe, knowing full well the prime minister was against it. The Tory party chairman, Sir Thomas Dugdale, regarded Beaverbrook at the time as 'a man utterly and completely untrustworthy, a crook of crooks, without principle or conscience'.[49] A rather more benevolent observer, one of his former civil servants, thought he was behaving 'very like a naughty schoolboy preparing for an escapade which he knows will earn him a caning from the head'.[50] The campaign for a second front made Beaverbrook popular with his friends on the left, including MPs like Aneurin Bevan, but even they were alarmed. Bevan told him that the way he was using his papers would have 'the most harmful effects on your political reputation. They will give rise to the unwholesome impression that a straight political line is not being followed but rather a series of unpleasant intrigues are being set on foot.'[51] Some of those intrigues included the minister of labour, Ernest Bevin. Bevin was on Labour's right wing and had little in common with Nye Bevan other than a confusingly similar surname. Bevin's biographer records Beaverbrook going to see him to propose the formation of an alternative government because 'Churchill was on the way out'.[52] Despite knowing what his old friend was up to, Churchill tried on many occasions to woo him back into the government. This may have been partly to have him inside the tent pissing out, but it's clear Churchill genuinely liked and valued him, no matter how mischievous he could be. When the prime minister finally convinced him that the second front, in the form of an Allied landing in France, was on the way, Beaverbrook returned to office in September 1943 as lord privy seal. He had significantly less power than he had enjoyed previously, which helped overcome the objections of Attlee and others, but the appointment still caused dismay among many of Churchill's supporters in parliament. According to Channon's contacts the prime minister was far too inclined to rely on his cronies like Bracken and Beaverbrook, who were said to 'rule the country when the PM is abroad, and dominate and fascinate him when he is at home'.

Churchill was well aware of the discontent at the 'Bracken–Beaver' axis but as the war news got gradually better he saw no need to change his friends or alter the construction of his government. The two men had guided him through the minefield of working with a largely independent media during the darkest months of the war and had helped the journalists in turn by restraining his more dictatorial instincts. Wars, like all crises, are good for newspapers and most saw their circulations rise significantly. The public wanted reports of the fighting but also craved some entertainment and distractions from the horrors of it. It's unlikely that many readers missed the absence of so much political news with party battles on hold for the duration of the war. The newspapers found plenty to argue about without leaving themselves open too frequently to the charge of undermining the war effort. The *Daily Mirror*'s postbag showed overwhelming support for its campaigning style even when Churchill and his ministers were savaging it. On occasion the papers even helped save the government from itself. Whitehall was no less leaky than in peacetime but when journalists obtained highly sensitive material they usually buried it rather than publish dramatic scoops that would have aided the enemy. The *Daily Telegraph*, for example, got hold of the most secret of state secrets, the Enigma decryptions of German transmissions, but nothing was published. The *Telegraph* was Churchill's most loyal defender and the prime minister told Barrington-Ward that he read 'the papers every morning, *The Times* "last but one"', finishing with the *Daily Telegraph*, "because I know that it will be all right!"'[53]

For most of the war Churchill was content to let press criticism go, no matter how much it irked him. Towards the end, however, he took another very public swipe at the media, this time in the form of *The Times*, a paper that had become far less malleable since the departure of Chamberlain's old friend Geoffrey Dawson. The issue was one dear to Churchill's heart, the civil war in Greece. The prime minister thought fighting the communist uprising justified the use of British troops; *The Times* disagreed. It wasn't the only paper to take this view: the *Manchester Guardian* took the same line, but that didn't matter in Downing Street. Churchill drafted an angry letter to Barrington-Ward, reminding him of his paper's history of appeasement. Beaverbrook and Bracken quickly intervened to stop him sending it. So instead

Churchill vented his fury in the House of Commons. 'There is no case in my experience', he told MPs, 'certainly not in my war experience, when a British government has been so maligned [loud and prolonged cheers] and its motives so traduced in our own country by important organs of the press among our own people. That this should be done amid the perils of this war now at its climax has filled me with surprise and sorrow.'[54] Barrington-Ward was shocked not just by the words but by the reaction in the House. He wrote in his diary, 'This – a direct and obvious reference to [*The Times*] – immediately touched off the loudest, largest and most vicious – even savage! – cheer that I have heard in the House . . . there could be no doubt it was almost wholly Tory . . . a vent for the pent-up passions of three years, a protest against all that has, wrongly or rightly, enraged the Tories in the paper during that time.'[55] Bracken warned that the paper would not be forgiven until it backed down. Barrington-Ward stuck to his guns, telling him, 'Very well, it will not be forgiven.'

With victory in Europe now only a matter of time, it was inevitable that thoughts in Downing Street as well as in Fleet Street were turning to post-war Britain and the very different challenges ahead. News of Hitler's suicide in the Berlin bunker was brought to Churchill during a strategy meeting at Downing Street called to discuss the Conservatives' propaganda needs once normal politics resumed. There had been no general election since 1935 and with all three major parties working together in government it was no easy matter trying to assess the mood of the country in conventional political terms. Beaverbrook thought public opinion had shifted leftwards but that Churchill would still win handsomely. Others were not so sure. Channon's contacts were divided: 'Robin Barrington-Ward, Editor of the *Times* . . . thinks that politically there is no serious swing to the left; and says the country is "centre of centre": so much for the foolish prophecy of that very nice ass Harold Macmillan who goes about saying that the Conservatives will be lucky to retain a hundred seats at the election.'[56]

The election came sooner than Churchill would have liked. After the German surrender on 7 May 1945 he hoped the coalition would stay together until there was victory in the Far East, too. Neither

Labour nor the Liberals were willing to give him such an open-ended commitment and so, on 23 May, the National government came to an end. Conservative party strategists were happy enough, believing it was better to cash in on Churchill's prestige before it became obvious that the country was broke and that living conditions were going to get tougher before they got better. So within weeks of 'Victory in Europe' Britain was back to politics as usual and plunged into one of the nastiest election campaigns ever. It was as if the democratic system itself was pent up after years of inactivity and bursting to flex its muscles again. That the machinery of democratic politics, including a free and vigorous press, had survived the war years in such robust health was a tribute to its inner strength. Despite all the rows, neither Downing Street nor Fleet Street had abused its powers sufficiently to inflict lasting damage on relations between the two. Beaverbrook and Bracken, two peculiarly colourful individuals with a foot apiece in each camp, had enjoyed considerable power and influence. Yet they had owed their positions solely to the authority of the prime minister. They now set about trying to help get him re-elected, only to fail ignominiously. Many Tories would later blame them both, for making his defeat more certain and more complete, although the worst misjudgements were Churchill's own.

Journalists anticipated the election with enthusiasm. The decade since Britain had last gone to the polls had been a very difficult one for their profession. They looked forward to the day when the brooding presence of Downing Street would no longer hover over their shoulders and when their patriotism would cease to be called into question. If the politicians were getting ready to start attacking one another at last, maybe, just maybe, they would leave the media to get on with their own jobs. No one party had governed Britain alone with a secure majority since 1929. The country was about to get a sharp reminder of just how rough politics could be.

5

OF MICE AND MEN: ATTLEE, CHURCHILL AGAIN (1945–55)

I'm with you on the free press. It's the newspapers I can't stand.
Tom Stoppard, *Night and Day*

Winston Churchill had every right to be proud of his rhetorical prowess. Time and again his instinct for finding the right words for the occasion had inspired the nation and steeled its people for yet greater sacrifices in the war against fascism. Having spent the past four years crafting powerful phrases to characterise the enemy, it was perhaps asking too much for him to pull his punches now the battle was political rather than military. It just wasn't his style. In his own words, 'If you have an important point to make, don't try to be subtle or clever. Use a pile driver. Hit the point once. Then come back and hit it again. Then hit it a third time, a tremendous whack.' Churchill threw himself into the 1945 election campaign with his customary fighting spirit. It didn't seem to occur to him that the voters might find it odd that he was now firing broadsides at the very same men who had given him such loyal and effective service as ministers until just a few weeks earlier.

Churchill's first election broadcast set the tone for what was to come. It was an extraordinarily ill-judged attack on the party of Attlee, Bevin and Morrison, accusing them of being undemocratic and of opposing both a free parliament and freedom of expression. 'No social-ist government conducting the entire life and industry of the country could afford to allow free, sharp or violently worded expressions of public discontent', he warned. 'They would have to fall back on some sort of Gestapo, no doubt very humanely directed in the first instance.'[1] Wiser heads around Churchill knew he had gone too far. His wife Clementine had tried to get him to take out the 'odious and invidi-ous' reference to the Gestapo but he had refused.[2] She clearly had a better sense than he did of how it would go down. The newspapers reported his warnings with varying degrees of disapproval and distaste. Only Beaverbrook's *Daily Express* took up the prime minister's theme with enthusiasm. 'Gestapo In Britain If Socialists Win' ran the head-line. Just in case the point was missed, the paper went on to warn, 'They would dictate what to say and do, even where to queue.'[3] Perhaps not surprisingly, many believed Beaverbrook must have been the inspiration for the phrase in the first place, but both his biographer and those of Churchill himself say not. All place responsibility for the words on the prime minister and the prime minister alone. Not every-body who heard the broadcast disapproved. Sir Henry 'Chips' Channon thought it had been 'heavy pounding, certainly' but nonetheless 'today the Labour boys seem very depressed and dejected by Winston's trouncing. I met Attlee in the lavatory, and he seemed shrunken and terrified.'[4] If so, he soon recovered. Attlee's response delivered the following evening was, by contrast, well judged and well received. He thanked the prime minister who he said 'clearly wanted the electors to understand how great was the difference between Winston Churchill the great leader in war of a united nation, and Mr Churchill, the party leader of the Conservatives'. And he went on, 'The voice we heard last night was that of Mr Churchill, but the mind was that of Lord Beaverbrook.'[5]

The Tory campaign became so bound up in people's minds with that conducted by Beaverbrook's papers that the excesses of the *Express*, including its most notorious headline that read simply 'The National Socialists',[6] did more damage to Churchill than anything he said himself. Arthur Christiansen, the paper's editor, acknowledged that it was held responsible for 'conducting the dirtiest election campaign of all time'.[7] Neither Labour nor the Tories would thank them for it afterwards, although Churchill's friend Brendan Bracken told Christiansen 'the Conservative party will never forget what you have done for us' and appears to have meant it kindly.

The first thing the paper did for them was to break the story of Harold Laski, the left-wing academic who happened to be chairman of the Labour party when the election was called. The paper claimed one of its reporters had heard him at an election rally in Newark say of Labour's policies 'if we cannot have them by fair means, we shall use violence to obtain them'. Laski was notably reluctant to issue a retraction and one had to be drafted for him in the offices of the *Daily Herald*. Laski had already caused something of a storm by suggesting that a Labour prime minister would be bound by the edicts of the party's national executive committee. This provoked one of Attlee's famous laconic put-downs, 'a period of silence on your part would be welcome'. The *Express* did its best to suggest it had discovered what life under Labour would really be like, but the public seemed distinctly unmoved.

For the first time in an election Labour was ready to make the conduct of the press an issue. Attlee declared that 'the power of great wealth exercised by irresponsible men of no principle, through newspapers with enormous circulations, is a danger to democracy and a menace to public life,'[8] although this was also the first election in which Labour enjoyed anything close to parity of press support. The regional media was still very heavily pro-Tory, but the first of the Nuffield College election guides that continue to this day reported that 'contrary to general opinion, the Labour party was nearly as strongly supported in the London daily press as was the Conservative party'.[9] This was stretching it more than a bit, as Roy Greenslade shows in his epic history of the post-war press,[10] but Labour did have its own big guns and, more importantly, they were better at hitting the right targets. The TUC-controlled *Daily Herald* was effectively part of the Labour campaign although Herbert Morrison, in charge at the party HQ, Transport House, found it too ready to follow the agenda of his rival, Ernie Bevin, who was closer to the trade-union movement. Morrison much preferred dealing with the *Daily Mirror*, the paper he'd threatened with closure only three years earlier, and its sister paper the *Sunday Pictorial*.* He even got Philip Zec, the man responsible for the notorious 'Price of Oil' cartoon, to do some propaganda drawings for the party. They had a common enemy now in the Conservative party and the *Mirror* had lost none of its campaigning zeal. 'Frauds, Cheats, Wrigglers Seek Power' it declared. It avoided the mistake of playing the *Express* at its own game and, unlike the communist *Daily Worker*, it never accused the Tories of being fascists. Instead, it ran a surprisingly sophisticated and effective campaign based on the slogan 'Vote for Him'. It featured pictures of servicemen, many of whom would be in transit and unable to vote themselves, and appealed to their loved ones back home to 'make up your mind what, in the circumstances of a general election, he would have been likely to do if he had been at home. And vote for HIM!' The paper didn't even need to suggest 'he' would have voted Labour. The *Mirror* judged the mood of the country far better than did the *Express*. People were in a rather sombre frame of mind, not jubilant after victory, and wanted serious men with a serious approach to the country's problems.

Churchill's triumphal tour around the country was conducted with far greater aplomb and accompanied with more soaring rhetoric than Attlee's more modest perambulations but it too struck the wrong note. Attlee was driven about by his wife in their family car, accompanied only by a *Daily Herald* journalist, H. R. S. Philpott, whom he found 'invaluable in dealing with the press and in reporting the meetings . . . Our rather unostentatious method of travel contrasted with the elaborate procession which accompanied Churchill on his journey. Quite unintentionally, this turned out to be somewhat of an asset as it was given a great deal of prominence in the press.'[11] After it was over Attlee was presented with a copy of *The British General Election of 1945* and noted with pleasure that the authors 'stated that I had the air of a sound and steady batsman keeping up his wicket with ease against a demon bowler who was losing both pace and length'.

---

*See p. 120.

The conduct of the election campaign was an early illustration of the change in both style and substance that was on its way with the election of the first ever majority Labour government. Clement Attlee entered Downing Street with 146 more MPs than the other parties combined. In his typically arrogant manner, the *Mirror*'s director Cecil King claimed the credit. 'We were what opposition the government had in the war years. Attlee was merely supine, and the opposition consisted of Nye Bevan in the House of Commons and ourselves outside it. Our assessment of the political mood of the country was correct; that of the government was not. The result was the Labour landslide in 1945, to which Messrs Attlee, Bevin and Co. had contributed nothing.'[12] Hugh Cudlipp, then working for King as editor of the *Sunday Pictorial*, was more realistic when he suggested that nothing in any of the newspapers had affected the nature of the result. 'If Churchill had suppressed the *Mirror* in 1942 instead of threatening to do so, there would still have been a Labour victory.' Although, even he thought they might have contributed to its landslide proportions. Had Churchill won, similar claims would undoubtedly have been made for the influence of the *Daily Express*. But he did not. Arthur Christiansen had been expecting the Tories to triumph right up until polling day and noted, 'It is a fault of newspapermen that they can be carried away by their own efforts and believe they are having the same effect on the readers as on themselves.'[13]

Attlee started his premiership with a relatively benign press ready to give him the chance to prove himself. Even *The Times* and *The Economist*, both of which had been strongly Tory in the past, were inclined to lean in his direction. Unfortunately for the media, however, Attlee had no inclination whatsoever to lean in theirs. He quickly appointed the former *Daily Herald* editor, Francis Williams, who had been working for the Ministry of Information, as his press secretary. Williams was an astute observer of both politics and journalism and the new prime minister had made a wise choice. Attlee wanted Williams to deal with the media so that he wouldn't need to. He declared himself 'allergic to the press' and recalled a favourite saying of his father that 'Only a fool buys a dog and barks himself.'[14] He almost never asked Williams whom he was talking to or what he was doing or, indeed, what he was saying about the government. He simply had no interest in the business of press relations and even less, if that were possible, in journalists themselves. Williams wrote many years later that 'Unlike later prime ministers he took no interest in what they might have to say about him, and although courteous to those journalists he met had no desire to seek out their company and no wish to bribe them with confidences. He took the old fashioned view that politicians and journalists were likely to do their best work if they were not in each other's pockets.'

Williams recognised that he would have to do his job with a boss who wasn't interested in the press and with a media that were interested in politics only when it was exciting. It came down, as so often, to the question of circulation. Williams quoted with approval the observation that 'newspapers . . . resemble fashionable ladies of the West End in that they are more concerned with their figures than with their morals'.[15] When he did tell Attlee about some particularly disagreeable article, the prime minister replied, 'That so? Suppose they've got to write something. Circulation slipping, you think?'[16] Far from being alarmed by Attlee's insouciance, Williams seems to have rather approved. His experience first as an editor and then within Whitehall convinced him that politicians credited journalists with far more influence than they deserved. 'Most cabinet ministers are indeed almost excessively sensitive to newspaper comment. During the war it was a constant source of wonderment . . . to find the amount of attention paid by ministers and heads of department to newspaper stories which our experience told us had no particular significance as an indication of general public feeling, but were merely the result of a not very bright idea by a harassed news editor trying to keep a junior reporter busy.'

Attlee was the least sensitive of all prime ministers to press criticism, mainly because he hardly ever saw it. He let it be known that he read the *Daily Herald* occasionally to keep up with what 'the chaps' in the Labour movement were thinking and he took *The Times* for its crossword and maybe the births, deaths and marriages, and that was about it. The story of Attlee and the Downing Street news wire has been told many times as evidence of his naïvety about press matters, but if any political anecdote bears repetition it is this one. Francis Williams wanted a telex machine so that he could get speedy access to what the news agencies were reporting and therefore what the lobby journalists were likely to be writing about. Had he told the prime minister it was essential in order to do his job properly, then Attlee might have agreed. But instead he told him it would useful for getting the cricket scores. A week after it was installed a worried-looking prime minister arrived at his press secretary's office. 'Francis, you know my cricket machine at the cabinet door? When I checked it just now for the lunchtime score at Lords, it was ticking out the decisions and subjects discussed at the cabinet meeting this morning. How can it do that?' Williams did his best to explain his job of briefing the press after cabinet meetings and was told, 'OK, Francis, I'll leave the show to you. Good work.'[17] Like many of the best stories about Attlee it seems a little too good to be true. It's hard to believe that a man whose name appeared in every newspaper every single day was so completely indifferent to what was being said about him, but perhaps it's enough to know that he was happy for people to think that he didn't care.

His parsimony with words was certainly no myth. Conversation with him was described as less like playing ping-pong and more like throwing biscuits to a dog. After the traditional meeting at the Palace to pass on the seals of office, King George VI is said to have remarked, 'I gather they call the new prime minister Clem. "Clam" would be more appropriate.'[18] Attlee would be just as tight-lipped with journalists on the rare occasions that he encountered them. 'Nothing in that' or 'can't say' would be his standard reply to their questions, or if he was feeling particularly chatty, 'you shouldn't listen to gossip; it's all poppycock'.[19]

Williams had the good sense to realise that he had to work with what he'd been given; there was no point trying to mould the prime minister into something he wasn't. He wrote that 'Attlee is one of the most difficult men in the world to publicise and possesses fewer of the political arts of self-presentation than any public man I know'. Professor Peter Hennessy goes further: 'On the Richter scale of charismatic leadership, the needle barely flickered. He had all the presence of a gerbil.'[20] Churchill called him a 'mouse', among many other put-downs. And yet, did it matter? He changed Britain for good, something very few prime ministers can claim to have done. He pushed through a more extensive and radical programme of reforms in his first five years than any other holder of that post, including Margaret Thatcher. He never lost a by-election and polled a higher popular vote in 1951 than he did in 1945. All of that was achieved with precious little help from the media. The goodwill that Attlee, like most new prime ministers, enjoyed on entering Number 10 was not to last and the next five years were to witness the 'most poisonous, bad tempered and embittered' relationship between Downing and Fleet Street that the veteran journalist James Margach ever experienced.[21] Attlee seemed to content to let it all wash over him.

Labour did have some senior figures who understood the need for good political communications better than their leader, most notably Herbert Morrison, whose grandson, Peter Mandelson, would later become the most notorious practitioner of the craft. In his earlier incarnation as editor of the *Daily Herald*, Francis Williams had judged that Morrison would make a better leader than Attlee and, funnily enough, Morrison agreed. Morrison had urged his colleagues as early as 1920 that 'generally speaking it is best to assume that newspapermen are your friends',[22] an assumption Attlee would never make. He went on to head the London County Council with a flair for publicity that encouraged his popularity. As wartime home secretary he would chide editors for being 'naughty', a word that came just as readily to his grandson's lips fifty years later. In 1945 Attlee asked him to chair the cabinet information committee and take over responsibility for the government's communications strategy. He enjoyed a reputation for getting on well with journalists without abusing their trust. According to his biographers, 'He was in advance of his time in his awareness that governments in the twentieth century must communicate to the people and that public relations had become an essential instrument of modern mass politics.'[23] Morrison's efforts were a bit obsessive at times and it wasn't always clear whether he was promoting his own interests or those of the government. His readiness to phone or write complaints about stories that offended him was clearly passed down in his genes, but at least he was willing to stand up to the press when he thought they were in the wrong. Attlee, by contrast, just wished they would go away.

A year after entering Number 10, Attlee opened the 6th Imperial Press Conference at Grosvenor House in London. Prime ministers have a habit of being more polite about journalists to their faces than behind their backs and Attlee used the occasion to declare that no freedom was more important than the freedom of the press. Although he couldn't stop himself from letting them know that politicians weren't always pleased to see them and that 'sometimes, seeing political correspondents awaiting them in the House of Commons, they are tempted to mutter in the words of Duncan in *Macbeth*: "What bloody man is this?"'[24] They were words the chancellor of the exchequer, Hugh Dalton, would have done well to remember the following year. Dalton was walking towards the Commons chamber to deliver his Budget speech when he bumped into a journalist he knew well, John Carvel of the now-defunct London *Evening Star*, and stopped for a brief conversation during which he revealed three or four of the main points that he was just minutes away from announcing in the chamber. Carvel dashed to a phone as soon as he could and his paper carried a short report in its next edition. The leak was held to have been such a serious breach of privilege and security that the chancellor was forced to resign. Attlee's judgement was as laconic as ever: 'Behaved like a fool. Can't see why anyone would want to talk to the press.'[25]

Attlee believed in employing professionals to do the talking. When Francis Williams wanted to return to life as a writer in 1947, he was replaced by Philip Jordan, a former information officer at the embassy in Washington. Attlee also had at his disposal the largest team of civil-service press officers and communications experts that peacetime Britain had ever seen. In part this was a hangover from the war, when government publicity had come of age. The number of press officers had increased massively from 1939 and the public were used to being told not just to 'Dig for Victory' but how to do it and which fertiliser to use. The Ministry of Information was disbanded with the coming of peace but thousands of public-relations officers survived all over Whitehall. The profession had proved its worth and was here to stay. Lord Reith recalled asking for a press officer when he was first made a minister in 1940 and being told by his permanent secretary that there would be nothing for such a person to do. He insisted on the appointment and when he came to change jobs asked for the man to come with him to his new department. 'Not on any account' came the reply; he was now too valuable to lose.[26] With such a large programme of economic and social reform, the Attlee government needed the help of such professionals to explain to the public what it would mean to them. But it was one thing telling people how to fit a gas mask properly and quite another informing them how the NHS would change their lives. Press officers had to learn how to distinguish between government information and party propaganda at a time when their own roles were a subject of heated political debate. The Tories accused ministers of using civil servants to manage the news and suppress information rather than simply to keep the public informed about government policy. Attlee defended the use of professional press officers to parliament but the row rumbled on until the Tories returned to power and, funnily enough, became converts to good government communications themselves.

The argument was just one element of the relationship between politics and the media that became the subject of a Royal Commission on the Press, set up in 1947. The main focus of the inquiry was the way in which the press was owned, controlled and managed. It would never have been set up had there not been an assumption by many on the Labour benches that the media was institutionally biased against them. The commission started its work at a time when Attlee and his ministers were getting an unprecedented battering not only from the traditional Tory press, but also from their own erstwhile supporters. The former opposed what the government was doing, regardless of its popular mandate, in particular the nationalisation programme and the plans for a National Health Service. The latter objected to how they were going about it and what they saw as weakness at the top. The *Daily Mirror* turned on the prime minister himself, accusing him of failing to offer real leadership: 'In effect he has contracted out the country's crisis. His cabinet should go. So should Mr Attlee.'[27] And papers of right and left joined forces in attacking food rationing and, an issue dear to their own hearts and pockets, the rationing of newsprint.

The Royal Commission was supposed to be looking at structural problems not day-to-day political skirmishes. But Herbert Morrison sent in a fat file of clippings designed to show how the press was guilty of distorting and suppressing the truth as well as, on occasion, telling outright lies. The commission already had the words of the government's senior law officer to consider. The attorney-general, Sir Hartley Shawcross, had publicly accused the 'Tory stooge press' of a 'campaign of calumny and misrepresentation'. Like Attlee he defended the principle of press freedom, but said 'the truth is there has never been a time when certain sections of the press have more seriously abused the freedom which is accorded them under our constitution. Freedom of the press does not mean freedom to tell lies.'[28] The newspapers had hit back, calling his words insulting and offensive among other things. One proprietor, Lord Kemsley, who owned the *Sunday Times*, issued a writ for libel after Shawcross accused him at a public meeting of distorting the news and suppressing the facts, and Attlee instructed his attorney-general to issue a grovelling apology. As Roy Greenslade points out, the incident was awash with irony given that the issue at stake was freedom of expression; 'a newspaper proprietor, able to exercise unlimited freedom of speech and so reach millions through his papers, was prepared to sue a man for exercising his freedom of speech in front of a couple of hundred people at a political meeting.'[29]

The media are never comfortable when politicians shine the spotlight on their behaviour for a change, which is the main reason why they do it. The tactic can have short-term benefits and often does, but it's unlikely to turn a surly and oppositional press into a supportive one, as Attlee's government learned to its cost. The Royal Commission had been set up at the urging of the many new Labour MPs who were also members of the National Union of Journalists, including Michael Foot. They had hoped it would expose the malign influence of unelected press barons. Nye Bevan declared that Britain had 'the most prostituted press in the world, most of it owned by a gang of millionaires'. One of those millionaires, Lord Beaverbrook, who regarded both Foot and Bevan as friends, considered the whole thing to be a personal attack on him but he had no intention of being cowed. With typical defiance he told the commission he ran the *Daily Express* 'for propaganda, and with no other purpose'.[30] He and other proprietors nonetheless insisted that they kept news and views separate and said the biggest threat to press freedom was government interference. Kemsley's brother, Lord Camrose, owner of the *Daily Telegraph*, took grave exception to the way the commission heard evidence from witnesses in private. It was, he said, 'a curious way of conducting an inquiry "into the best method of ensuring the freedom of the press"'.[31] It all provoked a public debate about journalistic ethics, which is just what Morrison and others had hoped for, but any relatively impartial observer would have been hard pushed to decide who was upholding the freedom of the press and who was endangering it. The Royal Commission report when it came wasn't much help in resolving the question.[32] It cleared the press of the worst charges, including that of following the political whims of wealthy owners. It concluded that 'complete fabrications' were 'seldom' published and that while there might sometimes be a 'political factor in the selection and presentation of news' more often than not there were just 'legitimate differences of opinion on news value'. The only recommendation of any substance was the establishment of a Press Council, a form of self-regulation that has continued to this day. The media had escaped pretty well unscathed. In Peter Hennessy's fine phrase the commission 'scarcely scratched the paintwork of a press Lord's Rolls-Royce'.[33]

If the Royal Commission had been intended to shame the press into mending its ways it failed. But, by the same measure, if all the ridicule and abuse heaped on Clement Attlee by journalists was designed to alter his manner of running the country it failed, too. He was sustained by a calm self-confidence that somehow never spilled over into arrogance. He told his ministers to get on with their jobs and if they weren't up to it he fired them with a minimum of fuss. He simply shrugged off an attempt to replace him halfway through the parliament with Ernest Bevin, the foreign secretary. Most prime ministers relish the chance to appear tough, especially when they are still in the process of establishing their authority. Margaret Thatcher, for example, gleefully adopted the soubriquet 'the Iron Lady', which had been intended by its Russian authors as an insult, at a time when her command even of the cabinet was uncertain.[34] Attlee, by contrast, was more powerful and had greater authority over his colleagues than his public image suggested. In the run-up to the 1950 general election the *Evening Standard* took to calling him 'Clem the Wimp' while at the other end of the political spectrum the *Daily Worker* said he was 'middle class and mediocre'.[35]

Nobody had ever called Winston Churchill a wimp. He was eight years older than the prime minister but was once again the dominant figure of the election. He made fewer big speeches than in 1945 and no big gaffes, but the Nuffield study found that he got the lion's share of the press coverage while 'Mr Attlee, on the other hand, slipped quietly away on his extensive tour by car and attracted a remarkably small quantity of space and oddly little prominence even at first in the *Daily Herald*.'[36] The press campaign was judged to have been 'overwhelmingly partisan, relatively demure and, so far as can be judged, politically ineffective'. The Tories had the support of a clear majority of national titles but there was little evidence of any direct relationship between newspaper endorsements and the subsequent results. Figures compiled for the Nuffield guide suggest Labour had 40 per cent of the national and regional newspaper circulation to the Tories' 49 per cent, yet the result in terms of votes cast was almost exactly the opposite, 46 per cent Labour, 40 per cent Conservative. The Liberals had both the *Manchester Guardian* and the *News Chronicle*, two well-respected titles, and yet they won just nine seats. The *Daily Mirror* was, as usual, Labour's most effective backer without overtly declaring itself for Attlee. During the campaign even the paper's popular cartoon family, The Ruggles, only ever came across people with good things to say about Labour. Cecil King said that 'with no great enthusiasm, the *Mirror* supported the Labour party in 1950 and was probably decisive in getting it a small majority'.[37] In fact Labour should have done much better. The party's support was very unevenly distributed around the country, giving it huge majorities in some seats while it lost others by just a handful of votes. A better-targeted campaign would have made far more difference than a more favourable press. Labour's slender majority of five seats was a poor reward for its share of the national vote and another election looked inevitable before long.

In preparation for going to the polls again, Herbert Morrison continued to chair the party's publicity committee. He had little doubt what Labour needed to do – 'modernise'.[38] He was more interested in what ministers said than how they said it. In his view the party had to concentrate on key marginal constituencies and direct policy at swing voters. This meant, among other things, an end to 'nationalisation for the sake of nationalisation'. When the left accused him of trying to water down the party's socialist creed Morrison mocked them for wanting to take Labour's most unpopular policies and feature them 'in bigger type than ever'. The resignation from the government in April 1951 of one of his fiercest critics, Nye Bevan, along with Harold Wilson and John Freeman, highlighted the growing divisions in Labour's ranks. At issue was the introduction of prescription charges and, more generally, whether the party was still committed to its principles. Attlee was unable to paper over the cracks. He was now sixty-eight and not in the best of health. Even at the height of his powers, Peter Mandelson, Morrison's grandson, would have had his work cut out to present the Labour party as a vigorous, modernising force with a fresh appeal to the middle ground.

Attlee called the second election in October 1951. It came as no surprise to anybody that he intended to tour the country in the same undemonstrative way that he always had. Another well-known Attlee story always brings a smile to the lips, but it is hardly a masterclass in how to use the media to communicate with the electorate. The following exchange with a television interviewer took place at the start of the campaign.

INT: Tell us something of how you view the election prospects.

CA: Oh, we shall go in with a good fight. Very good. Very good chance of winning if we go in competently. We always do.

INT: On what will Labour take its stand?

CA: Well, that is what we shall be announcing shortly.

INT: What are your immediate plans Mr Attlee?

CA: My immediate plans are to go down to a committee to decide on just that thing as soon as I can get away from here.

INT: Is there anything else you'd like to say about the coming election?

CA: No.[39]

Our weary familiarity with politicians who don't know when to shut up means we find Attlee's approach refreshing, although it can't have done much to win over any undecided viewers. But he couldn't have changed his style if he'd wanted to and wisely nobody tried to persuade him to do so. As the *Manchester Guardian* reported, 'He has never cheapened himself or his argument to gain applause. He has just been his quiet, assured self.'[40] Nevertheless the *Guardian* 'regretfully' advised its readers to vote for Churchill. *The Times* also came out explicitly for the Tories for the first time since the war. On the other hand, the *News of the World*, with a higher circulation than the two of them put together, went from being pro-Conservative to neutral. Only the *Daily Mirror* made a concerted effort to influence the result, portraying Churchill as a warmonger and a threat to world peace. Britain was now a nuclear power and the *Mirror* asked its readers to consider one question above all others: 'Whose Finger on the Trigger?' Churchill issued a writ for libel, but the case never came to court. He won the election with a majority of sixteen seats and allowed the matter to drop.

Labour had won over 200,000 more votes than the Tories, and the 1951 election is often cited as 'the most unfair in recent political history and . . . a serious indictment of our electoral system'.[41] Whether Attlee could have avoided defeat in 1951, or, better still, secured a workable majority in 1950, with a more proactive campaign, making better use of the media to generate some enthusiasm for the government's re-election, remains one of the great 'what ifs?'. The 1950s were to be a Conservative decade and Labour would be out of power for thirteen years. Attlee didn't complain about the result; it wasn't in his nature. The phrase 'good innings' could have been invented for him and he took well-justified satisfaction in having calmly withstood all the battering associated with being prime minister without making a fuss and without letting anybody, press baron or political rival, get the better of him.

Churchill re-entered Number 10 at the age of almost seventy-seven, having just won his first and only general election as leader of the Conservative party. He was already in decline physically and mentally and his friends expended a great deal of effort in the next four years to keep from the press and the public just how infirm he was. He stayed around too long for his own good or for the good of the country but, as he said himself, 'I always believed in staying in the pub till closing time.'[42] Those who do prop up the bar too long tend to find that their judgement is clouded by the time they have to leave and so it was with Churchill. Yet rather than expose the fact that the prime minister of Great Britain was no longer capable of doing his job properly, senior figures in Fleet Street chose instead to conspire with Downing Street to hide the truth from the public. The conspiracy was made up principally of Churchill's long-time friends and associates but that scarcely excused what happened. For weeks if not months, Downing Street's behaviour was akin to that of the Kremlin or the North Koreans, issuing mendacious bulletins to a compliant media about the health of a leader who could no longer lead.

Churchill's final decline was gradual and it would be wrong to suggest he was of unsound mind or body from the moment he returned to Downing Street. His behaviour could be erratic, certainly, and he spent a great deal more time issuing directives from his bed or his bath than most voters would have found comforting. Yet Jock Colville, who became his principal private secretary, recalled that 'at least until the midsummer of 1953 his mind was as clear and his reactions almost as prompt as in former days'.[43] According to Colville, Churchill abandoned his previous habits of napping in the afternoon and reading the first editions of the newspapers before going to bed, although other accounts suggest he continued to do both. He certainly said of the newspapers that he got 'far more out of them than the official muck'.[44]

Churchill's views of journalists and how to handle them hadn't changed since his wartime premiership. They were there to report his great speeches and statesmanlike actions, nothing more. If he had something of importance to say he would say it in the House of Commons or at a public meeting, never to a journalist. He didn't even see why Downing Street needed a press officer and the man he inherited from Attlee, Reginald Bacon, had a terrible time of it. The prime minister, on whose behalf he was supposed to speak, would barely acknowledge his existence. Ministerial responsibility for the burgeoning ranks of government press officers was handed to John

Boyd-Carpenter, who had been one of their fiercest critics while in opposition. Churchill sent out a clear signal that he didn't think the machinery of government communications served any real purpose, although little or nothing was done to dismantle it.

To his credit, he didn't even believe in using the media to further the nation's interests abroad. He feared the consequences of a nuclear conflict as much as any man, but when he read official papers outlining a proposal to deceive the Russians about Britain's atomic tests by feeding misinformation to the *Sunday Express* he was very uncomfortable about it. He wrote a memo saying, 'the idea of stimulating, through an inspired article, information both true and false, so mixed up as to be deceptive, to any particular newspaper, is not one hitherto entertained in time of peace. Certainly no departure from the principle that the government tells the truth . . . should be made except upon direct ministerial responsibility as an exception in the public interests.'[45]

Then came Churchill's stroke on 23 June 1953 and a very clear departure from that very same principle.

The prime minister had just finished an after-dinner speech at Number 10. The guest of honour was his Italian counterpart and Churchill was in 'sparkling form' talking about the Roman conquest of Britain.[46] As they were having drinks a short time later in an adjacent room Churchill slumped into a chair and was barely able to speak or move. Signor de Gasperi was discreetly ushered out without having the chance to say thank you or goodbye. Most of the guests apparently assumed the prime minister was drunk. Somehow Churchill managed to preside over the cabinet the following morning, although he said little and his face drooped. He was then taken straight to Chartwell, his Kent home, where his doctor expected him to die that weekend. When he didn't, there ensued one of the most audacious cover-ups in modern political history. Except that on this occasion the media weren't kept in the dark. Instead they pulled the covers over themselves in order to conceal the truth. Two days after the stroke, on 25 June 1953, *The Times* reported that 'The prime minister, who is particularly diligent in his attendance at the House of Commons to answer questions, was not there to do so yesterday afternoon. This was because

of pressure of work . . .' On 29 June, after a major international conference had to be postponed, it told its readers, 'The prime minister –
now in his seventy-ninth year – is not physically ill, but is suffering
from fatigue . . .'

Out of public view Churchill's condition deteriorated but not
before he had given Jock Colville strict instructions to keep the fact
that he was incapacitated from getting out. His medical bulletin was
duly altered, removing the reference to his 'disturbance of the cerebral
circulation' and reporting only that he was 'in need of a complete rest'.
Colville realised it would be a constitutional outrage for himself and
others at Downing Street to take over the reins of power on Churchill's
behalf, second-guessing what he would want them to do. He also
understood that the truth was bound to leak if he didn't take 'immediate defensive action'.[47] So he wrote to three of Churchill's friends,
all of them powerful men in Fleet Street, Lords Beaverbrook and
Camrose and the recently ennobled Brendan Bracken, now chairman
of the *Financial Times*. They rushed to Chartwell to confer about what
to do and, in Colville's words, they 'achieved the all but incredible, and
in peace-time possibly unique, success of gagging Fleet Street, something they would have done for nobody but Churchill. Not a word of
the prime minister's stroke was published until he himself casually mentioned it in a speech in the House of Commons a year later.'[48]

It wasn't until the end of July, a month after he was taken ill, that
'the prime minister was sufficiently restored to take an intelligent interest in affairs of state and express his own decisive views'. Even then he
moved to Chequers, where he convalesced until mid-August and spent
more time reading fiction than government papers. In all that time the
public knew nothing about his stroke, although some journalists suspected there had to be more behind the official statement that his
doctor's had advised him to rest. Churchill's friends couldn't manipulate the entire world's media. The *Daily Mirror* in particular was outside
their influence although by the same token it was outside the loop and
was never privy to private information about the prime minister's
health. All it could do was ask questions based on speculative pieces
that appeared in the American press, including a report in the *New York
Herald Tribune* that suggested he had made a near-miraculous recovery

from a stroke. 'What is the truth about Churchill's illness?' asked the *Mirror*. And, even more tellingly, was there 'any reason why the British people should not be told the facts about the health of their prime minister?' It was a very good question.

The public were not told, of course, although when Churchill did re-emerge in public it was obvious he was still well below par. He was frequently grumpy and depressed and his Commons performances were uncertain and ill judged. His friends in the media could protect him when he was shielded from view but once he was back on public display it was a different matter. There were more and more frequent references in the papers to his obviously waning powers and this, combined with a Labour revival at by-elections, led him to consult Lord Swinton, who had been in and out of government since 1918 and was now a close confidant of the prime minister's. Swinton told him to come down from his ivory tower and start treating journalists with respect for once in his life – not just the grand proprietors and editors, but those who actually wrote the articles that most people read. Churchill told him wearily that he was too old to learn new tricks. 'I suppose it's the new American style of trying to persuade journalists they're important,' he said and asked Swinton to take on the task for him instead.[49]

By 1954 the man who had waited patiently for years to succeed him, the foreign secretary Anthony Eden, was reported as saying 'this simply cannot go on; he is gaga: he cannot finish his sentences'.[50] Others, with less reason to draw attention to his weaknesses, also reported some decidedly odd behaviour. Both Rab Butler, the chancellor, and Harold Macmillan, minister of defence, would later paint extraordinary pictures of being summoned to see the prime minister to discuss serious matters of policy only to find him in bed with a parrot, Toby, on his head. Toby would fly around the room, poop on Butler's head and sip from Churchill's whisky and soda while occasionally uttering a few words with a voice like a husky American actress.[51] Needless to say such colourful scenes were not made public.

The electorate did get some sense of what was going on, with the *Daily Mirror* again leading the way. 'Twilight of a Giant' said the paper on its front page in April.[52] There would be more in the same vein, but still he held on, with remarkable tenacity, for almost a year. In early 1955 he reluctantly settled on Easter of that year for his departure, although he would later try to wriggle out of it. Both Beaverbrook and Bracken knew of his intentions in mid-January but there was no informed speculation in any newspaper before the end of March. To the very end his handful of close friends in the media looked after his interests and protected him. Never in the field of political reporting had one man owed so much to so few. He left Downing Street for the final time as prime minister on 6 April. One of his last utterances had been, with reference to Eden, 'I don't believe Anthony can do it.'[53] However accurate his prediction, it was too late to do anything about it. There was a final irony as he departed. A strike in Fleet Street meant that now the news was official there were almost no papers to report it.

6

GREAT EXPECTATIONS: EDEN, MACMILLAN, DOUGLAS-HOME (1955–64)

> *I read a great number of press reports and find comfort in the fact that they are nearly always conflicting.*
>
> Harold Macmillan

In many ways Sir Anthony Eden was the Gordon Brown of the mid-twentieth century – the heir apparent who feared that a stubborn prime minister with a singularly high opinion of his own talents might never make way for him. By 1955 Eden had been waiting in the wings for more than ten years, eyeing the party leadership with far greater patience and equanimity than Gordon Brown would ever display. Both men were certain they could do a better job, and each would be tested in the field they knew and understood best – Brown on the economy, Eden in foreign affairs. And they had similar strengths and weakness; hardworking but indecisive and too prone to interfering with the work of colleagues. The writer and publisher Nigel Nicolson, who was a Tory backbencher at the time, wrote that 'Eden was a bad prime minister. For one thing, he could never leave his ministers alone. He was always fussing them, ringing them up in the middle of the night to ask them had they done this? Had they seen this in the newspapers?'[1] Eden took over in far more favourable circumstances than Brown would do, but he managed to turn every advantage into a liability and resigned in failure after less than two years in office.

If all it took to be a successful prime minister was an outstanding CV and a good image then Anthony Eden should have been up there among the greats. He cut an exceptionally fine figure with film-star looks and an easy manner. Yet those who knew him well, and after so long near the top that included not only his political colleagues but most of Fleet Street too, sensed a weakness behind the confident exterior. Another backbencher, George Harvie-Watt, spoke of his entirely 'press-made reputation . . . mere platitudes and amiable generalities'.[2] Yet while the papers would occasionally mock his vanity, fancy clothes and perma-tan, they also reminded their readers that he had been a brave opponent of appeasement. He was widely perceived as a man of honour and integrity. Within two years that image would be destroyed. The same person who had resigned as foreign secretary in 1938 when he thought the British people were being misled about the threat from abroad showed himself capable of perpetrating a monumental deceit of his own over Suez. In the process he, like Chamberlain before him, would lecture the media about their 'patriotic duty' and try to bully them into supporting his misguided policy.

Eden became prime minister owing no great debt of gratitude to Fleet Street. No newspaper could claim to have put him where he was, although the *Daily Mail* had singled him out as 'politician of the year' for 1954. Nor would the media be responsible for his early demise – he managed quite well on that score by himself. Yet his cack-handed management of the press was symptomatic of a premiership that never came together. Lord Swinton, who shared Churchill's fears that Eden was the wrong man for the job, took little pleasure in concluding that 'he proved a *prima donna*, not a prime minister'.[3] Eden's friend Noël Coward could see the actor in him but also the reality behind the public performance, calling him 'a tragic figure who had been cast in a star part well above his capabilities'.[4]

It didn't take the media long to rumble him. Anthony Eden's honeymoon with the press was as short as Gordon Brown's, although he did at least manage to win his own mandate, calling an immediate general election and winning it comfortably. With Labour tired, weak and divided, the 1955 campaign was really no contest. Even the *Daily Mirror* could muster little enthusiasm for the attack, merely poking fun at the 'Miles and Miles of the Eden Smiles' and his Old Etonian smugness. The papers were more concerned about the new opposition they themselves faced from television. TV political coverage hadn't yet fully come of age, but Eden was much better placed to take advantage of the medium than the publicity-shy Clement Attlee. He appeared live in a fifteen-minute election broadcast speaking directly to the voters. It was an enormous success, especially after his advisers rejected the use of a tele-prompter on the grounds that it made Eden 'look mad'.[5] Having smiled his way to an easy win and a majority of sixty, Eden felt he had a right to the same reverence and support that Fleet Street was in the habit of according to Tory prime ministers. He didn't get it and was so thin-skinned that he allowed the press to get to him and to weaken him with their criticism.

The man Eden appointed to look after his press relations had a torrid time of it. William Clark was a former *Observer* journalist and radio and TV presenter. He was the first to hold the title of 'press and broadcasting officer' as Downing Street finally caught up with the changes taking place in the media. Clark was popular with journalists but probably a little too much so for his own good or that of the prime minister. He could be indiscreet and rather too ready to give his views to the press rather than Eden's. If at first Fleet Street thought it was being brought in from the cold with Clark's instinct for openness, they were in for a shock. Eden started looking into how Churchill had handled the release of official information. According to his biographer, the former Tory MP Robert Rhodes James, he was startled to learn that 'a small group met regularly to decide which confidential documents should be leaked to the press, and specifically to which newspapers and reporters'.[6] Eden ordered the practice stopped and 'One political correspondent in particular was at first bewildered, and then enraged, when his sources of information suddenly dried up, and became noticeably hostile to the Eden government as a result.'

Unlike Churchill, who didn't think he needed anybody to help him get his message across, Eden fussed endlessly over what Clark said to the press. When he didn't like what he read in the papers he would blame anybody – journalists, his colleagues, Clark – other than himself. He could have a terrible temper and his press secretary was often at the receiving end of it. And while future spokesmen would be criticised for briefing against other members of the government, Eden thought Clark was praising them too highly. 'It's no good you saying that everyone is all right except the prime minister, who just dithers.'[7] Eden's wife, Clarissa, who was Churchill's niece, wound him up rather than calmed him down, pointing out critical articles he might have missed. She had a particular contempt for one journalist in particular, the former prime minister's son, Randolph, whom she accused, with ample justification, of undermining her husband at every opportunity and of being a 'wholly horrid man'.[8] Randolph Churchill's own political career had been a flop, but he had his father's flair for writing. According to James Margach, who knew him, 'Randolph tried hard to orchestrate Fleet Street's attacks while himself writing hostile articles in Beaverbrook's London *Evening Standard*. But worse than this, he was frequently on the phone to his cousin Clarissa, Lady Eden, making it clear in his hectoring style, just how disastrous a premier he considered her husband to be. These personalised battering-ram onslaughts – and Randolph had a cruel and wicked tongue when he was trying to destroy anyone, which was often – added enormously to the anguish of Lady Eden, already at the point of exhaustion by worry over her husband's health.'[9]

As William Clark observed, 'the press does latch on to people's failings, and they soon latched on to Eden's'. By January 1956 it seemed as if Eden had no friends at all in the press. The *Daily Mail* and *The Times* made repeated references to the government's lack of direction and purpose. Clark's old paper, the *Observer*, picked up on the growing feeling among Tory backbenchers that Eden was a liability. These were all papers that had traditionally supported the Conservative party. Then, after a botched reshuffle, the most Tory paper of the lot, the *Daily Telegraph*, weighed in with an article that Eden took very personally indeed. The deputy editor, Donald McLachlan, was the author of an editorial under the headline 'Waiting For The Smack of Firm Government'.[10] It pointed out that the prime minister had a habit of clenching 'one fist to smash the open palm of the other' but that he almost never went through with the movement. The implication was obvious and, in his memoirs, Rab Butler recalled that the article 'drew from the prime minister a pained and pungent oath, with which I expressed warm sympathy. Anthony was very susceptible to such criticism.'[11] Word of his anger quickly leaked and there was a wave of speculation that Eden was even on the point of resignation. He made matters worse by allowing Clark to issue an official denial that he was about to quit, which inevitably gave the story renewed impetus. Butler then stirred the pot even more when he was 'door-stepped' by the media. It's another of those famous political quotations that were never made, along with Callaghan's 'Crisis What Crisis?' and Macmillan's 'You've never had it so good'. Butler never said that Eden was 'the best prime minister we've got', but it doesn't make a lot of difference. He didn't argue when it was it put to him. 'My hurried assent to this well meant but meaningless proposition was flashed round the world; indeed it was fathered upon me. I do not think it did Anthony any good. It did not do me any good, either.'[12]

Eden's diary at this time is full of references to 'torrents of abuse' in the press, some of which he attributed to another personal vendetta, this time between Clarissa and Lady Pamela Berry, whose husband owned the *Daily Telegraph*. Eden told Rab and others that he was unconcerned by it all, but that was clearly not the case. He showed his true feelings when he started a speech in Bradford by saying 'I do not have to advise this great Yorkshire audience not to believe everything they read in certain London newspapers. I know that one or two of these cantankerous newspapers claimed that they were reflecting public feeling. They were doing nothing of the sort. What they were doing was to try to make you think and feel what they wanted you to. I am sure you will always be on your guard against such methods. That way lies the denial of democracy.'[13] Despite the best efforts of the press, he said, he had every intention of serving a full term. Although *The Times* called the speech 'well proportioned' it was immediately obvious to the media that they were getting under his skin and, far from warning them off, the speech merely served to goad them on.

This was all before Colonel Gamal Abdel Nasser decided to take over the Suez Canal on 26 July 1956, provoking a military response from Britain and France that might have made Eden's reputation but instead destroyed it. It also destroyed his relationship with Clark, who resigned soon afterwards, having disagreed all along with the policy and resenting being dragged into a situation in which, in his words, 'news management became news invention'. It is the most devastating judgement by any press secretary on the prime minister he served. 'Parliament, the public and the bureaucracy were not only unconsulted, not only surprised, they were deceived . . .' he wrote. 'Public opinion at home and particularly abroad could not be ignored, it had to be fooled.'[14]

All the evidence suggests the public was genuinely divided over the rights and wrongs of the Suez expedition, as, indeed, was opinion in the leading newspapers. They were united in condemning Nasser's nationalisation of the canal. Most happily compared the colonel to Hitler and Mussolini, but their reactions to Eden's attempts to regain it were less gung-ho, increasingly so as the operation turned to disaster. The regional press was largely in favour, with the exception of the *Daily Record* in Scotland. The national media were much more supportive at first, although the *Observer* and the *Manchester Guardian* were hostile and *The Times* was ambivalent and erratic. By the time British troops were actually involved the London press was divided just about 50/50, generally along party lines. The weekly news magazines, more influential then than they are now, were almost all in the anti-war camp. The opposition of both *The Economist* and the *Spectator*, neither of them left wing or pacifist, caused particular concern in Downing Street. The problem was not so much the impact at home, but abroad. The Russians and the Americans saw a divided press as evidence of a divided country and no doubt Colonel Nasser took comfort in seeing Eden struggle to convince even such patriotic journals as these of the justice of his cause.

The affair exposed the prime minister's obsession with the media and ignorance of how they operated. After attending a cabinet meeting early in the crisis, Clark wrote in his diary, 'Then we got down to publicity. It was discussed with no sense of reality and no understanding of the working of the agencies – everyone agreed the press ought

not to say too much for patriotic reasons, and that was that . . . I tried
to intervene, without effect.'[15] Eden started by calling in groups of editors and giving them off-the-record briefings, including extensive
military information that he told them they couldn't use. He would
then lecture them on their duty to rally round the armed forces. Not
surprisingly they didn't find that approach unduly helpful and it did
nothing to help the government's case. He ruffled a few feathers at *The
Times* by telling the editor, Sir William Haley, that he was pleased the
paper was not 'repeating its own appeasing posture over the
Rhineland'.[16] Eden then took to telephoning proprietors and editors
from six in the morning as soon as he had seen the papers and read stories he didn't like. When that didn't help either he became increasingly
angry and frustrated. Clark would constantly try to calm him down as
he erupted several times a day over what the press was saying. Clark
himself put the bad press down to confusion within government over
what the policy actually was. Eden and others 'want the press to be
quiet about our military preparations because they are politically
embarrassing; but fool themselves into thinking they are only asking for
military censorship in the national interest.' When he listened to the
BBC the prime minister would ring Clark and ask him if they were
'enemies or just socialists'. He had hoped to use the BBC to speak to
the nation over the heads of the unhelpful newspapers and thought he
would have no problem because 'the director general was my fag at
Eton'.[17]

The corporation was in a difficult position. Its chairman, Sir
Alexander Cadogan, was not only a personal friend of the prime minister, but also a director of the Suez Canal Company. Yet Cadogan
made it clear to Downing Street that if Eden wanted to make a prime-
ministerial broadcast during the crisis, then time would also be made
available for Hugh Gaitskell, as leader of the opposition, to do the
same. Eden did broadcast, from a tiny, cramped studio at Lime Grove,
on 8 August. It was not the success he had hoped. He was forced to
wear glasses to read his notes and blamed 'those communists at the
BBC' for deliberately shining bright lights in his eyes.[18] Gaitskell, who
was then supporting Eden's stand against Nasser, chose not to take up
his right to reply.

Under instructions from Eden, William Clark then sought time for the Australian prime minister, Robert Menzies, to make a broadcast too but he was rebuffed. Eden exploded into a rage at the news and Clark warned the corporation that the PM was so angry that 'some drastic action' might be taken that would be 'permanently harmful to the BBC'.[19] The tradition of ugly spats between the government and the corporation whenever British troops go into action was thus initiated in the hot summer of 1956. This time Downing Street got the better of the argument and Menzies' broadcast eventually went ahead. Clark later said that Eden had instructed the lord chancellor 'to prepare an instrument which would take over the BBC altogether and subject it wholly to the will of the Government',[20] although Eden's official biographer disputes this.[21] In the event Suez would result in more freedom for the BBC to cover controversial events rather than less. Since 1944 the corporation had been operating under a rule banning it from discussing any subject due to be debated in parliament over the following two weeks or the subject of any legislation then going through the House of Commons. The ban was at first voluntary. It was made compulsory only in 1955 and during the debate Attlee had warned with characteristic prescience that 'There might come a time when major measures were introduced by a minister, not first in this House, but first on the wireless. That may sound absurd, but we have had examples of what happens when the wireless is used in totalitarian countries.'[22] Commercial broadcasting, then in its infancy, was subject to the same restriction. Both the broadcasters and the press united in condemning the restriction but reluctantly the BBC abided by it until its absurdity was convincingly exposed during Suez the following year. The BBC felt the crisis gave it strong enough cause to ignore the rule and the government didn't try to enforce it. It was abolished in July 1957.

The events that freed the corporation, but left the canal in the hands of Colonel Nasser, began in earnest on 29 October 1956. Israeli troops entered Egyptian territory in an operation secretly planned in London and Paris to justify a subsequent Anglo-French intervention 'to separate the combatants'. Eden had embarked on a strategy that would involve not only deceiving the British people and Britain's allies in

America and elsewhere, but also his own press secretary. William Clark was at home when he first heard of the Israeli military action. The Admiralty press office rang him to say they were getting calls from journalists inquiring about reports of an attack. As soon as he put the phone down it rang again. The *News Chronicle* asked if he knew about it and he said no. He then rang Downing Street only to be told that Eden was 'very surprised' to hear of the invasion. He duly passed this on to journalists although he already suspected it wasn't true. Two days later he was sure he was part of a conspiracy to deceive and considered resigning. 'This was really the first time I had realised that I couldn't stand the hypocrisy of the whole policy.'[23] Only a sense of duty convinced him to stay in his post until the operation was over. 'I am perhaps being useful in seeing that some truth between government and public remains.' One junior minister, Tony Nutting, did resign from the Foreign Office and Clark was dismayed to get a call from the Conservative whips' office 'asking if I couldn't hint that Nutting was terribly under the influence of his American mistress and anyway was not quite himself nowadays. I replied bitterly that I thought that was the sort of thing the party did, certainly not me.'[24]

After the British and French bombing campaign began on 31 October, Eden insisted on broadcasting to the nation to reassure the public that he was still 'a man of peace' but that military intervention was needed 'to put out the forest fire' of fighting between Israel and Egypt.[25] It was the first ever live prime-ministerial broadcast from inside Number 10 itself, and it was well received. The actor Dirk Bogarde sent a telegram of congratulations on his performance. On 5 November British paratroopers landed on Egyptian soil. Inside Downing Street there was quiet satisfaction that things were going according to plan, but Clark did not join in the sense of relief. He wrote in his diary, 'the week just past has been the worst by far of my life. The knowledge of collusion, the deception, the hypocrisy . . . I am really getting a bit hysterical myself. It seems to me that the PM is mad, literally mad.'[26] Clark suffered terrible mood swings and crises of conscience, writing 'I long to be free as a journalist to drive this government from power and keep the cowards and crooks out of power for all time.' By 6 November the operation was already going wrong and the defence secretary, Walter Monckton, who had never been in favour of it, complained angrily to Clark about a report in *The Times* saying the cabinet was totally united in support. Clark told him 'it was just one of the PM's lies' and sat down to write his resignation letter. As he was doing so, news came through that the United States was refusing to support Britain, leaving Eden with no option other than an ignominious retreat. Eden summoned Clark to the House of Commons and told him to issue yet another misleading statement. He was told to make it look as if the prime minister had made his own decision to withdraw the troops rather than being forced into it by President Eisenhower. Clark did so 'gladly', knowing it would be the last lie he would have to tell for Number 10.[27]

The press was in uproar. Contempt for Eden degenerated into ridicule when, a few days later, Downing Street announced that he would be flying to Jamaica to stay at Goldeneye, the home of the James Bond author Ian Fleming, because his doctor had ordered a complete rest. He never fully recovered and resigned as prime minister in January 1957, a broken and humiliated man. The true extent of his duplicity would only become public knowledge later, but the press knew they had been lied to and his credibility was destroyed more fully than his health. Even the Palace was concerned. With classic royal understatement, the young Queen Elizabeth II told her private secretary, 'I think the basic dishonesty of the whole thing was a trouble.'[28] It would fall to Eden's successor to try to repair the broken bond of trust between Downing Street, the media and the public beyond.

If Anthony Eden had sometimes been likened to a film star, Harold Macmillan was the true actor-premier. Only Tony Blair would ever outclass him in his ability to ham it up, turn on the charm, ooze sincerity and play shamelessly to the gallery. Lord Hailsham recalled 'the beautiful acting of Harold Macmillan',[29] Enoch Powell called him 'the great actor manager' and his biographer Anthony Sampson said that his performance as prime minister reflected the dramatic talent he had shown at Oxford and his love of musical theatre: 'like Disraeli, he seemed to see himself as part of a fashionable play'.[30]

He certainly dressed for the part and, again like Disraeli, he had a touch of the dandy about him. And he was the first prime minister that the public would be able to see in action on an almost daily basis. Television had finally come of age as a medium of political reporting and communication. By the time he left office it was the principle means by which most people formed their views of those in office or aspiring to it. Macmillan could see what was happening and while he pretended to be uneasy about it he made his way in the new television age with great skill. He spoke of 'The camera's hot, probing eye, these monstrous machines and their attendants. A kind of twentieth-century torture chamber, that's what it is,'[31] but the camera treated him kindly. Above all it reinforced his image of unflappability that did much to reassure the electorate after the obvious flappability of Eden.

Nye Bevan called him 'Macwonder' but it was the cartoonist Victor Weisz, better known as Vicky, who came up with the name that stuck, 'Supermac'. It tells us almost all we need to know about Macmillan's relations with the press. Vicky, a committed socialist, had meant it as cutting satire but Macmillan effortlessly turned it to his advantage and 'Supermac' took on a life of his own entirely favourable to the prime minister. According to Michael Foot, who knew him well, Vicky was dismayed. He had intended the cartoon character to portray 'the stunt merchant of all time who could still fall flat on his face'.[32] Macmillan did stumble eventually, but not because of any of Vicky's famous cartoons. By the end of his premiership many political reputations would be tarnished, his own included. That of Fleet Street would take even more of a battering. But while Eden had the shortest honeymoon with the press in modern times, Macmillan had one of the longest.

He was helped by a very good choice of press secretary in Harold Evans, a journalist turned career civil servant not to be confused with the future editor of the *Sunday Times* and *The Times*. Evans was perhaps the most successful and popular spokesman in the history of Downing Street. He was always fully briefed on every subject of importance – after Clark's experience he had to be – and treated the media with the right mixture of professionalism and understanding. He quickly gained a reputation for giving quick, straightforward answers to journalists' questions and never telling a lie, which is as good a reputation as a press secretary can ask for. He also had the great advantage that the prime minister let him get on with it with very little interference and never a tantrum. Macmillan may have known how to put on a show for the media but he wasn't terribly interested in what they said about him. His opinion of journalists was summed up in what he told Evans: 'They can hardly avoid behaving as they do. It's the same with painters. Unless their work is controversial, exaggerated, distorted, they arouse no interest.'[33] To provide ministerial oversight he appointed as information minister Charles Hill, who had first come to prominence as the 'radio doctor' during the Second World War and would go on to chair the BBC. Hill thought it was a thankless task, especially after Suez, when policy failure had been blamed, as it so often is, on poor communication. 'This technique is as old as the press officer. When things go well ministers puff out their chests and bask in the praise. When they go badly they look for an alibi – it can't be that the policy was wrong.'[34] Macmillan, who had been one of Eden's strongest supporters over Suez, although this inconvenient fact was quickly forgotten, needed Hill because he didn't know, or want to know, how to deal with the media himself. 'I gathered that he was not enamoured of the techniques of public relations – he made it pretty plain that he never used them himself and, despite that, he had become prime minister.' Macmillan may not have mastered the theory of public relations but he had an instinctive feel for how to influence perceptions. According to Evans, he was 'always completely alert to the niceties of presentation, whether in content, style or timing. He thought about them deeply and was usually a jump ahead of the rest of us.'[35]

Macmillan's immediate task, as is usually the case when a prime minister takes the reins between elections, was to signal a change in the style of government. He pinned a note in his own hand on the cabinet-room door. It was a quotation from Gilbert and Sullivan's *The Gondoliers* that could never have been used to describe his predecessor's way of working. 'Quiet, calm deliberation disentangles every knot'. He silenced the klaxon on the prime-ministerial car, which Churchill had fitted and Eden had overused. And he let it be known that at times of anxiety he was prone to reading the novels of Anthony Trollope. It was a class act and no mistake. Superficially he was from another age. Britain was only a few years away from the swinging sixties but

Macmillan was the last prime minister to have been born in the nineteenth century. He was all tweeds, moustache and Old Etonian reserve. Yet he made the techniques of the modern world work for him as no previous occupant of Number 10 had done. He was forever jumping on and off jet planes and cutting a surprisingly youthful figure as he did so. He dug out a particularly impressive fur coat and donned a borrowed white Russian hat for the first visit to the Soviet Union by any Western leader since the war. His meeting with Nikita Khrushchev caused even more of a stir than Margaret Thatcher's much-publicised visit to see President Gorbachev in the dying days of the USSR. Television lapped it up. Macmillan recognised that when he was on the box he had a direct line of communication with the voters. No press lords, editors, headline writers or satirists could get in the way of what he wanted to say or how he wanted to appear. Although the prime minister rarely if ever watched television, Evans believed the medium revealed the real man 'not the comic Edwardian dandy of the carica-tures'. Macmillan did use the tele-prompter although he wasn't comfortable with it and had to work hard at improving his perform-ance in set-piece broadcasts. After his retirement from office he said that for politicians of his generation television was still alien. They had developed their communication skills in a very different age. For most of his career, Macmillan had been more used to speaking at public meetings, which generated some reaction from the audience. Appearing on television, by comparison, was 'like playing lawn tennis and there isn't anybody to hit the ball back from the other side of the net'.[36]

The exception was the studio interview and it was Macmillan who agreed to initiate the now-familiar format. The BBC got first crack in 1958 on the programme *Press Conference*. Three journalists put restrained questions and he had an easy enough ride. Soon afterwards it was the turn of ITN's *Tell the People*, presented by Robin Day. It was a less comfortable encounter for Macmillan, who arrived in the studio and noted that his interviewer had a comfortable swing chair behind a desk while he was given a hard one. He complained that he felt 'on the mat'. When Day offered to swap chairs he refused, saying 'I know my place.'[37] The programme caused controversy because Day asked about newspaper criticism of the foreign secretary, Selwyn Lloyd. Macmillan knocked back the question with ease but the *Daily Telegraph* wondered whether he should ever have been put on the spot 'before a camera which showed every flicker of the eyelid. Who is to draw the line at which the effort to entertain stops?' The balance of power between prime ministers, the press and television was shifting in front of everybody's eyes.

If Macmillan was going to grant interviews to TV then he could scarcely refuse to offer them to the written press also. It seems remarkable now, but these on-the-record exchanges with journalists were seen as yet another dangerous innovation in Whitehall. They worried that the prime minister might make an announcement or indicate a change in government thinking without consulting his civil servants or his ministerial colleagues first. In other words, he might make news and if he did they wouldn't know what to do about it. Accountability to parliament, collective responsibility, the very foundations of parliamentary democracy, were at risk. Macmillan didn't spend much time worrying. The lucky recipient of the first ever formal sit-down interview with a serving prime minister was James Margach. The world didn't collapse; indeed, Margach claims it may have got a little better. 'Macmillan told me, for the record, that the future of the world depended on breaking down the barriers between east and west. The *Sunday Times* published his words and within forty-eight hours of the interview came a response from the Kremlin: an invitation to visit Moscow. The result was *détente*, an easing of the Cold War tensions for the first time since the war.'[38] Not bad for a mere interview. Margach got his scoop and the cameras soon got their pictures of the prime minister in a white hat and his father-in-law's fur coat.

Just as Margaret Thatcher would do almost thirty years later, Macmillan called a general election in the same year as his historic visit to the Soviet Union. Images of the prime minister on the international stage were still fresh in voters' minds. The election of 1959 was the first real television election. The percentage of voters with a TV in their home had risen from under 40 per cent to over 70 per cent since the country had last gone to the polls four years earlier. According to the Nuffield study of the 1959 campaign, image mattered more than ever before. This 'reflected an increased recognition that people's votes are influenced by general impressions . . . that characterise a party much more than any carefully drafted manifestos or speeches . . . The Conservatives' main contribution to the advancement of political warfare was to enlist professional public-relations men to shine the spotlight upon the most favourable aspects of the party's image, thus leaving defects in shadow.'[39] The party spent more than ever before on publicity to promote two things in particular – rising prosperity and Harold Macmillan. The experts even thought that the famous phrase 'You've never had it so good' was too backward-looking. Macmillan had never uttered the exact words anyway. On 20 July 1957, he said in a speech in Bedford that 'most of our people have never had it so good'. For the election it became 'You're having it good. Have it better. Vote Conservative'. Macmillan was happy to let the professionals get on with marketing him and his government. Their images successfully dominated the election, not least because Labour made little effort to compete. The party leader, Hugh Gaitskell, disliked the whole idea of public relations, which he thought was inherently false.

Harold Evans played no part at all in the campaign. He was very strict about keeping his role as government spokesman free from contamination by the polluting effects of party politics. Once the prime minister was safely back in Downing Street, however, Evans would have to deal with some far muckier things than a mere contest for votes. The second half of Macmillan's tenure in office was far less comfortable for all concerned than the first. It started with foreign affairs and ended with affairs of a rather more personal nature. With the former he was more than comfortable, with the latter extremely ill at ease. His attitude to sex was as Edwardian as his upbringing. It was simply not something you talked about. Unfortunately for him the Britain of the early 1960s was shaking off its inhibitions and getting ready for a sexual revolution that would take hold of the public imagination, even if the imagination was as far as it got for the vast majority of citizens. The newspapers would be full of sex and scandal in his last years in Downing Street, although Macmillan had reason to be thankful that one story Fleet Street voluntarily suppressed was of the long-running affair between his wife, Dorothy, and the former Tory MP Robert Boothby.

In the period immediately following the 1959 election, however, Macmillan seemed to have lost none of his touch or his ability to command the agenda and the headlines. He visited the newly elected John F. Kennedy in Washington and managed to avoid looking like a relic from another age beside the glamorous young president. Together they agreed on a programme of nuclear collaboration that continues to this day, and negotiated with the USSR the first partial test-ban treaty. In Cape Town he made the prophetic 'wind of change' speech acknowledging the right of African nations to independence from colonialism. He had less success trying to negotiate Britain's membership of the Common Market, but it was at home that things really started to turn sour as the 1960s began. The economic boom faltered. The sunny optimism of 'You're having it good' no longer rang true and the Conservative party began to suffer by-election losses. 'Supermac' seemed to be losing some of his powers. Television, which had started out by being so kind to Macmillan, suddenly turned cruel. It wasn't anything on the news bulletins, or even the efforts of Robin Day and his colleagues, that altered perceptions so much as the emergence of a new breed of comic talent, the television satirist. The likes of David Frost, Alan Bennett and Peter Cook managed to do what Vicky's cartoons hadn't. They made Macmillan look vulnerable. He scored a number of 'firsts' but one that he had cause to regret was being the first prime minister to be lampooned mercilessly, first on stage and soon afterwards on radio and television. Cook's portrayal of the slurring, doddery, forgetful Macmillan in *Beyond The Fringe* caused an uproar simply because it had never been done before. It was also very funny, often taking the form of a prime-ministerial address to the nation, something that Macmillan himself had developed into almost an art form.

'I have recently been travelling round the world on your behalf and at your expense visiting some of the chaps with whom I hope to be shaping your future', said Cook as Macmillan. Among the 'chaps' was President Kennedy. 'We talked of many things, including Great Britain's position in the world as some kind of honest broker. I agreed with him when he said no nation could be more honest, and he agreed with me when I chaffed him and said no nation could be broker.'[40]

Beyond The Fringe opened at London's Fortune Theatre in May 1961. Macmillan tried to show he could take a joke by going along to the theatre to see Peter Cook's impersonation himself, only to find his presence mocked in an ad lib: 'When I've a spare evening there's nothing I like better than to wander over to a theatre and sit there listening to a group of sappy, urgent, vibrant young satirists, with a stupid great grin spread all over my silly old face.'

While *Beyond The Fringe*, *Private Eye* and *That Was The Week That Was* all gleefully poked fun at politics and at the prime minister, the more conventional media were not short of material to make Macmillan's life uncomfortable. Cook's portrayal of a man in decline was effective because it seemed to reflect the reality. With his botched ministerial reshuffle of 13 July 1962, Macmillan by his own actions raised questions about whether his judgement and his unflappability were deserting him. The Night of the Long Knives, as it was dubbed, didn't look like the product of 'quiet, calm deliberation'. The planned reshuffle had to be brought forward after Rab Butler had lunch with Lord Rothermere after which the *Daily Mail*'s political editor, Walter Terry, revealed that big changes were on the way, including the departure of the chancellor of the exchequer, Selwyn Lloyd. The *Mail* had an embarrassing scoop but Macmillan allowed himself to be rushed into announcing an even bigger story, the sacking of a third of his cabinet, including some of his oldest friends. Some of them had wanted to go but others, including Lloyd and Charles Hill, had not. Prime ministers can usually get away with being portrayed as ruthless from time to time, but by appearing to allow the media to dictate the timing Macmillan laid himself open to the more damaging charges of panic and disloyalty. A young Liberal MP, Jeremy Thorpe, showed he could match the prime minister for theatricality when he said, 'greater love hath no man than this, that he lay down his friends for his life'. The Tory MP Nigel Birch congratulated him for keeping his own head while all around him were losing theirs. For the headline writers 'Supermac' had become 'Mac the Knife'.

The reshuffle brought into government Bill Deedes, who had inspired the journalist William Boot in Evelyn Waugh's novel *Scoop*. He would later edit the *Daily Telegraph* and be immortalised by *Private*

Eye as the recipient of the 'Dear Bill' letters from Denis Thatcher. In his memoirs Deedes said that his appointment as minister without portfolio in charge of the information services had made his heart sink. 'Will you return to the sinking ship?' asked Macmillan. He did his duty, reflecting that 'a sinking ship is my spiritual home'.[41] He soon realised that there was little that he could do to improve the government's relations with the press. 'The longer I worked in the job,' he remembered, 'the more clearly I came to see that I was superfluous.' He found work for himself, however, including a role that, in the hands of others, would become much more controversial forty years later: burying bad news. He ensured that 'if ministers had good news to tell, the day was kept clear for them. We had a weekly conference of chief press officers to co-ordinate that. If their news was bad, we tried to tie that in with some juicy distraction.'

Deedes was soon to discover that sometimes the news is so bad that nothing can be found to distract attention from it. In September 1962 John Vassall, a clerk at the Admiralty, was arrested and charged with spying for the Soviet Union. He had been blackmailed into espionage while on a posting to Moscow, where Russian agents had got him drunk and then taken explicit photographs of him enjoying the company of several different men. After he was convicted the press decided they had a homosexual spy ring on their hands, including other leading members of the Establishment, including Vassall's former ministerial boss, Tom Galbraith, by then at the Scottish Office. The first lord of the Admiralty, Lord Carrington, was accused of knowing he had a spy in his department but doing nothing. The media got into such a frenzy that Galbraith felt he had no choice but to offer his resignation, which Macmillan accepted. As John Major and Tony Blair will testify, when to stand by a minister accused of 'sleaze' and when to let one go is never an easy decision. Macmillan got it wrong. James Margach recalled that it seemed 'as though Galbraith was being offered as a blood sacrifice to assuage the gods of Fleet Street. But the gods were not appeased. Having hounded Galbraith without mercy or responsibility, the papers then switched their attacks to Carrington, as though the big fish had escaped while the small fry had been hooked.'[42]

Macmillan was furious and, for once, showed it in public, accusing

a Sunday journalist of 'lies, lies, falsehoods' and of being 'a disgrace to
the profession' during a meeting with political correspondents. In private the prime minister told his press secretary he detected 'the growth
of what I can only call the spirit of Titus Oates and Senator
McCarthy'.[43] Downing Street was to get its revenge soon enough. A
Royal Commission under Lord Radcliffe looked into the allegations
and after going though 250 separate newspaper stories concluded that
not one of them could be justified by the facts. Both Galbraith and
Carrington were vindicated and Fleet Street was in the dock instead,
in the case of two of the offending journalists quite literally. Brendan
Mulholland of the *Daily Mail* and Reg Foster of the *Daily Sketch* went
to jail for contempt after refusing to tell the inquiry the source of their
information. There was a half-hearted effort to turn them into heroes
for defending press freedom, but the denunciation of the media had
been so complete that there was little public sympathy. The government didn't quite have it all its own way, however. Ministers had
wanted to suppress a section of Radcliffe's report that contained the
embarrassing revelation of communist cells in the civil-service staff
associations. Once again the story leaked and Macmillan reluctantly
told the cabinet that 'in the new situation created by this disclosure . . .
the balance of advantage now lay on the side of including . . . a shortened version of this chapter' in the published document.[44]

The government had won the battle hands down and rightly so. It was
the biggest official slap down of media standards and truthfulness until
Lord Hutton sided so conclusively with Tony Blair and Alastair
Campbell after the invasion of Iraq. In both cases the media retreated
bruised and resentful, ready to go back on the attack at the first opportunity. In 1962 they didn't have to wait long. By the end of the year
the Profumo affair was in full swing and this time a minister was guilty
and Macmillan took too long to get rid of him. Although the war secretary, John Profumo, is remembered for 'sleaze', an affair with a
high-class prostitute who was also sleeping with the Russian naval
attaché, his real offence was lying to parliament about what he had
done. Christine Keeler, Yevgeny Ivanov, Mandy Rice-Davis and
Stephen Ward and the other protagonists in the story of society

shenanigans had been all over the papers for weeks by the time Profumo told the Commons there had been 'no impropriety whatsoever in my acquaintanceship with Miss Keeler'.[45] It was the British equivalent of Bill Clinton's 'I did not have sexual relations with that woman, Miss Lewinsky.' Except Clinton kept his job and Profumo didn't. If Macmillan had been less squeamish about talking about sex he might have got the truth out of Profumo sooner, but it seems they never had the discussion. Sources within MI5 tipped off the Labour opposition, now led by Harold Wilson, about what had really been going on and eventually, confronted with his dishonesty, Profumo resigned on 5 June. His departure only poured more petrol on the flames. The media was in a mood to throw Macmillan and the entire Tory party on the pyre and once again they went over the top. Lord Hailsham said 'a great party is not to be brought down because of a squalid affair between a woman of easy virtue and a proved liar.'[46] Macmillan was equally aghast at what was going on. On 7 July he wrote in his diary, '*The Times* was awful – what has since been called a "Holier than thou" attitude, which was really nauseating. The "popular" press has been one mass of the life stories of spies and prostitutes, written no doubt in the office. Day after day the attacks developed, chiefly on me – old, incompetent, worn out.'[47] He surveyed the press and saw only, '. . . the wildest rumour and innuendo against the most respectable ministers . . . more than half the cabinet were being accused of perversion, homosexuality and the like.' Harold Evans had seen nothing like it before, 'few prime ministers can have been subjected to such a sustained barrage of press criticism, much of it amounting to vilification. Yet he survived.'[48]

Macmillan set up another inquiry, this time conducted by the master of the rolls, Lord Denning. If he was hoping to get away unscathed a second time, he was out of luck. Denning concluded that 'It was the responsibility of the prime minister and his colleagues, and of them only, to deal with this situation: and they did not succeed in doing so.'[49] The newspapers publicly, and some Tory MPs privately, started to question how long Macmillan could go on. If there had been an obvious successor around whom the party could quickly unite he would almost certainly have been out that summer. Instead he held on until the party conference in October when he declared that health reasons prevented him remaining in office. He lived for another twenty-three years, long enough to look back and reflect on having experienced both the best and the worst of the British media. He had at least fought back against them and forced the spotlight with great success on the ethics of journalism. In that he did politics a favour, although he paid a price for it. On the day he set up the Radcliffe inquiry into the Vassall affair he told Evans, 'I have made a lot of enemies in the press today . . . But I am an old man and I don't really care.'[50] Between them Harold Macmillan and Harold Evans were a double act to rival Thatcher/Ingham and Blair/Campbell. If a reputation among both journalists and politicians for professionalism and integrity is the measure of success, and it's as good a measure as any, then they were the best of the lot.

Where Harold Macmillan had an instinctive feel for publicity, his successor, the aristocratic Sir Alec Douglas-Home, had little or none. He acknowledged as much in a brief TV statement after taking office. After the usual bit about wanting to serve the nation, he said, 'no one need expect any stunts from me, merely plain, straight talking.'[51] He was prime minister for only a year but has a surprising number of entries in the political record books. He was the last member of the House of Lords to become prime minister (and the first since Lord Salisbury in 1895), although he immediately renounced his peerage after being chosen by the 'magic circle' of Conservative party grandees. He was also the last person to be sent for by the Palace without having first been elected by his own party, at least until Gordon Brown became prime minister unchallenged in 2007. At the time of writing Douglas-Home shares with only James Callaghan and Neville Chamberlain in recent history the dubious honour of never having won a general election. He took greater pride in being the only prime minister to have played first-class cricket at an international level. Hard though it is to prove, he may also have been the only prime minister genuinely not to want the job. In the dramatic days after Macmillan resigned he told James Margach, 'there must be someone else, but please, please, not me!' and Margach, at least, believed he was totally sincere.[52]

Lord Home of the Hirsel would soon re-enter the House of

Commons as Sir Alec Douglas-Home but that wasn't enough to make him a commoner. His blue blood and hereditary title was a political weak point right from the start, although he did his best to make light of it. Harold Wilson commented that 'in this ruthlessly competitive, scientific, technical, industrial age, a week of intrigues has produced a result based on family and hereditary connections . . . After half a century of democratic advance, of social revolution . . . the whole process has ground to a halt with a fourteenth earl.'[53] Douglas-Home's response was witty but missed the point: 'as far as the fourteenth earl is concerned, I suppose Mr Wilson, when you come to think of it, is the fourteenth Mr Wilson'.[54] His daughter Caroline didn't help matters, telling the *Daily Herald*, 'he is used to dealing with estate workers. I cannot see how anyone can say he is out of touch.'[55] But that's exactly what they said. The *Sunday Mirror* called his accession to the top job 'Deplorable, Outrageous, Squalid', and commented, 'thus the processes of British democracy, decaying for years, receive the ultimate brush-off'.[56] It wasn't just the left in politics and the media; some senior Tories expressed similar views. Two, Enoch Powell and Iain Macleod, refused ministerial posts, telling him they didn't believe a man with his social background could win an election. But the anything-but-aristocratic Margaret Thatcher, then on the lowest rung of the ministerial ladder, saw it all as inverted snobbery of the worst kind and firmly blamed the media. She wrote later, 'the press were cruelly, ruthlessly and almost unanimously against him. He was easy to caricature as an out-of-touch aristocrat, a throwback to the worst sort of reactionary Toryism . . . By 1964 British society had entered a sick phase of liberal conformism passing as individual self-expression. Only progressive ideas and people were worthy of respect by an increasingly self-conscious and self-confident media class. And how they laughed when Alec said self-deprecatingly that he used matchsticks to work out economic concepts.'[57]

The quotation to which she referred – 'when I have to read economic documents I have to have a box of matches and start moving them into position to illustrate and simplify the points to myself' – was only the most famous of those in which Douglas-Home appeared to damn himself from his own mouth. He'd said it to a journalist on the

Observer six months before entering Number 10. As he recalled himself, 'It was a frightful bit of bad luck. I was having lunch with Kenneth Harris. He said do you think you could ever be PM and I said I thought not because I do my economics from a matchbox! While I was eating my mutton chop! I never gave another thought to it. I saw it in the draft and I ought to have taken it out. But then I never thought about being prime minister.'[58] The *Daily Mirror* headline on the day after he did get the job was 'Not Smart Alec – Just Alec'. Unlike 'Not Flash, Just Gordon', which an advertising agency recommended to Brown, it wasn't intended to improve his image, although some voters may have been attracted by a man who admitted to the same difficulty with economics that they had.

Douglas-Home couldn't afford to let people think he wasn't up to the job, not least because it was patently untrue. Once in Downing Street he would have to take more care over what he said and even how he looked, and he recognised he would need some expert help. Two journalists-cum-politicians were drafted in, Eldon Griffiths and the future chancellor, Nigel Lawson, while Conservative Central Office employed the director of Associated Television, Norman Collins, to work on presentation. Between them they did what they could. Collins told him that when he was in a TV studio he should imagine he was just talking to one or two people in a room. They tried to improve his appearance on public platforms, as these were often televised. The cartoonists had seized on his cadaverous head and half-moon glasses so an extra-tall lectern was built with a bright light attached in the hope that he'd be able to read his notes without them. But he was never at ease on the small screen. In his memoirs he admitted '[I] could not conceal my distaste for the conception that the political leader had also to be an actor on the screen.'[59]

He didn't always appear to be very well briefed for his media appearances. He told Robin Day that the economic outlook had never been stronger and 'exports are going up' on the eve of the official announcement of the worst balance-of-payments figures in Britain's history.[60] In another interview he referred to 'donations' for old-age pensioners when he meant benefits. Day himself thought criticism of Douglas-Home's TV manner unfair. He 'did not speak with the sonorous formality of Macmillan, or with the sharp-witted fluency of the young Harold Wilson. But he spoke crisply, lucidly and incisively.'[61] Nonetheless Downing Street detected just the kind of cultural bias in the media, and on the BBC in particular, that Margaret Thatcher would later abhor. Before he became prime minister, *That Was The Week That Was* had referred to Douglas-Home as a 'cretin'. Also in the name of humour, the TV serial *Swizzlewick* depicted a fictional Midlands town with a Tory council made up of the most pompous and unpleasant characters imaginable. Douglas-Home remembered that he had 'a terrible lot of that sort of stuff to contend with. It became fashionable, and was called "satire" . . . I think they probably did have an effect, and it was nasty.'[62] Some people at Conservative Central Office thought BBC producers were deliberately allowing the prime minister to look gaunt and tired. But he recounted one exchange with a make-up lady that suggests it wasn't all the BBC's fault:

Q. Can you not make me look better than I do on television?
A. No.
Q. Why not?
A. Because you have a head like a skull.
Q. Does not everyone have a head like a skull?
A. No.[63]

Because a general election couldn't be long delayed, Douglas-Home didn't waste time trying to court Fleet Street editors and proprietors. It was another world, like that of economics, in which he felt out of place. He turned down an invitation to lunch from Cecil King, the chairman of the newly created International Publishing Corporation (IPC), which owned the *Mirror* titles. King was vain and desperate for influence. He was also, despite the tribal loyalty of his papers to Labour, basically a conservative. Bill Deedes, who did agree to see him, was greeted with a tirade about the arrogance of ministers and their failure to consult him. King offered advice and support but he wanted something in return. 'Like Rothermere and Beaverbrook before him,' wrote Deedes, 'Cecil King was seeking a dangerous bargain . . . his newspapers would support policies on which he had been personally consulted – and such consultation would then become a condition of his support.'[64] Deedes learned that King had been making similar overtures to the Labour opposition and concluded his interest was purely selfish. He wanted the power to influence political events irrespective of who was willing to grant it.

While his minister of information dealt with the egos of Fleet Street, Douglas-Home toured the country tirelessly, allowing as many people as possible to see and hear the real man rather than relying on the media image. The run-up to the 1964 election saw a dramatic reversal in the two main parties' campaigning techniques. Labour, which had been outspent, outclassed and outspun in 1959, was now far more media-savvy and ready to use whatever market research and public-relations techniques it could. Party advertisements and slogans were put before focus groups before anybody had ever heard of the term. Spending on publicity was trebled and the views of the media experts consulted before any major announcement was made. The Tories, having pioneered professional political communications, now took a step back. Their advisers weren't given any clear direction from the party leadership and the man in charge of their publicity agents, Colonel Arthur Varley, admitted 'it's tricky trying to advertise a product if you don't really know what the product is'.[65]

During the election campaign itself the Conservatives poured money in, outspending Labour on advertising and propaganda by 9–1. Still the prime minister did his best to avoid the television studios, preferring to meet people face to face. His opening line at rallies was usually, 'I like to come and see you in person to show you that I'm not exactly what they make me look like on the TV screen.'[66] Douglas-Home might have felt more comfortable on the stump but it was a step backwards in terms of modern campaigning. One Central Office official blamed the party's media team for allowing him 'to exhaust himself talking to hundreds at farm gates instead of making effective use of television where he could talk to millions'.[67] So when the Conservatives managed to keep Labour's majority to a mere four it was rightly seen to be a tremendous achievement. Much of the credit had to go to the man that so many journalists had dismissed as unsuited to the modern media age of government. His campaign may have been old-fashioned and unexciting but in the year previously Douglas-Home had managed to put the sleaze and scandal headlines behind him with remarkable speed, not least because he was self-evidently honest and above reproach. Some voters no doubt prefer to be governed by a man of pedigree, and attacks on a leader's privileged upbringing rarely do much good, as David Cameron has shown. Others came to recognise what Harold Macmillan had seen in his successor: 'iron painted to look like wood'.[68]

Yet Sir Alec Douglas-Home wasn't steely enough to stand his ground against those in his own party who blamed him for the defeat rather than crediting him with turning around a near-hopeless position. Not having wanted the leadership in the first place he didn't try to hold on to it. Instead, the last aristocrat to have been prime minister devised a system of election for his successor as Tory leader and stood back while the party chose the son of a carpenter and a maid, Edward Heath. In a very short space of time, Douglas-Home had reshaped politics. He never confronted the media head-on and, though he came close, he never quite managed to throw their caricature of him back in their faces. As Peter Hennessy puts it, 'Douglas-Home's near miss, perhaps inevitably, was seen as failure and, ever since, parties have looked for supposed telegenic qualities in their leaders – no more aristocrats, skulls or half-moon glasses.' As the man who narrowly beat him put it, 'Most of politics is presentation and what isn't is timing.'

Enter, stage left, Harold Wilson.

7

BRAVE NEW WORLD:
WILSON (1964–70)

*For a politician to complain about the press is like a ship's captain
complaining about the sea.*

Enoch Powell

If there is one prime minister of whom it could be said that he owed
his job to the media it is Harold Wilson, although, in truth, only
because he said so himself. In the run-up to the 1964 general election
Wilson and his team were assiduous complainers to the media and to
the BBC in particular. Wilson objected personally to the director general, Hugh Greene, when he saw that an episode of *Steptoe and Son* was
due to be broadcast half an hour before the polls closed. Labour
believed its supporters were more likely to stay in and watch a comedy
about rag-and-bone men than Tory voters. The corporation postponed
the programme by an hour and Greene took a grateful call from the
leader of the opposition: 'Thank you very much, Hugh. That will be
worth a dozen or more seats to me.'[1] Wilson became prime minister
on 16 October 1964 with an overall majority of four.

Yet it needs more than the postponement of a popular television
sitcom to make the case that Harold Wilson became prime minister
only with the help of the media. To judge by his frequent accusations

of bias you might think the newspapers, and to a lesser extent TV and radio, were trying to keep him out of office rather than help him get elected. But like Tony Blair's New Labour, Harold Wilson's old Labour party complained incessantly at a time when most impartial observers believed the media were being *too* kind to them. At the outset Wilson didn't have much to complain about and he knew it. He dominated the political news throughout the brief premiership of Sir Alec Douglas-Home and he was portrayed in a very favourable light. While the Tory leader was being derided as an out-of-touch toff, Wilson was usually depicted as young and forward-looking. The Labour leader came across well on TV and not merely because he was blessed with a head that bore little resemblance to a skull. He was, as Sir Robin Day observed, 'the first PM to enter office with professional mastery of the techniques of television'.[2] He had an instinctive feel, much as Macmillan had, for how to mould his own image. When Wilson first crossed the threshold of Downing Street his father, Herbert, turned to some of the new press office team and advised them, 'Buy shares in Kodak. They'll sell a lot of film now because Harold will generate a market in photographs of himself.'[3]

The Nuffield guide to the election had given the Tories a slight edge in terms of newspaper support, but had concluded that 'The traditional complaint that Labour has a bad press could not be raised in 1964.'[4] The opposition had the backing of the newest title on Fleet Street, the *Sun*, then a very different paper than it is today, which had risen out of the ashes of the ailing *Daily Herald*. Traditional party loyalties in Fleet Street were in one of their periodic states of flux and even those papers that backed Douglas-Home regarded Wilson as the clear favourite. The *Daily Express*, eager for newer, younger readers, now called itself an 'independent, classless newspaper' although it still gave lukewarm support to the Tories. Lord Beaverbrook, who had used it time and again in the past to help his friends in the Conservative party, died four months before the election. The *Daily Mail* remained solidly Tory and the *Daily Mirror* campaigned for Wilson in its traditionally exuberant fashion. Cecil King, with his nose for power and his thirst for influence, now drove around London in his Rolls-Royce with a red flag on the bonnet saying 'Vote Labour'. His fellow director Hugh Cudlipp said 'our front pages had more power on one morning than a million pamphlets or a hundred speeches in drill halls, parks or schools in the provinces'.[5]

The media were kind to Wilson not because they felt like it; even less because they had a political agenda to see him in Downing Street. They were kind to Wilson because he and his party put in the effort, time and resources to make sure they were. Labour's success with the media was part and parcel of its success in the 1964 election but that is not the same as saying that Wilson entered Number 10 in debt to the journalistic profession. He got a good press because he worked at it, because he made news and because he was a credible prime minister-in-waiting leading a party that appeared to have put the worst of its divisions behind it. Like Blair, Wilson distracted the media from his own party's past while concentrating relentlessly on the future. With his speeches about the 'white heat' of the technological revolution and so on, he managed to identify himself with innovation and scientific progress, relegating the Tories to the past as he did so. He was talking of the 'new Britain' while Tony Blair was still in short trousers. The Conservatives tried to dismiss him as 'the slick salesman of synthetic science', but that was merely an admission that the Labour leader was running rings round them in terms of presentation. Wilson was the man of the moment. As an official at Conservative Central Office admitted after the election, 'slogans can't create moods; they can only capture them'.[6]

Whether or not the media helped put Harold Wilson into Downing Street, there is no doubt that his obsession with them, which eventually developed into paranoia, made him far less effective in office. Had he combined his talent for presentation with the indifference to press criticism of Attlee or Macmillan he might have been as good a prime minister as either of them. Instead, as James Margach, who reported on his premiership with growing horror, recalled, 'Government by public relations was the glittering prize after which he strove. He believed that political power and survival depended on his achieving ascendancy over the proprietors and editors of Fleet Street and their political writers at Westminster.'[7] They didn't ask him to accord them such influence, indeed they would have much preferred to be left to get on with their

jobs. He voluntarily gave them a power over the prime minister of
Great Britain that they did not deserve and should never have had. He
allowed them to distract him from what he should have been doing and
gave them control over the political agenda rather than seizing it for
himself. He was the first, but not the last, prime minister to mistake
good headlines for good government. And his experience should have
been enough to ensure that nobody went down the same road again.

Wilson ended up with the worst relations with the media suffered
by any prime minister but he started out with some of the best. His
first press secretary, Trevor Lloyd-Hughes, saw something deeply personal in his love-hate relationship with the media that seemed out of
character for a man who was normally self-controlled and the cool
master of his temper. 'He was like an over-passionate young man, madly
in love with a girl, pining for her affectionate attention, perennially suspicious, intensely jealous at any sign of coldness, alternately placing his
darling on a lofty pedestal and then, persuaded all at once that she was
no more than a dirty slut, over-reacting in violent disgust.'[8] He liked the
company of journalists and they liked him. Gerald Kaufman, who was
his political press officer, described him as a 'journalist *manqué*. He had
wanted to work for the *Manchester Guardian* but he didn't get the job.'[9]
In fact he probably could have had the job if he'd really wanted it. He
was offered a probationary position as a leader writer while he was still
at Oxford, but decided to stick to academia and went on to become a
don at the age of just twenty-one.[10]

Wilson dealt with reporters with an informality and intimacy that
had never been seen before, calling them by their first names, joining
them for a drink, remembering personal details of their families and
asking after them. He saw them regularly, often briefing the
Westminster lobby himself. He knew all about edition times and deadlines, he knew what journalists wanted and he made sure he gave it to
them. In short, he made news. During his first term, from October
1964 to March 1966, he was rewarded with generally positive and
sympathetic coverage, although there was constant speculation about
how long he could survive with so slender a majority. He continued
to dominate the news by constant activity, or at least the impression of
activity. There was a touch of 'initiativitis', with news plans, targets and

claims of success announced almost daily. It seemed Wilson was never off the TV. Quite apart from his appearances on the news, in the eighteen months of his first government he did no fewer than six prime-ministerial broadcasts and five long interviews on the BBC's *Panorama* alone. He was hardly being starved of the oxygen of publicity but the hostility towards the BBC that would become so vitriolic in his second term was already in evidence. During the 1965 Labour party conference in Blackpool he summoned the editor of the BBC's coverage to his hotel room to complain about the inclusion of an interview with an unhelpful trade-union leader, Clive Jenkins. There were veiled threats that if the BBC did not mend its ways the government would make sure that it did. Wilson wanted the BBC to be a counterweight to the perceived right-wing bias of the written press. His dominance of the airwaves was already drawing satirical comment. On *BBC3*, the successor to *That Was The Week That Was*, John Bird had Wilson off to a T as he addressed the nation: 'Good evening. It's more than a day since I last talked to you. I am sure you have been wondering . . .'[11]

The real Wilson was keen to ensure the Downing Street press operation had the capacity to keep up with his frenetic pace. In 1964 Number 10's only window on what the press were doing was the same PA wire machine that had been installed for Attlee, and a black-and-white TV in the prime minister's flat. Not much evidence there of the white heat of technology. The only paper that sent its first edition to Downing Street late at night was the *Daily Telegraph*, a legacy of Churchill's tenure. Wilson, on an early visit to the *Daily Mirror's* offices, asked for both the *Mirror* and the *Daily Herald* to be sent over too. At the same time he set about modernising the press office although not, at first, politicising it. Trevor Lloyd-Hughes, a Liverpool journalist he knew of old, had nearly become a Tory candidate, and his deputy was Henry James, who had done the same job under the Conservatives. In addition, there were now four information officers and three support staff as well as Kaufman working outside the civil-service machine on political communications. Lloyd-Hughes quickly had two new tape machines installed, one for Reuters and one for the Associated Press, as well as a TV in his own office. Later, he recalled, 'I had a battle royal to convince a parsimonious Treasury that the prime minister himself ought to be equipped with a modern, colour TV – if only to see if one of his ministers or an opposition spokesman had flushed or paled in a give-away reaction to some awkward question.'[12]

Wilson, who had criticised Bill Deedes's role under both Macmillan and Douglas-Home for blurring the boundaries between government and politics, could hardly appoint a minister of information of his own. He did, however, ask George Wigg, the paymaster-general, to oversee government communications. It was not a happy arrangement. Colonel Wigg, a larger-than-life former army officer, was a natural conspirator. A less excitable minister would have better served Wilson. The press office had to put up with Wigg taking over their precious TV to help him place bets on the horses and, when he had been watching the news, with his frequent calls at all times of the day and night demanding they take action on stories he thought were damaging.

Wigg may have exacerbated the prime minister's already worrying obsession with the media but it was clear Wilson did expect his staff to be one step ahead of the news. Henry James dined out for years on the story of getting a phone call from the prime minister, who was on holiday in the Scilly Isles but still worrying about a damaging story that was refusing to go away. 'Get it off the front page, Henry', he was told. 'I don't care how you do it, but get it off the front.' The following morning's newspapers led on a nasty murder in west London and Wilson was back on the phone. 'Henry, you've gone too far this time.'[13]

Murders aside, all the relentless activity paid off. According to Trevor Lloyd-Hughes, 'for the first two years or so as prime minister, Wilson enjoyed a reasonably, indeed, considering the natural anti-Labour bias of most national newspapers, a remarkably good press'.[14] It was an advantage he took for granted despite being warned that it could not last for ever. The journalist and television interviewer Kenneth Harris was among those who tried to warn the prime minister of the dangers ahead. During a private meeting in the summer of 1965 Wilson told him the lobby was 'the finest democratic instrument ever fashioned for use by a prime minister'. Harris warned him that their sympathy was unlikely to persist and predicted that the press proprietors would also turn against him before long. When, within a year, those predictions came true, Harris told Trevor Lloyd-Hughes that while he still admired Wilson's qualities, including his courage, intelligence and humanity, his suspicious nature 'makes him behave at times like a small boy in short trousers'.[15]

Wilson kept a wary eye on the IPC titles with, as it turned out, good reason. The *Daily Mirror* backed Edward Heath for the Conservative party leadership in July 1965. Privately Cecil King told Heath he was delighted when he won as 'we shall have in due course the right prime minister for this country in its present troubles'.[16] In December the paper produced a special on the crisis in Rhodesia, where Ian Smith had recently declared unilateral independence from Britain. The front-page headline was 'Watch It Harold!'. Hugh Cudlipp, King's deputy at IPC, was invited into Number 10 the very same afternoon and an interview with Wilson was arranged for that weekend at Chequers. The following Monday Cecil King was invited for lunch. In the *Spectator*, Alan Watkins observed that 'Really, world statesmen ought to be able to take a few knocks from Mr Hugh Cudlipp and Mr Cecil King without becoming rattled.'[17] Cudlipp received a knighthood a month later.

In the approach to the 1966 election, however, the tide of press opinion was still running powerfully in the prime minister's favour and Edward Heath found it hard to get a look-in. Wilson was the story and that's exactly how he wanted it. So when the inevitable election was called, to try to secure a workable majority, Wilson was the issue – for or against. A majority, based on what they had seen, heard and read were clearly for. Labour didn't have things all its own way, however. This time the BBC refused to reschedule an episode of *The Man From U.N.C.L.E.* on election night. Perhaps American secret agents didn't have the same pull as rag-and-bone men from Shepherds Bush. Despite the distraction of Napoleon Solo and Illya Kuryakin, Labour got 48 per cent of the votes cast and a majority of ninety-seven. Wilson had continued to manipulate his own image throughout the campaign, presenting himself as a sort of family doctor to the nation, in his own words 'the kind of man who inspires trust by his appearance as well as by his soothing words'.[18] One of his ministers, Richard Crossman, called him 'super-Harold', echoing Macmillan's success as 'Supermac'.[19] Wilson's ministers were great diary writers. Another of them, Tony Benn, then a moderniser and very much in favour with Downing Street, drew a different parallel with the past. He wrote that '. . . since his success in the eyes of the public, encouraged by the press, is greater than is perhaps justified by his real achievements, so, when the moment comes for mistakes and failures, these too may be made to seem far greater than they are. This is rather the same thing as happened to Harold Macmillan.'[20]

Those mistakes and failures came thick and fast after the 1966 election. Wilson's fall from grace with the media was faster than Macmillan's and far more painful. While Supermac, on the whole, had an insouciance about 'events, dear boy', super-Harold thrashed around for somebody – anybody – else to blame. The usual suspects were his own ministerial colleagues, guilty of leaking to the press, or the press themselves, guilty of conspiring to undermine and destroy him. It was true that some cabinet members were willing to take senior lobby journalists into their confidence from time to time, but hardly more so than under most governments. The only difference was that some, seeing how assiduously the prime minister worked the press, saw no reason for any particular restraint themselves, especially if they felt the Downing Street briefing machine was working against them. As for the media, there was too much competition and rivalry within their own ranks for them to conspire to do anything in unison. To the extent that there was any sentiment in common it was a feeling that Wilson had taken them for a ride for rather too long and it was time to start examining his strengths and weaknesses more objectively. As it became increasingly obvious that he was incapable of being objective about them, it did appear that some journalists became ill inclined to give him the benefit of the doubt about anything. Rather than feeling grateful for having had a good press for so long, Wilson came to believe he was due one as of right. Not unreasonably, most journalists found it hard to sympathise. That relations between Downing Street and the media went from bad to worse throughout his second term was almost entirely down to him. Trevor Lloyd-Hughes, who could see that Wilson's obsession with the media was making him less effective in office, later admitted, 'I

never succeeded in bringing him to what I regarded as a proper appreciation of how a prime minister should behave towards the press.'[21]

When he confronted a sterling crisis soon after being re-elected it
was clear that Wilson wasn't a political Houdini after all. Where he
went wrong was in trying to continue the pretence that he was. He
resisted devaluation for as long as he could. When it came on 18
November 1967 it reduced the value of the pound by 14 per cent, a
relatively modest drop compared to the fall in sterling under Gordon
Brown in 2008. Then as now, the devaluation had positive benefits for
the economy and could fairly have been portrayed as the right and
prudent thing to do. Instead, Wilson not only allowed the media to be
misled right up the last minute that no devaluation was on the way –
normal practice to avoid speculation making the situation worse – he
then seemed almost to pretend that it hadn't really happened at all. His
famous TV broadcast reassuring the public that 'it does not mean that
the pound here in Britain, in your pocket or purse or in your bank, has
been devalued' could also be justified as true so far as it went, but those
words, which he inserted himself into a carefully worded draft, gave the
impression that he was trying to talk himself out of failure. Even the
timing of the devaluation announcement had been made with press
deadlines in mind, although with the intention of frustrating the
denizens of Fleet Street rather than helping them. It came at half past
nine on a Saturday evening, just too late for the Sunday papers.

Devaluation was the most high profile of his policy reverses but
there were many others. When the media had the audacity to link his
name with failure he felt betrayed, as if he'd earned some sort of
exemption from personal criticism after giving the papers so many
good headlines in the past. Wiser heads around him, like his lawyer
friend Arnold Goodman, tried to point out that you couldn't bank
credit with the press, but to no avail. They were going for him personally so he would go for them in the same spirit. His obsession with
the media extended to keeping a mental note, as well as a drawer full
of newspaper cuttings, of every slight and hostile comment from the
Westminster press pack. These he would raise with editors and proprietors at any and every opportunity. Among the senior journalists he
tried to have sacked or moved were the *Observer*'s Nora Beloff, Harold

Hutchinson of the *Sun*, the political editor of *The Times*, David Wood, and Anthony Howard of the *Sunday Times*. Those journalists who weren't on his hit list started to wonder if they were doing their jobs properly. Wood's greatest offence had been to suggest that health checks then being proposed for MPs should also include the prime minister who had taken no proper holiday since getting the job and was troubled by a stye on his eye.[22]

'Relations with the Press' was frequently on the cabinet agenda and on at least one occasion was deemed so important as to be the first item of business discussed. The prime minister told the cabinet that it 'should now be made an established rule, to be vigilantly observed, that ministers should not give press interviews, whether attributably or unattributably, except in the presence of a reliable witness such as a public relations officer'.[23] Wilson saw Anthony Howard's appointment as Britain's first Whitehall correspondent as 'a new and potentially dangerous development' and succeeded in cutting off his sources to such a degree that the new position was abandoned. Howard took the job of Washington correspondent of the *Observer* and at least one troublesome journalist was out of the prime minister's hair for a while. Yet Wilson singularly failed to stop his ministers speaking off the record to journalists. Tony Benn, after one such lunch, recorded a view that was shared by many of his colleagues: 'I talked openly about all the issues that were current . . . I draw the line at any critical comment about any named colleagues but do not see why I should become a mere spokesman for the government on every private as well as public occasion.'[24] Had ministers been more discreet we would not know as much as we do about the severity of Wilson's media fixation. Anthony Howard recalls lunching Richard Crossman, who told him, 'you won't believe what we've just been through. Harold spent ten minutes at cabinet complaining about a disc jockey, I think they're called.'[25]

Barbara Castle, another great diarist, was among Wilson's most loyal and supportive cabinet members but even she was frequently dismayed by his obsession. Ten weeks after the '66 election she wrote: 'Harold . . . held forth about the iniquities of Nora Beloff . . . "She is a dedicated enemy of this government – takes everything straight to

Heath".'[26] Eleven months later: 'An astonishing outburst from Harold at cabinet about the press. He was writhing with annoyance at *The Times* . . . "We should refuse to talk to them: Ian Trethowan, for instance, is just a publicity man for Heath" . . . I think Harold is getting quite pathological about the press.'[27] Then the following year: 'Harold . . . was as usual obsessed with conspiracies . . . I begged Harold not to bother with these press comments – he could never prove anything anyway – but he kept repeating, "I've got them this time". I sometimes think he is going mildly off his rocker.'[28]

Castle's fears for her boss's mental health followed an incident that did more than any other to destroy any last vestiges of trust between Downing Street and Fleet Street. It became known as 'the D–Notice Affair' and was sparked off by a report in the *Daily Express* of 21 February 1967 by its defence correspondent, Chapman Pincher. Many of the details of the story – 'Cable Vetting Sensation' – weren't even new. It alleged that the government was able to spy on thousands of private cables and telegrams sent abroad by ordinary citizens, a 'Big Brother intrusion into privacy, which ranks with telephone-tapping and the opening of letters'. It was an overwritten 'sensation' that was not as sensational as the paper claimed, but that was nothing new for Fleet Street. Trevor Lloyd-Hughes advised Wilson to ignore it on the grounds that, 'in journalistic parlance, "it would have died a natural"'[29]. Instead, 'unnecessarily and on doubtful information', he went on the attack. He accused Pincher of defying a D–Notice, one of the instructions issued to protect sensitive defence information. Unfortunately the secretary of the D–Notice committee had already told Pincher that the story would not breach any such order. Wilson attacked the *Express* in parliament, set up a committee under the distinguished Lord Radcliffe to look into it, and, when Radcliffe came down in the paper's favour, refused to accept his findings. He went back to the Commons and rejected the report in a manner that Radcliffe himself likened to refusing to accept the result of the cup final. Wilson's own account of his time in office is generally as self-serving as most prime-ministerial memoirs, but on the D–Notice affair even he was forced to accept he'd blundered. The damage 'I can only describe as self-inflicted, in personal terms one of my costliest mistakes of our near six years in office . . . It was a very long time before my relations with the press were repaired.'[30]

And it was a very long time before he stopped brooding over the row. His closest staff, including Marcia Williams, his personal political secretary, worried that he was becoming so obsessed by the media that it was distracting him from the real business of government. He told Lloyd-Hughes not to go running after the lobby, but then 'without my agreement, against my advice, sometimes even without my knowledge' changed tack and decided to bring some of them in from the cold as best he could. Some of the more formal briefings were held in the warmth and comfort of the 'White Boudoir' at Downing Street where a small group of senior correspondents were invited to come and meet the prime minister for lengthy and informal discussions once a fortnight. This privileged group soon became known as the 'White Commonwealth' although some of its members were soon questioning whether it was such a privilege to be invited after all. The meetings tended to be dominated by long monologues from Wilson and the journalists rarely went away with what they regarded as a 'story' to justify their patience. Inevitably the system also alienated those journalists who hadn't been invited and felt they should have been. According to Lloyd-Hughes 'even his "trusties" increasingly came to mistrust his guidance, and could by no means be relied upon to produce the kind of stories he wanted'.[31]

Divide and rule can be a useful tactic for Downing Street to employ towards the media from time to time, but this was not the way to go about it. The normal operation of the lobby system, which, when it was working well, gave the Number 10 press secretary huge power to influence the media under the cloak of anonymity, was on the point of breaking down. Henry James, who regularly had the job of briefing the lobby, said that after the D-Notice affair Wilson 'wasn't taken seriously – an air of cynicism entered. It made my job harder.'[32] David Watt of the *Financial Times* put it down to the fact that journalists 'regard him as having abused the system and themselves'.[33] Whoever was to blame, there was, as Marcia Williams said, 'a new and nasty turn in press relations'.[34]

Relations with the BBC were scarcely any better. Wilson, who

could gnaw away at an old grievance, no matter how trivial, like a dog
with a bone, still hadn't forgiven the corporation for *The Man From
U.N.C.L.E.* Having once seen the broadcasters as a useful antidote to
a hostile press, he now regarded them as coming from the same poison
bottle. Senior executives at the BBC thought he was demanding on a
daily basis the kind of uncritical coverage they were used to prime
ministers expecting in wartime. They saw it as the corporation's job to
report on division between and within parties whereas to Wilson and
those who did the complaining on his behalf, 'broadcasting . . . was an
enemy because it was not on their side'.[35] He threatened to deny them
any increase in the licence fee, hardly a novel prime-ministerial tactic.
He complained bitterly about jokes at his expense and lines in news
reports that he thought undermined his authority. Then, in 1967, he
had the chance to teach the corporation a lesson. Despite its day-to-
day independence, the BBC has to accept whomever the government
decides to appoint as its chairman. It is the nearest a British prime
minister comes to appointing judges to the US supreme court, especially when, at its most pompous, the BBC tends to see itself as the
arbiter of public opinion. Lord Normanbrook, who had been
appointed by the Conservatives, died in office. Wilson chose as his
successor Lord Hill, who as Dr Charles Hill had been Macmillan's
minister of information. Nobody could accuse Downing Street of
political bias, but it was a slap in the face for the BBC because Hill
had, since 1963, been chairman of the Independent Television
Authority. David Attenborough is said to have remarked that it was
like appointing Field Marshal Rommel to command the Eighth Army
during the Second World War.[36] Hill was certainly a tough and combative leader, but he was no pushover for a prime minister on the
warpath and relations between the government and the corporation
saw little improvement.

Harold Wilson had no right to expect support from either the
broadcasters or the written press but he did have some claim to the loyalty of his own ministers. Unfortunately he believed many of them
were conspiring to undermine him as well, and, worse still, they were
compounding the offence by leaking to the media. Time and time
again Wilson complained to his inner circle, top civil servants and

ministers themselves about the unofficial disclosure of information to journalists. He even had the lord chancellor, Lord Gardiner, hold an investigation and interrogate members of the cabinet about their dealings with journalists. Some, like Roy Jenkins, refused out of hand to be treated in such in a way. Most knew that, as an aide to President Kennedy had once observed, 'the ship of state is the only ship that often leaks at the top', and that supposedly secret information was far more likely to find its way to the media via Downing Street and its press office than by any other route. Lord Gardiner's report showed he had at least as good an understanding of how journalists work as did the media-obsessed prime minister. The lord chancellor said, 'Apparent leaks frequently appeared to be no more than informed guesses by experienced journalists. Such journalists were, however, expert in acquiring separately and piecing together small items of intelligence, none of which might in themselves be important or explicit, but which in total often provided an informed and experienced man with sufficient material to make an accurate assessment of the Government's intentions.'[37] It was one of the most realistic assessments ever penned by a politician of how political correspondents work. Wilson responded by ordering a further investigation, this time extending to junior ministers and parliamentary private secretaries.

Wilson wasn't entirely off his rocker. His cabinet did leak, probably more than most. There were more 'big beasts' around the cabinet table then than there are these days and they seemed neither to trust nor even to like each other very much. Wilson's preference for discussing issues to the point of exhaustion didn't help either. Cabinet really did make major decisions in the 1960s and if no conclusion had been reached at one meeting it is not altogether surprising that ministers used their contacts in the media to try to win the argument in advance of the next one. Wilson knew that full well, which is why he would stay up late at night with Marcia Williams, Gerald Kaufman and others going through the stories in the first editions looking for ministerial fingerprints. When Barbara Castle was involved in a battle royal over her trade-union reforms, contained in the white paper 'In Place of Strife', he actually told her to 'leak like hell' in order to get her way.[38] She might reasonably have thought the prime minister could employ

more conventional means to push through a policy of which he was
supposedly in favour.

Nor was Wilson mad to suspect some of his cabinet of wanting to
get rid of him. His real problem was not that they talked too much to
the papers about their own ambitions, but that he was himself too
weak politically to discipline or sack them. Wilson dreaded finding
himself in the same position as Herbert Asquith in 1916, unable to prevent a determined rival from unseating him in a palace coup. It had
happened before so why shouldn't it happen again? His deputy, George
Brown, was often suspected, although Brown was no David Lloyd
George. An unstable man with a well-deserved reputation for alcohol
consumption excessive even by Westminster standards, Brown was
never seen as a prime minister-in-waiting except perhaps by himself.
But others were more credible rivals, notably Roy Jenkins and Jim
Callaghan, and Wilson detected numerous plots, some real, more
imagined, to replace him with one or other of them. Roy Hattersley,
then still on the lower rungs of the ministerial ladder, was identified by
Wilson as a key conspirator on behalf of the Jenkinsite wing of the
party. When the newspapers were tipping him for promotion, Wilson
warned him with a hint of menace that 'It's better to have one prime
minister on your side than ten editors.'[39]

Wilson let his sometimes fevered imagination run away with him
over the idea that the media were not only reporting and commenting on the threats to his leadership, but also actively supporting them.
Most of the time all they were doing was revealing the truth about a
cabinet of rivals. The nearest thing to evidence of a media plot lies in
the extraordinary behaviour of the *Mirror* chairman, Cecil King. King
had been given his first job in Fleet Street at the age of nineteen by his
uncle, Lord Northcliffe. Now sixty-six, he seemed to believe he too
could try to dictate who should run the country. At first Wilson had
tried to keep him sweet, offering him a life peerage almost as soon as
he became prime minister. King turned it down because he thought
he deserved a hereditary peerage. He then refused an important government job, minister of trade, because it didn't come with cabinet
rank. He did accept a directorship of the Bank of England but this certainly did nothing to buy his support for the government. The *Mirror*

was at best lukewarm towards Labour in the 1966 election and King maintained his private contact with Edward Heath. Wilson had personally tipped King off in advance about the likely polling date only to discover that the information was promptly passed on to his opponent. After Wilson won, an unembarrassed King wrote to him, just as he had in 1964, advising him what policies to adopt and which ministers to appoint. On this occasion, however, he added dark hints about the need for 'a British de Gaulle or a national government', a theme to which he would soon return.[40]

In early 1967, just a few months after the electorate had given Wilson a clear mandate, King was telling anyone who would listen that the prime minister was finished and that it was time to bring in some unelected outsiders and form a new coalition or an emergency government. When his comments appeared in print the communist *Morning Star* put the case for democracy, asking, 'Isn't it time the Labour movement told Mr Cecil King and his *Daily Mirror* to go and get stuffed?'[41] Yet ministers continued to be subjected to his views. Tony Benn had lunch with him and found him 'slightly unbalanced'. King told Benn he thought Wilson would be 'totally swept away. No one believes a word he says and he has no future whatsoever', and that Denis Healey, then defence secretary, was the only member of the cabinet capable of taking over.[42] Geoffrey Goodman, who worked on the *Sun*, another IPC paper, told Benn ten days later that Healey had been 'pouring stuff in to the *Daily Mirror*, including the voting figures on critical issues in the cabinet, to persuade Cecil King that Harold was weak'.[43] Clearly King didn't need much persuading. No cabinet member ever objects to being told he or she is prime-minister material, but in his memoirs Healey insists he rebuffed all King's advances until 'he finally accepted that I was not interested, and turned his attention instead to Mountbatten'.[44]

Although Lord Mountbatten, the Queen's cousin, had never met King he did know Hugh Cudlipp and agreed to a meeting. Before it took place he told Cudlipp, 'I don't want to appear to be advocating or supporting any notion of a right wing dictatorship – or any nonsense of that sort. Nor do I want to be involved at my age. But like some other people I am deeply concerned about the future of the country.'[45] Given that he already knew King's agenda, Mountbatten was very unwise to agree to a meeting at all, and although accounts differ it is clear that he was at least willing to support much of King's analysis of the problem if not his solution. The encounter took place at Mountbatten's London flat on 8 May 1968. Sir Solly Zuckerman, the government's chief scientific adviser, who was also thought to be disenchanted with Wilson, was there at Mountbatten's insistence. According to Cudlipp, King predicted a crisis just around the corner: '. . . there would be bloodshed on the streets, the armed forces would be involved . . . people would be looking to somebody like Lord Mountbatten . . . somebody renowned as a leader of men who would be capable, backed by the best brains and administrators in the land, to restore public confidence. He ended with a question to Mountbatten – would he agree to be the titular head of a new administration in such circumstances?' Mountbatten didn't give a direct answer but asked Zuckerman what he thought. The reply was emphatic: 'This is rank treachery. All this talk of machine guns at street corners is appalling. I am a public servant and will have nothing to do with it. Nor should you, Dickie.'[46] Cudlipp says Zuckerman and King then left within a minute or two of each other. King's own diary, however, suggests Zuckerman 'hurried away as soon as he decently could' while Mountbatten went on to reveal not only that morale in the armed forces 'had never been so low', but also that Queen Elizabeth was 'desperately worried over the whole situation'. King said Mountbatten 'had no wish to intervene' although Zuckerman later wrote that he 'was really intrigued by Cecil King's suggestion that he should become the boss man of a government'.[47]

In the event it was Cecil King not Harold Wilson who was brought down. Three days after his meeting with Mountbatten he insisted on printing a huge front-page editorial in his own name entitled 'Enough is Enough'. There was no talk of bringing in any outsiders or over-turning an elected government, but King proclaimed that Wilson had 'lost all credibility; all authority' and should be replaced.[48] There was an outcry and, predictably, Wilson's ministers closed ranks behind him. Richard Crossman, who had been one of Wilson's fiercest critics, said privately, 'we'll never get rid of the little man now'.[49] Publicly

Crossman turned on King the following day in *The Times*, saying he could not 'recollect an episode which has brought Fleet Street into such disrepute since the attempt of the *Daily Mail* and the *Daily Express* to drive Stanley Baldwin out of the premiership'.[50] The rest of Fleet Street was quick to distance itself, asking, with varying degrees of contempt, just who King thought he was. His fellow directors at IPC, deeply embarrassed by the whole affair, asked themselves the same question and Cudlipp was prevailed upon to force King from the chairmanship and take his place. King had proved himself to be no Northcliffe and no Beaverbrook either. His attempts to unseat the elected prime minister look almost laughable in retrospect, but for the fact that some serious people who should have known better were prepared to bide their time to see just how much support he could garner. Perhaps the best measure of the threat posed by this last attempt by a press grandee (albeit never a real baron) to change the country's political direction was that Harold Wilson was untroubled by it. He saw threats to his leadership everywhere but not, it seems, from the Mirror Group. According to Benn's diary, Wilson told him 'King was mad – a view with which I would not really disagree'.[51]

Wilson could afford to shrug off the attempted coup that never was, but what was being said and done elsewhere in Fleet Street still kept him up at night. Marcia Williams said the press's treatment of him 'hurt and hurt deeply'. The prime minister was depicted on a regular basis as, in her words, 'cunning, devious, a liar and a cheat'. It was time for another rethink about how to improve relations. Bringing in a new press secretary is generally an admission of defeat by Downing Street, although it is never presented as such. So it was when Joe Haines was recruited from the *Sun* to become deputy to Trevor Lloyd-Hughes. Haines replaced him a few months later when Lloyd-Hughes was kicked upstairs into the Cabinet Office to 'co-ordinate government information'. In Marcia Williams's estimation, Lloyd-Hughes had been simply 'far too nice for that job at such a time in politics', whereas Haines had a 'rougher, more direct style'[52]. One man who would work with Haines closely, Bernard Donoughue, 'felt he had the tension of a coiled spring and he reminded me of Humphrey Bogart about to flatten some Chicago hood'.[53] Lloyd-Hughes, whose own mantra had been 'never tell a lie; never mislead', looked askance at his successor. 'He made no bones about larding his briefings on behalf of the prime minister with some heavy doses of party propaganda, with the inevitable result that he steadily wrecked his credibility.' Gerald Kaufman, who recommended him for the job, eventually came to the view that Haines 'wasn't good for Wilson. He had vendettas.'[54] One of the bitterest vendettas would be with Marcia Williams and Haines's appointment certainly brought a new level of creative tension to Wilson's inner circle. He had a gift for sound bites, however, and is credited with Wilson's classic response to talk of plots to unseat him: 'I know what's going on – *I'm* going on.'[55]

Wilson could only go on if he won the next election and improving his image before that contest was Haines's first priority. He found it difficult to make headway while the cabinet tore itself apart over Barbara Castle's 'In Place of Strife'. There seemed a real possibility that raw politics rather than any form of media pressure might bring the prime minister down. 'Some people were saying,' recalled Haines, 'it doesn't matter who we have instead, Roy [Jenkins], Jim [Callaghan] or Denis [Healey].'[56] Wilson saw the trade-union legislation as crucial to his re-election; some of his cabinet rivals saw it as the opportunity to remove him as Labour leader. In the event he sacrificed the bill but kept his job. It would be for the Conservatives to reform industrial relations, with far more devastating consequences for the trade unions than anything threatened by 'In Place of Strife'. Curiously, Wilson looked tougher after his bruising battle. He had argued passionately for what he believed in and as the opinion polls started to turn in his favour the papers stopped speculating about his chances of survival. The economy was showing clear signs of recovery. Then Northern Ireland erupted into violence. The 'troubles' would not be resolved for three decades but in the short term Wilson's government was thought to have handled the situation well. Writing off the prospects of parties and prime ministers is a popular mid-term sport and one that is win–win for the media. If they are right they get somebody new to build up before knocking them down; if they are wrong they have a comeback kid. It makes for good copy whichever way it goes. At the end of the swinging sixties they got an even better story. The electorate seemed to swing in Wilson's direction only to swing back the other way at the last minute and bring his government to an end.

It very nearly didn't happen. The only person who seemed confident of Edward Heath winning the 1970 election was Edward Heath himself. Wilson ran a deliberately low-key, even dull campaign. He had no interest in helping Fleet Street. As the usual round of press conferences, visits and photo opportunities went on day by day without much excitement Labour bypassed the written press as much as possible by concentrating heavily on the broadcasters. Marcia Williams was credited with introducing the 'walkabout', enabling Wilson to be seen mingling with the crowds while Heath was usually set apart on a podium making speeches. A new political press officer, Will Camp, had been appointed after Gerald Kaufman became a parliamentary candidate. According to Camp, Wilson wanted to draw attention to the fact that Heath had never married.[57] The idea was to make the Tory leader look awkward and a little suspect while Wilson was reassuring and down to earth. Conservative Central Office worked out what was going on and decided to retaliate. Heath was a world-class yachtsman and so a photocall was arranged on his yacht, *Morning Cloud*, with a woman he had never met before. Not surprisingly the press wanted to know if romance was in the air. Foolishly Heath's advisers hadn't dared prepare him for that question and his answer, 'Of course not. She's only the cook', was music to Labour's ears.

Wilson exuded calm confidence but Camp worried that he was being too cautious. It reminded him of what he'd read about Stanley Baldwin's disastrous 'Safety First' campaign in 1931. Wilson had stopped talking about the future with any enthusiasm or imagination. He remained suspicious of the press, refusing to let Camp organise an informal session with journalists because there were 'too many enemies' on the list. And while he was good at making the most of the television coverage, he was still convinced the BBC was deliberately trying to help Heath. When, despite consistent and often sizeable leads in the polls, Labour lost by just over 3 per cent Wilson pinned much of the blame on the corporation's staff. They had made him sweat in overheated studios, ignored his key speeches, focused on hecklers when his public meetings were shown and been biased when editing news reports. There was little evidence for his complaints and the Conservatives believed his anger 'was just a smokescreen to divert attention from the corporation's left-wing bias'.[58] Marcia Williams was nearer the mark when she wrote that 'the trouble with the BBC is that it is even more buried in its own bureaucracy than the civil service'[59]. It was a description that many inside the corporation would recognise. The BBC is institutionally incapable of organising a coordinated misrepresentation and denigration of a political leader even if it chose to do so. It is quite capable of being carried along by a political mind-set that originates in the newspapers, but in 1970 the consensus was that Labour was heading for victory.

Wilson himself thought he had the election sewn up until the results started coming in. Either the polls were wrong from the outset or something happened to change voters' minds to an unprecedented degree during the campaign. But the margin of the Tory victory, which produced a majority of thirty-one, was too great to be attributed to media bias. There were many other factors that added to the mix and made the outcome more unpredictable than it seemed. The voting age had been reduced to eighteen. The Liberal vote collapsed, which undoubtedly helped Heath. And nobody was certain how the electorate, and in particular white working-class voters, might respond to Enoch Powell's campaign against Commonwealth immigration. He was still a Conservative, despite being sacked from the shadow cabinet after making a speech in Birmingham during which he had said, in a characteristic classical allusion, 'As I look ahead, I am filled with foreboding. Like the Roman, I seem to see "the River Tiber foaming with much blood".'[60]

If Wilson left office at a time when his relations with the media were at an all-time low, then the bulk of the responsibility for that state of affairs lay with him. Having started out as a good friend to journalists he finished his premiership barely on speaking terms with any of them. Reporters don't cold-shoulder prime ministers. They rely on them for so much that fills their papers and their news bulletins. Foolish premiers do try to make the media pay for sins real or imagined. Instead of accepting their criticism as part of the rough and tumble of politics, Harold Wilson chose to see it as a betrayal that could never be forgiven. He tried to punish them but ended up punishing himself.

Wilson got the best part of an extra day as prime minister in which to reflect on what had gone wrong. On the Friday after the election the Queen was at Ascot and he was unable to see her to tender his resignation until the evening. Perhaps Her Majesty had believed the polls as well and didn't think she would be needed in London. When Wilson did finally leave, a journalist asked him what he would miss most. He replied, 'Mainly the job.'[61]

8

THREE MEN AND A BOAT:
HEATH, WILSON AGAIN,
CALLAGHAN (1970–79)

*The government's policies are like cornflakes, if they are not marketed
they will not sell.*

Lord Young

Edward Heath was used to being written off. He had received few
of the panegyrics that the media so often confer on opposition
leaders when they sense the country tiring of the old administration.
During the election campaign he couldn't have failed to pick up the
vibes from the travelling journalists. They were all expecting him to
lose. Two were already working on books to explain the reasons for his
failure. On polling day his friend Lord Carrington advised him that he
should resign if Labour's majority was greater than twenty-five. When
he defied everybody's expectations but his own he felt vindicated, of
course, but also liberated. The press had done nothing to help him, not
that he had expected it to. His view that the media were essentially
frivolous, uninterested in the serious business of government and too
easily seduced by the superficiality of image had been confirmed. He
felt his old adversary, Wilson, had exactly the same failings and determined to be as different as he could be. 'Only one man has won this

election and that man is Mr Heath,' said *The Economist*. According to his biographer, John Campbell, 'Bugger them all – I won' crudely expressed the new prime minister's feelings.[1] Ted Heath was to be the least media-obsessed PM since Clem Attlee. Douglas Hurd, his political secretary from 1970, says, 'Ted has less interest in and more of a disdain for the press than any other prime minister I have known. I'm not saying it's a good thing. He was too detached.'[2] Unfortunately for Heath the world had changed a great deal since the mid-1940s. Disdain for the business of communicating your objectives and actions in government was a luxury no leader could now afford.

The paradox is that in preparation for the 1970 campaign Heath had brought in some very experienced and talented media advisers, most of them experts on advertising and television like Geoffrey Tucker, Barry Day and Bryan Forbes. He had taken their advice and as a result had fought what the BBC documentary maker Michael Cockerell called 'the most sophisticated TV campaign ever'.[3] He threw a party for them the Monday after the election and then effectively slammed the door to Number 10 in their faces. They found themselves excluded from the prime minister's inner circle or even his outer circle. And out with them, Day ruefully observed, went everything they had tried to teach him: 'how to compress a lot of information into a small space, keeping a message simple and relevant to as many people as possible – and giving it immediacy and impact. All the things a politician needs his utterances to achieve.'[4] Hurd, who had a lot of sympathy with them, felt powerless to help. 'There was no deliberate snub but the PR team found that Ted was too busy governing – that's what he was interested in. He spent a lot of time with civil servants and colleagues, less with the House of Commons and the press. He got rather impatient with anything that got in the way of that.'[5] Soon after taking office he had even cancelled the rental on Harold Wilson's television set.

If Wilson had been a journalist *manqué* Heath was a civil servant *manqué*. Government and the process of government fascinated him. He wanted, as a top priority, to reform the way the state did business, not an issue that was ever going to push many buttons with the electorate. In that sense he was the aloof, out-of-touch technocrat that his critics said he was. He loved the company of the mandarins with their first-class brains and their attention to detail. Many politicians and journalists are cut from the same cloth and can slip into each other's professions with relative ease. Heath was different. Very few senior civil servants have ever wanted to become journalists or have done so. And that made them all the more appealing to the prime minister. He knew where he felt at home and deliberately surrounded himself with those who shared his outlook. Government was a serious business and he wanted serious people. That few of them had much expertise or interest in translating the business of good governance into a language the voters at home could relate to was by all accounts no deficiency in his estimation.

His choice of press secretary exemplified the change of approach perfectly. In place of the abrasive, political, tabloid-minded Joe Haines came the reserved, calm, high-minded Donald Maitland. Maitland was a Foreign Office man and Heath brought him back from Libya, where he was British ambassador, to take up the role of spokesman. Maitland had previously headed the Foreign Office news department, a job often given to diplomats on the way up, but he was no expert on the ways of Fleet Street, never mind those of the broadcasters. Heath, who liked to introduce him to foreign leaders as 'the ambassador', gave him no real steer about how he was to do the job. In a brief interview in his flat at the Albany, Heath told him, 'You know what to do; get the facts out.'[6] Maitland was perfectly comfortable with the idea that communications should come a distant second or even third place behind policy and strategy. 'Successful government depends, first and foremost, on wise policies and then on the extent to which these are understood and appreciated by the public. [That] places the role of the press secretary in proper perspective.'

Maitland shared the prime minister's distaste for anything that smacked of populism. Along with Michael Wolff, Heath's main speechwriter, Douglas Hurd would try periodically to slip in what we would now call sound bites, but with little success. 'We often devised lines for the news,' recalled Hurd, 'but they usually got crossed out, rarely got used. He would go through drafts of speeches crossing out the interesting bits. He didn't like colour. He thought it was dangerous and he didn't see the point in trying to be colourful or to seize attention. He thought that was all ephemeral stuff.' Donald Maitland, the man in charge of communications, was almost as disdainful. 'My only regret is that I failed to persuade Douglas Hurd or Michael Wolff that the speeches they drafted for the prime minister would benefit from more references to the "high road" and less preoccupation with the "high street",[7] he wrote. Ted Heath's own memoirs, *The Course of My Life*, contain virtually no mention of the media or how he dealt with them. Margaret Thatcher, who, as we shall see, took a very different view of political PR, summed him up succinctly in hers: 'No one could describe Ted as a great communicator, not least because for the most part he paid such little attention to communication.'[8]

The idea that an incoming prime minister should use his first hundred days to put over something significant about his intentions, which has since become something a cliché of all new administrations, would have been inexplicable to Heath. In his first three months as prime minister he didn't make a single appearance on television to explain his policies. Throughout the first summer it was as if the government had all but shut down. In a stark and deliberate contrast to Wilson's domination of the headlines, virtually no news emanated from Downing Street at all. On his second weekend in office Heath had escaped to his beloved *Morning Cloud* for a spot of sailing. It was the only sense in which he could have been said to hit the deck running.

Not only did Heath not want to be blown off course by the media, he would have been equally happy not to have to waste his time with anything so trivial as politics. He had as little appetite for cultivating his own party in parliament or the country as he had for the press. If anything, this would prove an even graver weakness. He had no taste for the cut and thrust of debate in the Commons and seemed to resent the demands it made on his time. He thought he was entitled to the loyalty of his party and did little to build up any personal affection or bank of support that might otherwise have protected him when the going got tough. He was respected more than loved and was quite content with that. The same could be said for his cabinet. Heath presided over perhaps the most united and collegiate cabinet of the twentieth century. Although Margaret Thatcher and Sir Keith Joseph, in particular, emerged later as retrospective dissidents they caused him few problems while serving under him. Heath trusted his ministers to get on with their jobs and meddled relatively infrequently. The other side of the coin was that he could be both abrasive and autocratic. It was a combination they could live with and his colleagues repaid him by avoiding any serious acrimony, either in private or in public. Such disagreements as they had – and no cabinet could possibly be without them – they worked out among themselves, much to the enormous frustration of Fleet Street. Journalists had come to believe that cabinet splits, rivalries, jockeying for position, rows and recriminations were the normal by-products of government. They expected to be able to take a member of the cabinet out to lunch and get a bit of dirt on his or her fellow ministers. From 1970 to 1974 they were, for the most part, disappointed. There were no rivals to the crown, no real factions and no incentive strong enough for indiscretion or disloyalty. John Junor, the editor of the *Sunday Express*, complained over lunch to one senior minister that, unlike every other government he could remember, 'this one did not leak, did not gossip and provided no stories of plots against the prime minister'.[9]

While Heath avoided much of the negative press comment that had driven Wilson to distraction, he rarely won the plaudits and positive support that most new premiers enjoy, at least for a while. He seemed indifferent to their absence, perhaps on the grounds that what they don't build up they will find more difficult to knock down. By the end of his term, however, he found that, having failed to explain effectively what he was in office to do, it was commensurately harder to make the case for being given a chance to carry on doing it. And over the longer term he has paid a high price in terms of his reputation. The Heath government is now remembered for three things above all: entry into the Common Market, the three-day week, and the U-turn. Had he taken more trouble to communicate his *raison d'être* he might not have had to spend the last thirty years of his life in a monumental grump because he felt so misunderstood.

There was a good story to be told about his ambitions and his courage in pursuing them, but it has fallen to contemporary historians like John Campbell and Peter Hennessy to work out the narrative that Heath failed to articulate himself. He was a moderniser, hoping to shake Britain out of its malaise by equipping the economy with the investment and the degree of economic stability, and in particular low inflation, sufficient to set it on a new and competitive upward trajectory. He wanted Britons to cast off the chains of underachievement and low ambition. He hoped to do it with the grain of the post-1945 consensus of a mixed economy with strong but responsible trade unions if he could. He preferred to make progress through exhortation and agreement although he recognised that some legislation would be required to remove barriers to economic progress. Much of that was set out in his first, well-received party-conference speech as prime minister. It would, he said, be a 'quiet revolution'. Yet by definition quiet revolutions are unlikely to arouse the passions or the fighting spirit of a nation, and by temperament Heath was more inclined to calming passions than arousing them. Unwilling to make radical, never mind revolutionary, changes to the post-war economic settlement he soon found his task far harder to achieve than he had anticipated and it was not until the much noisier revolution of Margaret Thatcher that many of his own aims were finally achieved, although at what he considered too high a price.

By the first anniversary of Heath's election there were already signs of irritation in the papers at his reluctance to use them as a means of explaining his policies. There was a large measure of self-interest in their complaints, but they couched them in terms that suggested the voters were being short-changed, too. The *Observer* marked the occasion by saying, 'Mr Heath promised a new "style" of government . . . but in his desire to concentrate on the business of government – "deeds not words" – and his obvious anxiety to avoid Mr Wilson's obsession with publicity he seems to have forgotten that it is an essential part of democratic government to communicate with the electors, to carry them along as far as is possible'[10]. Individual journalists mixed their frustration with a very real sense of relief that Downing Street no longer divided them into bad guys and (a very few) good guys. Collectively the lobby had its nose put somewhat out of joint by the fact that both the prime minister and his chief press secretary clearly felt more at ease with the diplomatic correspondents than with them. But it was better to suffer neglect than paranoid contempt on any day of the week. In opposition Heath had shown occasional flashes of anger towards individual journalists, but they were rare and out of character. At a Stock Exchange lunch he shocked his hosts by pointing at the *Guardian's* financial editor, William Davis, and saying, 'Either he goes or I go!' The offence, it seems, was an article that had followed a two-hour discussion over lunch between the two men. It was a serious interview, mainly on economic policy, and, while Davis complained in print that Heath had promised to send him more details of the party's plans but had failed to do so, this was not the cause of the subsequent outburst. It seems Heath's fury was provoked by the observation that the interview had taken place at his home 'in exclusive Albany'.[11]

An incident of far greater importance in the early weeks of his pre-miership may have played a part in confirming Heath's disdain for the lobby. Many journalists, including James Margach, who was now on his tenth prime minister, certainly thought so. It concerned the arrest of a woman terrorist, Leila Khalid, who had taken part in the attempted hijacking of an Israeli plane on its way into London. Three other planes had been hijacked in the middle east and one was blown up in Cairo. The terrorists threatened to blow up the other two on Jordanian soil unless Khalid was released from jail in London. Parliament was not sitting and for two anxious weeks, Maitland was responsible for keeping the press and public informed. Not surprisingly he couldn't reveal everything that was going on and 'one thing which I did not reveal, because it could have had a very serious bearing on the case, was that we didn't know for certain at what precise point the terrorists took over the aircraft; was it in British air space or was it over international waters?'[12] With today's much tougher laws and treaties it may seem incredible that if, as the pilot reported, the hijacking took place 'south of Clacton' Khalid had committed no offence under British jurisdiction. After lengthy negotiations and once all the hostages had been allowed to go free she was released and flown to Egypt. The lobby quite properly reported the views of those on the Tory right, like Enoch Powell, who condemned what they saw as weakness in the face of terrorism. Heath was furious and according to Margach, 'from that moment onwards he more or less broke off relations with the politi-cal corps for their lack of cooperation and understanding.'[13]

When parliament returned, Maitland, with Heath's approval, set out to try to change the basis of the relationship between Downing Street and the lobby that had existed since the 1930s. The ways of parliamentary journalists bemused Maitland. Having dozens of them pack into his office at the front of Number 10 for his regular morning briefings 'sitting on settee arms and leaning against the wall, seemed to carry the British cult of amateurism to absurd lengths'[14]. Then there was the peculiarly British habit of editoralising so that 'the viewer, listener or reader would be told what opinion to form about some development before learning what it was'. What he had in mind was stories that started with words like 'The government suffered a setback today when ...' If Maitland wanted to put Downing Street's side of the argument at one of their meetings, then, under lobby conventions, he could do it only as an anonymous 'source close to the prime minister', whereas if any other reporter called him he was free to go on the record. Maitland wrote to the chairman of the lobby, Keith Renshaw, suggesting a rather modest step towards a more transparent system. He wanted to make some statements at lobby briefings on the record, not as a substitute for the non-attributable briefings but to supplement them.

Renshaw summoned the entire lobby to decide what to do, having already set out his own views in a memo. He thought the change might make it easier for Maitland to indulge in news management. 'What is favourable to his case he might pronounce with the full authority of the record. What is unhelpful he might prefer to leave for the correspondent to write on his own authority. Put slightly differently, there may obviously, on occasion, be pressure upon a correspondent to give prominence in his report to quotable information.'[15] By twenty-five votes to twenty-one the lobby said no to Maitland's suggestion. When I joined the lobby in 1989 everything that had so baffled him was still going on. We all crammed into the same room. Bernard Ingham, then speaking for Mrs Thatcher, was still referred to only as a source 'close to the prime minister'. And even at the BBC we happily told our viewers and listeners that the government had suffered 'setback' after 'setback'.

Having been rebuffed, Maitland decided instead simply to hand out government statements at lobby meetings in the form of press releases.

He rightly judged that no journalist was going to be perverse enough to refuse to read them. And he did manage to get some of the meetings moved to a more suitable room, although again the correspondents were reluctant to give up completely their right to walk through the famous black front door. He then tried another tack. Why should the prime minister continue with the curious tradition of giving press conferences only when he was abroad but never at home? Accordingly the media were called to a press conference in the grand surroundings of Lancaster House on the Mall on 12 July 1971. The purpose was to set out Heath's case for the legislation enacting Britain's accession to the European Economic Community.

Nobody can take away from Heath his achievement in securing British membership of the EEC, although some in his party would later come to see it as his greatest betrayal. It was undoubtedly a diplomatic triumph but it was also a dramatic coup in media terms. Although Heath had promised to keep the British public informed as the negotiations progressed – through parliament, of course, not the press – the final stages in May 1971 were conducted very much in private. The conditions were right. President de Gaulle, who had pronounced a firm 'non' to British membership as long ago as 1963, had now gone and been replaced by President Pompidou, who was far more amenable. Yet there was certainly no guarantee of success and the negotiations were protracted and sometimes difficult. Any other prime minister and press secretary would have been accused of deliberately downplaying expectations, and maybe they were, but when the papers reported 'deadlock' Heath and Maitland never sought to deny it. As the talks at the Elysée Palace dragged on into the Friday evening the media assumed things must be going badly. So when the prime minister and the president walked into the briefing room to announce an agreement Heath felt it was 'marvellous to see the looks of astonishment on the faces of so many of those present. The President and I looked across at each other with delight, for we had secured success and also triumphed over the media.'[16] That he had the media anywhere near the front of his mind at the moment of his greatest accomplishment would have pleased those in the room, who had decided by now that he didn't care what they thought about anything.

The Lancaster House performance on home turf two months later was not such an unqualified success, at least from the point of view of the lobby. Heath spoke without a note for an hour and a half and looked every inch the purposeful, confident leader on top of his job. It came across magnificently on television, but the written press were not so happy. They had felt like extras in a TV spectacular, something they were going to have to get used to. Heath had little sympathy. Television had been kind to him at last and he asked his staff to take things one step further by arranging for regular prime-ministerial 'fireside chats' to be broadcast on both the BBC and ITV. In Margach's phrase, '*Sunday Night at Number 10* was seen as a rival to *Sunday Night at the London Palladium*'[17]. The idea was abandoned when they realised the opposition would have to be given the same opportunity. The thought of a fireside chat with Harold Wilson was more than Heath could bear.

Instead Downing Street encouraged Granada Television to make a programme about his sailing that seemed almost an allegory about solitary and determined leadership. That summer Heath skippered *Morning Cloud* to victory in the Admiral's Cup, a remarkable achievement for any man, never mind one with a day job that involved running a powerful industrial nation. There he was again looking determined and energetic and talking about the importance of winning. The programme's producer was a young man by the name of John Birt who went on to become not only director general of the BBC, but also a special adviser to Tony Blair, the prime minister who thirty years later would both break open the lobby and formalise the idea of prime-ministerial press conferences.

While Blair would combine press conferences with a mind-boggling array of other appearances on any and every form of media available to him, Heath made the mistake of thinking they could be a substitute for regular and effective communication. In that respect his first performance at Lancaster House had been too good. The sequels, notably on his prices-and-incomes policy and then the miners' dispute that led to the three-day week, were less successful. They confirmed the impression that the press and public had by then formed of him, of an aloof and out-of-touch man, more given to lecturing than to listening.

All governments get mid-term blues but when the going got tough from 1972 onwards, the Heath administration suffered something much darker than the blues. Northern Ireland was on the brink of civil war, unemployment passed the psychologically important million mark, inflation continued to rise and the miners went on strike to demand a 47 per cent pay rise. The crises followed one after another with a relentlessness that nobody could have foreseen. On the economy, Heath decided a new approach was necessary, but once again he failed to use the media to make an effective case for it. Historians and economists still debate the extent to which the expansionary 'Barber boom', that carried the name of his chancellor but was really of his own devising, and the adoption of a statutory prices-and-incomes policy amounted to a total reversal of his initial approach. But certainly when Margaret Thatcher stood up as prime minister to declare, 'You turn if you want to, the Lady's not for turning',[18] it was a deliberate renunciation of the perceived U-turns by her predecessor. Either way, Heath's new policies needed public understanding and support to succeed and that was never going to be achieved by lectures alone. As Peter Hennessy, who was then just starting out in journalism, has observed, 'at such moments prime ministers need to call in debts from political supporters and media alike. Here Heath was very thinly endowed, partly for the creditable reason that he had no time for the charlatanries and hypocrisies which are often involved in the accumulation of such credits.'[19]

The trade unions had no compunction about using every media opportunity that came their way to make the case for strike action to protect the living standards of their members. Heath thought it was properly the job of the employers to make the counter-arguments but he was reluctantly persuaded that he would have to enter the arena, too. Television was the obvious medium but Heath had never mastered the art of talking through the camera and making himself understood in the living room. Douglas Hurd did his best. He sent the prime minister a memo describing 'Words to avoid because meaningless to the audience – regressive, relativities, anomalies, unified tax system, productivity, threshold agreements, deflation, realignment. Also avoid percentages where possible.'[20] He didn't have much success. 'He wasn't good at expressing himself. Most politicians like finding words, organising words, it's part of the attraction of the profession. He didn't.'[21]

Things went from bad to worse. In 1973 the Yom Kippur war put up the price of oil with further inflationary consequences that also added to the bargaining power of the miners. Heath headed for his final confrontation with the National Union of Mineworkers with his own physical reserves running dry. His friends, including Ian Trethowan, then managing director of BBC Radio, urged him to appeal to the nation for support. He took their advice and, having barely slept for four days because of the continuous negotiations to try to avert a crippling strike, made a prime-ministerial broadcast on 13 December. It was deliberately doom-laden. Heath said later, 'I don't think a miners' strike is the time to come on television and ooze charm'[22], as if that had ever been an option. Once again his television manner let him down. 'He didn't set himself to do it well,' said Hurd. 'Everybody can if they try but he didn't really.' One BBC reporter said he had 'never looked worse on television' and was 'so tired he could scarcely speak'.[23] What he did say was hardly inspiring. He declared that 'At times like these there is deep in all of us an instinct which tells us we must abandon disputes among ourselves. We must close our ranks so that we can deal together with the difficulties which come to us whether from within or from beyond our own shores.'[24]

His appeal did nothing to lessen the chances of what he predicted would be 'a harder Christmas than we have known since the war'. As the three-day week took hold and the lights started going out he and his colleagues began to consider a different kind of appeal, one direct to the people in the form of a general election. It was an intensely political decision and Heath was reluctant to take it. He recoiled from the idea of an election fought on the basis of industrial conflict. He wasn't ready to condemn the miners as 'the enemy within', as Margaret Thatcher would do. Had he been less squeamish and had he thought in media terms, which, as ever, he did not, he might have been able to find the words to appeal to the journalist's love of a good straightforward fight. With better politics and a better strategy Heath could have gone to the country with a far more favourable press than he did.

Throughout the early seventies, while Heath stayed aloof, the pre-vailing mood in Fleet Street had been overwhelmingly pessimistic. There was endless analysis of the fundamental weakness of the econ-omy and the 'British disease' of industrial unrest. The papers didn't like what they saw but they didn't have any radical ideas for how to change it. Many of the titles that would later become associated with the right-wing populism of Mrs Thatcher had yet to be convinced there was an alternative to the post-war consensus and a mixed economy. When Rupert Murdoch bought the *Sun* in 1969 it was neither 'super' nor 'soar-away' and nor was it a cheerleader for right-wing values. The first Labour leader to get the *Sun*'s endorsement was not Tony Blair but Harold Wilson. Throughout the Heath government the paper remained sympathetic to the trade-union movement, although it was far from alone. Even among the majority of national papers that con-tinued to support the Conservatives over Labour, the unions were not yet the bogeymen they would soon become. When the miners first went on strike in 1972 they were backed by both the *Daily Mail*, which had become a tabloid the previous year, and the *Daily Express*. By the second strike of 1974 sympathy for the miners had largely evap-orated but that had more to do with the actions of the NUM than any efforts on behalf of Downing Street to bring press opinion around.

Late in the day many of the same friends who advised Heath to use television more effectively also urged him to start trying to court the editors. Reluctantly, he agreed. They were duly summoned to Downing Street to be lectured by the prime minister about the national importance of supporting his prices-and-incomes policy. They weren't impressed by this belated attention. According to Margach: 'his manner was still cold and commanding. Heath did not like general dis-cussions, he preferred monologues, and many editors did not welcome what they saw as his efforts to manage the news and condition their opinions. To them it was clear that Heath was not interested in their views, only in the need for better understanding of his.'[25]

The government's relationship with the media would have been even worse had it not been for the diplomats in his press office. When Donald Maitland left Downing Street with a knighthood in 1973 he was replaced by another Foreign Office man, Robin Haydon. Maitland was able to say of the lobby, 'If I ever had a reservation about the way they covered the range of government activities, it was minor.'[26] He had never been the controversial figure that Bernard Ingham would become, and not least because, as he said himself, 'there was never any occasion when I commented on the performance of any member of the cabinet for the very good reason that the prime minister never discussed his cabinet colleagues with me'.[27] Maitland and Haydon were the least political press secretaries of modern times, but they and Heath would have regarded that as entirely right and proper. It may have handicapped Downing Street's efforts to make a strong case against the unions but so be it.

The prime minister had also been scrupulously fair in his dealings with the broadcasters. When the chance to appoint a new BBC chairman had come up in 1973, Heath had no particular reason or desire to punish the corporation as Wilson had done. He took the advice of Mrs Thatcher, then his education secretary, and selected an eminent scientist, Sir Michael Swann. Political considerations played no discernible part in the decision. Since 1970 there had been only one significant tussle between the government and the BBC, over a programme called *The Question of Ulster*. It was broadcast despite strong representations from ministers that it was potentially dangerous at such a delicate time, but Heath himself had kept out of the row. Harold Wilson had been embroiled in a much more acrimonious dispute over *Yesterday's Men*, a highly critical documentary about him and his frontbench colleagues. Joe Haines called it 'a deliberate, continuous and calculated deceit'[28], and in 1974 Wilson was in the unique position for a leader of the opposition of going into an election with worse relations with the BBC than the governing party.

For four years Edward Heath had done what he believed to be right with barely a nod to what the media might make of it. And in the first election of 1974 he had the satisfaction of enjoying strong support from the national dailies. Only the *Mirror* and the *Guardian* backed Labour. The *Sun* probably reflected the views of many of its readers when it declared it was sick of the 'Ted and Harold Show' and dismayed by a choice between 'the Devil and the Deep-Blue Sea'. And yet while Heath welcomed the endorsements of just about every other paper, he wasn't happy at Fleet Street's collective decision to make it the 'Who Governs Britain?' election. For their part the Tory-supporting titles were disappointed at his reluctance to come out with all guns blazing. He sounded moderate, admitted the miners were a special case and refused to go along with the idea that democracy was at stake. Had he done what they and many of his own advisers wanted, the result might have been different. The whole of Fleet Street, friend or foe, was predicting another comfortable Tory victory, but for the second election in a row they were wrong. Heath won more votes than Wilson but fewer seats. Predictably, he held the media partly to blame. 'Labour had fought the election on the most extreme platform of any party since the war, which had been more or less ignored thanks to the inevitable media focus on the miners' strike.'[29] Edward Heath gave the media one last story as PM, refusing to resign for four days while he tried and failed to negotiate some kind of coalition or agreement with the Liberals. Nobody had an overall majority but Wilson took office once again with the certainty of a second election hanging in the air.

While Wilson waited for Heath to pack his bags, he had a conversation with Barbara Castle that showed he was already thinking about the press, although promising to do things differently this time. 'No more lobby briefings,' she recorded him as saying, 'just the *Mirror*, the *Sunday Mirror* and the *People* will have access to me . . . Government decisions will all be on the record – preferably announced in the evening before the 9pm news.' She was relieved but unsure. 'So long as he doesn't renew that vendetta with the press!'[30]

Unlike in 1964 Wilson now had somebody to conduct vendettas on his behalf. In with him came Joe Haines, who had remained as his press adviser throughout the years of opposition. Haines was almost as controversial a figure as Alastair Campbell would become under Tony Blair. According to Bernard Donoughue, Wilson's senior policy adviser, Haines's role, like Campbell's, went wider than press relations: 'he possessed remarkable political insight and judgement and for most of the 1974–6 period he was effectively the prime minister's main political adviser.' He didn't always agree with his boss and wasn't afraid to say so. 'He strongly opposed many of Mr Wilson's less felicitous ideas in private – and then, if overruled, of course had to defend them in public to disapproving fellow journalists.'[31] Political and communications strategy were closely intertwined and the immediate objective was to secure a workable majority as soon as possible and thereafter to ensure that Downing Street communications did what Haines believed they were there to do, reinforce and promote the power of the prime minister. His approach could not have been more different to that of the diplomat-press secretaries whose office he took over. Politics was back and back with a vengeance. Haines started as he meant to go on, sacking five of the eleven press officers he inherited. The separation between the civil-service press office and the political operation, which had been run by first Gerald Kaufman and then Will Camp from 1964 to 1970, was effectively abolished and Haines became a temporary civil servant with an expanded role. According to Marcia Williams, who was back with at least as much vengeance herself, Haines 'wanted a Labour-orientated organisation'.[32] From what he said to Robert Harris some years later it is clear he wanted a Wilson-orientated organisation: 'The press secretary is employed by the prime minister and for the prime minister, not by or for Fleet Street. He has no function in helping Fleet Street. Everything he says and everything he does is designed to help the prime minister first, and after that the government as a whole. If, in the end, it means ditching another minister . . . then you ditch that minister.'[33]

The minister Haines probably had in mind was Tony Benn, industry secretary in the new administration. If Ted Heath was right and Labour had been elected on a red-blooded socialist manifesto then Benn saw himself as the man to keep Wilson to the words it contained. Indeed, he would walk into Downing Street with the document conspicuously under his arm for the cameras to see when he thought the cabinet was backsliding. Part of the re-election campaign in the summer of 1974 clearly involved reassuring wavering voters that Benn was not the power he liked to think he was. By mid-June Benn was used to a diet of headlines over breakfast along the lines of 'All Out Attack On Benn' and 'Wilson Rebuffs Benn'. He was astute enough to see the hand of Joe Haines behind the briefings and regarded him as a barrier to better relations. He wrote in his diary: 'The fact is there is a war between us and Number 10 at the moment and there's no point pretending there isn't.'[34]

When he wasn't undermining left-wingers like Benn, Haines was squaring up to the lobby journalists. Like Alastair Campbell, who hailed from the same Mirror Group stable, Haines's own experience in the lobby had left him with nothing but contempt for it. It is easier to set about trying to manipulate people if you have little respect for them in the first place, although, again like Campbell, he might have been better advised to mask his contempt a little, if only to make the job of manipulation more effective. Ian Aitken, who would soon take over as political editor of the *Guardian*, thought Haines's abrasiveness did him no favours. 'I don't think he did manipulate us frightfully well, because he was so hostile to us that if he told us the time of day we would look at our watches to make sure he was telling the truth.'[35]

Within weeks of his return to Downing Street, Wilson would have good reason to believe that some sections of the press were determined to go to almost any lengths to damage him. The 'slagheaps scandal' had threatened to break during the campaign but the *Daily Mail* held off until two weeks after polling day before publishing a lengthy article alleging links between both Marcia Williams and her brother, who had also worked under Wilson, and a highly dubious land-deal speculator, Ronald Milhench. Two weeks later the paper published a letter to Milhench on House of Commons notepaper with what appeared to be Wilson's signature. It wasn't exactly the Zinoviev letter of 1924 but it was a forgery and Milhench was eventually convicted of fraud and went to jail. Williams was only ever a sleeping partner in a deal that never came to fruition. She broke no laws and Wilson himself was blameless. Before that could be established, Williams had an unruly press pack camped outside her front door. Wilson told *World in Action* 'the whole thing is a pretty seamy, squalid press story. This doesn't happen to Conservative prime ministers. The aim is to destroy the Labour government.'[36] According to Haines, 'Harold Wilson's relationships with the press were never worse than at that time, and neither were mine',[37] and that was saying something.

Wilson decided to show the media just what he thought of them. First he set up another Royal Commission on the Press, charged with examining not only the economics of the newspapers, but also their ethics. Then he had an even more Wilsonian idea. Far from being disgraced, Marcia Williams would be ennobled. He told the Queen that it would 'do a Harvey Smith' at the press. He assumed she would know what he meant. Harvey Smith was a jockey who got into trouble for sticking two fingers up at the judges after winning the British show-jumping derby in 1971.[38] The *News of the World* spoiled his fun by getting holding of the news before the official announcement. Wilson denounced their story as a 'pack of lies' and told Haines not to speak to any lobby briefing where the guilty journalist was present. Then, despite the opposition of many of his advisers, including Haines, Marcia Williams duly became Lady Falkender on 23 July 1974. There was no apology to the *News of the World* or its correspondent. The prime minister had told his press secretary to lie, although Haines would claim his denial 'was right at the time'.[39] Wilson's promise to Barbara Castle to do things differently was already looking pretty threadbare.

Yet Harold Wilson had good reason to claim that he was more victim than assailant. That summer the British press was awash with conspiracy theories and alleged scandals that amounted to very little. Wilson defended his cabinet colleague, Ted Short, against untrue allegations of corruption and then became aware of stories involving himself. *Private Eye* thought it had evidence linking Wilson with both Soviet and Israeli intelligence, none of which stood up. The Conservatives failed to benefit from the media hoo-hah although they would have liked to have done. One official inside Central Office told the authors of the Nuffield guide to the October 1974 election: 'We don't really have anyone nasty enough and skilful enough to make the mud stick.'[40] To his credit Heath was more interested in making the most of another favourite media charge, that Wilson was in hock to the unions, and in deriding Labour's renegotiation of Britain's EEC membership, which Wilson was promising to put to a referendum as a fig leaf for divisions in his own government.

After a summer in which Wilson kept off the media as a deliberate tactic, he ordered the release of a series of white papers setting out his intentions on everything from sex equality and pensions to consumer protection and devolution. It was a cheeky use of the government machine and the public purse to trail key parts of the forthcoming Labour manifesto, but it was within the rules. As for Heath's attacks, Wilson knew he was trying to paint Labour as stuck in its bad old disreputable ways, but calculated that the public would not object either to relative peace on the industrial front or to being consulted on a new, and cheaper, deal with Europe. When the second election came it was a surprisingly low-key affair. Heath floated the idea of a unity government of all the talents. In reality it would be made up of Tories and the Liberals with a few outsiders because Wilson said Labour wouldn't join. The idea played into Wilson's hands. It was attractive to many commentators but sent out the message that the Conservatives didn't really believe they could win alone. Heath had already lost significant support in Fleet Street since the February election. Only the *Daily Telegraph* and the *Daily Express* came out firmly for him in October. Even the *Daily Mail* felt unable to endorse the Tories wholeheartedly, although fears that it would run an eve-of-poll smear story on Wilson's wealth and tax affairs had him in a panic during the last weekend of the campaign. He was convinced the paper was behind a break-in at his house when financial documents had been stolen. According to Bernard Donoughue, Marcia Williams 'wanted Harold Wilson to get the newspaper unions to strike and stop the *Mail* from coming out'.[41] Wilson listened to her, as he always did, but wiser heads, like Bernard Donoughue, advised caution. Donoughue was able to help persuade him this wasn't a wise course of action. 'On the press his reactions are always wrong,' he wrote in his dairy on the final Sunday. 'I said he must not get into an argument . . . He must dismiss it with contempt, like Baldwin. Joe agreed — but was pessimistic that this could lose us the election.'[42] Wilson's lawyer, Lord Goodman, spoke directly to the *Mail*'s proprietor, Lord Harmsworth, apparently to some effect. The front page of the following morning's paper was filled with a long open letter to the prime minister, claiming there was no truth in the 'incredible rumours' that it was planning a smear. The letter was so long and repetitive that it had clearly been written to fill the space left when the original story was pulled at the last minute.

The Tory press may have been in a sullen mood, but Wilson had the enthusiastic backing of the Mirror Group during the campaign although that was it. None of the 'heavies' supported him so when he was returned with a wafer-thin majority of three he had no reason to believe, as he had in 1964 and 1966, that the media had helped him on his way. He also knew, although few others did, that he would not be fighting another general election, which can only have encouraged his Harvey Smith instincts towards the press. Edward Heath, who had now lost three elections out of four, would soon lose the Tory leadership as well. Margaret Thatcher would eventually change the business of political communications out of all recognition and have a profound impact on Fleet Street, too, but in October 1974 Wilson believed the *Sun* could still be won back to the Labour camp. He quickly invited its editor, Larry Lamb, to Downing Street where the prime minister conspicuously drank Federation bitter while Lamb quaffed the burgundy.[43]

Harold Wilson was unable to shake off his obsession with the media, no matter what promises he might have made to Barbara Castle and others. It would colour his last administration as much as it had his earlier ones and would be exacerbated by signs of a paranoia that some believe may have had not just psychological but physical causes. Wilson died in May 1995, but was physically and mentally diminished by Alzheimer's long before that. There has been speculation, never proved and generally dismissed by all those closest too him, that a premonition of what was to come or even early signs of the illness may have prompted his decision to resign in 1976. In fact he told Joe Haines and one or two others after the February 1974 election that he would stand down when he turned sixty and that is exactly what he did. In the meantime, Haines had a rather different health scare to contend with. During a bumpy landing on an official visit to Paris Wilson felt the symptoms of a heart palpitation – the very same problem that Tony Blair would shrug off in 2003. His doctor put it down to overwork. 'I told the press, who believed me when I said it, that Harold had the flu', Haines admitted. 'We had an economic crisis and we had a majority of three. If I had said "He's got a heart problem", then the cabinet would have been queuing up to take over from him, and the Stock

Exchange would have fallen through the floor. So I didn't have the slightest compunction about not telling the truth.'[44]

They may have believed him on that occasion, but the media were getting increasingly frustrated and angry with the way Haines was treating them. Some journalists had started referring to him as the 'anti press officer'. He stopped allowing them to fly on the prime minister's plane during foreign visits, refused to give briefings on anything outside the direct remit of Downing Street and then, in June 1975, decided to finish the job that Donald Maitland had started but backed away from five years earlier. He wrote to the chairman of the lobby to say that he intended from now on to speak only on the record. It would, he wrote, 'eliminate the kind of extreme absurdity where, under the rules governing the present meetings, even the name of the annual poppy day seller who calls on the prime minister is given unattributably'.[45] There was a more important point: 'whether a daily meeting between the prime minister's spokesman and political journalists on a non-attributable basis is good for government, good for the press, and above all good for the general public which sustains us both. In my firm opinion, and in the view of the prime minister, it is not.'[46] Haines wasn't offering to negotiate. He stuck to his word and for the remaining months of Wilson's premiership, while conversations he had with individual journalists might be off the record, the Downing Street briefings were not.

Bernard Donoughue, while accepting that Haines's public argument had some validity, saw the real reason for the move as Wilson's 'paranoia about and hatred of the press'. He wrote in his dairy, 'It is now a year since I first heard him tell Joe to stop the lobby. HW has not himself seen the press, except after summit conferences, since he came to power. Not a single press conference in the UK, which is a bizarre situation. Rather like Richard Nixon, his relations with the press get worse as he gets older, and he stores up resentment from all the previous election campaigns, etc., where they have lied, misrepresented and criticized him. Yet he still reads every page of every newspaper, however trivial.'[47]

In fact, as we have seen, the tradition of domestic prime-ministerial press conferences was a relatively new one. By contrast the tradition of collective cabinet responsibility was not. It is almost unheard of for members of any government to be allowed to express opposing views on matters of policy, with the exception of issues of 'conscience' like abortion or the death penalty. On the renegotiated terms of Britain's EEC membership, however, Wilson knew there was no point trying to pretend that his colleagues saw eye to eye. By sixteen votes to seven the cabinet backed staying in the Common Market but he decided that in the run-up to the promised referendum on 5 June 1975 the minority would be free to express their disagreement. Wilson did his best not to hand the media the gift of seeing cabinet ministers tear into one another, red in tooth and claw. He warned them that in deciding on his post-referendum reshuffle he would 'judge people on the basis of whether they behaved in a spirit of comradeship'.[48] The tactic worked. The two-thirds majority won in the referendum by the 'yes' campaign was seen as 'quite frankly a triumph' for the prime minister by the *Daily Telegraph*, and the rest of the papers were in broad agreement.

His tactical skill had triumphed but he did not have long to bask in his success. Ten months later he would startle the country with the announcement of his resignation. In the time left to him he quickly cut Tony Benn down to size, demoting him from industry to energy secretary on 10 June. 'Wilson Gives Benn's Head to the City' declared the *Guardian*. Otherwise he was preoccupied, as Heath had been, with the economy and the fight against inflation, as well as Northern Ireland and foreign affairs. Not that he was too busy to forget iniquities of the press. At a dinner in Downing Street in June he 'dragged up every instance of injustice that had been meted out to him in his years of office'.[49] But he now believed far more serious injustices were being directed at him, a conviction that has contributed to the view that his mind was perhaps starting to go. He became paranoid that the security services were not only watching him, but also getting ready to support a coup. He would run taps while talking in the lavatory and point at the lights, suggesting they contained listening devices. Peter Hennessy recounts a conversation the prime minister had at this time with a civil servant. Wilson pointed to the Number 10 garden:

'Look. That's where they'll come. They'll come through there.'

'Who, prime minister?'

'Them. When they come to take over the government.'[50]

He also quotes George Bush, who would go on to be the first US president of that name, after a visit to Downing Street as director of the CIA, asking, 'Is that man crazy? He thinks there's a bug behind all the pictures.' A portrait of Gladstone, which Wilson identified as suspect, was eventually taken down to establish that all that lay behind it was an old hook used to hang a previous painting.

While there is no evidence of any plans for a coup, there seems little doubt that people claiming to have secret-service connections did approach not just *Private Eye* but some in the mainstream press, offering stories about the prime minister's alleged communist leanings. His biographer Ben Pimlott looked into it all as even-handedly as anybody could and concluded that, while Wilson's allegations, most of them made public only after his resignation, were hard to prove, some at least were 'supported by the recollections of a number of journalists who were on the receiving end of leaks'[51]. When he was no longer prime minister Wilson used the opportunity of his evidence to the Royal Commission on the Press, which continued to sit until 1977, to describe a series of suspicious break-ins at his home and those of his family and close political staff during which personal letters and bank statements were stolen.

Whatever else he had on his mind, Wilson's last months in office were clouded by his obsession with the media just as much as his first months had been. Right up to the end he was talking to his lawyer, Lord Goodman, about articles that had offended him. *The Times* had chosen to revisit the events surrounding Lady Falkender's ennoblement. On 1 March 1976 he wrote to Goodman, saying the article suggested that 'I had directed the press office in the past two years and earlier to put out information which, whether they knew it or not, was the reverse or a prevarication of the truth.'[52] The press-office staff believed the article impugned their reputations also and collectively sued for libel. The *Observer* then suggested Wilson had put them up to taking legal action and the row rumbled on during and after his resignation on 16 March. Although his departure had been the subject of periodic bouts of press speculation, the announcement when it came was a genuine 'hold the front page' moment. In Pimlott's words, 'the press reaction was like that of Talleyrand when told that the Turkish ambassador had died: "What does he mean by that?"[53]

The media would have their opportunity for a final crack at him with the publication of his resignations honours, the so-called 'lavender list' in May. The name was derived from the colour of Lady Falkender's notepaper. It was alleged that she had selected the names of those to be nominated although she always insisted she had not drawn up the list. Some of the recommendations looked like pay-back time for donations and other political services, but Joe Haines refused the offer of an honour for himself. He disapproved of the House of Lords and said his wife would disown any honour that made her Lady Haines as a result.[54] For the last time in office Wilson attacked the media for an 'orchestrated vendetta' of denigration. He might have added, if Richard Nixon hadn't come up with it first in his even more dramatic resignation two years earlier, 'you won't have Wilson to kick around any more'.

Of course Wilson delivered almost as many well-aimed kicks as he received during his decade of almost constant scrapping with the media. His staff and his ministerial colleagues could see how it distracted and weakened him, but he was incapable of letting go of his obsession. It wasn't the only thing that stopped him being a great prime minister, and it wasn't even the most important factor. Who can say what use he might have made of the time he wasted poring over newspapers and fretting about leaks and conspiracies. Had he been able to take press criticism more in his stride he would have been a different person in other ways as well, and the better for it probably. That he couldn't damaged his standing while in office and lessened his reputation after he left it.

James Callaghan, who was Wilson's preferred successor, comfortably won the ensuing leadership election and set about putting his own mark on the premiership. He knew he had relatively little time in which to do it and, following a number of by-election defeats, no majority in parliament on which to rely. With the help of an agreement with the Liberal party he managed to survive for three years until the 'winter of discontent' destroyed his hopes of getting his own mandate. That period of ugly and irresponsible trade-union excesses helped usher in not only Margaret Thatcher, but also a period of pro-market, large- and small-'c' conservatism that some commentators and many socialists maintain has persisted to the present day. Callaghan was the last prime minister to operate fully within the post-war consensus. In many ways he was a small-'c' conservative himself, more so than Wilson, and his *modus operandi* in Downing Street resembled that of Edward Heath more than it did that of his immediate predecessor. Straightforward dealings with the media were an important element of his approach and undoubtedly contributed to the fact that, in the words of his biographer Kenneth Morgan, he left Number 10 'with his public reputation significantly enhanced'.[55]

Even before he became prime minister, Callaghan signalled that he wasn't going to perform for the media just because they wanted him to or thought that he should. He did no interviews during the leadership election and was the only candidate not to take part in a *Panorama* special. A new era in political communication via television would soon overtake him, driven forward by Margaret Thatcher, but he had had a taste of what was to come and he didn't like it. There was no way, he said, that he was going to appear for the cameras 'dressed in a striped apron and pretending to wash up in the kitchen, as had happened during the Tory leadership election'.[56] His immense political experience – he had held all of the big three offices of state – meant he knew perfectly well how to handle himself in the media, and he came across very well, but there would be no jumping through hoops while he was in charge.

As ever, the choice of press secretary was a clear indication of how the prime minister intended to handle the media. Tom McCaffrey had been his head of information at both the Home Office and the Foreign Office. Callaghan's high regard for him dated back to the disastrous 1967 devaluation that had forced him to move from being chancellor to home secretary. Callaghan was angry, feeling that blame for the devaluation was being directed at himself to an unreasonable degree, and was making the lives of his ministerial colleagues and civil servants a misery. The department was on the point of rebellion and the media were picking up stories about his behaviour. McCaffrey decided he had to do something. 'One day in his Commons office I just shut the door and told him bluntly what was going on. From then on he totally trusted me and changed his whole attitude towards journalists.'[57] Callaghan in return admired McCaffrey's 'fierce Scottish integrity and his candour . . . It was thanks to him that I enjoyed a less barbed relationship with the press than I might have done.'[58]

McCaffrey had little time for the Joe Haines approach to media relations. He had no reason to mistrust journalists and they felt the same way about him. The parliamentary lobby had good cause to welcome his appointment. 'The first thing I did on arrival in Number 10 was to phone the chairman of the lobby and say the briefings start again tomorrow. From then on they were very kind to me, I think.'[59] McCaffrey saw Callaghan daily but he would never have presumed to offer political advice in the way that Haines had done. That was the responsibility of another Tom, the political secretary Tom McNally, and the two men forged a constructive alliance although both would suffer at times from being kept in the dark by officials. Callaghan may have trusted McCaffrey personally, but he opted for a Downing Street regime that often made it difficult for his press secretary to do his job properly. Even Bernard Donoughue, who stayed on as chief policy adviser, had to use backstairs contacts to find out exactly what was going on, most notably as the cabinet grappled with the terms of a massive loan from the International Monetary Fund. 'It is the old crazy fear of "leaks", which leads to only the civil servants having the information,' he wrote. 'So we get in the crazy position where McCaffrey, who must answer the press, McNally, who is Jim's closest adviser, and I, who briefs him on the cabinets (all of whom will be unemployed if the decisions are wrong), are not told what is going on.'[60] Even the minutes of cabinet meetings were kept from them. 'As if McCaffrey, after twenty years in the service, is going to start leaking cabinet minutes!'[61]

McCaffrey got 'very fed up' but recognised with relief that it was a symptom of the fact that Callaghan was very different from Wilson in so many respects. He was far more like Heath in wanting to make certain the right decisions were taken rather than ensure the right headlines were written. But, like Heath, while he didn't waste time

fretting about the press nor did he devote enough thought to working out how the media could be used to advance his political
objectives. McCaffrey was left to get on with his job, and while
Callaghan read the newspapers and often disliked what he found in
them, he didn't take it too personally or bear grudges against individual journalists. 'Jim wasn't like his predecessor. He didn't look at the
papers to see if there was the slightest criticism, wrong or bit of praise
here or there. He just didn't do that.' Tom McNally concurs: 'Jim
Callaghan would take care with the media, preparing for an interview,
but he was not obsessed with either what they thought about him or
the more scientific ideas of spin and media management. He was probably more brusque with the media than he needed to be. They often
thought he was a bit of a bully. He was very professional with them but
he didn't see it as part of his job to either manipulate the media or
dance to their tune.'[62]

There was a truce in the war between Downing Street and Fleet
Street with Callaghan's arrival, but nobody was naïve enough to believe
it would bring a permanent end to hostilities. Journalists did find him
brusque at times but they also recognised that the voters, their readers, found 'Big Jim', or 'Sunny Jim' as they called him when things
were going well, a reassuring figure. *The Times* welcomed his arrival
as 'the man the nation would trust'. When compared to the rather
shrill and unsettling image of Margaret Thatcher, in the years before
her image makeover, Callaghan appeared genial and relaxed, 'avun-
cular, reassuring, embodying the old values of neighbourhood, family,
and an orderly and law-abiding society'.[63] It is surprising, therefore,
that his first serious row with the media should have concerned
another man who personified a very traditional view of the world.

Edward Heath had appointed Sir Peter Ramsbotham British ambassador to the United States in 1974. The posting was expected to last
another two years, but Ramsbotham got a very rude shock when
Callaghan's first foreign secretary, Anthony Crosland, died suddenly
and was replaced by Dr David Owen. Owen, who was just thirty-
eight, wanted a much newer broom. Ramsbotham believed he had a
right to stay on. 'It was silly to change, but the fact was I was at Eton
and Magdalen, I was the son of a viscount, I wasn't his man. He was

very Labour, not SDP yet, but very Labour conscious at that time, and allowed it to spill over in his role as foreign secretary. So I can understand him wanting to get rid of me and persuading Callaghan as prime minister to approve it. Although after I retired Callaghan told my wife at a party that it was a wrong decision.'[64] What made the decision even more politically sensitive was that the man Owen chose to replace him was a young journalist, Peter Jay, who happened to be married to James Callaghan's daughter, Margaret (who would later, as Baroness Jay, be leader of the House of Lords under Tony Blair). 'I don't think it was Owen's fault, but I was smeared in London. They panicked. People roared with laughter when he announced to the press correspondents that Jay was going there. There were peals of hilarious laughter, which upset him very much . . . and they panicked, the PR people at Number 10, who put out stories, which appeared in identical terms in two tabloid papers, that I was a fuddy-duddy, that I was not serious, and all sorts of things. I didn't mind that at all because I knew I wasn't a fuddy-duddy, but I did object when they started saying I was, professionally, not very good. I know when I'm good and when I'm bad in my career, and I know that I was good in Washington.' The story was summed up by the *Evening Standard*'s headline: 'Snob Envoy Had To Go'.[65]

The man responsible for the 'smear' was not a political animal at all, but a fellow civil servant, Tom McCaffrey. He had spoken out of turn, and out of character, to two old friends, Robert Carvel of the *Standard* and John Dickinson of the London *Evening News*.

Added to the charge of nepotism, the charge against Callaghan's government of deliberately blackening an ambassador's reputation in this way was dynamite. McCaffrey put up his hands and offered to resign, but it wasn't his blood the press were out for. The papers were convinced that Callaghan had put his press secretary up to it. McCaffrey insists he had never heard such sentiments expressed by the prime minister. 'It was entirely me, I promise you. Jim knew nothing about it. He was pretty pissed off.'[66] Callaghan was obliged to make a statement in the Commons, denying a deliberate smear campaign. He told MPs that as a result of what had happened he was 'attracted . . . to having public briefings and not private briefings'.[67] There was a brief experiment with on-the-record lobby meetings once again but McCaffrey was so reluctant to be quoted saying anything at all remotely interesting that it was soon abandoned.[68]

The affair did little lasting damage not least because both Harold Wilson and Joe Haines were busy at the same time reminding people just how bad things had been before. Haines's book *The Politics of Power* was published in 1977 with what was considered indecent haste and confirmed what most people already believed about the rivalries and machinations in Wilson's Downing Street. Wilson himself talked with astonishing frankness to journalists about his fears of subversion and plots to unseat him. Compared to all that, and with the economy once again teetering on the abyss, the injudicious words of a press secretary who everybody knew to be as straight as anybody could be in such an exposed position was a storm in a rather old-fashioned tea cup.

Just as the Royal Commission into the Press, set up by Wilson, was coming to the end of its deliberations, the *Daily Mail* handed Downing Street a gift in the form of a front-page story alleging that the state-owned car manufacturer British Leyland had been using a 'slush fund' to pay bribes to help win foreign orders.[69] Unfortunately for the *Mail*, the letter at the heart of the story was a forgery, written by a disgruntled executive at the company who had been paid £12,000 for his trouble. Callaghan called it a 'contemptible display of political spite that has reduced journalism to a lower level than I can remember for many years'.[70] Wilson chipped in to remind everybody that from the Zinoviev letter on, the paper had been a 'peddler of forgeries' for decades. The industry secretary, Eric Varley, who had been implicated, successfully sued and the forger went to jail. It later emerged that there was more than a little truth in the basic story. Tony Benn's diaries revealed that the cabinet privately acknowledged that this kind of bribery went on all the time.[71] But the exposé did the *Mail* immense damage. The editor, David English, was forced to issue a swift apology, while denying that the story had been motivated by any anti-Labour bias. 'Does anyone truly believe that if we had had a Tory government for the past three years, this paper would have been a sycophantic lapdog, silently adoring our rulers with moist and worshipping eyes?'[72] Perhaps not, although it's a description some would recognise under the next Tory government. The Royal Commission stated the obvious when it said calling the *Daily Mail* a 'polemical and politically partisan newspaper' was old news. The journalist responsible for the story, Stewart Steven, lived to tell quite a few more tales. He was to become editor of the *Mail on Sunday* for ten years and then of the London *Evening Standard*. He finally retired from newspaper editing in 1995 after publishing an article critical of Tony Blair under the byline of the former Labour frontbencher Bryan Gould when it had actually been written by the teenage son of Michael Howard. The paper explained that faxes had become mixed up but Steven had no choice other than to publish a rare front-page apology.

Overall, however, the Royal Commission report was a disappointment to Labour. It concluded that the press was 'less partisan' than the party believed and the current balance against the government was 'not a strong one'.[73] Only the *Daily Mail*, *Daily Express*, *Daily Telegraph* and *Daily Mirror* were found to be consistently slanted politically. The report came just too soon to mark a dramatic shift in the stance of one newspaper that escaped its censure, the *Sun*. That same year Rupert Murdoch's fast-growing tabloid would harden both its style and its politics. Its Labour-supporting origins were finally cast off when it condemned Callaghan's 'tattered, discredited, disastrous government . . . bogged down by incompetence . . . drifting, rudderless' and said it was increasingly dominated by 'the fascist left'.[74] A year later, on 9 May 1978, official figures showed the *Sun* to be Britain's most popular daily paper for the first time. In March, after Labour was defeated in a by-election in Ilford, it had declared its change of political allegiance unambiguously. It said it was 'Margaret Thatcher, not Jim Callaghan, who speaks for Britain these days'.[75] It was a significant change for a paper that in 1976, at the end of her first year as Tory leader, had claimed she couldn't 'knock the skin off a rice pudding'. Having secured the *Sun*'s change of heart, Mrs Thatcher made sure she kept its backing. She became a frequent visitor to the paper's offices in the evening. There she would accept a whisky from Larry Lamb and expound her views on the issues of the day and even flatter him by asking for his.[76]

Although Labour lost the Ilford by-election as well as the *Sun*, the swing to the Conservatives was the lowest for two years, encouraging some in Number 10 to believe a general election was still winnable. Callaghan thought 'the tide was coming in.' By the middle of the year the newspapers, whatever their political stance, were all speculating on the date of the election. McCaffrey, McNally and Donoughue were busy speculating too, and with a greater degree of self-interest as their jobs were on the line, but even with them the prime minister was giving nothing away. He discussed the options with members of his cabinet but rarely with his staff. They assumed, partly because they thought it would be the right decision, that he would go to the country in the autumn. When he told them there would be an announcement on 7 September they, not unreasonably, concluded it would be the start of the campaign.

The *Daily Mirror* had been complaining for months that Downing Street was ignoring Labour's only true friend in Fleet Street. They had a point. Donoughue thought it was 'catastrophic and petty'[77] and blamed it on 'McCaffrey's hostility to the Mirror Group. He is out to demonstrate his difference from Joe Haines and his independence from the *Mirror*. The problem is that he is putting his own *amour propre* above the prime minister's and the government's political interests. The *Mirror* is the only paper which supports us and it is mad to alienate them.'[78] Tom McNally therefore thought he was doing the paper a favour and helping to undo some of the damage when he tipped them off that he believed the election would be on 5 October. The rest of the media, surmising that the *Mirror* must have had a reliable source, quickly built up public expectations for an autumn poll. Not for the first, or the last, time the *Mirror* had got a bum steer on election timing. Two days before informing any of his colleagues of his decision, Callaghan went to the TUC conference and in his only reference to the election date sang, or rather spoke, the words of an old music-hall song which concluded with 'can't get away to marry you today, My wife won't let me'. He had apparently intended it as a hint that the election wasn't coming after all but it was too opaque for most delegates or, indeed, the media to understand. So when on 7 September, as promised, he told the cabinet his decision but revealed that he had written to the Queen to say there would not be an election most of them were astonished.

The same day Callaghan sat down to write what has become known as the 'Jim'll Fix It' note. It was essentially an *aide-mémoire* for his personal benefit, possibly with his autobiography in mind. He had undoubtedly made the decision based on his own judgement that Labour was unlikely to win a workable majority that autumn, but the handwritten note suggests he also derived considerable pleasure from confounding the media. 'I've been written off more times than I care to remember,' he wrote. He then went through the various dates when 'they' had decided to fix the election date because 'they' had decided he wouldn't be able to carry on, before concluding: 'Neither the press nor the Tory party will fix it.'[79]

Politically it was a disaster and the media felt they had been played along. That needn't have mattered had Callaghan devised any clear strategy for the coming winter but he hadn't. Never did McCaffrey and McNally or anybody else sit down with the prime minister to plan how to manage the remaining months before a general election would have to be called. 'In a way it was an age of innocence in terms of the media,' reflected McNally. 'There was none of this rapid rebuttal or get your retaliation in first. In 1978, and it may have lessons for Gordon Brown, the strategy was that we had faced up to and taken the country through a crisis. It was a pretty strong message to take into an election, but the winter of discontent blew all that out of the water.'[80] Having made the fateful decision to soldier on, Callaghan had put the future of his government in the hands of the trade unions. He thought he could persuade them to act responsibly. Once it was evident that he could not, any attempt to convince the media that Labour was fit for re-election was effectively doomed. Even the *Mirror* joined the chorus of anti-union, if not overtly anti-Labour, coverage. In terms of the impact on the population as a whole, the crisis was arguably no more severe than the power cuts and other deprivations of Heath's three-day week, but to judge it from the pages of the newspapers it was ten times worse.

The only trump left in Labour's hands was the personality and image of Callaghan himself. Regardless of whether the Tories or Labour were ahead in polls, he continued to consistently outpoll Margaret Thatcher when the two leaders were compared head to head. Callaghan wanted to preserve his personal reputation at all costs, which is why he became so angry when the *Daily Mail* went to such lengths to undermine it. In early January 1979 the prime minister flew to Guadeloupe in the West Indies for talks with President Carter, Giscard d'Estaing of France and Chancellor Schmidt of Germany on the subject of nuclear-arms control. Guadeloupe had been chosen, in part, because it was easier to keep the journalists at bay than at a mainland venue. Undeterred, the *Mail* went all out to get a shot of the prime minister lapping up the sunshine and, eventually, they succeeded. Tom McNally held the paper responsible for destabilising Callaghan at a crucial moment. 'The *Mail* got a shot of Jim in his trunks while he was swimming. We were later told by our security people that they estimated the shot was taken at four thousand yards from a motor boat off shore. The rankling of that, the unfairness of that after what had been a very important international conference in which he'd played a key brokering role between the United States and Germany had been devalued by the *Mail* into a picture of him in his swimming trunks, implying that he was jollying while the country was freezing.'[81] Back at Downing Street, Donoughue was dismayed. 'It did not look good in a freezing London paralysed by strikes, when the newspapers frequently published huge photographs of the prime minister, McNally and McCaffrey basking in the Caribbean sunshine.'[82] Callaghan was aware of how it looked by the time he flew back to London. McNally believed, 'It was that that knocked him off his focus so he gave the famous "crisis, what crisis?" press conference.'[83]

Against the advice of McCaffrey, Callaghan decided to speak to the waiting journalists at Heathrow airport on his return. His normally measured and confident style when talking to the media deserted him and he messed up the encounter badly. He was jocular, when the mood in the country was anything but, and dismissive of questions about the growing disruption at home as a result of the wave of strikes. His actual words, that 'I don't think other people in the world will share the view that there is mounting chaos', were translated by the *Sun* into one of its most famous headlines, 'Crisis, What Crisis?'[84] Walter Terry, the political editor, wrote that 'Sun-tanned premier Jim Callaghan breezed back into Britain yesterday and asked Crisis? What

Crisis?' He added that 'Sunny Jim' had 'ticked off reporters' saying 'Please don't run down your country by talking about chaos.' The leader column insisted, 'it HASN'T all been cooked up by the press, Jim'.

Donoughue judged that the prime minister had 'tried to convey an "unflappable" image, but it came over as complacency in the sunshine and he never recovered from that'. A few days later, in the middle of a lorry drivers' strike, a Labour pre-election poster started appearing on the billboards with the slogan 'Keep Britain Labour and it will keep on getting better'. It was greeted with a mixture of incredulity and black humour, but it reflected the chronic weakness of the party's press and publicity operation. Callaghan had set up his own, supposedly secret, team including advertising and media experts known as the 'White Drawing Room Group' after the room in Downing Street where they met. This group came up with a far more effective poster showing a candle in the dark and the slogan 'Remember the last time the Tories said they had all the answers' but officials at Transport House, the party HQ, refused to let it be distributed. Countering the onslaught from the press was always going to be a massive challenge, but the rivalry and squabbles between the party and Downing Street-based campaign teams all but destroyed what little hope there was of an effective fightback. The mood inside Downing Street suggested to Donoughue 'a sense that the government had already ended its active life and was merely going through the final pre-burial preparations . . . McNally and McCaffrey complained to me that [Callaghan] did not discuss any serious issues with them . . . McCaffrey's "bottle" seemed to have gone, with him reminding me too often, though realistically, that "the game is over".'[85]

The Conservative party campaign had tensions and disputes of its own, but both Central Office and Margaret Thatcher herself were willing to listen to the polling and advertising experts they had hired. During regular visits to her home in Flood Street, Chelsea, Larry Lamb had been counselling her on the importance of getting through to the kind of people who bought the *Sun* and the *News of the World*. She listened carefully to what he had to say and in return gave Lamb an inside track on the campaign preparations.[86] Saatchi and Saatchi's 'Labour

Isn't Working' poster, with its line of supposedly unemployed men and women (in fact they were from Hendon Young Conservatives) is perhaps the most famous in British political history. Encouraged by Gordon Reece, the party's director of publicity whose previous clients had included Eamonn Andrews and Bruce Forsyth, Thatcher was seen doing everyday things like shopping and housework. During the election campaign itself there seemed to be nothing she would not do for the cameras. She cuddled a newborn calf for a full thirteen minutes until she was sure every photographer had the shot they wanted. Callaghan refused to follow suit, saying: 'It's not my style . . . I'll sound as phoney as she does.'[87] Before the campaign he had indicated to Roy Hattersley that he knew what was coming: 'That woman's going to be packaged; they are going to decide what she ought to be and she is going to be that. I wouldn't do that.'[88] Callaghan benefited from some good photo-opportunities, attending church with his grandchildren, for example, which oozed dependability and experience. According to Michael Sullivan, the BBC man assigned to cover his campaign, 'Jim's style was to treat his tour as a private affair between himself and the electorate, making no concession to the television age razzamatazz adopted by the publicity men at Conservative Central Office.'[89] On the eve of poll Callaghan had the following exchange with David Rose of ITN before taking off his microphone and refusing to continue with the interview. The questions had all been about the unions.

> CALLAGHAN: The media is always trying to find out what's wrong with something. Let's try and make it work.
> ROSE: What if the unions can't control their own militants, are there no circumstances where you would legislate?
> CALLAGHAN: I didn't say anything of that sort at all . . . I'm not going to take the interview further . . . This programme is not to go out.

And it didn't. Remarkably, ITN agreed not to broadcast it and recorded a new interview, something that would be unthinkable now.[90]

Contrary to the finding of the Royal Commission only two years earlier, the Nuffield study concluded that during the 1979 general election the tabloids were 'totally partisan'[91], with only the *Mirror* supporting Labour. Since 1977 the paper had a new leader writer with a crisp and acerbic style by the name of Joe Haines, and as usual the paper put its sense of grievance at the way Labour had treated it to one side for the election. Elsewhere in Fleet Street there were endless scare stories predicting a left-wing takeover of the party if Labour won. Tony Benn was often portrayed as the real prime minister-in-waiting. More than ever before the partisanship spread way beyond the comment pages and editorials and infected the news pages. The most notorious example was the *Daily Mail's* front-page news story, 'Labour's Dirty Dozen'. It listed '12 lies designed to frighten voters into staying with a bankrupt Labour government'[92] and was taken almost word for word from a speech by Tory frontbencher Angus Maude which had been reproduced in a Conservative party press release. The *Sun* probably did more damage to Callaghan if only because more of its readers would have supported Labour in the past. 'Vote Labour This Time' said its headline on polling day, although a subtle change had been demanded from the original 'Vote Labour Today' by none other than Rupert Murdoch. The leader, which ran to an extraordinary 1,700 words, claimed the *Sun* was 'not a Tory newspaper' but a radical one. It was self-consciously addressed to 'traditional supporters of the Labour party' and warned them the choice was between 'freedom and shackles'.[93]

Academic research suggests that people were more likely to take heed of the political advice offered by newspapers in 1979 than they are today, but the media didn't cost Callaghan his job. As ever there was a variety of factors, but the real honour must go to the trade-union movement, which had claimed its second prime-ministerial scalp in five years. But a new political media had shown its hand in the campaign. Mrs Thatcher would almost certainly have won even if Fleet Street had maintained the strictest separation between news and comment, but the fact is that it didn't. Labour would take a very long time to adjust to the new stridency in political reporting, preferring to cry foul than work out how to counter it or at least live with it. Tony Benn suffered more personal abuse than any other politician although he overstated the case when he recorded, 'The media were utterly corrupt in this election, trying to make it a media event.'[94] The following day he made the ominous observation that 'I am one of the few ex-ministers who enjoys opposition. I intend to take full advantage of it.' Of Callaghan's ministers only two, Margaret Beckett and Gavin Strang, would ever see office again. Eighteen years of impotent opposition lay ahead before the party, buoyed up by unprecedented media support, would storm back into government.

PART TWO

PRIME MINISTERS V. THE MEDIA:

TWENTY-FOUR-HOUR NEWS AND THE MEDIA DEMOCRACY

9

SHE: THATCHER (1979–90)

Politicians run on publicity like horses run on oats.

Matthew Parris

If any prime minister got it right when it came to handling the media it was Margaret Thatcher. Alone among the seventeen premiers who have sat in Downing Street since the First World War, Mrs Thatcher had a relationship with the newspapers, radio and television that was so successful it both enhanced her standing and effectiveness while in office and contributed to a lasting reputation at least equal to, and arguably greater than, her actual achievements. She had the extraordinary good fortune to be prime minister at a time when the political and economic circumstances favoured her unique brand of leadership, but she successfully exploited the media to strengthen her hold on power and further her objectives. She used her almost mesmeric grip over much of the popular press to build herself up and, crucially, to cripple her adversaries, whether the opposition parties, the trade unions, hostile foreign nations or those within her own government who failed to measure up to her expectations.

The relationship worked to her advantage for the best part of ten years. She came unstuck only when the gap between reality and the image she had crafted with the aid of a pugnacious press secretary and an often eulogistic media became too wide and she failed to see the danger signs. Having been praised for a decade for standing firm in order to defeat any and every foe, she lost sight of the value of the tactical concession that, before her supremacy was established, she had used to great effect. The media did not make Margaret Thatcher a successful prime minister but they used their powers of amplification and exaggeration and their reflex towards simplification to sustain and embolden her. Moreover, she got all of that in return for very little on her part. She never lay awake at night worrying about the headlines, nor did she use her daylight hours to obsess over what journalists were saying or writing. She variously courted them, flattered them and rewarded them but the effort cost her nothing. The period from 1979 to 1990 brought little credit on the popular press but many of their proprietors made a lot of money and she helped sell their papers. 'Maggie' was good copy and in backing her the majority of newspaper titles were undoubtedly in tune with a significant proportion of their readers. What was extraordinary about the period was that the campaigning zeal the popular press had often shown at election times was continued between elections with only slightly reduced force. As Hugo Young observed in one of the earliest biographies of her, 'the Thatcher era coincided with a broad retreat from the days when newspapers considered it a primary duty to make life difficult for those in power'.[1] It drove those out of power to distraction and the impact of those years on British politics is still being felt. Mrs Thatcher may not have paid a high price for the devoted support she received but others have and still are. She helped convince a generation of politicians that it is impossible to govern successfully without the backing of the popular press or at the very least its acquiescence. In so doing she gave the media greater status and influence than they have ever deserved or even asked for and only now, thirty years later, is that power finally in decline.

The Thatcher decade – she was in power for eleven and a half years – saw dramatic changes in many aspects of British society, and she could fairly be credited with responsibility for a large number of them. The relationship between the media and politics was transformed, too, although here her role was more tangential. She encouraged some developments when she saw they would be to her advantage, but others were driven by technological advances outside her control. The way James Callaghan and Edward Heath's press advisers handled the media looks haphazard and amateurish by today's standards. By the end of Mrs Thatcher's period in office, Number 10 had no choice but to become far more professional in its dealings with journalists. Harold Wilson kept an eye on all the main political news partly because he was able to do so. In 1979 the press office had only to monitor a dozen or so national and major regional newspapers, the *Today* programme in the morning and news bulletins on BBC television, ITV and Radio 4, at lunchtime, early evening and at the end of the day. Within a few years there would be many more calls on their attention. *Newsnight* was first broadcast on BBC2 on 23 January 1982. Channel Four went on air in November. BBC breakfast television started a year later. Rupert Murdoch's Sky News was launched in 1989, broadcasting twenty-four hours a day. The introduction of electronic news-gathering – video in place of film and satellite trucks able to transmit live from almost any-where – transformed the speed and appearance of broadcast news during the course of the eighties. By November 1990, when Mrs Thatcher was forced from power, no one individual, whether an obses-sive prime minister or even an overworked press secretary, could keep track of all the political news by themselves. Increasingly the public could see and hear it as it happened. Politicians had to adjust to the fact that they couldn't emerge from a door or appear on a platform with-out the possibility of it appearing live on air.

Changes in technology were transforming the economics of news-paper production, too. A new national tabloid, *Today*, hit the streets in March 1986, although it lasted less than a decade. In October the same year, the *Independent* was launched as a broadsheet with high ambitions to restore the reputation of serious journalism. The move of the News International titles to a new high-tech plant in Wapping, east London, led to a year-long industrial dispute that ended only in February 1987. Even before these changes Britain had enjoyed, if that is the right word, more national news outlets than any comparable nation. There were now many more pages and many more hours of broadcasting time to fill. And compared to almost every other form of news, pol-itics stories are inexpensive and plentiful. Only the *Sunday Sport*, also launched in 1986, found a cheaper alternative. It just made them up. 'World War Two Bomber Found On The Moon' and 'Space Aliens Turned My Son Into An Olive' were among its classic headlines.

Downing Street could ignore the *Sport* but not the rest and the demands on the press office grew commensurately. In the process the press secretary – his title had not yet caught up with the technological changes – became a much more significant figure in Whitehall, and so too in the history recounted here. Political communications were transformed for all parties, whether in government or opposition. And as they became more professional, and more proactive, the men and women employed to keep up with the appetite of the media became a bigger part in the lives of every political journalist. The process by which politicians communicated with the public through the media became news in itself. The phrase 'spin doctor' first appeared in print during the American presidential election of 1984. 'Spin' and those who practise it have been a journalistic obsession on both sides of the Atlantic ever since.

Mrs Thatcher made sure that her friends in the media, notably Rupert Murdoch, were able to capitalise on the new technologies available as much as possible. And she was always ready to help meet the demand for pictures and dramatic headlines if she could. No previous prime minister had made such good use of the opportunities inherent in the job for making news and shaping it. She did so despite having little real interest in journalism *per se*. In this respect, at least, she resembled Edward Heath, the man who would spend the Thatcher years playing the 'Incredible Sulk' and trying to distance himself from just about everything she stood for. Both were driven by policy not presentation. Thatcher, however, recognised that good presentation was necessary to help get public support for the policies she wanted to implement. For her it was simply part of the job to employ the latest techniques of professional communications to ensure she was presented as sympathetically as possible to the voters. As a woman she had fewer inhibitions than any of her predecessors, certainly since Macmillan, about using some cosmetic techniques to achieve that. But, so far as she was concerned, the less she had to concern herself with that directly the better.

Mrs Thatcher was remarkably relaxed even about who should do it for her. Before the election she had offered the job of press secretary to the former *Daily Mail* political editor Anthony Shrimsley, then assistant editor of the *Sun*, but he had turned it down, preferring to stay in Fleet Street. So for the first few months she brought back Henry James, whose Downing Street career had been as long as the novels of his namesake. Having worked for Sir Alec Douglas-Home as well as Harold Wilson and Edward Heath, he was invited to return from the private sector in 1979 on a short-term contract as a safe pair of hands. At the same time Angus Maude, whose speech about 'Labour's Dirty Dozen' had inspired the *Daily Mail*'s pre-election headline, was given responsibility for coordinating government information as paymaster-general. Neither was a very happy appointment. Maude set about trying to bring some discipline to the release of announcements and ministerial statements. He saw nothing whatever wrong with news management, which 'when it means representing the facts in a way that reflects most favourably on the government, is a perfectly fair process and it's one which has been undertaken by all governments since the beginning of time'.[2] And, like most people in his position, he counted burying bad news under the simultaneous announcement of good news as a legitimate part of that process. Unfortunately for Maude, Mrs Thatcher's first cabinet was neither in tune nor in harmony so any attempt to get them to sing from the same hymn sheet was doomed to failure. He wasn't even a true believer himself. He left the government in 1981, an early victim of the tension between Mrs Thatcher and the 'wets', those ministers she suspected of being too wedded to the consensus politics of the past.

Henry James left even sooner, as soon as his six-month contract was up. According to the man who took his place, James 'could not bear the thought of leaving Number 10' and clung on to the bitter end.[3] Thatcher hadn't really taken to him and yet she still seems to have given scant thought to whom she did want in a position that involved such a close working relationship with her personally. She had heard good things about a civil servant by the name of Bernard Ingham, a former *Guardian* journalist who had been a highly rated information officer for many years before taking charge of the conservation section

at the Department of Energy. She decided he was the right man after
the briefest of meetings during a tour of government offices. When he
was called into Downing Street for what he thought was an interview,
he was surprised to discover that she assumed he'd already been offered
the job and had accepted it.

If no prime minister made more effective use of the media than
Margaret Thatcher, then no press secretary served his employer better
than Bernard Ingham. He was the first holder of that post that I knew
personally, just as she was the first serving prime minister that I interviewed. Had either of them bothered to take much notice of this
junior member of the lobby they would have found little to recommend him. When Mrs Thatcher was first elected I was at Oxford, a
university that would later refuse her an honorary degree. As editor of
the student paper I had urged my fellow undergraduates to vote against
her. Now I worked for the BBC, an institution she considered riddled
with closet lefties just like me. Long after she was forced from office
I would go on to work inside Downing Street for Tony Blair, a man
Ingham believes reduced the post of prime minister to nothing more
than government by manipulation of the media and public opinion.
He and I have had our run-ins and he once refused to have anything
to do with me ever again, although he eventually relented. If we have
little else in common we can at least agree on this point, that he was
the most successful press secretary of any covered in this book.

During the time that he occupied the bow-fronted office that looks
out over Downing Street itself Ingham was a highly controversial
figure. He may not have been the first press secretary to become 'part
of the story', a dubious honour that goes to Joe Haines, but Ingham
was the first to be the focus of persistent comment and criticism from
parts of the media, the political opposition at Westminster and even
members of the cabinet, all of whom thought he was going beyond the
proper limits of his job description. He was the first to be a big enough
figure to warrant a biography, *Good and Faithful Servant* by Robert
Harris. He didn't entirely welcome all the attention. Some was
inevitable thanks to the increased importance of the role he filled. His
larger-than-life appearance and character were also a factor. He was a
big, ruddy-faced Yorkshireman with untamed eyebrows who could

Herbert Asquith 'Squiffy', His last year as PM, 1916 (*Left*)

David Lloyd George 'The Welsh Wizard', 1916–22 (*Right*)

Andrew Bonar Law 'The Unknown Prime Minister', Inside Downing Street, 1922 (*Left*)

Stanley Baldwin 'Power Without Responsibility', Outside Downing Street, October 1926 (*Right*)

Ramsay MacDonald 'Moss Bros socialism', Re-elected PM, October 1931 (*Left*)

Neville Chamberlain 'Peace in Our Time', Heston aerodrome, London, 30 September 1938 (*Right*)

Lord Northcliffe compared himself to Napoleon and thought
nothing of dictating to mere prime ministers like Lloyd George.
The Passing Show, 5 January 1918

'The price of petrol has been increased by one penny – Official'.
4 March 1942. The cartoon that led Churchill to threaten the *Daily Mirror*
with closure

(Left)
Winston Churchill
'Never Surrender',
In RAF uniform,
1948

(Right)
Clement Attlee
'Clam', Reluctant
communicator, 1945

Sir Anthony Eden
'The best PM we've got', On
becoming PM, 7 April 1955

Harold Macmillan
'The great actor manager' meets Nikita Kruschev,
Moscow, 22 February 1959

Sir Alec Douglas-Home
'Iron painted to look like wood',
12 August 1964

Harold Wilson
'Journalist manqué', Scilly Isles,
10 August 1965

Clement Attlee and Winston Churchill claimed to want a clean fight. Outside the ring
Ernest Bevin, Lord Beaverbrook and Brendan Bracken were accused of taking the
gloves off. Public opinion didn't approve. *Daily Mail*, 14 June 1945

Victor 'Vicky' Weisz
intended to portray
Macmillan as a stunt
merchant but the
prime minister
turned 'Supermac' to
his advantage.
Evening Standard,
6 November 1958

Edward Heath
'Bugger them all – I won!'
Polling day, 18 June 1970

James Callaghan
'Crisis, What Crisis?' 10 January 1979

Margaret Thatcher
'You turn if you want to', On manoeuvres,
17 September 1986

John Major
'Back me or sack me',
Resigns as Tory leader,
22 June 1995

Tony Blair
With Catherine Tate, 'Am I bovvered?'
Comic Relief video, 16 March 2007

Gordon Brown
'YouTube if you want to', 21 April 2009

Harold Wilson as Don Quixote tilting at windmills in the media. *Daily Telegraph*, 22 May 1969

Margaret Thatcher and the 'vegetables'. Her *Spitting Image* puppet did her real image no harm. 5 June 1989

Steve Bell's addition of external underpants did nothing to propel John Major to victory. *Guardian*, 4 February 1997

Lord Northcliffe

C.P. Scott

Lord Beaverbrook

Cecil King

Rupert Murdoch

Tony Blair was accused of dancing to the tune of
Rupert Murdoch and his business interests. *Sunday Telegraph*,
29 March 1998

Gordon Brown and Peter
Mandelson, spin doctor
turned political life saver.
Sunday Times, 14 June 2009

easily have been cast in a Dickensian costume drama. And then, of course, there was what he said and did. The common complaint of all his critics was that he was too close to the mistress of the house and too ready to do her bidding. It is often said of ministers that when they get their feet under the desk in their departments they 'go native' and start thinking and behaving more like civil servants than politicians. With Ingham the opposite was true. As the 1980s went on he became less and less the civil servant and more and more a member of Mrs Thatcher's personal court. It is hardly surprising that in doing so he increasingly took on her political views and sympathised with her policy objectives. When he was pressed some of both would come out, but the occasions on which he flagrantly overstepped the mark for a civil servant were fewer and further between than his enemies maintained. Cabinet ministers, from Francis Pym on the left to Nigel Lawson on the right, had good grounds for complaint, as we shall see. Journalists, on the other hand, had more reason to be grateful to him than resentful. Even when he was undermining members of the government his off-the-record briefings were an accurate reflection of the prime-ministerial mind.

The occasion that led to our temporary estrangement is a case in point. In March 1989, along with my colleague Martin Dowle, I took him to lunch at his favourite restaurant, Beotys in St Martin's Lane. Towards the end of the meal, when conversation started to flag a little, I searched around for something to ask him and mentioned a story that had been running for a few days but seemed to be petering out. Who, I wondered, had Mrs Thatcher been referring to when she said that the privatisation of the water industry had been 'badly handled'? He volunteered the name of Michael Howard, then the middle-ranking environment minister responsible for the policy. He said he had no doubt Howard was a good barrister but his political skills were lacking. With, I fear, undue haste and enthusiasm, we made a big story out of his remarks. It was the lead story on the *Six o'Clock News*. Howard went into overdrive to defend himself and Ingham denied having briefed against him. In his memoirs Ingham says he was 'stitched up' and that our story 'had no foundation whatsoever in fact'[4]. In other words two BBC correspondents had lied on air about what they had been told by a man upon whose professional services they depended. We may have been stupid but we weren't that stupid. Perhaps Ingham's recollection of the lunch was not as good as he thought. Either that or he thought he could remember what he said better than whom he said it to. The first edition of his book named somebody else in my place as having impugned his integrity. Years later a book by another of Mrs Thatcher's ministers, Norman Fowler, confirmed what Ingham had told us, that she had 'underestimated Howard and saw him more as a skilled barrister'.[5] He had accurately reflected her views over our lunch, however angry he might have been to see those views broadcast so openly to the nation.

Robert Harris, who attended Ingham's briefings for a while as political editor of the *Observer*, thought he spent his time 'trying to reconcile the objectivity of Trevor Lloyd-Hughes with the partisan style of Joe Haines'[6] but that he came unacceptably close to the latter for a civil servant. 'It was often impossible, in this torrent of Yorkshire grit, to work out which were Ingham's opinions and which were Mrs Thatcher's.'[7] That was undoubtedly the case but none of us felt we were being misled. On his retirement the *Sun*'s Trevor Kavanagh, then chairman of the lobby, spoke for the overwhelming majority when he said 'very few of us recognise the . . . manipulative character portrayed by Robert Harris . . . I believe it is important to understand that Mr Ingham's first duty was towards the prime minister and not the media . . . But I believe I speak for my colleagues when I say he was unfailingly straight, honest and fair.'[8] Mrs Thatcher's judgement was succinct: 'He's the greatest.'[9] Edward Heath, by contrast, believed her government used 'the press office in Number 10 in a way that can be described as corrupt'.[10] That surely went too far. Harris got it right, however, when he observed that: 'Between them, Margaret Thatcher and Bernard Ingham were to use the Downing Street press office in a way that her predecessors – even men as astute and manipulative as Neville Chamberlain and Harold Wilson – would never have dared attempt.'[11]

Chamberlain, as we have seen, found many allies in Fleet Street willing to work with him to promote a specific policy, appeasement, having persuaded them there was no alternative. Margaret Thatcher found allies willing to support her overall political stance for a much longer period. A year after becoming prime minister she told the Conservative women's conference, 'There's no easy popularity in what we are proposing, but it is fundamentally sound. Yet I believe people accept that there is no real alternative.'[12] For the best part of a decade the majority of newspaper proprietors and editors agreed. The level of distortion and deliberate misinformation by the press was arguably greater and certainly more sustained than in the late 1930s. Nobody had to be coerced into it or lied to; they did it entirely voluntarily although many would be richly rewarded. When one of her ministers commented on what a good press she was getting she replied, 'That's because I've been so kind to them.'[13]

The clatter of honours falling on the shoulders of newspaper editors could be heard shortly after her arrival at Number 10. Sir Larry Lamb became the first tabloid knight in 1980 and similar rewards soon went the way of the editors of both the *Daily* and *Sunday Express*, the *Financial Times* and, of course, the *Daily Mail*. Proprietors tended to get peerages, although Rupert Murdoch, now an American citizen, wasn't eligible. She might have won over the men at the top, but not all rank-and-file journalists were impressed with the direction their profession was taking. Not long after Mrs Thatcher won her first majority an unprecedented revolt took place at the *Daily Mail*. With the 'Labour's Dirty Dozen' headline still fresh in everybody's mind, members of the National Union of Journalists overwhelmingly passed a motion condemning the paper's biased coverage of the campaign.[14] If they hoped to discourage anything similar from appearing in the future they were to be disappointed. The *Mail's* editor, David English, dismissed any attempt to interfere in his power as 'unacceptable'. He wasn't alone in asserting the right to use his paper to defend Mrs Thatcher and all that she stood for. The *Express* titles were now owned by Victor (soon to be Lord) Matthews. He was already the largest individual donor to the Conservative party, and the papers were even more reliably Tory than they had been under Lord Beaverbrook. Matthews also owned a Labour-leaning downmarket newcomer to Fleet Street, the *Daily Star*, although he said he would never have it in his house.[15] The *Star* even went so far as to back Michael Foot for the leadership of the Labour party after James Callaghan's resignation. The Conservatives were not content to see even this chink in their tabloid armour if they could help it. According to Sir Jocelyn Stevens, who was then the Express Group's managing director, the prime minister made a personal appeal to Matthews after which he decreed that the *Star* must stop attacking her.[16] The *Sun* had no such crisis of identity and continued its rapid lurch to the right, although it would have to await the arrival of a new editor, Kelvin MacKenzie, in 1981 before it descended into the depths of vulgarity and crude political bias with which it became synonymous. Among the tabloids, only the *Mirror* retained its traditional role as a whole-hearted and no less partisan supporter of the Labour party. At the other end of the market, what MacKenzie liked to call the 'unpopulars', support for Mrs Thatcher was more measured but scarcely less potent. Bernard Ingham, who shared MacKenzie's views about which papers mattered most, had little enough to worry about. The *Guardian* never fell for her charms but the mass-circulation *Daily Telegraph* and, after an initial hiccup, *The Times*, more than made up for any lingering liberal sentiments elsewhere.

The government may have enjoyed a solid base of editorial support among the national papers but that didn't mean the journalists working for them were content to churn out propaganda for a decade. Comment infected the news pages too frequently, but correspondents continued to search out stories that Downing Street wouldn't like, many of them provided over lunch and in other private discussions by ministers themselves. There was always more than enough to provoke the ire of Bernard Ingham on a daily basis and, almost as frequently, earn his trademark putdown of 'bunkum and balderdash'. Before long he would start to take pleasure in lecturing the media in more detail on their many failings. Ingham was given to military metaphors – his memoirs were entitled *Kill the Messenger* – and he believed in going into battle well armed. 'I sometimes compare press officers to riflemen on the Somme – mowing down wave upon wave of distortion, taking out rank upon rank of supposition, deduction and gossip,' he told them.[17]

Margaret Thatcher thought journalism 'the haunt of the brittle, the cynical and the unreliable'[18]. Although she was a regular listener to the

BBC's *Today* programme, Ingham found that 'she was quite simply not interested in the press, radio and television unless she came to feel that the government's message was not getting over. It was not that she pretended not to read newspapers; she did not read them at all, except the front page of the *Evening Standard*.'[19] She might flick through the weekend papers while at Chequers, but otherwise she relied almost entirely on the press summary, an innovation that Henry James had started for her benefit but on which Ingham was to stamp his own very personal style.[20] Ostensibly a brief written report of the main political news, this document came to be seen as part of Ingham's Rasputin-like influence over his boss. Nigel Lawson, a former journalist who went on to become chancellor, claimed that the press summary had 'a selection and a slant that was very much his own. It would usually start with the *Sun*, the paper he himself was closest to and which he had taught Margaret represented the true views of the man in the street.' A dangerous circularity was thus produced. 'Margaret would sound off about something, Ingham would then translate the line into *Sun*-ese and feed it to that newspaper, which would normally use it. This would then take pride of place in the news summary he provided for Margaret, who marvelled at the unique rapport she evidently enjoyed with the British people.'[21]

Early in her premiership, however, the press summary contained plenty to concern her. She was right to tell the Tory women that her approach didn't bring 'easy popularity'. The Tory manifesto had not been a particularly radical document and, while her campaign rhetoric had been all about changing Britain before its greatness became 'a footnote in the history books', few people were prepared for the initial shock brought about by her economic policies. Income tax was cut but VAT went up dramatically to compensate. At the same time she started looking for ways to reduce public spending as a share of national income and, with it, the size and scope of the state itself. She did her best to make a virtue of the fact that there would be a lot of economic pain before anybody saw the gains she was convinced would follow. As if to prove her point inflation, interest rates and unemployment all rose quickly. The steelworkers went on strike and after sixteen weeks secured a 16 per cent increase. Round one had gone to the trade-union movement. The 'wets' in the cabinet became increasingly restless and talkative with journalists, and the press was full of stories about the divisions in Mrs Thatcher's own ranks, hence her assertion of the TINA principle – 'there is no alternative' – which Hugo Young called 'a famous acronym that became a beautiful propaganda weapon'[22].

Political propaganda was properly the responsibility of Conservative Central Office not the Downing Street press team and Ingham knew the limits to his role very well. 'I considered myself bound, as my predecessors had been, by the civil service rules, which required us to maintain political impartiality, never to lie or mislead or indulge in favouritism in the dissemination of news, to respect confidences and parliamentary privilege and to observe a backroom role, avoiding becoming the story.'[23] Even the clearest of rules allow for some interpretation, however, and Ingham certainly wasn't impartial when it came to any conflict between the prime minister's interests and those of members of her cabinet with barely concealed doubts about where she was heading. Jim Prior, the employment secretary and a leading 'wet', saw Ingham's hand at work in undermining the doubters soon after his appointment when: 'Margaret developed a technique of getting the right wing popular press to have a major lead story on some matter coming up for decision in cabinet that morning. The headline would be along the lines of "Battling Maggie Under Attack From Wets". The issue would then be unfolded in terms of being pro- or anti-Maggie.'[24] Often the coverage would be downright misleading. 'In October 1980, at the time of the cabinet discussion on public spending, the *Sun* proclaimed: "Premier Margaret Thatcher routed the 'wets' in her cabinet in a major showdown . . ." This was not what had happened.' Prior was not alone in having few doubts about where the paper had got its inspiration.

That same October the prime minister scored a major propaganda coup at the Conservative party conference in Brighton. Using words written for her by the playwright Ronald Millar, who had worked previously for Ted Heath, she not so subtly recalled the way her predecessor had buckled under pressure, as she saw it, and declined to go down the same road. 'To those waiting with bated breath for that favourite media catchphrase, the "U" turn, I have only one thing to say. "You turn if you want to. The lady's not for turning."[25] It was made for the headlines and almost every news bulletin and national newspaper obliged by leading with it.

Whatever reservations Thatcher may have had about Heath's policy shifts she made little complaint while serving in his government and certainly no evidence of any unease on her part made its way into the newspapers. Heath had a remarkably leak-free cabinet, but the same could not be said for Mrs Thatcher's. She decided she had no choice but to assert her authority. In January 1981 Norman St John-Stevas, an arch (in more than one sense of the word) 'wet', became the first minister to lose his job specifically for talking to the press. According to the *Daily Telegraph*, 'sources close to the prime minister' had revealed that St John-Stevas had gone because of 'concern about open and at times inaccurate portrayals in the press of what had been going on in government'.[26] On the same day as Ingham was speaking off the record, Mrs Thatcher came close to saying much the same in public. So while this was the first example of one of her senior colleagues being briefed against personally by Downing Street, on this occasion at least Ingham could claim political cover for his remarks. Mrs Thatcher accepted her responsibility and even felt moved to apologise subsequently to her now ex-minister, a rare event in itself. She had told Judith Chalmers on Thames TV's *Afternoon Plus*, 'Leaks there have been, yes. This shouldn't happen, because . . . it doesn't make for efficient cabinet government if you feel that anything you say might be repeated outside. It should not happen, it shouldn't happen in any government. I hope it will happen less and less, I think people are very much aware of the damage that it's done.'[27]

Margaret Thatcher was now engaged in a deliberate campaign through the media to improve her public image. It had two seemingly contradictory aims: to convince people that she was a strong leader, very much in charge of her government, but also a warmer, more caring person than they might have thought. Before the election, with the help of Gordon Reece at Central Office, Tim Bell at the advertising agency Saatchis and a voice tutor at the National Theatre she had worked hard on both her appearance and her delivery. She now tried to put what she had learned to good effect by going on the softer kind of programmes that prime ministers had traditionally avoided. *Afternoon Plus* was only the beginning. In June of the same year, in an extraordinarily frank interview with Angela Rippon for the BBC, she talked about having made her hair look less fussy and about trying to sound less shrill. 'What you learn is: bring it down, bring it down. You have to think for the first time in your life not only about the impression that you make in the flesh but what it is going to look like on the news on television.'[28] She wasn't the first prime minister to think about such things. Harold Wilson had puffed on his pipe when the cameras were on him, although he preferred cigars in private. What was different about Margaret Thatcher was the sheer professionalism of her efforts to improve her image. She had no patience at all for anything she considered trivial or time-wasting. Good presentation, of herself and through herself of the government, on the other hand, was an essential part of the job and she took it very seriously. In other areas she was absolutely certain she had all the answers, but when it came to presentation she was willing to look, listen and learn. Tim Bell found her approach refreshingly realistic: 'The Tories were good clients in the beginning because they let the professionals get on with it . . . Mrs Thatcher took the view that communication was important . . . She has got past the stage of whether it should or shouldn't happen. The fact is it does.'[29] Gordon Reece went further. Although he acknowledged that 'she's responsible for her own image' he admitted that 'Mrs Thatcher is being wrapped like a commodity . . . When this job is over I suppose I will go back to my own business. I will have produced the product I set out to produce.'[30] The job would not be over for a long time. Reece continued to offer advice right to the end and was with Mrs Thatcher in her last days as prime minister.

Internationally as well as domestically this was the start of the age of the professionally packaged political leader. In February 1981 Mrs Thatcher was the first foreign head of government to meet the newly elected President of the United States at the White House. In the years to come she and Ronald Reagan would enjoy a formidable bond of trust and friendship. She admired his gut political instincts and his remarkable ability to convey them in a language everybody could understand. Not for nothing was he called 'the great communicator'.

During the visit she had a chance to exhibit her own talent for reducing dry economic arguments to the bread-and-butter language of household budgets. The American media pointed to the appalling levels of joblessness and bankruptcies in Britain and asked if they weren't evidence of an economic failure that could yet prove terminal. Her response was to say 'that news of a requiem for my policies was premature. There was always a period during an illness when the medicine was more unpleasant than the disease, but you should not stop taking the medicine.'[31]

Back in Britain there were still plenty of people who thought the cure was worse than the disease. Michael Foot's Labour party offered a stark alternative, although not one that earned much support in the press. Then in the spring of 1981 a new remedy became available, one that many appeared to find extremely palatable. On 26 March, the Social Democratic Party, led by former Labour ministers Roy Jenkins, David Owen, Shirley Williams and Bill Rodgers, had a glitzy launch that proved the Tories didn't have a monopoly in effective presentation. Almost five hundred journalists packed into the baroque-style Grand Hall at the Connaught Rooms in London. I was then a BBC news trainee and joined the throng. Like most of those present, I had never seen such razzmatazz at a British political event. It was a made-for-television occasion complete with girls in blazers and red-white-and-blue rosettes and a compere to introduce the leading players. The SDP soon chalked up some dramatic by-election results and continued to be something of a media sensation. The *Guardian* became known as the SDP house journal and a number of its leading columnists, including Polly Toynbee and her husband, the late Peter Jenkins, were closely identified with the party. The very fact that the Social Democrats appealed most to *Guardian*-reading liberals made the Tory tabloids wary but the opinion polls in all the papers recorded leads so huge as to suggest the SDP could go from nowhere to forming the next government. Margaret Thatcher's view of the kind of politics espoused by the new centre party was characteristically dismissive: 'Standing in the middle of the road is very dangerous; you get knocked down by traffic from both sides.' She declared that she had no intention of changing her policies just for the sake of popularity. The political world would undergo another dramatic change before she would have to appeal for the support of the electorate at the next general election. By then the SDP had turned out to be less of a juggernaut capable of flattening the Tories than a very useful vehicle for splitting the opposition.

The emergence of the SDP was part of the background to a clash that would produce a high-profile casualty not in politics but in the world of journalism. What happened at *The Times* was highly significant for the future balance of power between Downing Street and the media, and the consequences are still being felt. On 22 January 1981 Rupert Murdoch appeared at a press conference to announce that he was taking over both *The Times* and the *Sunday Times*. As Roy Greenslade says in his history of the press, the news created 'a greater concentration of national paper ownership than had previously existed, arguably greater than Northcliffe's. Any impartial reading of the 1973 Fair Trading Act suggested that Murdoch's takeover must be referred to the Monopolies and Mergers Commission.'[32] It was not. The government intervened to protect Murdoch's interests, something that was to become a habit under both the Conservatives and Labour. The trade secretary, John Biffen, used his powers to exempt those businesses that were deemed to be 'uneconomic'. He insisted he had come under no pressure from Downing Street to reach such a conclusion, an assertion that was greeted with widespread incredulity in parliament and in those parts of Fleet Street that Murdoch didn't already control. Suspicions of a political fix were later confirmed by Woodrow Wyatt, a newspaper columnist who was personally close to Mrs Thatcher and frequently acted as a go-between with Rupert Murdoch. In his journals he revealed that 'she stopped the *Times* acquisition being referred to the Monopolies Commission though the *Sunday Times* was not really losing money and the pair together were not'.[33] A member of the cabinet at the time, Lord Prior, confirmed to a less adoring journalist, Bruce Page, that it was 'a political decision, cynically made to supplement the government's press support'.[34] From that moment on Murdoch knew he was in Mrs Thatcher's debt. He would prove more than ready to repay it when the going got tough.

Even the prime minister couldn't give her supporters in the media a completely free rein. Rupert Murdoch had to sign unprecedented guarantees as part of the takeover process, including a promise not to interfere in the editorial independence of either paper. They were enough to persuade a wary Harold Evans to swap the editor's chair at the *Sunday Times*, where he had been a legendary success, for that at *The Times*. Evans had no illusions about the new proprietor: 'Murdoch's wish that *The Times* should be valiant for Thatcher in Britain and stalwart for Reagan in the United States had been obvious from the start of my editorship.'[35]

Evans had no intention of allowing the paper to become a paid-up member of anybody's fan club, as Downing Street soon discovered. That September he received a gold-embossed invitation to Number 10 for a dinner in honour of President Mitterrand and was seated at the prime minister's table. A week later *The Times* carried a front-page story detailing how Denis Thatcher had written a letter to the environment secretary on Downing Street notepaper asking for a planning appeal in which he had an interest to be accelerated. By chance Evans and Murdoch were having dinner with Woodrow Wyatt when the first edition containing the story was delivered. Murdoch 'looked miserable and said nothing' when he saw the front page.[36] Ingham did his best to dismiss the story on the grounds that anybody could write to ministers from their home address and Mr Thatcher's home address was 10 Downing Street. There would be plenty more stories in the months ahead to show that so long as Evans was in charge *The Times* was going to assert its independence. Lengthy features highlighted the misery of unemployment and linked it to the inner-city riots that had broken out that summer. In October, after the SDP won another by-election in Croydon, Murdoch was appalled to see a front-page comment piece by Shirley Williams attacking the government. He accused Evans of 'lacking all political conviction', a view shared by the prime minister[37], and relations between the two men never recovered.

Evans didn't get the chance to decide whether to endorse the SDP at a general election. In March 1982 Murdoch called him into his office and demanded his resignation. *The Times*'s flirtation with the Social Democrats wasn't the only reason. There had been long-running arguments over the paper's finances and poor staff morale. Murdoch has always been a businessman first and a political player a distant second, but now his business interests and his political instincts coincided neatly and both required Evans to go. Under the terms of his purchase Murdoch had no right to sack him and Evans considered taking a defiant public stand. In the end he concluded he would be unable to do the job the way he wanted to even if he won and reluctantly agreed to resign. His successor, Charles Douglas-Home, returned the paper to the Tory fold, as might have been expected of the nephew of the former prime minister. He was quite comfortable doing his boss's bidding and later described Murdoch as 'one of the main powers behind the Thatcher throne', adding that 'Rupert and Mrs Thatcher consult regularly on every important matter of policy'.[38]

Bernard Ingham seems to have played little part in these manoeuvrings. It was better for all concerned if somebody outside the confines of Downing Street was used to look after Mrs Thatcher's interests in a less official capacity. Woodrow Wyatt, who had lengthy conversations with her by telephone most weekends and who knew the big beasts of Fleet Street far better than Ingham, was more than happy to oblige. Until Wyatt's journals were published after his death in 1997 few people were aware just how closely involved he had been, and even then some thought that he exaggerated his influence. Ingham wasn't suited to the kind of wining and dining that accompanied Wyatt's lobbying on Mrs Thatcher's behalf. Millionaire businessmen were not his cup of tea. In any case he had more than enough to do dealing with the journalists who actually wrote the news, although he too preferred to do much of his work under a cloak of secrecy or, to be more accurate, anonymity. Another man who seemed dangerously close to sympathising with the SDP was in Mrs Thatcher's sights and this time 'sources close to the prime minister' were used to fire a warning shot.

Francis Pym, the leader of the House of Commons, was one of the wettest of the wets in the cabinet and among those least convinced that there was no alternative to the painful economic medicine being administered. His offence was to be honest with the public, saying in a speech that they should not expect 'an early return to full or nearly full employment, or an early improvement in living standards generally'.[39] Given what he really thought, Pym probably regarded his comments as admirably restrained. Mrs Thatcher praised it as 'an excellent speech'[40] when challenged about it in the Commons but privately she was furious. By now the official line was that the signs of recovery were starting to be seen. So within minutes of her sitting down after prime minister's questions, Ingham was telling the lobby unattributably that Pym was like the wartime radio character Mrs Mopp with her catchline 'It's being so cheerful as keeps me going'. He got it wrong (the character was Mona Lott), but it wasn't his memory for radio shows that mattered. 'Never before,' said Robert Harris, 'had the government's official spokesman, a civil servant, deliberately disparaged a minister for speaking what he saw as the truth – and done it, moreover, to the entire lobby only moments after the prime minister had given an entirely different version of events.'[41] It was the earliest example of a habit that Nigel Lawson later described from bitter experience. Mrs Thatcher, he said, 'could let off steam in private in a thoroughly indiscreet and intemperate way going far beyond the rather attractive outspokenness that marked her utterances in public. Ingham frequently failed to discern the distinction, and relayed to a wide audience sentiments that should never have been given a public airing.'[42] In his own memoirs Ingham made no attempt to justify what he'd done. 'I should not have made such remarks and I wish I never had. But I did.'[43] Although he was right to add that he wasn't exactly misleading anybody, as what he'd said 'was all the more offensive for being accurate'.

Pym was a marked man so far as Thatcher was concerned, but far from sacking him within a few weeks she would give him one of the three great offices of state. Not because she wanted to but because, in the circumstances, she had little choice. On 5 April 1982 Lord Carrington resigned as foreign secretary after Argentinian forces invaded the Falkland Islands. Thatcher chose Pym to replace him because he had foreign-affairs experience and would be 'just right in a crisis'[44], although his vigorous pursuit of a diplomatic solution, which was nothing less than what his job required, meant she later came to regret appointing him.

The military campaign to retake the islands was the defining moment of the Thatcher premiership. It strengthened immeasurably her position and her image both at home and across the world. She would invoke the 'Falklands spirit' for the rest of her time in Downing Street and exploit the political windfall for all it was worth, although that is not to take away from her the credit for winning a war that many, including Francis Pym, thought unwinnable. The press and television pictures from the conflict would prove invaluable to her later, but at the outset she was more concerned about the need for effective propaganda as a means to victory. She made the Conservative party chairman, Cecil Parkinson, a member of the war cabinet because of his skills as a communicator. She then left him and Bernard Ingham to get on with it and took little or no day-to-day interest in what was being written or broadcast. She would deliver the occasional reprimand to journalists, most famously her insistence that they should 'Rejoice!'[45] at the news of the first British victory, and generally treated them as an irritant more than anything else.

As ever at times of war, the relationship between the government and the broadcasters came under strain, with the BBC once again bearing the brunt of attacks for its alleged lack of patriotism. Yet there were as many battles over presentation within Whitehall, notably between Downing Street and the Ministry of Defence, as there were between the government and the media. The Falklands conflict showed in microcosm how the laws of supply and demand work to the advantage of Downing Street. For once, and it will probably never happen again, the government even had the mechanics of news-gathering under its own control. Test-tube conditions don't always reflect what happens under more normal circumstances but they do help us strip away extraneous factors and see how elements react. As the task force set sail with its small band of select journalists on board, none of them with independent access to the outside world, it was the start of an experiment the media would hope never to repeat.

Bernard Ingham had to fight hard to get the Ministry of Defence to accept that journalists should be allowed to travel with the fleet at all, and then harder still to get enough places to accommodate most British news organisations. It wasn't the last of his battles with the department. He thought its head, Sir Frank Cooper, was 'barmy'[46] to suspend background briefings for the duration of the hostilities. Ingham himself continued to give off-the-record guidance to those journalists covering the conflict from London because he thought it was the best way to influence what they wrote. Those on board the task force were subject to official censorship of every story they filed as well as restrictions over which pictures were released and when. Michael Nicholson of ITN, who was on HMS *Hermes*, had the clear impression 'that Mrs Thatcher expected us to report the "good news war". You remember how Gaumont British News used to put it: "and there goes Tommy climbing over the trenches and he's going to give the Argies another black eye" and up comes the music.' Nicholson had been told by one of the MoD press officers on board, 'you must have been told when you left you couldn't report bad news. You knew when you came you were expected to do a 1940 propaganda job.'[47]

Sir Frank Cooper left Whitehall soon after the conflict and was then free to say publicly what he had thought of Ingham's role. 'The aim now is the management of the media with a very much higher degree of central control from Number 10 Downing Street and with the connivance of part of the media,' he said. 'There is now public relations – which I would define as biased information. I suggest that the post of chief information officer at Number 10 Downing Street is in fact a political job in a party sense and is not a job which it is proper for a civil servant to fill unless he or she resigns from the civil service on appointment.'[48] Ingham said he found Sir Frank's attitude inexplicable but noted wearily that the press secretary is often 'a convenient repository for blame in the heat of battle'.[49]

The House of Commons' defence committee report into the media handling of the crisis revealed many of the tensions both within Whitehall and between the government and the media. The principal complaint from journalists was not of political bias but of excessive restrictions on their freedom to report. Some of their objections were upheld and MPs were critical of the MoD's lack of understanding of how journalists worked and the poor communications between the department and Number 10. Overall, however, it concluded that 'the government were generally successful in the information war'.[50] In its evidence, the BBC had expressed 'deep concern that the Ministry of Defence has come very close to the "management" or "manipulation" of news, an idea that is alien to the concept of communication within a free society'. Some of its journalists implied as much during the fighting. On *Newsnight*, Peter Snow observed that 'we cannot demonstrate that the British have lied to us but the Argentinians clearly have'.[51] That led to the corporation being accused of coverage that was 'totally offensive and almost treasonable' by a Tory MP. Mrs Thatcher responded by saying that from what she had been told, 'the case for our British forces is not being put over fully and effectively. I understand that there are times when it would seem that we and the Argentines are almost being treated as equal.'[52] Most of the tabloids knew whose side they were on. The *Daily Mail* said Mrs Thatcher's criticisms had been 'quite right' and the *Sun* said Peter Snow was 'among the traitors in our midst'.[53]

Never was the gulf between the two different traditions of British journalism more evident. While the BBC attempted a degree of detachment and was howled down for it, the mass-market tabloids reached levels of bad taste that had never been seen before. For the *Sun*, now under Kelvin MacKenzie, no amount of gung-ho triumphalism was ever too extreme. 'Gotcha!',[54] after the sinking of the Argentine cruiser *General Belgrano* with the loss of 323 lives, is only the most notorious example. The paper reproduced another of its headlines, 'Stick It Up Your Junta' on T-shirts for sale at £2 a time. 'Hero Bayonet Troops Kill 50' and 'Argies Blown Out Of The Sky' were just par for the course.[55] The *Private Eye* spoof headline 'Kill An Argie And Win A Metro' was all the more effective for being so close to the reality. The *Daily Mail* was more temperate in its choice of words but no less committed to victory at all costs. The opposition leader, Michael Foot, who supported the military action, sought to defend the BBC and criticised 'the hysterical bloodlust of the *Sun* and the *Daily Mail*', which he said 'brought disgrace' on British journalism. Mrs Thatcher replied that while the media were free to publish what they wished 'we are free to say what we think about them'.[56] The only ones she ever criticised publicly were those that expressed reservations about the conduct of the war. Alone among the tabloids, the *Daily Mirror* took a critical position. It launched its own assault against the *Sun* after an editorial on 7 May levelled the charge of treason against not only the BBC but the *Guardian* and the *Mirror*, too. Joe Haines wrote a leader entitled

'The Harlot of Fleet Street' which said, 'the *Sun* today is to journalism what Dr Josef Goebbels was to truth'.[57] The Falklands conflict was not Fleet Street's finest hour.

On 14 June Downing Street used its powers to impose a total blackout on all news coming out of the Falkland Islands. For nine hours journalists there could file nothing back to London. Then, in time to be carried live during *News at Ten*, Mrs Thatcher appeared at the despatch box to announce that the Argentinian forces had surrendered.[58] Whether the censorship imposed from London throughout the campaign had made any material difference to the outcome is impossible to prove but it seems unlikely. Bernard Ingham was unapologetic in any event, arguing that 'wars, if they must be fought, are there to be won'.[59] He would indulge in one more bit of news management six months later when Mrs Thatcher made an unannounced visit to the Falklands. Ingham told the lobby on the Friday that her weekend schedule said 'Chequers', which indeed it did, although she had no intention by then of sticking to it. A BBC team that was already in Port Stanley didn't take much persuasion to stay on for a few extra days, although BBC management were harder to convince that their footage of the prime minister's visit should be made available to their competitors. Ingham knew the answer to that one. He told them that no film would be leaving the islands unless they agreed.

Victory in the Falklands produced an immediate and lasting political dividend. From May 1982 until the election in June 1983 the Conservative party slipped below 40 per cent in the polls only once. At the end of 1981 the Tories had been on 23 per cent while the SDP, by now in alliance with the Liberals, had 50 per cent.[60] Pictures from the conflict would be used over and over again during the subsequent election. Preparations for the campaign were well under way by the time the prime minister paid her visit to the islands and Bernard Ingham was playing a part in them despite his status as a civil servant. He attended the 'liaison committee' that brought together Downing Street and Conservative Central Office staff responsible for coordinating presentation.[61] However careful he might have been to stay silent during overtly party-political discussions, Ingham was sailing close to the wind.

His activities were already drawing unwelcome attention to the messenger rather than the message. In January 1983 he was accused in the House of Commons of trying to manipulate coverage of the Franks Report into the events leading up to the Argentine invasion.[62] The same week *Channel Four News* broadcast a radio ham's recording of him browbeating the BBC over the film of Mrs Thatcher's visit to Port Stanley. So on 6 February he took the highly unusual step of allowing an on-the-record interview to be published in the *Sunday Telegraph* in which he insisted 'I play no part in politics.' It led to more complaints by opposition MPs, to which the leader of the House, John Biffen, had to respond. 'One would begin to imagine,' he said, 'that we have in Mr Bernard Ingham some sort of rough-spoken Yorkshire Rasputin who is manipulating government and corroding the standards of public morality.'[63] Whether deliberately or not, Biffen didn't go so far as to say the image was unfounded. John Nott, who was defence secretary during the Falklands, told *Panorama* some years later that what was needed was 'a new edition of Machiavelli's *The Prince* to explain the way the lobby has been used by Number 10 to raise the cult of personality so far as the prime minister is concerned, at the expense of colleagues who have happened to disagree at the time'.[64]

Detailed planning for the 1983 election began on 5 January with a strategy meeting at Chequers. Everything from who should type up the speeches to whether to allow a leaders' debate was on the table. On the latter Mrs Thatcher had a rare disagreement with her publicity guru, Gordon Reece, who thought she would wipe the floor with Michael Foot. Her view was that 'arguments were too important to be reduced to a sound bite or a gladiatorial sport'.[65] As they looked ahead to the election the Conservatives had every reason to be confident of success but they recognised that, while the Falklands had changed the way many people looked at the prime minister and her party, some hard political realities remained and would have to be overcome by good presentation. The conflict had distracted attention from other problems but they had not gone away. In May, when Mrs Thatcher called another Chequers gathering, unemployment rose above three million for the first time. Before the 1979 election she had predicted she would be drummed out of office if it were above a million.[66] That

the Tories could contemplate an election in 1983 against such an economic background shows just how much had changed. This time
around the image and personality of Margaret Thatcher would be an
advantage not a handicap. It was no accident of timing that, for the first
time, an ITV documentary team was allowed to film inside Downing
Street. *The Woman at Number Ten* was broadcast nine weeks before
polling day.[67] Political advertising is banned in the UK so this was in
every sense the kind of publicity money could not buy. She used the
occasion to show the cameras the portraits of British heroes that she
had ensured now hung on the walls, remarking, 'I thought of
Wellington very much during the Falklands.' She clearly intended that
people should think of the Falklands very much during the election.

The Conservatives could have sat on their hands and still won the
1983 election. The media would have done their work for them without being asked. The coverage was at times almost painful to watch,
whether you believed Michael Foot was a credible alternative prime
minister or not, and scarcely anybody did. In the Nuffield study of the
campaign, Martin Harrop observed that in most of the tabloids the
Labour leader was portrayed 'as a sad old man in the wrong place at the
wrong time'.[68] Election coverage had never been so crude or so partisan and the contamination of the news pages by overt political bias
was so severe that: 'In many cases, this amounted to a rejection of any
professional standards of journalism.' The 'heavies' took the issues more
seriously but only in the context of the challenges that would confront
the next Tory government, whose election was regarded as a foregone
conclusion. The *Observer* recommended its readers to vote Labour but
only just. Its owner, Tiny Rowland, changed his mind at the last
moment. Anthony Howard reminded the editor, Donald Trelford, that
a BBC TV crew had not only filmed the editorial meeting at which
the original decision was made but had taken a photocopy of the original leading article away with them.[69]

Mrs Thatcher successfully dominated most of the set-piece television
exchanges of the campaign. She had clearly not forgiven the BBC for
its lack of patriotism. She appeared to strip Sir Robin Day of the
knighthood she had conferred on him by calling him 'Mr Day' five
times during their interview. Then came *Nationwide* and her most

uncomfortable moment of the campaign. In a segment of the programme given over to viewers' questions, aptly entitled 'On The Spot',
Mrs Diana Gould, a teacher from Cirencester, proved better able to
take the prime minister on than any of the professionals. She repeatedly pressed Mrs Thatcher over the sinking of the *Belgrano*.[70] Why had
it been sunk when it was outside the naval exclusion zone? Mrs
Thatcher replied that it had been sailing towards the task force, only
to be reminded by Mrs Gould that it had actually been sailing away
from it. 'When it was sunk it was a danger to our ships – you do accept
that, don't you?' retorted the prime minister. 'No,' said Mrs Gould, 'I
don't.' Mrs Thatcher was furious but knew better than to vent her
anger on a grey-haired geography mistress. 'Only the BBC could ask
a British prime minister why she took action to protect *our* ships
against an enemy ship that was a danger to our boys,'[71] she said afterwards, conveniently forgetting that it hadn't been the BBC that had put
the question at all. Clearly not every invocation of the Falklands was
to be welcomed.

Away from the TV studios there was an important battle on for
second place in terms of votes and seats. Had it gone the other way it
would have turned the Liberals, along with their partners in the SDP,
into serious contenders for power for the first time since the days of
Lloyd George. Labour won a victory of sorts merely by surviving as
runners-up. The only other question to be resolved was how big Mrs
Thatcher's majority would be. If the name of Francis Pym had ever
been pencilled in against a cabinet post in Thatcher's second term,
which seems improbable, then it was swiftly erased after he told the
audience on the BBC's *Question Time* that 'landslides don't on the
whole produce successful governments'.[72] The following day Mrs
Thatcher told a press conference, 'I think I could handle a landslide
majority all right.' On 9 June she was given the chance to try when her
party was re-elected with a majority of 144.

The administration elected in 1979 had been a Conservative government backed decisively but not uncritically by the Tory press. The
administration returned in 1983 was a Thatcher government sustained
enthusiastically by the larger and more reliable Thatcher press. The
appointment of Andrew Neil as editor of the *Sunday Times* a few days

after the result made it larger still. He told Rupert Murdoch the paper should become 'the champion of a market-led revolution that would shake the British establishment to its knees'. While Neil didn't object to being identified as being on the radical right he noted that 'Rupert was well to the right of me'.[73] Mrs Thatcher hadn't needed the support of News International to win but she would be immensely grateful for it as she embarked on a truly Thatcherite agenda for the first time, confronting the trade unions, privatising public assets (or, as Harold Macmillan put it, 'selling off the family silver') and extending home ownership. When she was at her most vulnerable Rupert Murdoch didn't let her down. They were in it together as 'the Thatcherite revolution and the Murdoch revolution strode hand in hand across the decade'.[74] Murdoch had the briefest of doubts only once, at the end of 1983, when she failed to give wholehearted support to President Reagan's invasion of the Caribbean island of Grenada. 'She has gone out of her mind,' he told the *Melbourne Age*.[75]

The following year he gave her unstinting support as she squared up for her biggest battle with the unions. The year-long miners' strike, which started in January, was more than a dispute over the future of one industry. Newspaper proprietors and editors had been engaged in sporadic battles with the trade unions themselves for most of the twentieth century. Murdoch was not alone in recognising that the government's success was very much in their interests, too. More than once during the miners' strike the print unions sought to use their own industrial muscle. In May, they refused to print a *Sun* front-page picture of Arthur Scargill giving what looked like a Nazi salute under the headline 'Mine Führer'.[76] In September another headline, 'Scum Of The Earth', led to the paper being kept off the streets for four days by strike action. From the miners' perspective the entire British media were against them and TV crews were physically attacked in retaliation for the scenes of picket-line violence that were being played out on the news night after night. Nicholas Jones, now a prominent critic of 'spin' in all its forms, was then a BBC industrial correspondent covering the strike. In retrospect he accepts that he and his colleagues were 'ensnared by the seeming inevitability of the Thatcherite story line that the mineworkers had to be defeated in order to smash trade union militancy' and so 'most radio and television journalists became, in effect, the cheerleaders for the return to work'.[77] Consciously or unconsciously journalists were helping the employers and the government achieve their objectives. Public opinion was never monolithic on this issue or any other, but the images people were fed daily by the media helped undermine the miners' cause. Arguably the tactics of the NUM, and in particular Arthur Scargill's refusal to hold a national strike ballot, damaged that cause to a far greater degree but the media played their part. Mrs Thatcher had tried at first to pretend that the strike had no political dimension, but after the miners returned to work she made no complaint when it was portrayed as a victory for her against what she described as 'the enemy within'.

There were other enemies to be tackled during her second term, armed with very different weapons. In the case of Ken Livingstone, leader of the Greater London Council, they included a talent for political communications and the use of the media that exceeded even hers. In the end the power that really mattered rested with her. She had the votes in parliament to abolish the council no matter how good its PR campaign might have been. In October 1984 she confronted a much more dangerous adversary. The Irish Republican Army came close to killing her, and claimed the lives of five others, when a bomb went off in the Grand Hotel in Brighton during the Conservative party conference. She had been working on her speech with, among others, Ronald Millar, shortly before it exploded at three o'clock in the morning. Her coolness in the wake of such a terrifying ordeal was extraordinary. 'It touched me,' said her private secretary, Robin Butler, 'because it was one of those moments where there could be no playacting.'[78] She later walked through the rubble and told John Cole of the BBC that the conference would go on uninterrupted and so it did.

At the end of the year Mrs Thatcher welcomed the new leader of the old Soviet enemy, President Gorbachev, to London and concluded, in another interview with John Cole, that 'we can do business together'.[79] Cole used the opportunity to ask her about her 'domineering, strident style'. 'I cannot change my style,' she told him. 'There are many, many people who are reasonably pleased that one gives a firm lead. My job also is to persuade and I do that.' It was a style that the

ITV programme *Spitting Image* had homed in on to great effect during 1984, its first year on the air. She was regularly portrayed by a latex puppet dressed as man and puffing on a very Churchillian-looking cigar. It did her no harm at all. Mrs Thatcher shared with Harold Macmillan the ability to turn even images designed to undermine her to her own advantage. The programme's most memorable sketch had her seated at a restaurant table surrounded by her fawning cabinet:

WAITRESS: Would you like to order, sir?
THATCHER: Yes. I will have the steak.
WAITRESS: How would you like it?
THATCHER: Oh, raw, please.
WAITRESS: And what about the vegetables?
THATCHER: Oh, they'll have the same as me![80]

One of the puppets seated round the table depicted the chancellor, Nigel Lawson. In real life Lawson had enough on his plate. Unemployment remained stubbornly high and the Treasury also had to decide what to do about the falling value of the pound. Mrs Thatcher, supported by her own economics adviser, Sir Alan Walters, didn't generally believe in 'bucking the market' but Lawson wasn't so sure. These were the days before Bank of England independence and on 11 January the chancellor secured her approval for a 1 per cent increase in interest rates to support the currency. At his briefing for the Sunday papers that same afternoon Bernard Ingham, who had not consulted the prime minister, repeated what he had heard her say many times, that 'throwing money at the pound' would be a waste of time. The journalists decided this meant, in the words of the *Sunday Times* headline: 'Thatcher Ready To Let £1 Equal $1'. The BBC, after getting broad confirmation of the story from Downing Street, started broadcasting a similar line but when the prime minister heard it on the radio she was alarmed. She knew it was wrong and that such widespread media speculation could move markets. She was right, but it was too late to do anything about it. On the Monday rates had to be raised again and it was estimated that Ingham's briefing had cost the country around £100 million in lost reserves. He recognised that he had made a mistake, 'I took it on the chin. I accepted responsibility. I did not blame the media for misreporting.'[81] The incident showed the dangers of a press secretary who thinks he knows the prime minister's mind without asking. Lawson was furious. He knew there were limits to Thatcher's monetarist orthodoxy, that she 'deeply disliked a falling pound' and 'was most definitely not Milton Friedman in drag'.[82] He summoned Ingham to his study and gave him a dressing-down. 'Had anybody else made that mistake he'd have been out.' Instead at a lobby party at the House of Commons the following day she escorted him around declaring 'Bernard's marvellous. Isn't he marvellous? He's great. He's the *greatest*.'[83]

He may have had no grounds to complain on this occasion, but 'marvellous' was not a word Ingham would use about the press. A couple of months later he was invited to speak to the International Press Institute. He used the occasion to attack the satirists, confrontational interviewers and journalists with conspiracy theories and asked, 'Can you honestly say that British journalism, even acknowledging its right to take a political standpoint, strives to be fair?'[84] Over at Labour party headquarters they shook their heads in bemusement and answered 'no'.

Ingham was starting to make news in his own right and to become 'part of the story'. The events surrounding the helicopter company Westland, which came to a head in early 1986, would bring him even greater name recognition. 'The Westland Affair' was one of those long-running stories that people saw every night on their TV screens and every morning on the front pages of the newspapers but which often left them wondering what all the fuss was about. Why should an argument about the ownership of a small company on the point of bankruptcy be tearing Mrs Thatcher's government apart? Mercifully the finer details, which were complex and confusing enough even at the time, need not detain us here. Suffice it to say that the defence secretary, Michael Heseltine, and the trade secretary, Leon Brittan, took different views about who was best placed to take over the company. The prime minister sided with Mr Brittan. Heseltine felt that the odds were being stacked in favour of the American company, Sikorsky, and he wasn't being given an adequate opportunity to present his case for a European consortium. So he did what ministers who find themselves losing the argument around the cabinet table often do: he decided to use the media to strengthen his case. When the decision went against him, Heseltine saw to it that a letter to the consortium's bankers setting out his views found its way into *The Times* on 4 January 1986. Mrs Thatcher's view, as recalled in her memoirs, was that 'cabinet collective responsibility was being ignored and my own authority as prime minister was being publicly flouted. This had to stop.'[85] The solicitor-general, Patrick Mayhew, one of those curious British hybrids, part politician and part law officer, was brought in. Mayhew was by no means unsympathetic to Heseltine but he agreed that there had been some 'material inaccuracies' in the letter. At the request of Number 10, Mayhew put his view in writing and with, at the very least, the connivance of Ingham and Downing Street, it was leaked to the press. We have come to think of leaks as commonplace and unexceptional, but the unauthorised release of advice from one of the law officers is in a different league. 'You Liar!' was the *Sun*'s verdict on Heseltine the following morning, with or without a nudge from Ingham in the right direction.[86] Mrs Thatcher, who admitted she wanted the contents of the advice made public as quickly as possible but was 'not consulted' and 'would not have approved of the leaking of a law officer's letter'[87], won the argument. But she paid a high price. Heseltine went first, walking out of cabinet and announcing his decision to the cameras in the street before his colleagues were even aware that he was resigning. Then, in the wake of the row over the leaked advice, Brittan had no choice but to go, too. Even Mrs Thatcher faced the outside chance of losing her own job. Whether half-jokingly or not – and Mrs Thatcher didn't tell many jokes – on the afternoon she had to defend what had happened in the Commons she told colleagues, including the foreign secretary, Sir Geoffrey Howe, she might be out of office by six o'clock.[88] Neil Kinnock, now leader of the opposition, failed to deliver a killer blow in the debate and she lived to fight another day.

That evening Rupert Murdoch rang Woodrow Wyatt as he was driving through the picket lines at Wapping. Wyatt recorded that, 'He thinks Mrs Thatcher has done well and says that the *Times* is favourable for tomorrow.'[89] Once again Murdoch and Thatcher found their interests coincided completely. Two weeks earlier as the Westland crisis mounted Murdoch had told Wyatt, 'We've got to get her out of this jam somehow. It's looking very bad.'[90] His concern was not entirely altruistic; he needed her just as much as she needed him. The Conservatives' trade-union laws had already given News International the legal powers to take on the print unions but a change of prime minister was the last thing he wanted. So he appears to have done what he could to help her out of her jam. Bruce Page has described a web of influence whereby TNT, the Australian freight company that helped Murdoch get his papers through the pickets every night, bought 2.6 million shares in Westland on the day of the crucial Commons debate. It is unlikely to be a coincidence that the chairman of TNT, Sir Peter Abeles, was an old school friend of Murdoch's. The balance of power within the company was thus tipped in favour of the deal Mrs Thatcher wanted, although it was still up to her to win the political battle at Westminster. As Page notes, her personal future had been on the line in a way that Murdoch's had not. And while Michael Heseltine's resignation would eventually help precipitate Mrs Thatcher's downfall four years later, Murdoch went from strength to strength, 'casting interesting light on the relative advantages of media power and political power'.

The bitter dispute at the Wapping plant strengthened the Murdoch–Thatcher alliance and led Neil Kinnock into a trap, souring his relations with some of the best-selling papers in Britain for years to come. Labour's national executive voted to boycott all News International titles and Kinnock wrote to the chairman of the lobby, Chris Moncrieff, to say he would not accept questions from their journalists at his weekly briefings. Roy Greenslade was then assistant editor of the *Sun* and one of those who crossed the picket lines to work at 'Fortress Wapping', despite being an ex-communist and union activist. Murdoch's 'friendly relationship with prime minister Margaret Thatcher had paid off,' he wrote later. And with her support 'Murdoch transformed the British newspaper industry, heralding a new industrial revolution which was to lead directly to the electronic super-highway . . . Wapping marked the beginning of the end of Fleet Street.'[91]

Without Wapping there would have been no *Independent*. The paper had a highly successful launch in October 1986 using non-union labour and employing many ex-News International journalists. The paper contrasted its own political independence with the strongly Thatcherite line now being taken by the *Times* and *Sunday Times* and, despite its modest sales, went some way to redressing the overwhelming pro-Tory bias in the written press. One way it tried to be different was by announcing publicly that it would not participate in the lobby system. The *Guardian* and later the *Scotsman* took the opportunity to announce that they would be pulling out also. Peter Preston, the *Guardian*'s editor wrote to Bernard Ingham to say that 'the customary and increasingly threadbare circumlocutions'[92] used to hide the author of official briefings would be abandoned. He cited the most recent case of Ingham using the anonymity of his office to denigrate a member of the cabinet, when he had called John Biffen 'semi-detached' after the leader of the house had dared to say on television that Mrs Thatcher had limitations and was unlikely to 'be prime minister throughout the entire period of the next parliament'.[93] If Ingham was going to make statements like that the *Independent* and its new allies wanted to let their readers know that 'Mrs Thatcher's spokesman' had spoken. Ingham was furious and said it would happen 'over my dead body'. He took a diametrically opposite view of the lobby system to that expressed by Joe Haines under Wilson and by Donald Maitland under Heath. Invited by Moncrieff to give his views he said the current system not only respected the primacy of parliament but that it also facilitated 'the flow of information and guidance'.[94] What he didn't say in so many words was that unattributable briefings were a very effective tool in the hands of a skilful press secretary who wanted to retain his power to 'guide' journalists to his version of the truth. The rest of the lobby were now put on the spot and after much soul-searching voted by 67 to 55 to stick to the old way of doing things. Ingham simply froze out those journalists who refused to comply. When Margaret Thatcher flew to Moscow in March 1987, newspapers that remained outside the lobby were given no briefings, no transport and no sympathy. Colin Brown of the *Independent* reported watching the official coach carry the lobby journalists from the airport while he tried to bribe the driver of a taxi 'with bald tyres'.[95] Although the *Mirror* hadn't left the lobby, Joe

Haines, who was also on the trip, stayed true to his beliefs and voluntarily accepted pariah status. Ingham wouldn't even tell his predecessor
as press secretary where the official party was staying in Moscow.
'When I said "Why not?" he said, "Because I look after my friends".
I said, "You mean the lobby?" He said, "Yes".'[96]

The spat did little to take the shine off a spectacularly successful visit
to the Soviet Union for which Ingham got much of the credit.
Cheering crowds greeted Mrs Thatcher in carefully chosen and pho-
togenic locations. According to the *Observer*, 'the Einstein of the
photo-opportunity had pulled off the big one – the most successful
exercise in public relations that has been mounted for years'.[97] The TV
news bulletins lapped it up and for the tabloids it was 'Maggiemania!'
For Ingham, as a civil servant, the fact that the prime minister was
almost certain to call an election sometime soon was clearly of no rel-
evance whatever. The cycle was repeating itself. In the run-up to the
election the softer side of Mrs Thatcher was once more carefully put
on display alongside pictures that showed her strength of leadership.
Back in Britain, she was photographed on the beach with a cute
spaniel. In a BBC documentary, *An English Woman's Wardrobe*, she
talked about the problems of choosing what best to wear and expressed
her fondness for Marks & Spencer underclothes. Just for good measure she pulled out one outfit and said 'This came through the Falklands
War all right.' She found time to be interviewed by *Woman*, *Woman's
Own*, *She* and even *Smash Hits*. On *Saturday Superstore* with the DJ
Mike Reid she gave her views on the latest pop videos.[98] Sadly the
Central Office of Information transcript omitted her observations,
confining itself to what it called 'the relevant parts'.

While the prime minister was using television to such great effect
her party chairman, Norman Tebbit, had been doing some softening-
up of the broadcasters in his own, somewhat more abrasive, style. As
ever it was the BBC that was the prime target. In October 1986 Mrs
Thatcher had appointed a new chairman, Marmaduke Hussey, apparently on the advice of Rupert Murdoch. She told Woodrow Wyatt,
who thought it was a disastrous choice, 'I wouldn't have done it if I
hadn't had a strong recommendation from Rupert.'[99] Tebbit wanted
Hussey 'to get in there and sort it out – in days and not months'. At

the party conference just before Hussey took the helm, Tebbit made it clear what he thought needed sorting out. He lambasted the corporation for a multitude of sins, from its coverage of the US bombing of Libya in April to an interview with an IRA leader, Martin McGuinness, and a *Panorama* programme, 'Maggie's Militant Tendency', on the alleged links between the Tory right and neo-fascists.[100] It was the usual pre-election softening-up exercise but this time it took a more serious turn. In January 1987 the director general, Alasdair Milne, was forced out by Hussey. Mrs Thatcher denied having anything to do with it, but that wasn't how it looked to the BBC's journalists.

The Tories went into the 1987 campaign in worse organisational shape than they had in either of the two previous elections. There was no director of publicity at Central Office and Tebbit failed to convince Mrs Thatcher that she needed one. Lord Young, whom Tebbit described as 'a persuasive, indeed compulsive, talker to the press'[101], was brought in to take responsibility for briefing Fleet Street editors and a press officer was poached from Ingham's team at Number 10. Tebbit looked across at Labour HQ where a new, young director of communications by the name of Peter Mandelson had been at work since 1985, and he was alarmed. Neil Kinnock was a more formidable opponent than Michael Foot and Tebbit was right to be worried. The Tory campaign would be beset with difficulties. Mrs Thatcher clearly didn't have full confidence in her party chairman, preferring to take private advice from Lord Young and others. The Tories could still rely on the enormous stock of goodwill they had built up with the popular press and with Murdoch's titles in particular. Labour's campaign manager, Bryan Gould, complained that 'Norman could pick up the phone whenever he wanted and launch a story, however unfounded, on the front pages of half of the nation's newspapers. Even if we could show that the story had no foundation, the mere fact that it dominated the front pages of so much of the press would compel the broadcast media and the rest of the press to follow it. So much for the independent media.'[102] The Nuffield study described it as 'Mrs Thatcher's election' with seven out of the eleven national dailies supporting her, and the *Sun*, true to form, being 'basic, bigoted and brilliant'.[103]

During the campaign both major parties found themselves knocked off their chosen ground by comments made by their own leaders, but the press were generally kinder to Mrs Thatcher when it happened. So when Neil Kinnock told David Frost on TV-AM that under Labour Britain's response to a Soviet attack would be to use 'the resources you've got to make any occupation totally untenable'[104] it became 'Dad's Army Kinnock' in the *Daily Mail*. When Mrs Thatcher told a press conference she used private health care so she could go to a hospital 'on the day, at the time and with the doctor I choose' it was 'Thatcher: I don't jump NHS Queues' in the *Daily Telegraph*.[105] Woodrow Wyatt was with Rupert Murdoch as the election results started coming in. 'When Ken Livingstone appeared on the screen and put down the Labour defeat to the dreadful lies and smears of the media, Rupert cried out "That's me!" and was delighted.'[106] Mrs Thatcher was returned with an overall majority of 102.

On the morning after the election Rupert Murdoch agreed a tentative deal to purchase yet another national newspaper, *Today*. The downmarket tabloid, launched by Eddie Shah, had helped prepare the ground for the Wapping revolution but was now losing money. The network of influence that had helped smooth Murdoch's purchase of *The Times* and *Sunday Times* was reactivated as Woodrow Wyatt told Mrs Thatcher there was no need for a referral to the Monopolies and Mergers Commission and that 'we look like having another pro-Margaret newspaper'.[107] Lord Young, now trade secretary, approved the sale without a referral. There were howls of protest from Labour MPs and from elsewhere in the media, but to no avail, and Murdoch had his fifth national title.

Thatcher did not need another pro-Margaret newspaper. Yet during her third term many things that had helped her achieve a position of such personal political authority were to become liabilities that would contribute to her downfall. Both Ingham and her foreign-policy adviser, Sir Charles Powell, remained fiercely loyal within Downing Street although Ingham had offered to resign after so long in the job. Some, including her loyal deputy, Lord Whitelaw, urged her to agree.[108] She did not and instead Ingham became even more influential, taking over, as head, the whole Government Information Service two years later.

The judgements of those who left her cabinet in painful circumstances clearly need to be tempered with caution, but Nigel Lawson was far from alone in believing that Ingham's loyalty had become 'self-defeating' and that his departure would have been to her advantage. 'He reinforced all her worst characteristics and, unwittingly, did her a profound disservice.'[109] Lawson watched from next door at Number 11 as 'she started to live up to her caricature'. I joined the lobby as a BBC political correspondent in 1988 and found Conservative ministers and backbenchers surprisingly willing to confide even in a newcomer like me that she was becoming blinkered and stubborn and reluctant to listen to the advice of anybody outside her immediate circle of support.

In the wake of the election victory Mrs Thatcher consolidated her position with the removal of some unreliable supporters, among them John Biffen, who was sacked finally because she thought 'he had come to prefer commentary to collective responsibility'.[110] But she rejected consolidation as a political strategy. Encouraged by the support of such a large proportion of the print media she believed the British people really had embraced Thatcherism. She was determined that her third term would not be an occasion to take the foot off the accelerator but the opposite. Harold Wilson used to say that leading the Labour party was a bit like driving a car. It was OK so long as you kept your speed up. If you stopped everybody would get out and start arguing about the best direction to take. In 1987 the only direction was the prime minister's and that meant further tax cuts and privatisation, renewed market-based reform in housing, education and health, and an overhaul of the domestic rating system. Not long after the election she told *Woman's Own* that 'there is no such thing as society . . . the quality of our lives will depend upon how much each of us is prepared to take responsibility for ourselves'.[111]

Her belief in self-reliance and independence extended to the international scene, too. She put it succinctly in her Bruges speech of 1988: 'We have not successfully rolled back the frontiers of the state in Britain to see them reimposed at a European level with a European superstate exercising a new dominance from Brussels.'[112] The sustained and often hysterical support of the popular press, led by but not confined to Murdoch's News International, helped convince her that she was in tune with the public mood. It wasn't just Europe. The tabloids, even at times the Mirror Group, would happily ridicule Mrs Thatcher's least favourite institutions at home and abroad and exaggerate, if not fabricate, their threat to 'common sense' British values. Conservative Central Office and, in a less overtly political way, the Downing Street press office helped supply the ammunition but the will to fire it was already there. 'Loony left' local councils were a frequent target, along with those they sought to protect from the worst effects of the 'no such things as society' culture, like ethnic minorities, gays, single mums and welfare recipients.

She received less support from the papers for the poll tax or 'community charge', her preferred replacement for the rates. Both *The Times* and the *Sunday Times* said the idea was wrong. Even Kelvin MacKenzie warned Rupert Murdoch that she was making a mistake. Murdoch took notice because 'He's a much more grass-roots man.'[113] MacKenzie's views were passed via Woodrow Wyatt to the prime minister who 'took it all without flinching'. The anti-poll-tax rioters in London and elsewhere would give the papers another target to attack, but her stubborn refusal to listen even to those who most supported her was causing increasing alarm within her own party. Tory MPs were shocked by the public anger and, while it was her attitude to Europe that would precipitate her fall, it was her refusal to compromise on the poll tax that lost her more votes when the time came. As Simon Jenkins put it, 'Like Al Capone she was brought down by an act of tax evasion.'[114]

No set of institutions has ever suffered such a sustained barrage of misinformation and distortion as those of the European Community at the hands of the Conservative party and its friends in the British press. In February 1986 Mrs Thatcher had agreed to the Single European Act, the biggest step towards closer union in the community's history. It came into effect just after the 1987 election but was swiftly airbrushed out of her political record as effectively as any comrade-turned-traitor in the old Soviet Union. In Mrs Thatcher's lexicon 'Europe' was an external menace, not something of which Britain was a fundamental part. 'Brussels' was not a rather dull city in a dysfunctional neighbouring state; it was the bastion of foreign notions of governance and culture that threatened British independence as surely as Nazi Germany ever had. Mrs Thatcher was at her most Churchillian in her resistance to 'Europe' and when Bernard Ingham told her how closely her views were echoed in the media it confirmed her belief that the nation supported her. The extent to which the media influenced rather than reflected the public's views of the European Community is, as ever, impossible to prove either way. But it is reasonable to assume that such strong press support emboldened the prime minister and freed her from any restraint in her language of condemnation. Even as she delivered her fatal Commons speech which said 'no, no, no' to closer political integration in 1990 and led directly to her fall from power,[115] she was sure she was right and no less certain that her views were popular.

Some colleagues who had stood by her from the start now had their doubts. Cabinet ministers who would never have been described as 'wet' believed she, and Bernard Ingham on her behalf, were using the press not just to close off discussion of an alternative view of Europe but also to undermine them personally in the process. The circularity in the Thatcher–Ingham–media relationship now seemed to be operating against people who had always been thought of as on her wing of the party. A year after the election Nigel Lawson, now in his sixth year as chancellor, made a speech to the Institute of Economic Affairs that was open to the benefits of exchange-rate regulation within Europe. Ingham's summary of the press coverage it generated found its way to the chancellor's desk. It started with 'I'll do it my way – Lawson puts job on line in row with Maggie' and Ingham then went on to tell the prime minister that the speech was 'an amazing challenge to your authority and a massive gamble over his future'. The chancellor clearly believed this was not a judgement that fell within the remit of a press secretary and 'the effect of this sort of poison, week in, week out, month in, month out, on Margaret's attitude towards me is not hard to gauge'.[116]

A year later Mrs Thatcher reshuffled her cabinet and Sir Geoffrey Howe, who had been her first chancellor, was moved from the Foreign Office. His crime had been to ally himself with Lawson in an effort to push her towards agreeing to British membership of the European

exchange-rate mechanism, the ERM. In her memoirs she wondered
if perhaps she should have sacked him altogether but she did not, offering him instead the job of leader of the House and the title 'deputy
prime minister'. Lobby journalists wanted to know what this grand-
sounding title meant and Ingham told them it meant very little. The
following morning the *Daily Mail* called it a 'constitutional fiction' and
the *Daily Telegraph* 'a courtesy title with no constitutional status'.[117]
Ingham was unrepentant about his briefing and laid the blame for the
ensuing row on 'those who had so ridiculously talked up the role of
deputy prime minister and revealed a private conversation between the
prime minister and Sir Geoffrey Howe about what post he might fill
in the Government'[118]. He certainly hadn't misled the lobby about her
views but he had used the anonymity of his post to make an enemy
who would prove to be lethal in revenge the following year. The man
who replaced Sir Geoffrey as foreign secretary was a relative newcomer
to cabinet rank with almost no experience of foreign affairs by the
name of John Major.

At the end of October the unresolved tension over the ERM was
a major factor in Nigel Lawson's sudden resignation. 'Ingham's black
propaganda machine was already fully cranked up'[119], he noted. The
following morning the *Sun*'s front page had the blunt headline 'Good
Riddance'.[120] John Major barely had time to make sure his passport
hadn't expired before his tenure at the Foreign Office ended after
ninety-four days and he became the new chancellor. Major was by
now Mrs Thatcher's protégé, the man she saw as her preferred successor, although she hadn't the slightest intention of handing over any
time soon. Politically he was in a much stronger position than Lawson
or Howe. Mrs Thatcher couldn't afford to lose another chancellor. In
June of the following year he used that strength to secure the prime
minister's agreement that the pound should enter the ERM. She found
that 'I had too few allies to continue to resist and win the day. There
are limits to the ability of even the most determined democratic leader
to resist what the cabinet, the parliamentary party, the industrial lobby
and the press demand.'[121] It was the only occasion in her premiership
when she conceded any power to the press to force her to do what she
didn't want to, and it lacked credibility. Whatever pressure she was

under, the press was the least of it, except to the extent that stories about splits at the top made Tory MPs even more jittery. Britain entered the ERM on Friday 5 October. She may not have liked it but she wouldn't have long to worry about it. On 22 November she would herself resign in the most dramatic transfer of power since Lloyd George unseated Asquith.

The Murdoch–Thatcher show would have one final, controversial scene before she departed. His last meeting with her at Downing Street was to discuss the merger of his Sky satellite company with its rival BSB. The prime minister was a big fan of Sky, which had started broadcasting in February 1989. As her previous guest was leaving she introduced him: 'Here is Mr Murdoch, who gives us Sky News, the only unbiased news in the UK.'[122] She sympathised with his desire for a quick merger and it was rushed through in advance of changes to the regulations governing independent broadcasting that were due to come into effect in a matter of days. Technically the merger might actually have been illegal, as the home secretary, David Waddington, conceded in the Commons.[123] But by then it was too late. Murdoch claimed that the success of BSkyB, as it became, was more important to him than beating the unions at Wapping. It was the last chance Mrs Thatcher had to be helpful to him and the last example of what her biographer John Campbell called 'the grubbiest face of Thatcherism'.[124]

The events leading up to her departure from Downing Street – her 'no, no, no' speech to the Commons followed by the resignation of Sir Geoffrey Howe and the subsequent leadership challenge from Michael Heseltine – have been written about many times and turned into TV dramas and political fiction. Michael Heseltine had not wasted his time exiled on the back benches. He had cultivated political correspondents assiduously. I, like most lobby journalists, had lunch with him several times and while he always steered clear of outright disloyalty there was never any doubt in my mind that one day he would make his move. When he did, his excellent relationship with the media and his star quality as a television performer arguably did him as much harm as good. Many of his colleagues had long concluded he was 'unsound' and not to be trusted. John Major, who had kept a much lower profile and cultivated fewer press contacts, went on to win. As the leadership crisis erupted he conveniently absented himself from the political scene alto-gether for a wisdom-tooth operation. Once Mrs Thatcher was out of the race, he did get press support, but mainly because he was her chosen successor. The *Sun* urged Major to run and advised Tory MPs to remember 'it was *Sun* readers that put you in office'[125] and that if they wanted to keep the paper's support they had better not back Heseltine.

As Mrs Thatcher fought for her political life those of us reporting on events were swept along by the biggest political story of our careers. Her fate was sealed behind closed doors at Westminster, not in any newsroom. It was the desertion of her cabinet that did for her. To the end *The Times, Telegraph, Mail, Express, Sun* and *Today*, along with most of their Sunday equivalents, stayed loyal to her, although the *Mail on Sunday* did not. Heseltine was convinced that Bernard Ingham was behind stories designed to undermine him as 'glamour without sub-stance' and that the Downing Street press secretary had directly encouraged a *Times* editorial which stated that 'Mr Heseltine is at pres-ent merely helping the Conservatives to lose the next election. He should either put up or shut up.'[126]

The nearest thing to an argument that the media helped remove Margaret Thatcher from office concerns the *Sunday Times*. Its editor, Andrew Neil, had been an enthusiastic Thatcherite, although with a streak of independence that had greatly annoyed and upset her in the past. He now believed Heseltine was the best man to lead the Tories into the next election and, despite pressure from Rupert Murdoch and entreaties from the prime minister's most loyal supporters, he was ready to say so. After Heseltine declared his candidacy Neil took a call from Murdoch in which he said, 'Heseltine would be disastrous. We owe Thatcher a lot as a company. Don't go overboard in your attacks on her.'[127] He didn't, but on the weekend before the first round of voting he wrote an editorial saying Heseltine's programme 'reads like an agenda for the 1990s that the *Sunday Times* could support'. It acknowl-edged that Margaret Thatcher was 'possibly the greatest peacetime prime minister of this century' but concluded that keeping Neil Kinnock out of office 'requires saying a reluctant goodbye to Mrs Thatcher and the endorsement of Michael Heseltine'.[128]

Two days later Margaret Thatcher narrowly failed to get a sufficient majority to avoid a second leadership ballot. Neil says that 'I learned later that Thatcher thought the *Sunday Times* played a crucial part in her downfall: she needed only two more votes to survive and believed the *Sunday Times* editorial swung at least that number of Tory MPs against her.'[129] In the years to come, however, when she took every opportunity to condemn those she held responsible for her removal, she never mentioned the *Sunday Times*. And, in any case, Neil had mollified Murdoch as best he could by providing equal space in that Sunday's paper for pro- and anti-Thatcher comment.

It would be nice at this point if I could claim the credit for breaking the news of Mrs Thatcher's resignation. Unfortunately I cannot. I was the only political correspondent outside Downing Street when Bernard Ingham emerged with a piece of paper announcing that she would not, after all, be standing in the second ballot. My producer, Don Brind, phoned Television Centre and asked for me to be put on air. These were still the days before 24-hour news channels on either BBC television or radio. BBC1 was showing a cookery programme and somebody decided the show couldn't be interrupted. By the time it finished at 10.00 a.m. I had been joined in the street by Adam Boulton of Sky News and Michael Brunson of ITN. My scoop was no longer an exclusive. Mr Ingham, if he'd had the time to notice, would have been delighted.

Mrs Thatcher left Downing Street on 28 November 1990. Her principal private secretary, Andrew Turnbull, presented her with a short-wave radio, so 'wherever you are in the world, you can continue to be cross with the BBC.'[130] Bernard Ingham, who had played a conspicuously political role at the last hurdle in trying to help her avoid defeat, resigned a week later. He had become so closely identified with everything she stood for that it would have been impossible for him to stay and work for anybody else. Of course he regretted 'the political passing of a phenomenon' but by his own account he retired happy and fulfilled, as well he might.[131] He had helped demonstrate how, with sufficient determination and professionalism, combined with a clear ideological drive and a healthy measure of luck, the office of prime minister wields far more power and influence than those of all the editors and proprietors put together. She rewarded her friends in the media and, in the case of Murdoch in particular, used the law (and occasionally ignored it) in order to help his business interests. Had the official scrutiny committee not blocked it she would have offered him an honorary knighthood as well.[132] Her departure from Downing Street with moist eyes earned her the final *Sun* headline 'Mrs T-ears', not one of their best but then maybe the subs were too upset themselves at losing their heroine to come up with anything better. She was giving them good copy right up to the end. 'I shall be a very good back seat driver,' she promised. To John Major it sounded more like a threat.

10

DECLINE AND FALL:
MAJOR (1990–97)

The trouble is newspapers will bring anybody down just for the hell of it these days. They think it shows their power, titillates their readers and helps to sell their newspapers.

Woodrow Wyatt

John Major's term as prime minister saw the political world turn on its head. Only now, almost two decades after he took office, is it showing signs of righting itself. During Major's seven years in the job many of the easy assumptions that had underpinned British political life for much of the twentieth century crumbled. They had never been set in concrete, as lazy minds, most of them in journalism, had chosen to believe, but they had been a sturdy enough basis on which to build a working model that came close to reality. By 1997 talk of 'the Tory press' or of loyalty as 'the Conservatives' secret weapon' or of Labour's natural instinct for division and a culture of betrayal made little sense any more. 'It's a funny old world,'[1] Mrs Thatcher had remarked as power slipped from her hands. By the time it was wrenched from John Major's it looked a whole lot funnier.

The experience would leave Major more resentful than any other prime minister in history about his treatment by the media. The testimony of almost everybody who worked with him confirms that he was the most thin-skinned of premiers, whose obsession with what was written and said about him exceeded even Harold Wilson's. It unambiguously weakened him and made him less effective in office. It was arguably his greatest failing and everybody, from friends to advisers to political colleagues, tried to warn him of the damage it was doing. Time and time again they urged him to shrug off the criticism but he couldn't do it. He had good grounds for being upset. He was derided and patronised and insulted. Like playground bullies, once the media realised they were getting to him, the more they piled on the pressure. When he compared the way he was treated to how Mrs Thatcher had been idolised he despaired at the injustice of it all. Had he known what was to come, he would have enjoyed more than he did the initially good press he received after replacing her. Journalists weren't quite sure what to make of him but they were willing, for now, to give him the benefit of the doubt.

'The image-makers will not find me in their tutelage,'[2] he pledged in November 1990. If they had been asked they would have told him to avoid words which ordinary people never use. But there I go, mocking him already. His curious use of the English language had that effect on commentators and was, inevitably, exaggerated by the satirists. The way he spoke in private was much more earthy and that made his public utterances sound all the more contrived, as if he was trying a little bit too hard to be prime-ministerial. It is a difficult criticism to make without sounding patronising and therein lies much of the early tension between Major and the media.

John Major believed that he deserved more credit for not being Mrs Thatcher, or at least for avoiding her failings. He set the tone he hoped to maintain on arriving at Number 10 when he expressed the wish to 'build a country that is at ease with itself'.[3] It had a ring of Stanley Baldwin about it. It suggested that, like Baldwin, he wanted to avoid conflict where he could, and while that reassured some it alarmed others. After the upheavals of the past eleven years he might simply have repeated Mrs Thatcher's 'Where there is discord let us bring harmony' with the added rider 'we mean it this time', but he wanted to look to the future not dwell on the past. As he went inside, the media tried to work out just who this man really was that they would now be writing about on a daily basis. Journalists were wary of Major in part because they knew so little about him. His rise through the ministerial ranks had made few waves. Edward Pearce, who as a parliamentary sketch writer had seen more of him than most, summed up his colleagues' attitude: 'Clearly anyone capable of moving shyly through the alcoholic mists, evading a snake-eyed, white-hot press must be a dull little number, one of life's engine number collectors.'[4]

In the days before Google, when journalists wanted to become instant experts on somebody or something they reached for the drawers of newspaper cuttings. These contained everything that has ever been written on the subject by people just like themselves. In John Major's case the files proved depressingly thin. He appeared never to have said or done anything terribly interesting or significant except rise inexorably and swiftly to the top. As for his political instincts there was little to help define him in the old right/left, dry/wet shorthand. The *Sunday Telegraph* had once called him 'a more moderate version of Norman Tebbit' while a *Times* profile thought he was 'in the mould of Kenneth Clarke'.[5] In escaping detailed press comment for so long he had also managed to escape press criticism. His brief period as foreign secretary had exposed him to some ridicule as Mrs Thatcher's bag carrier but he had never needed to develop the thick skin that protects most senior politicians. As chancellor he had succeeded where Nigel Lawson and Geoffrey Howe had failed and persuaded Thatcher to allow Britain to join the European exchange-rate mechanism, but even then he was seen as having given the final kick to a door that was already on its last hinges.

Major's personal story, that of the poor boy from Brixton in south London who made it to the top despite little formal education, should have been a huge political strength. He threw away the advantage it proffered by equating any reference to his humble beginnings and, in particular, his interrupted education with the sneering of snobs who had had it so much easier. When the media tried to investigate his education and even to find out how many O-levels he had passed, they found it very difficult. He had deliberately covered his tracks. According to Penny Junor, who interviewed him for an early biography, he asked for his school records to be hidden in the archives as late as 1989, although he later realised this had been a mistake. He 'hated the intrusion' into his privacy and that of his wife Norma, 'hated the snobbish tone of the writers, who were snide and patronising by turns, and hated total strangers talking with authority on things they knew nothing about'.[6] But that is what journalists do. 'He couldn't shrug it off any more than he could stop reading it. In the early days he was obsessed by it, he read everything first thing in the morning. He became angry at the inaccuracies, hurt by the unkindness, worried by the effect it was having on his family, whom he didn't consider fair game. But most wounding of all were the quotes from nameless colleagues.'[7] His political secretary, Judith Chaplin, made frequent references to his sensitivity in her diaries. 'So much of our time is wasted looking at what all types of media say. He cannot bear to be criticised and takes it as a personal slight: he is obsessed by his image and will have to get a tougher skin about it all. Not only does it thoroughly depress all of us who work for him, it wastes so much time – better spent dealing with the problems.'[8]

As Major sought to establish his authority, all manner of baseless innuendo about his marriage and his private life swirled around the newsrooms of London. Every journalist had heard stories of an affair between Major and the Downing Street caterer Clare Latimer. The stories weren't true and Major successfully sued both the now-defunct magazine *Scallywag* and the *New Statesman* for libel after they referred to them. Neither had a large readership but the prime minister's lawyers argued that it was a serious attack on his reputation to accuse him of adultery. Only in 2002, long after he left office, did it emerge that he was indeed an adulterer, but that the magazines had named the wrong woman. The former minister Edwina Currie revealed in her diaries that they had been lovers for four years in the 1980s and that she had broken off the relationship only when he became a cabinet minister, because 'for John to give his bodyguards the slip, would have been to put him into a seriously dangerous situation. It just wasn't worth it.'[9] Ms Latimer told the BBC that she had been used as a 'decoy' and that Downing Street had allowed her name to be circulated to cover his real affair with Mrs Currie. 'He or they or whatever. I'd been planted to hide a story, which is the most extraordinary thing to me when you work in a place like Downing Street, to be put into this position.'[10] Major had taken an enormous risk by authorising the legal action and the strain of not knowing when, if ever, the truth would be revealed is cited by many of those who worked closely with him as one factor that helps explain his endless paranoia about the media.

Fortunately the man who joined Major in Downing Street as his first press secretary was known for his great patience and good humour. He would need every ounce of both. Gus O'Donnell was probably the best liked, both by journalists and officials, of any holder of that post. His integrity is admired as much as his affability and there has never been any suggestion that he knew anything about the affair with Mrs Currie. O'Donnell was a civil-service high-flier who would go on to reach the top of his profession, as cabinet secretary under Gordon Brown. The nearest thing to a criticism ever made of him during his time as press secretary was that maybe he was just too nice for the job. On a personal level he and Major were closer than Thatcher and Bernard Ingham had ever been. O'Donnell had already been Major's spokesman at the Treasury. They both came from south London and shared common interests like cricket. His arrival – or rather Ingham's departure – gave the *Independent*, *Guardian* and *Scotsman* the excuse they needed to rejoin the lobby eight months later and get the benefit of his briefings, which were certainly more low key than his predecessor's. The papers were helped by O'Donnell's willingness to allow his words to be directly attributed to Number 10. As a broadcaster I was free to use phrases like 'Downing Street says . . .' for the first time. O'Donnell endeared himself to journalists by being both more forthcoming with the facts and less touchy about the comment. Where Ingham was as outspoken and confrontational as Thatcher, so O'Donnell was as inclined towards understatement and consensus as Major. Where Ingham would attack a journalist for writing 'bunkum and balderdash', O'Donnell would look puzzled and patiently give the reasons why a different interpretation might be justified. Or, in the words of Charles Reiss, former political editor of the *Evening Standard*, 'Bernard would go red with rage. Gus would go red with embarrassment. But that didn't stop them both being very effective press secretaries in their different ways.'[11]

O'Donnell was an economist who happened to find himself as press secretary rather than an expert in government communications and he lacked the ability to spot political minefields in the way Ingham or Alastair Campbell could do so effectively. Major's first publicity disaster was wholly avoidable, although scarcely O'Donnell's fault. Mrs Thatcher's cabinets were usually all-male affairs, with the obvious exception of the person at the top. She could get away with it; John Major could not. His first cabinet included no women at all and it seems it hadn't even occurred to him. He was forced into a rather humiliating photocall with the most senior woman outside the cabinet, Gillian Shepherd, whose importance he played up for all it was worth.

It was another woman, Margaret Thatcher, who presented a far more serious problem. It was personal, it was political and it polluted Major's relationship both with his parliamentary party and with the media. Thatcher refused to relinquish her grip on either and every time he tried to prise her fingers open she resisted. Norman Fowler was a Thatcher loyalist, having served in her government from 1979 to 1990, and had the rare distinction of being equally valued by her successor. He believed Major had every justification for suspecting her of systematically briefing the press against him. Almost immediately 'she became one of Major's most influential critics, telling politicians and journalists who visited her at home about the defects of the new administration. She complained of the failure to control spending, she characterised the administration as a government without beliefs and, of course, she complained about the new more constructive stance towards Europe.'[12] Fowler knew, from having being invited to her home himself, just how deadly her criticism could be. 'Conservatives regarded her as a political giant so when she spoke other Tory politicians, editors and leader writers listened and many followed.'

Edward Heath's criticisms of her when she was prime minister were harmless in comparison to the way she spoke about Major. Heath had attacked her directly and unambiguously and he could be confronted head-on. She was much more dangerous for her tactic of using private

conversations to disparage him mercilessly while in public either damn-
ing him with faint praise or suggesting he'd like to live up to her record
but didn't quite have it in him. At his first appearance for prime minister's questions her entry into the chamber produced an eruption of
hand-clapping from the Tory benches, some of it no doubt motivated
as much by guilt as appreciation. She had to be dissuaded from sitting
three rows behind Major 'in full view of the TV cameras, looking like
the back-seat driver'.[13]

Watching from the officials box was Sarah Hogg, a former journalist, whom Major had made his head of policy. In a book she wrote
with Jonathan Hill, later his political secretary, she acknowledged what
the media were looking for in those early days: 'journalists, reasonably
enough, wanted to know whether to tick the box marked "continu-
ity" or the one marked "change". Was Margaret Thatcher the
back-seat driver of the new government? Or was the new prime minister not only from a different generation, but a different kind of
Tory?'[14] He was certainly different in that he believed in genuine cabinet discussion and was keen to find agreement where possible. He
didn't go out looking for enemies in the way she had done, and that
was one reason the media found him less interesting. Consensus does-
n't make for good headlines. Prime ministers need enemies and
preferably not ones within their own ranks. Six days after taking office
he tried to show that he was passionate in his beliefs. 'First and foremost, I loathe inflation,'[15] he said. But who didn't? There were no
Labour MPs, trade unionists or local councillors chanting, 'What do
we want? Inflation! When do we want it? Now!'

One immediate task was to lance the boil of the poll tax and Major
asked Michael Heseltine to take on the job. Thatcher was furious both
at the reappointment of her nemesis and the rejection of her cherished
policy, although everybody else could see the political necessity of
both. Major had shown he was his own man, but to Judith Chaplin
and others that wasn't enough. 'It is worrying that he has no underlying conviction about the way he wants policy to go – pragmatic to
a fault. He is also in a state because the papers are saying there should
be firm leadership over poll tax whereas he has promised consultation.
He is too worried about what the papers say.'[16]

Major had inherited one very real enemy whom he was as resolute in defeating as his predecessor would ever have been. Although the war in the Gulf was not strictly his war, he conducted it with great skill. Saddam Hussein had sent his troops into Kuwait on 2 August and the week before Major became prime minister the cabinet had decided to send nearly 30,000 British troops to the Gulf to help remove him. While he and Douglas Hurd, who had been reappointed foreign secretary, sought to avoid war they recognised that it was all but inevitable. Major wasn't blind to the political advantages the conflict brought; no prime minister ever is, despite what they must claim. 'Before I became prime minister Labour were well ahead in the opinion polls, but my election had turned them around. Now, when [Neil Kinnock] must have wished to sink his political teeth into a new prime minister, he was forced to support him.'[17]

On the eve of hostilities starting, 15 January 1991, Major made a thoughtful statement to the Commons, praised by the *Guardian* for 'an absence, even perhaps a deliberate repudiation, of that triumphalism, that vainglory, that sense of international centre-stage, which was Margaret Thatcher's hallmark'[18]. The following evening he decided to do a prime-ministerial statement from Downing Street, a form of address that Thatcher had abstained from even during the Falklands conflict. Against the advice of his immediate staff he ended it with the words 'God Bless', a touch that resonated to a remarkable degree. Conservative Central Office, whose job it is to worry about the politics, tested the broadcast with a group of voters and a device that allowed them to register their reactions as it progressed. 'All through the Gulf broadcast,' Sarah Hogg and Jonathan Hill were pleased to note, 'the reaction line was extremely positive.' Overall the conclusion from a similar analysis of a number of Major's TV appearances was that the public approved of his 'quiet effectiveness' and the fact that he let 'everyone else do the shouting'.[19]

His reputation for calmness was reinforced when, before the ground war in the Gulf could begin, the IRA launched an attack of its own, firing three mortars into the Downing Street garden from a stolen van. Only one exploded but Major's comment to his cabinet, which was sitting at the time – 'I think we had better start again somewhere else'[20] – quickly became emblematic of his unflappable resolve. The public were not getting the full picture. They heard little of his private anger and frustration, often accompanied by a range of expletives and frequently provoked by what the media had said about him, but what they did see they seemed to like. With the Gulf war successfully concluded after a ground battle lasting only four days, the government's prospects were looking good and an early election was widely predicted in the press. Major considered the option but, according to his head of policy, 'the prime minister was never keen on a "khaki election", and the poll lead soon melted away again'[21].

In May 1991 I had the pleasure of leaving Westminster to report on a by-election in the agreeable surroundings of Monmouth in Wales. Peter Mandelson had taken personal charge of the Labour campaign, desperate for a win that would in all probability delay an election and give Kinnock time to regroup. He was not disappointed. There was a 13 per cent swing away from the Tories and they lost the seat. On polling day, 16 May, back in London the chief whip, Richard Ryder, held the first meeting of the 'Number 12 Committee' designed principally to coordinate the government's message but also to 'put the government on a political war footing'.[22] The committee included ministers, political advisers from Number 10 and from Central Office the new director of communications, Shaun Woodward, a former producer on *That's Life* who would later be a high-profile defector to the Labour party. Gus O'Donnell also took part, just as Bernard Ingham had done with the 'liaison committee' in Thatcher's time. It was otherwise a predominantly party-political gathering but his presence could be justified as it met in one of those grey areas between party and government where a civil servant could legitimately attend so long as he minded what he said.

Now an election was out of the question, at least until the autumn, there was the business of a full legislative agenda to attend to. Much had been inherited from Mrs Thatcher's last Queen's Speech, but new bills would be added, too. Among them was a particularly unfortunate piece of legislation, one of the most glaring examples of media hysteria pushing ministers into passing a bad law. The home secretary, Kenneth Baker, rushed the Dangerous Dogs Act through parliament, after a feeding frenzy involving mainly young children appeared to have taken hold of Britain's population of pit bull terriers. When the media gets its teeth into this kind of story its pack instinct can be savage. All kinds of incidents that might normally have made no more than the inside pages of a local newspaper were national news and the headlines demanded that the government 'Act!' Act it did, passing the bill into law through all its main stages on one day. Baker promised it would 'rid the country of the menace of these fighting dogs'.[23] He was grateful that pit-bull owners helped his case by 'appearing in front of TV cameras . . . usually sporting tattoos and earrings while extolling the allegedly gentle nature of their dogs, whose names were invariably Tyson, Gripper, Killer or Sykes'.[24] And yet no sooner had the legislation been passed than the tabloids changed tack. Sad-eyed crossbreed pooches on 'death row' were featured as the courts struggled to decide which of them had enough pit bull in their genes to be proscribed under the law. Understandably, John Major's lengthy memoirs make no reference to what, at the time, was supposed to be a significant piece of legislation. In reality it was little more than pandering to press panic. Some lessons do get learned, and when the *News of the World* returned to the fray with its 'Devil Dogs Campaign'[25] in 2006, by which time the focus had shifted to Rottweilers, Downing Street wisely let it run out of steam.

The Dangerous Dogs Act was the clearest example of media pressure affecting policy, but, according to the foreign secretary, Douglas Hurd, it wasn't the only one. Major would leave cabinet discussions to go and read the copy of the London *Evening Standard* that was put in an ante-room as soon as it was delivered. 'He would dash out at the end of cabinet and snatch it up and look at it to see what errors it might contain and then come back in and suggest we should consider the whole thing again, whatever it was we had been discussing, because they were getting it wrong.'[26] Hurd arranged for the paper to be placed out of harm's way after a while. He feared his colleagues were starting to be infected with the same obsession. 'Nowadays ministers . . . fret infinitely about the media. A huge amount of time is given to this fretting . . . the cabinet may no longer have to worry about India but it may, from time to time, worry itself sick about the *Daily Mail*.'[27] The

Mail was one of those newspapers that happily retained an open line to Margaret Thatcher. This was partly ideological, but what Major, like many other prime ministers, tended to forget was that even a politically outspoken newspaper like the *Mail* is primarily interested in news not influencing politics. And Thatcher continued to make news.

In June Major received some good news and some bad from the Thatcher front. She announced her intention to take a seat in the House of Lords, where at least she would no longer be available to those Tory MPs who hoped she might yet make a comeback as prime minister. But then, in a long interview with Simon Jenkins in *The Times*, she warned, 'I am not going to change my views and I shall go on propagating them.'[28] At the suggestion that Major might want to redraw the political map she replied, 'I most earnestly hope not.' She was reported in the *Daily Telegraph* to have started calling him 'the grey man' with 'no ideas', although she denied it.[29] According to Judith Chaplin's diary, his press secretary was left in no doubt what he thought of her: 'he says to Gus, who mentions Mrs T, "I want her isolated, I want her destroyed." He has been to see her but obviously says one thing to her face and something quite different behind her back. He says things like "she's bonkers", "over the top" etc to other people.'[30]

What most distressed Thatcher was Major's attitude to Europe. She later wrote: 'I could well understand that after the bitter arguments over Europe which preceded my resignation he would want to bind up the wounds in the party. But I was not prepared for the speed with which the position I had adopted would be entirely reversed.'[31] Over the summer Major and Hurd were busy preparing for the inter-governmental conference that would meet in Maastricht at the end of the year to shape Europe's future. The consequences of the treaty signed there would dominate Major's remaining time as prime minister. 'What if there had been no Maastricht Treaty?' is another of those fascinating but ultimately fruitless questions. There was. And it helped destroy Major's reputation and left the Conservatives unelectable for over a decade. What is too often forgotten is that, far from being pushed around by the media over Europe in general and Maastricht in particular, John Major refused to do what the bulk of the 'Tory press' demanded. Time and time again he could have transformed his image

in their eyes by remodelling himself as a sceptic in the Thatcher mould
but he wouldn't do it. Whatever his personal convictions, it would
have cost him the support of pro-Europeans in his cabinet such as
Heseltine, Hurd and Kenneth Clarke, and they mattered more than the
headline writers. When we ask what power the press has, the Major
years once again show its limitations. The media had the power to
unsettle him, to enrage him, to wound him deeply, but on the most
important issue of all it did not have the power to make him change
his mind.

That is not quite the same as saying that Major stuck to his principles. What the Euro-sceptic press hated most was that Major appeared
to have none. He was, in the words of his biographer Anthony Seldon,
'above all a Euro-pragmatist, convinced that Britain should be a
member of the community, and play a central role in its deliberations,
but content to go with the flow on how far to travel down the feder-
alist path at different times'.[32] As a strategy it made a lot of sense, and
it played to his determination, every bit as urgent as Harold Wilson's,
to keep his party from splitting apart over the issue if he possibly could.
Compared to 'no, no, no', however, it didn't make for exciting headlines. Labour, who would follow a broadly similar policy after 1997,
now painted him as a weak man blowing in the wind. The shadow
foreign secretary, Gerald Kaufman, called him 'the man who came to
dither'. Thus, unlikely allies on the right and the left came together to
condemn Major as weak and vacillating. It may not have been fair but
it was devastatingly effective.

Major played into the hands of those who wished to ridicule him
when he produced the nearest thing he could manage to a 'big idea'.
The Citizen's Charter was launched at the party's 1991 spring conference in Southport. Designed with the simple aim of raising standards
in public services, it came across as well-meaning but inconsequential.
Despite the huge amount of political capital that Major sank into it, the
Citizen's Charter never caught the public imagination. The ever-loyal
Daily Express may have greeted it as 'Power To The People' but the
people were underwhelmed. The idea never recovered from one tiny
component of the Charter that became a national joke. The 'Cones
Hotline', set up so that drivers could complain about unnecessary

traffic cones, kept stand-up comedians in good material for months. Gyles Brandreth, then a Tory backbencher but always a man with an eye for the popular and a nose for the ridiculous, came away from a lunch with the prime minister and wrote in his diary, 'Of course, he believes in it, passionately, believes it will change the quality of life of ordinary people. Inevitably, though we must all have thought it, not one of us dared say, "No one gives a toss about the Citizen's Charter, prime minister!"'[33] Yet once again, Major dismissed the derision in many of the newspapers as much as the taunts of the opposition and kept on with what he believed to be right.

That mocking continued to upset him, nonetheless. Nobody, not even his wife Norma, could dissuade him from picking up any newspaper he saw lying around. Like Harold Wilson, whom he resembled in a surprising number of ways, he would often read the first editions of the newspapers late at night before going to bed. He was painfully aware of what the satirists were doing to him, too. *Spitting Image*, which had shown Thatcher as a cigar-puffing Churchillian strongman, portrayed Major as a pathetic figure all in grey pushing peas around his plate. At first they put an aerial on his head to suggest she still controlled him. The cartoonists were no less dismissive. The most famous image by far was a reworking of the 'Supermac' character created for Harold Macmillan. In it Steve Bell of the *Guardian* had Major flying through the air with his underpants outside his trousers. Bell had hit on the Y-fronts as 'a metaphor for uselessness and awkwardness'.[34] Once again the comparison with Thatcher was deliberate and demeaning and, unlike Macmillan, Major could not turn it to his advantage.

It all gave the Tories a huge presentational challenge ahead of Major's first annual conference as prime minister. They could see that a week of speculation about an autumn election – 'will he, won't he?' – could be fatal and would play into the image of the ditherer. I remember sitting at dinner with John Humphrys of the *Today* programme during the Labour conference that preceded the Tories'. A call came through from London to say that several of the papers closest to the government had been briefed that there would be no election. Humphrys remarked immediately that Major had avoided Callaghan's PR disaster of 1978. It looked as if Richard Ryder's Number 12 committee had done its work. The Tory press had benefited from a classic bit of spin, Neil Kinnock's speech had been successfully upstaged, and the rest of us were left running around playing catch-up. In fact, Major hadn't yet made up his mind and Number 10 was far from happy. John Wakeham, a member of the Number 12 committee, who did the briefing, was thought to have overegged the story or, if not, to have given it to the political editors too early in the day so that it took on a life of its own and became more robust by the time it was published.

The effect of the spin operation was double-edged. Had the steer gone the other way there is little doubt that the papers Wakeham had rung, the *Sun*, *Mail*, *Express*, *Telegraph* and *Times*, would have gone into full pre-election mode, downplaying Labour's gathering and then going on to laud every ministerial speech at the Tory conference for its vision and statesmanship. They might even have discovered the true virtues of the Citizen's Charter. Instead, relieved of the obligation to help keep the spectre of a Labour government at bay, they were generous to Kinnock and started to speculate instead about the role Thatcher would play the following week. Would she appear? Would she overshadow the prime minister if she did? The answers were yes and no. Party managers allowed her on the platform and she was greeted with rapturous applause, but they persuaded her not to speak and for once she kept her own counsel. Major's own speech was improved by the return of Sir Ronald Millar, who had scripted so many of Thatcher's best lines, and earned him generous reviews. He promised 'wealth cascading down the generations', and even managed a joke about what the papers said about him: 'A great deal has been written about my education. Never has so much been written about so little.'[35] But a good conference week in Blackpool wasn't enough to propel the Tories into an election-winning lead in the opinion polls. The prospect of an autumn election faded further, although just in case there was the customary pre-election spat with the BBC. The Tories believed, with some justification, that the corporation had given too much credence to Labour claims that the Tories wanted to privatise the NHS. Chris Patten, the party chairman, not an instinctive BBC-basher under normal circumstances, told the assembled representatives that if

they thought programmes were biased they should complain immediately and 'If necessary, jam the switchboards.'[36]

With the election delayed, Major was now free to devote his attention to a very different kind of fight – getting the kind of deal he
wanted from the Maastricht negotiations. Failure was not an option,
not least because it would have united the Thatcherite right in his parliamentary party and in the media against him. It was a fate he would
suffer in any event, but his success at Maastricht held it off until he was
safely back in Downing Street with his own mandate. Only later would
his enemies decide that the deal he secured was a betrayal of Britain's
proud heritage as an independent nation. At the time, to judge by what
they said, they thought he'd done extraordinarily well. The British delegation went to Maastricht with clear 'red lines'. The UK would not
be railroaded into monetary union with the rest of Europe, defence
and foreign policy must remain at the national level and the provisions
of the so-called 'Social Chapter', which among other things would
have undermined much Tory legislation on the unions and employment rights, must not be imposed on Britain. He got everything he
wanted. It was 'game, set and match'. Boris Johnson, then the
European Community correspondent of the *Daily Telegraph*, correctly
predicted that 'The headlines today, and not just in the popular press,
will read that Britain has slain the dragon of the social chapter.'[37] Under
the headline 'Major Wins All He Asked For At Maastricht', *The Times*
said it was 'an emphatic success'. The *Daily Mail*'s headline was 'Major
Wins By A Knock-Out'. Even Margaret Thatcher was caught on
camera saying he had done 'brilliantly.' She later claimed this was a
'misunderstanding' and that she knew already that 'I would have to
oppose it root and branch'.[38] Fortunately for Major she started 1992
resolved to get down to work on her memoirs rather than causing
trouble in the run-up to the election.

John Major was conscious that he was governing with Thatcher's
mandate and not his own. 'I had the sneaking feeling that I was living
in sin with the electorate. I wanted to change that.'[39] Prime ministers
suffer higher-than-usual levels of anxiety about when to go to the
country and in what circumstances when they know the maximum
five-year term of a parliament is about to expire. Jim Callaghan got it

wrong and, in retrospect, John Major did, too. Following the first
Commons vote on the Maastricht treaty, which he won comfortably
with only a handful of votes against (led by Norman Tebbit) and
abstentions (including Margaret Thatcher), the prime minister weighed
up whether to pass its provisions into law on a shortened parliamentary timetable. Had he done so it would have avoided many of the
agonies of the next parliament, although the combined might of the
foreign-exchange markets and a virulent alliance of right-wingers in
parliament and the media would still have made life hell.

Instead, the early months of 1992 saw the final legislation to replace
the poll tax take centre stage while at party headquarters all energies
were focused on election planning. There the key players largely
accepted the conventional wisdom that, while Labour had lost the previous election in 1987, it had won the campaign. The Tories vowed
not to cede the battle for news management and control of the media
agenda again. Sarah Hogg and Jonathan Hill, who were closely
involved in the preparations, acknowledged that the aim was 'to reduce
risk, to eliminate spontaneity, to curtail the cut and thrust of political
debate. Words should be written down on autocue, photographs plot-
ted in advance, sound-bites pre-cooked and wrapped in clingfilm: for
Britain was bound to follow the Americans further and further down
the path of candy-floss politics.'[40] They quoted one of their colleagues
at Central Office as saying, 'What you have to understand is that the
prime minister is just wallpaper. All he's got to do is provide the pictures.' In other words the demands of the media campaign were to take
precedence at every turn.

From the start of the New Year what the Conservatives called their
Near Term campaign was already on. Early January saw the launch of
the simple but devastatingly effective 'Labour's Tax Bombshell' poster.
This would develop into 'Labour's Double Whammy': higher prices
and higher taxes. It was designed by Maurice Saatchi and was very
much in the style of the Saatchis' groundbreaking 'Labour Isn't
Working' of 1979. As the polls showed the campaign was taking effect
the Tory strategists were justifiably pleased with themselves. Unwisely,
however, they let their satisfaction show. The papers were full of stories about the mechanics of the campaign, the spin doctors and

strategists and the rest of the Central Office 'brat pack'. Among the advisers who were so proud of their media skills was a young man by the name of David Cameron. Within a few years the Conservatives would be trying to imply that 'spin' was a wicked invention of New Labour, conveniently airbrushing out their own highly effective use of many of the same techniques.

Shaun Woodward acknowledged the importance the Conservatives attached to political 'branding' as the 1992 election approached. In a revealing insight, given his later defection to New Labour, he felt that for most voters there was nothing much to choose between the two parties. 'So what we were confronted with was very much like a marketing exercise trying to establish differences between brands that were basically alike. The answer was obvious – packaging. From the packaging point of view the obvious difference was Major and Kinnock.'[41] Chris Patten calculated that the best single weapon in their armoury was 'trust'. Woodward, however, recognised its limitations for positive campaigning. 'A slogan like "You Can Trust John Major" just invites people to start discussing Major's credibility in a way that causes as many problems as it solves.' Negative campaigning, turning the attack on Labour and on Neil Kinnock in particular, was the obvious answer.

Major knew by now he couldn't count on the automatic adulation that Thatcher had enjoyed from so much of the press. He wasn't good at charming the editors and proprietors, not least because he had no interest in telling them what they wanted to hear. Rupert Murdoch had come away from a meeting with him believing 'he is paranoiac about the press'.[42] Patten agreed but had had no more success than anybody else in convincing Major to take the day-to-day criticism in his stride. The prime minister didn't like journalists and they knew it, but now, with the polls showing the parties neck and neck, he needed their help like never before. When it came to bending editorial ears Patten and Woodward realised they would have to do it themselves.

Parliament was dissolved in the middle of March with election day set for 9 April. The polls showed Labour with a narrow lead. They were, in the words of the *Guardian*, 'the least favourable circumstances for a sitting government since Harold Wilson ended the last 13-year tenure in 1964'.[43] The general election of 1992 is remembered for many things – John Major on his soapbox, bitter arguments over the NHS, Labour's triumphalist rally in Sheffield – but above all perhaps for the claim after the Tories won against expectations that 'It's The Sun Wot Won It'.[44] Never have so many column inches and so many hours of academic research been given over to seeking to establish whether the media, and the Tory tabloids in particular, determined the outcome of an election. That the case has never been decisively proved one way or the other simply reinforces the central dilemma at the heart of this book. Proprietors, editors and political journalists as well as prime ministers, campaign managers and spin doctors all know that the media has the power to influence public opinion and consequently voting intentions. What none of them can know for certain is whether that influence is sufficient, irrespective of everything else that helps the individual voter to make up his or her mind, to alter the result. If it could be shown that the popular-newspaper campaign had saved Major from defeat in 1992 then every prime minister would be justified in believing in the power of the media to determine their fate. Sadly the reverse is not true. Even though it almost certainly wasn't the *Sun* wot won it, the temptation is for party leaders to continue to behave as if it was, just in case. And in so doing they cede to the media a power to influence political behaviour that they don't deserve.

Kelvin MacKenzie, then editing the *Sun*, got 'the biggest bollock-ing of his life' from Rupert Murdoch after the headline appeared.[45] Much as they love to have prime ministers chasing after their favour, today's proprietors and editors know the risks of extravagant claims that appear at best boastful and at worst anti-democratic. Sir Nicholas Lloyd at the *Express* and Sir David English at the *Mail* were equally quick to disavow any such power to influence the outcome of an election. MacKenzie pointed out that the headline referred to somebody else's view, not necessarily the paper's. That somebody was none other than the defeated candidate for prime minister, Neil Kinnock. In a terse speech after the result he said: 'I make, and I seek, no excuses, and I express no bitterness, when I say that the Conservative-supporting press has enabled the Tory party to win yet again when the Conservative party could not have secured victory for itself on the basis of its record, its programme or its character.'[46] Kinnock himself then quoted another man's judgement to back up his assertion. This was the former Tory party treasurer and arch-Thatcherite, Lord McAlpine, who had said: 'The heroes of this campaign were Sir David English, Sir Nicholas Lloyd, Kelvin MacKenzie and the other editors of the grander Tory press. Never in the past nine elections have they come out so strongly in favour of the Conservatives. Never has their attack on the Labour party been so comprehensive . . . This was how the election was won.'[47] Margaret Thatcher herself told Lloyd, 'You won it, Sir Nicholas, you won it!'[48] Joe Haines, former press secretary to Wilson and now *Daily Mirror* leader writer, agreed: 'if Kinnock had been able to persuade four newspaper proprietors who don't even have a vote to support him, he would have been in Number 10 today.'[49] What McAlpine, Thatcher, Haines and indeed Kinnock all had in common was a reluctance to give John Major the credit for winning on his own merits. Naturally he resented that and arguably treated the press with even greater contempt as a result. When, five years later, he suffered a catastrophic defeat, many people drew the wrong conclusion again. He didn't win in 1992 because the headline writers helped him, nor did he lose in 1997 because they switched their affections to Tony Blair.

The '92 campaign started badly for Major. His early appearances, sitting on a stool surrounded by audiences of safe Conservative supporters, were mocked as 'Val Doonican without the guitar'. Once again Labour seemed on course to win the campaign. Kinnock looked prime-ministerial as he swept around the country in smart suits and even smarter cars. The shadow chancellor, John Smith, had presented his own alternative Budget just before the election was called and visually he too looked the part, although drawing attention to the tax issue, never a winner for Labour, was a tactical mistake. At first the *Sun* seemed more bored by the campaign than anything else. Only towards the end did it pull out the stops on Major's behalf. The soapbox helped. John Major's decision to break out of the confines of the pre-planned campaign and go back to the oldest form of political campaigning had a disproportionate effect on the modern media. A week before polling day he told *The Jimmy Young Show* he'd done it because elections were 'not about hiding away in photo opportunities and striking an image'[50], although Major speaking directly to the crowds was itself a striking image. It gave the press an opportunity to reassess him and to face up to the consequences of his defeat. The *Sun*, in common with the other Tory tabloids, now praised his decent qualities but had more fun vilifying Kinnock. It reached its climax on the eve of polling day with a special 'Nightmare On Kinnock Street' edition with eight pages of dire warnings of what would happen if Labour won. Readers were warned that they would need the approval of lesbian and gay groups on left-wing councils before they could install a loft conversion. The paper's psychic revealed from beyond the grave that Mao and Trotsky would vote Labour if they could while Queen Victoria and Elvis Presley were Tories.[51] It was easy to dismiss as harmless fun, but on polling day itself the front page was a picture of Kinnock's head inside a light bulb with the headline 'If Kinnock Wins Today Will The Last Person In Britain Please Turn Out The Lights'[52]. In case its readers didn't get the point the paper helpfully went on: 'We do not want to influence your choice of prime minister but if it's a bald bloke with wispy red hair and two K's in his surname, we'll see you at the airport.'

Detailed analysis of the shift in voting intentions during the campaign by the polling organisation MORI suggested that 4 per cent of *Sun* readers switched their preference in the last week. Martin Linton, then a *Guardian* journalist and now a Labour MP, used other polling data to put the figure at 8 per cent and was at the forefront of those arguing that this was enough to swing the election for Major[53]. He was supported to a degree by academics like Ivor Crewe who thought as many as six seats could have gone Tory as a result.[54] They pointed out that many of the key marginals won by the Tories had a high percentage of *Sun* readers. In Basildon, for example, it was estimated at 50 per cent. David Hill, one of Labour's most experienced and respected media advisers, argued that 'it doesn't require many *Sun* readers in that town to be marginally influenced by a constant diet of vitriol for it to have some effect on the result'.[55]

And yet this must be weighed against some salient facts that point the other way. The Conservatives did less well in the marginals than in their national share of the vote. And according to one academic study,

support for the Conservatives *fell* by 3 per cent among readers of the
Tory tabloids in the course of the campaign and by 1 per cent among
readers of the Tory broadsheets. Fewer than 40 per cent of *Sun* readers ended up voting Conservative.[56] If there was a late swing to Major
it was among readers of pro-Labour papers like the *Daily Mirror* and
among those who weren't regular newspaper readers at all. Shaun
Woodward thought Labour was just desperately looking for somebody
to blame and 'it is naïve to assume that the British public are so unsophisticated that they would do what newspapers tell them to do'.[57]
Ultimately David Hill agreed. Despite the biased coverage and the evidence that the Tory papers were in collusion with Conservative
Central Office once again, he didn't believe that the *Sun* had won it.
'Any sensible analysis of the result shows that we lost because we did
not have the necessary trust of the key swing voters. But that is not to
underestimate the power of the press.'[58] Neil Kinnock himself later
agreed that, while he detested having his head stuck in a light bulb,
what lost him the election was the culmination of a much longer
process in which he had been vilified by the media.[59]

While the long-term campaign of denigration by the Tory tabloids
is indisputable, it doesn't mean that, had the media been scrupulously
fair to Kinnock at all times, he would have gone on to become prime
minister. Nobody has yet devised a method for isolating the impact of
sustained press distortion from all the other factors that contribute to
the judgements voters make about a politician's fitness for the highest
office. A more likely explanation for Major's victory is that, while there
were enough voters who *wanted* to believe Kinnock was ready to be
prime minister, when it finally came to casting their vote they didn't.
Daniel Finkelstein, who was director of the Conservative research
department under Major and now writes for *The Times*, calls it the
'Kinnock Test' and argues that it can be applied to all general-election
results. It relies on a belief that instinctively the voters get it right. 'The
proposition is that in every contest in these last 80 years the party that
was more fit to govern has been victorious. Sometimes both of the
main offerings were weak and unappealing, often the winner wasn't
much good, but always the winner was better able to conduct the business of government than was the loser.'[60] So just because the tabloids

treated Kinnock outrageously it doesn't mean he was the better man for the job. Ultimately, of course, that comes down to a matter of opinion. Newspaper editors and proprietors can ensure their opinions are conveyed with far greater force than those of the rest of the population. Their views do have an influence, but even in 1992 it does not appear that they alone were able to determine who should be prime minister.

John Major was returned to power with a parliamentary majority of just twenty-one, desperately small given the number of his MPs who continued to identify more with the Euro-scepticism of his predecessor than with his own more pragmatic approach. Many of his friends had lost their seats, including Chris Patten. Nevertheless, it should have been a decisive boost to his confidence and authority. But any sense of personal satisfaction was short-lived and his sensitivity to the media was, once again, a debilitating factor. The debate over the influence of the press continued and Major was stung by suggestions that he was still prime minister only because Rupert Murdoch had thrown his weight behind him, or because he was seen to be the better of two poor contenders. Max Hastings, then editor of the *Daily Telegraph*, wrote that 'it was Neil Kinnock who made it possible for the *Telegraph* and the Tory party, to fall in behind John Major during the campaign'.[61] According to Charles Lewington, who took over as the Tory director of communications during Major's second term, 'he certainly thought the media were more important and influential than they actually were and I think part of this was to do with the folklore and the role of the *Sun* in the 1992 election. He didn't have any way of disproving the theory that the *Sun* had won it for him.'[62] Sir Christopher Meyer, his press secretary from 1994, agrees: 'Like Tony Blair and Gordon Brown he exaggerated the power of national newspaper editors and thought they could swing elections.'[63]

Regardless of how it had been achieved, Major barely had time to savour his victory. Within a week Margaret Thatcher was at it again, using the media to take the shine off his success. She told *Newsweek*, 'I don't accept the idea that all of a sudden Major is his own man . . . There isn't such a thing as Majorism.'[64] The new Queen's Speech included the ratification of the Maastricht treaty, so hated by Thatcher and her followers. There was plenty of other legislation, including the establishment of the National Lottery, and to Major's satisfaction the papers acknowledged the Tories hadn't run out of steam. Not everything in politics can be legislated for, however, and the most significant event of 1992 was not the election or anything put before parliament, but the events of Wednesday, 16 September. Black Wednesday.

The eviction of the pound from the European exchange-rate mechanism, after a massive run on sterling that the Treasury had been powerless to resist, destroyed in a few hours the Conservative party's reputation for economic competence. John Major was closely identified with the ERM. He was the chancellor who had finally persuaded Thatcher to join against her own instincts. It is for economists to argue whether the reverse was in Britain's long-term interests. In the short term it was a hugely expensive political and public-relations disaster. The chancellor, Norman Lamont, appeared outside the Treasury, with his special adviser David Cameron at his side, and promised that sterling would rejoin 'as soon as circumstances allowed'. They never did. Rumours swirled around newsrooms that the prime minister had come close to a breakdown although everybody who was with him that day denies it. Major knew he had to take personal responsibility and 'went to bed half-convinced my days as prime minister were drawing to a close'[65]. Writing after he left office he said: 'On that day, a fifth consecutive election victory . . . became remote, if not impossible.' That evening Major did something he had rarely done before and would rarely do again. He rang some of the newspaper editors to see how they planned to cover what had happened. The most colourful reply, not surprisingly, came from Kelvin MacKenzie at the *Sun*. 'Prime minister, I have on my desk in front of me a very large bucket of shit which I am just about to pour all over you.' There was a pause. Major said, 'Oh Kelvin! You are a wag!'[66] The headline, recalling a recent sex scandal involving a minister, was 'Now We've *ALL* Been Screwed By The Cabinet'. The rest of the press coverage was not much better and it went on for days. Norman Fowler, who had replaced Patten as party chairman, wrote in his diary that Major was 'very down about the press comment. He fears he is "damaged to the point of not being able to recover".'[67] As Bruce Anderson observed in the *Guardian*, relations between the Tory leader and the Tory press were worse than at any time since Baldwin had taken on Rothermere and Beaverbrook in the 1930s.[68]

In Major's own assessment ejection from the ERM changed his relations with both the media and the Euro-sceptic right of his party for ever. 'Political journalists and politicians have always dined from the same table, but from Black Wednesday on, the Conservative press enmeshed itself closely with the more active elements on the Euro-sceptic cause,'[69] he wrote. 'Such daily opposition ripped into my premiership, damaged the Conservative party and came close to destroying the government. Some of those involved would protest their genuine horror at the effect of what they were doing. "Those news-paper people are all small men and small women with large powers," said Margaret Thatcher privately. But, alas, not publicly.'[70] The chan-cellor, whose private views were closer to Thatcher's than to Major's, came under even greater pressure. Max Hastings told Lamont to his face on the day after Black Wednesday that he should resign, warning him, 'if you stay, you'll simply be hounded out sooner or later'. Hastings believed it was 'the only unequivocally wise political coun-sel I ever tendered'[71] and the *Telegraph* continued to hound Lamont until he was finally sacked a year later.

The only resignation in the weeks that followed, however, had nothing to do with the ERM. The *Sun*'s 'we've all been screwed' headline was a reference to the heritage secretary, David Mellor. His affair with an actress had been exposed by the *People* in July but he had managed to keep his job, partly because Major didn't want to lose him and thought his personal life was his own business and partly because many of the more lurid stories were pure invention. Now it emerged that he had enjoyed a holiday over the summer as the guest of the daughter of an official of the Palestinian Liberation Organisation. This time Major reluctantly accepted that he had to go. Once again the prime minister was accused of having dithered. The *Sun* asked 'Is It Time For Mrs T?'[72]

It was all manna to the newly elected Labour leader, John Smith, who looked every inch a credible alternative. In their first Commons clash he called Major the 'devalued prime minister of a devalued government'.[73] And it was poison ahead of the Conservative party conference in October. Throughout the week the *Sun* ran a telephone poll on whether Lady Thatcher, as she now was, should be brought back. By chance I took a morning off from reporting on the conference to go and see her at her Chesham Street home in London. I wanted to record a farewell tribute to John Cole who was retiring as political editor of the BBC. She did her best for John, a man she considered to be a lifelong socialist, and then spent the best part of an hour regaling me with the inadequacies of John Major and the iniquities of the Maastricht treaty. I still have the photocopy she gave me of the text with her own handwritten criticisms in every margin. I had a good story but hardly an exclusive. She would say the same to anybody who asked her.

Europe overshadowed the conference. Norman Tebbit received a rapturous reception for a speech condemning the treaty in its present form. Kenneth Baker, the former home secretary, quoted Martin Luther saying he could 'do no other' but oppose Maastricht. Thatcher told the *European* of all newspapers it was a 'straitjacket . . . [which] would be ruinous' and on Spanish TV demanded a referendum. The media lapped it all up, although when she appeared on the platform they couldn't help notice that her reception was rather more subdued than the year before.

Major now had ranged against him a resurgent Labour party, the bulk of what had once been the Tory press and a large enough rump of diehard Euro-sceptics to overturn his slender parliamentary majority. He would be forced to threaten a snap election more than once before he could get the treaty through. And he was not above using the media himself to give vent to his frustration. Norman Fowler, who thought the threat to call a suicidal election was 'unsustainable', was dismayed to hear it given prominence on the BBC while the prime minister was on a visit to Egypt in October. Major had already made 'back me or sack me' noises when he gave an off-the-record briefing to journalists in his Commons office the week before. The latest story went further, suggesting that it was not just the prime minister's job that might be put on the line, but the future of the whole government. Fowler tried to play it down until he received a call from Gus

O'Donnell that confirmed 'wearily' that Major himself had once again been the source during another briefing on the plane to Cairo. O'Donnell told Fowler 'He had not thought what message he wanted to get over and as a result the agenda was set for him . . . Did a defeat mean there would be an election? "You must draw your own conclusions," John replied. John thus never used the word "election" himself but had failed to guide them off the prospect.'[74]

O'Donnell tried forlornly to keep Major from speaking to correspondents off the record on foreign trips and advised his successor, Christopher Meyer, to do the same. Meyer told the prime minister on many occasions to stop because 'sooner or later you tell them something and that's their lead for the following morning and it obliterates whatever was the purpose of the visit, so stop doing it'[75]. According to Meyer, Major knew the risks but 'it was the moth and flame thing. He knew the press could burn him but he couldn't resist going in closer. It was as if one last briefing could fix it.'

The prime minister wasn't alone in his enthusiasm for off-the-record briefings. Members of his cabinet, some of whom thought of themselves as potential replacements if he ever did resign, were speaking to journalists with less and less regard for either collective responsibility or the rules of confidentiality. Those on the Euro-sceptic right, Michael Howard, Peter Lilley and Michael Portillo in particular, were those most often blamed but they were far from alone. A common theme, apart from the running sore of Maastricht, was the lack of any unifying theme or strategy for the government as a whole. After one illuminating lunch Michael Howard sent me a note: 'I hope it served at least to get across the seething sense of frustration which so many of us feel!'

Major tried to answer all the criticism in a series of interviews at the start of 1993. He told *Breakfast With Frost* that he recognised the need for 'strong government' and that his would be based on 'choice and opportunity'.[76] It wasn't enough. The pace of leaks quickened and on 21 January he read the riot act to the cabinet. His words duly appeared in the papers within days. With such indiscipline government communications were in disarray. O'Donnell lacked the political authority to knock heads together. If the prime minister couldn't do it, how could he? Drift, muddle and incompetence became the media watchwords for the Major administration. Every attempt at a fresh start ran into the ground. The *Daily Telegraph* recalled the criticism it had made of Anthony Eden in 1956 and called again for the 'smack of firm government'.[77]

It was the *Sun*'s turn to echo its own judgement when the chancellor produced a tax-raising Budget, including VAT on fuel. It was, the paper said, 'Nightmare On Lamont Street'.[78] As the Maastricht bill made its tortuous way through the Commons the *Sun* and its allies kept up the pressure, fed on a daily basis with warnings from the Eurosceptics that Britain's very future as an independent state was under threat. When the prime minister sought to reassure them he was ignored or derided. And at times the picture he painted of the Britain he wanted to defend seemed wildly out of touch with the experience of most voters. It was 'the country of long shadows on cricket grounds, warm beer, invincible green suburbs, dog lovers and pools fillers, and as George Orwell said, old maids bicycling to holy communion through the morning mist'.[79] The people of Brixton where he had been brought up must have wondered what planet he had been living on since he left.

In May the government did disastrously in the local elections in England and Wales and lost the safe seat of Newbury in a by-election. Talk of a leadership challenge in the autumn began to surface on a regular basis as the opinion polls suggested John Major was now the least popular prime minister on record. Something had to be done and on 27 May Major sacked his chancellor who, declining a more junior job, returned to the back benches. Norman Lamont's resignation speech didn't have the same impact as Sir Geoffrey Howe's three years earlier, but it was wounding nonetheless. His target was the prime minister but he started by aiming at the pollsters and party managers. 'The trouble is that they are not even very good at politics, and they are entering too much into policy decisions. As a result, there is too much short-termism, too much reacting to events, and not enough shaping of events. We give the impression of being in office but not in power. Far too many important decisions are made for 36 hours' publicity.'[80] Given that the government was proving so inept at presentation it was a curious charge, but the central message that the Major government lacked any sense of direction struck home. The two men never spoke again.

John Major now had another enemy on the back benches. Not one who was ever likely to be an alternative candidate for the leadership, but a powerful irritant nonetheless. He didn't want any more. In June 1993 he had another crisis of confidence. He told Fowler he would resign if he thought it was in the national interest. 'If I went we would be able to turn over a new page. Even the blood lust of the press would be satisfied.'[81] The party chairman told him they had a year to turn things around and they both knew the biggest challenge lay in restoring discipline to the parliamentary party. Major unintentionally revealed his dilemma the following month in the least private of environments, a television studio. He was interviewed by Michael Brunson of ITN after a night of high drama at Westminster. On 23 July, Major had finally got parliament's approval for the Maastricht treaty. It had been a close-run thing. He lost the first vote when some of his Eurosceptic rebels voted with the opposition and got his way only after calling a confidence vote to reverse the decision under the threat of an immediate general election. When the interview was over Major unclipped his microphone and, thinking he could now speak privately, said, 'what I don't understand Michael, is why such a complete wimp like me keeps winning everything'.[82] Brunson then put to him the rumours that three members of his cabinet (he didn't name them but they were Michael Portillo, Peter Lilley and John Redwood) were threatening to resign over Europe. Major was blunt about why he hoped to keep them in office 'Where do you think most of the poison is coming from?' he asked. 'From the dispossessed and the never-possessed. You and I can think of ex-ministers who are causing all sorts of trouble. Do we want three more of the bastards out there?'

Within days the *Daily Mirror* helpfully set up a phone line so that readers could hear the prime minister's words for themselves. It had been possible because the ITN studios at Millbank, close to the Houses of Parliament, are linked to the other broadcasters by a network of wires that enable journalists to share material to which they are all entitled. Upstairs at the BBC one of my colleagues, Nicholas Jones, was still listening to the sound feed. It hadn't been switched off after the formal interview was over. As is his habit he was making a full short-hand note. Only much later, in his book *Trading Information*, did Jones, who is an outspoken critic of how governments manipulate the media, admit to having leaked what he heard. Politicians aren't the only ones to pass on information unattributably when it suits them. Major was intensely irritated when the row over his comments distracted attention from his victory. The rebels appeared delighted to learn that they had got under his skin and did everything to show it, short of wearing lapel badges proclaiming 'I'm a Bastard'.

As 1993 went on Major found he was fighting on two fronts simultaneously. When the Euro-sceptic press wasn't attacking him over Maastricht, it was taking part in the most sustained assault on the integrity and responsibility of government ministers ever launched by the media. Here, too, Major's own words would be used against him. It has become one of the myths of the Major years that he opened the floodgates on intrusion into ministerial private lives himself with his 'Back to Basics' speech to the party conference in October of that year. The truth is that most of the stories would have been run in any case. The speech merely gave the papers the opportunity to tar the prime minister personally with the sins, real, imagined or exaggerated, of his colleagues.

The 'Back to Basics' speech was designed as another fresh start after yet another difficult pre-conference period. In September, Major's visit to Japan was overshadowed by his response to talk of a leadership challenge. Yet again he spoke to journalists on the plane and gave vent to his frustration. Once on the ground he did another briefing and said he heard 'the flapping of white coats' whenever one of the rebels was mentioned. Collectively they were 'barmy'. When John Sergeant of the BBC asked about the party splits in a TV interview, Major was livid and even O'Donnell's patience snapped. Uncharacteristically he called Sergeant 'a jerk' in front of other journalists[83]. Major's victory in July was as good as forgotten. His war with the rebels in his own party and with the media, who lapped up their every utterance, continued unabated.

At first Major was pleasantly surprised to find that the Blackpool conference went better than expected. Even Lady Thatcher was persuaded to delay the serialisation of her memoirs until the following weekend. The prime minister got the longest standing ovation of his career and his speech was well received. The call to 'go back to basics' gained notoriety only later. At the time it was largely dismissed as woolly and wishful thinking. *The Economist* called it 'comically uninspiring'.[84] The basics he outlined were 'sound money; free trade; traditional teaching; respect for the family and the law'[85]. He even made a point of saying it wasn't the government's job to make people good: 'That is for parents, for churches, for schools.' But the chief whip, Richard Ryder, hadn't been consulted about the wording and he was nervous. It was part of his job to know what mischief his colleagues got up to in their private lives and he knew that 'any initiative with even a hint of moralising about it would give the press an excuse to hunt down Tory MPs'.[86] The party chairman, Norman Fowler, regretted that the speech had been finalised so late. 'There was no time for collective examination of the words before they were spoken. Questions and answers could not be prepared; press officers could not be properly briefed.'[87] He was clear, however, that Major was not launching a campaign about sexual morality, 'and following the revelation of Major's affair with Edwina Currie it can now be seen to be so. Major was never a fool. He was not likely to start a campaign that could leave him as the chief victim.' The initial cause of the misinterpretation was attributed to Tim Collins, then the party's director of communications, who was asked if Major meant to include 'moral basics' and replied that he did.

In his memoirs Major acknowledges that he should have seen the risk. Editors could now claim a 'public interest' justification for running all sorts of stories. 'From that day forward, any tittle-tattle about a parliamentary colleague could be published as a serious political news story, under the "nose" (as I believe editors call it) of an opening paragraph along the lines of: "Prime minister John Major was last night severely embarrassed in his call for a return to moral basics by the shock disclosure that Mr X, now junior minister for paper clips, once spent a steamy night . . ." – and so on. I could write such stuff myself. Any fool could. Many fools did.'[88] Perhaps it is time to add John Major to the list of prime ministers who could have built an equally successful career in journalism.

The broadcasters, as ever, were able to follow a step or two behind. We would tend to play down or ignore the initial allegations against a minister, but as soon as any political consequences could possibly be seen to follow, including the likelihood of a resignation, we were on the case. At the beginning of January 1994 the BBC sent me to Suffolk, where Tim Yeo, a local MP and middle-ranking environment minister, was revealed to have fathered a 'love child'. He, quite reasonably, hoped to hang on to his job. The leader of the Liberal Democrats, Paddy Ashdown, had held on to his after being labelled 'Paddy Pantsdown' by the *Sun*, and Steve Norris, a junior transport minister, had been able to shrug off reports of multiple affairs just a few months earlier. But Yeo wasn't to be so lucky. An attempt by Norman Fowler to say it wasn't for the government or for the media to pry into the private lives of individuals was written up by the *Sun* as 'Carry On Bonking, Fowler Tells Tories'[89]. Although Yeo had never been a moraliser, the paper attacked MPs for 'not practising what they preach'. The charge was one of hypocrisy and papers at both ends of the spectrum joined in. There was politics mixed up in it, too. Yeo was a pro-European supporter of Michael Heseltine; his loudest critics in the party and in the press were on the right. He eventually resigned on 5 January when it was obvious his local party wasn't standing by him. 'Tory Chaos As Back To Basics Backfires' said the *Sunday Telegraph*.[90] Three days later the *Sun* declared, 'What fools we were to back John Major.' The prime minister tried forlornly to hold back the tide, insisting on the day after accepting Yeo's resignation that 'back to basics' was 'not a crusade about personal morality and was never presented as such'[91], but the waves of 'sleaze' stories would crash over him for the rest of his premiership.

Gus O'Donnell would not be at his side to help him through the storms to come. He left Number 10 at the beginning of 1994 to resume his career at the Treasury. His send-off was enough to remind him of everything he'd be leaving behind. At his farewell dinner in Downing Street, to which ten journalists were invited, Major was reported as saying to Michael Brunson of ITN, 'I'm going to fucking crucify the right for what they have done and this time I will have the party behind me.'[92] The reports were in two newspapers whose political editors hadn't been invited to the dinner, presumably because of their hostility to Major, the *Sun* and the *Daily Mail*. They insisted they had their story from an 'absolutely reliable' source who was there. Major denied ever using the words and O'Donnell left Downing Street less willing to trust the integrity of journalists than when he had arrived.

The prime minister's new press secretary was Christopher Meyer, a former and future diplomat. He was brasher than O'Donnell and more of a bruiser when he needed to be. His model for the job was Bernard Ingham and, while Meyer lacked the Yorkshire grit and avoided getting too closely identified with the prime minister's politics, he too was a little larger than life. By his own definition, a press secretary required 'quick wits, sense of humour, histrionic skills, self-confidence and a thick skin'.[93] He had them all and he was going to need them. O'Donnell left him in no doubt about the size of the task he faced. Not merely in the almost blanket hostility of the media, which he could see for himself, but in Major's acute and unhealthy sensitivity to it.

Meyer recalled: 'I was worried when I came in that he would ask me to produce a summary of the press like Bernard had done for Margaret Thatcher, but he was so concerned about what was in the actual newspapers and suspicious that officials were trying to hide bits of the press from him that he insisted on reading the authentic thing. I tried to convey to him the notion that a lot of this stuff didn't matter and that if you showed the lobby you were sensitive to what was going on it was like throwing blood into the water when the sharks were circling. I never succeeded. He might have believed it intellectually but he couldn't do it emotionally.'[94]

Major's closest cabinet confidants gave him the same advice. Michael Heseltine, who knew how brutal the Thatcherite press could be, had developed a thicker skin. 'John was continuously at the receiving end of adverse press comment, which he was finding increasingly difficult to bear. I told him simply not to read it. But such advice ran counter to his character. He was a man who had to know.'[95] The foreign secretary, Douglas Hurd, found the contradictions in Major's approach curious. 'He's the only PM I know that laughed at himself quite consistently but was also extremely sensitive, particularly of the written press. He would ring me early in the morning – "have you seen this, have you seen that?" – and I never had. He worried about it and talked about it endlessly. He agrees now that this went too far and he was over-concerned with it. He tried to remedy it with all the off-the-record stuff but it bounced back and the remedy was worse than the disease. He just got it wrong. And it made his own life unhappy as a result. By reading too many papers, worrying about tiny things. I just find it very odd. I said it all to him at the time and he accepted it all but he went on worrying.'[96]

If Meyer couldn't change the prime minister's personality he could at least set about organising drinks and dinners with editors and proprietors to try to improve relations. Rupert Murdoch was among those invited. According to one witness Major 'almost pleaded with Rupert to give him a fair wind. When John had gone Rupert said, "He's a nice guy, but is he strong enough?"'[97] Looking back much later, Meyer acknowledged that the relationship with Murdoch never prospered. 'With his unerring eye for winners, the only way you could win over Rupert was to convince him that the Tories stood a good chance of winning the next election and John Major was an effective leader, but neither of those things was present.'[98] Meyer tried to stop the prime minister talking to journalists on aeroplanes after being warned by O'Donnell of the pitfalls. Correspondents, including Alastair Campbell, then on the short-lived *Today* newspaper, complained that Major had become the 'invisible man'. But it seemed to be working. After a visit to Moscow in February the *Daily Telegraph* said, 'For the first time since the general election he has completed a gaffe-free trip.'[99] At home the scandals, although few really warranted the term, continued. Some were sexual, others financial, but Major refused to give a running commentary on them. Norman Fowler, himself a former *Times* journalist, reflected the collective view in Downing Street and Central Office when he said, 'The truth about this period is that the media suddenly became hysterical and balanced judgement simply went out of the window.'[100]

Extraordinarily Major chose this time to consider legislation to protect the privacy of individuals, including politicians, from media intrusion. Fowler thought the idea absurd as it 'would be seen as clearly

self-serving – to say nothing of alienating the press'[101]. A taste of what
might come was served up by Kelvin MacKenzie. He revealed that a
member of the cabinet had approached him during the previous
election campaign offering false allegations about other alleged affairs
involving Paddy Ashdown. Fowler questioned every cabinet minister
and all denied it but his personal view was that it had happened. Major
was eventually persuaded to drop the idea. He had new allegations to
deal with and this time they had nothing to do with anybody's private
life.

Major was called to give evidence into the lengthy inquiry into the
Arms-to-Iraq affair which included the allegation, first revealed by the
Sunday Times, that ministers in Mrs Thatcher's government had been
prepared to see three businessmen go to jail rather than admit their
own wrongdoing. Major was not directly involved, although some of
his ministers were, but that didn't stop some papers claiming that his
integrity was on the line. The Scott Inquiry largely exonerated those
still in office, but Major narrowly avoided losing two of his cabinet,
William Waldegrave and Nicholas Lyell. The precariousness of his parliamentary position was exposed again when the Commons voted to
support the government on the issue by 320 to 319 at the end of
another confidence debate.

Arms–to-Iraq soon gave way to 'cash for questions', and this time
ministers would be caught in the net. The first allegations arose from
a controversial sting operation by the *Sunday Times*. Two Tories on the
lowest, unpaid, rung of the ministerial ladder, David Tredinnick and
Graham Riddick, had agreed to take money from a reporter posing as
a businessman in return for asking questions in the Commons. Their
actions couldn't be justified and Major didn't try. They were quickly
suspended from their jobs. Three months later the *Guardian* revealed
that two middle-ranking ministers, Tim Smith and Neil Hamilton, had
taken money and gifts while they were still on the back benches from
the owner of Harrods, Mohamed Al Fayed, without declaring them.
The editor of the *Sunday Express*, Brian Hitchen, had already been to
Downing Street to warn the prime minister personally that Fayed was
advancing stories not just about Smith and Hamilton, but also Michael
Howard and another minister, Jonathan Aitken. According to Major,

Hitchen 'said that Fayed wanted to see me himself to ask for a report by the Department of Trade and Industry into his take over of Harrods to be withdrawn or reviewed. Fayed was threatening to pass his allegations to the opposition. I responded that it would be impossible for me to see Fayed in such circumstances and Hitchen went away.'[102] The cabinet secretary, Robin Butler, had already investigated the allegations against Howard and Aitken and found them to be false. The allegations against Michael Howard were nonsense and his career was unscathed. Tim Smith resigned and would later confess to accepting cash from Fayed in return for asking questions. In their different ways Jonathan Aitken and Neil Hamilton chose to stand and fight, with disastrous consequences for the Conservative party.

Major reported to parliament on what had gone on, hoping that by exposing some of the dealings between the newspapers and Fayed he could both fire a shot over the bows of the media and show the public that not everything they read over their cornflakes was quite what it seemed. Whatever ministers might or might not have done before he became prime minister, he wasn't going to allow his administration to be accused of a cover-up. When Hamilton declined to stand down pending an investigation of the allegations, Major was forced to sack him. The *Guardian* refused to let the accusations against Aitken drop and he too stood his ground, promising to sue and 'cut out the cancer of bent and twisted journalism in our country with the simple sword of truth and the trusty shield of British fair play'[103]. He later resigned from the cabinet to pursue his legal case. In January 1999 Aitken went to jail, having been found guilty of perjury and perverting the course of justice. There were genuine issues of journalistic ethics to be addressed. The *Guardian* had used a forged letter on House of Commons notepaper to help pursue its investigation and the editor, Peter Preston, was called to account for himself in front of a Commons committee. What stuck in the minds of the voters, however, was the blanket allegation of 'sleaze'. Major's government would never shake it off. Tony Blair, elected Labour leader after John Smith's death in 1994, exploited the issue for all it was worth. Major had set up a Committee on Standards in Public Life under Lord Nolan but acknowledged in his memoirs, 'There is a good chance that, when many of the achievements of the last Conservative government . . . [of the twentieth] century have been forgotten, people will still remember one word: sleaze.'[104]

Blair's election coincided with a new bout of leadership speculation in the Tory party. The press contrasted the confident young Labour leader with his embattled opponent. Major had a word of warning for Blair: 'Don't believe what they say about you now . . . and don't believe what they say in eighteen months.'[105] Blair's honeymoon was to last a great deal longer than the prime minister predicted. Labour successfully dominated the 1994 conference season. Michael Portillo did his own party no favours by using his speech to the Tory conference to promote his prospects of succeeding Major if a vacancy arose. There was no direct leadership challenge, despite all the speculation, but in the autumn the government faced another big vote on Europe to reform the finances of what was now, thanks to the Maastricht treaty, called the European Union. The prospect of another rebellion loomed. Once again both sides of the European argument were happy to oblige the media with a constant stream of claims and counter-claims that infuriated Major and Meyer in Downing Street. Factions were also starting to emerge at Conservative Central Office, where the new chairman, Jeremy Hanley, struggled to establish his authority after a series of media gaffes of his own. The communications director, Tim Collins, was suspected of allowing his own Euro-sceptic views to colour his briefings, which were sometimes out of step with those from Downing Street. It all made Christopher Meyer's job harder than ever. 'Each morning I was forced to look the lobby in the eye and say that I saw absolutely no contradiction between these different positions,' he recalled.[106]

Even though the EU finance bill passed with relative ease, Major authorised the chief whip to retaliate against eight Tory MPs who failed to support the government. By withdrawing the whip, Major effectively suspended them from his parliamentary party and in so doing deprived his own government of its overall majority. It was a bold but, in the event, futile gesture. The 'whipless wonders', including a ninth MP who joined them voluntarily, were emboldened rather than chastised and became fixtures on the television and radio for months. Downing Street's fragile hold on the news agenda was weakened still further. The tactic had misfired badly and when the rebels were readmitted the following April they had suffered nothing more painful than the glare of the media spotlight. It gave Tony Blair the cue for another of his made-for-TV attacks at prime minister's questions when he taunted Major: 'I lead my party. He follows his.'[107]

The turn of the year into 1995 brought Major some respite. There was strong praise across the media for his handling of a new framework agreement for peace in Northern Ireland. But there were soon more ministerial resignations and Major suffered the humiliation of seeing his own youthful relationship with an older woman splashed over the front pages. More serious was renewed evidence of splits in the cabinet over Europe, with the chancellor Ken Clarke and the employment secretary Michael Portillo disagreeing publicly about the single currency. Major would lecture his cabinet about disunity and leaking to the media but the appeals went unheard. In May, Margaret Thatcher's second book of memoirs, *The Path to Power*, appeared. In it she criticised the government for lacking 'a sense of purpose' and seemed to hint at her support for a leadership challenge, echoing the speech by Sir Geoffrey Howe that had precipitated her own fall. 'I offer some thoughts about putting . . . things right', she wrote. 'It is now, however, for others to take the action required.'[108] In an interview to promote the book she called Blair 'the most formidable Labour leader since Hugh Gaitskell'.[109]

By the summer of 1995 the Conservatives were trailing Labour by almost 40 per cent in the polls. The media were still eating out of Blair's hands and the only story they seemed interested in on the Tory side was the prospect of an autumn leadership crisis. On another flight home, this time from Canada, with a disgruntled press corps again denied access to the prime minister, he decided on one last throw of the die to regain the initiative. 'I thought, "I am not prepared to tolerate this. If they wish to have a change, then they must vote for a change." So I decided to go for a leadership election.'[110]

The idea earned the prime minister plaudits for his courage and audacity. It even helped restore some of the Tories' former reputation for effective news management. Although the only voters were Tory MPs at Westminster, the campaign was a national media spectacle. The resignation of the Welsh secretary, John Redwood, to challenge Major was a surprise, but he proved incapable of looking like an alternative prime minister. Norman Lamont joined a motley crew of colourful Euro-sceptics to help launch his campaign. Margaret Thatcher helped by refusing to say any more than that both candidates were 'good Conservatives'. The Tory papers, having ridiculed Major for so long, couldn't bring themselves to support him now. Paul Dacre, editor of the *Daily Mail* since 1992, wrote later that under Major he 'could smell the decay. I was determined to break the kind of umbilical cord between the Tories and the *Mail*, which in my view was offensive; it was so obsequious and sycophantic.'[111] Major's memoirs reveal that he was told that 'the proprietors of three traditionally Conservative newspaper groups – Rupert Murdoch (News International), Vere Harmsworth (Associated Newspapers) and Conrad Black (Telegraph Group) – had met, armed with a black spot apiece. Whether this is true or false, it was widely believed to be credible, and spoke volumes for the extent to which it was presumed that the press was prepared to influence the domestic political process.'[112]

Major had only to read the headlines to confirm his suspicions. The *Sun* said it was 'Redwood Versus Deadwood' having previously commented, 'If John Major is the answer to the country's problems, then heaven knows what the question was.'[113] The *Daily Mail* said, 'Time To Ditch The Captain'.[114] The *Times* and *Sunday Times* were scarcely more helpful and hoped other heavyweight candidates would emerge. The *Telegraph* and its Sunday equivalent backed Redwood. Only the *Daily Express* and the *Daily Star* stayed loyal. Major remained confident he could win despite the media and he did. More than that, by orchestrating a swift and effective spin operation on polling day, his campaign team made what in normal circumstances would have been a damaging rebuff – a third of his party had voted against him or abstained – look like a crushing victory. Major was quoted afterwards as saying 'We're going to get the millionaire press,'[115] but others knew better than to crow about their victory over the newspapers. Norman Fowler, who had returned to the back benches, noted that the victory was not a knockout. 'Even now in the internet age you can never entirely defeat the people who control the printing presses. The proprietors, editors, the leader writers will always have the last word. Their view would be that if the party had taken their advice then the catastrophe of 1997 might have been avoided.'[116]

The leadership election bound some of his Euro-sceptic critics closer to the prime minister for a while but he failed to capitalise on his win. According to Meyer, 'as soon as things got a little bit comfortable Major eased off and fell back into the old habits.'[117] There were some significant changes at Downing Street, however. Michael Heseltine was brought closer to the centre and made deputy prime minister. This time, unlike in the case of Sir Geoffrey Howe, the title really meant something. Earlier that year Heseltine received reports from a colleague of 'conversations he had had with David English, the editor-in-chief of the *Daily Mail* and the *Mail on Sunday* and on another occasion with Rupert Murdoch. Both were now doubting if they would support John in a general election but told him they would back me for leader, if a contest developed.'[118] Heseltine never fully gave up his own hopes of succeeding, but pledged himself to work loyally for Major as long as he remained prime minister. Heseltine took charge of trying to coordinate the government's message and communications. The Number 12 committee was superseded by one of his own which met every morning at 8.30 in his vast office. One participant called them 'Cecil B. De Mille affairs'. 'There was a cast of thousands. Every civil servant involved in media work thought he had to be there. Hezza had a chair that was much higher than everyone else's so he was at least a foot above the rest of them.'[119]

Heseltine and Major put huge efforts into making the 1995 conference a success. The defection to Labour's ranks of the Tory MP Alan Howarth in a flurry of publicity carefully orchestrated by Tony Blair's press secretary, Alastair Campbell, took some of the shine off the event, but Major's speech was the best-received of his time in Number 10. 'Today,' he said, 'we meet united, healed, renewed and thirsting for the real fight with Labour.'[120] The substance, including a promise to reduce public spending to below 40 per cent of national income, seemed to offer what many of the traditionally Tory papers had been calling for. In the words of the *Daily Telegraph,* it 'put clear blue water between the Tories and Labour while at the same time retaining the government's claim to the middle ground.'[121] But the mood didn't last. The opinion polls remained dire and Tory MPs played into Labour's hands by resisting proposals from the Nolan committee for all outside earnings relating to parliamentary affairs to be disclosed. Major failed to stand up to them and was widely condemned for it. In November Hugh Colver ended a brief stint as Conservative party director of communications, where he had replaced the controversial Tim Collins, and complained in the *Sun* that while the leadership election should have been the spring-board for a political recovery 'everything has turned sour.' Why, he asked, 'with all the advantages of a well-oiled government machine at our fingertips' did the party 'continually snatch defeat from the jaws of victory?'[122]

Colver was himself replaced by a former *Express* journalist, Charles Lewington. Lewington arrived at Conservative Central Office just as a Gallup opinion poll showed the party an extraordinary 39.5 per cent behind Labour. Lewington had no illusions about the difficulty of the task he was taking on. Journalists who were inclined to be helpful, or who wanted to turn the attack onto Blair, were in a minority and feeling beleaguered themselves. Peter Oborne, who joined the *Sunday Express* in 1996, recalls that 'there was no point putting up anti-Labour stories to news desks in 1994-7. They just wouldn't run. All stories have to fit a narrative and the narrative then was "Tories in new sleaze crisis as . . .".'[123] Inside Downing Street they were well aware what they were up against and nerves got increasingly frayed as they struggled to deal with it. The prime minister wasn't the only one capable of losing his temper as Lewington discovered at his first meeting with Major and Christopher Meyer, who was about to leave to resume his diplomatic career. After an unproductive discussion about Downing Street's dealings with the media, Meyer 'slammed his papers down and said to Major "I don't know why I give you all this advice" and walked out on the prime minister, which he admitted afterwards was a rather unprofessional thing to do, but he was at the end of his tether at that point.' Meyer confirmed that 'I think it did happen once. I got quite angry. He just wouldn't take advice.'[124]

In early 1996 Major got his third press secretary, Jonathan Haslam, who had many years experience in government communications and had been Meyer's deputy. None of his experience could help Major with his party-political difficulties, however. There were more defections, more by-election defeats, more sleaze stories, more leadership speculation and more unhelpful comments from Lady Thatcher. In January, she acknowledged 'It is no secret that between John Major and me there have been differences . . . on occasion,' and went on to describe herself as the party's 'Chief Stoker', there to make sure the government didn't run out of steam. She advised against trying to move onto the centre ground which was 'as slippery as the spin doctors who have colonised it' and said the party was unpopular 'because the middle classes – and all those who aspire to join the middle classes – feel that they no longer have the incentives and opportunities they expect from a Conservative government'.[125] The billionaire businessman and MEP, Sir James Goldsmith, offered an alternative home to those on the right who were disillusioned with Major's leadership. In March he formed the Referendum Party with an avowedly anti-European and xenophobic agenda. Goldsmith threatened to run candidates again any MP he considered unsound on the Europe issue.

The threat from the right rattled many on the Tory benches whose seats were already vulnerable to Labour's massive opinion-poll leads. The pressure on the prime minister to move in a more Euro-sceptical direction was growing by the day. Major had no desire to take Lady Thatcher's advice and abandon the centre ground to Tony Blair, but he did want to show he could get tough with the European Union. In May he launched the ill-fated 'beef war' in defence of the nation's farmers. Britain, he announced, would refuse to cooperate with day-to-day EU business until the ban on exports of British beef, imposed after reports of a possible risk of a link with the human brain disease CJD, was lifted. It meant a veto on all measures requiring the unanimous support of member states. Major thought the EU was responding to 'media hysteria', but his sabre-rattling was reminiscent of his response to the 'whipless wonders'. Once again there was tough talk followed by a humiliating climb-down. 'Major Goes To War At Last'[126] said the *Daily Mail* when hostilities were declared. Jonathan Haslam briefed journalists that there would have to be a clear 'timetable' for the lifting of the ban before Britain would be satisfied.

It was a choice of words that reportedly annoyed Major and which would be thrown back at Downing Street when the prime minister lifted the veto at the end of June with no timetable in place. Most journalists didn't bother to look into the details of what Major had achieved in negotiating progress towards an end of the ban. The headlines, which were all about climb-downs and retreats, infuriated him. He told the *Sunday Times* the stories he read 'were from *Alice in Wonderland*'.[127]

Against the discouraging background of the beef war, a new committee started meeting at Central Office to plan the political war against Labour. It brought together the party's policy, media and advertising experts and the heads of Downing Street policy and political units. According to Lewington, Maurice Saatchi believed 'the public would see behind the smiles and through the PR and glitz of Labour. It was a bit like what Labour tacticians have been saying about David Cameron.'[128] The result was the 'New Labour, New Danger' campaign which led on to a poster showing Blair with 'demon eyes'. It was controversial. The poster was banned by the Advertising Standards Authority. But at least the Tories appeared to be gearing up for the fight.

Major steadfastly refused to do one thing that many of his advisers thought could transform the political situation: rule out Britain's membership of the single currency in the next parliament. Those who advocated the strategy thought Major too beholden to Heseltine and his pro-single-currency chancellor, Ken Clarke. The tensions surfaced in September when a Foreign Office minister told the BBC that Clarke was 'out of line with government policy'.[129] Major insisted on sticking to his 'wait and see' policy, but his senior ministers continued to talk to journalists and tell them that even if the prime minister hadn't made up his mind on the currency issue, they had. They eyed each other warily and scoured the press to see what those on the other side of the Europe fault-line were saying and doing. When they didn't like it they said so, sometimes publicly. Not for nothing was Norman Fowler's book on the period called *A Political Suicide*.

Haslam and Lewington encouraged the prime minister to take selected newspaper editors and proprietors into his trust. It wasn't an idea that appealed to him. 'The media had been cavalier in their treatment of the government, and brutal to some of its members, myself included. I was contemptuous of the way Labour were flatter-ing the egos of the proprietors, and did not wish to compete with them. During my time in Downing Street I had not used the honours system to reward journalists and newspaper proprietors; I owed them nothing, and did not wish to fall into debt now.'[130] He had little faith in his advisers' hope that, having given Major a good kicking, the Tory papers would support him in the run-up to an election rather than see Labour have it all their own way. Efforts to re-establish relations with News International proved difficult. Murdoch had met Major again earlier in the year but had been more concerned to talk about the impact of the proposed Broadcasting Bill on his ownership of Sky than to hear the prime minister's complaints about the coverage of sleaze or Europe.[131] Now Murdoch was said to be 'furious' that his rights to monopoly distribution of digital set-top boxes was under scrutiny by the telecommunications regulator OFTEL.[132] An 'amiable but unpro-ductive' dinner took place at which, according to Major, Murdoch 'made no offer of support, and I asked for none'.[133]

At the *Daily Mail*, the editor, Paul Dacre, showed no interest in being courted but Major was intrigued when Lord Rothermere and the *Mail* group chief editor David English told him over dinner that they thought they could help him win the election 'as though they were wholly on-side. Events were to prove otherwise.'[134] Major had a better relationship with Dominic Lawson, the son of the former chan-cellor, who edited the *Sunday Telegraph*. There was less of a rapport with Charles Moore, editor of the *Daily Telegraph,* who was known to be a Euro-sceptic and suspected of being too readily influenced by Lady Thatcher. Major invited Moore for a breakfast meeting at Downing Street. He used the occasion to send out a signal that he was dubious about the single currency, but was furious when the *Telegraph* said that he was planning to drop his 'wait and see' stance. 'I do not believe I gave him any grounds to imagine that I planned to abandon a policy I thought right for the country.'[135] On the *Today* programme Clarke called the story 'preposterous' and the papers concluded that he had blocked what Major wanted to do, something he denied. 'This was what the Euro-sceptic press wished to believe, and what Euro-sceptic ministers and MPs were telling them. It was part of the unceasing campaign to shift policy from the pragmatic centre-ground the cabinet had settled on.' Just months away from the general election and once again the prime minister appeared unable to control his own government or his party. *Today*'s editor, Roger Mosey, couldn't believe his luck when time and again cabinet ministers would appear on his programme to pursue their own agendas. 'The Downing Street machine was completely ill-disciplined. We had times when we knew that the reason Ken Clarke was appearing on the programme was because he'd been annoyed by what Michael Howard had said the day before . . . You had a government that was falling apart live on your air-waves.'[136]

At a lunch with two BBC journalists in December Clarke called the comments the *Telegraph* had attributed to Major 'a boomerang laden with high explosives'. It was naïve of him not to expect them to report the words, along with his advice to the party chairman Brian Mawhinney, in an apparent reference to Lewington and others, to 'Tell your kids to get their scooters off my lawn.'[137] Haslam, like Meyer before him, had to keep a straight face and deny that ministers were at each other's throats. Major was furious but powerless to impose collective responsibility. 'When cabinet debated European policy, ample and accurate reports of who said what found their way into the morning papers with depressing regularity.' When in January Blair taunted him in the Commons with the words 'weak, weak, weak'[138] Major looked as pained as he must have felt.

The prime minister might have been cheered by the news that he had come top of the *Today* programme's poll for 'Personality of the Year' but even this worried him. Lewington was in a hotel bar in Dorset with his wife when news of the award appeared on Ceefax on Christmas Day. The BBC's teletext service was Major's favourite source of news when he was at home in his Huntingdon constituency. Lewington's mobile rang and 'to everyone's amusement' it was the prime minister. 'Major was hugely exercised and thought that the Labour party and their friends in the BBC would twist the story and try to accuse the Tories of fixing it. Did I have any thoughts on the matter? My answer was "get a life please".'[139]

A touch of gallows humour was understandable, but the situation Major faced could scarcely have been more serious. With his gift for understatement he noted 'This was no way to go into a general election.'[140] It was clear that the splits over Europe would haunt him right up to and through the campaign. Journalists combed through every candidate's personal election address, not their usual habit, to see how many would defy the official line. Dozens, including a number of Major's middle-ranking ministers, obliged. They became heroes in the *Sun* and in the *Mail,* which praised them for being ready 'to stand up to be counted in the Battle for Britain'.[141]

No previous Conservative prime minister had fought an election with less support in the newspapers. No Labour leader had ever before secured the endorsement of more than half the national titles. The *Sun* made a huge splash out of its decision to back Blair on the day the election was called. It was a big news story for the broadcasters, although it hardly came as a surprise. Yet diehard Conservatives like Woodrow Wyatt were dismayed. 'Rupert has behaved like a swine and a pig,' he wrote in his journal. 'He doesn't like backing losers and he thinks Major will lose.'[142] In addition Labour had the *Mirror, Star, Guardian, Independent* and *Financial Times*. More surprising, perhaps, was that the Tories retained the *Telegraph* and *Daily Mail*, as well as the *Express*, although all three continued to berate Major for refusing to rule out the single currency. *The Times* opted out, urging its readers to vote for Euro-sceptic candidates from whatever party. Overall the Nuffield study calculated that in terms of daily newspaper readership, Labour had 21.6 million to the Tories' 10.6.[143] The Sunday papers all followed their daily stablemates, although the *Sunday Times* opted for the Conservatives 'warts and all'[144].

And there were warts aplenty on display throughout the campaign. Aside from the divisions over Europe, the Tories were hit with another batch of embarrassing personal stories and Neil Hamilton's defiant stand against the non-party 'anti-sleaze' candidate, Martin Bell, the former BBC correspondent, was a sideshow that ran all the way to his ignominious defeat on polling day. At Conservative Central Office there was anger at what they saw as media collusion with the opposition to build up 'sleaze' as more of an issue than it really was, but they were powerless to do anything about it. The decision to have a longer-than-usual campaign, in the hope that Labour would unravel, was also a factor. The media get bored easily and the sideshow brought variety and unpredictability to an otherwise safe and tightly managed election.

By mid-campaign Europe was again the most reported issue in the papers and on the airwaves. On 16 April, Major used one of the Conservatives' election broadcasts to urge his MPs not to wreck his policy. As Fowler noted, 'It was one of the most effective broadcasts he ever made – but whoever heard of a party leader having to appeal to his own party for loyalty in the middle of an election campaign?'[145] The Tories' best card was an economy that had strengthened significantly since Black Wednesday, but they rarely had the chance to play it effectively. They scored a modest coup when Mawhinney revealed that he had been leaked a copy of Labour's 'war book' for the election, detailing plans for some misleading negative campaigning, but Labour soon regained the initiative with a scare alleging Major wanted to abolish the state pension. It was a scrappy end to a campaign that Major had by now concluded was irretrievably lost. He hoped to limit Labour's majority to eighty or ninety.[146] On 1 May 1997, Tony Blair became the first Labour leader to win a general election since Harold Wilson twenty-three years earlier. He had an overall majority of 179.

Despite his obvious disappointment, Major left office convinced he had been right to hold firm to what he believed in. He had every reason to feel badly let down by many of his parliamentary colleagues and to observe that the media had treated him more harshly than any other prime minister of the twentieth century bar none. In the short term he received little sympathy. Those outside his party thought the idea of a Tory leader complaining of press bias was pitiable. Many Conservatives, not all of them Euro-sceptics, felt that if he had shown a clearer sense of direction and given the Tory papers some worthwhile causes to salute he might have fared much better. And yet, while it may not have been in his best interests or those of his party, he had stood up to the media with greater courage than any prime minister since Stanley Baldwin. He neither flattered them nor allowed them to dictate to him. He stood his ground and defended it tenaciously. Like Baldwin, however, he consistently failed to convey what made his territory worth defending. Compared to Labour's promise of 'change', more of the same was an unattractive offer. Having watched John Major swing in the wind, stripped to the bone by the vultures in the media – and having done all he could to encourage the feeding frenzy – Tony Blair was resolved not to let it happen to him.

11

A MAN FOR ALL SEASONS: BLAIR (1997–2007)

The press, like fire, is an excellent servant, but a terrible master.
James Fenimore Cooper

Tony Blair had been prime minister only a few days when he returned from an evening engagement to be met by an apologetic doorman at 10 Downing Street. When he asked what was wrong he was told that although staff had been sent to both nearby mainline stations, Charing Cross and Victoria, they had failed to return with the first editions of the newspapers. 'We'll try to make sure it doesn't happen again, prime minister.' Blair looked perplexed. The doorman explained that John Major had always wanted to know what was in the papers before he went to bed. The new prime minister reassured him. 'I never want to see the first editions before I go to bed. There are people who work for me whose job it is to do that.'

The anecdote, which Blair related many times, tells us more about him than it does about his predecessor. People said he was too obsessed by the media so he had a story to hand to show it wasn't true. In the long history of an office held by people of extraordinary vanity and self-obsession, none cared more about how he was perceived than Tony Blair. Even more so than Harold Macmillan, for whom the term was coined, Blair was 'the great actor manager'. The effects of ten years in office would temper his thirst for popularity, a fortunate development given the fall in his personal ratings, but it didn't lessen his ability to put on a bold performance when he chose to. Nobody who saw his role in a video for the charity *Comic Relief* in the year he was forced to take his final bow could doubt his dramatic talent. He played his part opposite the comedian Catherine Tate, complete with the catchphrase 'Am I bovvered?', almost to perfection.

Another of Catherine Tate's characters would rise to any challenge saying, 'I can do that!' It could have been written for Blair. For over ten years journalists, academics and political opponents struggled to identify the real Tony Blair. None succeeded. In desperation many concluded he was 'all spin and no substance', an easy jibe that missed the real point. He didn't lack substance but he did have an infuriating ability to remould it to suit almost any audience. If he was aware of Walter Mondale's observation that political image was like cement* he was determined never to let it dry fully in case the result was unflattering. 'You want a man of the people? I can do that. Determined war leader? That's me. Family man? Conviction politician? Pragmatist? Moral guardian? Social liberal? Fiscal conservative? Pluralist? Statesman? Ordinary bloke? I can do that!' His biographer John Rentoul called him 'an Augustinian preacher–politician, always promising the virtue of clarity, but not yet'.[1]

While still at the BBC I had seen many of these personae played out for the cameras as Blair sought to win power and then come to grips with what to do with it. I joined his staff at Number 10 in June 1998, just over a year after he took office. Like most people, I still wasn't quite sure what to make of him. The question I was asked most frequently by friends and former colleagues was 'what's he really like?' Out of sight of the media Blair couldn't be bothered with play-acting. None of us would go round to his 'den', the surprisingly small prime-ministerial office overlooking the Downing Street garden, unsure which Tony Blair we might find there. The reality was more consistent than the image and, it seemed to me at least, more impressive. But

---

*See p. 14.

then I'd just given up a good career as a journalist to work for him. I had a stake in his success so maybe I wasn't the most detached observer. Nonetheless I found him focused and invariably serious about what really mattered, which for him was policy not presentation. He was affable and unstuffy, ready to take advice and criticism, but he expected commitment and dedication in return. He was conscious of the rare opportunity he had as a Labour leader with an impregnable majority and determined not to blow it. He worked hard but knew how to pace himself. He got frustrated when he found he didn't have the power to make things happen as fast as he wanted, and irritated by anything that he thought wasted his time. Like Mrs Thatcher, whom he admired in many ways, he recognised the need to use the media to explain and win support for what he wanted to do, but could get exasperated when his press team demanded too much of him. 'Why do I have to do this?' he would ask when we told him there was one more interview, one more photocall, or one more visit to be made.

Tony Blair had an instinctive feel for how to make effective use of the media and there's no doubt he got a kick out of celebrity, but he was never wholly at ease with the relationship. It was if he knew he'd flirted a little too much and come across as a bit too easy. Now he wanted to be taken seriously but he wasn't quite sure how to do it. A more significant problem confronted him at the same time. He knew he wanted to be a good prime minister – that much was obvious – but he wasn't yet certain what it took to become one. In opposition there had been few such doubts. As early as 1994, when he was putting his bid for the Labour leadership together, he was quoted by one colleague as saying, 'You have got to understand that the only thing that matters in this campaign is the media. The media, the media and the media.'[2] It is a sentiment familiar to those running for high office at a relatively young age. Before going into national politics Barack Obama observed that, 'For the broad public at least, I am who the media says I am. I say what they say I say. I become who they say I've become.'[3]

New Labour, created in Tony Blair's own amorphous image, used every trick in the communications book to help win power. It worked in spectacular fashion and he wasn't ready to throw away the book once he got there. Peter Mandelson, Blair's most accomplished manipulator of the media and the man closest to him intellectually and emotionally, argued that 'spin – or presentation – bought us the time and space to change the underlying reality'.[4] Throughout Blair's first term, reality was still playing catch-up. He was performing the role of prime minister until he had time to work out what kind of prime minister he actually wanted to be. Eventually reality would gain on him and overtake the carefully crafted impression but by then it was too late. Tony Blair's name would be for ever associated with 'spin'. He and his first press secretary, Alastair Campbell, couldn't fail to notice the damage done. In Blair's own words: 'We paid inordinate attention in the early days of New Labour to courting, assuaging, and persuading the media. In our own defence, after 18 years of opposition and the, at times, ferocious hostility of parts of the media, it was hard to see any alternative.'[5]

Blair, Mandelson and Campbell had used the years from 1994 to 1997 to build up a bank of support in the media that no previous Labour leader had ever enjoyed. It was not a bank of goodwill, anything but, but the reserves would last a remarkably long time nonetheless. Blair was reluctant to run them down too soon and realised only belatedly that trying to retain all the press backing he had enjoyed was not only impossible, it was counter-productive. By then many of his personal ambitions for his first term, things that would have given his government better definition and clarity, had been abandoned. Some of those who shared his ambitions and were disappointed to see them fade came to the conclusion that powerful figures in the media had been granted an effective veto over aspects of policy dear to the prime minister's heart. As ever with Blair, appearance and reality do not always accord. Strong political pressures, mainly within his own party, kept him from being as radical in action as his rhetoric promised. It was easy to blame the media and Blair would sometimes imply that they were indeed a factor in making him more cautious than he might have been. In his last year in office, when he was asked why he had courted them, he replied, 'They've got power.'[6] Yet much of that power he had ceded to them. More than any prime minister in history, Tony Blair allowed the media to influence the pace and direction of his government. In doing so he stayed closer to public opinion, to the extent that the popular press truly reflected it, than he might have done, but he sacrificed much of the opportunity he'd been handed to lead public opinion in a new direction. Significantly, however, the choice was his. The 'real' Tony Blair was more of a small-'c' conservative than he was willing even to admit to himself. He was capable of using the fear of how the media might react as a cover for his own caution or uncertainty. As a result he looked like a supplicant at the court of the newspaper proprietors more often than he really was.

Nobody holds court quite like Rupert Murdoch. Despite having no vote in the UK, carrying an American passport and living abroad, Murdoch's vast media holdings have allowed him to become accustomed to British political leaders seeking his benediction. He tends to view politicians as little more than a barrier to his commercial interests; there to be overcome by whatever means necessary. They see him as a man with whom they have no choice but to do business. They seek his favour and do all they can to impress. Margaret Thatcher succeeded; John Major failed; Tony Blair looked at the experience of both and knew which he wanted to follow. Symbolically the most dramatic gesture of courtship was his decision to fly to Australia in July 1995 as leader of the opposition to speak at a conference hosted by Murdoch for his corporate executives. Blair's speech was less of a capitulation to News Corporation's right-wing agenda than political folklore suggests. He praised both Margaret Thatcher and Ronald Reagan for having 'got certain things right. A greater emphasis on enterprise. Rewarding not penalising success. Breaking up some of the vested interests associated with state bureaucracy.'[7] But he said they were better at destroying what was bad than building what was good. On the sensitive subject of Europe, Blair challenged his audience to accept that closer integration was inevitable and at the time the *Guardian* detected 'no discernible concessions to the Murdoch world view'.[8]

As an exercise in mutual aggrandisement the visit was a tremendous success. Blair and Campbell took to heart the advice of the Australian prime minister, Paul Keating, on how to deal with Murdoch: 'He's a big bad bastard, and the only way you can deal with him is to make sure he thinks you can be a big bad bastard too. You can do deals with him, without ever saying a deal is done. But the only thing he cares about is his business and the only language he respects is strength.'[9] Blair and his team believed they had achieved exactly that. A deal had been done, although with nothing in writing. If Murdoch were left to pursue his business interests in peace he would give Labour a fair wind.[10] When the time came Murdoch duly instructed the *Sun* to throw its weight behind Blair and the endorsement set the seal on the campaign to show that New Labour was now a safe bet for all those who had mistrusted the party in the past. 'The *Sun* Backs Blair'[11] was just the headline they wanted to see, although it was clearly an endorsement for the man not the party. After the election was won Blair wrote a personal note to the paper's editor, Stuart Higgins, saying 'You really did make a difference',[12] but it was self-evidently not the difference between victory and defeat. Murdoch had done what he liked to do and backed a winner in his own commercial interests. But, as Chris Patten observed, the help Murdoch provides to political leaders 'is only available if you don't need it'.[13] And it was conditional on future good conduct. One of Murdoch's editors, the late Richard Stott, said the *Sun* reflected its proprietor's personal views more clearly than any other of his titles but it never really believed in New Labour, 'just the parts it could bolt on to its unshakeable belief in the remnants of Thatcherism'.[14]

Campbell and Mandelson were realistic enough to realise that winning over the entire Thatcher press would not be so easy. They were erecting a big tent but it couldn't be expected to accommodate everybody. Blair's assistant and close personal friend, Anji Hunter, who did much schmoozing on his behalf before and after he became prime minister, put out feelers to Lord Rothermere, owner of the *Daily Mail*. There was none of the high-profile courting that Murdoch enjoyed but Rothermere and Associated Newspapers' editor-in-chief David English met Blair for discreet lunches at Claridge's in London.[15] These would continue after the election and had some success. Rothermere even went so far as to sit on the Labour benches in the Lords, but he left the *Daily Mail*'s editor, Paul Dacre, to determine his own, frequently hostile, political line. When Rothermere declared that Blair's government was 'doing all the things the last one should have done and failed to do'[16] it said more about the parlous state of the Conservative party than anything else. Even the most loyal of Labour loyalists like David Hill, who would later replace Campbell as director of communications, recognised that the party had moved further than the newspapers to reach a new accommodation. There was, he suggested, 'a closer conjunction of opinion between Labour and the tabloids than ever before . . . so in that sense the tabloids have got what they wanted'.[17]

The other end of the newspaper market mattered less. Labour was disappointed not to get the explicit backing of *The Times* at the election, although once Blair was in power it became more like the New Labour house journal than any of the traditional left-of-centre titles. The *Daily Telegraph* was never going to back Labour and its editor Charles Moore said the extent of the attention he received was limited to 'lunches, handwritten notes, Alastair Campbell being matey'.[18] After four years of Labour government Moore concluded that Campbell was 'the most pointlessly combative person in human history'.[19] Those who had more regular contact with the new Downing Street press secretary were, on the whole, more generous. Combative he may have been, but he did it with style. He gave the media what they wanted whenever possible and gave them hell whenever he could. Trevor Kavanagh, who as political editor of the *Sun* was never comfortable with his paper's conversion to Blair, said Campbell's 'hatred of the press was not reciprocated. We revelled in his insults, compared our scratch marks, ignored the venom and found him thoroughly likeable.'[20] I attended Campbell's lobby briefings for over a year as a BBC journalist. I then sat alongside him for a further two as a member of the political wing of the Downing Street press office. They were indeed, as Kavanagh called them, 'virtuoso performances' rivalled only by Bernard Ingham at his best. Traditionally the lobby liked to establish its own rules but now they were playing by his. Before he left Number 10 Campbell would have a more dramatic impact on the relationship between his office and the political lobby than any man who had held the job before him. He started out as he meant to go on, doing it his way.

Alastair Campbell's twin-track approach to the media – simultaneous manipulation and denigration – sprang from his mixed feelings towards his former profession. He still delighted in finding a good story and writing it up for publication. Some appeared under the byline 'Tony Blair' and in jest the prime minister was named Freelance of the Year in 1998 for his prolific output of signed articles, many of them also written by the former *Daily Mirror* journalist David Bradshaw, now part of the Downing Street Strategic Communications Unit. On other occasions Campbell would dictate stories over the phone to political editors, complete with punctuation marks and suggested headlines. They were never printed word for word, but Campbell had lost none of his skills as a writer and he had the satisfaction of seeing many of his own phrases appear in print under the byline of senior correspondents. At the same time he genuinely loathed the way the lobby operated and had a low regard for many of its members as individuals. The strategy was pure Campbell, although Blair was more than aware of how it functioned. The prime minister would occasionally suggest a gentler approach. 'We can't be at war with them all the time. We're going to have to work with these guys again at some point,' he would say. But Campbell was not to be deflected.

Lobby correspondents continued to troop into Downing Street at eleven each morning as they had done for decades. The initial read-out they were given of the prime minister's day and the forthcoming business of government was not so very different from what had gone before. When it came to questions and answers, however, they had seen nothing like it. Campbell had been given unprecedented powers for a special adviser. Under an order in council, which didn't require parliament's consent, he could issue instructions to civil servants, although he was not exempted from the requirement to avoid political controversy and to 'observe discretion and express comment with moderation, and avoid personal attacks'.[21] It suited everybody in the room that the rules were never strictly enforced, although Campbell did try to restrain himself from expressing his strong private views on the Tory leadership and their policies. He felt no such restraint when it came to many of the journalists who attended his briefings. They, and their profession, would receive abuse on a regular basis. When it came to using attack as a form of defence, Campbell showed that Bernard Ingham had been nothing but an amateur league player.

A dramatic example followed the revelation in *La Stampa* on 24 March 1998 that the Italian prime minister Romano Prodi had taken a call from Blair in which they discussed Rupert Murdoch's multi-billion pound offer for Mediaset, a powerful television, newspaper and publishing company owned by Silvio Berlusconi. Prodi had said he preferred an Italian bidder and, claimed the paper, Blair had passed the information back to Murdoch. It led Roy Hattersley in the *Guardian* to refer to Blair as the new 'European sales representative for Mr Rupert Murdoch'.[22] Asked about it at the lobby, Campbell called the story 'baloney'. In case the journalists hadn't got the message he spelt it out for them. It was 'balls that the prime minister "intervened" over some deal with Murdoch. That's c.r.a.p.'[23] Robert Peston, then political editor of the *Financial Times*, which had led on the story, was told it was a 'complete joke'. *The Times* then reported that its own proprietor had 'used information obtained directly from Tony Blair to inform his business decisions' and quoted Murdoch saying he had called Blair personally with a 'perfectly innocent request for information'.[24] The former *Sunday Times* editor Andrew Neil had revealed that while in opposition Blair had told him: 'How we treat Rupert Murdoch's media interests when in power will depend on how his newspapers treat the Labour Party in the run-up to the election and after we are in government.'[25] The Tory spokesman Francis Maude accused Campbell of statements that were 'at best misleading and at worst deliberately false'.[26] This led to what the *Guardian* called 'a dramatic confrontation with political correspondents' during which Campbell's officially anonymous status 'crumbled'. Nicholas Jones of the BBC called it a 'ten-minute tirade' of which the highlights were: 'Francis Maude said I was lying. But everyone in this room knows that I haven't lied . . . Blair's relationship with Murdoch is a legitimate matter of interest but it's a non-story . . . There are certain things the media are neuralgic about. One is Murdoch. One is Labour party spin doctors. Put the two together and you can have an orgy of self-indulgence lasting for days.'[27]

The Murdoch relationship was indeed a matter of legitimate interest but if Campbell could distract attention from it, then he very much wanted to do so. Some papers owned by Murdoch's rivals had already reminded their readers that New Labour had a record of looking after the interests of News International. Plans to limit cross-media ownership in a way that would have restricted Murdoch's empire had been quietly dropped within six months of Blair's visit to Australia in 1995. Since the election ministers had rejected calls to outlaw 'predatory pricing', subsidised price cuts that were illegal elsewhere in Europe but which had helped both the *Sun* and *Times* boost circulation. Blair told Campbell that 'he didn't fancy a sustained set of questions about whether Murdoch lobbied him'[28] in the Commons that afternoon. Instead at prime minister's questions he succeeded in ensuring that Campbell's conduct remained the big story when he said, 'There is one reason why the opposition attack the press spokesman: he does an effective job in attacking the Conservative party.'[29] But he had gone too far. It was no part of Campbell's job to attack the opposition directly. Blair was on safer ground when he turned a question about Murdoch from the specific to the general: 'As for the newspaper proprietors, I meet all of them regularly; I know all of them. I regard that as a sensible part of being the leader of a major political party. As a matter of fact, I have no illusions about any of them. They are all highly able, highly ruthless and dedicated to the success of their business, as I am dedicated to the success of mine.'

Campbell had one more spat with the lobby that afternoon. Liam Halligan, another *FT* correspondent raised what Blair had said about attacks on the Conservatives. Nick Jones watched as 'Campbell looked away. He pretended to fall asleep and started snoring. Halligan tried again, reminding him that he was paid nearly £90,000 a year by the taxpayer. Once roused, Campbell resorted to belligerence: 'I do a good service for you all . . .' He paused, and then turned to face Halligan '. . . and your eight readers. The answer to your question is that the order in council changed it. As well as being able to instruct civil servants I can also put the government's case in a political context. So get a grip on yourself.'[30]

Blair had been prime minister just over a year and already his press secretary was a highly controversial figure. In June 1998 the House of Commons select committee on public administration opened an inquiry into government communications and Campbell was the star witness. Sir Bernard Ingham appeared a few days earlier and used the opportunity to condemn both New Labour for its way of feeding the press and journalists for their 'astonishingly poodle-like' behaviour in being fed.[31] The committee chairman, Rhodri Morgan, suggested Ingham had been 'the original professor of rotational medicine', or spin doctor, but he denied it and condemned Campbell for politicising the job he had once held. The cabinet secretary and head of the home civil service Sir Richard Wilson then reassured the committee that he looked carefully at the records of Campbell's briefings to the lobby. In his view 'Campbell is overtly political so everyone knows where he is coming from . . . But I do not think his job is to go over the top and attack the opposition with bricks and bottles . . . if he were to go wrong, I would go along and say "watch it".'[32] Campbell's own evidence was confident and unapologetic. He dismissed talk that he was too powerful as 'a media obsession' and insisted he not only stuck within the rules that allowed him to 'set things in a political context' but tried 'to err on the side of caution'. Afterwards he wrote in his dairy that the MPs had failed to 'sustain a line of questioning' and that he felt he had 'shafted' the Conservative David Ruffley, the only one who had really tried to put him on the spot.[33]

Campbell's extraordinary self-confidence was one reason for him becoming far and away the most powerful press secretary in the history of Number 10. The new dispensations he'd been given by the order in council were just the start. The real power he had was stripped, sometimes brutally, sometimes discreetly, from others. From departmental heads of information, from the Downing Street policy unit, from the prime minister's private office and even the chief of staff, Jonathan Powell, who preferred to work in a more low-key and consensual way. In a crisis, and in Downing Street the next crisis is never far off, it was Campbell's decisiveness and clarity of thought that Blair most valued. As a result the prime minister too ceded some of his power to his press secretary, and not simply because Campbell had the authority to put words into Blair's mouth. Privately Campbell would joke to some of us in his team that the prime minister's 'indecision is final', and Blair often did prefer to keep his options open as long as he could. When the crunch came and a decision could be postponed no longer, Campbell's judgement, informed by how he thought the media would react, often held sway.

An early and dramatic example came just three months after the election with the revelation in the *News of the World* that the foreign secretary, Robin Cook, was having an affair with his secretary, Gaynor Regan. After the years of 'sleaze' under John Major, Blair was unsure how to react. 'What the hell do I do about this?' he asked.[34] Campbell famously telephoned Cook, who was at Heathrow about to leave for a holiday with his wife, and told him that 'in pure media terms, and I think in political terms too, the most important thing was clarity.' In other words he should choose between the two women. According to Campbell, Blair 'backed my line'. The prime minister wanted the story dealt with quickly and then forgotten as fast as possible. I remember the weekend well because I was BBC TV's duty political correspondent. One of my jobs was to go through the first editions of the Sunday papers as soon as they were available on Saturday evening. I found an unusually rich array of possibilities to follow up. Not just the news that the foreign secretary was leaving his wife in the *News of the World*, very sympathetically written up thanks to Campbell's intervention, but also a *Sunday Times* report claiming that Chris Patten, now governor of Hong Kong, could be prosecuted under the official secrets act. Another, in several papers, suggested the Royal yacht *Britannia* might not be scrapped after all. The stories were classic smokescreens designed to distract media attention away from the Cook revelations and they had some short-term success. The BBC was, as ever, wary of stories that intruded into private lives with no obvious public interest. I duly followed the Patten story after having it confirmed, off the record, by Peter Mandelson, now 'minister without portfolio' but in effect minister of information. The strategy was cack-handed and counter-productive. By the Monday it was clear neither story had any foundation and many of us realised we had been taken for a ride. The BBC took the only kind of revenge in its power. It carried a detailed report on *The World At One* on Radio 4 about the weekend of spin.

Three weeks later Blair told Campbell he was worried about a new attitude he detected in the media. 'TB was onto the notion that our biggest enemy was cynicism. Once the mood really turns, they'll all turn together.'[35] Stories about how the government was managing the news, rather than about the news itself, were becoming a regular occurrence. Questions were also being asked about what was going on in the Government Information Service, which encompassed all departmental press officers. The heads of communication in the various ministries were well known to journalists and their concern at what was happening was bound to filter out. Campbell wanted a shake-up. They had all received a letter from him in September saying that the change of administration was a chance for the GIS 'to raise its game and be right at the heart of government'.[36] What he really thought was that the service was sluggish, unimaginative and too passive. He wanted to modernise the whole structure and that meant not just new ways of working but fresh blood, too. Many of those who had worked in Downing Street under John Major agreed with the need for a thorough overhaul, although they didn't say so now. It suited them that the story became one of a 'great purge' of long-standing civil servants and the subsequent politicisation of the service. Three heads of information had already left and several more were to follow. Many saw their jobs taken by outsiders, often journalists suspected by the people they replaced of having New Labour sympathies. Once their civil-service careers were over they were free to say what they thought, and some did so in language that suggested that they knew how to put a message across when they wanted to. Jill Rutter was an early casualty, forced out of the Treasury by Gordon Brown's special advisers with little ceremony. She thought she was a victim of politicisation, saying, 'It's fine if the Labour party want to spend their money on publicity but it's an entirely different matter for the state to provide a huge government machine for Labour.'[37] Romola Christopherson, who retired from the Department of Health, described Alastair Campbell as the real deputy prime minister and suggested Blair 'turns to him on policy as much as presentation'.[38] Another of those who refused to go quietly was Andy Wood, the respected head of information at the Northern Ireland Office, who had fallen foul of his new secretary of state Mo Mowlam. Wood was replaced by an ex-BBC journalist, Tom Kelly, who went on to become Tony Blair's spokesman after the 2001 election.

Campbell got his way, although not as quickly as he would have liked. The GIS was renamed the Government Information and Communications Service and did become more efficient and better able to respond to the growing demands of the media. It was also better attuned to what ministers expected of it. Whether that amounted to politicisation was a debate that rumbled on for years. 'Yes' said those who believed Blair was less interested in civil-service neutrality than in 'government by headline'. 'No' said others who thought professional communications were a prerequisite for good government and wondered only why the Tories hadn't done something about it when they had the chance.

Nobody doubted Blair's ability to deliver carefully crafted phrases that sounded as if they had been written just for the headlines. Even when he was being sincere and had something of great importance to convey, Blair could sometimes undermine it by appearing a little too glib and well packaged. When Princess Diana was killed at the end of August 1997 his observation that 'she was the people's princess'[39] was judged apposite. Only through constant repetition in the media has it come to sound cheesy. The same cannot be said for his words in Belfast to mark the Good Friday peace agreement the following April. Blair had achieved something that had eluded every prime minister since Gladstone but he allowed himself to make a badly judged remark that haunts him still. With Alastair Campbell and Tom Kelly beside him, he declared: 'A day like today is not a day for sound bites really – we can leave those at home – but I feel the hand of history upon our shoulders, I really do.'[40]

In November 1997 it was not just Blair's sincerity that was challenged. The question was whether the British prime minister could be trusted to tell the truth. The issue was the Ecclestone affair. The government had announced that Formula One motor racing, which was effectively owned by Bernie Ecclestone, had been exempted from the ban on tobacco sponsorship in sport. When it emerged that Ecclestone had previously donated a million pounds to the Labour party, it looked like too much of a coincidence. Denials from both Downing Street and the party sounded hollow and the questions kept on coming. Peter Mandelson appeared on the *Today* programme to assert that the government had acted with 'great scrupulousness and great transparency'[41] but it failed to kill the story. Blair was forced to put his personal credibility on the line and to use the media to ask voters to look him in the eye and believe him. Campbell believed the only way to deal with the 'innuendo' that the government had acted improperly was for the prime minister 'to do a few rounds with John Humphrys on TV and remind the people who elected him of the big picture, of better schools, hospitals, jobs and industry, on which the government is delivering'.[42] In the course of the interview on the BBC's *On The Record*, Blair said, 'most people who have dealt with me think that I am a pretty straight sort of guy, and I am'.[43] Those words would be thrown back at him many times before he left office. It was the first example of what, in the wake of the Iraq war, would become known as the 'masochism strategy', taking a pounding, surviving the assault and hoping to win back some credibility in the process. Campbell had argued for it and, in his own assessment, 'It did the job.'[44]

Blair and Campbell were learning the hard way that what worked in opposition didn't always work in government. Most journalists had played along when New Labour was setting the agenda on a daily basis. Now they were getting difficult. Embarrassing stories couldn't be consistently buried or deflected. And trying to do so often did more harm than good by provoking yet more column inches and hours of broadcast time devoted to spin. Being in opposition is about making friends; being in government involves making enemies. The trick is to ensure that your enemies are well defined and unpopular and, crucially, too weak or inept to win the sympathy of the majority on whose backing you depend. The problem for Blair was that the constant criticism of spin gave his enemies common cause and a vehicle for eroding his central core of support. The success of New Labour had weakened and demoralised both the right and the old 'socialist' left. Neither had a policy platform that could appeal to the centre ground but both had an interest in claiming that the government had no programme and no substance. It was an unholy alliance designed to chip away at the government's popularity and, if possible, make it harder for Downing Street to carry on using all the communications techniques that had proved so effective until now. Blair was aware of the dangers but he also knew that, in the words of Professor Colin Seymour-Ure, 'the prime minister's formal powers often guarantee only the minimum of success: good public communication can produce something better'.[45] He didn't intend to let his enemies deprive him of one of the most valuable tools of his trade.

Not every attempt to weaken and demoralise the prime minister came from his opponents to the right and to the left. Gordon Brown was a co-architect of New Labour and had few if any serious policy differences with Blair. But by insisting on the right to run his own wholly independent operation for briefing the press he, too, contributed to the narrative that the government was obsessed with spin and counter-spin. Downing Street had never before faced such an autonomous and combative rival source of news and 'guidance' for journalists and no previous prime minister would have tolerated it. Where John Major had constantly to look over his shoulder to see what his predecessor was up to, for Tony Blair it was the man who was determined to succeed him who caused him endless trouble. Brown had brought his own larger-than-life spin doctor into the Treasury with him, the former trade-union official Charlie Whelan. Whelan and another of Brown's special advisers, Ed Balls, had helped pull off one of the most spectacular coups of the new administration with their deft handling of the announcement that the Bank of England was to be given the freedom to set interest rates. The government had been made to look decisive and radical and Blair had been delighted with the results. Within a year he would be forced to recognise that the talents of Whelan and Balls were being employed not to promote the interests of the government as a whole but the personal political ambitions of Gordon Brown, who believed he would make a better prime minister and intended to prove it as soon as he possibly could.

By the time I joined the Downing Street press office in June 1998 it felt as if I was being employed to work for a coalition government of two parties, each with their own structures, loyalties and agendas. They worked together as best they could because they had a mutual interest in doing so. But they knew there was likely to come a time when they would have to go their separate ways and a disproportionate amount of time and energy was spent in preparing the ground for that eventuality. For the Brown party much of that preparation was being done by Whelan and Balls. Their counterpart on the Blair side was always more Mandelson than Campbell. Like Whelan, Mandelson had his own band of journalists who could be relied upon to print pretty much whatever he told them. As Mandelson later admitted: 'Everyone was divided, the government was divided, the party was divided, MPs were divided, the media was divided, into camps.'[46] From Downing Street's point of view the situation had nothing but downsides. Blair already had the job and nothing would have pleased him more than to be allowed to get on with it, while his cabinet ministers, including Brown, got on with theirs. He had nothing to gain from a decade of sniping with the Treasury. He had everything to gain from dissuading Brown from taking such a well-known bruiser as Charlie Whelan with him into government in the first place. According to Whelan he tried to do just that on the day he became prime minister. 'Tony phoned Gordon at 5 p.m. on the first of May and spent an hour trying to persuade him to sack me. Then back in London he tried again with Gordon in the garden of Number 10. Gordon came back furious because Tony Blair wasn't interested in the Bank of England becoming independent. He just spent ages telling the new chancellor I should be sacked. How pathetic can you get?'[47] Whelan probably flatters himself if he thinks the newly elected prime minister devoted quite so much time to him on a day like that, but if that's what he believed, or was told by Brown, it helps to explain why loyalty to the leader of his party would come so low down on his list of priorities. Blair had more time for Balls, whose intellectual stature and grasp of policy he respected, although it was clear that his ambitions too were tied inextricably with Brown's hunger for the top job.

Once Brown had made clear he was keeping his special adviser, relations between Whelan and Campbell were rarely easy. They reached crisis point in January 1998 with the publication of a book by the *Independent on Sunday* correspondent Paul Routledge entitled *Gordon Brown: The Biography*. Routledge made little effort to disguise the fact that he was firmly in the chancellor's camp and on the inside flap it stated baldly that the book had been written with Brown's 'full co-operation'. A pre-publication copy fell into the hands of the *Guardian* while Blair was on his way to a summit meeting in Japan. The paper's story, 'How Blair Broke Secret Pact',[48] made much of Brown's continued resentment that Blair and not he was now prime minister. It was an exaggerated account of what the book contained but that scarcely mattered. Whelan attempted to distance himself and his boss from the book but journalists close to Mandelson, including Andy Grice on the *Sunday Times* and Patrick Wintour on the *Observer*, were told it had in effect been 'commissioned' to promote Brown's ambitions. Campbell said it was Whelan's 'denial of all knowledge that really got my goat'.[49] According to his diary entry for 14 January: 'I totally lost it with him, and in between screaming abuse at him' told him his 'efforts to pursue a pure GB agenda were pathetic and doing GB more harm than good.' The row reached its peak on 18 January when the *Observer* columnist Andrew Rawnsley wrote that 'According to someone who has an extremely good claim to know the mind of the prime minister, he still regards Brown as "a great talent" and a "great force". But he is wearying of the chancellor's misjudgements, of which this was a "classic". It is time, in the words of the same person, for Brown to get a grip on his "psychological flaws".'[50] Not surprisingly Brown took the remark badly and its publication was seen as evidence that Downing Street was willing to brief viciously against the chancellor. Rawnsley has not yet said who gave him the quotation, although he has ruled out Mandelson. Most subsequent accounts have tended to finger Campbell, although he too has denied it.

In January 2007 I appeared on an obscure internet television channel hosted by the Conservative blogger Iain Dale. In the course of a lengthy interview I said that 'someone very close to the chancellor' had named another culprit. I had handed Dale a publicity coup and at prime minister's questions the following day Tony Blair was asked about my comments:

> **Jeremy Wright (Rugby and Kenilworth) (Con):** Following yesterday's television interview with the prime minister's former spin doctor Lance Price, will the prime minister confirm that he has not called the chancellor of the exchequer psychologically flawed?
> **The Prime Minister:** I certainly do confirm that, yes.[51]

My source had been Charlie Whelan, which suggests Gordon Brown too believed Blair to have been personally responsible. In the course of researching this book I learned that another person, this time somebody very close to Blair in 1998, also claimed the words were the prime minister's.[52] Either way Brown thought he had good grounds for resentment and the words took on a disproportionate significance in the battle of wills that was to last until Blair was finally forced to relinquish power almost a decade later.

Whelan was no stranger to controversy. In October 1997 he was seen on his mobile phone in the Red Lion pub opposite the Treasury briefing journalists that Gordon Brown had ruled out British membership of the single currency, or EMU, before the next election. The episode cast light on how New Labour media management worked, and how badly it could backfire. On this occasion Campbell and Whelan had been working together. *The Times* had been fed quotes from the chancellor to try to kill the kind of stories about government splits over Europe that had so damaged the Tories. Campbell dictated the words to the paper's political editor, Phil Webster. 'I spoke to Webster and agreed that the intro was that he was effectively ruling it out for this parliament while saying it would be folly to close options.'[53] Whelan spoke to the *Sun* and urged them to run a 'Brown Saves The Pound' headline. The flaw in the spin operation was that the prime minister didn't agree with such a hard line and he told Campbell as much in no uncertain terms as soon as heard about it. Campbell 'suddenly realised that because I had not really checked and double-checked with TB, we had briefed an enormous story on the basis of a cock-up'. He even admitted that 'I was keen to push my instinctive anti-EMU feelings because I didn't want TB outflanked.' The event had rarity value – Campbell didn't normally allow his own views to influence his briefings and it was almost as unusual for him to work in consort with Whelan – but it was telling nonetheless. Once announced, the policy couldn't be un-announced and the prime minister was stuck with it.

The two Murdoch papers had been handed yet another scoop designed to appeal to their Euro-sceptic views. And while the importance of the economic decision was lost on nobody, much of the rest of the media saw the way it became public as little more than blatant appeasement of News International. But was it more than that? Had Rupert Murdoch succeeded in doing what the press barons of the twenties and thirties, Lords Northcliffe, Beaverbrook and Rothermere, had failed to do? Had government policy been changed because of what he believed and what his papers said?

Shortly after I joined Number 10 I was startled to be told by somebody in the know that 'We've promised News International we won't make any changes to our Europe policy without talking to them.'[54] From conversations I had with Tony Blair at the time I know he would have liked to take Britain into the single currency if he could.[55] He didn't. The temptation to conclude that he was dissuaded by his fear of how the media would react is strong, although ultimately I believe it would be wrong. To a thoughtful and avowedly pro-European observer like Hugo Young of the *Guardian*, however, Blair's weakness in the face of the Euro-sceptic press was his Achilles heel. In an article under the deliberately provocative title 'It's the *Sun* wot really runs the country',[56] he said the prime minister would have 'to face down the screaming and the bullying, which is the British tabloids' matchless contribution to democracy' or face the charge of putting 'soft-soaping the editors and readers of the *Sun*' above the interests of the nation as a whole. 'Who,' he asked 'is running the country?' Hugo Young died in September 2003 while Blair was still in office, Britain was no closer to joining the euro and the question continued to hang in the air.

The *Sun* has never run the country and nor has Rupert Murdoch. If Tony Blair really had given them a veto over the euro he wouldn't have objected as he did to headlines about 'saving the pound'. Of course Blair took into account the likely reaction of the media and it played heavily on his mind, but it was only one factor that determined the government's attitude to the euro. The chancellor was opposed to British entry, the balance of opinion among senior Treasury officials and the prime minister's own economic advisers was tilted heavily against, and in academic circles no argument had been produced establishing that membership was unquestionably in Britain's interests. All the polling evidence, both public and private, suggested that a referendum on the euro would be lost heavily. In party-political terms, it was about the only issue on which the majority of voters strongly supported the leader of the opposition, William Hague. Years of negative headlines about the European Union in general and the single currency in particular had undoubtedly influenced public opinion. The attitude of the media may also have been one reason Gordon Brown was sceptical. And Blair didn't completely rule out the possibility that he could alter the public mood. According to his adviser on Europe, Roger Liddle, who favoured entry, the prime minister had 'a touching innocence about his own powers of persuasion. He still genuinely thinks he can persuade . . . Murdoch of the virtues of the euro.'[57] He continued to make positive noises about the single currency from time to time, knowing the reaction of the press was likely to be swift and over the top. On one occasion the *Sun* printed his photo and asked 'Is This The Most Dangerous Man In Britain?'[58] It is doubtful whether many of its readers would have answered in the affirmative, but in his heart Blair probably knew this was an argument he was unlikely ever to win. Once again it is impossible to isolate the impact of the Eurosceptic press from his calculations. Had every newspaper in Britain spent the past ten years arguing enthusiastically for the euro then perhaps other elements of the equation would have been different, too. But the fact is that while passionate supporters of Britain's membership of the single currency are inclined to single out the media for the failure of their dream, nothing is ever quite that simple.

Another aspiration dear to the prime minister's heart but which never came to fruition was a realignment of centre-left politics involving a merger with the Liberal Democrats and the introduction of some kind of proportional representation. Whether any of the reforms he toyed with could have prevented the disillusionment with politics that set in during 2009 is another great 'what if?' although it seems improbable. Once again those disappointed with his lack of progress were tempted to blame the media. Robert Maclennan, a former Labour MP turned Liberal Democrat, was involved in numerous discussions with Blair on the subject. In his view the prime minister was 'very concerned that the Murdoch press will rend him apart if he speaks in favour of electoral reform . . . They might tolerate him for one term, but not if they knew he was interested in a project that was arranged to put the progressive left in power for a long time, excluding the Tories by a new voting system.'[59] There's no doubt Blair was interested in just such a project and invested a great deal of time and thought in it. Yet here again political forces more powerful than the press prevented him pursuing his ambition. Quite apart from anything else, the hostility of so many in his cabinet and party, including the deputy prime minister, John Prescott, and the home secretary, Jack Straw, both of whom were more tribal in their politics than Blair had ever been, made any fundamental realignment of the centre-left all but impossible.

By itself the populist, right-wing agenda of much of the press didn't keep Britain out of the euro or scupper electoral reform but it certainly exercised a pull on government policy. A significant proportion of the stories generated by Downing Street for the sake of headlines were designed to suggest that New Labour understood and even sympathised with the socially conservative instincts of most of the tabloids. Only rarely did they try to challenge the mindset of the *Sun* or the *Daily Mail*. Tim Allan, whose place I took after his early and much-lamented departure from the press office, accepted that 'the government wasted far too much time trying to turn the *Mail* around'.[60] Under Margaret Thatcher the media summary produced by Bernard Ingham had encouraged her to believe that the country agreed with her basic instincts. Under Tony Blair the focus groups and other research carried out by his polling expert Philip Gould sent the opposite message. Gould would sit down with small groups of 'swing' or uncommitted voters and tease out their views. He told Hugo Young that 'every time I do a focus group I get the *Daily Mail* coming back at me. It's terrible.'[61] Some of the memos he wrote at this time were later leaked to the *Sunday Times*. A common theme was that: 'TB is not believed to be real. He lacks conviction, he is all spin and presentation, he says things to please people, not because he believes them.'[62] Professor David Marquand described a new circularity that gave the media, not Downing Street, the upper hand. 'Media storms fed into focus groups; focus-group discussions fed into the prime minister's office; and ministerial reactions fed back into the media.'[63] The number of hours I spent with ministers planning new 'crackdowns' on drugs, asylum seekers and benefits cheats testifies to the accuracy of his assessment, but only in so far as I was doing the prime minister's bidding.

In April 2000 I was copied into a memo he had written entitled 'Touchstone Issues'. He was worried that the government was look-ing 'out of touch with gut British instincts'. Among his suggestions was that 'we should think now of an initiative, e.g. locking up street mug-gers. Something tough, with immediate bite . . .' The memo was leaked to the *Times* and the *Sun*[64] and prompted John Rentoul of the *Independent* to observe that it 'rendered a striking impression of Blair as a fearful and headline-driven politician'.[65] But such ideas appealed to him not just because he thought the *Daily Mail* and the *Sun* would like them. He liked them too. On other issues, notably race and gay rights, he refused to follow the tabloid agenda and even succeeded in pulling them in his direction. When the papers tried to embarrass gay members of his cabinet, including Peter Mandelson and Nick Brown, by 'outing' them, Blair gave them his personal backing. When it was clear he was more in tune with their readers than they had thought, the *Sun* made a rare public about-turn and the rest of the tabloids followed in their wake. Having asked 'Tell us the truth, Tony. Are we being run by a gay mafia?'[66] the paper's editor, David Yelland, was forced to announce three days later that it was 'no longer in the business of destroying closest gays' lives by "exposing" them as homosexuals'.[67]

The way Blair responded to media pressure on different issues tells us a great deal about the power of the press to influence policy. On Europe he disagreed with the view of most of the tabloids but he recognised that they reflected majority public opinion and he knew he lacked the necessary political support to take them on. He conceded tactically but continued to make his case when he felt it might have an effect. On crime and asylum seekers he instinctively agreed with them and had no reservations about aligning himself with their views. On gay rights he fundamentally disagreed and had all the political support he needed to stand his ground. He was convinced they were out of touch with the country's mood and was proved right. They backed off, not him. In every case it was his judgement both of what the public wanted from him and of what he could achieve politically that was the determining factor.

When it comes to the use of military action abroad the instinct of the popular press is almost always to offer support, unless and until things start to go wrong. Tony Blair's strong leadership on the international stage to avert a catastrophe in Kosovo was widely and justifiably praised. I travelled with him to Chicago in April 1999, where he outlined the case for humanitarian intervention in a speech that has been much quoted in the light of subsequent events. His focus was on getting the arguments right, and in particular, on convincing President Clinton to back the threat of a ground invasion to protect the civilian population from Serb attacks. The media were the last thing on his mind. It is a mark of the reputation Downing Street had already earned for effective communications that NATO, which was responsible for coordinating the military response, had invited Alastair Campbell to restructure its entire media machinery. Several of Number 10's best people were seconded to NATO headquarters for the purpose and Campbell noted that not only had coverage for Blair personally been 'terrific' but that 'the press were also beginning to say the media operation was improving.'[68] Blair's strategy worked and the defeat of the Serbs under Slobodan Milosevic did much for his self-confidence and his reputation. Campbell's strategy had also worked. Relations with the media weren't always easy during the conflict. When, on more than one occasion, NATO missiles hit the wrong targets and civilians were killed Blair struggled to make the case that moral responsibility for the deaths lay with Milosevic and nobody else. There was a familiar war of words between Downing Street and the BBC over its coverage of the collateral damage caused by air strikes. The corporation's foreign-affairs editor John Simpson became a personal *bête noir* for both Campbell and Blair. The prime minister called him a 'precious arsehole' who would 'swan around criticising as he pleases but if anyone speaks back it is an attack on civilisation as we know it'.[69] He expressed his frustration in similar terms many times in private and in more diplomatic language on occasion in public. Blair did not have the same luxury of controlling access to the images of the conflict that Margaret Thatcher had enjoyed during the battle to regain the Falklands. His only recourse, apart from periodic words of admonition to the likes of John Simpson,

was to ensure that NATO could compete effectively in the market-
place of wartime communications.

Alastair Campbell had exported to NATO's Brussels HQ techniques
that were already proving their worth domestically. In private
Westminster-based correspondents were often ready to express their
admiration for the new professionalism that had transformed Number
10's dealings with the media. The press office responded more quickly
and with more information to journalists' questions. The strategic
communications unit dramatically improved relations with specialist
magazines, the regional media and other journalists outside the
Westminster village. In public, however, the discussion was almost
always in the context of spin. The simultaneous attacks from left and
right on the government's exaggerated claims and poor delivery were
having the desired effect. And some intractable if, in retrospect, tangential presentational problems showed the limit to what even the best
communications can be expected to achieve. As the end of the twentieth century approached nothing could convince a sceptical press or
the public that the Millennium Dome was a triumph of British inge-
nuity. Tony Blair's reluctant agreement to travel to the site by tube
produced some embarrassing photographs of a man being studiously
ignored by his fellow passengers but did little to convince anybody that
he understood the everyday concerns of the electorate. The visit was
the product of one of an endless cycle of internal meetings designed
to show that the prime minister was 'on the side' of ordinary voters.
In the first few months of 2000 the discussions became more urgent.
The next general election was in all probability little more than a year
away. Tony Blair believed he now had no choice but to tackle the spin
question head-on.

In June the prime minister used a speech in London to reflect publicly on the apparent lack of trust in him and his government. Trust, he
acknowledged, was a two-way process: 'I think we in government – and
that means me – have to trust people more. We don't need to fight over
every headline.'[70] Alastair Campbell had already persuaded him to agree
to another, far riskier, idea. The BBC documentary maker Michael
Cockerell was given unprecedented access to Downing Street to make
a film about how the press office worked. *News From Number 10* was

broadcast on 15 July 2000. Campbell hoped it would show up the lobby journalists as self-obsessed, trivial and living in 'medialand', cut off from what people really cared about. Most attention, however, focused on a sequence in which the prime minister wandered into Campbell's office while the cameras were running. Blair hadn't been warned they would be there because his press secretary wanted him to act naturally. It was a disaster. The prime minister was asked about press cynicism and gave an honest answer: 'what is important for me is that it doesn't disturb me from doing the things that are really important. Y'know for the country. Otherwise there is no point in doing this. You can believe it or not, but that's what I spend my time doing.'[71] Campbell then interjected to say 'that's why you've just spent seven minutes talking to Michael Cockerell'. Those words and the body language between the two men played straight into the image of a vacillating prime minister bullied by his domineering press secretary. The satirist Rory Bremner had been portraying just such a relationship on his weekly TV show. Now it had been confirmed without the use of actors. The papers all picked up on it, as Campbell noted in his diary: 'The *Mirror* leader said I could take over, several said TB looked weak, but at least it wasn't meltdown and people thought we came out better than the press. Peter M felt we had to sue for peace now. TB ditto.'[72]

Another tactic to try to counter the obsession with spin was for Campbell to do fewer lobby briefings himself and allow his deputy, an unflappable and popular civil servant, Godric Smith, to face the journalists instead. Once again the results were mixed. No matter how good Smith was, the correspondents complained they weren't getting the access to the mind of Tony Blair that Campbell could provide. 'God, I hate these people', he wrote in his diary. 'First they say we spin them too much and then when we take it away they say they need more spin.'[73]

When they couldn't get what they wanted from Campbell many journalists still spoke to Peter Mandelson. He had given up his unofficial role as minister of information in 1998 when he was promoted to the cabinet as trade and industry secretary. In his first party conference speech he promised delegates 'no more spin – honest'.[74] But he continued to speak to those journalists he trusted and to give them the impression that he knew what the prime minister was thinking as well as anybody, which was generally true. It caused tension in his personal relations with Campbell and when, not once but twice, Mandelson had to resign from the cabinet he had good reason to believe that Campbell had advised Blair it was the right course of action.

At the end of 1998 the issue was a secret home loan from a fellow minister, and loyal supporter of Gordon Brown, Geoffrey Robinson. The arrangement was revealed in another book by Paul Routledge, this time a biography of Mandelson himself. Once again Charlie Whelan was suspected of collaborating on the book and this time he couldn't evade responsibility. Mandelson fought to keep his job, arguing that he had done nothing wrong as a minister, but eventually Blair told him he would have to go. Brown was finally persuaded to dispense with Whelan's services also. Campbell was genuinely sorry to see Mandelson out of government but no tears were shed in Downing Street for Whelan. Campbell wisely avoided twisting the knife in public, saying merely that 'press officers simply are not as important as the media make out . . . There is an obsession about them which goes way beyond their real importance.'[75]

Mandelson was soon rehabilitated as secretary of state for Northern Ireland, a job he held for just over a year. At the same time his skills were deployed in planning for the next general election, already pencilled in for May 2001. But in January he was in trouble again, accused of having misused his ministerial position to lobby for a Labour donor, Srichand Hinduja, to be granted a British passport. He was later exonerated after an independent investigation by Sir Anthony Hammond, but by then he was once again a backbencher. Mandelson resigned a second time not because of the original allegation, which dated back over two years, but because Alastair Campbell and Godric Smith believed he had misled them about what had happened and caused them in turn to mislead journalists. Peter Mandelson became the first cabinet minister effectively to be sacked during a lobby meeting. While he was still upstairs in Tony Blair's study pleading for his job, downstairs in the briefing room Campbell pointedly refused to tell journalists that he still had the confidence of the prime minister. That could only mean one thing and they knew Mandelson was out before he did. By this time I was the party's director of communications and reluctant to lose a talent like Mandelson from the campaign. Tony Blair told me, 'If I wasn't convinced he'd fibbed . . . then I'd have kept him, whatever the shit I had taken, but I was convinced he had fibbed.'[76] The need to protect the integrity of what Downing Street said took precedence over personal friendship. With an election so close Number 10 could not afford to be accused of misleading anybody.

In the weeks running up to the election Blair worried that the obsession with spin would distract attention from and undermine his government's real achievements. There was much in the first term of which he could justifiably be proud: devolution, his leadership over the conflict in Kosovo, Bank of England independence, the equalisation of the age of consent, to name only the least contentious. He knew the allegations of media management mattered more to journalists than they did to the voters and the improvements to government communications were something else of which he was proud. For every negative headline about Alastair Campbell there had been hundreds more that, often thanks to his efforts, told a very different story. William Hague and the Conservatives tried to use 'spin' to undermine Labour's popularity and deny its successes, but it didn't do them much good. Nevertheless, as Professor Raymond Kuhn argued, 'In the run up to the 2001 general election, New Labour's obsession with news management had arguably become counterproductive as journalists filed stories critically unpacking the spin for their audiences. For some commentators "spin" was becoming for the Blair premiership what "sleaze" had been for the Major government – a critical label used as shorthand to sum up the perceived deficiencies of an administration.'[77]

The country first learned of the election date, 7 June, thanks to a lead story in the *Sun*. It had been postponed following an outbreak of foot-and-mouth disease and speculation about when it might be held had become intense. Alastair Campbell denied having given the story to the *Sun* but few people believed him, least of all Piers Morgan, editor of the *Daily Mirror*. So far as he was concerned, Downing Street had form. The *Mirror* had uncovered a genuine exclusive two years earlier, the fact that Cherie Blair was pregnant. That story too had mysteriously found its way to the *Sun* before the *Mirror* hit the streets. Now it seemed the *Sun* had been told when the election would be even before the prime minister had told the Queen. Her Majesty's reaction isn't known, but Piers Morgan has never been a man to keep his opinions to himself. When, after the election, word leaked out from a private seminar that I had said 'having the *Sun* on board was a sufficiently important prize to take [the] risk' of alienating the *Mirror*, Morgan called it 'treacherous', led the paper with a story called 'A Spin Too Far' and even berated Blair in person about it.[78] My judgement on the balance of risk on that occasion was almost certainly wrong. Although Campbell had guessed correctly that the *Mirror* would back Labour in the election regardless, the paper's support was so grudging that at the end of the campaign he wrote to Morgan to tell him how 'pathetic' he thought it was.[79] More importantly the incident appears to have hardened Morgan's resolve to oppose as aggressively as he could Blair's post-election policy towards Iraq.

Campbell had no reason to complain about the *Sun's* election coverage. It announced that 'Hague Hasn't Got a Prayer' and backed Labour once again with only one qualification. The paper supported the Tories' line on Europe. Despite all that had gone before, Labour had more press support in the 2001 election than it had enjoyed four years earlier. Murdoch's *Times* also came out for Labour, as did the *Daily Express*, which was going through a rare non-Tory phase after being purchased by Richard Desmond, a man better known until then for somewhat racier titles, including *Asian Babes*. The Conservatives had just the *Daily Telegraph* and *Daily Mail* and their Sunday editions. News coverage of the Labour campaign was hardly enthusiastic, however, and the Nuffield guide concluded that the press had been de-aligned but not re-aligned. Praise for Blair 'fell far short of the adoration of Maggie that had accompanied the Conservative successes of the 1980s. New Labour had disarmed and contained the press but not converted it.'[80]

There was no question of the press eating out of Labour's hands this time around and the election did not go all the party's way even if the result was never in doubt. The media reacted to the studiously cautious campaign by making the most of any unexpected event. The day of Labour's manifesto launch alone provided more than enough

unplanned excitement. It started with the prime minister being publicly harangued outside an NHS hospital, was followed by a slow
hand-clap from police officers for the home secretary and culminated
in John Prescott throwing a punch at a protester in Wales. This last
event, recorded for posterity by *Sky News*, led to an angry war of
words between Campbell and *Sky's* political editor, Adam Boulton,
who thought the deputy prime minister should resign. Prescott kept
his job and Tony Blair managed to win the sympathy of most of the
papers, and much of the public, with his wry comment that 'John is
John . . . He's got very, very great strengths, not least in his left arm.'[81]

As usual at election time it was the BBC which, among the broadcasters, took most of the flak. Producers were accused of packing
studio audiences with hostile questioners and of encouraging public
confrontations when Tony Blair and other ministers were on the
stump. Campbell returned to his theme that the corporation was too
easily influenced by the '*Daily Mail* agenda'. If I ever felt uncomfortable at being asked to attack my former employers on behalf of my
current ones I had only to remind myself that no general election
would be complete without rows of this kind. Not that any of it made
any discernible difference to the result. Labour's majority of 167 was
only twelve lower than in 1997 and the Tories made a net gain of just
one seat. The voters had told Blair to go back to Downing Street and
get on with the job, preferably with a bit more to show for it this time.
I chose not to go with him, little realising how soon I would witness
from the sidelines the biggest battle in history between those who had
kept me in work for the past twenty years.

It was a more confident and determined Tony Blair who now began
his second term. He thought it might well be his last and he didn't
want to be accused of wasting another four years. Alastair Campbell
returned to work with less enthusiasm and with the intention of withdrawing from front-line briefing or even resigning altogether. The
prime minister picked up on his mood, but didn't want to lose a man
on whose judgement he relied to such a degree. In a conversation in
the Downing Street flat they discussed how to put their communications strategy on a better footing. According to Campbell's diary, 'He
said he was worried that I was confusing downspin – the right thing –

with non-communication – the wrong thing. Spin is not the same as communication, he said. Clinton had told him "Never stop communicating," and "He was right".[82] As part of a broader reform of the Downing Street structure a new role was designed for Campbell as 'director of strategy and communication'. As always, his every move fascinated journalists. His biographers Peter Oborne and Simon Walters said, 'Campbell had been afforded the unique privilege of being able to write his own job description – because the prime minister was terrified of losing him.'[83] In the words of the lobby's historian, Andrew Sparrow, he 'celebrated his promotion by doing even less direct communicating with the media than before'.[84] Godric Smith and Tom Kelly, both of them civil servants, would now take the daily lobby briefings.

The new communications directorate moved into much more spacious quarters on the ground floor of Number 12 Downing Street, linked to the main building by a connecting corridor through Number 11. The idea had been much discussed in the past and postponed because of the fear that the media would react just as they did. Number 12 had traditionally been the base of the chief whip. Oborne and Walters saw great symbolism in the move, arguing that the party whips 'had no place in the presidential style of government which Tony Blair and Alastair Campbell were eager to impose. The decision to evict the chief whip from her historic office was an unambiguous sign that the real government enforcer was . . . Campbell and his information machine.'[85] In fact Number 10 for many years been too small to house the number of staff required for a modern premiership and the extra capacity of Number 12, which had been underutilised in the past, was badly needed. Campbell was aware of the cynicism that greeted anything and everything he now did but, short of resigning, felt unable to prevent it. On arriving at Number 10 Tom Kelly found that feelings were 'still very, very raw between Downing Street and the media' and that Campbell's withdrawal made little difference as 'they still saw his hand behind everything'.[86] Far from improving, relations swiftly deteriorated further and within a year Number 10 was engaged in the biggest battle it had ever fought with the media.

Any hope Blair and Campbell had of escaping the constant barrage of criticism over spin was destroyed on the day two airliners crashed into New York's twin towers. On the afternoon of the 9/11 attacks a special adviser in the transport department, Jo Moore, sent an email to the press office saying 'it was a very good day to get out anything we want to bury.'[87] A month later as the first American missiles rained down on Afghanistan it was leaked to the press. In calmer times, the former *Guardian* editor, Peter Preston could look back on what she had written and conclude that 'spin of this kind isn't new, it's as old as politicians in a jam.'[88] At the time there was justifiable outrage. Blair regarded it as out of character for a woman he knew well and admired. He told Campbell it was 'a bit much to destroy her career over one leaked email that she should never have written or sent . . . it was not a hanging offence.'[89] But her televised apology only made matters worse and within seven months three careers were destroyed. Moore resigned on 15 February 2002. In May her former boss, the transport secretary Stephen Byers, a close political of ally of Blair's, was driven out. The email scandal wasn't the only reason but the decision to get rid of the department's communications director, Martin Sixsmith, at the same time made it look like it was. Sixsmith refused to go quietly and was convinced Campbell had 'fed smear stories to the papers' about him.[90] The second term was already starting to resemble the first with a succession of embarrassing events that called into question not only the professional integrity of government communications but also the personal integrity of the prime minister and his press secretary.

In February 2002 Blair was accused of writing to the Romanian prime minister to try to help another major party donor, Lakshmi Mittal, with a commercial steel contract. He denied it vigorously, telling the Commons 'it's not Watergate it's Garbagegate.'[91] Campbell wasn't sure it could be dismissed quite so easily, but the prime minister told him they 'just had to ride it out and tell them to get stuffed'.[92] A few years earlier that would have been Campbell's attitude too but he was now starting to wonder if he still had the mental and physical reserves to go on fighting battles with the media day after day. He agonised over whether to resign. Blair picked up on his mood and asked if he thought he was clinically depressed. When Campbell said he thought he was, Blair urged him to 'see the press as the inevitable downside of a job that had a huge upside, namely doing an important job and being part of a huge process of change for the country'.[93] It was a familiar argument but one that was starting to lose its persuasive power.

Blair was only a few months into his first term when Princess Diana had died; nine months into his second the Queen Mother passed away at the age of 101. This time around Number 10's handling of the event was less sure-footed. Downing Street was accused of trying to 'muscle in'[94] on her funeral. Strenuous denials were accompanied by the unusual decision to take the authors of the most damaging stories to the Press Complaints Commission. The names were familiar. They were the two journalists most reviled by Blair and his press team, Peter Oborne of the *Spectator* and Simon Walters of the *Mail on Sunday*. As it turned out, the PCC would never have to adjudicate because Alastair Campbell withdrew his complaint without explanation. The parliamentary official in charge of the arrangements, Lt.-Gen. Sir Michael Willcocks, better known as Black Rod, had told Downing Street privately he wouldn't back up their version of events. He finally broke his silence on the affair in 2009 when he told the BBC that he had 'refused to lie' on behalf of Number 10. He said they had wanted to turn the funeral into a 'political football' and 'kept on and on' in an effort to secure a bigger role for the prime minister.[95]

Philip Gould's polling showed that Blair's 'trust ratings' had taken another dive. The focus groups were 'jittery' and he was convinced the government had to do something about 'spin and sleaze'.[96] Blair agreed that there was a need for a new media strategy and on 2 May political editors were called into Downing Street to be told what it would be. The traditional morning lobby meetings would be held outside Number 10, in a much larger venue, and non-lobby journalists would be invited to attend if they wished. Ministers and policy officials would be made available, the prime minister would do more press conferences and it would all be on the record. Predictably, it provoked a storm of protest from some of those who saw their exclusive access to information being thrown wide open. According to the *Daily Mail*, 'For 118 years, ministers have faced scrutiny by the lobby system. Yesterday, at barely a moment's notice, Blair scrapped it.'[97] Others feared the new system would make it easier for the prime minister's spokesman to deflect difficult questions and commensurately more difficult for one or more correspondents to pursue an issue and refuse to let go until they had an answer. The new-style briefings, which started that October, were indeed less intimate affairs and reporters complained that they rarely got to ask more than one question each. The afternoon lobby meetings at the House of Commons continued unchanged and, of course, senior correspondents could still talk to Campbell or one of his deputies on the phone. According to Oborne and Walters, 'Traffic between Downing Street and its favoured political editors became more intense and fruitful than ever . . . In the name of openness and transparency the changes tended to make reporting more secret.'[98]

Blair claimed he was now the most accessible prime minister in history. As well as giving monthly press conferences he agreed to be questioned by a joint select committee comprising some of the most senior backbench MPs of all parties. At the first encounter he said he intended 'to try to engage in the public debate in a different way',[99] by which he meant he hoped to avoid having his words constantly interpreted by the correspondents and commentators even before the public had the chance to hear them. Some lobby journalists, who were deeply suspicious of Blair's desire to cut out the middlemen, argued that 'an end to spin' was spin in itself. The war of words became ugly, as Blair and Campbell had known it would. The pugnacious Labour party chairman Charles Clarke said that a lot of the criticism levelled at ministers was 'pious and hypocritical, sometimes entirely manufactured, coming from parts of the media which themselves have done their best to bring democratic politics into disrepute'.[100] The most determined counter-attack came from Peter Oborne who claimed that 'not since Baldwin in the early 1930s has a government squared up to the press' in such a determined way. Their real objective, he believed, was 'to evade scrutiny. That is the motive that causes it to whinge at every opportunity about the cynicism of the press. But the government has no moral right of any kind even to make the accusation. The hypocrisy is quite breathtaking. The government wants a timid, controlled media and will resort to any argument that lies to hand to promote this agenda.'[101]

Having turned what he saw as the media's self-obsession to his advantage by provoking the most extensive debate about journalistic ethics in over thirty years, Campbell unveiled a new tactic – uncharacteristic even-handedness. He appealed for both sides to recognise where they had gone wrong and the damage they were doing to themselves and to the reputation of politics. Competition within the media had 'eaten into standards of accuracy, fairness and judgement',[102] he wrote. That much they had heard before. Historically the press had been biased against the left but, he conceded, New Labour had over-reacted. 'We appeared, and perhaps we were, over-controlling, manipulative. People stopped trusting what we had to say. I think what we underestimated was the extent to which the changes we made in our relationships with the media, and in getting our media act together, would itself become an issue and a story. That's in part because we carried on for too long in government with some of the tactics of opposition.' He hoped the media would admit to behaving as if 'it was their job actually to stand up and try to do the job the opposition was failing to do – conveniently overlooking the fact that you are supposed to get elected to do that'. They should become 'less superficial, less defensive, less clubbish' and join with the government in trying to find better ways of working as 'cynicism, ultimately, will damage the media as much if not more than us'.

As he wrote those words Campbell knew that events were in train that were likely to put more strain on government–media relations than anything that had happened since Labour came to power. Earlier that summer Campbell had taken part in a meeting at Number 10 to review the diplomatic, military and intelligence situation in Iraq. There had been speculation in the media both in the United States and Britain that President Bush had already decided to extend his 'war on terror' from Afghanistan to Iraq. Minutes of the Downing Street meeting on 23 July were later leaked to the *Sunday Times* and published in the approach to the election of 2005. These minutes would be central to the charge that Tony Blair misled the British public, media and parliament in the run-up to the invasion of Iraq. Over much of the next eight months the prime minister would argue that war was not inevitable but that clear evidence existed that Saddam Hussein possessed weapons of mass destruction and had to be disarmed. The Downing Street minutes appear to tell a different story.

Sir Richard Dearlove, or 'C', the head of MI6, had just been to America to be briefed by his opposite number, George Tenet, director of the CIA. According to the minutes: 'C reported on his recent talks in Washington. There was a perceptible shift in attitude. Military action was now seen as inevitable. Bush wanted to remove Saddam, through military action, justified by the conjunction of terrorism and WMD. But the intelligence and facts were being fixed around the policy. The NSC [National Security Council] had no patience with the UN route, and no enthusiasm for publishing material on the Iraqi regime's record. There was little discussion in Washington of the aftermath after military action.'[103] The foreign secretary, Jack Straw, told the meeting, 'It seemed clear that Bush had made up his mind to take military action, even if the timing was not yet decided. But the case was thin. Saddam was not threatening his neighbours, and his WMD capability was less than that of Libya, North Korea or Iran.' Tony Blair appeared already to be thinking about how UK support for military action could be sold to the electorate. In his view, said the minutes, 'If the political context were right, people would support regime change. The two key issues were whether the military plan worked and whether we had the political strategy to give the military plan the space to work.'

Campbell was in no doubt about the significance of the discussions. 'The tough question is whether this is just regime change or is the issue WMD?'[104] he wrote in his diary the same day. It was clear to him that 'the US had pretty much made up their minds' and that Blair was 'pretty clear we had to be with the Americans'. The option of not supporting Bush had been posed by the foreign secretary. But 'when Jack raised the prospect of not going in with the US, TB said that would be the biggest shift in foreign policy for 50 years and I'm not sure it's very wise. On the tactical level, he felt maximum closeness publicly was the way to maximise influence privately.' Blair was clearly acutely aware of how difficult it would be to convince both his parliamentary party and the public, but nobody at the meeting was left in any doubt about his determination to go ahead. At one point he told them, 'it's worse than you think, I actually believe in doing this.' In communications terms the dilemma was now stark. On the basis of what was said at the Downing Street meeting this was a war that couldn't be spun. No communications strategy could sell the argument that Britain was giving unqualified support to America because it always had or in order to retain the greatest influence behind the scenes. The argument that war was right because Tony Blair believed it was would never be sufficient either. The only alternative was the threat posed to world peace by Saddam and his weapons of mass destruction. As the foreign secretary had pointed out, this case was 'thin'. It was going to have to be made a lot more substantial.

While Blair used the influence that was so precious to him to persuade a reluctant Bush to exhaust the diplomatic options through the United Nations, Campbell took up the task that had already begun in Washington: aligning the facts and the policy. On 24 September, Downing Street published a document entitled 'Iraq's Weapons of Mass Destruction – The Assessment of the British Government'. The intelligence services had been put under considerable pressure to come up with convincing evidence to go in the dossier. According to Lord Butler, who would later chair an inquiry into the intelligence-gathering, 'Blair said, in effect, "you may not have much evidence but for goodness sake go out and find it." So MI6 and GCHQ went out to find it.'[105] Most of Campbell's time was spent on the dossier and when it was published he felt it 'ended up convincing those who wanted to be and not those who didn't'.[106] The 'fact' that grabbed the headlines, as it was clearly intended to do, was contained in the prime minister's own foreword and said that Saddam's 'military planning allows for some of the WMD to be ready within forty-five minutes of an order to use them'. Downing Street made no objection to the London *Evening Standard* reporting '45 Minutes From Attack'[107] or to the *Sun*'s headline the next morning: 'Brits 45 Minutes From Doom'[108]. Blair had told the Commons that 'Saddam's WMD programme is active, detailed and growing'.[109] It wasn't, but it may be that the prime minister had convinced himself that it was. He also said intelligence contained in the dossier was 'extensive, detailed and authoritative' when it was anything but.

Campbell had every reason to be pleased with the initial reaction of the media. With the exception of the *Mirror* and the *Independent*, which would remain the only papers consistently to oppose the war, the rest of the press was supportive. *The Times* and the *Guardian* went beyond anything contained in the dossier to claim that Saddam's agents were scouring Africa in search of uranium to build a nuclear bomb. It is unlikely that either paper did so without first putting in a call to Downing Street. Whether or not they were advised that this was an avenue worth pursuing, the claims turned out to be false.

The events of that autumn put everybody in Downing Street under enormous stress, whether or not it was compounded by the knowledge that they were stretching the truth to breaking point. The last thing anybody needed was another story that put intense strain not just on individuals but on their personal relationships. That autumn Campbell was forced to take time away from persuading the media of the case against Saddam in order to defend somebody the tabloids delighted in condemning even more than they did the Iraqi dictator. Whatever her foibles, and she had her fair share, Blair's wife Cherie was in his view frequently the target of unfair media criticism as a way of getting at him. The longer it went on, however, the more Blair realised that this was one part of his life where he could not rely on his press secretary always to be ready to turn things around. Campbell and his partner, Fiona Millar, who looked after Mrs Blair's press relations, couldn't understand why she insisted on retaining the friendship of her 'lifestyle coach', Carole Caplin. Campbell became convinced that Cherie hadn't been giving him all the facts, and there was nothing he hated more than that. The press wanted to know if Caplin's lover, Peter Foster, a convicted con man, had been involved in Mrs Blair's purchase of two properties in Bristol. She told Campbell that Foster was not her financial adviser and the press office duly relayed that to any journalist who asked. When emails emerged that proved the contrary there were angry rows in the Downing Street flat. The Blairs wanted to stick to their line and Campbell had to tell them 'they were deluding themselves if they thought we could persuade people of that'.[110] Campbell resented being described as 'Liar In Chief' by papers like the *Mail* and *Telegraph*. He finally persuaded Mrs Blair to admit, in an emotional speech live on television, to giving incomplete answers to media inquiries, which had led to 'misunderstandings in the press office'. 'I am not superwoman'[111], she

added. The saga was significant because, in the estimation of Peter
Stothard, the former editor of *The Times*, who was given special access
to spend a month in Blair's company as the Iraq war unfolded: 'The
sight of his wife being pilloried for weeks in the press caused miserable
stress to Tony Blair. If anyone asks what has hardened him in the last few
months, this certainly did not soften his soul.'[112]

Having spent more than two weeks on little other than the problems of the prime minister's wife, Campbell started the Christmas
holiday in a sour mood. He felt no more motivated when he returned
to Downing Street in the New Year with the immediate task of rein-
forcing the case for the prime minister's determination to pursue the
Iraq crisis to its now-inevitable conclusion. In Washington at the end
of January Campbell and his deputy, Tom Kelly, found themselves
having to persuade the British press not just to accept that Blair was
committed to working through the United Nations but that Bush was
too. After a joint press conference during which Bush's body language
made clear his lack of enthusiasm for the task of getting another vote
by the Security Council to authorise war, Campbell's deputy had work
to do. 'Tom managed to spin our lot to a more positive position by
saying Bush was making clear he was open to a second resolution.'[113]
In the meantime work had been going on to complete a second
dossier, one that would soon earn the epithet 'dodgy'.

The following morning journalists attending the summit found a
document had been slipped under their hotel doors during the night.
It was entitled 'Iraq: Its Infrastructure of Concealment, Deception and
Intimidation'. Once again it secured some good headlines in those
newspapers whose editorial line already favoured military action if it
proved necessary, but they were to be the costliest headlines imaginable in terms of Downing Street's credibility. Once back in London
Blair told parliament the contents of the dossier were the work of the
security services who were 'not publishing this, or giving us this information and making it up. It is the intelligence they are receiving and
we are passing on to people.'[114] It was another highly misleading statement. Privately officials described the document as 'an Alastair
Campbell stunt'.[115] Its credibility lasted less than a week. *Channel 4
News* dubbed it the 'Dodgy Dossier' after discovering that much of it

had been lifted from a twelve-year-old post-graduate thesis on the internet, grammatical errors and all. Campbell called it 'a bad own goal'.[116] In the judgement of Godric Smith: 'We suffered very badly. The public thought that we were playing fast and loose with the intelligence, and lacked appropriate checks and balances. That perception went straight into the public bloodstream.'[117] A communications blunder had done disastrous damage to Blair's efforts to persuade the public of his sincerity. It seems clear from Campbell's diaries and the evidence of those like Peter Stothard who saw him at close hand that Blair did believe Saddam was capable of launching chemical and biological weapons, although perhaps not in forty-five minutes. Yet a huge number of people who had only the media to help form their judgements were now convinced their prime minister was either a liar or that he was willing to ignore any evidence that didn't support his convictions. As the build-up to war continued, hundreds of thousands of them took to the streets in demonstrations across Britain, some carrying placards with the one word: BLIAR.

The debacle over the 'Dodgy Dossier' contaminated anything the government said from that point on, and called into question the reliability of everything it had said before. In many people's minds it became confused with the earlier September document which, although it contained some tendentious claims, had been a much more robust piece of work. Yet by now most people, like the leader writers, had made up their minds one way or another. They didn't have access to the raw intelligence material that crossed the prime minister's desk and they had to make a gut decision whether to trust him or not. The continued support of the majority of newspapers heartened Downing Street and once again the Murdoch stable had remained loyal. Campbell fumed about those that did not – 'e.g. the *Mirror* front page with a dying Iraqi child and the headline "March For Him" as if he was starving because of us'.[118] Nevertheless, when Blair made his final plea for parliamentary support on 18 March, Campbell acknowledged that 'TB got the best press he had had for ages'.[119] Even the *Independent* conceded that it was 'the most persuasive case yet made by the man who has emerged as the most formidable persuader for war on either side of the Atlantic'.[120]

Persuasive it might have been but 139 Labour MPs voted against the war and the former foreign secretary Robin Cook resigned from the cabinet. Had every Labour MP, including those with ministerial jobs, voted with his or her conscience it is almost certain that Blair would have been the one to go. His resignation papers were ready for him to sign back at Downing Street. He survived thanks to the Conservative party's backing for the war. It was not a comfortable position for a Labour prime minister. Two days later, in a televised address, he announced that British forces had gone into action in an American-led operation 'to remove Saddam Hussein from power, and disarm Iraq of its weapons of mass destruction'.[121]

The twin-track approach to the media continued. In the first flush of military success sympathetic journalists were given favoured access for profiles that portrayed Blair as a decisive war leader in the Thatcher mould. Those who questioned the effectiveness of the invasion came under enormous pressure. As ever in wartime, that meant, above all, the BBC. Campbell had already had cause to complain about BBC coverage, first in Kosovo in 1999 and more recently in Afghanistan. Correspondents in the field of battle were, in his view, too prone to focus on the consequences of war rather than on the crimes that made war necessary. Now it was happening again in Baghdad. Andrew Gilligan, defence correspondent on the *Today* programme, reported that 'Baghdad may in theory be free but its people are passing their first days of liberty in greater fear than they have ever known'.[122] Extraordinarily, on the same day back in London Alastair Campbell was helping Tony Blair prepare for a cameo appearance in *The Simpsons*. It still left time to organise a telephone call of complaint to the BBC news centre.

When, at 6.07 on the morning of 29 May, Andrew Gilligan went live on to the *Today* programme with his latest 'scoop', Campbell was heading for Iraq for Blair's first visit. Gilligan was broadcasting from his home. John Humphrys introduced him by saying 'The government is facing more questions this morning over its claims about weapons of mass destruction . . . This in particular, Andy, is Tony Blair saying they'd be ready to go within forty-five minutes?' Gilligan replied, 'That's right, that was the central claim in his dossier which he published in

September, the main case if you like against Iraq, and the main statement of the government's belief of what it thought Iraq was up to and
what we've been told by one of the senior officials in charge of drawing up that dossier was that, actually, the government probably knew
that that 45-minute figure was wrong, even before it decided to put it
in.' Downing Street, said Gilligan, had 'ordered the dossier to be sexed
up', to be made more exciting and ordered more facts to be discovered.'[123] Word of what Gilligan had said was passed on to Campbell and
while he thought it was 'ghastly' he concluded it was 'clearly a repeat
of the stories at the time'.[124] And yet the report was to become, as the
Financial Times columnist John Lloyd wrote: 'a central fact in the battles about the media and their relationship with power'.[125] Lloyd's
objection was that Gilligan had played into the 'cynical assumption that
politicians are born liars and rogues'.[126] Campbell, who was named by
Gilligan in the *Mail on Sunday* as the man who had ordered the sexing
up,[127] had a more serious objection. He appeared before the Commons
foreign-affairs committee and said: 'Let's get to the heart of what the
allegation is: that the prime minister, the cabinet, the intelligence agencies, people like myself, connived to persuade parliament to send British
forces into action on a lie.'[128] Although his initial reaction had been
more measured, now, a month later, he wanted the BBC to admit its
error. 'Until the BBC acknowledges that that is a lie, I will keep bang-
ing on.' The prime minister had been wary of his press secretary going
so public with the demand for an apology but he agreed to the strategy and afterwards told Campbell he 'did superbly'. Campbell was
pleased with his performance and noted 'Flank opened on the BBC'.[129]

As the flank lengthened and the BBC stood its ground, believing its
independence was under attack, it was clear Campbell was leading
from the front. He was so incensed by the corporation's counter-attack
accusing him of 'conducting a personal vendetta against a particular
journalist whose reports on a number of occasions have caused you discomfort'[130] that he headed straight for the next available news studio.
Live on *Channel Four News*, Jon Snow announced the arrival of the
prime minister's press secretary, 'a rare moment'.[131] Blair learned that
he was going on just a few minutes in advance and warned him to stay
calm. He didn't. His seething anger was obvious even to those who

believed his battle with the BBC was nothing more than a smokescreen to hide the failure to uncover any weapons of mass destruction. The appearance was a serious misjudgement and if Campbell hadn't already decided it was time for him to leave it would have raised questions about his ability to do the job effectively for much longer. He was way out ahead of Blair who, in his estimation, 'lacked the killer instinct. His rationale was that he didn't want every single media organisation against him. I said we had to get it absolutely proven that we were right and use that to force a rethink of the political/journalism culture. I could see he was up for suing for peace.'[132]

At the beginning of July it emerged that Gilligan's source was a weapons scientist by the name of Dr David Kelly. He was not, as Gilligan had claimed in his broadcast, 'one of the senior officials in charge of drawing up' the dossier. It was clearly in the government's interests for that fact to become known – in Campbell's phrase it 'would fuck Gilligan'[133] – and they made sure that it did. Kelly had been a regular contact for a number of journalists but he had never sought the limelight. On a flight to Tokyo two weeks later, Blair received a call telling him that Dr Kelly had taken his own life. The prime minister was deeply shocked and announced an inquiry as soon as he landed. Campbell, who wasn't with him, wept. Friends and colleagues dissuaded him from resigning immediately. Neil Kinnock told him not to let 'the bastards take you as a scalp.'[134] Even the editor of the *Sun*, Rebekah Wade, a personal friend, said 'you've done nothing wrong, told the truth . . . Just hang in and don't give them the satisfaction.'

It seemed Campbell might suffer the fate he had predicted for Andrew Gilligan. His own picture was published alongside that of the prime minister and defence secretary in the *Daily Mail*, under the headline 'Proud Of Yourselves?' In Campbell's own judgement, 'The only person who came out well was Kelly. There was not nearly enough directed towards the BBC.'[135] A gaunt-looking Blair asked people to allow the inquiry, under Lord Hutton, to establish the facts. 'In the meantime, all of us, politicians, media alike, should show some restraint and respect.' He looked aghast when asked at a press conference with the Japanese prime minister, 'Have you got blood on your hands?'[136]

Anthony Seldon, who spoke to many of those around Blair at the time, believes the prime minister concluded then that it was time to accept Campbell's wish to resign. 'Campbell's value was long past. His aggression with the media, if necessary once, was no longer needed and it damaged Blair. So too did Campbell's obsession with the short-term when what Blair needed was someone at his shoulder urging him to think about policy not presentation. With Campbell still there, Blair would never blossom fully as a person or as prime minister.'[137] Blair was clear that Campbell couldn't go immediately, but agreed that as soon as Lord Hutton had finished interviewing witnesses it would be time for a formal parting of the ways. First Campbell had not only to give evidence to the inquiry but also, at the request of the judge, submit the relevant sections of his private diaries. These showed that Campbell had indeed wanted Dr Kelly's name to be made public but provided no evidence that he had been complicit in its release. When he appeared in person on 19 August it was a huge media event in itself. Blair had prayed for him in advance and said afterwards that he had been 'word-perfect'.[138] He recognised that once his press secretary's departure was announced 'he would have lost his main lightning con-ductor'. On 29 August Blair himself gave evidence. He said that, had Gilligan's allegation been true, 'it would have merited my resignation'. The following day he finally accepted that of Alastair Campbell. Publicly Blair said of him, 'He is a strong character who can make ene-mies, but those who know him best like him best.' Privately Blair warned him: 'You do realise I will phone you every day, don't you?'[139]

With Campbell gone, the high point in the power of the Downing Street press secretary was passed. No holder of that post either before or since has come remotely close to the influence he wielded and it unlikely that any future appointee would either wish to match it or be allowed to. The strength of the Blair–Campbell relationship was unique. At its most effective it enhanced and extended the power and influence of the prime minister himself. When Campbell's determination to fight for every story and every headline ran away with him, he inadvertently damaged the man he sacrificed so much to defend. Campbell helped define the Blair premiership for good and for ill. He won Labour new friends in the media but, as Blair had been frank enough to admit, he made many enemies, too. And he hadn't finished yet.

On 28 January 2004 Lord Hutton published his report. It came down almost exclusively for the government and against the BBC. Hutton concluded that Gilligan's allegation was 'unfounded'; the September dossier had not been 'embellished with intelligence known or believed to be false'; and 'There was no dishonourable or underhand or duplicitous strategy by the government covertly to leak Dr Kelly's name to the media.'[140] The report contained everything Blair and Campbell could have hoped for and more. The mood in Downing Street shifted from relief to jubilation and back again. In retrospect some realised the findings had actually been *too* helpful. 'If I had looked at it from a purely PR perspective,' said Tom Kelly, 'my view on the morning of the publication of Hutton was that I wish he had put the boot into us a bit more because frankly I knew that people were going to see it as a whitewash.'[141] Campbell saw it as the total vindication he had been looking for and went public, in another strident televised statement, to say so. He made it clear he thought heads should roll at the BBC as they would have done in government if the findings had gone the other way. He was not disappointed. First the corporation's chairman, Gavyn Davies, and then – reluctantly – its director general, Greg Dyke, resigned. If Blair had hoped to avoid further recriminations after the report, Campbell's reaction had made that impossible. Dyke, who received an extraordinary display of support from BBC staff after he went, later described Campbell as 'a deranged, vindictive bastard'.[142] As for the Hutton Report, it was, in Dyke's estimation, 'a crude whitewash of the government and yet another example of Number 10 spin'.

That wasn't the official BBC line. With Gavyn Davies gone, the acting chairman was Lord Ryder, who had been John Major's chief whip. He apologised without reservation for the mistakes made. The corporation set up a lengthy re-examination of its own editorial culture and processes and in the short term appeared to suffer an acute crisis of confidence. Richard Sambrook, the head of news, reflected later with admirable equanimity: 'The government was defending its integrity and the BBC was defending its independence. For each side, those two principles are non-negotiable, and it could only end badly. Part of the tragedy is that the BBC didn't set out to accuse the government of bad faith and I don't believe the highest levels of government set out to threaten the BBC's independence. It just seemed that way.'[143] Tom Kelly acknowledged that 'we were too ready to declare victory rather than have a sober assessment of what we had got right and what we had got wrong.'[144] One thing hadn't changed: both sides still needed each other. Ministers relied on the BBC to get their message across, and the corporation had no choice but to report what they were doing. There was no time for bearing grudges.

At Downing Street the task of rebuilding the media's trust fell to David Hill, who replaced Campbell as director of communications. It was an ideal choice. He had worked for the party since before Blair had even become an MP and was well respected by journalists for his straightforward approach to communications. His observation that 'the perception of Number 10 as a place of spin had to change and be put on a calmer footing'[145] was indicative of his gift for understatement. Hill's arrival coincided with the publication of a report by a former BBC executive turned chief executive of the Guardian Media Group, Sir Bob Phillis, into 'the three-way breakdown in trust between government and politicians, the media and the general public'. It criticised the 'increased use of selective briefing of media outlets, in which government information was seen to be being used to political advantage' and acknowledged journalists' complaints about information 'being used as the currency in a system of favouritism, selective release and partisan spinning'. Among its recommendations were the creation of a new civil-service post, at permanent-secretary level, to oversee government communications along with a new career structure and better training for information officers. The rules governing special advisers should be clarified and 'all major government media briefings should be on the record'.[146] That the report had ever been necessary was an indictment of what had gone before, but its main conclusions were quickly accepted by the government and seen as an opportunity to draw a line and move on. The *Independent* noted wryly that the report had been leaked in advance. 'The end of spin has been pre-announced, announced and re-announced many times. The Phillis report is unlikely to deliver a fatal blow to off-the-record conversations between politicians and journalists. It might, however help to end some of the worst excesses of the culture of spin.'[147] David Hill was clearly the right man at the right time. Alan Rusbridger at the *Guardian* reflected the views of most editors when he said that under Hill there was 'less sense of favourites and a political agenda'.[148]

Hill did not inherit Campbell's powers to instruct civil servants, a change he was more than happy to accept. He had neither the personality nor the desire to dominate Downing Street in the same way. The influence of the press office declined as Blair turned increasingly to his policy experts for advice. According to Kelly, 'the press office didn't have less access or less influence when it mattered but it wasn't the constant factor in every discussion' in the way that it had been.[149] The Iraq invasion and its consequences had diverted attention from the rest of the government's agenda but that was something Blair wanted to put right as soon as he could. The growing realisation that weapons of mass destruction were never likely to be found provided a powerful additional incentive to get back to something akin to normal politics as quickly as possible. The former cabinet secretary Lord Butler was asked to carry out a second inquiry, this time into the intelligence material that had preceded the war. Hill acknowledged that this was in no small part a response to the mood in the press. 'The media pressure was so great that we had to find a way of lancing it. We did it in the belief that the prime minister had acted responsibly and would be cleared.'[150] Butler's report, in July 2004, did indeed clear Blair of the most serious charge against him. It found 'no evidence of deliberate distortion or of culpable negligence', although the prime minister was found to have exaggerated the strength of the evidence in his Commons statement in September 2002 when, said Butler, he had 'misled the public, parliament and the world'.[151] The Butler report was less of a political and media event than Hutton had been. Despite the criticism it had the desired effect, in classic Downing Street parlance, of 'providing closure'.

'Politics as normal', as if politics is ever normal, had already resumed and in New Labour terms that meant familiar tensions over issues like the euro and the pace of reform in the public services and, hanging over all of it, Gordon Brown's ambitions to supplant the prime minister. At the party conference in 2003 the chancellor had made his most audacious bid for the leadership in a speech remembered for his reworking of a Blair line into a new refrain. 'We are best when we are boldest', the prime mister had declared a year earlier. 'Best when we are Labour,'[152] said Brown. The briefing wars had never really gone away; there had just been more important things to worry about. Brown had largely kept his head down during the Iraq controversy. It was a familiar tactic. Without saying or doing anything much publicly he was able to signal to those disenchanted with Blair in the parliamentary party and more widely that he understood their concerns. The signals were broadcast via private conversations with MPs, trade unionists and trusted journalists. The ripple effect created the impression that a Brown government would be very different, more 'Labour', whatever that meant, but without ever explaining how.

Brown could not speak out against any specific policy without appearing disloyal, but in January 2004 the House of Commons was due to vote on university tuition fees and the chancellor had a decision to make. The fees had been specifically ruled out in the Labour manifesto. Blair wanted to pass a bill to introduce them but not until after the next election. Technically by then the 2001 manifesto would no longer be binding, but still it looked like a breach of trust. Leading the rebels was the former chief whip Nick Brown, one of the chancellor's closest political allies. Journalists couldn't fail to see the battle lines being drawn and, for once, they were right to say that Blair's future as prime minister was on the line. Many of his key advisers believed he would be fatally wounded if such a high-profile vote went against him. But at the last minute the chancellor reined in his troops and the 'Brownite' rebels withdrew. The government won by five votes. In the Downing Street press office they tried, as so often before, to work out his motives. The fact that Murdoch's News International titles had supported the bill was seen by some as a factor. Brown would need their support if he were to become prime minister. Others believed Brown had 'bottled it'[153] and lacked the killer instinct. The papers were not slow to point out, however, that it had taken Brown's intervention to save Blair's neck.

On the issue of Europe the importance of the media was unambiguously part of the political calculations, as it always was. When the EU started seriously to consider rewriting its rules in the form of a new 'constitution' the Conservative opposition saw their chance to rebuild alliances with those parts of the press that had once supported them so enthusiastically. Michael Howard, who had become the third Tory leader to face Blair as prime minister in November, demanded a referendum on any changes. The *News of the World* called Blair a 'traitor'[154] for undermining British democracy and Murdoch himself reportedly chose the word.[155] Strongly pro-European cabinet ministers like Patricia Hewitt, a former press secretary to Neil Kinnock, urged Blair to adopt a referendum as Labour policy too and, in time-honoured fashion, it was the *Sun* that broke the story on 15 April that a U-turn was indeed on the way. Very few people had been consulted and cabinet ministers were dismayed once again to learn of such a significant change of policy through the press. Blair confirmed his change of heart to the Commons five days later. He said he had done it so as to take the fight to those who sought 'to persuade Britain that Europe is a conspiracy aimed at us, rather than a partnership designed for us and others to pursue our national interests properly'[156]. But with a general election expected within a year the convenient side effect of muting the growing press campaign was too obvious to be ignored.

The imminence of the election created a pressing need for good stories to show that Labour had not forgotten the domestic policy agenda on which it had been elected the last time around. In September the *Sunday Times* reported that Whitehall departments were once again feeling the heat. The paper had a leaked memo that revealed private discussions at a conference of government communications directors. Julia Simpson, head of press at the Home Office, complained that 'Number 10 think they can rugby-tackle you. They have made an announcement before you have thought through the policy. One time, the prime minister was making a visit. His people said he needed to make an announcement. The people around him wanted a snappy line.'[157] Siân Jarvis, a former GMTV reporter who would once have been grateful for those snappy lines, was now in charge of communications at the health department. She was reported as saying, 'This is the Number 10 problem: they are asking for announcements before we have a policy.' Those quoted were furious at seeing their words in print and it was a sufficiently embarrassing leak to warrant an investigation that included going through the phone records of some of those who attended the meeting. Only five years later was the probable culprit publicly named. An investigation by Patrick Wintour of the *Guardian* into what he called 'one of the most infamous incidents in the long-running Blair-Brown spin wars' revealed that the then head of the civil service, the cabinet secretary Andrew Turnbull, and the permanent secretary at the Treasury, Gus O'Donnell, 'came to believe that the source of the story was Damian McBride'.[158] At the time McBride's name would have meant nothing to the public. He was Gordon Brown's communications director, a civil servant and supposedly apolitical. But not for long. O'Donnell became increasingly concerned that he was engaged in systematic political briefing on the chancellor's behalf and insisted his status be changed to that of a special adviser. By the time Brown became prime minister O'Donnell had taken over as cabinet secretary himself. Once again he spoke to Brown and advised him not to bring McBride with him. Had his advice been heeded the name of Damian McBride might never have been known beyond the Westminster cognoscenti and Downing Street could have avoided one of the worst spin scandals in its history.★

All that was for the future. In 2004 McBride and his boss were still directing a guerrilla war from within the Treasury bunker and it wasn't going well. Blair came back from his summer holiday looking refreshed and showing every sign that he was determined to carry on. What's more he was bringing in reinforcements. The chancellor was horrified to learn that a man he regarded as an 'uber-Blairite', the former health secretary Alan Milburn, was to return to the cabinet with overall responsibility for planning the election campaign. The media correctly reported it as a snub for Brown, but worse was to come. In October, after a relatively harmonious party conference, Blair went into hospital to be treated for an irregular heart beat. When he came out, rather than allow his health to be used for a flurry of renewed leadership speculation, he called the television crews to Downing Street. He announced that he was 'absolutely fine' and intended leading the party into the next election. Not only that but 'if I am elected I would serve

---

★See p. 424.

a full third term – I do not want to serve a fourth term.'[159] One of
Brown's supporters was quoted in the *Observer* as calling it 'an African
coup'[160], a curious phrase given that Blair was already in power.
Brown's own feelings were revealed with the publication of a book by
the journalist Robert Peston, then on the *Sunday Telegraph*. Once again
Brown and his closest supporters had collaborated on a book, one that
they had assumed would be published after he became prime minister. *Brown's Britain* was serialised at the beginning of January 2005. In
it the chancellor was quoted as routinely saying to Blair, 'There is
nothing that you could ever say to me now that I could ever believe.'[161]
It rang so true that any efforts to deny it would have been pointless.

Relations between the two men were as bad as they had ever been
but as the election approached it was in the interests of both of them
to pretend the opposite. Just as he had threatened to do, Blair had kept
in regular contact with Alastair Campbell and he was now back advising the Labour party, although without any formal role at Number 10.
His judgement, and that of Philip Gould, was that Blair and Brown
must campaign as a team. No matter what people might have read or
heard, Gould's polling showed a significant increase in the party's support when the two men were seen as working together. On 6 April,
the day after he announced the election date of 5 May, the prime minister made it clear that Brown would not be sacked or moved if he
won. 'He is the most successful chancellor in 100 years. We would be
crazy to put that at risk,' he said.[162] For months Brown had been sulk-
ing over the way Milburn's arrival had effectively sidelined not just him
but his closest allies. At the last possible moment a peace of sorts was
re-established to give the media and the public an impression of harmony even if the underlying reality remained discordant. Pictures of
Blair buying Brown an ice-cream cone on the eve of polling day were
the peak, or perhaps trough, of the audacious camouflage strategy.

For the Tories, Michael Howard sought to make Blair's honesty a
campaign issue. Posters proclaimed that 'If He's Prepared to Lie to Take
Us to War, He's Prepared to Lie to Win an Election'[163], omitting to
add that the Conservatives had supported the war themselves. Labour
found the media far more hostile than in any election since 1983,
although it came as no surprise. The launch of the official campaign

had been preceded by what became known as the 'masochism strategy'. Blair had appeared on as many different kinds of broadcasts as he could, and agreed to answer readers' questions in the papers and online, with the aim of taking as much heat out of the public's anger over Iraq and other issues as possible. Running in parallel was what one academic called the 'Heineken strategy' in which Blair 'ruthlessly exploited his notoriety and incumbency to reach parts of the public that didn't usually engage with politics'.[164] The low point was an appearance on *Ant and Dec's Saturday Night Takeaway* during which Blair was asked 'if you make an ugly smell do people pretend not to notice because you is the prime minister?'[165] Those who believed Blair had devalued the authority of his position by his willingness to court popularity through the media were given powerful new ammunition.

The print media were in a churlish mood throughout the campaign and neither major party inspired much enthusiasm. In terms of endorsements, the *Daily* and *Sunday Express* returned to the Tory fold, as did the *Sunday Times*. Yet Labour still retained the support, albeit grudging, of five of the ten national dailies and four of the nine Sundays. The *Daily Mirror*, historically Labour's most reliable cheerleader, was in a truculent mood. Relations had soured with the paper's opposition to the Iraq war. At the time Campbell had told the paper's political editor, James Hardy, 'the only message the prime minister has for *Daily Mirror* readers is: don't buy it'.[166] Hardy regarded it is as typical of his 'arrogant and contemptuous' attitude towards the *Mirror* resulting from the 'obsessive chase of the *Sun*'. The *Sun* stuck with Blair but with little enthusiasm, offering him 'One Last Chance'. The *Mail* had no inhibitions about echoing the Tory campaign claim that 'Blair Lied And Lied Again'. The formal endorsements made less of an impact than they had in earlier elections and the Nuffield study rightly felt that 'Traditional displays of press partisanship seem out of place in an era in which many voters (including newspaper readers) no longer even take the trouble to vote.'[167]

The final week of the campaign was once again dominated by Iraq following the leak of the attorney-general's opinion on the legality of the war on *Channel Four News*. Lord Goldsmith's view that 'while a "reasonable" case could be made for going to war, he was not confident that a court of law would necessarily agree'[168] was not fatal but it was a massive distraction from what Labour wanted to be talking about. Blair's subsequent appearance on a *Question Time* special on BBC1, in front of an angry and vocal audience, was one of the worst moments of the campaign for him personally. Labour emerged battered and bruised but with a majority of sixty-six seats. Any previous Labour leader would have seen that as a very comfortable margin but Blair felt 'demoralised' and 'rejected'. Number 10 was convinced Brown immediately broke the fragile truce by briefing the press that the results were a setback for the party and its leader. 'There was a pretty big rubbishing of it from the Brownites,' said one. 'That is what they do.'[169] The chancellor was more than happy to see Andrew Rawnsley in the *Observer* rewrite the *Sun* headline of 1992 to conclude, 'It Was Brown Wot Won It'.[170]

Later that month the voters in France released Blair from his promise to fight another campaign, and one that it's unlikely even Gordon Brown could have helped him win, assuming he wanted to. By a narrow majority they voted in a referendum to reject the European constitution. The need for Blair to confront Rupert Murdoch, the *Daily Mail*, and the rest of the Euro-sceptic press by recommending a 'yes' vote in Britain effectively evaporated overnight. He found himself in the more comfortable position of vigorously defending the rebate to Britain's EU contributions first negotiated by Margaret Thatcher and predictably those same papers applauded. But having declared publicly that he would not fight another general election, Blair no longer felt driven to appease them in the same way. His aides thought he had been 'liberated' from the media at last. According to Tom Kelly, who returned as official spokesman, 'it wasn't that he didn't think about presentation, because he wanted his ideas to have an impact. He wanted to get his thoughts across. But the first thought wasn't "Is this going to be popular or unpopular?" The first thought was "Does this make sense?".'[171]

For a few months at any rate he continued to enjoy popularity whether he sought it or not. London's success in winning the 2012 Olympic Games in July was attributed in large part to his personal diplomacy. His pleasure was cut brutally short by the tube and bus bombings in the capital the very next day. Once again he found the right words for the occasion. 'When they try to intimidate us, we will not be intimidated. When they seek to change our country or our way of life by these methods, we will not be changed.'[172] The attacks happened while Blair was chairing a G8 meeting of world leaders and by now he was the longest-serving of all of them. Yet his position was inevitably weakened by the knowledge that, whatever he had said about serving a full third term, he could not be around very much longer. He had admitted as much when in May he promised his MPs 'a stable and orderly transition' to his successor.[173] Speculation about when he would stand down and whether anybody would challenge Brown for the leadership provided a continuous background noise to his last two years in office. He could hardly complain if the media obsessed about it.

Blair was determined to avoid being labelled a 'lame duck' and rushed ahead with the kind of speed and determination that not even a duck in the very best of health could hope to match. Journalists often need a deadline to concentrate the mind and it seemed as if the prime minister was being energised in much the same way. He had a new message for the media and for his own party: it's better to lose on what you believed to be right than to win and be wrong. Most controversial was the proposal to detain terrorist suspects for up to ninety days without trial. Blair suffered his first ever parliamentary defeat on the issue on 9 November. In other areas of policy – education, pensions, health – he was intent on laying out ambitious proposals and 'five-year plans' that everybody knew he wouldn't be around to see through. It was a political battle for the future and Downing Street now faced a number of rival claimants to the territory. With the election of David Cameron as Conservative leader in December 2005, the opposition at last had a leader who could match Blair for charisma and made-for-the-media sound bites. Cameron even claimed to be the 'true heir to Blair' and during their first exchange in the Commons he taunted the prime minister with a line that was as good as any Blair could have come up with himself: 'You were the future once!'[174]

Gordon Brown wasn't ready to let David Cameron claim the future, but there were others in the Labour party who doubted whether the

chancellor was the right man to take him on. It was all a gift to the
political correspondents, who enjoyed the spectacle of the rival camps
vying for their attention. Remarkably, the Blair brand still had great
resilience. All the rivals wanted to be seen as the ones to take it forward; nobody proposed reversing the changes he had presided over for
the past decade. Once again at a time of political flux, the different
camps used the newspapers to play out their strategies and to look for
evidence of what the others were up to. In that respect this transfer of
power was little different from the one that had seen David Lloyd
George replace Herbert Asquith ninety years earlier. At the Treasury,
where Brown had the most to lose, the papers were scanned with
greater care than ever. The chancellor knew that ex-ministers like
Stephen Byers, Alan Milburn and Charles Clarke wanted to frustrate
his ambitions if they could. These men could fairly claim to have
shown more loyalty to Blair over the years than Brown had done and
that gave them a currency with journalists that they would otherwise
have lacked. It also meant that not every story that was attributed to
'Blairite' sources could be traced back to Number 10. Damian
McBride recognised that it was no longer a simple case of TB versus
GB. 'In the later years you would get all sorts of mischievous stories
coming out not necessarily from Number 10 but from people who
could call themselves "Downing Street sources". David Hill and Tom
Kelly wasted a lot of energy having to damp down stories that had
been briefed with some authority by "ultras" claiming to have the
prime minister's ear.'[175]

Inside Downing Street discreet contact was being maintained with
the 'ultras' but not by Hill or Kelly. Benn Wegg-Prosser, formerly Peter
Mandelson's special adviser and now in charge of strategic communications at Number 10, became a pivotal figure. Blair had told Brown
he would not support any alternative candidate for the leadership and
this time he appeared to be keeping his promise. Whatever doubts he
may have had about the chancellor's suitability as a replacement he had
no intention of making them public. The Treasury's use of the media
to draw attention to its differences with Number 10 was as infuriating
as ever, but it was hardly new. In November 2005 a letter making clear
Brown's opposition to radical reforms to pensions being pushed by

Number 10 was leaked to the *Financial Times*.[176] According to Anthony Seldon's account, Brown was suspected of being behind an even more serious leak the same month while the prime minister was negotiating with other EU leaders over the union's budget. 'Blair was having breakfast in his hotel when David Hill walked in with a copy of the *Daily Telegraph*. Its headline announced 'Day Of Surrender'. Underneath was laid out in considerable detail Britain's whole negotiating strategy, including its willingness to make a concession on the rebate. '"We believed it was the Treasury that leaked it to the press. The detail clearly meant it had come from a very close inside source," said one official . . . Number 10 regarded it as a betrayal and, coming on the heels of the pensions leak, as outrageous: they held Brown personally responsible, believing he wanted to undermine Blair for conceding too much, as well as to impress Paul Dacre of the *Mail* and Rupert Murdoch with his Euro-sceptic credentials.'[177]

Like Lloyd George, Brown was suspected of supping with the devil, entering into an alliance with his party's traditional enemies in the press to undermine the prime minister. It was a journalist on a paper with no interest in seeing Labour prosper who said, 'we were all implicated in the dirty business of Gordon Brown . . . we all colluded in advancing Gordon Brown's interests'.* The last months of Blair's premiership were dominated by a scandal that again had people reaching for the history books and looking up David Lloyd George. 'Cash for honours' was a long, debilitating affair. No proof of wrongdoing was ever found but Downing Street was shackled by a lengthy police investigation and a succession of damaging leaks to the media. 'Who was pushing us on that?' asked the same journalist. 'Gordon Brown.'

Tony Blair found himself having to defend the fact that those who gave large sums of money to the Labour party stood a disproportionately high chance of being elevated to the House of Lords. He argued that any party was entitled to have its supporters in the Upper House and inevitably some of them would be donors. But the sale of honours is illegal and Blair became the first prime minister in history to be interviewed as a witness in the course of a criminal investigation into

---

*See p. 6.

possible offences committed by his own staff. The press office had to erect 'Chinese walls' so that Tom Kelly could tell journalists in all honesty that he had no idea when the prime minister was being interviewed. The fact that a civil servant was briefing the lobby was now a distinct advantage. Had either Alastair Campbell or David Hill claimed not to be in the loop over something as significant as the prime minister giving evidence to a detective they would not have been believed.

No proof of wrongdoing was ever established. Nor could Downing Street prove that Brown had a role in exacerbating the affair. At best the evidence was circumstantial. The story had first come to light when the party treasurer, Jack Dromey, went public with his concerns. Dromey is married to Harriet Harman who was closely identified with the chancellor and already fighting an unofficial campaign to be his deputy should he make it to Number 10. Never had Blair felt so powerless in response to a story that seemed to go on and on, and relations with Brown were as bad as they had ever been. The two men were still talking but the conversations were hardly productive. After one meeting the prime minister said, 'We didn't get down to any substance: all he would say is "When are you going to fuck off out of here?"'[178]

In his frustration Blair once again looked for other ways to get his message across. Ben Wegg-Prosser advocated making much better use of the 'new media' now that the conventional media were interested only in leadership and scandal stories. The internet, podcasts, YouTube and the Downing Street website became the preferred means of prime-ministerial contact with the public. Blair's grasp of the technology was never extensive but he was willing to try his hand at whatever his staff thought would work. A memo written by Wegg-Prosser at this time later fell into the hands of the *Daily Mirror.* Entitled 'Reconnecting With the Public – A New Relationship With the Media', it said of the prime minister, 'He needs to go with the crowd wanting more. He should be the star who won't even play that last encore.'[179] Blair needed to reach over the heads of the Westminster journalists. Both *Blue Peter* and *Songs of Praise* were mooted as possible venues for the farewell shows. And then, for good measure, Wegg-Prosser added that 'the more successful we are, the more it will agitate and possibly destabilise [Brown].'

One thing the prime minister was not prepared to do was to moderate or conceal his views. His conviction that it was better to be right than popular did as much to destabilise his own position as anything coming out of the Treasury. If people didn't like those whom he chose to support or do business with, then that was too bad. His refusal to criticise Israel's invasion of Lebanon in July 2006 infuriated even some of his most loyal ministers. When in the middle of the middle-east crisis President Bush greeted him with the words 'Yo, Blair!' at a summit in St Petersburg, the image of a prime minister subservient to a deeply unpopular American president was reinforced.[180] At the end of July he saw Bush again, this time in the United States. But this time it was his detour to Pebble Beach in California to address a meeting of News Corporation executives that excited most comment. As Michael White in the *Guardian* pointed out, 'Mr Blair knows from experience that he will pay for the applause: his enemies at home will see it as yet further proof of a "poodle" relationship with the Australian-turned-American media tycoon, scarcely less malign than the servility he supposedly gives President George Bush'.[181] The symmetry of his attendance at a Murdoch gathering in his last year as prime minister, just as he had done in his first year as party leader, was almost too neat. In fact he made no reference to the media until the very end of his speech on 'leadership'. He advised the wide array of other leaders present in the hall, not to 'let your ego be carried away by the praise or your spirit be diminished by the criticism and look on each with a very searching eye. But for heaven's sake, above all else, lead.'[182] Blair then went off on holiday to Cliff Richard's villa in Barbados with the key question still left unanswered: How much longer did he intend to go on leading?

When he returned to Britain his response came in one of the most extraordinary interviews he ever gave as prime minister. Phil Webster and Peter Riddell of *The Times* were invited to Chequers for the occasion. They knew he wanted to draw a line under the Lebanon controversy but it was the leadership issue that they expected to provide the front-page news. They had been warned in advance that he planned to signal that the coming party conference would be his last. Webster recalled, 'Two minutes into the interview I asked the question and he said precisely the opposite of what I had been expecting. I wanted to be sure and when we listened back we counted nine times that I asked more or less the same question. He had been hardened up that morning not to give way. We even stayed for a spot of lunch, so there was no possibility that we had misunderstood what he wanted to say.'[183] Webster and Riddell's article appeared on 1 September declaring that 'Defiant Blair' was ready to take on his party. 'Tony Blair remains completely unmoved by the frenetic speculation about his future in the political and media worlds. Talking in the calm of Chequers yesterday lunchtime, he brushed aside the queue of Labour MPs and commentators angrily calling for his resignation and the demands by union leaders for sweeping changes in policy.'[184]

Even more extraordinary scenes followed that day with key members of the Downing Street media team telephoning editors and correspondents to inform them that, whatever the prime minister may or may not have said to *The Times*, he would be leaving office the following year. The damage had been done, however, and the interview was enough to convince Brown's allies that the time to move had come. It led directly to what became known as 'the Curry House plot'. On the day Blair's interview was published a group of West Midlands MPs sympathetic to Brown met at the Bilash Bangladeshi restaurant in Wolverhampton to discuss tactics. Three days later one of them, the defence minister Tom Watson, visited Brown at home in Scotland, where he was looking after his newborn son Fraser. Given that the baby was only a few weeks old the public explanation for the visit – to hand over a *Postman Pat* video – seemed implausible to say the least.

Downing Street knew by now that formerly loyal backbenchers were gathering signatures on letters calling on Blair to resign. One had Tom Watson's name on it. On 5 September the environment secretary David Miliband was deputed to appear on the *Today* programme and confirm that it was 'reasonable' to assume that Blair would be gone within a year. The same morning the *Guardian* published details of the letter Watson had signed and the *Mirror* printed the Wegg-Prosser memo at a time calculated to do most damage to Blair. The following day Blair and Brown had two face-to-face meetings in the prime minister's office, the first at 7.45 in the morning. In the interval between them Tom Watson resigned and Downing Street then told journalists they'd been about to sack him anyway. Five unpaid ministerial advisers also resigned. They all called on Blair to step down. As Brown returned to Number 10 the threat was clear. More resignations would follow if Blair didn't go public with a commitment that even he couldn't wriggle out of. Wegg-Prosser told contacts in the lobby it was a 'coup' and amounted to 'blackmail'.[185] He was right but it worked. While Brown was being driven away from his second meeting the waiting photographers caught him with a look of delight on his face so obviously heartfelt that it at least showed he could manage a genuine smile when it suited him. Twenty-four hours later the prime minister appeared before the cameras at a school in north London and said that, while he would have preferred to make the announcement in his own time, the forthcoming party conference would be his last.

What Blair didn't do was to endorse Brown as his successor and, in the days that followed, advisers like Wegg-Prosser believed they had his permission to use private discussions with journalists to question the chancellor's suitability for the job. Others, like the former home secretary Charles Clarke, went public with their doubts. Clarke told the *Daily Telegraph* that Brown was a 'control freak' with 'psychological issues'[186] who should not assume he would succeed to the top job without a contest. In the circumstances the party conference in Manchester passed off relatively calmly, although speculation continued about whether Brown would face a challenge. It certainly seemed that Mrs Blair, if not her husband, hoped that he would. She was overheard by a journalist saying, 'That's a lie!' as the chancellor told delegates what a 'privilege' it had been to work 'with the most successful Labour prime minister'.[187]

Blair's last Queen's Speech on 15 November was best remembered for a prime-ministerial sound bite that was not quite as explicit as it first sounded. He warned David Cameron that he would soon 'come within reach of a big clunking fist'.[188] Brown thought it was, at last, a public endorsement of his succession. But some papers reported sources 'close to Blair' suggesting it could have referred to any one of the other cabinet heavyweights who might take over. By the New Year it was increasingly evident that, whatever doubts Blair might have had,

Brown would not face a serious challenger. Those who considered taking him on, John Reid, Charles Clarke, Alan Milburn, David Miliband, decided they either could not win or could not face the consequences of trying. One later told Alice Miles of *The Times*, 'When I considered challenging him for the leadership, people warned me it would be a very unpleasant campaign; and it would have been an unpleasant campaign because Gordon's people would have run it in an extremely vicious way.' Ms Miles said she 'remembered being told at the time by a number of journalists that one potential candidate was having a mental breakdown, and there was some embarrassing story involving him and a woman doing the rounds. The tales seemed obviously to have been invented by Mr Brown's muck-spinners. In place of ideas, smears: that contest should have been conducted by open debate, not whispered poison. But Mr Brown was afraid of the debate.'[189] As the assumption grew that his succession was all but inevitable, attention shifted to what kind of prime minister Gordon Brown would actually make.

Blair promised not to do anything to undermine his successor. He told *The Times*, 'When you get a new leader, the last thing I'm going to be doing, I can assure you, is making mischief for whoever comes afterwards. I think that the worst form of vanity that anyone can ever have after they leave the job, is thinking that anyone is interested in what you say afterwards, other than causing trouble for your successor.'[190] He was true to his word and avoided the accusations of disloyalty that both Edward Heath and Margaret Thatcher earned by their conduct. Although, according to the *Guardian*, 'In 2006, shortly before Brown finally clambered over him to become prime minister, Blair told a journalist who prefers not to be named, "If he [Brown] is going to make a fist of being PM, he's got to change his way of operating. Can he change? Probably not".'[191] Brown's character came under public attack the following month from a very unusual source. Lord Turnbull, who had been both permanent secretary at the Treasury and cabinet secretary, told the *Financial Times* the chancellor possessed 'Stalinist ruthlessness', 'a very cynical view of mankind and his colleagues' and that he had 'played the denial of information as an instrument of power'.[192]

Blair had one bit of unfinished business before he went. He wanted to say what he thought about the state of British journalism. His aides, including David Hill, cautioned him against allowing his anger at more recent controversies to influence unduly his argument. The resulting 'feral beasts' speech, written by Blair in longhand, was a curious affair. It was spoiled by a headline-grabbing phrase that distracted attention from his real argument and then went on to single out for blame one of the least influential of the national newspapers. He delivered it in June 2007, just a fortnight before he was due to stand down. He conceded that the relationship between politics and the media had always been fraught, 'as it should be', but argued that it had now changed to such a degree that it was 'seriously adverse to the way public life is conducted'.[193] He was frank about how much of his time in Downing Street had been dominated by it. 'A vast aspect of our jobs today – outside of the really major decisions, as big as anything else – is coping with the media, its sheer scale, weight and constant hyperactivity. At points it literally overwhelms.' Any political leader had to employ people to defend their interests. 'Not to have a proper press operation nowadays is like asking a batsman to face bodyline bowling without pads or headgear.'

The media faced more competition, he argued, and so were interested only in stories that had real impact. The consequence was lower standards of reporting, more sensationalism, cynicism and a tendency to exaggerate any error made by those in public life. He then gave the assembled journalists what he must have known would be their headline quote: 'Today's media, more than ever before, hunts in a pack. In these modes it is like a feral beast, just tearing people and reputations to bits.'

Blair then switched his argument to criticise the media for mixing fact and comment as a matter of course – describing the *Independent* as 'a metaphor for this kind of journalism' – and for sacrificing balance in favour of exaggerated extremes of black and white. 'It's a triumph or a disaster. A problem is "a crisis". A setback is a policy "in tatters". A criticism, "a savage attack".' He concluded by acknowledging the power of the media and decrying its lack of accountability. 'This relationship between public life and media is now damaged in a manner that requires repair. The damage saps the country's confidence and self-belief; it undermines its assessment of itself, its institutions; and above all, it reduces our capacity to take the right decisions, in the right spirit for our future.' Blair suggested that the media might need better, statutory regulation although clearly he wouldn't be around to put it into law.

Sadly Blair didn't give his views on those newspapers that had done most to frustrate his own ability to take what he believed to be the right decisions. There was no mention of the *Sun* or any of the News International titles and not a word about the *Mail*, the paper most hated and feared within Downing Street throughout his time as prime minister. Adam Boulton, political editor of *Sky News*, wrote later after a conversation with the now-former prime minister that: 'out of office, Blair conceded that it was a mistake to single out the *Independent*. His real target had been the *Daily Mail* but he feared what the paper would do to him and his family should he have targeted it. Blair said he had thought long and hard about whether it had been wise to be so friendly in the early days with senior executives at Associated Newspapers, but he argued that the tone of the group had grown much worse with the rise of Paul Dacre.'[194]

Despite pulling its punches, the speech hit home. For months to come journalists would turn up to Number 10 lobby briefings wearing badges proudly identifying themselves as 'feral beasts'. More seriously it provoked, as it was intended to do, much soul-searching by editors, columnists and leader writers. The *Telegraph* found his argument 'deeply disturbing, founded on false premises and worthy of the strongest refutation'.[195] The *Guardian* hoped 'nothing will ever come of any attempts to place the press under any kind of statutory regulation. The British press is all the things Mr Blair says it is. But it must remain free to be both awful and, on its day, magnificent.'[196] *The Times* saw some merit in his argument about the blurring of news and comment. 'Journalists are right to hold politicians and companies to account, but journalists should not be afraid of being held to account themselves. Readers are intelligent and thoughtful, and hardly able to be fooled by an individual article or an individual politician, but if the traditional media exist as a separate, self-serving universe, then the distance from readers will grow and the size of the audience will shrink.'[197] The *Mirror* thought New Labour should look to its own failings. 'Mr Blair and his army of spin doctors severely warped relations between media and politics . . . If politicians really believe the media fails to accurately reflect the facts as they see them shouldn't they start the house-cleaning by promising to tell the truth.'[198] The *Independent*'s editor, Simon Kellner, asked if Blair would have made the same attack on his paper's journalism if it had supported the war in Iraq and concluded 'of course not'.[199]

Less than two weeks later Blair stood up in the House of Commons to face prime minister's questions for the last time. His final words as a member of parliament were a defence of politicians against those who sought constantly to criticise them. 'Some may belittle politics but we know, who are engaged in it, that it is where people stand tall and although I know it has its many harsh contentions it is still the arena that sets the heart beating a little faster. And if it is on occasions the place of low skulduggery, it is more often the place for the pursuit of noble causes. And I wish everyone, friend and foe, well, and that is that. The end.'[200] MPs of all parties broke with tradition to stand and applaud him as he left. Up in the press gallery overlooking the chamber some lobby journalists fought the temptation to do the same. They all knew he had been a class act. Like most other people they watched Blair depart with mixed feelings. He had infuriated many. Some had come to despise him; others believed he would eventually be recognised as one of the few prime ministers who had changed Britain fundamentally and for the better. None could deny that, as Philip Stephens of the *Financial Times* put it, 'Like Margaret Thatcher, he filled almost all the available political space.'[201]

Simply by dint of the time he spent in office it was inevitable that comparisons with Thatcher would be drawn. In terms of his relationship with the media there were more similarities than at first appeared. Like her, Tony Blair was prepared to perform, indeed to ham it up to the rafters, in order to get his message across. It was part of the job, although he probably enjoyed it more than she did. He also took more of an interest in what journalists said about him, although he still preferred to let others do most of the worrying and the cajoling on his behalf. As he had tried to explain in his 'feral beasts' speech, the demands of the media had grown massively since Mrs Thatcher left office. Under Blair, Downing Street's approach was to try to meet those demands insofar as they possibly could. They – I should say 'we' for the relatively brief time I was there – probably tried too hard. Nobody can keep up with a 24-hour media disseminating news and comment across a multitude of channels and websites simultaneously. According to Professor Peter Hennessy, by 1997 the attempt to try 'represented the largest single change in the day-to-day conduct of the premiership. Mr Attlee would not only have found the media life of Mr Blair incredible, he would have recoiled from it absolutely. Indeed, he almost certainly could not have existed within it.'[202] Mrs Thatcher would have found the amount of time and effort Blair gave over to the media disproportionate to their importance and tangential to the real responsibilities of the job. With the possible exception of Harold Wilson, no previous prime minister would have sanctioned the kind of media-management techniques that Blair regarded as necessary. He didn't know about everything that was being done in his name. No prime minister ever does. But none of us who worked for him felt in any way inhibited by the sense that he might disapprove of what we were up to. Only when the political damage being done by spin became too great did Blair insist that things would have to change. But by the time Downing Street signalled that it wanted to play straight with the media, most journalists doubted it would know how to if it tried. Every attempt to draw a line under the past, every declaration of *mea culpa*, every new 'media strategy' failed. Trust is like virginity. Once lost, there is no getting it back. Gordon Brown, no babe in arms when it came to the dark arts of spin, would now have his opportunity to do things differently.

12

SUNSET SONG:
BROWN (2007−)

If a government policy cannot be presented in a simple and attractive
way, it is more likely than not to contain fundamental flaws and prove
to be the wrong policy.

Peter Mandelson

Standing on the front step of Downing Street for the first time as prime minister, Gordon Brown promised to lead 'a new government with new priorities'. Before turning and disappearing inside he declared 'Now let the work of change begin.'[1] The message he wanted to convey was unambiguous. This prime minister was going to do things very differently to his predecessor and changing the way Downing Street dealt with the press was a high priority. Even before the expenses scandal of 2009, Brown knew that the public's faith in politics generally, and in New Labour in particular, was at a low ebb. He believed Tony Blair's use of the media was a contributory factor, but his attempts to change the culture were very quickly disappointed. According to Damian McBride, who was the nearest thing Brown had to an Alastair Campbell figure, 'It was a noble experiment but probably doomed to failure in the age we live in.'[2] Others who have worked inside Number 10 at a senior level since 2007 and have seen the media operation at work are less charitable. They were unable to give their views on-the-record while Brown was still prime minister, but they said he and his closest advisers must take responsibility themselves for seeing the reputation of 10 Downing Street sink still further so quickly.

Gordon Brown entered Downing Street with the best intentions, sincerely held. Above all he wanted to rebuild the public's trust through an open and honest dialogue about the problems facing Britain and what he hoped to do to address them. Many correspondents who had worked at Westminster over the previous decade were doubtful. In their experience Brown had been no more straightforward in his dealings with the media than Tony Blair, indeed in many ways less so. Whenever the chancellor had something he wanted to say or had a big statement to make to parliament, including his annual Budget, the details had been leaked in advance and its significance heavily spun on the day. When things were going badly he had a remarkable capacity to disappear from view and refuse to say anything at all that earned him the nickname 'Macavity'. Having finally secured his ambition Brown had only a narrow window of opportunity to show that he could now afford to do things differently.

Gordon Brown's views on his predecessor's approach to the media had been revealed to the journalist Robert Peston as long ago as 2004 when Brown wrongly believed he was about to take over. According to his analysis, Blair's response to an unpopular issue was too often to 'take a step to the right' and set himself deliberately in opposition to his own party. Brown thought that was bad policy-making and bad government. 'You may have moved the press headlines so that they support you,' Peston was told by 'one minister', almost certainly Brown himself, 'but you have not shifted fundamental opinion in a way that would allow you to sustain the policy over a period of time. It's an initiative simply taken for presentational reasons.'[3] Brown wanted to put policy first, with presentation a distant second. He had said as much when he launched his campaign for the leadership. 'As a politician I have never sought the public eye for its own sake. I have never believed presentation should be the substitute for policy. I do not believe politics is about style.'[4] His promise was summarised by the media as 'an end to spin' although he never used those words. One of those who joined Brown in Number 10 six weeks later now believes there was less to the pledge than at first appeared. 'No more spin was the new spin. Almost everything they did in the initial phase was simply about delineating themselves from what Blair and Campbell had done.'

Among the many changes, some real, some more symbolic, that Brown announced on taking office was that the unusual powers given to Alastair Campbell to instruct civil servants would not be accorded to his own special advisers. It practice it was little more than a gesture. When David Hill replaced Campbell he had not been given the same dispensation and had never felt the need for it. The announcement was important to Brown, however, because he rightly judged that the media had no intention of letting him shake off his reputation for aggressive media management that easily. Two days before he entered Number 10 the BBC broadcast a *Panorama* programme entitled 'Trust Me I'm Gordon . . . not Tony'. It included material from an earlier documentary in which his former spokesman, Charlie Whelan, was brutally frank about how he operated and his willingness to be 'economical with the truth'. 'You should never lie, but it's very difficult. They understand. They will certainly understand tomorrow and forgive me.'[5] Whelan, who had been forced to resign after less than two years at the Treasury, was reinterviewed for *Panorama*. Reporter John Ware asked him about leaks of sensitive Budget information to the *Financial Times*. Had he been responsible? 'I might well have been, I can't remember, to be honest. Probably was me. It could be Ed Balls, it could be me.'[6] Balls, now an MP who was about to be appointed to Brown's first cabinet, denied any such leak had taken place. But Whelan's honesty about the business of revealing Budget details in advance was guileless:

> Whelan: That was my job. I wouldn't call it leaks. You're briefing people what the sort of . . . the thinking of the chancellor and what's probably going to be in it.
> Ware: You'd have done that, though, with the chancellor's authority?
> Whelan: Of course, yeah.

Gordon Brown knew he could not erase history. His best hope lay in trying to convince people that the future would be different. To help give his media operation an unimpeachable public face he brought with him the head of the Treasury press office, Michael Ellam, as his director of communications and official spokesman. Ellam, who would take almost every lobby briefing until his departure in 2009, was the archetypal 'straight bat', uncharismatic but reliable. He was sufficiently close to the prime minister to be able to brief with authority, but as a civil servant rather than a special adviser he refused resolutely to get involved in politics. At the outset that responsibility fell to another man who had been part of the team at the Treasury, Brown's political spin-ner Damian McBride. In fact all three of the highly combative and intensely loyal special advisers from his decade as chancellor remained close at hand. Ian Austin, McBride's immediate predecessor, was now an MP and the prime minister's parliamentary private secretary. Whelan, too, was a regular visitor to Downing Street. Although not on the Number 10 staff, he had been found a job with the trade union Unite which allowed him free reign to work as an unofficial media adviser to Brown. But it was McBride who was by far the most impor-tant of the three and the man on whose judgment the prime minister relied more than any other until he was forced to resign in 2009 in the single most spectacular display of self-destruction in the history of the Downing Street press office.

The brief period of public notoriety that followed McBride's res-ignation saw him painted as the worst kind of thug-like political operator working under the cover of anonymity to brief against any-body who stood in Brown's way. Even his strongest defenders admit there is a bit of him that does resemble the image that earned him the nickname 'McPoison', but insist that was always far from the whole picture. McBride retained a small group of trusted journalists, many of whom would join him in karaoke bars and pubs after their stories had been filed. One political columnist who was part of the group said, 'He could be brilliant and he could be very bad. He could be utterly charming and he could play rough.' Another who admits 'we trusted each other completely' said, 'he can drink like a trooper and can be incredibly brutal in his assassinations of people. He has done plenty of dark business in his time. But he is also an incredibly thoughtful, brilliant political analyst who could generate insights that were fascinating. Behind the image of a hard-drinking football fan was somebody with an incredible intellect.'

A Cambridge-educated economist, McBride turned his analytical skills on the media on Brown's behalf and understood better than most how journalists operate and how best to influence them. 'We tried to transport from the Treasury the idea of having much more discipline about who could speak for Downing Street or who could speak for the prime minister,' he said. So only Ellam and McBride would be licensed to brief on a daily basis. The inevitable down-side was that as soon as negative stories did start to appear, including thinly veiled attacks on government ministers, the conclusion was almost invariably drawn that McBride must have been responsible. The reluctance of journalists to reveal their sources added to the suspicion that he was abusing his position. He came to accept that 'if you're any good at your job as a press secretary, it's easy for people to blame you for anything in the press they don't like . . . It's the easiest thing in the world if a minister is not getting a good press for them to think someone is briefing against them.'[7]

Brown and McBride wanted to end the practice of offering 'exclusives' to individual newspapers to try to keep them sweet. The objective was to 'kill the idea that there were factions within the one government rather than one team working together', although even McBride didn't have the chutzpah to deny their own responsibility for creating the problem in the first place. 'We were probably guilty of it in the Treasury, selective briefing and playing favourites. But it ends up pissing off every other paper.' In its place they wanted a level playing field 'where papers could no longer complain, and feel entitled to complain, that very significant stories were given out selectively. You might get a good hit in one paper but that invited a backlash in all the other papers.'

Even those outside the inner circle gave McBride credit for his readiness to treat almost all journalists with due respect, not a quality for which Alastair Campbell had been famous. One beneficiary was the *Daily Mirror*, which Campbell and his team had taken for granted. The paper's political editor, Bob Roberts, recalled, 'We were always the loyal wife and never the mistress. We were never the mistress being taken out for dinner, wined and dined and given treats, because the Downing Street operation knew that they could rely on us. We were not an important player in their eyes because we would always back Labour. And they were entirely correct in that.' Under Brown, said Roberts, things changed for the better. 'Partly because they thought it was the right thing to do. But also the politics was different. And anyway Labour couldn't expect the same support from the *Sun* and the *Times* that they had had before.'

Rupert Murdoch's stable was not to be ignored but nor was it to be wooed to the exclusion of its rivals. The change had been signalled while Brown was still chancellor. At the end of November 2006 the *Sun*'s political editor, George Pascoe-Watson, called McBride and told him the paper had discovered that Brown's young son had cystic fibrosis. Rather than give the impression that the paper was being given special treatment Brown and his wife, Sarah, decided to issue a public statement announcing the fact, so effectively depriving the *Sun* of its exclusive. The gesture was appreciated by, among others, the *Daily Mail*. In an extraordinary reversal, the *Mail*, which was loathed under Blair for its devotion to conservative values and the Conservative party, became the nearest thing Brown had to a favourite among the daily papers. Eyebrows had already been raised when its editor, Paul Dacre, had been invited to the funeral of the Brown's first child, Jennifer Jane, who died shortly after her birth in 2002. The following year, on the occasion of Dacre's tenth anniversary as editor, Gordon Brown recorded a video tribute in which he said, 'Paul Dacre has devised and delivered one of the great newspaper success stories. He also shows great personal warmth and kindness as well as great journalistic skill.'[8] That wasn't the view of most people at the top of the Labour party over the past decade. They were more inclined to agree with the *Guardian* journalist Nick Davies, who described in his book *Flat Earth News* how the *Mail* 'more than any other newspaper in Britain . . . deals in falsehood and distortion'.[9]

Those most cynical about Brown's motives accused him of targeting a paper openly critical of Blair for his own benefit. But there was clearly more to the relationship between the two men than that. Dacre, like Brown, has an austere streak to him. One person who knows them both says they have much in common. 'They are both big men, workaholics, driven, prone to towering rages.' And each had his own reason for establishing a close relationship. 'Dacre knows how to form strategic alliances that are useful to him. He saw that one of the benefits of an alliance with Brown was that it would be an alliance against Tony Blair. And one of the many things Tony Blair has good cause to be angry about is the way in which his chancellor worked hand in hand with the *Daily Mail* to do him in.' As for Brown, 'Paul to Gordon was a way for him to understand middle England. Gordon has a complete tin ear for anything to do with England and the English middle classes in particular.' It is one reason Brown has always relied heavily on polling advice. According to Philip Gould, even when Brown had been chancellor he had taken more interest in the findings of focus groups than Blair had done because they were 'the only way he can keep in touch with the British, especially the English, mind'.[10]

Brown's desire to understand the country he hoped soon to be governing encouraged him to court another paper that had been all but frozen out under Blair, the *Daily Telegraph*. Given the paper's well-earned soubriquet the *Torygraph*, Brown and his advisers went out of their way to ensure the paper had a direct line to their thinking. Brown's passion for the concept of 'Britishness', another attempt to show that he could connect with a culture that went beyond his native Scotland, was particularly well received at the *Telegraph*. And so Gordon Brown entered Downing Street on 27 June 2007 enjoying better relations with newspapers most of whose readers were thought to be already politically committed – the *Mirror* on the left and the *Mail* and *Telegraph* on the right – than with those more likely to be read by 'swing voters'. It was unmistakably a change from what had gone before, born in part of necessity and in part of calculation. One very senior civil servant who has seen both the Blair and Brown press offices at work said he found it 'much harder to understand the strategic value of Gordon's media relationships. Blair and News International struck me as an entirely rational relationship. You could exactly see the calculation was about what you get in return. With Gordon and the *Mail* it's much harder to see what the pay-back is.'

At first it seemed there might be a dividend. In 2007 Paul Dacre was reported to have told a group of students that the *Mail* wouldn't necessarily support David Cameron's Tories at the next election.[11] The prospect of the paper backing Labour was never realistic but Brown believed that if its outright hostility could be tempered it would make him more acceptable to middle England. Early policy announcements overturning Blair's plans for 'super-casinos' and reviewing proposals for 24-hour drinking in the inner cities chimed in very neatly with the views expressed by the *Mail*. Dacre wasn't dictating policy for the simple reason that Brown and Dacre's views on such matters happily coincided. But one adviser to the governments of both Blair and Brown was uneasy. The new administration seemed to be coming in with a media-management plan that struck him as 'all tactics and no strategy, scarily so'.

Ellam, McBride and their colleagues moved straight into the same open-plan 'War Room' that had been used by Blair's press office. There would be less space available thanks to another early promise to allow the chief whip to move back into his traditional accommodation at Number 12. Once again it was more symbolic than practical. Geoff Hoon, Brown's first chief whip, rarely used the building and the press-office staff found themselves with too little room, all, according to one of those squeezing in, 'for a small story on page 12 of the *Telegraph*'. The open-plan layout suited Brown who liked to be able to come through from his own office in the main building and see all his key media advisers in one place. The frequency with which he did so, especially in the first few months, astonished those who weren't familiar with his obsessive attention to detail. The large plasma television screen outside Brown's office – the same 'Den' in which Blair used to work – is permanently tuned to *Sky News* with its tickertape of the most recent headlines running across the bottom. If Brown saw something he didn't like he would rush round to the press office and demand that it be corrected or that a response be issued immediately. His personal intervention helped Downing Street look very much in control when the first crises hit, including terrorist attacks in Glasgow and London, summer flooding in the north of England, and an outbreak of foot-and-mouth disease in Surrey. At times, however, he

seemed to want to direct every minute detail of policy and presentation himself. One person who witnessed it said, 'he would come
racing round and stand over people saying "You've got to get this bulletin changed" or "We've got to get this corrected for six o'clock. I've
got to do a clip". On one occasion during foot and mouth it was about
a cracked pipe on a farm and I thought to myself, that's probably a bit
below the job of a junior minister at DEFRA [Department of the
Environment, Food and Rural Affairs].' Another recalled him 'storm-
ing into the press office dictating a press release in response to
something he'd seen on the television, except he'd misread it. It was
embarrassing.' Those who knew him better were less shocked.
'Everything about Gordon is being across what's going on so you are
not taken by surprise,' said McBride.

Brown likes to start the day with an early briefing over the phone
on what the media are reporting. This is followed by a wider conference call with his other key advisers at 7.30. He is not an avid reader
of newspapers, although he will look at the front pages and the main
political stories. His preference is for regular verbal updates during the
day. 'He will regularly ask, "What's going on? Everything under control?"' When he believes a story is running out of control or that – the
worst sin of all – the press office has been caught unawares he can react
with extraordinary flashes of anger. Stories of mobile phones being
hurled across the room in fury have regularly appeared in the press,
although it rarely gets to that stage. Shouting at staff, jabbing an angry
finger, throwing down papers, even kicking the furniture are far more
common. His behaviour towards relatively junior members of staff can
be 'unforgivable' according to one person who has witnessed it. 'It isn't
a very nice place for people to work. However bad it sometimes looks
from the outside, it's far, far worse from the inside. And the atmosphere
is very much set by him.' Those in the press office more used to dealing with the daily onslaught of unpredictable news put it down to
Brown's ten years in the Treasury, where events could be carefully
planned and the phone never rang in the middle of the night with
another crisis to be handled.

As reports of Brown's erratic behaviour began to emerge, the media
looked for psychological explanations. In the *Guardian* David

Runciman, who lectures in politics at Cambridge University, argued that the personal qualities that helped make him a good chancellor were ill suited to the job of prime minister. 'Brown is an almost pathological version of a closed-off politician. That kind of personality is clearly very good at politicking behind the scenes. Chancellors are meant to be closed off. They keep secrets from us, go into purdah – it's the least democratic office of state. But the relentless exposure of being prime minister makes that sort of closed-off politician vulnerable.'[12] Others were less charitable. It is Brown's misfortune that he is forever being assessed in the light of the observation that he is 'psychologically flawed'. Those who have witnessed his behaviour refer back to it constantly without being prompted. 'It doesn't come close,' said one. Another said Brown was always looking for somebody else to blame when things went wrong. 'It's this self-pity thing. There's a pathetic side to him that is really unbecoming.' A third said the problems have got no better with time, concluding that 'He is psychologically and emotionally incapable of leadership of any kind.' McBride, however, thinks those who know Brown less well misunderstand his moods. 'In the entire time I've been working with him I've never seen him throw anything. I've seen him do lots of other things. I've seen him shout and swear, but that is always quite a superficial thing, to release a bit of frustration, and then he settles down and can be normal again. The times when he's really angry are not when he shouts but when he's very quiet. So sometimes people, civil servants, will come out of meetings and think, "oh that went OK", because they had been expecting him to explode when actually he'd be very quiet. But it's then that you know he's really angry.'

During his first summer in Number 10 the less attractive aspects of Brown's personality were rarely in evidence. He was enjoying being in control and demonstrated a flair for leadership that genuinely surprised many of those who had harboured doubts about his capacity to take on the challenge. He received a very positive press, even by the standards of early praise that all new prime ministers receive. In the *Spectator* Matthew d'Ancona said: 'This PM's greatest triumph to date has been to persuade the world that he is not an exhausted traveller, limping and grey after 10 years in office, but a man at the very start of

a journey . . .' Alice Thomson in the *Daily Telegraph* described his performances at prime minister's question time as 'masterly'. 'Brown is
wrongfooting Cameron,' wrote Fraser Nelson in the same paper.
'Brown could be a great PM,' wrote Peter Oborne in the *Daily Mail*.[13]
Two years later there was barely a journalist in the land with a good
thing to say or write about him. Neville Chamberlain's observation
that 'few men can have known such a tremendous reverse of fortune
in so short a time' applied even more forcefully to Brown.

While his fortunes were still good, pictures of Brown welcoming
Lady Thatcher back to Downing Street in mid-September 2007
helped reinforce the idea that decisive, principled leadership had been
restored. Most opinion polls showed Labour with a comfortable lead
over the party she once led. The conditions were right for a conference season that Brown intended to follow swiftly with a general
election that he hoped would secure his personal mandate. Preparations
were well advanced. The American political strategist, Bob Shrum,
who had been a regular general-election adviser to New Labour since
1997, was in and around Downing Street from late August onwards.
Damian McBride worked closely with the election coordinator,
Douglas Alexander, the cabinet-office minister Ed Miliband and the
Number 10 political secretary, Spencer Livermore, to prepare the
ground for a November election. The party met for its annual conference in Bournemouth in a confident mood. Brown's speech was a
direct appeal for support from the uncommitted middle ground that
determines every election result. In the offices of the *Daily Mail* they
ticked off the various themes they thought were designed to appeal to
their readers. Recalling the terror attacks and floods he said 'Britain has
been tested and not found wanting' because 'our spirit is indestruc-
tible'.[14] He spoke of his 'moral compass' saying, 'This is who I am. I
am a conviction politician.' Among those convictions was his belief that
immigrants to Britain should 'learn our language and culture' and 'play
by the rules'. His promise to 'create British jobs for British workers'
even reminded some commentators of the rhetoric of the far-right
British National Party. There was plenty too, on education, health and
opportunities for all, to please the *Daily Mirror* and Labour's more traditional supporters, but it was unmistakably a pre-election speech, and

the *Times* among others found many echoes of speeches Shrum had written for Democratic presidential candidates in the past.[15]

Everything was ready for an election on November 1, although publicly Brown denied it. The party's general secretary at the time, Peter Watt, confirmed that 'No matter what anyone says, the election had been called and was then cancelled. We had been working on it for weeks. We spent £1.2m in immediate preparations.'[16] The plans were abandoned only when the Conservatives bounced back strongly in the polls during their own conference a week later. A combination of David Cameron's confident leader's speech, which he made without notes, and a promise to cut inheritance tax by the shadow chancellor, George Osborne, burst Labour's election bubble almost overnight. The mood in the media swung away from Brown with equal speed. The prime minister's visit to Iraq on the day the Tories were debating defence was widely condemned and he was accused of manipulating government business for party advantage, notably by bringing forward announcements on health, troop cuts, London's Crossrail, and public spending. The shine came off Brown's conference speech with remarkable speed. One commentator described it as 'a pick and mix of poses and attitudes generated by focus groups, pollsters and clever but inexperienced advisers. It was predicated on the view that Brown had regained the confidence of *Guardian*-reading liberals and could now embark on capturing the confidence of *Daily Mail*-reading conservatives. It was entirely tactical rather than strategic. It took people for granted. That is why it backfired and why it let Cameron back into the game.'[17] Having concluded that the polls were too volatile, Brown recorded an interview at Chequers with Andrew Marr of the BBC to say he had decided against an election. His uncertain performance led the *Mail on Sunday* to announce 'Brown Bottles It'.[18] Privately some of his closest advisers used the very same words.

By giving his interview exclusively to the BBC and briefing it to selected journalists in advance, the prime minister infuriated the rest of the media. The head of *Sky News*, John Ryley, made an official complaint to Downing Street saying, 'Much has been made by Gordon Brown of how, under his premiership, relations with the media would be handled without spin or favour. On this evidence, at least, he has failed to honour his word.'[19] The director of the Society of Editors said, 'It shouldn't be left to a journalist to make this announcement outside Downing Street. Brown should have either announced it in a press conference or in a pooled interview.'[20] Brown hurriedly brought forward his next scheduled news conference but it did little to repair relations. The chairman of the lobby journalists, *Sky*'s Adam Boulton, said, 'It shows the same old spin. I don't accept bringing forward the news conference is anything more than a continued attempt to spin the news agenda.'[21] An ICM poll for the BBC's *Newsnight* showed that 61 per cent of respondents thought Brown's government was just as likely to spin as Blair's and another 15 per cent said 'more likely'.[22]

Jackie Ashley, who happens to be married to Andrew Marr, revealed in the *Guardian* that Murdoch himself had been at Chequers on the weekend the election was called off. Ashley contended that it was no coincidence and that 'the *Sun*'s threat to use Europe against Brown during an autumn campaign was a factor in his decision not to call [an election].'[23] Murdoch's demands were quite specific. The latest treaty on the functioning of the European Union was due for signature in Lisbon in just a few months' time. Murdoch and his papers believed it would fundamentally alter Britain's constitutional position and insisted that it be put to a referendum. The government did not agree. A few days later Irwin Stelzer, a commentator and friend of Rupert Murdoch's who is often referred to as his 'representative on earth', confirmed that Brown's attitude to Europe would be a decisive factor in deciding who both the *Sun* and the *News of the World* would support whenever the election came. And Stelzer had more bad news for Brown. He said he knew from 'discussions at the highest level of News International' that Murdoch was reassessing his attitude to the main party leaders. His earlier view that 'Cameron was kind of a lightweight toff', not as agreeable to Murdoch as Brown, the hardworking Presbyterian Scot whose father had a similar background to Rupert's grandfather . . . changed and it changed very recently, around Cameron's speech, to where it is my impression that the *Sun* and the *News of the World* – to the extent they take direction from Murdoch – feel that Cameron is worth a look, whereas before he was not worth a look. And I know that to be a fact.' Brown's volte-face on the election date was, said Steltzer, 'an appalling blunder'.[24] Murdoch's intervention was a distinctly unsubtle shot across Brown's bows, as Martin Kettle observed in the *Guardian*: 'In essence, Murdoch and Stelzer's view is that Brown can be forced to concede a referendum by the danger that the *Sun* will otherwise embrace the Tories. This is power politics – nothing else. To me, the question here is not whether the EU or a referendum is good or bad. The question is whether the elected government or the Murdoch press should prevail on a matter of national interest.'[25] By refusing to agree to a referendum Brown ensured that the Murdoch press did not prevail, although political calculations and the near certainty that any referendum would be lost weighed more heavily on the prime minister's mind than any desire to spike the guns of News International.

Since becoming prime minister Brown has continued to see Rupert Murdoch whenever possible during his visits to the UK. He meets other proprietors and editors on a regular basis too, with the exception of Richard Desmond of the *Express*, who is considered too hostile to warrant cultivation. Brown will normally spend time with them alone, with no officials or advisers present. And after a big announcement or event he will sometimes telephone editors to see how their papers are likely to cover the story, something he did as chancellor after every Budget. But he didn't need Murdoch or anybody else to tell him that the non-election had been a disaster both politically and in terms of his standing with the media and the public. Brown's immediate reaction, according to Peter Watt, was typical of his style of leadership. 'Publicly, Gordon talks about values and his moral compass, but actually the way he conducts himself behind the scenes is anything but that – it's brutal.'[26] The immediate casualties were those who had most strongly advocated an election. Livermore and Alexander, in particular, found their names appearing in articles analysing what had supposedly gone wrong. 'There was clearly briefing against me,'[27] said Alexander, a long-standing ally of the prime minister's. When the going got tough nobody was immune.

Having anticipated an election Downing Street was left with a vacuum as the summer of confidence turned into an autumn of recriminations. Brown's loss of political authority prompted exactly the kind of stories about government divisions that Downing Street had been determined to avoid. Brown's internal party critics had remained silent for four months but were now ready to offer 'helpful advice' from the sidelines. Every story in the press suggesting that the government had lost its way was manna to the Conservatives. David Cameron still judged it tactically convenient to claim the true mantle of Blairite centre-ground politics. Number 10 seemed to have little idea how to respond. 'There was no exit strategy when the election was called off,' said one civil servant. 'They were left with nothing. The autumn was a shambles.' Another put it down to a lack of strategic vision that left the press office unsure what they were supposed to be selling. Brown had promised change but it was unclear what that change was supposed to have brought about. 'What was missing was an overall narrative. Nobody knew what the big picture was. Ultimately that has to come from the boss.'

In an effort to fill the gap and regain some momentum Brown embarked on a series of big policy speeches. One of the first, on 'liberty' at the University of Westminster, contained much that appealed to those in the media who had long argued that the state should be more open, not least to the inquiries made by journalists. Plans to raise the cost of making requests under the freedom-of-information laws and proposals to restrict media access to coroners' courts were scrapped. Brown said he didn't want to see 'an unacceptable barrier between the people and public information'.[28] A three-man panel was appointed to look at ways of relaxing the rules on the release of historical government documents and one of those appointed to it was Paul Dacre. The next speech, on education, was less successful. Several local papers were briefed in advance that schools in their area would be singled out for praise. When none of them was mentioned at all *The Times* said they had been victims 'of a sophisticated government spin operation',[29] although an unsophisticated cock-up was a more plausible explanation.

The Queen's Speech a week later did little to improve the government's standing. Most commentators found it uninspiring and thin. Once again Brown struggled to find the language to explain what his government was seeking to achieve and another round in the public-relations battle went to the Tories. David Cameron accused Brown of stealing Tory policies and of being a 'weak' leader compared to Tony Blair. When Brown sought to impose discipline on his government, however, it looked as if he couldn't trust his own ministers to say the right thing. Lord West, a former admiral brought in by Brown to be security minister, was summoned to see the prime minister after saying on the *Today* programme that he was 'unconvinced'[30] about the need to extend the 28-day limit for detaining terrorist suspects without charge. By the time he emerged from Number 10 the minister was back 'on message'. It was then the turn of the foreign secretary, David Miliband, to be told what he should be saying. A speech on Europe that had already been briefed to the media was then delivered with some pro-European sentiments removed on Brown's insistence. Despite public claims that the speech had been subject only to the normal process of discussion within government, Downing Street told journalists that Miliband had indeed been overruled. In an effort not to let the incident damage relations further, McBride made a rare private apology, telling his opposite number at the Foreign Office that he had been responsible for the briefing. Miliband had let it be known that he was unhappy at the way he had been treated and one of his aides was quoted as saying 'I think he is watching out to be sure that he is not knocked down by people who want to ensure he is not Gordon's successor.'[31]

At the end of November Brown was forced to issue an equally rare apology of his own when it emerged that discs containing the personal financial information of 25 million people had gone missing. The loss had nothing at all to do with either the prime minister or Downing Street but the incident added to the impression that somehow the government was incompetent. The acting leader of the Liberal Democrats, Vince Cable, scored a palpable Commons hit when he spoke of Brown's 'remarkable transformation in the last few weeks from Stalin to Mr Bean'.[32] The previous weekend Peter Watt had resigned as Labour's general secretary after the *Mail on Sunday* revealed that the party had accepted over £600,00 in hidden donations from a Tyneside businessman, David Abrahams. Only after a lengthy police investigation was Watt cleared of breaking the party funding laws. Watts believed he had been 'hung out to dry' by Brown. He told the *Sunday*

Times, 'This is Gordon's politics: when things go wrong you find someone to blame.'[33]

As the year drew to an end Brown faced the decision that he had been warned would have a powerful influence over his treatment by many of the best-selling newspapers. Despite his best efforts, and those of David Miliband, to argue that the Lisbon treaty was more a tidying-up exercise than a new constitution for the European Union, it continued to be opposed root and branch by the Euro-sceptic press. Rather than allow himself to be photographed signing the treaty along with all the other EU heads of government, Brown deliberately set in train what proved to be another PR disaster. He claimed that pressures on his diary wouldn't allow him to attend and sent Miliband instead. He then turned up later in the day and signed the document away from the massed ranks of the media. It was a clumsy manoeuvre that impressed nobody. At the final Downing Street press conference of 2007, journalists were handed free mince pies, paid for by the prime minister personally. When one asked if they could have mulled wine as well next time, Brown observed ruefully, 'You're never satisfied.'[34]

If the autumn of 2007 had been miserable for Downing Street, the first half of 2008 was to feel a whole lot worse. Brown's well-intentioned efforts to restructure his staff and bring in outside expertise led to a prolonged and debilitating period of infighting, briefing and counter-briefing that only damaged further both the image and effectiveness of his administration. Within little more than six months of his succession, Brown's insistence that Number 10 should be disciplined and speak only with one voice was being flagrantly ignored. One of his most loyal lieutenants, the political secretary Spencer Livermore, the most high-profile casualty of the non-election debacle, left. A new duopoly of power was created at the top of the Number 10 administrative structure with the arrival of Stephen Carter as head of strategy and 'principal adviser' to work alongside Jeremy Heywood, the principal private secretary. Heywood was a widely admired civil-service high flier with many years experience working for both Brown and Blair. By keeping his own views of their relative merits private he had managed to win the trust and respect of both. Stephen Carter was more of an unknown quantity. He too was a high flier, having been the first chief executive of the media regulator, Ofcom, but had little direct experience of government or, crucially, Labour politics. The new appointments brought significant organisational improvements but it was never made clear who was actually supposed to be in charge and there were significant territorial battles too. The biggest threat to Carter came not from Heywood, however, but from Brown's political allies, including McBride and the two Eds in the cabinet, Balls and Miliband, who were used to being the prime minister's main source of strategic advice. The arrival of a non-political outsider as 'principal' adviser was bound to be seen as a threat by men who had enjoyed unrestricted access to Brown until now. Carter, who had been tempted away from the job of chief executive of one of the world's largest PR agencies, Brunswick, had been promised a virtually free hand. According to the *Independent*: 'Carter drove a hard bargain during the series of intense meetings he had over Christmas with the prime minister, whose self-confidence had been shaken over a disastrous autumn. He extracted a deal that gave him complete control of the political side of operations in Downing Street, including the decisions on whom to hire or fire, and over the prime minister's speeches and statements made in his name.'[35]

Whatever powers he had been promised they were not enough. In the press office, neither Ellam nor McBride was prepared to go along with having a new layer of authority imposed between them and Brown. When a detailed diagram showing the Downing Street chain of command, with Carter at the top, appeared in *PR Week*, they became convinced that he was doing some briefing of his own.[36] For a while the magazine, hitherto little read outside the public-relations industry, became essential reading at Westminster as the two sides fought out their disagreements through its columns. One member of the media team who tried hard not to take sides said it was clear from early on that while Carter was a talented and confident administrator, he was outgunned politically. 'Communications wasn't his thing. He was completely kippered. It fell apart for him within about two months. It was like taking candy from a baby.' Another said, 'Carter never really changed Gordon's mind on anything. All his efforts would be undone if Ed Balls or Ed Miliband came on the phone. Damian especially was thrown off balance by Stephen's arrival but he soon recovered. Gordon knew that stories criticising him were going out but he did nothing to stop them. He showed real cowardice over it.' McBride insisted he was not acting out of pique. Carter's arrival had undermined one of the objectives they had set themselves in order to get a better press. 'It let the genie out of the bottle. Once it was credible that there were different voices coming out working within the same team, then the Sunday papers especially could get away with running stories [about divisions] that we might deny, but . . . there were differences of view within the operation and journalists could get away with writing those kinds of stories.'

As ever, the tensions mattered more to those working inside the building than to the public as a whole, most of whom probably discounted the stories, if they read them at all, as the usual Westminster backbiting. Events of far greater significance were taking place in the real world, and in the financial world in particular. In February the Northern Rock bank was nationalised, having already received a massive bail-out from public funds. The crisis at the bank, one of Britain's top five mortgage lenders, was the first evidence that the turmoil in the American financial system might threaten the very economic stability at home that Gordon Brown claimed as his greatest achievement before reaching Number 10. The true effects of the 'credit crunch' would take time to be felt but Downing Street was well aware that they now had to defend his record both as prime minister and as chancellor. And it was one his last acts at the Treasury that provoked the next political controversy. Brown's final Budget in March 2007 had cut the basic rate of income tax to 20p from 22p but, to help pay for it, had also abolished the lower 10p starting rate that benefited the least well off in particular. The change was deferred by a year and came into effect on 1 April 2008. Somewhat belatedly the media, the public and a significant number of Labour MPs woke up to the fact that many people on low incomes would suffer. Both publicly and privately the prime minister insisted that because of other tax and benefits changes there would be no losers. 'Gordon said it was all a media creation. He was in denial. Everybody looked at their shoes when he did it,' according to one civil servant. 'Even Jeremy Heywood wouldn't meet anybody's eye.'

Eventually, faced with a growing backbench rebellion, the government would be forced into an expensive volte-face, but not before the row had become very personal and very public. The leader of the rebellion, the former welfare-reform minister Frank Field, said it was a 'tragedy – on a personal level as well as for a party, government and country level – that somebody whose real aim in life is to be prime minister, now has the task and seems so lacking in enjoyment in trying to carry it out.'[37] Field said he would be 'very surprised' if Brown was still leading the Labour party at the time of the next election. Although he later apologised for allowing their disagreements to become personal, the media now had the ammunition they required for a summer of sniping over Brown's fitness for the job and the desire of some in his own party to try to remove him from it.

The prime minister and his allies correctly anticipated a newspaper-led campaign exaggerating the strength of opposition to him within his own party. Their views were reflected by relatively sympathetic columnists like Jackie Ashley in the *Guardian*, who wrote that 'Rupert Murdoch's journalists have been at the forefront of those suggesting that Gordon Brown is clinically depressed, on the edge of resignation, and in general a loathsome Caledonian vacuum. Most are long-time, enthusiastic Conservatives. Those who are not simply want a new story to report.'[38] Ashley detected a shift within News International that boded ill for the prime minister. 'Brown, like Blair, spent too long oiling up to Murdoch and therefore probably deserves everything he gets. But let's just recall that Cameron's Tories have now promised not only a referendum on the European constitution, but also to allow a version of the politically loaded *Fox News* into Britain, both policies designed to appease Murdoch. So the "next story" that the media are now assiduously promoting is that Brown will be challenged by panicking Labour MPs to stand down before the election.' The weakness in the analysis was that Cameron preferred to face a weakened Brown than a fresh new leader. And while it may have been true that it now suited Murdoch to destabilise rather than support Brown, it was equally true that others, who certainly didn't have Murdoch's interests at heart, had concluded for wholly different reasons that Brown was a liability.

Labour's lamentable performance in local elections and a parliamentary by-election in Crewe and Nantwich in May provided the trigger for further attacks on his leadership. Less than a year into his premiership some of his most loyal defenders in the press now gave up on him. The *Guardian's* Jonathan Freedland wrote that 'A settled view, among the electorate as well as the commentariat has formed, one that will take an earthquake to shake. I can see its distortions and exaggerations and yet, no matter how much I would like to, I cannot depart from the substance of it. I find myself in sympathy with those who admired Brown through his 10 long years as chancellor and who keenly awaited his premiership, and yet now conclude that they got Brown wrong – that, on the current evidence, he is simply not up to the job.'[39] Freedland identified several weaknesses but concluded that 'The most obvious skill gap is in communication . . . He does not seem able to deliver three or four plain, human sentences that anyone could understand. The result is an empathy gap: he does not seem able to show any to the electorate and so they don't feel any for him. None of this should have come as a surprise: the lack of presentational skills was visible a year ago. But plenty of us thought it might not matter. We reckoned Brown could make a virtue of his lack of glitz, offering himself as a figure of rocklike solidity in a fast and often fake world: "Not flash, just Gordon." That approach could have worked. But it was fatally undermined by Brown himself.'

Freedland's article caused particular despondency among Brown's advisers. Not because one commentator can change the political weather, but because they knew that among the constituency that really mattered, Labour MPs, his shift could very well act as a weather vane. His views could not be brushed aside as easily as those of others, and here I must include myself in their number, who had never been Brown sympathisers, and who now argued publicly for his replacement. Downing Street watched carefully for signs that the most likely challenger, the foreign secretary David Miliband, was ready to make his move. Once again Brown and his team studied the media to try to divine what was going on in the rival camp. In the wake of the election reverses Miliband told Sky News he was 'not in the market for any job other than the one I have got at the moment'[40], hardly a cast-iron promise not to stand against Brown. When, at the end of July, Labour lost one of its safest seats in Scotland, Glasgow East, to the Scottish National Party he wrote a lengthy article in the *Guardian* calling on the party to be 'more humble about our shortcomings but more compelling about our achievements'.[41] It made no mention at all of Gordon Brown but set out a detailed case for how Labour could recover. Interviewed by Jeremy Vine on Radio 2, he said. 'I am not running a leadership campaign. I have always wanted to support Gordon's leadership.'[42] The significance of his careful use of the perfect tense was lost on nobody and in two days of high-profile media appearances he avoided ruling out a challenge. Publicly Downing Street tried to appear relaxed. Off the record, 'the prime minister's allies' told journalists that Miliband was being 'self-serving and disloyal'[43] and that the 'nuclear option' of dismissing him had not been ruled out.

McBride's hand was again suspected. Given the evidence of at best questionable loyalty from the foreign secretary, some kind of reaction from Brown's political staff was understandable and arguably justifiable. But McBride insists they chose not to react so as to avoid inflaming the situation. 'David's people were making lots of overtures to us, saying they didn't want it to go this big. Whatever the truth in that, it was one of those occasions where the newspapers, because they couldn't get a strong reaction out of Downing Street, started calling MPs known to be close to Brown and doing that as "Downing Street". They were trying to generate a row story and to some extent they succeeded.' The story refused to go away because the discontent among Labour MPs was not a media invention. It soon became clear, however, that while some backbenchers were willing to go public with their concerns, those actively seeking a change in the leadership were too few in number to pose a serious threat. The Mili-band-wagon failed to gather sufficient momentum and his challenge stalled. Number 10 remained ever vigilant, however, ready to cut off any evidence of rebellion at the pass. They believed, with ample justification, that the media were ready to jump on anything that called into question the prime minister's authority.

Damian McBride was not the only one ready to go on the offensive. Although journalists are always careful to protect their own sources, several correspondents pointed to a number of individuals willing to provide them with an unattributable quote to undermine anybody who stepped out of line. Ian Austin had a reputation for negativity that earned him the nickname 'the Abominable No-Man'; the deputy chief whip, Nick Brown, delivered his rebuffs with 'a mixture of charm and bile', and from within the government at least two ministers, Ed Balls and Tom Watson, were prepared to criticise ministerial colleagues with journalists they trusted. One political editor who was called regularly with stories said, 'they were totally unscrupulous about damaging whoever they saw as Gordon's enemies. They didn't seem to care about anything but short-term survival.'

McBride insists that nobody can 'point to specific circumstances, specific instances where individuals had been smeared, attacked in a personal way' by him.[44] There is no doubt that, whoever was responsible, the merest trace of disloyalty could lead to ministers being undermined in the press. One of the names most often cited is Ivan Lewis, then a junior health minister. In August 2008 he wrote in the *Sunday Times* that 'credible economic strategy cannot be shaped by political dogma, selective press briefings or the pursuit of one day's or one week's positive headlines.'[45] Later that month embarrassing details of text messages he had sent to a woman in his office were leaked to the *News of the World*.[46] No formal complaint had ever been made but Lewis apologised unreservedly to the woman concerned and kept his job.[47]

Mr Lewis was small fry compared to another alleged victim, the chancellor of the exchequer, Alistair Darling. If Downing Street was in denial about the severity of the economic situation, Darling was anything but. In an interview with Decca Aitkenhead for the *Guardian Weekend* magazine he said the prospects were 'arguably the worst they've been in 60 years'.[48] Soon afterwards Darling and his advisers quickly became convinced that they were victims of a deliberate and sustained negative briefing campaign and they suspected Damian McBride. There were many people in the Treasury press office who had witnessed his activities at first hand while Brown was still chancellor. Not unreasonably they were convinced that he had not mended his ways. McBride acknowledged that negative comments about

Darling did appear but insisted that the prime minister had issued specific instructions after the *Guardian* interview that there should be no attacks on him. Nevertheless, 'you could not get something appearing in the press in any way critical of Alistair without them thinking "it must be Damian, he must have wound this up." It was all a complete myth but it became a very convenient thing for everybody to blame it all on this one person or the Number 10 operation.'

Thanks to the *Observer* columnist Nick Cohen, an alternative source for at least some of the comments was revealed. Cohen described events at the Pillars of Hercules pub in Soho during a book launch for a novel by Emma Burstall, the wife of the *Daily Mirror* journalist Kevin Maguire. 'We were all rubbing along until for no reason Charlie Whelan, Brown's point man in the unions, turned to the journalists and started laying into the chancellor of the exchequer. As he was speaking in a public place and did not ask to go off the record, the etiquette of journalism allows me to say that I was astonished. Darling had been a loyal friend of Brown's, but that did not stop Whelan from denigrating him. More pertinently, it was obvious even then that we were indeed facing the gravest economic crisis of our lifetimes; obvious to everyone, that is, except the Brownites. Because Darling had implied, however obliquely, that Brown's stewardship of the economy had been less than magnificent, Whelan and his friends were willing to betray an ally, make an unnecessary enemy and undermine the chancellor at a moment of national danger. The result was predictable. Darling could barely contain his contempt for the deviousness of a man he once considered his friend.'[49]

The impact of Alistair Darling's interview was still reverberating when Brown mounted what had been trailed as a 'relaunch' of his government; a package of economic measures including the suspension of stamp duty on house purchases. It was a flop, although Darling was hardly to blame. The former editor of the *Observer* Donald Trelford observed that 'as far as the press was concerned, the relaunch was dead in the water before it had even been announced . . . That simply isn't the story the press wants to hear or that it thinks the public wants to hear. It won't sell . . . One cannot help feeling some sympathy for the government's public relations plight, even if it has brought much of this on itself by "spinning" the news so blatantly and so deviously over the past 11 years. But when a government believes it cannot trust the media to present basic facts fairly on such serious matters, or without turning every crisis into a popularity or beauty contest, something has clearly gone badly wrong.'[50]

By the time of the party conference in Manchester at the end of September the belief that Number 10 was mounting a systematic campaign of destabilisation against any MP critical of Brown was widely held at all levels, from members of the cabinet down to the backbenches. In his speech, Brown had a brutally effective shock in store for David Miliband. At the end of a passage drawing attention to the inexperience of David Cameron, the prime minister said that the economic downturn meant that 'this is no time for a novice'.[51] The BBC, who had been told what to expect in advance, immediately cut to a shot of the youthful foreign secretary. Any ambitions Miliband might still have harboured of supplanting Brown that autumn quickly disappeared as much of the media spent conference week treating him more as a figure of fun than a potential prime minister. He was seen to have brought it on himself, having cooperated with lengthy and flattering profiles in both the *Daily Mirror* and the *Times.* The power of the press photograph to damage a political career was exposed dramatically as the week progressed and Miliband was shown first grinning inanely after his own conference speech and then, bizarrely, clutching a banana. All politicians are familiar with the selective use of photographs. Two pictures taken within a split second of each other can convey very different impressions of the subject and the choice of which to use has a dramatic effect. Brown had suffered from just such a technique many times but this week it was Miliband's turn. The foreign secretary learned to his cost that week that if he ever were to mount a serious challenge he couldn't expect to be supported by an adoring media.

Party conferences bring together ministers, advisers, trade unionists and party members who rarely get a chance to rub shoulders at other times of the year. The hot-house atmosphere, not to mention the late nights in the bars and restaurants, is ideal for plotting and the exchange of gossip. Downing Street had no intention of sitting back and letting the threat to Brown grow unchecked. They were determined to identify and deal with any MP thought likely to criticise the prime minister even before the delegates gathered in Manchester. On 12 September a junior member of the whips' office, Siobhain McDonagh, was sacked after calling for a debate on the leadership to clear the air. Other backbenchers with similar views found their names appearing in the papers in what they believed was an attempt to flush out opposition ahead of the conference. Every secretary of state was told to speak to his or her ministers to ask if any was likely to resign or call for a change at the top. The Scottish secretary, Des Browne, reported back that one of his team, David Cairns, fitted the bill. Cairns reached an agreement with Downing Street by which he would make a brief statement of resignation, record one interview for broadcast, and then keep his counsel. When he spoke to *Sky News*, however, he made it clear he wasn't happy at the way other critics of Brown had been treated. 'What really depressed me is that somebody somewhere leaked their names.'[52] Rather than engage in a proper debate he said the leakers, whoever they were, 'chose to diminish the claims, chose to say that these people were malcontents, that they were stupid, that they didn't speak for anyone.' Cairns kept to his word not to elaborate further until, during conference week itself, he was called by a journalist with what he described as a totally untrue smear. He called a member of Brown's team and threatened to denounce the leadership from the conference floor unless the briefing stopped. It did.

On the Tuesday of conference week the BBC's *Newsnight* broadcast the news that Ruth Kelly, the transport secretary, was ready to resign. Earlier that day McBride had heard rumours about the story and checked with Kelly's advisers, who said it wasn't true. He passed that information on to journalists only to discover later that Kelly did intend to stand down and that she had said as much to the prime minister but not to her own spokeswoman. McBride wanted to correct his earlier statement and try to ensure that the journalists didn't add her name to those known to be unhappy with Brown's leadership. He hastily arranged a briefing in the bar of the Midland Hotel at 3.15 in the morning and, with Ruth Kelly's adviser sitting beside him, explained that she would be going for family reasons. It was certainly an unconventional end to a cabinet career, and not the one that Ms

Kelly had planned, but McBride can be acquitted of any 'dark arts'. His reputation was so compromised by now, however, that, as Nick Cohen wrote, 'it says much about the levels of hatred at the top of the government that every minister I spoke to believed Kelly was the victim of a Brown dirty trick.'[53] Benedict Brogan, in the *Daily Mail*, judged that, 'It is an explosive charge, which Number 10 denies, but such is the poison now contaminating relations at the very heart of Labour that, to some, it appears truth no longer matters.'[54]

It had been a bruising week for all concerned. Back in London McBride spoke to Brown and told him he felt it was no longer possible for him to continue in his current role because of the widespread assumption that he was behind every negative story. The fairest assessment would appear to be that while McBride was far from wholly blameless, nor was he guilty of everything of which he had been accused. His reputation was now such, however, that several ministers, including some genuinely loyal to Brown as well as those who were not his natural allies, passed on the clear message that he would have to go. Brown had one last *coup de théâtre* planned to help secure his leadership, but it would succeed only if McBride was removed from front-line briefing. On 3 October he was transferred to a backroom job working on 'long-term strategy'. Stephen Carter's departure was announced on the same day. Carter was made a lord and a minister, in charge of broadcasting. But it was another new peer that claimed most of the headlines. Peter Mandelson, who had barely been on speaking terms with Brown for most of the past decade or more, was recalled from his job as European commissioner to become secretary of state for business. It was an astonishing political comeback for a man who had had to resign twice from Tony Blair's cabinet. From Brown's point of view it was a masterstroke. Quite apart from his extensive experience and acumen in trade and business affairs, the newly created Lord Mandelson brought a much-needed political strategist to the cabinet table. It was also a classic example of the famous dictum of President Lyndon Johnson that when it comes to a dangerous rival it is 'better to have him inside the tent pissing out, than outside pissing in'. Mandelson was congenitally incapable of resisting the temptation either to give his outspoken views to trusted journalists or to engage in private gossip with senior politicians in his own party or others. One journalist who remained in regular contact said 'Peter was not averse to dripping poison into the ears of anybody who wanted to hear about how awful Gordon was or, more particularly, how awful his operation was.'

If the prime minister had had his way there would have been another ex-spin doctor to add to his team of ministers. Alastair Campbell had also been offered a peerage and a job in government but he turned it down preferring to help out in a less formal capacity. Mandelson, by contrast, was delighted to be back in the cabinet. When his political fortunes were at their lowest ebb he had described himself as 'a fighter not a quitter'[55] and now his resilience had paid off. His return temporarily muted opposition to Brown from those most frequently referred to as 'Blairites', whether in parliament or the media. Gordon Brown would come to owe his old rival an enormous amount – including his ability to survive in his job when many of those closely identified with Blair turned against him once more – but in the autumn of 2008 Mandelson's resurrection was only one factor in the revival of the prime minister's fortunes. Far more significant was Brown's effective leadership in the face of the growing economic crisis that now threatened national economies across the globe. Stories about spin and political infighting didn't disappear altogether but they faded well into the background. Two men untarnished by allegations of media manipulation, Michael Dugher and John Woodcock, took over as Brown's special advisers responsible for dealing with journalists. Neither had the ear of the prime minister in the way that Damian McBride had done but while the economic story was so huge it made little difference.

Away from the full glare of the spotlight, however, the debate over the Brown administration's use of the media continued. Towards the end of October the cabinet secretary, Sir Gus O'Donnell, gave evidence to the House of Lords communications committee. He told them that in his estimation one change signalled by the new prime minister on coming to office had not materialised. When Brown had promised to 'restore power to parliament in order to build the trust of the British people in our democracy', journalists were told that would mean no more advance notice of announcements that should properly be made first to MPs. Sir Gus said parliamentary statements continued to be pre-briefed. 'The media want to jump the gun and be ahead of the game . . . I recognise the evidence about briefings being given off-the-record.'[56] Michael Ellam told the same committee it was 'inevitable that some information will get out'. In fact it was not just inevitable; it was deliberate. Ellam and McBride had concluded some time before that the government was losing out in the struggle to dominate the news agenda. According to McBride the Conservatives were out-doing them, 'operating a play book of giving exclusive stories to one paper or another, having lines running on the radio in the morning and generally running a complete spin operation at the same time as decrying Labour as the party of spin. We had too many bruising exam-ples where we had a big statement in parliament or whatever but the day had been taken over by something else that was running in the papers or on the *Today* programme and *Sky* so that by the time we got to what we regarded as the important statement of the day the coach had already moved on.' Having decided to get back in the game, Downing Street went to the opposite extreme and played it too vig-orously. In December the head of the UK Statistics Authority, Sir Michael Scholar, accused Number 10 of deliberately releasing selec-tive figures on knife crime in a way that contravened protocols Brown himself had supported while at the Treasury. It had been done for pure political advantage and Sir Michael described Downing Street's involvement in the 'premature, irregular and selective release' of the figures as 'corrosive of public trust'.[57]

No story, however big, can fill all the available media space, but the economic and financial crisis was about as big as they come. The sit-uation presented Brown with the opportunity he craved to play to his strengths and in the process to set the agenda and dominate the head-lines. This was the Brown premiership at its best. His boldness in confronting the challenge to the world economy kept him 'ahead of the curve' both domestically and on the international stage. The Conservative opposition struggled to keep up and, for once, seemed at a loss to find a convincing alternative narrative. Colleagues reported that Brown had never seemed happier or more comfortable in the job.

There was no conceivable threat to his leadership and he felt in control of his own destiny for the first time since the aborted election the previous year.

Gordon Brown's New Year message for 2009 was not a parliamentary statement nor was it subject to the rules on the release of statistics. So there were no grounds for official complaint, at least, when it was spun in advance in a curiously misleading way. Number 10 wanted to make sure it got the maximum impact but succeeded only in reminding people that when they read in the papers that 'the prime minister will say later today . . .' it could not be taken as fact. The final Sunday papers of 2008 revealed that Brown would be delivering an almost Churchillian message to the nation. 'Brown: we need Dunkirk spirit in 2009'[58] said the *Observer.* 'The Blitz spirit will save us, insists Gordon Brown'[59] was the *Mail on Sunday* headline. After Brown delivered his actual words the *Guardian* described the advance briefing as 'utter pups. There is no reference to Dunkirk in the message at all. None to the Blitz either. The so-called Churchillian echoes presumably refer to some rather pedestrian stuff in the message about Britain overcoming worse crises in the past.'[60] As ever the spin was not all down to Downing Street. The papers had asked for some advance notice of what to expect and had been given a briefing before the final message had been signed off by the prime minister.

Downing Street may have hoped to present Brown as a national leader in the mould of Winston Churchill but the opposition was not prepared to let him escape all responsibility for Britain's plight. Questions were asked about his own responsibility for the lax regulation of banks and other financial institutions during his time as chancellor. In early 2009 the prime minister met several groups of editors, leader writers and commentators to explain why his expensive rescue package for the economy was so vital. More than one asked about his repeated promise that under Labour there would be 'no more boom and bust' and were astonished when he told them, 'I actually said: No more Tory boom and bust.'[61] There were demands for Brown and his chancellor to say sorry for past mistakes, but the prime minister steadfastly refused to do so. Journalists reported his angry reaction to the calls during a visit in March to the newly elected President

Obama. The political editors of both the BBC and ITN were at the receiving end of his ire. Nick Robinson of the BBC said Brown's reaction was 'Apologise for what?' Tom Bradby of ITN said that 'Off camera, the mike was ripped off and we exchanged a few tart remarks. He has a bad temper.'[62] Back in London Alistair Darling seemed more willing to offer an apology of sorts. He told an interviewer that 'If there is a fault it is our collective responsibility. All of us have to have the humility to accept that over the last few years things have got out of alignment.'[63] The chancellor's staff continued to suspect that those close to Brown, either with or without his knowledge, were telling journalists that the prime minister was thinking of replacing him. It seems they had good reason to be suspicious. According to three separate accounts given privately, both Ed Balls and Damian McBride were guilty of briefing against the chancellor. 'Darling had good cause to be worried,' said one political editor. 'Damian was slagging him off and arguing for Ed to be given the job.' Another described it as a 'freelance' campaign being conducted without Brown's direct knowledge. 'There has always been this separate operation, which is the Ed Balls operation. The Ed Balls for chancellor operation.' And one person who witnessed it from within Number 10 confirmed that 'Ed Balls was working to his own agenda, which was not always the same as Gordon's, and he and Damian were thick as thieves.'

Whatever bad feeling there now was between the chancellor and prime minister, the two men worked effectively together in preparation for the meeting of the G20 group of industrialised nations in London in April. One senior official involved in the summit said Brown was 'brilliant'. He said Downing Street was already mapping out a political route map that led them out of the mess they were in. 'You could see a trajectory whereby success at the G20 coincided with signs of the economy turning around. That would have an impact in the polls and political and economic recovery would go hand in hand.' Some within the Number 10 media team who had doubted whether Brown would ever be able to turn things around said he was now on top of his game. According to one, 'He was in a very good mood up to and during the G20. He was decisive and effective.' The same person added with regret, 'unfortunately it didn't last.'

Little over a week after the end of the summit Brown's second honeymoon with the media was cut brutally short. 'Guido Fawkes', the pseudonym of the internet blogger Paul Staines, revealed that on 13 January Damian McBride had sent an email from his Downing Street computer containing what most newspapers referred to as 'vile and false allegations' against leading Conservatives, including David Cameron and the shadow chancellor George Osborne, and their spouses. The email was sent to Derek Draper, a former adviser to Peter Mandelson who was now editing a Labour-supporting blog and considering setting up another more scurrilous one alongside it. It was copied to, among others, Charlie Whelan. Draper, whose reply describing the suggestions as 'brilliant' was also published, insisted: 'The idea that this was some great smear campaign gives me and my internet work far too much credit, and the idea that it was a big project orchestrated in Downing Street is ridiculous . . . it was all just a batting around of ideas.'[64] McBride said he had been 'at a bit of a loose end after [stepping back] from day-to-day briefing' and got involved 'as a personal favour to Derek'.[65]

At first Number 10 tried to dismiss the email as 'a storm in a teacup', although it conceded that its contents were 'juvenile and inappropriate'.[66] The storm refused to subside, however, and Brown had no choice but to accept the resignation of his most loyal and trusted adviser on the media. In a statement on his departure McBride said he had never wanted the allegations to be in the public domain and blamed Staines for the fact that they now were. He said he was resigning because, 'we all know that when a backroom adviser becomes the story, their position becomes untenable.'[67] Brown said there was 'no place' in public life for the kind of conduct McBride had been guilty of. Privately he went into what one observer described as 'one of his very quiet, smouldering furies. He could not understand how people could be so ill-disciplined.' Another said McBride's departure was 'like a death in the family'. McBride said when he told Brown what he'd done 'he was just so angry and let down he could barely even speak to me.'

Ed Balls had welcomed McBride's support for his own ambitions but now distanced himself from him as swiftly as he could, calling him

'Mr McBride' and his actions 'vile, horrible, despicable'.[68] The *Sun* later paid substantial libel damages to another minister, Tom Watson, after alleging he was part of the 'motley crew' responsible for 'grisly lies'.[69] The resignation provoked a flurry of insider accounts in the newspapers by current and former ministers who claimed to have been smeared by McBride in the past and journalists who had been party to his negative briefings. The former cabinet minister Stephen Byers wrote: 'I have been the victim of Mr McBride's aggressive and hostile media briefing on a number of occasions. As a result I have to admit that I made little effort to suppress a smile when I heard about his enforced departure.'[70] The former home secretary Charles Clarke said 'there had been a pattern of behaviour with Damian over a long period, and I am glad that the prime minister has been decisive and got rid of him yesterday when this evidence came into the open.'[71]

In the *Independent* Andy McSmith, himself a former Labour party press officer, listed off-the-record attacks attributed to McBride against the deputy leader of the Labour party, Harriet Harman, fellow cabinet ministers James Purnell and Douglas Alexander as well as familiar names like Alistair Darling, David Miliband and Ivan Lewis.[72] Many of the stories had appeared in Conservative-supporting Sunday newspapers. Those papers joined in the blanket condemnation of McBride and what the *Mail on Sunday* called 'New Labour's toxic culture of spin'.[73] What they failed to report was that their own journalists had helped provide McBride with the gossip about Tory leaders that then appeared in his notorious email. One political commentator rang McBride after his resignation to ask if his own name was in the email or liable to be linked with it. Having been reassured that it was not, he then wrote one of the most detailed accounts of the background to the affair without, naturally, mentioning his own involvement. Some of McBride's contacts rang to apologise for what they had been required to write by their news desks. One could offer only the small consolation that he had managed to ensure McBride's Cambridge education was mentioned before his ruddy complexion and love of beer.

Paul Staines offered his own views on 'The Lobby's Shameful Complicity' on his blog. 'Cowardice and cronyism runs right through the lobby. Fear of being taken off the teat of pre-packaged stories served to them. That is not journalism, that is copy-taking. The many stories filed this week which reveal just how horrible Brown's cabal have been are of mere historical interest. They would have been brave if they had been written before McPoison was toppled. You all knew and said nothing. You knew and went along with it. Your revelatory articles are merely confessions of previous personal cowardice.'[74]

Some journalists had the courage to agree. In *The Times*, Alice Miles wrote: 'The media are all chorusing now: we knew, we called him McNasty and McPoison, we had nothing to do with him, he sent us foul messages, we didn't like him. But the point is, we did know. We may not have known the detail of the nasty smears about senior Conservatives that Mr McBride was dreaming up, but we knew about the smears against his own side. We knew what he was up to, and we knew that he was being paid more than £100,000 a year of public money to do it – and we did nothing to stop it.'[75] Miles confirmed that: 'There has long been a "dirty tricks" cabal around Mr Brown that any Westminster journalist or minister could name – Ian Austin, Tom Watson, Ed Balls, Mr McBride and, formerly, Charlie Whelan,' but that 'the keys to the system are held by journalists. It is only through the collusion of journalists that underhand and anonymous attacks on political colleagues can have any effect.' Whelan himself tried to argue that not just the media but the Tories too were implicated, writing in his local paper: 'Now just in case you think that political "dirty tricks" are the prerogative of the Labour party, [you] may be interested to know who runs the Tory party spin machine. His name is Andy Coulson, the former *News of the World* man who was forced to quit his job there. And why? Well, just the little matter of paying £100,000 for someone to tap the mobile phones of the royal family. So next time you hear a Tory spokesperson talk about Labour dirty tricks, just think about the sort of people they employ. Apart from the utter hypocrisy of the Tories, what was just as sickening about the email scandal was the way the Westminster media attacked Damian McBride, despite the fact that they had spent the previous ten years relying on him for their stories.'[76]

Downing Street understood that trying to deflect blame was bound to fail and that the prime minister's own integrity was at stake.

McBride himself had advised Number 10 to cut him loose and depict him as a loose cannon rather than allow what had happened to damage Brown himself, but it didn't work. Trevor Kavanagh in the *Sun* wrote that: 'There's no such thing as a badly behaved dog – only a badly trained dog. Damian "Mad Dog" McBride was bred to kill. And he was obedient to one master – Gordon Brown.'[77] The editor of the *Spectator*, Matthew d'Ancona said 'plausible deniability' was Gordon Brown's middle name.[78] In the *Guardian*, Jackie Ashley said: 'The truth is that Brown has always been double-sided in his political personality and now the whole country knows it. The ideologically serious, morally driven statesman, whose steely determination was most recently on view in his successful handling of the G20, has lived his life with a sinister twin, spinning and dealing. McBride has been an extension of that other self.'[79]

The response of the 'serious' Brown was to ask the cabinet secretary to rewrite the code of conduct for special advisers to make clear that 'if they are ever found to be preparing and disseminating inappropriate material they will automatically lose their jobs.'[80] There was justifiable scepticism as to whether the change would make any practical difference. In a clear reference to the prime minister, one former cabinet minister told *The Times*: 'These changes to the rules about special advisers are completely and totally irrelevant. It's not about rules, it's about the moral compass of those involved.'[81] Michael Ellam confirmed to the lobby that there was 'huge frustration' within Downing Street that the prime minister's agenda of fighting the recession was being overshadowed by a controversy that ran for days and days. On day six Brown finally apologised for what had happened, but the tactic failed to put an end to the stories. The following weekend the *Sunday Times* reported that 'a senior Downing Street adviser who has never spoken out before' had revealed 'an operation within an operation at Number 10 . . . a leadership campaign in all but name'.[82] According to the paper's source, Ed Balls was 'McBride's puppet master'. 'Ed identifies someone as a potential rival and gets Damian to brief against that person to the media. Gordon, who's an avid reader of the papers, then reads that so-and-so is being disloyal to him. Gordon then freezes that person out. Thus that person is weakened and Ed's objective is achieved.' The report put Brown into a fury and he spent most of the day trying to identify the leaker, even personally telephoning former Downing Street employees at home. Predictably the source was never found. A spokesman for Balls called the allegations 'completely fabricated and malevolent nonsense without any foundation in fact'.[83]

The continuing controversy threatened even to overshadow the Budget the following week. Attention was finally shifted by Alistair Darling's announcement that the highest rate of income tax would be increased to 50 per cent, something that went against the long-standing New Labour pledge not to increase the basic or top rates. Economic commentators cast doubt on the likely benefits of the move to the exchequer, prompting *The Times* among others to observe that 'it looks suspiciously like a ploy to distract attention from the scale of the crisis in Britain's public finances revealed by the chancellor.'[84] Brown's efforts to shake off the politically lethal allegations of spin and dishonesty had been so comprehensively undone that the prime minister was in the worst possible position when, just a week later, the biggest scandal in Britain's political history broke.

It usually takes a little time for the true significance of political crises to be assessed fairly. Many that appear serious while they are in train are forgotten by the media and the public with remarkable speed. But the severity of the earthquake that shook parliament in May 2009 was evident as soon as it struck. The media, in the form of the *Daily Telegraph*, showed their true and legitimate power to expose wrongdoing and hold politicians to account. With the abuse of the parliamentary expenses system dominating the front pages for the best part of a month, MPs were rendered powerless to fight back. The innocent, or less guilty, were tarnished along with those whose offences were genuinely inexcusable. Amongst themselves MPs complained about the conduct of the media, the purchase of stolen information by the *Telegraph*, the recycling of all manner of unrelated stories about their private lives and other failings, but in public such arguments only inflamed the anger of the voters. Never before had the political classes been rendered so impotent by media revelations. Never had they earned the contempt of such a large proportion of the population, including many who habitually took little interest in affairs at

Westminster. The scandal led directly to a swathe of resignations that included the Speaker of the House of Commons, the home secretary and more than a dozen members of parliament from both sides of the House. But it did not come out of the blue. Ministers, with the support of MPs from all parties, had tried to exempt parliamentary expenses claims from the provisions of the Freedom of Information Act. When they failed, the Act had been used by campaigners and journalists to force the authorities to reveal what parliamentarians had been claiming from public funds. Civil servants and specially hired temporary staff at the Stationery Office in south London were given the laborious task of blacking out home addresses and other personal information from all the claims. It was supposed to be a highly secret and secure operation, but in early 2009 Downing Street picked up rumours that an unexpurgated copy of the claims was being offered for sale to newspaper editors. Yet despite being forewarned Number 10 and the parliamentary authorities seemed pitifully unprepared for the events of 8 May when Michael Ellam was first alerted by a text message from the deputy political editor of the *Daily Telegraph* asking him to call back 'ASAP'.[85] The paper contacted no fewer than thirteen other cabinet ministers that day with questions about their expenses. The team that had been studying the claims in great secrecy had no doubt it was 'the story of a lifetime. Even for such a cynical world-weary breed as national newspaper journalists, the details of what MPs had been claiming on their expenses had been startling.'[86] It was a central tenet of Labour's media strategy never to be taken by surprise and always to respond to potentially damaging stories quickly and robustly, yet in the weeks to come the government was constantly on the back foot and reduced to playing catch-up.

The scandal undermined the public's trust in politics as never before. It also tested the ability of the party leaders to respond to the voters' anger and meet demands for the offenders to be punished and the system swiftly reformed. It was a test that saw Gordon Brown repeatedly trailing behind both David Cameron and the Liberal Democrat leader, Nick Clegg. Brown had tried to preempt the inevitable outcry by proposing to abolish the allowance for second homes altogether, but having failed to consult on his ideas he found himself with no choice but to withdraw them or face defeat in the Commons. Then when the first *Telegraph* story appeared it was his own integrity he sought to defend rather than that of parliament as a whole. The newspaper revealed that he had claimed for payments for a cleaner that he shared with his brother. It was a trivial charge compared to those that were made against other MPs. These included avoiding capital-gains tax, claiming for mortgages that had been paid off, and repeatedly redesignating or 'flipping' second homes to maximise the amounts that could be reimbursed under the allowances system. Yet one of those who saw him several times on the day the story broke said he 'behaved as if the only story that mattered was the one about himself. He was in a furious sulk for thirteen hours.'

In the Downing Street press office, Michael Dugher tried unsuccessfully to dissuade the broadcasters from over-playing the story about the prime minister's own expenses. A copy of the Browns' cleaning contract was sent to all media organisations to show he had done nothing wrong. Dugher pursued the *Telegraph* for an apology, but the prime minister concluded he would have to intervene personally. On the morning of Friday 8 May Brown was put through to the mobile phone of the paper's editor, William Lewis. Lewis refused to disclose the contents of the call even to his own staff but joked afterwards that he was now 'off the prime minister's Christmas card list'.[87] All the pressure did eventually secure what amounted to a partial retraction. It appeared in the leader column of the *Sunday Telegraph* in terms that reflected some though not all of what Downing Street had been demanding: 'There are those MPs who, despite their good intentions, have none the less fallen victim to an overly complex expenses system that has served to portray their actions in an unflattering light. For example, the receipts submitted by Gordon Brown for the cost of a cleaner, shared with his brother Andrew, fall into such a category. There has never been any suggestion of impropriety on the part of the prime minister or his brother.'[88] Still Brown wasn't satisfied. He was furious that the BBC didn't give what he considered adequate coverage to the *Sunday Telegraph*'s editorial.

David Cameron knew that his party would soon be drawn into the scandal and told his staff to go through his own expenses and those of his senior colleagues to ensure they weren't taken by surprise in the same way. It wasn't until Monday 11 May, four days into its series of exposés, that the *Telegraph* turned its full fire on the Tories. Cameron announced that eight of his shadow cabinet, including himself, would be repaying money they should not have claimed. His MPs would be forced to obey tough new rules and those who had transgressed most seriously could find themselves deselected and unable to stand again for parliament. Labour's deputy leader, Harriet Harman, used her position as leader of the House of Commons to announce that a committee of MPs would quickly report on new rules that would apply to all parties.

At the *Telegraph* they concluded that 'Gordon Brown had dithered and dodged; Cameron was grasping the nettle with both hands. In short he was showing ruthless decisive leadership.'[89] Far more worrying for the prime minister was that so many journalists on previously supportive newspapers agreed. Brown's vacillation was the final straw for the *Guardian*'s leading columnist Polly Toynbee. She used it as an example of what had gone wrong for Labour since his arrival at Number 10. Politics, she wrote, was a test of character. 'The one character who has been tested to final destruction is Gordon Brown. The music stopped on his watch, first for the economy and now MPs' sleaze, for which the government of the day takes most blame . . . Gordon Brown has been tested and found in want of almost every attribute a leader needs. Squalid dealings by his poisonous inner circle were exposed to the light of day; yet at the same time he lacks a leader's necessary political cunning. Many hoped that the end of the rivalry with Blair would see Brown cast off his myrmidons. He didn't. In the tussle between his better and his worse selves, too often the lesser man won. That he was no great public orator or warm telegenic talker would never have mattered had he gained a reputation as a gruff, unspun man of honour, vision and purpose. I thought it an asset after Blair's glibness and Cameron's suavity. It wasn't the medium that did for him, but the message. There wasn't one. What was Labour for?'[90] Toynbee contrasted the Tory leader's response to the crisis with the prime minister's and concluded 'Cameron triumphed: it hardly mattered what he said or if his plan made sense – it too may unravel – when he showed himself forcefully decisive in a crisis and his words answered the wrathful spirit of the times: "Politicians have done things that are unethical and wrong. I don't care if they were within the rules – they were wrong." Compare and contrast that with Gordon Brown days later: "Where there is irregularity it has to be dealt with." This is the mindset and the language of a bunker under siege where dwindling trusted advisers lose touch with the daylight world outside.'[91]

Polly Toynbee was neither the first nor the last influential columnist from the left and liberal press to announce that she had given up on Brown, but her comments were a profound psychological blow to the prime minister. His allies tried to downplay the loss of support from columnists they had tried so hard to court. 'They tend to take it very personally when the things they'd been talking about to Gordon before he became prime minister – and which he had probably nodded his head to – then weren't his top priority when he came into power. So with Polly it was child poverty. With Freedland, constitutional reform. When they do these articles baring their souls about how disappointed they feel it always comes back to their old hobby horses.' But some in Brown's own communications team said Toynbee had identified a very real weakness. 'What Gordon lacks most,' said one, 'is any sense of what a normal person might think in any given situation.' Brown came back with better language in an article for the *News of the World,* in which he said: 'The bottom line is that any MP who is found to have defied the rules will not be serving in my government.'[92] It sounded tough until, two days later, he described the failure of one of his cabinet, Hazel Blears, to pay capital-gains tax on the sale of a second home as 'totally unacceptable' but then failed to sack her. Once again Cameron, who had forced his principal parliamentary aide, Andrew Mackay, to resign, appeared ahead of the game. Peter Riddell, one of Westminster's least excitable columnists, wrote in *The Times* that 'David Cameron has won all the tactical battles on the expenses row, leaving a frustrated Gordon Brown and his government trailing well behind. Yet there is more than a whiff of populist gimmickry about the "I am more a reformer than you" competition between politicians at present. The Conservative leader has displayed a steely mixture of ruthlessness and opportunism in his response to the public revulsion over the stories about MPs' expenses. He recognises the demand for blood and has been willing to sacrifice MPs via summary execution . . . Mr Brown has moved more slowly, suspending only two MPs . . . He has criticised the conduct of some ministers (such as Hazel Blears) as unacceptable but has seemed inconsistent and indecisive in his treatment of others.'[93]

The prime minister tried to appeal directly to the voters over the heads of the Westminster journalists at the end of April when Downing Street issued a video on the YouTube internet site. In it Brown set out his proposals for legislation to deal with the abuse of parliamentary expenses. The broadcast was a disaster for two reasons, one trivial, one rather more significant. When he tried to smile it looked more like an agonised grimace and comedians were soon doing mocking imitations all around the country. Even the normally loyal former deputy prime minister John Prescott was caught by photographers mimicking him.[94] More seriously there was the obvious question as to why he had made such an important announcement directly affecting parliament on the internet rather than in the Commons. In early May the communities secretary Hazel Blears used an article in the *Observer* to criticise Labour's 'lamentable' failure to get its message across. Harking back to Margaret Thatcher's 'you turn if you want to, the lady's not for turning', she said that while she was not against the use of the new media, 'YouTube if you want to. But it's no substitute for knocking on doors . . .'[95]

Brown told his staff that he had no intention of eschewing the use of YouTube and was 'not going to let the media tell me whether I can smile or not'.[96] He was proud of the way Downing Street had improved its use of the internet. Led by a former commercial radio manager, Mark Flanagan, now director of the strategic communications unit, Number 10 had modernised its own website and developed an effective presence on many of the most popular networking sites like Twitter and Facebook. When a Tory MP raised it at prime minister's questions Brown said 'YouTube is one of the most important mediums of communication and, even if the opposition will not use it, I shall continue to do so.'[97] In the event it was to be his wife, Sarah, who made the most effective use of the new media. Her posts on the Twitter site made her far and away the most popular political 'tweeter' in the UK.

For Gordon Brown his internet performances were the least of his worries. The contempt for all mainstream politicians that was being expressed so noisily in on-line communities was equally evident in real communities in every corner of Britain. MPs who, like Hazel Blears, were out knocking on doors and braving the fury of their electorates reported back to Downing Street that they had never experienced anything like it. Brown enjoyed the briefest of breathing spaces only because the pressure in parliament and the media was directed temporarily at the Speaker. Michael Martin had never enjoyed nor sought the high public profile of his predecessor, Betty Boothroyd. His brief period in the public eye was to prove the most painful of his political career. Constitutionally the Speaker is the ultimate authority responsible for the conduct of parliament. Martin had faced considerable criticism about his lack of authority, as well as his own use of public funds, since he was elected to the job in 2000. MPs are reluctant to speak out against the Speaker but when on 11 May he stood up in his chair and launched an extraordinary attack on two members of the House for making comments in the media about the crisis his fate was sealed. He turned first on the Labour backbencher, Kate Hoey, saying 'I listen to her often when I turn on the television at midnight and I hear her public utterances and pearls of wisdom on *Sky News* – it is easy to talk then . . . but it is a wee bit more difficult when you have to do more than just give quotes to the *Express* – or the press rather – and do nothing else.'[98] The Liberal Democrat Norman Baker was then castigated for saying 'to the press whatever the press wants to hear'. His outburst freed many MPs from their usual constraints and it quickly became clear that Martin had lost the confidence of the Commons. After a meeting with Brown at which both men agreed that he no longer had sufficient support in parliament to carry on he announced his resignation on 19 May, the first holder of that office to do so since 1695.

Martin's resignation left Brown even more exposed and, with elections to the European parliament and local councils in England fast approaching, speculation about his own position soon resumed. Opinion polls put support for Labour at its lowest ebb for a quarter of a century or more. He was asked by the BBC's Andrew Marr if he would resign if he thought it would improve his party's prospects and answered, 'No, because I am dealing with the issues at hand. I am dealing with the economy every day.'[99] Three days later the *Sun* endorsed the Conservatives in a national election for the first time since 1997. The following day the *Guardian*, the most widely read newspaper among Labour MPs and activists, said of Brown that the party should 'cut him loose'. 'The truth is that there is no vision from him, no plan, no argument for the future and no support. The public see it. His party sees it. The cabinet must see it too.'[100]

Some in the cabinet did indeed see it, but few were ready to say so. Nor did sufficient backbenchers feel inclined to follow the siren calls of the media, which many believed were motivated not by the best interests of the Labour party but by the desire for a good story. The fact that so many editorials and columnists were now calling for his head may even have helped Brown cling on. Ministers and MPs who spoke privately of their despair at Brown's leadership were unwilling to add their names to what looked like a media-driven campaign to get rid of him. The home secretary, Jacqui Smith, announced that she would be standing down from the cabinet but gave Brown her full support. She had been under intense media pressure since it had been revealed that claims for adult films viewed by her husband had inadvertently appeared on her expenses. Then Hazel Blears, who was still fuming at having been singled out by the prime minister, resigned on the eve of polling day. She did not criticise the prime minister either, although she made the mistake of wearing a brooch with the words 'Rocking the Boat' on it when she was photographed the same day. If her resignation had been intended to undermine Brown it had the opposite effect. Walking out of a job that carried responsibility for local government on the eve of local elections was seen by Labour MPs, no matter what they thought of Brown, as unforgivable disloyalty to the party. James Purnell, the work and pensions secretary, had a better sense of timing. He resigned just as the polls closed and he did have the courage to say what he really thought. He told Brown that his continued leadership made it more likely the Conservatives would win the general election and called on him 'to stand aside and to give our party a fighting chance of winning'.[101] The BBC's political editor, Nick Robinson, called the resignation 'a game-changing event'[102], but in the end the game remained the same. The foreign secretary, David

Miliband, considered following his good friend Purnell out of the cabinet but decided against it. Other ministers below cabinet rank did leave the government and some were highly critical of Brown and in particular what they perceived as his use of the media to damage his critics. Jane Kennedy, who resigned as environment minister, said 'the undermining of colleagues and friends orchestrated by Number 10' was the 'kind of politics that I've fought against all my life and I can't support it'.[103] Brown, however, survived.

The results delivered the worst Labour showing in a national contest since Lloyd George called his first general election in 1918. The party's support was at little more than 15 per cent and Brown was at his most vulnerable. His premiership was saved in the space of little more than two hours by the man he had barely spoken to for a decade before bringing him into his cabinet in October. Lord Mandelson was inside Downing Street as James Purnell made his announcement. He knew that one more top-level resignation could finish the prime minister off. Immediately he hit the phones. With somebody beside him getting each minister on the line in turn, he spoke to the likely waverers. The most important was David Miliband. Mandelson was in no mood for lengthy discussions. He told them all that for the good of the party they must declare their public support for Gordon Brown and do it quickly. The powers of persuasion mixed with icy menace that had worked so well on journalists for years were now focused on some of those closest to him politically. The newspapers, with the exception of the *Daily Mirror*, had written Brown off. One man then showed he had the power to defy their efforts to promote a cabinet insurrection.

Mandelson was richly rewarded for his efforts. The reshuffle that followed demonstrated Brown's weakness and Mandelson's strength. The prime minister was unable to make the changes he wanted because both Miliband and Alistair Darling refused to be moved to other jobs. Ed Balls's burning ambition to become chancellor was therefore frustrated. The job Mandeslon had craved all his political life was that of foreign secretary, the post to which his grandfather, Herbert Morrison, had risen under Clement Attlee. He got the best consolation prize available when Brown made him deputy prime minister in all but name. As 'first secretary of state', a title resurrected for him personally, he would come to wield extraordinary power. His reach extended into almost every area of policy and his influence was brought to bear to reinvigorate the government's communications efforts once more. Comparisons with the role Michael Heseltine had played in the final period of John Major's government were both obvious and apt. If anything Mandelson was even more powerful and he used the opportunity presented to him to great effect, coming close to achieving what Tony Blair had said he always wanted him to do – winning the love of the Labour party.

Mandelson's loyalty was now complete, but the same could not be said for every minister who remained in the government. Many still harboured bitter resentment against the treatment they felt had been meted out to their colleagues. In the run-up to the reshuffle fresh allegations about the expenses claims of both Alistair Darling and Hazel Blears had appeared in the *Daily Telegraph*. The paper's political editor, Andrew Porter, was known to have been close to Damian McBride, Ed Balls and others in the Brown inner circle. Angry ministers who spoke off the record to the *Guardian* were convinced the stories had been a deliberate attempt to undermine the chancellor so that Balls could take over and to punish Blears for her resignation. One called it a 'McBride-style dirty trick'.[104] Michael Ellam told the paper that the prime minister had been 'very annoyed' and if there had been a leak of information from Downing Street 'it would be something he did not authorise, did not know about and would condemn.'

On 16 June Brown announced personnel changes that he hoped would see him through to the next general election. Michael Ellam was to return to a senior post at the Treasury. The new director of communications was an old friend of Mandelson's, Simon Lewis, a former press secretary to the Queen who also happened to be the brother of the *Daily Telegraph*'s editor, William Lewis. Before taking up the job he said, 'As a civil servant in Downing Street I shall be communicating on behalf of the government, not on behalf of a political party. I only accepted the job on that basis. Being a civil servant gives me more credibility and a sense of pride to be joining a much under-rated civil service . . . It is important there are people in the civil service who bring neutrality to communications . . . Authenticity in communications is the key, the more authentic the more likely the message will be received.'[105] Lewis had no illusions about the challenge he was taking on. He had, in the words of one senior civil servant, 'no Whitehall experience and no real experience of the lobby'. Nor was he versed in the intricacies of Labour politics and he had no time to learn on the job. His first major crisis was over the souring of relations between Britain and the United States following the release of the man convicted of the Lockerbie bombing in 1988, Abdelbaset Ali Mohmed Al Megrahi. When President Obama made his feelings clear to Brown in a lengthy telephone call, lobby journalists learned about it only from the White House as Lewis's briefing on the call had failed to mention the rebuke.[106] Senior figures in Whitehall feared that Brown had once again appointed a 'very smooth top-class PR man' rather than the political heavyweight that the communications team still lacked.

The prime minister faced a familiar dilemma. If the Downing Street press office is too political it runs a far greater risk of generating controversy and drawing unwelcome attention to its activities. If it is not political enough, then its ability to communicate the prime minister's objectives and ambitions effectively will be hampered. Given the battering he had taken, it is perhaps understandable that Brown chose to play safe. In the last year left to him before he would have to call an election he told his staff he wanted to return to the principles he had hoped would underpin his relationship with the media from the outset. Once again equality of access for all journalists and an end to both negative briefing and the 'trailing' of parliamentary statements were to be the order of the day. Privately Brown continued to assert that he had never wavered from those standards. The implication was that others, like Damian McBride, had let him down and behaved in ways that he had known nothing about and would never have condoned. One official who had witnessed the prime minister and his media team in action since 2007 described that as 'typical self-delusion' on Brown's part. Whether he had been let down or had let himself down, the prime minister had little time left to restore his reputation. Over the summer the government did enter calmer waters and comparisons with the dying days of the Major administration were shown to be misplaced. Misgivings about Brown's leadership did not disappear – that would have been too much to ask – but his opponents within his own party recognised that their best chance had passed. There were no fundamental policy disagreements to divide the party in the manner of Major's Conservatives and the will to win again remained strong, however improbable it had come to seem.

There were fundamental questions of strategy to be resolved, however, and here too Mandelson proved the decisive influence. Shaun Woodward, who had been promised a new strategic role to compensate for his disappointment at not being promoted out of the Northern Ireland office in the reshuffle, wanted the government to stick to a trusted formula. Woodward believed he understood the Tories' vulnerabilities better than most, having once been their communications director. He argued that 'Labour investment versus Tory cuts' would continue to be the key dividing line to hit his old party where it hurts. Mandelson disagreed. It wouldn't play in the media, he argued, because it wasn't sustainable. Mandelson won the day. He also wanted to do what he could to make Brown appear more confident and convincing in public. He told journalists he wished the prime minister had more 'razzamatazz'[107] but he knew Brown's real strengths were his grasp of policy and his position as a leader who had been tested under fire. Labour planned to use its last party conference before the election to showcase those qualities and remind the voters once again of David Cameron's comparative lack of experience.

The party's leaders gathered in Brighton during the last week of September, anticipating a hostile media. Many complained that the papers behaved as if the Conservatives already had the election in the bag and they saw it as their task to remind the voters they still faced a real choice and it wasn't for journalists to say who would be the next prime minister. Labour's relations with the media were already at their lowest ebb for twenty years or more but by the end of the week they would be a whole lot worse. The 2009 conference produced significant changes in the relationship between Downing Street and the media, all of which looked certain to have a lasting impact. In the process the relative power and influence of the newspapers, broadcasters and internet bloggers shifted perceptibly too. And as a consequence the terrain on which the 2010 general election would be played out began to take shape.

On the first full morning of the conference Gordon Brown took his seat in the Grand Hotel for the traditional Sunday television interview with the BBC. Party leaders always hope to make news from these encounters but this time it was the interviewer, Andrew Marr, who was to dominate the subsequent headlines. Marr startled both the prime minister and the many journalists and political professionals who were monitoring the programme when he asked Brown if he was, like 'a lot of people', one of those who 'use prescription painkillers and pills to help them get through'.[108] Marr thought it was 'a fair question'. Brown deprecated it as 'the sort of questioning that is all too often entering the lexicon of British politics'. The prime minister said it wasn't true, while away from the cameras his advisers immediately asked what right the BBC had to air the allegation in the first place. Although Marr said it was something 'everybody has been talking about', the source turned out to be a retired advertising executive, John Ward, who wrote an obscure but provocative blog from his home in the South of France. Tracked down by *Channel Four News*, Mr Ward said he had 'no more proof, and I stress proof, than anyone else that Gordon Brown is actually taking anti-depressants'.[109] The basis of his blog had been a conversation at a drinks party with a senior civil servant who had merely said that Brown couldn't eat certain kinds of food that Mr Ward knew from his own experience were incompatible with a rarely used prescription drug. The allegation had already been picked up by columnists in the *Daily Telegraph* and *Independent* and denied by Downing Street. It was the first example of an unsubstantiated internet rumour being catapulted to prominence by the BBC without any independent corroboration. Although the Corporation stood by its presenter, the incident confirmed the fears of those who worried that the explosion in political blogging, with its predilection for gossip and unchecked speculation, was contaminating both politics and journalism.

Gordon Brown was furious at the distraction caused by the question. Unusually for a serving prime minister he allowed his more general irritation with the media to show in a brief aside during his leader's speech on the Tuesday afternoon. He joked that he would like to praise Alistair Darling as Britain's best ever chancellor but if he did, the media would say 'Brown snubs Brown.'[110] For the most part, the prime minister used the speech to stick to his chosen dividing line with the Conservatives. His government, he said, had made the right choices on the economy while David Cameron had made the wrong call on every big question. On policy, Brown's announcements were directed once again at the issues so often raised by papers like the *Mail* and the *Sun* – teenage pregnancies, drunken young tearaways in city centres, immigration and support for the armed services. It was a good but not a brilliant speech and immediately afterwards even Lord Mandelson conceded on television that there was what he called a 'filter' between the prime minister and the public. 'It's a filter perhaps he contributes to himself. I don't know. Or it's something that the media put in between him and the public.'[111] Either way Brown was still failing to communicate his beliefs and aspirations effectively, even in the estimation of his closest allies.

That evening Brown and Mandelson learned that they had lost one of the vehicles through which New Labour had sought to get its message across to millions of people for the past twelve years. Despite everything in the speech that had played to the paper's agenda, the *Sun* used it to justify the decision to switch its support to the Conservative party. 'Labour's Lost It'[112] wasn't a memorable headline but it confirmed what the party had long suspected, that Britain's best-selling tabloid would no longer be giving it the benefit of the doubt. The loss of the *Sun* was no surprise but the timing was. Mandelson made his feelings abundantly clear in an angry phone call with News International's chief executive, Rebekah Brooks. Brooks and the man who had replaced her as editor of the *Sun*, Dominic Mohan, strongly supported the shift of allegiance but most commentators assumed it had been dictated once again by Rupert Murdoch. In fact power had been shifting within the Murdoch empire too and it was his son, James, now chairman of the News Corporation parent company, who had made the final decision. The most recent biographer of Mr Murdoch senior, Michael Wolff, revealed that during a number of conversations with his subject he had come to the conclusion that 'Rupert Murdoch really adores Gordon Brown . . . in spite of the fact that there is much they disagree about, not least of all Europe. But when it comes to Gordon, political positions are beside the point. It's temperament and heart that are important. Rupert believes Gordon is all the things a proper man should be: serious, unaffected, unpretentious, down to earth, square (really square). Even his dubious qualities – his remoteness, dullness, inarticulateness and indecisiveness – are, for Rupert, signs of Gordon Brown's good value.'[113] Yet as early as 2008 Murdoch had acknowledged that his son liked Cameron and when it came to deciding who News International would support, 'It will be James's decision . . . it's got to be.'

Except to avid Murdoch-watchers it didn't really matter. The *Sun* had achieved what it wanted. The BBC and most of the rest of the media led their political news on the decision and the paper secured well over twenty-fours of valuable free publicity. Coverage of what the prime minister had actually said was overshadowed as a result. Gordon Brown showed his anger in a series of tetchy broadcast interviews the following day, even while he and his colleagues sought to argue that the political impact of newspaper endorsements mattered little. They were right in their assessment, although the prime minister conceded that 'Obviously you want newspapers to be for you. We would have liked everybody to be on our side, but the people decide.'[114] He added for good measure that 'I've got an old-fashioned opinion that you look to newspapers for news not opinions.' The *Sun* was doing what it always did, backing what it thought was a winner in its own commercial interests. Significantly in Scotland, where the Conservatives remained a minority taste, the *Scottish Sun* made clear it would not be following suit. The change of editorial policy south of the border mattered only in so far as it was a very high-profile confirmation that the Tories were now well entrenched as the party widely expected to emerge from the 2010 election with a majority. As the YouGov opinion pollster Peter Kellner argued, 'Although the *Sun* newspaper is a great weather vane, it doesn't decide the direction of the wind.'[115]

Labour now faced the prospect of going into the election with the lowest level of newspaper support since 1979. The possibility could no longer be ignored that only the *Mirror* group titles would give Brown their unambiguous endorsement. At the *Guardian,* with its long tradition of internal democracy, senior staff would be given a vote on whom to support, but with so many of its leading columnists and leader writers on the record as vehement critics of the prime minister it could not be relied upon to return to the fold. More than any prime minister before him, Gordon Brown would be relying on the broadcasters to compensate for the overwhelming hostility of the print media. And the weekend after the conference Brown gave the broadcasters what they most wanted.

For months Lord Mandelson had been advocating a bold departure for an incumbent prime minister. He argued privately and hinted publicly that Brown should be willing to take part in the first ever televised leaders' debates in the run-up to the election.[116] An announcement that Brown would take up the challenge had been removed from his speech for fear that it would overshadow his policy announcements. As it turned out the *Sun* had done that anyway, but even after its intervention Brown insisted that whether or not to have debates was 'a question which has got to be dealt with nearer the election'.[117] Well, not much nearer. Three days later he posted a letter on Labour's website announcing his support for 'a wide ranging series of television and radio debates with party leaders'.[118] Brown clearly believed such debates were one way of breaking through the 'filter'. He said he relished 'the opportunity of making our case directly to the people of this country'. It was a strategic shift that would last well beyond his own tenure in Downing Street. It is unlikely that any future prime minister would be able to muster a convincing argument for refusing to participate on principle. By calling for a series of debates both before and during the election campaign, Brown sought to avoid the danger of broadcast confrontations playing a disproportionate role in the electoral process. By suggesting that debates should also take place between other ministers and their opposition counterparts, he hoped to deflect criticism that they would make British politics more 'presidential'. But it was a fundamental shift nonetheless.

Gordon Brown faced the final few months before his fate would be decided at the ballot box with trepidation. Mastery of the media, once New Labour's not-so-secret weapon, was now in other hands. It was little consolation that the newspaper industry itself was in the midst of its biggest crisis since most of Fleet Street had broken free from its financial dependence on the political parties in the 1920s. Political communications mattered as much as ever, and every party was struggling to get its message into those places where people increasingly went for their news. The share of that news market held by the national newspapers was in steady decline. Labour could hope only that the parallel weakening and fragmentation of party loyalties meant also that voting intentions were now less predictable than ever before and that the media were wrong to think the contest had already been settled. The days when the overwhelming majority of the electorate supported one or other of the two main parties were clearly long since gone. The impact of a shift of support towards the minor parties, including the Greens, UKIP and even the BNP, exacerbated by the 'plague on all your houses' response to the expenses crisis, was hard to gauge. Labour was in a terrible position as it entered the final straight, but even its most sophisticated polling and focus-group analysts couldn't say with any accuracy just how bad it was.

One thing was certain, however. Power no longer lay where it had been traditionally thought to lie. No prime minister sitting in Downing Street in the years to come would need to concern him- or herself with flattering and placating the owners of British newspapers to anything like the degree that their predecessors had done. Nor could they expect the luxury of exercising as much untrammelled power as that enjoyed by previous incumbents. The system that Brown had grown up in and learned to dominate had changed dramatically and was changing still. He had come to the job he had always coveted just when his own political skills were becoming redundant and his discomfort was often painful to observe. Yet however inglorious his premiership may have looked, from its many tribulations has emerged the possibility of a healthier relationship between the government and the governed and even, perhaps, between Downing Street and the media. Both sides have had to learn a little humility and to look afresh at how they operate. How far-reaching the change will be has still to become clear, but business as usual is no longer an option. So as Gordon Brown said on 27 June 2007, 'Now let the work of change begin.'

CONCLUSION: ATONEMENT

An able, disinterested, public-spirited press, with trained intelligence to know the right and courage to do it, can preserve that public virtue without which popular government is a sham and a mockery. A cynical, mercenary, demagogic press will produce in time a people as base as itself.

Joseph Pulitzer

On my first day as a journalist at Westminster I was taken to one side by the BBC's political editor, John Cole, and given some invaluable advice. John was a man you listened to. The first prime minister he interviewed was Clement Attlee and he had known most of the giants of post-war politics and journalism personally. He had a genuine respect for both professions that was based on a belief that those who go into public life and those who endeavour to understand and explain it do so, for the most part, with the best intentions. His enthusiasm was infectious but it was his ability to put fast-changing events into a perspective that could come only with experience that I found most admirable. It would go against everything he believed in to put what he said into quotation marks when I didn't keep a note at the time, but the gist was this: always do your best to keep ahead of the story, you're a journalist after all, but whatever you do don't be tempted to follow the latest fashion.

The fashion as we enter the second decade of the twenty-first century is to decry not only the state of our politics but of our media also. Many apocalyptic words have been written about the parlous health of

British democracy and the failure of both politicians and journalists to uphold the standards to which they claim to aspire. The public feel let down and they have a right to do so. It is hard to say which has fallen furthest or fastest, confidence in politics or the circulation of newspapers. A powerful vortex of cynicism and negativity constantly threatens to drag both down still further. Public disengagement from what goes on at Westminster serves only to reinforce a readiness by the media to replace serious debate with a kind of info-tainment that barely passes for news. It is an alarming prospect but there is no inevitability about it. Escape from the vortex is possible if the arguments about how to fix our democracy are extended to cover the relationship between the media and politics that so colours our perceptions of everything else. If each side can acknowledge its mistakes, then the tensions between them – tensions that are essential for a healthy politics – could, just maybe, become creative rather than destructive.

The struggle with the media, which has always been in truth a struggle for influence over public opinion, has been fought with a greater intensity during the Labour governments of Tony Blair and Gordon Brown than in any other period in British political history. Ten years ago I worked in Number 10 when its power to influence, control, manipulate – choose the verb according to your point of view – the media was at its peak. A decade later and Downing Street was left impotent as the press used its power to expose, to humiliate and to condemn to deadly effect. It seemed as if every journalist who had ever been flattered, cajoled or threatened into reporting the news the way New Labour wanted had decided it was pay-back time for the humiliation they had suffered. The boot may have been on the other foot, but had the balance of power really shifted? No. What had shifted was public opinion and for the usual complex mix of reasons that has always influenced political fortunes. The media were no more the undoing of New Labour than they were its making and journalists overstate their own importance – a professional failing that has been evident throughout the period covered by this book – if they believe otherwise. It was Clem Attlee's press secretary who said they 'have to go with the prevailing mood. They cannot deflect the wagon of public opinion once it has started to roll, and certainly cannot reverse its course. But they can enormously increase its weight and velocity.'[1] Those words are as true today as they were then.

The media band-wagon effect may have boosted a prime minister's majority by a few seats from time to time but there is no evidence that it has ever made enough difference to determine who gets the job. In between elections the power of the media is harder to quantify but its limits have been demonstrated more often than its potency. In 1925 Lord Beaverbrook delivered a lecture in Liverpool on the power of the press in which he said that 'when skilfully employed at the right psychological moment no politician of any power can resist it,'[2] but he was to be proved wrong. Lengthy and vigorous popular press campaigns demanded economic protectionism in the 1920s and a referendum on Europe in the 1990s and 2000s. Neither happened. Most of Fleet Street wanted the King to stay in 1936. He abdicated. In 1969 Harold Wilson had to abandon his 'In Place of Strife' union reforms although every national newspaper supported them. In 1995 John Major won his leadership battle despite the vocal opposition of almost all the papers, including his party's traditional backers. Gordon Brown survived in 2009 in similar circumstances. The power of the media to secure political change is greatly inferior to their ability to stand in its way. The Euro-sceptic press added considerably to the weight of opposition to the single currency, although it undoubtedly reflected the prevailing mood. In many other policy areas the media, whose cry is so often 'something must be done', are an impediment to action. The fear of how the papers might react makes politicians timid. The dread of headlines about party 'splits' and cabinet 'divisions' encourages even the most creative of political minds to stick to the current script. Polly Toynbee identified the problem when she wrote that, 'ministers are not allowed to raise interesting questions. If they say anything beyond the anodyne mantras of the day they will be crushed by the same negative forces that complain that modern politicians are uninspiring, never tell the truth and never engage honestly with the public. This is not a partisan point: any Tory saying anything out loud that is mildly speculative but off-script will be mangled just as fast by media that are, paradoxically, eager for politicians to say something even slightly original – yet squash the breath out of them if they do. Thinking aloud is not allowed. Indeed, thinking of any kind is dangerous. It was not always so at Westminster, or not to this degree.'[3]

It need not always be so. A recognition that the media are weaker than both politicians and journalists seem to think, and are likely to get weaker still, would be healthy for democracy. Power lies today just where it lay when Lloyd George was in Number 10, primarily in the hands of the prime minister. If he or she feels impotent then they should look to themselves for the solution. If a prime minister has a good story to tell there will be journalists ready to help tell it. The media may be more impatient, less reverential and more inclined to cynicism but so too is the public. It is too late to argue about who is to blame. Attention spans are shorter in newsrooms but in living rooms also. Traditional party loyalties count for little in most editorial offices just as they do in the majority of households. The politicians may not like it but they must work out how to deal with it. Lashing out at the media is the political equivalent of kicking the cat. It may make you feel better for a short time but it's not going to make life any easier.

Let politicians criticise media ethics and behaviour by all means. They can and should demand a fair hearing. They have every right to complain about being treated like serial sex offenders every time they appear on the *Today* programme or *Newsnight*. If they are misrepresented they should be able to seek redress. If they are confronted by sneering, supercilious interviewers they should say as much and let the public decide whether they deserve it. When they see comment dressed up as fact they can point out the difference. The opportunities for doing so are now far more various and readily available than they were just a short time ago. The traditional media no longer have the stranglehold on public debate they once did. Not only are newspaper circulations falling, but viewing figures for the main news and current-affairs programmes are on a steady downward slide. At the next election more people will get their news about what is being said and by whom from the internet than ever before. And many of those most likely to switch their vote, the uncommitted but politically engaged, are also the most likely to go looking for news and views with the click of a mouse. Politicians serious about communicating with the electorate are now heavily engaged in blogging and using networking sites.

The complaint that they can't get a hearing in a hostile media environment no longer rings true.

New technology alone will not offer an escape from the vortex. Nor will exhortations for politicians and journalists to treat one another with a bit more respect. Combined with other changes, however, they may contribute to a more constructive relationship. It would be whistling in the wind to ask governments, any more than opposition parties, to stop using whatever methods of persuasion are available to them to get a better press. Why should they? And it would be asking too much to expect journalists to give every piece of information they receive its true value, never to turn a disagreement into a 'row', a disgruntled has-been into a 'senior backbencher' or a bad patch into somebody's 'worst week in politics'. A press that religiously balanced every political opinion and never again carried a headline that went over the top might be worthy but it would be deadly dull. In any case, you do not revitalise democracy by stifling lively debate and argument. That debate will serve its true purpose, however, only when the public feel once again that they can believe what they hear from politicians, up to and including the prime minister, and have confidence in what they read, see and hear in the media.

For once the interests of the two professions of politics and journalism coincide. A fractured, disengaged and mistrustful population will be harder for either one to reach. The 2009 crisis for parliament did at least capture the public's attention, so now is not the time for Augustinian procrastination. Those who work at Westminster may not be ready to pledge themselves to a life of virtue, but they have little choice other than to change their ways. Walter Bagehot, who described much of the hidden wiring of politics in *The English Constitution* in 1867, warned against letting too much 'daylight in upon the magic'.[4] Bagehot had the monarchy in particular in mind, but almost a century and a half since he wrote those words Westminster was still trying to discourage prying eyes. Today the option of keeping the curtains drawn, even if it were desirable, is no longer available. The light is now shining in and it has exposed the methods not just of the spin doctors who Clare Short famously described as 'the people who live in the dark'[5] but many others too. They may not be enjoying the experience but their discomfort is to be welcomed. The tried and tested way of improving behaviour is through public exposure. The threat of being named and shamed is sufficient to encourage all but the most hardened delinquents to think before they act. It was the parading of the guilty through the pages of the newspapers that ensured MPs will never again claim more than they can justify in public on their expenses. Simon Lewis, Downing Street's director of communications since the summer of 2009, believes 'the media and the body politic need to become more transparent,'[6] and he is right. That transparency, much of it generated by the internet, a phenomenon Bagehot could never have imagined, is turning into a powerful force for good in the reform of our traditionally secretive democracy.

This is not an argument for the equivalent of a CCTV camera in every corridor and office in London SW1. Journalists will continue to have private conversations with those in and around positions of power and that is all to the good. A great deal of information that the public deserves to know is divulged under the cloak of anonymity. That is quite different from 'client journalism', or what the first Lord Rothermere called 'cap in hand' journalism. If a correspondent relies to a disproportionate degree on one politician or faction for information, then only if that relationship is understood can due weight be given to the stories he or she writes. Here the new media are already providing part of the answer. Political bloggers, some openly committed to one party, others more independent, are bound by none of the old traditions of professional secrecy and have no hesitation in pointing out who is going cap in hand to whom. The journalists, many of them under instruction from their editors to blog themselves, are increasingly under pressure to respond and to justify what they write. Little dog eat big dog it may be, but it's already having an effect.

Simon Lewis took over a Downing Street press office that has had no choice but to embrace greater openness. 'Over my dead body' was Sir Bernard Ingham's response to the idea that what he said should be directly attributed to Number 10. Thankfully he lived to see it happen. Today what is said at the once-secret lobby briefings is speedily available on the Downing Street website and journalists routinely quote the prime minister's spokesman and frequently identify him by name.

Those briefings should now be televised and broadcast live both on television and the net. The public should be able to take the measure of both the media's questions and the responses they receive. No justification remains for excluding the electorate from such a significant part of daily political discourse. The argument that less information would be divulged as a result has withered to nothing as the proceedings have gone on the record. The objection that it would turn the spokesman into too much of a public figure is merely to say that the reality should continue to be hidden behind an out-dated and unsustainable fiction that only ministers can and should represent the government in public.

Now the light is shining in on the magic, many of the old tricks won't work anymore. The audience was getting more than a little bored with them anyway. Political communications shouldn't rely on smoke and mirrors and no longer can. Pretending that those who speak for the government are mere cyphers has always been a sleight of hand so let's stop pretending. The absence of the cameras did nothing to prevent Joe Haines, Bernard Ingham or Alastair Campbell becoming more influential than most members of the cabinet. Each of them in turn became bigger players than the role properly requires and their value to the prime minister they served was undermined. Greater transparency about the activities of the press secretary or communications director would help minimise that risk. So too would a recognition that once a prime minister thinks the spokesman is indispensable, the opposite is probably true. Every PM should be free to choose whoever he or she wants to speak for them, although this history suggests civil servants are better able to retain the credibility necessary to be believed at all times. No matter whether the spokesman has a civil-service or political background, however, the risk of becoming too much 'the story', and of being seen as a threat by jealous ministers, would be greatly reduced if they were limited to one parliamentary term. It would be impractical to legislate but the assumption should be that after every general election the spokesman would change, even if the prime minister did not. They should also be required to appear at least once a year before the House of Commons committee on public administration to account not just for their own conduct but for that of the Downing Street press office as a whole.

Under Gordon Brown those changes would have made Michael Ellam and Simon Lewis familiar faces but left the likes of Damian McBride in the dark and that cannot be right. When I was at Downing Street I proposed that the names, photographs, biographies and job descriptions of all special advisers employed in the building should be posted on the internet. Only two of my colleagues, both former journalists, Geoff Mulgan and Andrew (now Lord) Adonis, agreed. Everybody else came up with variants on 'over my dead body'. When we read about 'Downing Street sources' we should at least have an identity parade of the usual suspects. Those who do speak on a regular basis to journalists should not only be identified, they should be accountable. Not just the director of communications, but the director of forward strategy (or whatever title is dreamed up for special advisers like McBride), the head of the strategic communications unit, and others in similar positions should also be called to answer MPs' questions. If any of them wish to say that they never pick up the phone to a journalist, then fine, but it had better be true. They should also be free to appear on television and radio to present their arguments about the prime minister's message and what Downing Street believes to be the real issues of the day. Viewers of *The West Wing* will know what I'm talking about. These are our equivalents of Josh Lyman, Sam Seaborn and Toby Ziegler. Defenders of the traditional ways of working at Westminster argue that allowing the prime minister's staff to talk publicly in this way would further diminish parliament and enhance the powers of unelected officials at the expense of ministers. But if transparency about our political system means anything it means acknowledging the reality of where power lies and not hiding behind constitutional myths that obscure the truth. The prime minister's director of communications already is a significant figure. He and his staff provide ministers with their 'lines to take', preferred sound bites and pre-packaged arguments so they can speak with one voice and defend a common cause. Had the post existed in Bagehot's day it would have been listed as one of the 'efficient parts' of the constitution, 'those by which it, in fact, works and rules'.[7] If public trust in how government works is to be restored, then it is time to be open about who does what and when. The former cabinet secretary Lord Turnbull revealed an uncomfortable truth when he said that 'the sovereignty of parliament has become a myth. The control of parliament by the executive has grown to such an extent that we now, in reality, have sovereignty of government.'[8] And government is not just those who owe their positions to being members of the House of Commons or the Lords. It is also those civil servants, temporary or otherwise, appointed to positions of great influence by the prime minister.

The former Speaker Lady Boothroyd and the other redoubtable defenders of parliamentary privilege have done a proud job. In her final words to the Commons Betty Boothroyd said 'I have taken action to ensure that those who advise ministers should never overlook the primacy of parliament. This is the chief forum of the nation − today, tomorrow and, I hope, for ever.'[9] It was a hope but it was not then, and is even less so now, the reality. It is to the media that the public turn for debate. The current Speaker, John Bercow, described what he saw as the problem. 'In an age of 24-hour news, ministers are the lead suppliers of items for news coverage. Aided and abetted by the departmental machine, and with no power to instruct that parliament be the first to be informed, a debate on policy or events is essentially a joust between the media and the minister. MPs become at best bit-part players in the problem, struggling to catch up with what has been released and to probe the minister about it.'[10] The answer, however, is not to try once again to constrain the use ministers can make of the media, but to recognise that the media have a valuable role to play in the effective functioning of our democracy.

Gordon Brown tried to enforce what Lady Boothroyd wanted, with major announcements preserved for the chamber of the House of Commons, but it simply didn't work. Downing Street conceded that it had no choice but to 'trail' what was coming up or those announcements would be overlooked in the welter of other news. The only institution in the world that seems able to keep its secrets until it wants to unveil them is the Apple Corporation. If the next version of the iPhone were to be unveiled in a Commons debate, the audience would be immense. The truth − call it the sad truth if you wish − is that the British parliament must compete for attention like everybody else and that means using the media more effectively not treating them as dangerous rivals. The time has come for the Speaker and the Commons authorities to embrace a system of advance notification of statements and debates that would help generate interest in the proceedings of parliament, not the reverse. Important government announcements should not be traded for favours or distributed selectively but even the biggest blockbuster at the cinema benefits from a good trailer and the more people who see it the better. If a film is good enough, people will still go and watch it whether they have already seen the highlights or not. And if the trailer does its job properly it will have whetted the appetite of potential viewers not made them feel they no longer need to sit through the big picture.

So let announcements be trailed on an even-handed basis, with any information released in advance also posted on the internet. Even the Budget need not be sacrosanct. It has been parcelled out to selected journalists ahead of time for years now and the effect has often been to undermine its credibility. A more rigorous approach could have the opposite effect. We already have a pre-Budget report so, if handled responsibly, advance discussion through the media of such an important package of measures could help increase the public's understanding and acceptance of what is being proposed. Clearly changes to tax rates and other market-sensitive announcements have to be kept secret but if the chancellor wants to give appropriate warning of other parts of his economic strategy let him do it openly and on an equal basis.

None of the proposals above is designed to shift power from one institution to another, merely to be honest about where power already lies. For that reason I have deliberately not touched on privacy legislation, changes to the rules on cross-media ownership, or even freedom of information. These too need to be re-examined and, above all, debated on their merits and not to protect the interests of either secretive governments or powerful proprietors. News laws can, of course, make a difference to how Westminster functions, but more power has been transferred by behavioural changes on the part of both prime ministers and the media than anything legislation has ever achieved. When journalists queue up to be spun they hand those in power something no parliamentary majority, however large, could provide. When prime ministers allow the views of Rupert Murdoch or Paul Dacre to have more influence than those of their cabinet colleagues they weaken themselves and their governments by choice.

In answer to Tony Blair's attack on the 'feral beasts' of the media John Cole wrote that journalists should look to their own behaviour before complaining. 'Journalism is a serious trade,' he said, 'and broadcasters and journalists have a duty to audiences and readers not to allow politicians to manipulate them. Some of my best friends are politicians, but never forget that they and we exercise different crafts.'[11] The job of restoring the credibility of both professions would be made easier if prime ministers stopped trying to write headlines and newspapers stopped trying to make policy. Atonement for past sins and a pledge to operate, both separately and together, with greater integrity in the future would do a lot to help. But promises alone will no longer be enough. Only by shedding yet more light on the murky places where power lies can we be sure that it will be exercised more responsibly. Neither side need have anything to fear. Dedicated journalists and elected prime ministers would still be free to get on with what they are employed to do. After all, the relationship between a dog and a lamp-post is no different whether the lamp is lit or not.

NOTES

Introduction: The Power and the Glory

1 17 May 2009, *Sunday Times*
2 15 May 2009, *Guardian*
3 2 March 2009, *Guardian*
4 21 July 2009, *Guardian*
5 12 April 2009, *Mail on Sunday*
6 Margaret Scammell, *Designer Politics*, p. 19
7 6 February 1852, *Times*
8 John Keane, *The Life and Death of Democracy*, p. xxii
9 Peter Oborne, *The Triumph of the Political Class*, p. 233
10 17 January 1994, *Guardian*
11 Charles Hill, *Both Sides of the Hill*, p. 202
12 Kennedy Jones, *Fleet Street and Downing Street*, p. 341
13 Ibid., p. 329
14 James Harding, *Alpha Dogs*, p. 222–3
15 Jones, op. cit., p. 341
16 Harding, op. cit., p. 6
17 1 June 2009, *GMTV*
18 David Marquand, *Britain Since 1918*, p. 401
19 19 October 1976, Dimbleby Lecture
20 Hugh Cudlipp *Publish and be Damned*, p. 225
21 12 May 1991, *Independent on Sunday*
22 Bob Franklin, *Packaging Politics*, p. 24
23 Peter Hennessy, *The Prime Minister*, p. 85
24 23 April 1996, James Cameron Memorial Lecture, City University, London
25 24 June 1968, Barbara Castle, *The Castle Diaries*, p. 468
26 11 April 1992, *Sun*
27 August 1960, *Catholic Digest*

1. War and Peace: Lloyd George (1916–22)

1 Stephen Koss, *The Rise and Fall of the Political Press in Britain* (1990), p. 683
2 Bernard Ingham, *The Wages of Spin*, p. 200
3 William Douglas Home (ed.), *The Prime Ministers*, p. 194
4 Koss, op. cit., p. 745
5 Lord Beaverbrook, *Politicians and the Press*, p. 108
6 A.J.P. Taylor, *Beaverbrook*, p. 60
7 17 July 1912, Cabinet meeting
8 J.A. Spender, *Life, Journalism and Politics*, p. 169
9 A.J.P. Taylor, *English History 1914–45*, p. 55
10 25 September 1915, Bruce Page, *The Murdoch Archipelago*, p. 38
11 Ibid., p.41
12 Taylor, *English History 1914–1945*, p. 61
13 Spender, op. cit., p. 43
14 Bentley Brinkerhoff Gilbert, *Lloyd George*, p. 253
15 Ibid., p. 32
16 Koss, op. cit., p. 683
17 23 October 1915, Frances Stevenson, *Lloyd George: A Diary*, p. 71
18 8 May 1916, *Daily News*
19 Gilbert, op. cit., p. 316
20 John Turner, *Lloyd George's Secretariat*, p. 168
21 Unpublished until it surfaced in the *Times Literary Supplement*, 12 March 1971
22 A.J.P. Taylor, *English History 1914–1945*, p. 92
23 11 December 1916, *Times*
24 Kennedy Jones, *Fleet Street and Downing Street*, p. 12
25 Koss, op. cit., p. 744
26 Koss, op. cit., p. 745
27 28 January 1918, Sir George Riddell, *The Riddell Diaries*, p. 216
28 27–28 June 1917, Trevor Wilson (ed.), *The Political Diaries of C.P. Scott*, p. 296
29 Koss, op. cit., p. 773
30 Ibid., p. 776
31 Ibid., p. 779

32 A.J.P. Taylor, *Beaverbrook*, p. 160
33 30 November 1918, Riddell, op. cit., p. 250
34 16 April 1919, *Hansard*
35 27 September 1919, Riddell, op. cit., p. 301
36 James Margach, *The Abuse of Power*, p. 16
37 11 February 1918, cabinet papers
38 19 March 1922, Taylor, *Beaverbrook*, p. 192
39 13 July 1921, *Times*
40 4 September 1922, Riddell, op. cit., p. 374
41 22 June 1922, Stevenson, op. cit., p. 242
42 6 October 1922, *Times*

2. 'Tis Pity She's a Whore: Bonar Law, Baldwin, MacDonald (1922–31)

1 6 September 1922, *Daily Herald*
2 A.J.P. Taylor, *Beaverbrook*, p. 199
3 J.C.C. Davidson, *Memoirs of a Conservative*, ed. Robert Rhodes James, p. 135
4 Ibid., p. 139
5 William Douglas Home (ed.), *The Prime Ministers*, p. 201
6 A.J.P. Taylor, *English History 1914–1945*, p. 263
7 Stephen Koss, *The Rise and Fall of the Political Press in Britain* (1990), p. 861
8 A.J.P. Taylor, *Beaverbrook*, p. 210
9 Op. cit., p. 161
10 17 July 1923, Leo Amery, *The Leo Amery Diaries*, p. 334
11 A.W. Baldwin, *My Father: The True Story*, p. 154
12 James Margach, *The Abuse of Power*, p. 23
13 Koss, op. cit., p. 862
14 William Douglas Home (ed.), *The Prime Ministers*, p. 206
15 Roy Jenkins, *Baldwin*, p. 62
16 Koss, op. cit., p. 864
17 Davidson, op. cit., p. 167
18 Jenkins, op. cit., p. 73
19 Stephen Koss, *The Rise and Fall of the Political Press in Britain*, vol 2, p. 427
20 13 November 1923, *Times*
21 28 November 1923, *Manchester Guardian*
22 Koss, op. cit., p. 439
23 Taylor, *English History 1914–45*, op. cit., p. 271
24 Margach, op. cit., p. 37
25 14 December 1923, *New Leader*
26 Harold Nicolson, *King George the Fifth*, p. 387
27 Koss, op. cit., p. 437
28 15 March 1924, Beatrice Webb, *The Diaries of Beatrice Webb*, p. 427
29 Margach, op. cit., p. 38
30 Hamilton Fyfe, *My Seven Selves*, p. 258
31 *Workers' Weekly*, 25 July 1923
32 David Marquand, *Ramsay MacDonald*, p. 378
33 Ibid., p. 381–3
34 17 May 1924, *People*
35 Koss, op. cit., p. 438
36 Davidson, op. cit., p. 201
37 John Evelyn Wrench, *Geoffrey Dawson and Our Times*, p. 245
38 John Murray, *The General Strike of 1926*, p. 121
39 Ibid., p. 122
40 Roy Jenkins, *Churchill*, p. 409
41 Davidson, op. cit., p. 246
42 Koss, op. cit., p. 468
43 Richard Cockett in *Conservative Century*, ed. Seldon and Ball, p. 551
44 *Institute of Journalists Journal*, December 1928
45 9 December 1928, *Sunday Despatch*
46 Marquand, op. cit., p. 487
47 Koss, op. cit., p. 488
48 Taylor, *Beaverbrook*, p. 247
49 23 January 1930, to E.M. Young, Taylor, *Beaverbrook*, p. 275
50 19 February 1931, East Islington by-election
51 Margach, op. cit., p. 23
52 BBC poll, 1995
53 17 March 1931, Queen's Hall, Westminster
54 Anne Chisholm and Michael Davie, *Beaverbrook*, p. 304
55 Anthony Jay (ed.), *Oxford Dictionary of Political Quotations*, p. 214
56 Robert Skidelsky, *Politicians and the Slump*, p. 238
57 Marquand, op. cit., p. 576
58 Ibid., p. 576
59 Andrew Sparrow, *Obscure Scribblers*, p. 73

3. A Farewell to Arms: MacDonald Again, Baldwin Again, Chamberlain 'never again' (1931–40)

1 Stephen Koss, *The Rise and Fall of the Political Press in Britain*, vol. 2, p. 496
2 John Evelyn Wrench, *Geoffrey Dawson and Our Times*, p. 291
3 L. McNeill Weir, *The Tragedy of Ramsay MacDonald*, p. 441
4 David Marquand, *Ramsay MacDonald*, p. 671

5   Andrew Sparrow, *Obscure Scribblers*,
    p. 76
6   A.J.P. Taylor, *English History
    1914–1945*, p. 387
7   Margaret Scammell, *Designer Politics*,
    p. 35
8   K.D. Ewing and C.A. Gearty, *The
    Struggle for Civil Liberties: Political
    Freedom and the Rule of Law in Britain,
    1914–1945*, p. 217
9   R.D. Blumenfeld, *The Press in My
    Time*, p. 124
10 10 March 1934, *Astor Papers*
11 Koss, op. cit., p. 533
12 Stevenson, *Lloyd George*, p. 297
13 Koss, op. cit., p. 525
14 *Hansard*, 12 November 1936
15 'Cato', *Guilty Men*, p. 137
16 W.F. Deedes, *Dear Bill*, p. 58
17 Davidson, *Memoirs of a Conservative*, ed.
    Robert Rhodes James, p. 411
18 5 November 1936, *Chips, The Diaries
    of Sir Henry Channon*, ed. Robert
    Rhodes James, p. 75
19 23 November 1936, ibid., p. 85
20 28 November 1936, ibid., p. 86
21 Wrench, op. cit., p. 349
22 Hugh Cudlipp, *Publish and Be Damned!*
    p. 100
23 3 December 1936, *Diaries and Letters
    1930–39*, Harold Nicolson, p. 281
24 A.J.P. Taylor, *Beaverbrook*, p. 370
25 King Edward VIII, *A King's Story*,
    p. 402
26 James Margach, *The Abuse of Power*,
    p. 50
27 Robert Self, *Neville Chamberlain*, p. 1
28 Ibid., p. 150
29 Richard Cockett in *Conservative
    Century*, ed. Seldon and Ball, p. 549
30 J.C.C. Davidson, op. cit., p. 273
31 Ibid., p. 274
32 Richard Cockett, *Twilight of Truth*,
    p. 11
33 Margach, op. cit., p. 52
34 Cockett, op. cit., p. 48
35 Self, op. cit., p. 338
36 'Cato', *Guilty Men*, p. 59
37 30 August 1938, Cockett, op. cit., p. 64
38 30 September 1938, *Daily Express*
39 Cockett, op. cit., p. 81
40 A.J.P. Taylor, *English History
    1914–1945*, p. 512
41 Cockett, op. cit., p. 56
42 Letter to Lord Lothian, Margach, op.
    cit., p. 54
43 German memo, quoted in Cockett,
    op. cit., p. 67
44 R.A. Butler, *The Art of the Possible*,
    p. 69; see also Koss, op. cit., p. 580
45 Foreign Office papers, Cockett, op.
    cit., p. 39
46 Telegram to Foreign Office, 16 August
    1939, HM Stationery Office, 1953,
    vol. VII, no. 37
47 27 April 1939, Donald McLaughlin, *In
    The Chair*, p. 103
48 Cockett, op. cit., p. 51
49 4 October 1938, *Times*
50 Ronald Tree, *When the Moon Was High*,
    p. 76
51 Cockett, op. cit., p. 85
52 Margach, op. cit., p. 55
53 22 November 1938, Hansard
54 Halifax papers quoted in Cockett, op.
    cit., p. 105
55 16 March 1939, *Times*
56 2 July 1939, *Sunday Pictorial*
57 13 July 1939, *Times*

4. Put Out More Flags: Churchill (1940–45)

1   3 November 1939, cabinet minutes
    quoted in Margach, *The Abuse of Power*,
    p. 62
2   J.C.C. Davidson, *Memoirs of a
    Conservative*, ed. Robert Rhodes
    James, p. 425
3   Francis Williams, *A Prime Minister
    Remembers*, p. 5
4   Ian McLaine, *Ministry of Morale*, p. 27
5   Michael Balfour, *Propaganda in War
    1939–1945*, p. 60
6   3 January 1940, John Colville, *The
    Fringes of Power*, p. 45
7   A.J.P. Taylor, *Beaverbrook*, p. 396
8   7 January 1940, Colville, op. cit., p. 47
9   29 March 1940, interview with W.P.
    Crozier
10 9 April 1940, Colville, op. cit., p. 76
11 6 May 1940, *Times*
12 6 May 1940, Colville, op. cit., p. 91
13 7 May 1940, *Hansard*
14 13 May 1940, *Hansard*
15 14 June 1940, Sir Henry Channon,
    Chips, ed. Robert Rhodes James,
    p. 257
16 Taylor, op. cit., p. 411
17 Lt.-Gen. Sir Ian Jacob, future director
    general of the BBC, 11 August 1940,
    Colville, op. cit., p. 182
18 Kenneth Young, *Churchill and
    Beaverbrook*, p. 12
19 Stephen Koss, *The Rise and Fall of the
    Political Press in Britain*, vol. 2, p. 601n
20 Balfour, op. cit., p. 64

21 McLaughlin, op. cit., p. 194
22 Arthur Christiansen, *Headlines All My Life*, p. 220
23 18 June 1940, Colville, op. cit., p. 135
24 30 June 1943, Guildhall speech
25 9 June 1940, McLaine, op. cit., p. 89
26 Koss, op. cit., p. 604
27 Francis Williams, *Press, Parliament and the People*, p. 35
28 Hugh Cudlipp, *Publish and Be Damned!*, p. 143
29 7 June 1940, King diary entry, ibid., p. 146
30 8 October 1940, ibid., p. 149
31 12 October 1940, ibid., p. 152
32 30 January 1941, ibid., p. 164
33 25 January 1941, ibid., p. 163
34 11 February 1941, ibid., p. 167
35 4 March 1942, *Daily Mirror*
36 Williams, Francis Williams, *Press, Parliament and the People*, p. 35
37 Cudlipp, op. cit., p. 180
38 Koss, op. cit., p. 607
39 13 May 1941, *Daily Express*
40 28 May 1941, McLaine, op. cit., p. 235
41 Balfour, op. cit., p. 65
42 McLaine, op. cit., p. 7
43 Balfour, op. cit., p. 70
44 Often quoted with reference to the D-Day landings but unsourced
45 Kenneth Harris, *Clement Attlee*, p. 194
46 13 February 1942, Channon, op. cit., p. 321
47 9 February 1942, Taylor, op. cit., p. 511
48 Taylor, op. cit., p. 518
49 Koss, op. cit., p. 611
50 David Farrer, *G – for God Almighty*, p. 92
51 Taylor, op. cit., p. 531
52 Alan Bullock, *Life and Times of Ernest Bevin*, vol. 2, p. 177
53 McLaughlin, op. cit., p. 194
54 18 January 1945, *Hansard*
55 McLaughlin, op. cit., p. 253
56 6 September 1944, Channon, op. cit., p. 393

5. Of Mice and Men: Attlee, Churchill Again (1945–55)

1 4 June 1945, *BBC*
2 Roy Jenkins, *Churchill*, p. 791
3 5 June 1945, *Daily Express*
4 5 June 1945, Robert Rhodes James (ed.), *'Chips': The Diaries of Sir Henry Channon*, p. 408
5 5 June 1945, *BBC*
6 12 June 1945, *Daily Express*
7 Arthur Christiansen, *Headlines All My Life*, p. 238
8 Hugh Cudlipp, *Publish and Be Damned!*, p. 229
9 R.B. McCallum and Alison Readman, *British General Election of 1945*, p. 181
10 Roy Greenslade, *Press Gang*, p. 34–6
11 Clement Attlee, *As It Happened*, p. 167
12 Cecil King, *Strictly Personal*, p. 118
13 Christiansen, op. cit., p. 241
14 Francis Williams, *Nothing So Strange*, p. 215
15 Lord Burnham to students at London University, Francis Williams, *Press, Parliament and People*, p. 165
16 Francis Beckett, *Clem Attlee*, p. 208
17 Ibid., p. 208
18 Ibid., p. 198
19 James Margach, *The Abuse of Power*, p. 89
20 Peter Hennessy, *The Prime Minister*, p. 148
21 Ibid., p. 86
22 Dominic Wring, *The Politics of Marketing The Labour Party*, p. 22
23 Bernard Donoughue and G.W. Jones, *Herbert Morrison*, p. 359
24 Kenneth Harris, *Clement Attlee*, p. 324
25 Williams, op, cit., p. 226
26 Marjorie Ogilvy-Webb, *The Government Explains*, p. 55
27 28 July 1947, *Daily Mirror*, Greenslade, op. cit., p. 37
28 30 July 1946, speech in Battersea
29 Greenslade, op. cit., p. 33
30 18 March 1948, A.J.P. Taylor, *Beaverbrook*, p. 185
31 Lord Camrose, *British Newspapers and their Controllers*, p. 3
32 26 July 1949, H.M.S.O
33 Peter Hennessy, *Never Again*, p. 329
34 First used by the Soviet news agency TASS in 1976
35 Beckett, op. cit., p. 279
36 H.G. Nicholas, *The British General Election of 1950*, p. 153
37 King, op. cit., p. 119
38 22 March 1950, memo to the NEC, Donoughue and Jones, op. cit., p. 455
39 Hennessy, *The Prime Minister*, op. cit., p. 170
40 8 October 1951, *Manchester Guardian*
41 Beckett, op. cit., p. 293
42 Hennessy, *The Prime Minister*, p. 178
43 John Colville, *The Fringes of Power*, p. 596
44 Hennessy, *The Prime Minister*, p. 183
45 16 August 1952, ibid., p. 201
46 23 June 1953, Colville, op. cit., p. 626

47 Ibid., p. 626
48 Ibid., p. 627
49 Margach, op. cit., p. 68
50 To his PPS, Evelyn Shuckburgh, Roy Jenkins, *Churchill*, p. 877
51 Hennessy, *The Prime Minister*, p. 183–4
52 1 April 1954, *Daily Mirror*
53 Colville, op. cit., p. 662

6. Great Expectations: Eden, Macmillan, Douglas-Home (1955–64)

1 David Carlton, *Anthony Eden*, p. 376
2 David Dutton, *Anthony Eden*, p. 462
3 James Margach, *The Abuse of Power*, p. 105
4 Peter Hennessy, *The Prime Minister*, p. 247
5 Michael Cockerell, *Live From Number 10*, p. 36
6 Robert Rhodes James, *Anthony Eden*, p. 412
7 William Clark, *From Three Worlds*, p. 155
8 Ibid., p. 157
9 Margach, op. cit., p. 110
10 3 January 1956, *Daily Telegraph*
11 Rhodes James, op. cit., p. 425
12 R.A. Butler, *The Art of the Possible*, p. 184
13 18 January 1956, Rhodes James, op. cit., p. 426
14 Margach, op. cit., p. 108
15 3 August 1956, Clark, op. cit., p. 169
16 Iverach McDonald, *The History of* The Times, vol. V, p. 263
17 David Harvey postscript, Clark, op cit., p. 283
18 Cockerell, op. cit., p. 45
19 Grace Wyndham Goldie, *Facing the Nation*, p. 177
20 Harman Grisewood, *One Thing at a Time*, p. 193
21 Rhodes James, op. cit., p. 569
22 3 November 1955, *Hansard*
23 Clark, op. cit., 203
24 Ibid., p. 207
25 Cockerell, op. cit., p. 49
26 Clark, op. cit., p. 208
27 Ibid., p. 212
28 Hennessy, op. cit., p. 218
29 Interview with Peter Hennessy, ibid., p. 251
30 Anthony Sampson, *Macmillan*, p. 170
31 24 January 1962, Conservative party political broadcast
32 Michael Foot et al., *Supermac*, p. 16

33 Sir Harold Evans, *Downing Street Diary*, p. 63
34 Charles Hill, *Both Sides of the Hill*, p. 179
35 Evans, op. cit., p. 27
36 Cockerell, op. cit., p. 55
37 Sir Robin Day, *Grand Inquisitor*, p. 1
38 Margach, op. cit., p. 118
39 David Butler and Richard Rose, *The British General Election of 1959*, p. 18
40 Peter Cook, *Tragically I was the Only Twin*, p. 51
41 W.F. Deedes, *Dear Bill*, p. 148
42 Margach, op. cit., p. 122
43 Evans, op. cit., p. 66
44 29 March 1962, cabinet minutes
45 22 March 1963, *Hansard*
46 13 June 1963, TV interview
47 Harold Macmillan, *At The End of the Day*, p. 442
48 Evans, op. cit., p. 70
49 Margach, op. cit., p. 124
50 Evans, op. cit., p. 229
51 John Dickie, *The Uncommon Commoner*, p. 193
52 Margach, op. cit., p. 129
53 Dickie, op. cit., p. 193
54 21 October 1963, TV interview
55 21 October 1963, *Daily Herald*
56 20 October 1963, James Cameron, *Sunday Mirror*
57 Margaret Thatcher, *The Path to Power*, p. 130
58 Kenneth Young, *Sir Alec Douglas Home*, p. 173
59 Lord Home, *The Way The Wind Blows*, p. 201
60 17 February 1964
61 Day, op. cit., p. 221
62 Young, op. cit., p. 214
63 Home, op. cit., p. 201
64 Deedes, op. cit., p. 190
65 David Butler and Anthony King, *The British General Election of 1964*, p. 92
66 Wyndham Goldie, op. cit., p. 270
67 Ibid., p. 271
68 D.R. Thorpe, *Alec Douglas-Home*, p. 8

7. Brave New World: Wilson (1964–70)

1 Philip Ziegler, *Wilson*, p. 157
2 Sir Robin Day, *Grand Inquisitor*, p. 222
3 Sir Trevor Lloyd-Hughes, unpublished draft memoirs
4 David Butler and Anthony King, *The British General Election of 1964*, p. 201
5 Ruth Dudley Edwards, *Newspapermen*, p. 339
6 Butler and King, op. cit., p. 92

7   James Margach, *The Abuse of Power*, p. 140
8   Lloyd-Hughes, op. cit.
9   Interview with the author
10 Ben Pimlott, *Harold Wilson*, p. 60
11 Michael Cockerell, *Live From Number 10*, p. 117
12 Lloyd-Hughes, op. cit.
13 Michael Cockerell, Peter Hennessy and David Walker, *Sources Close to the Prime Minister*, p. 123
14 Lloyd-Hughes, op. cit.
15 Lloyd-Hughes, op. cit.
16 Dudley Edwards, op. cit., p. 345
17 10 December 1965, *Spectator*
18 30 April 1966, *Guardian*
19 20 March 1966, Richard Crossman, *Crossman Diaries*, p. 191
20 13 March 1966, Tony Benn, *Out of the Wilderness*, p. 397
21 Lloyd-Hughes, op. cit.
22 4 July 1967, *Times*
23 22 February 1965, cabinet minutes
24 2 June 1966, Benn, op. cit., p. 421
25 Interview with the author
26 9 June 1966, Barbara Castle, *Castle Diaries 1964–70*, p.132–3
27 11 May 1967, ibid., p. 254
28 24 June 1968, ibid., p. 468
29 Lloyd-Hughes, op. cit.
30 Harold Wilson, *The Labour Government 1964–70*, p. 478
31 Lloyd-Hughes, op. cit.
32 Interview with Pimlott, op. cit., p. 447
33 26 January 1968, *Financial Times*
34 Marcia Williams, *Inside Number Ten*, p. 182
35 Grace Wyndham-Goldie, *Facing the Nation*, p. 298
36 Lord Windlesham, *Broadcasting in a Free Society*, p. 35
37 21 September 1967, cabinet minutes
38 Margach, op. cit., p. 153
39 Ziegler, op. cit., p. 295
40 Dudley Edwards, op. cit., p. 348
41 30 September 1967, *Morning Star*
42 6 February 1968, Tony Benn, *Office Without Power*, p. 30
43 17 February 1968, ibid., p. 37
44 Denis Healey, *The Time of My Life*, p. 337
45 Dudley Edwards, op. cit., p. 369
46 Hugh Cudlipp, *Walking on the Water*, p. 356
47 15 July 1970, diary entry, Dudley Edwards, op. cit., p. 372
48 10 May 1968, *Daily Mirror*

49 Cudlipp, op. cit., p. 371
50 11 May 1968, *Times*
51 6 February 1968, Benn, *Office Without Power*, p. 31
52 Williams, op. cit., p. 181
53 Bernard Donoughue, *The Heat of the Kitchen*, p. 118
54 Interview with the author
55 4 May 1969, May Day rally, Festival Hall, London
56 Interview with Pimlott, op. cit., p. 535
57 Interview with Ziegler, op. cit., p. 349
58 Ian Gilmour, quoted in David Butler and Michael Pinto-Duschinsky, *The British General Election of 1970*, p. 200
59 Williams, op. cit., p. 190
60 20 April 1968
61 20 June 1970, *Daily Express*

8. Three Men and a Boat: Heath, Wilson Again, Callaghan (1970–79)

1   John Campbell, *Edward Heath*, p. 290
2   Interview with the author
3   Michael Cockerell, *Live from Number 10*, p. 156
4   Ibid., p. 171
5   Interview with the author
6   Donald Maitland, *Diverse Times, Diverse Places*, p. 176
7   Ibid., p. 192
8   Margaret Thatcher, *The Path to Power*, p. 162
9   Robert Carr, interview with Campbell, op. cit., p. 486
10 20 June 1971, *Observer*
11 James Margach, *The Abuse of Power*, p. 158
12 11 December 1997, British diplomatic oral-history programme
13 Margach, op. cit., p. 161
14 Maitland, op. cit., p. 176
15 Andrew Sparrow, *Obscure Scribblers*, p. 134
16 Edward Heath, *The Course of My Life*, p. 372
17 Margach, op. cit., p. 161
18 10 October 1980, Conservative party conference, Brighton
19 Peter Hennessy, *The Prime Minister*, p. 353
20 Cockerell, op. cit., p. 191
21 Interview with the author
22 Cockerell, op. cit., p. 184
23 Ibid., p. 193
24 Campbell, op. cit., p. 573
25 Margach, op. cit., p. 166
26 Maitland, op. cit., p. 190

27 Robert Harris, *Good and Faithful Servant*, p. 92
28 Cockerell, op. cit., p. 179
29 Heath, op. cit., p. 517
30 3 March 1974, Barbara Castle, *The Castle Diaries 1974–76*, p. 32–3
31 Bernard Donoughue, *Prime Minister*, p. 25
32 Lady Falkender, *Downing Street in Perspective*, p. 98
33 Harris, op. cit., p. 70
34 12 June 1974, Tony Benn, *Against The Tide*, p. 173
35 Michael Cockerell, Peter Hennessy, David Walker, *Sources Close to the Prime Minister*, p. 45
36 Cockerell, op cit., p. 207
37 Joe Haines, *The Politics of Power*, p. 202
38 Interview with Martin Gilbert, Zeigler, op. cit., p. 409
39 Haines, op. cit., p. 205
40 David Butler and Dennis Kavanagh, *The British General Election of October 1974*, p. 24
41 6 October 1974, Bernard Donoughue, *Downing Street Diary*, p. 211
42 Donoughue, op. cit., p. 211
43 Peter Chippindale and Chris Horrie, *Stick It Up Your Punter!* p. 61
44 27 February 2004, *Daily Telegraph*, interview with Michael Cockerell
45 Sparrow, op. cit., p. 144
46 Ibid., p. 145
47 19 June 1975, Donoughue, op. cit., p. 420
48 8 April 1975, Benn, op. cit., p. 361
49 Ziegler, op. cit., p. 456
50 Hennessy, op. cit., p. 372–3
51 Pimlott, op. cit., p. 711
52 Goodman papers, quoted by Ziegler, op. cit., p. 472
53 Pimlott, op. cit., p. 681
54 19 June 2001, *Daily Telegraph*
55 Kenneth Morgan, *Callaghan*, p. 486
56 James Callaghan, *Time and Chance*, p. 392
57 Interview with the author
58 Callaghan, op. cit., p. 406
59 Interview with the author
60 7 December 1976, Bernard Donoughue, *Downing Street Diary*, vol. 2, p. 114
61 8 December 1976, ibid., p. 115
62 Interviews with the author
63 Morgan, op. cit., p. 476
64 9 January 2001, interview, British diplomatic oral-history programme

65 12 May 1977, *Evening Standard*
66 Interview with the author
67 16 May 1977, *Hansard*
68 Sparrow, op. cit., p. 146
69 19 May 1977, *Daily Mail*
70 Margach, op. cit., p. 183
71 22 May 1977, Tony Benn, *Conflicts of Interest*, p. 146
72 21 May 1977, *Daily Mail*
73 Royal Commission on the Press. Final Report, 1977. Cmnd 6810
74 James Thomas, *Popular Newspapers, the Labour Party and British Politics*, p. 76
75 3 March 1978, *Sun*
76 Chippindale and Horrie, op. cit., p. 67
77 6 March 1978, Donoughue, op. cit., p. 297
78 10 March 1978, ibid., p. 300
79 7 September 1977, cabinet papers, national archive
80 Interview with the author
81 Interview with the author
82 Bernard Donoughue, *The Heat of the Kitchen*, p. 308
83 Interview with the author
84 11 January 1979, *Sun*
85 Bernard Donoughue, *The Heat of the Kitchen*, p. 313–4
86 Shawcross, op. cit., p. 211
87 David Butler and Dennis Kavanagh, *The British General Election of 1979*, p. 172
88 Hugo Young and Anne Sloman, *The Thatcher Phenomenon*, p. 94
89 May 1979, *Listener*
90 Cockerell, op. cit., p. 251
91 Butler and Kavanagh, op. cit., p. 237
92 16 April 1979, *Daily Mail*
93 3 May 1979, *Sun*
94 3 May 1979, Benn, op. cit., p. 494

9. She: Thatcher (1979–90)

1 Hugo Young, *One of Us*, p. 510
2 Michael Cockerell, Peter Hennessy, David Walker, *Sources Close to the Prime Minister*, p. 52
3 Bernard Ingham, *Kill the Messenger*, p. 166
4 Ibid., p. 331
5 Norman Fowler, *A Political Suicide*, p. 57
6 Robert Harris, *Good and Faithful Servant*, p. 141
7 Ibid., p. 162
8 Bernard Ingham, *The Wages of Spin*, p. 119–20
9 Harris, op. cit., p. 126
10 2 February 1989, *Hansard*

11 Harris, op. cit., p. 82
12 21 May 1980, Festival Hall, London
13 Young, op. cit., p. 510
14 Roy Greenslade, *Press Gang*, p. 452
15 Ibid., p. 324
16 28 October 1985, *UK Press Gazette*
17 February 1990, speech to press-gallery lunch, Westminster
18 Ingham, *Kill the Messenger*, p. 168
19 Ibid., p. 170
20 John Campbell, *Margaret Thatcher: The Iron Lady*, p. 407
21 Nigel Lawson, *The View From Number 11*, p. 467
22 Young, op. cit., p. 204
23 Ingham, *The Wages of Spin*, p. 102
24 Jim Prior, *A Balance of Power*, p. 135
25 10 October 1980, Brighton Conference Centre
26 7 January 1981, *Daily Telegraph*
27 6 January 1981, *Thames Television*
28 15 September 1981, *The Image Makers*, BBC
29 Margaret Scammell, *Designer Politics*, p. 68
30 Cockerell, Hennessy, Walker., op. cit., p. 194–5
31 Margaret Thatcher, *The Downing Street Years*, p. 160
32 Greenslade, op. cit., p. 377
33 14 June 1987, Woodrow Wyatt, *The Journals of Woodrow Wyatt*, vol. 1, p. 372
34 Bruce Page, *The Murdoch Archipelago*, p. 271–2
35 Harold Evans, *Good Times, Bad Times*, p. 19
36 Page, op. cit., p. 306
37 Evans, op. cit., p. 19
38 Greenslade, op. cit., p. 384
39 1 February 1982, speech to Allied Brewery Trades Association
40 2 February 1982, *Hansard*
41 Harris, op. cit., p. 92
42 Lawson, op. cit., p. 467
43 Ingham, *Kill the Messenger*, p. 323
44 Thatcher, op. cit., p. 187
45 25 April 1982, outside Downing Street after the recapture of South Georgia
46 Ingham, *Kill the Messenger*, p. 289
47 Michael Cockerell, *Live From Number 10*, p. 270
48 1986 lecture, Harris, op. cit., p. 99
49 Ingham, *Kill the Messenger*, p. 294
50 8 December 1982, *The Handling of Press and Public Information During the Falklands Conflict*
51 2 May 1982, *BBC 2*
52 6 May 1982, *Hansard*
53 7 May 1982, *Sun*
54 4 May 1982, *Sun*
55 Robert Harris, *Gotcha!*, p. 54
56 11 May 1982, *Hansard*
57 8 May 1982, *Daily Mirror*
58 Cockerell, op. cit., p. 275
59 Ingham, *Kill the Messenger*, p. 297
60 David Butler and Gareth Butler, *British Political Facts*, p. 264
61 Harris, op. cit., p. 100
62 18 January 1983, *Hansard*
63 8 February 1983, *Hansard*
64 5 January 1988, *BBC 1*
65 Thatcher, op. cit., p. 287
66 May 1977, party political broadcast, Young, op. cit., p. 140
67 29 March 1983, *ITV*
68 David Butler and Dennis Kavanagh, *The British General Election of 1983*, p. 206
69 August 2009, Anthony Howard, letter to the author
70 24 May 1983, *BBC 1*
71 Cockerell, op. cit., p. 283
72 19 May 1983, *BBC 1*
73 Andrew Neil, *Full Disclosure*, p. 26
74 William Shawcross, *Murdoch*, p. 210
75 24 November 1983, *Daily Mirror*
76 16 May 1984
77 Granville Williams (ed.), *Shafted: The Media, the Miners' Strike and the Aftermath*, p. 82
78 Carol Thatcher, *Below the Parapet*, p. 219
79 17 December 1984, *BBC News*
80 Campbell, op. cit., p. 471
81 Ingham, *Kill the Messenger*, p. 339
82 Lawson, op. cit., p. 468
83 Harris, op. cit., p. 126
84 14 March 1985, Caledonian Club, London
85 Thatcher, op. cit., p. 431
86 7 January 1986, *Sun*
87 Thatcher, op. cit., p. 434
88 27 January 1986. Ingham's account says she was joking, Howe's does not
89 27 January 1986, Wyatt, op. cit., p. 76
90 14 January 1986, ibid., p. 55
91 Greenslade, op. cit., p. 469–78
92 Ingham, *Kill the Messenger*, p. 199
93 11 May 1986, *Weekend World*
94 Ingham, *Kill the Messenger*, p. 202
95 Harris, op. cit., p. 156
96 Ibid., p. 155
97 Cockerell, op. cit., p. 319
98 10 January 1987, *BBC*
99 4 October 1986, Wyatt, op. cit., p. 201
100 Norman Tebbit, *Upwardly Mobile*, p. 323
101 Ibid., p. 333

102　Bryan Gould, *Goodbye to All That*, p. 188

103　David Butler and Dennis Kavanagh, *The British General Election of 1987*, p. 163 & 168

104　24 May 1987, *TV–AM*

105　Thomas, Popular Newspapers, the Labour Party and British Politics, p. 96

106　11 June 1987, Wyatt, op. cit., p. 366

107　14 June 1987, ibid., p. 371

108　Campbell, op. cit., p. 449

109　Lawson, op. cit., p. 468

110　Thatcher, op. cit., p. 589

111　31 October 1987, *Woman's Own*

112　20 September 1988, College of Europe, Bruges Belfrey

113　9 April 1990, Woodrow Wyatt, *The Journals of Woodrow Wyatt*, vol. 2, p. 271

114　Simon Jenkins, *Thatcher & Sons*, p. 3

115　30 October 1990, *Hansard*

116　Lawson, op. cit., p. 855

117　27 July 1989

118　Ingham, *Kill the Messenger*, p. 333

119　Lawson, op. cit., p. 968

120　27 October 1989, *Sun*

121　Thatcher, op. cit., p. 722

122　Page, op. cit., p. 419

123　Shawcross, op. cit., p. 511

124　Campbell, op. cit., p. 411

125　26 November 1990, *Sun*

126　5 November 1990, *Times*

127　Neil, op. cit., p. 248

128　18 November 1990, *Sunday Times*

129　Neil, op. cit., p. 251

130　Campbell, op. cit., p. 747

131　Ingham, *Kill the Messenger*, p. 398

132　Campbell, op. cit., p. 461

10. Decline and Fall: Major (1990–97)

1　Alan Watkins, *A Conservative Coup*, p. 26

2　John Jenkins (ed.), *John Major*, p. 7

3　28 November 1990, outside 10 Downing Street

4　Edward Pearce, *The Quiet Rise of John Major*, p. 161

5　Sarah Hogg and Jonathan Hill, *Too Close to Call*, p. 7

6　Penny Junor, *John Major From Brixton to Downing Street*, p. 215

7　Ibid., p. 216

8　12 April 1991, Chaplin diaries quoted in *Sunday Telegraph*, 19 September 1999

9　2 October 2002, *BBC Radio 5 Live*

10　29 September 2002, *BBC News Online*

11　Interview with the author

12　Norman Fowler, *A Political Suicide*, p. 96

13　29 November 1990, Woodrow Wyatt, *The Journals of Woodrow Wyatt*, vol. 2, p. 411

14　Hogg and Hill, op. cit., p. 84

15　4 December 1990, speech, Queen Elizabeth Conference Centre, London

16　24 March 1991, Chaplin, op. cit

17　John Major, *The Autobiography*, p. 224

18　16 January 1991, *Guardian*

19　Hogg and Hill, op. cit., p. 43

20　Ibid., p. 43

21　Ibid., p. 54

22　Ibid., p. 110

23　10 June 1991, *Hansard*

24　Kenneth Baker, *The Turbulent Years*, p. 453

25　1 October 2006, *News of the World*

26　Interview with the author

27　Peter Hennessy, *The Prime Minister*, p. 474

28　29 June 1991, *Times*

29　Anthony Seldon, *Major*, p. 254

30　3–7 June 1991, Chaplin, op. cit

31　Margaret Thatcher, *The Path to Power*, p. 474–5

32　Seldon, op. cit., p. 163–4

33　28 September 1992, Gyles Brandreth, *Breaking the Code*, p. 120

34　Interview in Seldon, op. cit., p. 204

35　11 October 1991, Winter Gardens, Blackpool

36　9 October 1991

37　11 December 1991, *Daily Telegraph*

38　Thatcher, op. cit., p. 480 & 488

39　Major, op. cit., p. 291

40　Hogg and Hill, op. cit., p. 164

41　Interview in Margaret Scammell, *Designer Politics*, p. 240

42　8 May 1991, Wyatt, op. cit., p. 510

43　12 March 1992, *Guardian*

44　11 April 1992, *Sun*

45　James Thomas, *Popular Newspapers, the Labour Party and British Politics*, p. 4

46　Ibid., p. 4

47　11 April 1992, *Sunday Telegraph*

48　19 April 1992, *Sunday Telegraph*

49　David Butler and Dennis Kavanagh, *The British General Election of 1992*, p. 208

50　Hogg and Hill, op. cit., p. 233

51　Butler and Kavanagh, op. cit., p. 182

52　9 April 1992, *Sun*

53　30 October 1995, *Guardian* lecture

54　Heath, Jowell and Curtice, *Labour's Last Chance?*, p. 43

55　28 April 1993, *Independent*

56　Heath et al., op. cit., p. 44–8

57　15 April 1992, *Independent*

58 28 April 1993, *Independent*
59 Letter to Roy Greenslade, *Press Gang*, p. 607
60 14 August 2008, *Times*
61 Max Hastings, *Editor*, p. 296
62 Interview with the author
63 Interview with the author
64 27 April 1992, *Newsweek*
65 Major, op. cit., p. 334
66 Peter Chippindale and Chris Horrie, *Stick it Up Your Punter!*, p. 442
67 26 September 1992, Fowler, op. cit., p. 129
68 12 October 1992, *Guardian*
69 Major, op. cit., p. 359
70 Ibid., p. 360
71 Hastings, op. cit., p. 299–300
72 3 October 1992, *Sun*
73 24 September 1992, *Hansard*
74 25 October 1992, Fowler, op. cit., p. 147
75 Interview with the author
76 3 January 1993, *BBC 1*
77 25 February 1993, *Daily Telegraph*
78 17 March 1993, *Sun*
79 22 April 1993, Speech to the Conservative Group for Europe
80 9 June 1993, *Hansard*
81 14 June 1993, Fowler, op. cit., p. 166
82 Seldon, op. cit., p. 389
83 Ibid., p. 395
84 20 November 1993, *Economist*
85 8 October 1993, Winter Gardens, Blackpool
86 Seldon, after a private letter from Ryder, op. cit., p. 403
87 Fowler, op. cit., p. 154–5
88 Major, op. cit., p. 555–6
89 Fowler, op. cit., p. 157–9
90 9 January 1994, *Sunday Telegraph*
91 Major, op. cit., p. 556
92 Seldon, op. cit., p. 436
93 Nicholas Jones, *Soundbites and Spin Doctors*, p. 112
94 Interview with the author
95 Michael Heseltine, *Life in the Jungle*, p. 472
96 Interview with the author
97 2 May 1994, Woodrow Wyatt, *The Journals of Woodrow Wyatt*, vol. 3, p. 359
98 Interview with the author
99 18 February 1994, *Daily Telegraph*
100 Fowler, op. cit., p. 158
101 Ibid., p. 160–1
102 Major, op. cit., p. 568
103 10 April 1995, outside his London home
104 Major, op. cit., p. 550
105 13 June 1994

106 Interview with the author
107 25 April 1995, *Hansard*
108 Thatcher, op. cit., p. 469
109 28 May 1995, *Sunday Times*
110 Interview in Seldon, op. cit., p. 568
111 *British Journalism Review*, vol. 13, no. 2, 2002
112 Major, op. cit., p. 639
113 9 May 1995, *Sun*
114 4 July 1995, *Daily Mail*
115 9 July 1995, *Independent on Sunday*
116 Fowler, op. cit., p. 179
117 Interview with the author
118 Heseltine, op. cit., p. 478
119 Interview with the author
120 13 October 1995, Winter Gardens, Blackpool
121 14 October 1995, *Daily Telegraph*
122 9 November 1995, *Sun*
123 Interview with the author
124 Interviews with the author
125 11 January 1996, Sir Keith Joseph Memorial Lecture, London
126 22 May 1996, *Daily Mail*
127 23 June 1996, *Sunday Times*
128 Interview with the author
129 28 September 1996, *World At One*, BBC Radio Four
130 Major, op. cit., p. 709
131 12 February 1996, Wyatt, op. cit., p. 602
132 24 December 1996, ibid., p. 698
133 Major, op. cit., p. 709
134 Ibid., p. 709
135 Ibid., p. 698
136 Tim Luckhurst, *This is Today*, p. 146
137 5 December 1996, *World At One*, BBC Radio Four
138 30 January 1997, *Hansard*
139 Interview with the author
140 Major, op. cit., p. 700
141 15 April 1997, *Daily Mail*
142 17 March 1997, Wyatt, op. cit., p. 721
143 David Butler and Dennis Kavanagh, *The British General Election of 1997*, p. 156
144 Ibid., p. 173
145 Fowler, op. cit., p. 183
146 Seldon, op. cit., p. 734

11. A Man For All Seasons: Blair (1997–2007)

1 John Rentoul, *Tony Blair, Prime Minister*, p. 580
2 Ibid., p. 230
3 Barack Obama, *The Audacity of Hope*, p. 121
4 Speech to the parliamentary press

gallery, Nicholas Jones, *Sultans of Spin*, p. 129–30

5 12 June 2007, speech to Reuters Foundation

6 29 July 2009, *Independent*

7 17 July 1995, NewsCorp 'Leadership Conference', Hayman Island, Australia

8 17 July 1995, *Guardian*

9 15 July 1995, Alastair Campbell, *The Blair Years*, p. 74

10 Private information

11 18 March 1997, *Sun*

12 Peter Chippindale and Chris Horrie, *Stick It Up Your Punter!*, p. 478

13 Interview with Bruce Page, *The Murdoch Archipelago*, p. 430

14 Richard Stott, *Dogs and Lampposts*, p. 349

15 Anthony Seldon, *Blair*, p. 253

16 21 May 1997

17 James Thomas, *Popular Newspapers, the Labour Party and British Politics*, p. 162

18 Seldon, op. cit., p. 255

19 6 June 2001, Campbell, op. cit., p. 537

20 *British Journalism Review*, vol. 13, no. 2, 2002

21 *The Role and Duties of Special Advisers*, schedule 1, part 1 (viii)

22 2 April 1998, *Guardian*

23 25 March 1998, Jones, op. cit., p. 200–1

24 Ibid., p. 201

25 19 March 1997, *Daily Mail*

26 1 April 1998, *Guardian*

27 Jones, op. cit., p. 203

28 1 April 1998, Campbell, op. cit., p. 287

29 1 April 1998, *Hansard*

30 Jones, op. cit., p. 215

31 2 June 1998, evidence to Public Administration Select Committee

32 17 June 1998, ibid.

33 23 June 1998, Campbell, op. cit., p. 308

34 1 August 1997, Campbell, op. cit., p. 226

35 26 August 1997, Campbell, op. cit., p. 230

36 Rentoul, op. cit., p. 395

37 Jones, op. cit., p. 217

38 10 January 1999, *Sunday Times*

39 31 August 1997, Sedgefield

40 10 April 1998, Stormont

41 15 November 1997, *BBC Radio Four*

42 Jones, op. cit., p. 120

43 16 November 1997, *BBC 1*

44 Andrew Rawnsley, *Servants of the People*, p. 104

45 Colin Seymoure-Ure, *Prime Ministers and the Media*, p. 7

46 25 April 2009, *Times*

47 Interview with Seldon, op. cit., p. 670

48 9 January 1998, *Guardian*

49 12 January 1998, Campbell, op. cit., p. 271

50 18 January 1998, *Observer*

51 17 January 2007, *Hansard*,

52 Private information

53 17 October 1997, Campbell, op. cit., p. 252–3

54 Private information

55 Lance Price, *The Spin Doctor's Diary*, p. 56

56 30 October 1997, *Guardian*

57 Hugo Young, *The Hugo Young Papers*, p. 626

58 24 June 1998, *Sun*

59 Young, op. cit., p. 514

60 John Lloyd, *What the Media are Doing to Our Politics*, p. 94

61 Young, op. cit., p. 603

62 11 June 2000, *Sunday Times*

63 David Marquand, *Britain Since 1918*, p. 364

64 17 July 2000, *Times* and *Sun*

65 Rentoul, op. cit., p. 568

66 9 November 1998, *Sun*

67 12 November 1998, *BBC News on-line*

68 21 April 1999, Campbell, op. cit., p. 380

69 Ibid., p. 380

70 7 June 2000, Wembley Arena

71 15 July 2000, *BBC 2*

72 14 July 2000, Campbell, op. cit., p. 464

73 14 June 2000, Campbell, op. cit., p. 460

74 28 September 1998, Winter Gardens, Blackpool

75 Jones, op. cit., p. 275

76 24 January 2001, Price, op. cit., p. 292

77 Anthony Seldon (ed.), *The Blair Effect 2001–5*, p. 98

78 24 October and 29 November 2001, Piers Morgan, *The Insider*, p. 303 and 310

79 6 June 2001, Campbell, op. cit., p. 537

80 David Butler and Dennis Kavanagh, *The British General Election of 2001*, p. 156

81 17 May 2001, press conference, Millbank Tower

82 5 July 2001, Campbell, op. cit., p. 554–5

83 Peter Oborne and Simon Walters, *Alastair Campbell*, p. 271

84 Andrew Sparrow, *Obscure Scribblers*, p. 195

85 Oborne and Walters, op. cit., p. 272

86 Interview with the author

87 9 October 2001, *Independent*

88 Bob Franklin, *Packaging Politics*, p. 3
89 9 October 2001, Campbell, op. cit., p. 578
90 30 August 2003, *Daily Mail*
91 13 February 2002, *Hansard*
92 11 February 2002, Campbell, op. cit., p. 606
93 13 February 2002, ibid., p. 606
94 11 April, 2002, *Spectator*
95 14 June 2009, *Politics Show*, BBC 1
96 7 March 2002, Campbell, op. cit., p. 608
97 3 May 2002, *Daily Mail*
98 Oborne and Walters, op. cit., p. 301
99 16 July 2002
100 12 June 2002, *Times*
101 *British Journalism Review*, vol. 13, no. 4, 2002
102 *British Journalism Review*, vol. 13, no. 15, 2002
103 1 May 2005, *Sunday Times*
104 23 July 2002, Campbell, op. cit., p. 630
105 14 July 2004, www.directgov.co.uk
106 19 September 2002, Campbell, op. cit., p. 638
107 24 September 2002, *Evening Standard*
108 25 September 2002, *Sun*
109 24 September 2002, *Hansard*
110 5 December 2002, Campbell, op. cit., p. 649
111 10 December 2002, Department for Education Awards, London
112 Peter Stothard, *30 Days*, p. 73
113 31 January 2003, Campbell, op. cit., p. 661
114 3 February 2003, *Hansard*
115 Anthony Seldon, *Blair Unbound*, p. 150
116 7 February 2003, Campbell, op. cit., p. 664
117 Seldon, op. cit., p. 151
118 15 February 2003, Campbell, op. cit., p. 667
119 19 March 2003, ibid., p. 682
120 19 March 2003, *Independent*
121 20 March 2003
122 11 April 2003, *BBC Radio Four*
123 29 May 2003, *BBC Radio Four*
124 29 May 2003, Campbell, op. cit., p. 698
125 Lloyd, op. cit., p. 4
126 Ibid., p. 11
127 1 June 2003
128 25 June 2003
129 25 June 2003, Campbell, op. cit., p. 709
130 Letter from Richard Sambrook, BBC head of news, 27 June 2003
131 27 June 2003, *Channel 4 News*
132 30 June 2003, Campbell, op. cit., p. 711–12
133 4 July 2003, ibid., p. 713
134 18 July 2003, ibid., p. 723
135 19 July 2003, ibid., p. 723
136 19 July 2003, Tokyo
137 Seldon, op. cit., p. 220–1
138 23 August 2003, Campbell, op. cit., p. 752
139 29 August 2003, ibid., p. 757
140 26 January 2004, Lord Hutton, *Report of the Inquiry into the Circumstances Surrounding the Death of Dr David Kelly C.M.G.*, HMSO
141 Interview with the author
142 Greg Dyke, *Inside Story*, p. 31
143 *British Journalism Review*, vol. 15, no. 4, 2004
144 Interview with the author
145 Seldon, op. cit., p. 224
146 *An Independent Review of Government Communications*, January 2004
147 20 January 2004, *Independent*
148 Facebook message to the author
149 Interview with the author
150 Seldon, op. cit., p. 284
151 *Review of Intelligence on Weapons of Mass Destruction*, 14 July 2004
152 29 September 2003, Brighton International Conference Centre
153 Private information
154 28 March 2004, *News of the World*
155 15 April 2004, *Independent*
156 20 April 2004, *Hansard*
157 26 September 2004, *Sunday Times*
158 21 April 2009, *Guardian*
159 1 October 2004, *BBC News*
160 3 October 2004, *Observer*
161 Robert Peston, *Brown's Britain*, p. 349
162 6 April 2005, *BBC News*
163 David Butler and Dennis Kavanagh, *The British General Election of 2005*, p. 79
164 Dominic Wring (ed.), *Political Communications*, p. 10
165 2 April 2005, *ITV 1*
166 Osborne and Walters, op. cit., p. 194
167 Butler and Kavanagh, op. cit., p. 144
168 Ibid., p. 76
169 Seldon, op. cit., p. 346
170 8 May 2005, *Observer*
171 Interview with the author
172 11 July 2005, Gleneagles
173 12 May 2005, meeting of the Parliamentary Labour Party
174 7 December 2005, *Hansard*
175 Interview with the author
176 23 November 2005, *Financial Times*

177 Seldon, op. cit., p. 411
178 Ibid., p.429
179 6 September 2006, *Daily Mirror*
180 17 July 2006, St Petersburg
181 31 July 2006, *Guardian*
182 30 July 2006, Pebble Beach, California
183 Interview with the author
184 1 September 2006, *Times*
185 Seldon, op. cit., p. 490
186 9 September 2006, *Daily Telegraph*
187 26 September 2006, Manchester
     Conference Centre
188 15 November 2006, *Hansard*
189 15 April 2009, *Times*
190 1 September 2006, *Times*
191 3 June 2009, *Guardian*
192 23 March 2007, *Financial Times*
193 12 June 2007, *Reuters Institute*
194 Adam Boulton, *Memories of the Blair
     Administration*, p. 180
195 13 June 2007, *Daily Telegraph*
196 13 June 2007, *Guardian*
197 13 June 2007, *Times*
198 13 June 2007, *Daily Mirror*
199 13 June 2007, *Independent*
200 27 June 2007, *Hansard*
201 Anthony Seldon (ed.), *Blair's Britain*,
     p. 133
202 Peter Hennessy, *The Prime Minister*, p. 86

12. Sunset Song: Gordon Brown (2007–)

1   27 June 2007, 10 Downing Street
2   Interview with the author
NOTE: To avoid repetitive references, all
quotations in this chapter are from
interviews with the author unless otherwise
stated. Those that were conducted
attributably are sourced in the text. Those
without attribution are from interviews
granted on the basis of anonymity.
3   Robert Peston, *Brown's Britain*, p. 321
4   11 May 2007, Imagination Gallery,
    London
5   30 September 1997, *Scottish Television*
6   25 June 2007, *BBC 1*
7   20 July 2009, *Guardian*
8   14 March 2003, *UK Press Gazette*
9   Nick Davies, *Flat Earth News*, p. 336
10 Hugo Young, *The Hugo Young Papers*,
    p. 673
11 24 January 2007, *Daily Telegraph*
12 3 June 2009, *Guardian*
13 3 June 2009, quoted by Andy Beckett,
    Guardian
14 25 September 2007, Bournemouth
    International Conference Centre
15 27 September 2007

16 10 May 2009, *Sunday Times*
17 8 October 2007, Martin Kettle, *Guardian*
18 7 October 2007
19 12 October 2007, *UK Press Gazette*
20 Ibid.
21 Ibid.
22 12 October 2007, *BBC 2*
23 15 October 2007, *Media Guardian*
24 Ibid.
25 15 October 2007, *Guardian*
26 10 May 2009, *Sunday Times*
27 15 July 2009, *New Statesman*
28 25 October 2007
29 6 November 2007, *Times*
30 14 November 2007, *BBC Radio Four*
31 18 November 2007, *Observer*
32 28 November 2007, *Hansard*
33 10 May 2009, *Sunday Times*
34 19 December 2007, 10 Downing Street
35 5 April 2008, *Independent*
36 13 March 2008, *PR Week*
37 11 May 2008, *BBC World Service*
38 14 April 2008, *Guardian*
39 18 June 2008, *Guardian*
40 24 May 2008, *Sky News*
41 29 July 2008, *Guardian*
42 29 July 2008, *BBC Radio 2*
43 1 August 2008, *Times*
44 20 July 2009, *BBC Radio Five Live*
45 8 August 2008, *Sunday Times*
46 7 September 2008, *News of the World*
47 7 September 2008, *BBC News*
48 30 August 2008, *Guardian*
49 29 May 2009, *Standpoint*
50 8 September 2008, *Independent*
51 23 September 2008, Manchester G–
    Mex Conference Centre
52 15 September 2008, *Sky News*
53 28 September 2008, *Observer*
54 25 September 2008, *Daily Mail*
55 8 June 2001, Hartlepool
56 22 October 2008
57 12 December 2008, *BBC News*
58 28 December 2009, *Observer*
59 28 December 2009, *Mail on Sunday*
60 2 January 2009, Martin Kettle,
    Guardian
61 15 October 2008, *Times*
62 8 March 2009, *Mail on Sunday*
63 3 March 2009, *Daily Telegraph*
64 12 April 2009, *Mail on Sunday*
65 20 July 2009, *Guardian*
66 11 April 2009, *BBC News*
67 11 April 2009
68 15 April 2009, *Today programme, BBC
    Radio Four*
69 28 October 2009, *UK Press Gazette*
70 14 April 2009, *Evening Standard*

71 11 April 2009, *Sky News*
72 18 April 2009, *Independent*
73 12 April 2009
74 15 April 2009, www.order-order.com
75 15 April 2009, *Times*
76 16 April 2009 *Strathspey and Badenoch Herald*
77 13 April 2009, *Sun*
78 11 April 2009 *Daily Telegraph*
79 13 April 2009, *Guardian*
80 13 April 2009, letter to Sir Gus O'Donnell
81 15 April 2009, *Times*
82 19 April 2009, *Sunday Times*
83 19 April 2009, *BBC News*
84 23 April 2009, *Times*
85 Robert Winnett and Gordon Rayner, *No Expenses Spared*, p. 3
86 Ibid., p. 5
87 Ibid., p. 146
88 10 May 2009, *Sunday Telegraph*
89 Winnett and Rayner, op. cit., p. 206
90 12 May 2009, *Guardian*
91 15 May 2009
92 17 May 2009, *News of the World*
93 27 May 2009, *Times*
94 6 May 2009, *Daily Mail*
95 3 May 2009, *Observer*
96 Private information
97 29 April, 2009, *Hansard*
98 11 May 2009, *Hansard*
99 31 May 2009 *Sunday AM*, BBC 1
100 3 June 2009, *Guardian*
101 4 June 2009, resignation letter
102 4 June 2009, *BBC Radio Five Live*
103 8 June 2009, *Sky News*
104 3 June 2009, *Guardian*

105 1 July 2009, Reform Club debate
106 11 September 2009, *Times*
107 24 September 2009, *Daily Mirror*
108 27 September 2009, *The Andrew Marr Show*, BBC 1
109 28 September 2009, *Guardian*
110 29 September 2009, Brighton Conference Centre
111 29 September 2009, *Sky News*
112 30 September 2009, *Sun*
113 4 October 2009, *Independent on Sunday*
114 30 September 2009, *Today* programme, BBC Radio Four
115 29 September 2009, *Sky News*
116 30 July 2009, *Daily Telegraph*
117 30 September 2009, *Today* programme, BBC Radio Four
118 3 October 2009, www.labour.org.uk

Conclusion: Atonement

1 Francis Williams, *The Right to Know*, p. 153
2 Anne Chisholm and Michael Davie, *Beaverbrook*, p. 276
3 24 June 2008, *Guardian*
4 Walter Bagehot, *The English Constitution*, p. 100
5 9 August 1996, *New Statesman*
6 1 July 2009, Reform Club debate
7 Bagehot, op. cit., p. 61
8 2 June 2009, *Financial Times*
9 26 July 2000, *Hansard*
10 2 June 2009, John Bercow, *The Speakership in the Twenty First Century*
11 *British Journalism Review*, vol. 18 No. 3, 2007

BIBLIOGRAPHY

Adams, R. J. Q., *Bonar Law*, John Murray, 1999

Amery, Leo, *The Leo Amery Diaries*, Hutchinson, 1980

Anderson, Bruce, *John Major*, Fourth Estate, 1991

Attlee, C. R., *As It Happened*, Odhams Press, 1954

Bagehot, Walter, *The English Constitution*, Fontana, 1963

Baker, Kenneth, *The Turbulent Years*, Faber & Faber, 1993

Baldwin, A. W., *My Father: The True Story*, George Allen & Unwin, 1955

Balfour, Michael, *Propaganda in War 1939–1945*, Routledge & Kegan Paul, 1979

Barnett, Steven, and Gaber, Ivor, *Westminster Tales*, Continuum, 2001

Bartle, John, and Griffith, Dylan, eds, *Political Communications Transformed*, Palgrave Macmillan, 2001

Beaverbrook, Lord, *Politicians and the Press*, Hutchinson, 1926

—— *Politicians and the War*, Collins, 1928

—— *The Decline and Fall of Lloyd George*, Collins, 1962

Beckett, Francis, *Clem Attlee*, Richard Cohen Books, 1997

Benn, Tony, *Out of the Wilderness, Diaries 1963–67*, Arrow, 1988

—— *Office Without Power, Diaries 1968–72*, Arrow, 1989

—— *Against the Tide, Diaries 1973–76*, Arrow, 1990

—— *Conflicts of Interest, Diaries 1977–80*, Arrow, 1991

Birkenhead, Lord, *Lord Halifax*, Hamish Hamilton, 1965

Blake, Robert, *The Unknown Prime Minister*, Eyre & Spottiswoode, 1955

Blumenfeld, R. D., *The Press in My Time*, Rich and Cowan, 1933

Boulton, Adam, *Memories of the Blair Administration*, Simon & Schuster, 2008

Bower, Tom, *Gordon Brown, Prime Minister*, Harper Perennial, 2007

Brandreth, Gyles, *Breaking the Code*, Weidenfeld & Nicolson, 1999

Bullock, Alan, *The Life and Times of Ernest Bevin*, William Heinemann, 1960–82

Butler, D. E., *The British General Election of 1951*, Macmillan, 1999

—— and Rose, Richard, *The British General Election of 1955*, Macmillan, 1999

—— *The British General Election of 1959*, Macmillan, 1999

—— and King, Anthony, *The British General Election of 1964*, Macmillan, 1999

—— *The British General Election of 1966*, Macmillan, 1999

—— and Pinto-Duschinsky, Michael, *The British General Election of 1970*, Macmillan, 1999

Butler, David, and Butler, Gareth, *British Political Facts 1900–85*, Macmillan, 1986

—— and Kavanagh, Dennis, *The British General Election of February 1974*, Macmillan, 1999

—— *The British General Election of October 1974*, Macmillan, 1999

—— *The British General Election of 1979*, Macmillan, 1999

—— *The British General Election of 1983*, Macmillan, 1999

—— *The British General Election of 1987*, Macmillan, 1999

—— *The British General Election of 1992*, Macmillan, 1999

Butler, R.A., *The Art of the Possible*, Hamish Hamilton, 1971

Campbell, Alastair, *The Blair Years*, Hutchinson, 2007

Campbell, John, *Edward Heath*, Jonathan Cape, 1993

Campbell, John, *Margaret Thatcher*, vol. 2, *The Iron Lady*, Vintage, 2004

Camrose, Lord, *British Newspapers and their Controllers*, Cassell, 1947

Carlton, David, *Anthony Eden*, Allen Lane, 1981

Castle, Barbara, *The Castle Diaries 1974–76*, Weidenfeld & Nicolson, 1980

—— *The Castle Diaries 1964–70*, Weidenfeld & Nicolson, 1984

'Cato', *Guilty Men*, Victor Gollancz, 1940

Chippindale, Peter, and Horrie, Chris, *Stick It Up Your Punter!*, Pocket Books, 1999

Chisholm, Anne, and Davie, Michael, *Beaverbrook*, Hutchinson, 1992

Christiansen, Arthur, *Headlines All My Life*, Heinemann, 1961

Churchill, Winston, *The Second World War*, vols 1–6, Cassells, 1948–54

Clark, William, *From Three Worlds*, Sidgwick & Jackson, 1986

Cockerell, Michael, *Live From Number 10*, Faber & Faber, 1988

Cockerell, Michael, Hennessy, Peter, and Walter, David, *Sources Close to the Prime Minister*, Macmillan, 1984

Cockett, Richard, *Twilight of Truth*, Weidenfeld & Nicolson, 1989

Cole, G. D. H., *A History of the Labour Party from 1914*, Routledge & Kegan Paul, 1948

Cole, John, *The Thatcher Years*, BBC Books, 1987

Colville, John, *The Fringes of Power*, Phoenix, 2005

Cook, Peter, *Tragically I was an Only Twin: The Complete Peter Cook*, ed. William Cook, Century, 2002

Cooper, Duff, *Old Men Forget*, Rupert Hart-Davis, 1955

Cowling, Maurice, *The Impact of Labour*, Cambridge University Press, 1971

Crossman, Richard, *The Crossman Diaries*, Magnum Books, 1979

Cudlipp, Hugh, *Publish and Be Damned!*, Andrew Darkers, 1953

—— *Walking on the Water*, Bodley Head, 1976

—— *The Prerogative of the Harlot*, Bodley Head, 1980

Curran, James, and Seaton, Jean, *Power Without Responsibility*, Routledge, 2003

Davies, Nick, *Flat Earth News*, Chatto & Windus, 2008

Day, Sir Robin, *Grand Inquisitor*, Weidenfeld & Nicolson, 1989

Deedes, William, *Dear Bill*, Pan, 2006

Dickie, John, *The Uncommon Commoner*, Pall Mall Press, 1964

Donoughue, Bernard, *Prime Minister*, Jonathan Cape, 1987

——— *The Heat of the Kitchen*, Politico's, 2003

——— *Downing Street Diary*, Jonathan Cape, 2005

——— *Downing Street Diary*, vol. 2, Jonathan Cape, 2008

——— and Jones, G. W., *Herbert Morrison*, Phoenix, 2001

Dorril, Stephen, and Ramsay, Robin, *Smear! Wilson and the Secret State*, Fourth Estate, 1991

Dutton, David, *Anthony Eden*, Arnold, 1997

——— *Douglas-Home*, Haus Publishing, 2006

Dyke, Greg, *Inside Story*, HarperCollins, 2004

Eden, Sir Anthony, *Full Circle*, Cassell, 1960

——— *Facing the Dictators*, Cassell, 1962

Evans, Harold, *Good Times, Bad Times*, Weidenfeld & Nicolson, 1983

——— *My Paper Chase*, Little, Brown, 2009

Evans, Sir Harold, *Downing Street Diary*, Hodder & Stoughton, 1981

Ewing, K. D., and Gearty, C. A., *The Struggle for Civil Liberties: Political Freedom and the Rule of Law in Britain, 1914–1945*, Oxford University Press, 2001

Falkender, Marcia, *Downing Street in Perspective*, Weidenfeld & Nicolson, 1983

Farrer, David, *G – for God Almighty*, Weidenfeld & Nicolson, 1969

Feiling, Keith, *The Life of Neville Chamberlain*, Macmillan, 1946

Fisher, Nigel, *Harold Macmillan*, Weidenfeld & Nicolson, 1982

Foot, Michael, *Debts of Honour*, Davis Poynter, 1980

——— *Loyalists and Loners*, William Collins, 1986

——— *Supermac: The Cartoons of Victor Weisz*, Park McDonald, 1996

Fowler, Norman, *A Political Suicide*, Politico's, 2008

Franklin, Bob, *Packaging Politics*, Arnold, 2004

Fyfe, Hamilton, *My Seven Selves*, Allen & Unwin, 1935

Gannon, Franklin, *The British Press and Germany 1936–1939*, Clarendon Press, 1971

Giddens, Anthony, *Over to You, Mr Brown*, Polity Press, 2007

Gilbert, Martin, *Churchill*, Heinemann, 1991

Gould, Bryan, *Goodbye to All That*, Macmillan, 1995

Grisewood, Harman, *One Thing at a Time*, Hutchinson, 1968

Haines, Joe, *The Politics of Power*, Jonathan Cape, 1977

——— *Glimmers of Twilight*, Politico's, 2003

Hargreaves, Ian, *Journalism*, Oxford, 2003

Harris, Kenneth, *Attlee*, Weidenfeld & Nicolson, 1982

Harris, Robert, *Gotcha!*, Faber & Faber, 1983

——— *Good and Faithful Servant*, Faber & Faber, 1990

Harrop, Martin, and Miller, William L., *Elections and Voters*, Macmillan, 1987

Hastings, Max, *Editor*, Pan, 2003

Healey, Denis, *The Time of My Life*, Michael Joseph, 1989

Heath, Anthony, Jowell, Roger, and Curtice, John, *Labour's Last Chance?*, Dartmouth, 1994

Heath, Edward, *The Course of My Life*, Hodder & Stoughton, 1998

Hennessy, Peter, *Never Again*, Jonathan Cape, 1992

—— *The Prime Minister*, Penguin, 2001

—— and Seldon, Anthony, eds, *Ruling Performance*, Blackwell, 1987

Heseltine, Michael, *Life in the Jungle*, Hodder & Stoughton, 2000

Hill, Charles, *Both Sides of the Hill*, Heinemann, 1964

Hogg, Sarah, and Hill, Jonathan, *Too Close to Call*, Little, Brown, 1995

Home, Lord, *The Way the Wind Blows*, Fontana, 1978

Horsman, Mathew, *Sky High*, Orion, 1998

Howe, Geoffrey, *Conflict of Loyalty*, Macmillan, 1994

Hurd, Douglas, *Memoirs*, Little, Brown, 2003

Ingham, Bernard, *Kill the Messenger*, Harper Collins, 1991

Ingham, Bernard, *The Wages of Spin*, John Murray, 2003

Jay, Anthony, ed., *The Oxford Dictionary of Political Quotations*, Oxford University Press, 1996

Jenkins, John, ed., *John Major: Prime Minister*, Bloomsbury, 1990

Jenkins, Roy, *Baldwin*, Collins, 1987

—— *Churchill*, Pan, 2002

Jenkins, Simon, *Thatcher & Sons*, Allen Lane, 2006

Jones, Kennedy, *Fleet Street and Downing Street*, Hutchinson, 1919

Jones, Nicholas, *Soundbites and Spin Doctors*, Cassell, 1995

—— *Sultans of Spin*, Gollancz, 2000

—— *Trading Information*, Politico's, 2006

Junor, Penny, *John Major: From Brixton to Downing Street*, Penguin, 1996

King, Cecil, *Strictly Personal*, Weidenfeld & Nicolson, 1969

—— *With Malice Towards None*, Sidgwick & Jackson, 1970

—— *The Cecil King Diary*, Jonathan Cape, 1972

Koss, Stephen, *The Rise and Fall of the Political Press in Britain*, vol. 2, Hamish Hamilton, 1984

—— *The Rise and Fall of the Political Press in Britain*, Fontana, 1990

Lamb, Richard, *The Macmillan Years*, John Murray, 1995

Lamont, Norman, *In Office*, Little, Brown, 1999

Lawson, Nigel, *The View from No. 11*, Bantam Press, 1992

Lloyd, John, *What the Media are Doing to Our Politics*, Constable, 2004

Luckhurst, Tim, *This is Today . . .*, Aurum Press, 2001

McCallum, R. B., and Readman, Alison, *The British General Election of 1945*, Macmillan, 1999

McDonald, Iverach, *The History of The Times*, vol. V, *1939–66*, Times Books, 1984

McLachlan, Donald, *In the Chair: Barrington-Ward of 'The Times'*, Weidenfeld
& Nicolson, 1971

McLaine, Ian, *Ministry of Morale*, Allen & Unwin, 1979

Macmillan, Harold, *Riding the Storm*, Macmillan, 1971

—— *At the End of the Day*, Macmillan, 1973

McNair, Brian, *Journalism and Democracy*, Routledge, 1999

Maitland, Donald, *Diverse Times, Sundry Places*, Alpha Press, 1996

Major, John, *The Autobiography*, HarperCollins, 1999

Margach, James, *The Abuse of Power*, WH Allen, 1978

—— *The Anatomy of Power*, WH Allen, 1979

Marquand, David, *Ramsay MacDonald*, Richard Cohen Books, 1997

—— *Britain since 1918*, Weidenfeld & Nicolson, 2008

Martin, Kingsley, *The British Public and the General Strike*, L. & V. Woolf, 1926

—— *The Press the Public Wants*, Hogarth Press, 1947

Moncrieff, Chris, *Living on a Deadline*, Press Association, 2001

Morgan, Austen, J. *Ramsay MacDonald*, Manchester University Press, 1987

Morgan, Kenneth, *Labour in Power 1945–1951*, Oxford University Press, 1984

—— *Callaghan*, Oxford University Press, 1997

Morgan, Piers, *The Insider*, Ebury Press, 2005

Murray, John, *The General Strike of 1926*, Lawrence & Wishart, 1951

Neil, Andrew, *Full Disclosure*, Macmillan, 1996

Nicholas, H. G., *The British General Election of 1950*, Macmillan, 1999

Nicolson, Harold, *King George the Fifth*, Constable, 1952

—— *Diaries and Letters 1930–39*, Collins, 1966

Oakley, Robin, *Inside Track*, Bantam Press, 2001

Oborne, Peter, *The Triumph of the Political Class*, Simon & Schuster, 2007

—— *The Rise of Political Lying*, Free Press, 2005

—— and Walters, Simon, *Alastair Campbell*, Aurum Press, 2004

Ogilvy-Webb, Marjorie, *The Government Explains*, George Allen & Unwin,
1965

Page, Bruce, *The Murdoch Archipelago*, Simon & Schuster, 2003

Parkinson, Cecil, *Right at the Centre*, Weidenfeld & Nicolson, 1992

Pearce, Edward, *The Quiet Rise of John Major*, Weidenfeld & Nicolson, 1991

Pearce, Robert, *Attlee's Labour Governments*, Routledge, 1994

Pelling, Henry, *A Short History of the Labour Party*, Macmillan, 1972

Penrose, Barrie, and Courtoir, Roger, *The Pencourt File*, Secker & Warburg,
1978

Peston, Robert, *Brown's Britain*, Short Books, 2005

Pimlott, Ben, *Harold Wilson*, 1992

Price, Lance, *The Spin Doctor's Diary*, Hodder & Stoughton, 2005

Prior, Jim, *Balance of Power*, Hamish Hamilton, 1986

Ramsden, John, *The Age of Balfour and Baldwin*, Longman, 1978

—— *The Making of Conservative Party Policy*, Longman, 1980

Rawnsley, Andrew, *Servants of the People*, Penguin, 2001

Rentoul, John, *Tony Blair, Prime Minister*, Little, Brown, 2001

Rhodes James, Robert, ed., *'Chips': The Diaries of Sir Henry Channon*, Weidenfeld & Nicolson, 1967

—— *Anthony Eden*, Weidenfeld & Nicolson, 1986

Riddell, Lord, *War Diary*, Ivor Nichols and Watson, 1933

Roberts, Andrew, *'The Holy Fox' – The Life of Lord Halifax*, Weidenfeld & Nicolson, 1991

Rogers, Simon, ed., *The Hutton Inquiry and Its Impact*, Politico's, 2004

Routledge, Paul, *Gordon Brown*, Simon & Schuster, 1998

Sampson, Anthony, *Macmillan*, Penguin, 1967

Scammell, Margaret, *Designer Politics*, Macmillan, 1995

Seaton, Jean, and Pimlott, Ben, eds, *The Media in British Politics*, Avebury, 1987

Seldon, Anthony, ed., *The Blair Effect*, Little, Brown, 2001

—— *Blair*, Free Press, 2004

—— ed., *The Blair Effect 2001–5*, Cambridge University Press, 2005

—— ed., *Blair's Britain 1997–2007*, Cambridge University Press, 2007

—— *Blair Unbound*, Pocket Books, 2008

—— and Ball, Stuart, eds, *Conservative Century*, Oxford University Press, 1994

Self, Robert, *Neville Chamberlain*, Ashgate, 2006

Seymour-Ure, Colin, *The British Press and Broadcasting since 1945*, Blackwell, 1966

—— *The Political Impact of Mass Media*, Constable, 1974

—— *Prime Ministers and the Media*, Blackwell, 2003

Shawcross, William, *Murdoch*, Pan, 1993

Skidelsky, Robert, *Politicians and the Slump*, Macmillan, 1967

Stothard, Peter, *30 Days*, HarperCollins, 2003

Stott, Richard, *Dogs and Lampposts*, Metro, 2002

Taylor, A. J. P., *English History 1914–1945*, Oxford University Press, 1965

—— ed., *Lloyd George: A Diary, by Frances Stevenson*, Hutchinson, 1971

—— *Beaverbrook*, Hamish Hamilton, 1972

Taylor, H. A., *The Strange Case of Andrew Bonar Law*, Stanley Paul, 1932

Taylor, Philip M., *The Projection of Britain*, Cambridge University Press, 1981

Tebbit, Norman, *Upwardly Mobile*, Weidenfeld & Nicolson, 1988

Thatcher, Carol, *Below the Parapet*, HarperCollins, 1996

Thatcher, Margaret, *The Downing Street Years*, HarperCollins, 1993

—— *The Path to Power*, HarperCollins, 1995

The History of The Times, vol. IV, *1912–48*, Times Books, 1952

Thomas, James, *Popular Newspapers, the Labour Party and British Politics*, Routledge, 2005

Thorpe, D. R., *Alec Douglas-Home*, Politico's, 2007

Tree, Ronald, *When the Moon Was High*, Macmillan, 1975

Tunney, Sean, *Labour and the Press*, Sussex Academic Press, 2007

Tunstall, Jeremy, *Newspaper Power*, Clarendon Press, 1996

Turner, John, *Lloyd George's Secretariat*, Cambridge, 1980

Watkins, Alan, *A Conservative Coup*, Duckworth, 1992

Webb, Beatrice, *The Diaries of Beatrice Webb*, Virago, 2000

Weir, L. McNeill, *The Tragedy of Ramsay MacDonald*, Secker & Warburg, 1936

Williams, Francis, *Press, Parliament and People*, Heinemann, 1946

—— *A Prime Minister Remembers*, Heinemann, 1961

—— *The Right to Know*, Longmans, 1969

—— *Nothing So Strange*, Cassell, 1970

Williams, Granville, ed., *Shafted*, Campaign for Press and Broadcasting Freedom, 2009

Williams, Marcia, *Inside Number 10*, Weidenfeld & Nicolson, 1972

Wilson, Harold, *The Labour Government 1964–70*, Penguin, 1974

—— *A Prime Minister on Prime Ministers*, Weidenfeld & Nicolson, 1977

—— *Final Term*, Weidenfeld & Nicolson, 1979

Wilson, Trevor, ed., *The Political Diaries of C. P. Scott 1911–28*, Collins, 1970

Windlesham, Lord, *Broadcasting in a Free Society*, Blackwell, 1980

Windsor, Edward, *A King's Story: The Memoirs of the Duke of Windsor*, Putnams, 1947

Winnett, Robert, and Rayner, Gordon, *No Expenses Spared*, Bantam Press, 2009

Wrench, John Evelyn, *Geoffrey Dawson and Our Times*, Hutchinson, 1955

Wring, Dominic, *The Politics of Marketing the Labour Party*, Palgrave Macmillan, 2005

—— ed., *Political Communications*, Palgrave Macmillan, 2007

Wyatt, Woodrow, *The Journals of Woodrow Wyatt*, vol. 1, Macmillan, 1998

—— *The Journals of Woodrow Wyatt*, vol. 2, Macmillan, 1999

—— *The Journals of Woodrow Wyatt*, vol. 3, Macmillan, 2000

Wyndham Goldie, Grace, *Facing the Nation*, Bodley Head, 1977

Young, Hugo, *One of Us*, Macmillan, 1989

—— *Supping with the Devils*, Atlantic Books, 2003

—— *The Hugo Young Papers*, Allen Lane, 2008

Young, Hugo, and Sloman, Anne, *The Thatcher Phenomenon*, BBC Books, 1986

Young, Kenneth, *Churchill and Beaverbrook*, Eyre & Spottiswoode, 1966

—— *Sir Alec Douglas-Home*, J. M. Dent, 1970

Ziegler, Philip, *Wilson*, HarperCollins, 1995

INDEX